ROOSEVELT
AND
CHURCHILL

Their Secret Wartime Correspondence

ROOSEVELT AND CHURCHILL

Their Secret Wartime Correspondence

EDITED BY

FRANCIS L. LOEWENHEIM

HAROLD D. LANGLEY

MANFRED JONAS

NEW PREFACE BY THE EDITORS

A DA CAPO PAPERBACK

Library of Congress Cataloging in Publication Data

Roosevelt, Franklin D. (Franklin Delano), 1882-1945.
   Roosevelt and Churchill: their secret wartime correspondence / edited by
Francis L. Loewenheim, Harold D. Langley, Manfred Jonas: new preface by
the editors.
     p.   cm. — (A Da Capo paperback)
   Reprint. Originally published: New York: Dutton, 1975.
   Includes bibliographical references.
   ISBN 0-306-80390-9
   1. Roosevelt, Franklin D. (Franklin Delano), 1882-1945 — Correspondence.
2. Churchill, Winston, Sir, 1874-1965 — Correspondence. 3. World War, 1939-
1945 — Diplomatic history. I. Churchill, Winston, Sir, 1874-1965. II.
Loewenheim, Francis L. III. Langley, Harold D. IV. Jonas, Manfred. V.
Title.
E807.A4   1990   89-26030
940.53'22 — dc20   CIP

This Da Capo Press paperback republication of *Roosevelt and Churchill: Their
Secret Wartime Correspondence* is an unabridged republication of the edition
published in New York in 1975, here supplemented with a new preface and
corrections by the editors, by arrangement with whom it is reprinted.

Published by Da Capo Press, Inc.
A Subsidiary of Plenum Publishing Corporation
233 Spring Street, New York, N.Y. 10013

Photographs 1, 2, 5, 6, 9, 10, 11, 14, 16, 19, 20, 21, 22, 27, and 31 are reproduced courtesy the Franklin D. Roosevelt Library, Hyde Park, N.Y.
Numbers 7, 8, 12, 15, 17, 18, 23, 24, 25, 26, 28, 29, and 30 are reproduced
courtesy the U.S. Department of the Army, Signal Corps, Public Information Division. Numbers 3 and 4 are reproduced courtesy UPI; and
number 12 is a Wide World Photo.

Maps by George Buctel.

Preface to the
Da Capo Edition

There can be few more satisfying experiences for scholars than to have their work well received on initial publication and then to see it appropriately reissued some years later. So it is with us and *Roosevelt and Churchill: Their Secret Correspondence*, which was first published in the United States and Great Britain in 1975, and in Italy in 1977.

Well over a decade has passed since then, and, not surprisingly, other books on the same general subject have appeared, and they continue to appear. Not even the publication of Warren F. Kimball's edition of the "complete" correspondence in 1984, however, has changed the essential story of the relations between the President and the Prime Minister during the Second World War from what we reported it to be in 1975, and it seems unlikely to be altered in the future.

Some of the more recent scholarship has emphasized the wartime stresses and strains between London and Washington. *Roosevelt and Churchill* treated those disagreements at some length, as well as the disappointments Churchill encountered in his dealing with Roosevelt, something perhaps disconcerting those who believed then that the relationship between the two wartime leaders had been a long, virtually uninterrupted love feast.

As became clear only later, the war was a decisive period in the seemingly irreversible shift of power from the European to the non-European world, a subject thoughtfully discussed in D.C. Watt's *Succeeding John Bull: America in Britain's Place, 1900-1975* (Cambridge, 1984). Under those circumstances, the

i

surprising element remains not that Roosevelt and Churchill—with their advisers—disagreed on a variety of important questions, but that they did not disagree more often and more publicly.

Churchill, we now know, was highly sensitive to the imperfections in the relationship, but sought to minimize them as best he could. On November 1, 1940, for example, John Colville, then one of the Prime Minister's private secretaries, recorded in his diary: "[Churchill] said he quite understood the exasperation which so many English people feel with the American attitude of criticism, combined with ineffectual assistance; but we must be patient and we must conceal our irritation."

The passage of time did little to change Churchill's mind. In 1952, while working on *Triumph and Tragedy,* the last volume of his history of the Second World War, Churchill dictated this note—plaintive, rather than complaining —to the young Oxford historian F.W. (now Sir William) Deakin, then one of his research assistants: "The death of President Roosevelt. . . . Three months of Roosevelt's failing health. Three months before Truman could form his own views. Roosevelt's great error in not having a deputy ready to succeed, who knew everything. . . . These six months were the most eventful."

Indeed, as we learn from the final volumes of Martin Gilbert's official biography (1986 and 1988), Churchill was determined to remain publicly silent about the disagreements and disappointments. Doubtless recalling the bitter resentments and recriminations that followed the First World War, that continued silence was understandable. But now that the record of the Roosevelt-Churchill relationship is virtually complete, we do no honor to the wartime leaders by glossing over the difficulties they encountered with each other, or failing to concede that the "special relationship" so fervently sought by Churchill was never fully realized.

One important subject that *Roosevelt and Churchill* left untreated was Anglo-American code breaking, usually referred to as Enigma or Ultra. Churchill well understood the importance of this operation for the course of the war. In a Top Secret minute dated May 19, 1945, he wrote of it: "The services rendered, the incredible difficulties surmounted, and the advantages in the whole course of the war, cannot be overestimated."

So sensitive was the breaking of the supposedly unbreakable German codes, however, that the President and Prime Minister never mentioned it directly in their correspondence for fear that the enemy might somehow learn one of the Allies' most invaluable secrets. Indeed, Churchill only gradually shared the secret with Roosevelt, and, according to the late Ronald Lewin, it was not until the approaching invasion of Europe in June 1944 that "the American involvement in Ultra was virtually complete."

Moreover, until the publication of F.W. Winterbotham's *The Ultra Secret* in 1974, it was a topic banned from discussion on both sides of the Atlantic. The lips of former participants remained firmly sealed, as did the voluminous official records. As F.H. Hinsley and his associates have pointed out in the final volume of their *British Intelligence in the Second World War* (1988), because of the continued "need for security," the story of that unprecedented operation cannot be fully told even today.

Important as this subject may be, however, it is clear that the breaking of the German codes was not the decisive element in the ultimate defeat of the Axis powers, but only one of the many factors that eventually enabled the United States, the British Empire, and the Soviet Union to marshal military forces that Germany, Italy, and Japan were unable to match.

* * *

It was perhaps inevitable that a work of such length and scope as *Roosevelt and Churchill* would not be entirely free of minor typographical or other slips. We are grateful to friends, colleagues, critics, and readers for bringing a number of these to our attention, and we have done our best to correct them in this new edition.

Beyond that, we should like to believe that *Roosevelt and Churchill* stands — as when it first appeared — as a balanced account and assessment of the greatest war of modern times, and of the remarkable friendship between the President and the Prime Minister who, though they sometimes failed grievously, successfully directed the victorious coalition.

F.L.L.
H.D.L.
June 1989   M.J.

Acknowledgments

We are indebted to:

Barton J. Bernstein, who first suggested to us the idea of publishing an edition of the Roosevelt-Churchill correspondence.

Eliot Fremont-Smith, for his personal interest and intercession at a crucial phase of our work.

The Franklin D. Roosevelt Library for the copies of the messages and supporting materials.

The Controller of Her Britannic Majesty's Stationery Office for permission to print the messages of Sir Winston S. Churchill.

George M. Elsey, former assistant to the naval aide to the President, for permission to quote from his papers at the Harry S Truman Library.

The University of Virginia Library for permission to use and quote from the papers of Edward R. Stettinius, Jr.

The Yale University Library and President McGeorge Bundy of the Ford Foundation for permission to use and quote from the diary of Henry L. Stimson.

The Hoover Institution Library and the Library of Congress for permission to use the papers of Stanley K. Hornbeck, Cordell Hull, and Harold L. Ickes.

The staffs of the Franklin D. Roosevelt Library, the Library of Congress, the Fondren Library of Rice University, the Mullen Library of the Catholic University of America, the Schaffer Library of Union College, the Columbia University Law Library, the Colorado College Library, the Elmer Holmes Bobst Research Library of New York

University, the Harry S Truman Library, the Hoover Institution Library, the National Archives, the National Museum of History and Technology, the Northwestern University Library, the Ohio State University Library, the Roosevelt University Library, the St. Xavier University (Cincinnati) Library, the Smithsonian Institution, the State University of New York at Albany Library, the University of Cincinnati Library, the University of Denver Library, the University of Houston Library, the University of Virginia Library, and the public libraries of Boston, Chicago, Cincinnati, the District of Columbia, Houston, New Orleans, Seattle, and of Arlington County, Virginia.

Fredrick Aandahl, W. W. Abbot, Barton J. Bernstein, James MacGregor Burns, A. Fryar Calhoun, G. M. Richardson Dougall, Herbert A. Fine, William M. Franklin, Arthur G. Kogan, Walter LaFeber, Richard M. Leighton, Philip K. Lundeberg, Kathleen M. Murfin, Forrest C. Pogue, Lisle A. Rose, William Slany, and Joan Oren Strickler, for reading all or parts of our manuscript and making numerous valuable suggestions.

Our editor, Thomas J. Davis, III, and the staff of Saturday Review Press and our literary agent, Donald R. Cutler of the Sterling Lord Agency.

Mr. Loewenheim: I wish gratefully to acknowledge the personal interest and encouragement of my colleagues at the Department of History, Rice University; the substantial assistance of Professor Katherine Fischer Drew, chairman of that department; Professor John L. Margrave, Dean of Advanced Studies and Research; Professor V. W. Topazio, Dean of Humanities and Social Sciences; and Professor Frank E. Vandiver, Provost of the University; and Linda M. Quaidy, secretary of the Department of History; as well as the invaluable technical help of Mr. C. W. Murphy (formerly) of the Department of Buildings and Grounds, and the manifold assistance of the superbly competent and helpful staff of the Fondren Library, Rice University. Above all, I am deeply indebted to my mother, Mrs. Lilly Loewenheim, who, as for so many years, has continued to be a source of boundless interest, encouragement and support.

Mr. Langley: I offer special thanks to Fredrick Aandahl and Philip K. Lundeberg for assistance at critical times. My portion of the manuscript was typed by Marsha Sitnik, Kay McMarlin, Patricia Farrar, and by my wife, Patricia. To my wife and children, who have borne many inconveniences, vexations, postponements, and sacrifices in the course of preparing this book, I owe a debt of gratitude that no mere word of thanks can convey. I hope that the book will stand as a testament to their contributions.

Mr. Jonas: I am grateful to the Humanities Faculty Development Fund of Union College for a grant that made possible the acquisition of copies of the Roosevelt-Churchill correspondence. Cynthia Young and Peter Slavis rendered valuable editorial assistance, and Albert Gilewicz and Guy Pultz helped in various ways with the preparation of the manuscript. I owe a special debt to Ann F. Sweet, who not only typed portions of the manuscript but also, through her managerial skills and plain hard work, enabled me to meet a number of crucial deadlines, including the last one. My wife, Nancy Greene Jonas, contributed to the completion of this book in ways that can neither be fully described nor adequately acknowledged.

Needless to say, none of the above are responsible for any surviving errors in the text; and for the selection and annotation of material and for the views expressed in this volume we assume joint responsibility.

For

Lilly Loewenheim

Patricia, Erika, and David Langley

Andrew, Katie, Emily, and Matthew Jonas

Contents

List of Illustrations

(Photographs follow page 400)

Preface

This volume includes the heart of one of the most extraordinary collections of letters in modern history—the more than 1,700 messages exchanged between Franklin D. Roosevelt and Winston S. Churchill during World War II.

Initiated by President Roosevelt in September 1939, the correspondence continued at an unflagging pace until the President's sudden death in April 1945. It was a correspondence so truly top secret that its substance was known to only a handful of the President's and the Prime Minister's closest advisers; and it was almost certainly never intended to be published in this form.

Roosevelt and Churchill were strikingly different personalities, and they differed notably in their attitude toward correspondence and written records in general. Shortly after becoming Prime Minister, Churchill issued instructions that all his orders would be in writing and that no orders from him were to be obeyed unless received in such form. Evidently he made it a practice to keep remarkably clear and complete records of all his important activities, military, political, and diplomatic.

The President, on the other hand, had a considerable dislike of written and formal records. In 1943, for instance, he instructed the Department of State not to publish at that time the minutes of the Big Four during the Paris peace conference of 1919 on the ground that such records ought never to have been kept and certainly should not be published. In his own case, during World War II, he bore ultimate responsibility for the absence of formal written records of many of his most important political, diplomatic, and military conferences, decisions, and policies. Moreover, it is by no means certain that, had he lived, he would have approved the publication during the lifetime of many of his leading associates and contemporaries of so vital and personal a correspondence as his messages to the Prime Minister.

It is our hope that this edition of the Roosevelt-Churchill correspondence will be of interest and use to general readers—to those who lived through World War II and those who did not—as well as to interested students and scholars. We have sought to make each section of the present volume self-explanatory, with separate introductions to each part and summary notes on the wartime summit conferences, and we have provided the reader with a general introduction assessing the correspondence in its personal, military, diplomatic, and political aspects.

A word about editorial practices and annotations. When possible, we have based our text on the copies of the correspondence located in the files of the Franklin D. Roosevelt Library at Hyde Park, New York. In the footnotes we have identified all important and many not-so-important personages, and, without cluttering the page excessively, we have sought to provide an adequate amount of background information and bibliographical detail. To make the correspondence easier to follow, we have also provided a chronology of the war, keyed to the documents printed in this volume, as well as maps of both the European and the Pacific theaters.

As the reader of this exciting correspondence will observe, there were few aspects of the war—from grand strategy to logistics to diplomatic negotiation to censorship—that escaped Roosevelt's and Churchill's attention. It was doubtless a mark of their breadth of vision, and of their remarkable energy, that they were able to take in and attend to so much and to record it all in messages to each other.

This volume is not, of course, intended to be a duo-history or biography of Roosevelt and Churchill. It is not a complete record of how they fought the war. It is an edition of their unprecedented and magnificent wartime correspondence, which we believe tells a story and paints a portrait all its own. If Roosevelt and Churchill live again in these pages, we shall have done our job.

F.L.L.
H.D.L.
M.J.

General Introduction

1. The Personal Relationship

ONE OF THE most extraordinary aspects of World War II was the high degree of cooperation achieved between Great Britain and the United States. That cooperation began long before America actually entered the conflict and continued, despite tensions and disagreements, to the very end. Never before in history had two allies come as near to success in pooling their resources, in meshing their military and diplomatic efforts, and in planning and carrying out a common strategy as did the two great English-speaking nations between 1939 and 1945.

The common heritage of the two countries, the history of increasingly amicable relations between them since the 1890s, and the necessities imposed by a battle against a powerful and dangerous combination of enemies help to account for this remarkable development. But they are only part of the story. As more and more of the documents of the period are opened to public view, it becomes increasingly clear that much of this unique instance of cooperation resulted from the accident of history that brought Franklin D. Roosevelt and Winston S. Churchill to positions of leadership at a critical juncture in world history and from the personal relationship that ripened between the two men during a time of common emergency. Seldom have two world leaders worked together so closely or attained such a degree of intimacy. In World War I President Woodrow Wilson and Prime Minister David Lloyd George had been antagonists as much as allies, and their personal relationship was distant, formal, and often strained. In World War II Roosevelt and Churchill became friends.

The friendship between the two men first developed through one of the most extensive and comprehensive correspondences between world leaders in all history. In the five and a half years between the outbreak of war in Europe and the death of Roosevelt more than 1,700 letters, telegrams, and other messages—over 700 from Roosevelt and over 1,000 from Churchill—passed between the two men, an incredible average of nearly one each day. While some were, to be sure, one-liners—Roosevelt's retort "Some Baby!" on March 30, 1943, is a fine example—others ran for five pages and more. Churchill, who usually ranged wider than did the President and wrote less tersely, needed fifteen pages—plus an appendix—to describe the war situation on December 7, 1940.

As always with respect to the statements and writings of political leaders, there is a question of actual authorship. Internal evidence, particularly the tone and style, as well as what is known about Churchill's work habits, strongly suggests that the Prime Minister dictated or drafted the overwhelming majority of his messages personally. For Roosevelt, much of the correspondence after 1942 was drafted by Admiral William D. Leahy, his personal Chief of Staff; his close friend and adviser Harry Hopkins and others may also have had a hand in the process. Nevertheless, there is abundant evidence in the correspondence files that the President approved all the messages, made additions and corrections of a substantive nature on a great number of them, and drafted many of the personal and some of the not-so-personal letters alone. He apparently did so even after his health had begun to decline, a factor not reflected in the contents of the correspondence but clearly evidenced by a deterioration in Roosevelt's handwriting as early as September 6, 1944. There seems little doubt, therefore, that the entire exchange can properly be called the Roosevelt-Churchill correspondence.

In these letters the basis for Anglo-American cooperation was established and the means for implementing it devised long before the United States actually entered the war. As early as February 1940 Roosevelt expressed his desire for a personal meeting; and in August 1941, while America was still technically neutral, the first of nine conferences was held, during which the two leaders cemented their relationship. This historic meeting took place aboard two warships in Argentia Bay, off the coast of Newfoundland. After the United States had entered the war, Churchill traveled to Washington several times to meet with the President: in December 1941, June 1942, and May and September 1943. Both men went to Casablanca in January 1943, to Quebec in August 1943, to Cairo and Teheran in November of that year, to Quebec again in September 1944, and to Yalta in February 1945. All in all, they spent some 120 days in each other's company, and what success they achieved in conference owed not a little to the groundwork, both substantive and personal, which had been laid in their correspondence.

The correspondence is not necessarily an entirely accurate mirror of the concerns of the two men. Much was added in oral communication relayed by various emissaries, in many transatlantic telephone conversations, and, of course, in the face-to-face meetings between the two leaders. The letters do not, for example, cover the all-important conferences themselves, and they are silent on the events of D Day and other equally important matters. A disproportionately small amount of space is devoted to the Far East, reflecting perhaps the Europe-first strategy of the authors. The correspondence says virtually nothing about the development of the atomic bomb, and it is relatively short on information relating to postwar plans.

At the same time, considerable space is devoted to relatively minor matters. There are lengthy discussions about Argentine beef and the disposition of the Italian navy, along with the problems of selecting sites for the meetings with Stalin. Nonetheless, the correspondence ranges widely, sometimes probes deeply, and reveals a great deal. It throws considerable light not only on the wartime relationship between the two countries and the two men but on a host of issues that shaped the postwar world.

The contact thus established and maintained between Roosevelt and Churchill—most of it official, but much of it nevertheless intensely personal—underlay the cooperation between the two countries they represented and led. It helped to maintain a common sense of purpose and common plans for action even in the face of sometimes vexing disagreements over strategy and tactics. It also cut through mountains of red tape on both sides of the Atlantic to make fuller and more effective implementation of these plans possible. Yet, surprisingly, the two leaders did not really know each other at all at the time the war broke out.

They had met only once, at Gray's Inn, London, on July 29, 1918. Roosevelt, then Woodrow Wilson's Assistant Secretary of the Navy, was on a mission to Europe and had stopped in London to attend a dinner for the War Cabinet. Another guest at the dinner was Lloyd George's Minister of State for War and Air Minister, Winston Churchill. Despite some later polite disclaimers, neither man then made a particular impression on the other. Although Churchill was already well known because of his exploits in the Boer War, his literary output, his services in several prewar Cabinets, and his activities as First Lord of the Admiralty, Roosevelt made no mention of the meeting in a detailed report on his European trip, which he compiled some months after the event. And Churchill, much to the President's dismay, had forgotten the encounter altogether by the time of the Atlantic conference.

For more than twenty years after this first meeting, the two men had no direct contact with each other. As early as the 1920s Churchill was enamored of the idea of Anglo-American unity, fostered perhaps by the memory of his American mother and at least implicitly revealed in portions of *The World Crisis*, published between 1923 and 1929. But although he crossed the Atlantic on several occasions, he made no effort to see Roosevelt, then governor of New York, on his visit to New York City in 1932. Roosevelt did not return to England between the wars. Even so, from a distance the two men came to admire each other.

When Roosevelt became President in 1933 and launched his New Deal programs to pull America out of the depression, his attempts were applauded by Churchill as "a valiant effort to solve the riddle of the Sphinx." "His impulse," wrote the future Prime Minister, "is one which makes toward the fuller life of the masses of the people in every land, and which, as it glows the brighter, may well eclipse both the lurid flames of German Nordic self-assertion and the baleful unnatural lights which are diffused from Soviet Russia."[1]

Roosevelt, for his part, admired Churchill's role as Britain's political gadfly during the 1930s. In particular, he listened with increasing respect, even if not always with sympathy, to the Englishman's often lonely warnings against the dangers posed by Adolf Hitler. Especially after the Munich conference of September 1938—during which Britain's Prime Minister Neville Chamberlain and France's Premier Édouard Daladier formally gave Hitler the Sudeten districts of Czechoslovakia in return for a paper promise of future good behavior—Roosevelt recognized the folly of appeasement and came to look upon Churchill as the kind of leader Britain and the democratic world needed. The "My dear Churchill" letter of September 11, 1939, which opened the wartime correspondence, appropriately reflected both official pleasure and personal admiration.

The correspondence, which moved into high gear after Churchill became Prime Minister on May 10, 1940, is noteworthy from the outset for its openness and relative informality, unusual in political exchanges.[2] Churchill was convinced that Britain would need massive help in its battle against Hitler's Germany and was deeply committed to the notion that he propounded eloquently in his *History of the*

1 Winston S. Churchill, "The Bond Between Us," *Collier's,* November 4, 1933, and "While the World Watches," *Collier's,* December 29, 1934.

2 On the transmission of Churchill's and Roosevelt's messages, see Richard J. Whalen, *The Founding Father: The Story of Joseph P. Kennedy* (New York, 1964), pp. 309–310; William M. Rigdon, *White House Sailor* (New York, 1962), pp. 7–13.

English-Speaking Peoples, written between 1936 and 1939, of a fundamental unity of interest and purpose between Great Britain and the
United States. He regarded Roosevelt as enlightened and sympathetic,
and never hesitated to communicate both Britain's problems and its
needs in the bluntest terms. Roosevelt, who had invited the correspondence initially, continued to encourage it, and from the outset he
responded sympathetically, even to requests that political considerations at home made it impossible for him to meet.

When France surrendered to Germany on June 22, 1940, the shock
moved Churchill to more eloquent pleas for American material aid; it
also caused both Roosevelt and a major segment of the American
public to fear for the safety of America in a world that might well be
dominated by Hitler and his allies. The United States reacted to the
events in France in the spring and summer of 1940 by moving to
prevent the Germans from taking French possessions in the Western
Hemisphere and by freezing the American assets of the countries overrun by Germany. Congress approved massive increases in defense
spending and passed the Selective Service Act of 1940, and Roosevelt
and Canadian Prime Minister Mackenzie King agreed to study common defensive problems. Most important, the "deal" sending fifty over-
age U.S. destroyers to Britain in return for leases in British possessions
on the American side of the Atlantic was consummated, and thus the
basic meeting of minds between Roosevelt and Churchill was clearly
demonstrated. When Roosevelt was reelected in November, the Prime
Minister could state in all honesty that he had prayed for that event.
And Roosevelt's letters now began ever more frequently with the
informal "Dear Churchill."

By 1941, after the President's speech promising to make the United
States into the "great arsenal of democracy" and after the subsequent
introduction and passage of the Lend-Lease Act, both Roosevelt and
Churchill regarded a mutual commitment as an established fact. Yet
how this commitment would translate itself into practice depended
more than ever on the relationship between the two men. By July both
were seeking a face-to-face meeting, yet neither could have been entirely unconcerned about the possibility that their apparent meeting
of minds, so laboriously developed in nearly two years of correspondence, might be strained by personality conflicts. Even Roosevelt,
usually confident of his ability to deal with anybody, was not free from
such doubts; and Harry Hopkins, who knew both men, feared a clash
of "prima donnas."

But the fears proved to be groundless. The two men greeted each
other warmly and enjoyed each other's company from the very beginning. Before the Atlantic conference ended, Roosevelt had begun
calling his visitor "Winston" and had, on occasion, been called

"Franklin" in return. Though the more stiff and proper Churchill did not succumb to using this form of address in his correspondence for another two years, and used it only sparingly after that, the pattern for all future meetings had been established.

Indeed, it turned out that, quite aside from their joint interests in Anglo-American cooperation, the two had much in common. They both loved the sea and the Navy, read avidly in history and biography, and enjoyed the outdoors. More than that, each quickly realized that his respect for the ability and determination of the other was fully warranted. Roosevelt returned from Argentia Bay with the feeling, as his wife later recalled, that he and Churchill had had the chance to begin to know and like each other, that the ice had been broken, and that Churchill was a man with whom he could really work. The Prime Minister in turn was charmed by Roosevelt's easy and friendly manner, impressed by his ingenuity, and fully persuaded that the United States would even enter the war should that become necessary. From the personal point of view, the first meeting had been a grand success.

So close had the relationship become after only one meeting that Churchill, upon hearing of the Japanese attack on Pearl Harbor in a news broadcast on December 7, 1941, at once telephoned Roosevelt for confirmation and made immediate plans to go to Washington. Roosevelt promptly invited him to stay at the White House, expressing both his delight at the prospect and his concern over the Prime Minister's safety during the voyage.

Churchill's first visit, interrupted briefly by a Florida vacation, lasted for more than three weeks and set a pattern for future contacts. The Prime Minister was given a room across the hall from Harry Hopkins' bedroom and very close to the President's quarters. The three men visited one another with considerable frequency, and they often talked on long into the night, not always about urgent matters of state. The lunches at the White House were informal and small; even the dinners, usually including only members of the Roosevelt family, were in no sense state occasions. Roosevelt enjoyed mixing drinks for his guest, and Churchill in turn insisted on wheeling the President out of the drawing room.

The degree of informality and genuine comradeship that prevailed is perhaps best suggested by Harry Hopkins' favorite story, which, though possibly apocryphal, is significant for its very existence. According to Hopkins, the President was wheeled into Churchill's room one morning only to find the Prime Minister emerging stark naked from his bath. When Roosevelt apologized and turned to go, he was allegedly dissuaded by the statement: "The Prime Minister of Great Britain has nothing to hide from the President of the United States." Churchill's later disclaimer to the effect that he always had at least a bath towel wrapped around him when meeting the President does nothing to dispute the general tenor of the story. "It is a joy," Roosevelt wrote in a personal note to Mrs. Churchill, "to have Winston with us. He seems very well. I want you to know how grateful we are to you for letting him come."[3]

By the time of Churchill's second visit in June, Roosevelt felt sufficiently relaxed about the relationship to ask the Prime Minister to stop first at his home in Hyde Park, New York. When Churchill cheerfully complied, the President met the plane at the New Hackensack airport and drove his visitor home in his own car. Nor was Churchill less relaxed. He appeared at dinner the first night in his famous siren suit and was observed the next morning walking barefoot on the lawn and—still barefoot—into Harry Hopkins' room. On subsequent visits to Hyde Park, in September 1943 and September 1944, he was accompanied by Mrs. Churchill, who was welcomed with the same easy informality. The warm receptions at airports or railroad stations were repeated at Quebec and at Cairo.

The evidences of a close personal relationship do not end there. The presents the two families exchanged on numerous occasions included, to be sure, such staple items of diplomatic gift giving as paintings of and by Churchill, photographs of the President (sent even to the Churchill children), a complete set of Churchill's writings, some unpublished works by Rudyard Kipling, a map case, a pottery bowl, and two electric typewriters, novelties at the time. But other gifts suggest something far stronger and more personal than mere diplomatic courtesy. These included a Virginia ham, accompanied by suitable amounts of honey, given to the Churchills in October 1942; informal snapshots of the two men fishing at Shangri-la, the President's retreat in the hills of Maryland, exchanged in July 1943 along with some delicious trout the Prime Minister had caught in Canada; a Christmas tree for the Churchill home at Chequers, flown over by bomber in the same year; portraits of the two men destined for their respective bedrooms, exchanged in May 1944; and, in December, three bow ties as well as a quotation from Lincoln, suitable for framing, inscribed "For Winston on his birthday—I would go even to Teheran to be with him again."[4]

It was more often Roosevelt who expressed his warmth and friendship through these tokens. The President also enjoyed innocent teasing, which, though sometimes annoying to the Prime Minister, marked him as "one of the family." The teasing carried over even into the

<hr />

[3] Roosevelt to Clementine Churchill, December 25, 1941, FDR Library, President's Personal File: Great Britain.

[4] Roosevelt to Churchill, November 20, 1944, FDR Library, President's Secretary's File: Churchill.

correspondence. The President liked to refer to his counterpart as a bricklayer, twitted him about the assumed name under which he painted, and accompanied the official statement ending the "Bundles for Britain" campaign with the reassurance that "if you personally long for a seven-to-one Martini, I will send it across pronto."[5] Even the Prime Minister's interest in Basic English did not escape the Roosevelt wit. "I wonder what the course of history would have been," he wrote in June 1944, "if in May 1940 you had been able to offer the British people only 'blood, work, eye water, and face water,' which I understand is the best Basic English can do with five famous words."[6]

More formal than the President, Churchill was never quite able to strike the same note, though on May 1, 1944, he unbent sufficiently to describe a portrait he was sending the President as "a tit for your tat." But assurances of a genuine friendship abound in his letters. "I cannot tell you how sorry I was to leave the White House," he wrote on February 1, 1942. "I enjoyed every minute of it." "It is lovely working with you," he added on July 6, 1943. In one of his few "My dear Franklin" letters, sent on September 13, 1943, he confided: "You know how I treasure the friendship with which you have honoured me and how profoundly I feel that we might together do something really fine and lasting for our two countries and, through them, for the future of all." "Our friendship," he wrote on June 4, 1944, on the eve of the Normandy invasion, "is my greatest standby amid the ever increasing complications of this exacting war." "I cannot tell you," he repeated on December 3, 1944, "how much I value your friendship or how much I hope upon it for the future of the world, should we both be spared." Perhaps the exchange of Christmas greetings tells the story best. The one to London on December 25, 1942, was worded: "The Roosevelts send the Churchills warm personal Christmas greetings. The old teamwork is grand. [signed] Roosevelt." On December 24, 1944, the message from London read: "Clemmie and I send you and Elinor [sic] our warmest wishes for a happy Christmas and a triumphant New Year. [signed] Winston."

The relationship, of course, was not unmarred by differences, both large and small. Neither man shied away from expressing his annoyance with the other, on occasion even to third parties. There is ample evidence that Roosevelt found Churchill's visits wearing, particularly because the Prime Minister took long naps in the afternoon and then worked late into the night, disrupting the schedule and taxing the

5 Memorandum for WSC, July 9, 1942, FDR Library, President's Secretary's File: Churchill.

6 Roosevelt to Churchill, June 17, 1944, FDR Library, President's Secretary's File: Churchill. In his first speech as Prime Minister to the House of Commons on May 13, 1940 Churchill had said: "I have nothing to offer but blood, toil, tears, and sweat."

energies of his host. The President also found Churchill's tendency to speechify disconcerting, and the Prime Minister, for his part, frequently complained of Roosevelt's discursiveness.

From the beginning Roosevelt thought of Churchill as "John Bull" —he even called him that to Stalin on one occasion—crediting him with all the solidity and determination the name implies but also looking on him as something of an anachronism. On occasion he amplified this idea by referring to Churchill as an unreconstructed Tory or as the last of the Victorians. Such feelings underlay the often acrimonious discussions between the two men over the future of the British Empire, which began with the first meeting in Washington and continued, both in the correspondence and in subsequent conferences, to the very end. The implication in Roosevelt's attitude that he, the man of the present, better understood the needs of the future than Churchill, the man of the past, led to even more serious difficulties between the two, both at Teheran and at Yalta.

On the whole, the relationship developed most effectively in the period before the Casablanca conference of January 1943. During that time, the British bore the brunt of the war in Western Europe and thus gave Churchill a position of strength from which to deal with his American counterpart. That strength allowed him to be magnanimous in his dealings with Roosevelt, to whom he was always intensely grateful for standing by Britain in its time of greatest need. He never forgot that the President, as head of state as well as of government, technically outranked him, and he took pleasure in referring to himself as Roosevelt's lieutenant, which surely flattered the American leader.

Behind this attitude, however, was Churchill's confidence in the importance of the British contribution to the common cause. He expected that his friendship with Roosevelt would contribute substantially not only to Anglo-American wartime unity but to the development of a special relationship between the English-speaking peoples. Churchill went so far as to express his hope, in a speech at Harvard University on September 6, 1943, that the relationship "may well some day become the foundation of a common citizenship."[7]

Roosevelt never shared the belief in a special relationship to the same extent, and his reservations led to substantial difficulties, particularly when the Roosevelt-Churchill collaboration itself was tested in dealings with Stalin. When the first meeting with the Russian leader was scheduled for December 1943, Churchill insisted on a prior conference with Roosevelt at Cairo so that the Anglo-American partners could coordinate policy and present a united front. But Roosevelt

[7] Charles Eade, ed., *The War Speeches of the Rt. Hon. Winston Churchill*, 3 vols., 2nd ed. (London, 1965), 2: 513.

did not want such an arrangement. Though he agreed to come to Cairo, he also invited Generalissimo Chiang Kai-shek of China and some Russian representatives to the meeting, hoping in this way to disassociate himself from Churchill and the British sufficiently to gain a freer hand with Stalin.

Churchill was hurt by these developments, which suggested that Roosevelt now regarded himself as the senior partner. Further, it looked as though the President attached no deeper meaning to his nation's relationship with Britain than he did to its relationship with China and the other Allies, including the Soviet Union. Increasingly, Churchill became aware that Britain was now dependent on the United States for the implementation of strategies he regarded as necessary to the security of the British Empire after the war. He noted with a certain dismay the unwillingness of Roosevelt and his advisers to revise their strategy to accommodate British concerns. When, at Teheran, Roosevelt turned down an offer to stay at the British legation and moved into the Russian enclave; when he met privately on several occasions with Stalin but only briefly toward the end of the conference with Churchill; and when he tried to ingratiate himself with Stalin by indulging in the old American political game of "twisting the lion's tail," the Prime Minister could not help but be further irritated by his American colleague.

Differences over the launching of a second front in Europe, over the invasion of southern France, over the future regimes in Italy and Greece, and even over the areas of Germany to be occupied by Great Britain and the United States kept this irritation alive. The events at Yalta in February 1945 did little to soothe it. The President once again turned down Churchill's request for thorough military and political coordination prior to the conference and held only a token meeting with him at Malta. The conference dealt mainly with military matters, and the coordination of political positions was scarcely considered. At Yalta a visibly tired Roosevelt, acting as chairman of the conference, assumed the role of mediator between Britain and Russia on global issues and made a private arrangement with Stalin about the Far East without involving Churchill at all. The "special relationship" on which the Prime Minister counted so heavily was nowhere in evidence.

Yet there is ample evidence that the personal friendship remained unbroken. "Throughout these events," Churchill's physician, Lord Moran, concluded in a book that made much of the differences between the two men, "Winston was moved only by a growing concern about the conduct of the war; there was nothing personal in his differences with the President. He always maintained that Franklin Roose-

velt was a very great man, and became angry when he heard criticism."[8]
Churchill's own letters seem to confirm this. "I have a feeling," he
wrote to the President on January 7, 1945, just before the Yalta meeting, "this is a time for an intense new impulse, both of friendship and
exertion, to be drawn from our bosoms and to the last scrap of our
resources." On March 17, after Yalta and just before the German
surrender, he added: "Our friendship is the rock on which I build for
the future of the world so long as I am one of the builders. . . . I
remember the part our personal relations have played in the advance
of the world cause now nearing its first military goal."

Perhaps these appeals to personal friendship were nothing more
than a rather desperate effort to salvage what could not be gained by
more formal and official pleading, but this is not likely. Churchill was
not a devious man, and he was surely too proud to try to manufacture
a friendship when none existed. The two men simply had shared too
much, had accomplished too much together, and had come to know
each other too well for them not to remain friends. Despite his doubts
concerning the wisdom of some of Churchill's proposals, despite his
confidence that he knew better how to deal with the Russians than the
Prime Minister, and despite his continued annoyance over what he
took to be Churchill's unwarranted concern over the future of the
British Empire, Roosevelt valued the alliance and cherished the
friendship. The President's declining health made him more irritable
and probably also less tolerant than ever of Churchill's concern for
England's glory. Perhaps it also made him more jealous of the Prime
Minister, who though older than he possessed and hugely enjoyed a far
greater mobility. But it did not shake the mutual affection and trust
that the years had produced. "I shall, of course," he wrote to Churchill
in a message dated April 10, 1945, two days before his death, "take no
action of any kind, nor make any statement, without consulting you,
and I know you will do the same."

Indeed, the differences between the two men over strategy and
tactics and their not infrequent disapproval of each other's actions
only prove how necessary the personal relationship between them was
for the effective continuance of the alliance. Given the strains and
burdens that the war imposed on both countries and the basic disagreements that existed between the two leaders, the degree of cooperation and coordination actually achieved seems ample evidence of the
importance of the Roosevelt-Churchill friendship. Without it, the
establishment of joint planning and joint command would have been
far more difficult, the meshing of national priorities even less effective,
and the cost and length of the war almost certainly far greater.

[8] Lord Moran, *Churchill* (Boston, 1966), p. 837.

2. The Military Relationship

THE WARM FRIENDSHIP and close collaboration between Churchill and Roosevelt were unique in international affairs. Alike as the two men were in a number of respects, they were very different in their knowledge of and approaches to military affairs. Ultimately these differences changed the tempo and direction of the war, and undoubtedly they helped to bring the conflict to an earlier end than might have been the case.

When Churchill became Prime Minister in May 1940, he brought to that office a rich and diverse background that included expertise in military and naval affairs as well as politics. Following his graduation from the Royal Military College at Sandhurst in 1895, he gained experience as a soldier, war correspondent, and member of Parliament and later as Minister of Munitions, Minister of War and Air, and Colonial Secretary. In both World War I and World War II he served for a time as First Lord of the Admiralty, an office that gave him a deep and abiding love for the Navy. But he remained essentially a Victorian soldier. He loved the dash, the gallantry, the esprit de corps associated with military life prior to World War I. His experience as a war correspondent gave him a particular interest in the kind of military action that made for a good story. Churchill also had a keen sense of history—and this combined with his strong journalistic sense often helped to produce very readable, popular, and entertaining histories. Churchill's lectures and books about his experiences in the Sudan and South Africa won for him a popular following in the United Kingdom, Canada, and the United States.

Not surprisingly, Churchill had a high respect for his own compe-
tence in military, naval, and political affairs. In both politics and war
he had won a reputation for being a fighter. And it was appropriate
that as the head of a coalition government he was serving both as
Minister of Defense and as Prime Minister. Indeed, he would not have
had it otherwise. "I was entirely resolved to keep my full power of war-
direction," said Churchill in his memoirs. "It is most important that at
the summit there should be one mind playing over the whole field,
faithfully aided and corrected, but not divided in its integrity. I
should not of course have remained Prime Minister for an hour if I
had been deprived of the office of Minister of Defence."[1]

Yet Churchill's varied life meant that his actual experience with
military and naval affairs was sporadic at best. And military practice
changed rapidly: even World War I was not the kind of land war that
Churchill had known as a young officer. In 1914–1918 the tremendous
valor and enormous endurance of the men in the trenches brought few
lasting gains. As First Lord of the Admiralty, Churchill was determined to break the costly stalemate on the western front in 1915, and
he conceived a plan to attack the Central Powers through the Dardanelles. This attack on Gallipoli failed. The disaster was blamed on
Churchill for having overridden the objections of professional military
men, and his dismissal from the Admiralty followed. In the years after
1915 Churchill remained convinced that his plan was essentially
sound, and that only its execution had been faulty. But when he
returned to the Admiralty in 1939, he was determined not to repeat
his past mistake of overruling competent military authority. He might
question, argue, or suggest alternative courses, but in the end he deferred to the judgment of Admiral Sir Dudley Pound, the First Sea
Lord; and he made sure that all orders were issued in Pound's name.[2]
Later, as Prime Minister, he continued to work in close harmony with
his military advisers.

A second lesson of World War I that Churchill never forgot was the
price in blood Britain and the Empire paid in that conflict. He was
determined that Britain would never again fight under conditions like
those on the western front. Mobility, flexibility, limited operational
areas, and advances along a narrow front—these were the ingredients
of campaigns that Churchill deemed essential. Also, the ability to seize
the moment and the wisdom to ensure an avenue of escape if things
went wrong were fundamental to his approach to war. Churchill liked
to gamble, but only with limited resources and for specific goals. These
considerations were underscored by the very real problems of diminish-

---

[1] Winston S. Churchill, *The Hinge of Fate* (Boston, 1950) , p. 91.
[2] Arthur J. Marder, " 'Winston Is Back': Churchill at the Admiralty, 1939–40," *The
English Historical Review*, supp. 5 (1972) , pp. 6, 29.

ing manpower and resources and the lack of ocean transport. His objective always was to strike the enemy in an unexpected quarter and knock it off balance. In modern warfare, this procedure is the closest equivalent to the old cavalry charge. Both maneuvers assume that a bold thrust will put the rascals on the run. War, like politics, is the art of the possible, and for Churchill both required drama to maintain public interest and support.

While Britain was fighting with its back to the wall, Churchill's inspiring leadership and careful use of resources served his nation well. The attack on Pearl Harbor brought the United States into the war on Britain's side, but it also added Japan to the list of Britain's enemies. The war was no longer limited to Western Europe and the Mediterranean. The United States pledged to continue its support for Britain, but it had to respond simultaneously to developments in the Pacific. Global thinking was required, and with it came a system of priorities. All these developments limited the flexibility of leaders and lessened their options. It became imperative for Churchill to seek a harmony of interests with the United States by working with President Roosevelt. Yet the President's military background, attitudes toward warfare, and methods of operation were quite different from the Prime Minister's. In the contrast between these two men lay the challenge, the frustration, and the hope of their collaboration.

During his formative years Franklin Roosevelt had no particular interest in the military life, but he did show an interest in geography. His sole experience with public schools took place one summer in Germany where he learned map reading and military topography. Later, as a young man, he made bicycle trips through parts of Western Europe, and his memory of that terrain stood him in good stead in World War II. When Churchill wrote to him in the early part of December 1944 expressing disappointment at the slow rate of the Allied advance, Roosevelt replied that he had anticipated that approaching the Rhine would be very difficult: "Because in the old days I bicycled over most of the Rhine terrain, I have never been as optimistic as to the ease of getting across the Rhine with our joint armies as many of the commanding officers have been."[3]

As a youth, Roosevelt developed a great love for the sea and for sailing. During the summers with his family at Campobello Island, off the coast of New Brunswick in the Bay of Fundy, Roosevelt gained an extensive knowledge of the tides and currents of the region. At fifteen, in 1897, he read Alfred T. Mahan's *The Influence of Sea Power upon History*, and for his sixteenth birthday he received the same author's *The Interest of America in Sea Power*. These books were important in

3 See below, Doc. 481.

shaping Roosevelt's ideas about control of the oceans. They also provided material for debates in his high school years at Groton. In fact, his love for the sea led him to contemplate a career in the Navy. But his parents disapproved of this ambition, and Franklin, a dutiful son, bowed to their wishes. After graduating from Harvard in three years, Roosevelt spent time at the Columbia University Law School and "clerked" without much enthusiasm for a Wall Street law firm.

Franklin Roosevelt had always followed with great interest the career of his cousin Theodore, who rose through the ranks of Assistant Secretary of the Navy, colonel of the Rough Riders, governor of New York, and Vice President to the presidency. But in his early life Franklin had had no desire to emulate him; it was only after the older Roosevelt left the presidency that Franklin decided to enter politics. In 1910 he ran successfully as a Democrat for a seat in the New York State senate representing Hyde Park and adjacent areas. Then the Democratic party came into power in the fall of 1912 with the election of Woodrow Wilson as President. Roosevelt was offered the post of Assistant Secretary of the Navy, and he accepted.

Roosevelt's background, personality, and interests made him a splendid complement to the Secretary of the Navy, Josephus Daniels. As a son of a shipwright, a former chief clerk in the Department of the Interior, and the editor of a leading Southern newspaper, Daniels was conservative in attitude; he was both a firm believer in pacifism and prohibition and a firm opponent of protocol and ceremonies. Roosevelt, the son of a wealthy Northern businessman and a former Wall Street lawyer, held moderate views on pacifism and alcohol, and he loved ceremonies and protocol, in which he saw news value. These formalities were means of dramatizing the Navy for the voters, and also of promoting his own career. Roosevelt's ideas in this area covered minor points as well as major ones; when he discovered that the Assistant Secretary had no official flag, Roosevelt designed one himself.

As a believer in a navy of big battleships and in the sea power doctrines of Mahan, Roosevelt was popular with naval officers in World War I. He fell under the influence of the senior officers comprising the Navy's General Board, chaired by Admiral George Dewey, and he urged that the United States begin making annual additions to the fleet, working toward a goal of forty-eight battleships. Secretary Daniels promptly cut in half Roosevelt's recommended number. Nevertheless, Roosevelt became an important link between Daniels and the officers concerned about naval preparedness.

The outbreak of World War I found Roosevelt arguing for preparedness well before President Wilson and Secretary Daniels embraced that view. The Assistant Secretary also favored universal military training along with a national census of the skills of men and women for a potential labor draft. Although Roosevelt was still a young man and new on the Washington scene, he had grasped some of the realities of modern warfare well in advance of his more experienced seniors.

When the United States entered World War I in April 1917, Roosevelt warmed to the challenges posed by large-scale mobilization and the expenditure of large sums of money. He tried, though unsuccessfully, to get a larger voice in the administration and operation of the Navy. Always he was receptive to new ideas, especially strategic and technological innovations. For example, he agreed with the young naval officers who saw as the Navy's greatest challenge the control of the German submarine menace, and he urged the building of a mine barrier between Scotland and Norway. The British had already virtually closed the English Channel, and it was thought that a string of mines across the North Sea would seal the Germans in their own waters. Both President Wilson and Secretary Daniels approved the project. Actually, the barrier was not finished at the time of the armistice and was not a decisive factor in winning the war, but Roosevelt and some naval officers liked to think that it was.

All in all, the wartime years were a maturing, exhilarating, and demanding period for Roosevelt; he showed that he had the ability to get things done. Throughout the war he observed Wilson's farsighted leadership, and that image made an indelible impression. In many respects Wilson superseded Theodore Roosevelt as Franklin's political and presidential idol.[4]

By 1919 some of the patterns that were to characterize his own years as President were already visible. Roosevelt had reached the national stage without any intense or overriding ambition and without a particular course of studies to qualify him for high office. Once there, however, his quick mind and voracious reading habits stood him in good stead. Always, he was a very popular and personable man; and his warm, friendly, outgoing attitude charmed many people. But his learning tended to be superficial. Also, throughout his early life he tended to be deferential to authority figures—parents, school and college officials, senior naval officers. In World War I he tended to reflect the ideas of the last person to whom he talked.

But the next two decades saw great strides in political and personal maturity for Roosevelt, highlighted by his unsuccessful vice presidential bid, his struggle against the effects of infantile paralysis, his years as governor of New York, and his election as President in 1932. But still his early experiences continued to be important. Even in the first-

4 Frank Freidel, *Franklin D. Roosevelt: The Apprenticeship* (Boston, 1952), chaps. 1–12. See also Robert A. Divine, *Roosevelt and World War II* (Baltimore, 1969), pp. 50 ff. and Kenneth S. Davis, *FDR—The Beckoning of Destiny, 1882–1928* (New York, 1972), chaps. 11–17.

term New Deal programs for domestic recovery Roosevelt drew upon his experiences and observations in his Navy Department years. Then, in his second term, foreign affairs became increasingly important. The outbreak of World War II obliged the President to devote increasing amounts of time to foreign and military affairs.

Roosevelt's chief military adviser was General George C. Marshall. A year and a month older than the President and a graduate of the Virginia Military Institute, Marshall became the Acting Chief of Staff of the Army in the summer of 1939; a regular appointment to that office came in the fall. Just a few hours before Marshall took his oath of office, Hitler invaded Poland and World War II began. During his first months in office Marshall felt isolated from the President; the General's calm, reserved, and selfless manner did not encourage the bantering first-name approach the President preferred. Gradually, though, Roosevelt came to know and appreciate the talents and qualities of his Chief of Staff. Marshall was always conscious of the fact that the service closest to the President's heart was the Navy—he could not change that. But the General did gradually convince Roosevelt that he should not refer to the Navy as "we" and the Army as "they." It was Marshall who was primarily responsible for expanding, training, equipping, and deploying the Army. On Marshall's recommendation, Douglas MacArthur, Dwight D. Eisenhower, and other officers received major commands. Thus, both directly and indirectly, Marshall was the major architect of the victory of the Anglo-American forces.[5]

When Roosevelt went to Argentia, Newfoundland, in August 1941 to meet with Churchill, he took with him a number of ranking officers, including Marshall; General Henry H. ("Hap") Arnold, Deputy Chief of Staff for the Army Air Force; Admiral Harold R. Stark, Chief of Naval Operations; and Admiral Ernest J. King, commander in chief of the Atlantic Fleet. The President was content to leave to his military and naval advisers the details of how much war material could be allocated to Great Britain in its struggle with Germany. But Churchill arrived at the Atlantic conference with great plans for American assistance in the form of increased convoying in the Atlantic, occupation of the Azores, and an attack on French North Africa—all ideas that had to be rejected by the American service chiefs as being too ambitious. Neither the U.S. military leaders nor their services were ready for war, and they wanted as much time as possible to prepare for action. At Newfoundland the British argued that a combination of blockades, bombing, and propaganda might undermine the German people's resistance and make an invasion of the Continent unnecessary. If landings did

5 Forrest C. Pogue, *George C. Marshall: Ordeal and Hope* (New York, 1966), pp. 1-24.

have to be made, the burden of the effort would fall on armored forces rather than infantry. General Marshall, on the other hand, doubted that the war could be won without an invasion of the Continent and without large land armies. The President talked, listened, and took the measure of Churchill. At the end of the four-day conference the two leaders issued the statement of principles known as the Atlantic Charter. But the tangible commitments were few. Coming out of this first meeting, Churchill failed to get the pledges he wanted of active intervention by or increased support from America.[6]

Churchill returned to Great Britain to lead a nation fighting for its life. Personally, he possessed the vitality, spirit, confidence, and determination the situation required. At his best in adversity, he showed a never-say-die attitude that was infectious. Yet working with Churchill could be difficult. His night working habits meant long hours for the bright men around him who had other duties in other departments during the normal day. Eventually the strain became too great for the Chief of the Imperial General Staff, General Sir John Dill, and he was sent to the United States to head the British military mission in Washington. There he became a close friend of General Marshall and did a great deal to harmonize Anglo-American military relations.

In November 1941 Churchill invited General Sir Alan Brooke to succeed Dill as Chief of the Imperial General Staff. Brooke accepted and in this role became the operational head of the British Army and the principal military adviser of the Prime Minister. Ten days after he took up his duties the Japanese attacked Pearl Harbor and the United States found itself at war with both Germany and Japan. Brooke and his colleagues now had to think in terms both of mounting a joint Anglo-American effort and of giving the Soviet Union as much help as possible in its struggle with Hitler. Brooke responded magnificently to his enlarged responsibilities, and he so impressed his colleagues that three months after he joined the staff he became its chairman. The position carried no authority over the two other members of the Imperial General Staff, the First Sea Lord and the Chief of the Air Staff; Brooke was simply designated the first among equals. But Brooke saw that it was vital for the three service chiefs to agree among themselves on strategy in order to present a united front to the Prime Minister and to the Americans. Above all, he had great confidence in the Imperial General Staff as the most efficient organization to coordinate Allied war strategy.[7]

Throughout the rest of the war Brooke was with Churchill almost daily. He soon learned that the Prime Minister had both massive

---

6 Pogue, *Marshall: Ordeal and Hope*, pp. 121–145.

7 Arthur Bryant, *The Turn of the Tide* (New York, 1957), pp. 3–28, 253–255.

virtues and tremendous flaws. Churchill had a strong temper; he was impetuous, stubborn, and subject to sudden changes of mood; sometimes he showed arrogance and petulance. In various ways the spirit of the Victorian cavalryman was always present in his thinking; this cast of mind showed up in his preference for audacious, small-scale actions against weak spots, taken before engaging the enemy in a major way. Given the realities of twentieth-century warfare and the need for long-range plans to coordinate shipping, supplies, and manpower, Churchill's devotion to a flexible policy posed problems for his advisers. But in Churchill's view: "An operation of war cannot be thought out like building a bridge; certainty is not demanded, and genius, improvisation, and energy of mind must have their parts.[8] Churchill's own career made him well aware of the conservatism of military and naval men. He tended to feel that his military advisers could never think of anything but what might go wrong in an operation. "I do not want any of your long-term policies," he told Brooke. "They only cripple initiative."[9] Yet he was not willing to go ahead with any scheme that did not have the blessing of the Imperial General Staff. Although he often argued with Brooke and sometimes showed bitterness, he never held any grudges or manifested any hard feelings or lack of respect. He could have removed Brooke but came instead to appreciate his great ability. Despite the strain and the problems, Brooke considered the association with Churchill a thrilling experience he would not have missed.[10]

Meanwhile the attack on Pearl Harbor and America's entry into the war aroused Churchill's concern that in responding to the Japanese the United States would put the bulk of its forces in the Pacific and would curtail further aid to Britain. Such a course would create tremendous problems, weakening critically the efforts to strengthen British forces. Churchill hurried to Washington late in December 1941 for a conference with Roosevelt about joint strategy. With him came his service chiefs—General Sir John Dill; Admiral of the Fleet Sir Dudley Pound, who was First Sea Lord and Chief of the Naval Staff; and Air Chief Marshal Sir Charles Portal, Chief of the Air Staff—as well as other ranking officers and Lord Beaverbrook, Minister of Supply.

Churchill's major fear was not well founded; in Washington General Marshall and Admiral Stark had already decided that the United

8 Winston S. Churchill to Sir Hastings Ismay, March 3, 1943, quoted in Churchill, *Hinge of Fate*, p. 935.

9 John Ehrman, *Grand Strategy*, vol. 5, *August 1943–September 1944* (London, 1956), pp. 424-427.

10 Bryant, *Turn of the Tide*, pp. 257-276, and *Triumph in the West 1943-1946* (London, 1959).

States would follow a Europe-first strategy for winning the war. But they could not overlook the acute needs of the Pacific theater, where for the time being the United States could do little but hold its own. Marshall and the other American service chiefs had their own worries about strategy; they were concerned that Churchill, stopping at the White House, would use his forceful personality and skill at argument to persuade the President to follow a British plan for winning the war. Marshall was convinced that unless the United States had its own strategy, its forces would be dissipated in a series of disparate operations. In his view, America ought to husband its resources and concentrate on goals that would make a direct contribution to the early defeat of the enemy. Specifically, this meant landing an Allied force on the Continent as soon as possible.

The day before Churchill arrived in Washington, Roosevelt read a memorandum from Secretary of War Henry L. Stimson outlining the views of the War Department on the questions to be taken up at the conference. The department recognized the North Atlantic as the principal theater of operations and the preservation of communications with the British Isles as a first essential in the conduct of the Allied war effort. In line with this emphasis, the memo urged that a start be made in building up American forces in Great Britain. In effect, this document assuaged Churchill's principal worry; it also marked the first stage of implementing Marshall's grand strategy.

Once he was reassured about the primacy of the European front, Churchill presented to Roosevelt some strategic proposals he had worked out with his military advisers while traveling to the United States. Assuming that the Russians could hold back the German onslaught in the east, Churchill thought it likely that the Nazis would open another theater in North Africa by way of Spain and Portugal. To forestall this, he wanted the United States to land in northwest Africa and eventually link up with the British forces pushing the German Afrika Korps westward from Egypt. Perhaps the French authorities in North Africa would cooperate with the American landings and perhaps not. Roosevelt seemed to favor the plan with or without French assistance.

The next day Churchill found Roosevelt following another track. This time the President took the initiative and proceeded to outline the points in Stimson's War Department memorandum. First, he was willing to have American troops relieve the British in Northern Ireland. Second, Churchill had stressed the importance of controlling islands in the eastern Atlantic, especially the Azores, to protect convoys; Roosevelt considered the Cape Verde Islands more significant than the Azores. Third, the President pledged that the United States would do its best in the Pacific to save the Philippines or, if that was not possible, the Dutch East Indies. He agreed that Singapore must be held. Churchill continued to argue the merits of the North African venture, but for the time being he accepted the judgments of Marshall and Stimson. By the time the conference ended both the President and the Prime Minister were determined to launch a North African operation, but they had to postpone it to until ships diverted to the Pacific became available.[1]

Out of this first Washington conference came an early but short-lived instance of Allied cooperation. To insure the effective coordination of the naval, air, and ground forces of Great Britain, the Netherlands and the United States in the Southwest Pacific, General Marshall proposed that a unity of command be established. After much discussion agreement was reached to name General Sir Archibald Wavell as the Supreme Commander of the ABDA (American, British, Dutch, Australian) area. Wavell would receive his orders from a joint body responsible to Roosevelt and Churchill. But the Allied forces under Wavell were unable to halt the Japanese advance, and on February 23, 1942 ABDA was ordered dissolved. Subsequently the United States accepted the responsibility for operations in the Pacific. The Southwest Pacific Area was established on April 18, 1942 under the command of General Douglas MacArthur. Two days later the Pacific Ocean Area was established under the command of Admiral Chester W. Nimitz, the commander in chief of the United States Pacific Fleet.

The President's meeting with Churchill had been generally satisfactory from the American point of view, but neither Marshall nor Stimson was prepared to congratulate the other. They had heard that in the course of the discussions between the two leaders Churchill had proposed that if the Philippines could not be reinforced, the American troops slated for the islands would go on to Singapore. Secretary Stimson told Harry Hopkins that he would resign if such a policy prevailed, and Hopkins delivered this message to the President in Churchill's presence. Both Churchill and Roosevelt denied that any such decision had been reached. Later the President gave assurances to his military advisers that the supplies earmarked for General Douglas MacArthur in the southwest Pacific would indeed go to him. Stimson confided in his diary that "this incident shows the dangers of talking too freely in international matters of such keen importance without

[1] Henry L. Stimson and McGeorge Bundy, *On Active Service in Peace and War* (New York, 1948), pp. 413–416; Pogue, *Marshall: Ordeal and Hope*, pp. 261–270; and Herbert Feis, *Churchill, Roosevelt, Stalin* (Princeton, 1957), pp. 38–40, 47–50; Maurice Matloff and Edwin M. Snell, *Strategic Planning for Coalition Warfare 1941–1942* (Washington, 1953), pp. 97–119.

the President carefully having his military and naval advisers present.[2]

In this instance Stimson's worries were calmed, but the situation pointed up the inefficiency of the President's approach to military matters in contrast to that of the Prime Minister. Churchill briefed his military advisers regularly, and they were always conscious of his policies and of his direction whether he was present or not. Roosevelt had no regular meetings with his Chiefs of Staff, and at his direction no record was made of their discussions. He saw the chiefs at various times when they could be fitted into his schedule. Obviously this haphazard arrangement could not continue, if only because there were too many decisions to be made on short notice. The President had to have closer contact with his military chiefs.

Drawing on their experience at the first Washington conference, the Allied military chiefs moved to increase coordination, and they created the Combined Chiefs of Staff in December 1941. Deputies of the senior commanders of the British armed services were assigned to Washington as the British joint staff mission, and a committee system paralleling the British system was set up for the Combined Chiefs of Staff. This complex system made it possible to achieve the high degree of coordination that was vital for the rest of the war. From the time of their first meeting on January 23, 1942, into the postwar years, the Combined Chiefs of Staff met regularly every Friday. Out of this close association there emerged a spirit of personal and professional respect that made easier the work of developing a combined strategy.

On the other side of the Atlantic Churchill presided over the Cabinet Committee of Imperial Defense, a group that met once a week, or sometimes more frequently, to prepare for eventualities and to determine policies. On the basis of these decisions the various government departments drew up more detailed plans.

To improve his own coordination and control, President Roosevelt turned to Admiral William D. Leahy. Roosevelt had met Leahy before the war, while he was serving as Chief of Naval Operations, and when Leahy retired from the Navy the President named him governor of Puerto Rico. In November 1940 Roosevelt sent Leahy to France as ambassador to the Vichy government, and he served there until May 1942. After his return, Roosevelt recalled him to active duty in July 1942 and named him to the newly created post of Chief of Staff to the Commander in Chief of the United States Army and Navy. In its relationship to the President, the post was similar to that held by Sir Hastings Ismay as Chief of Staff to Churchill in the latter's capacity as

[2] Stimson diary entry for December 25, 1941, quoted in U.S. Department of State, *The Conferences at Washington 1941–1942 and Casablanca 1943* (Washington, 1968), p. 95.

Minister of Defense for Britain. (But unlike Leahy, who presided over meetings of the American Joint Chiefs, Ismay was not a member of the British Chiefs of Staff.)

The Joint Chiefs of Staff kept the President informed on all common Army and Navy matters of policy, including manpower needs, munitions production and distribution, and strategy. Then, further down the hierarchy, there were subsidiary groups and specialized committees that dealt with a wide range of problems; and they briefed the Joint Chiefs on matters in their areas of expertise. It was Leahy's job to summarize for the President the findings of these groups as well as the actions of the Joint Chiefs, who sometimes met with the President in his private study to discuss concepts and grand strategy. Most often it was Marshall who maneuvered the other Joint Chiefs into a unified position on particular issues. With the President's approval, the Joint Chiefs issued the directives that sent men, ships, and planes into motion. In effect, the President determined the general objectives, while the Joint Chiefs worked out the policies and logistics and individual area commanders determined details. As individuals and as representatives of the points of view of their respective branches, the Joint Chiefs worked well together, providing the President with the support he needed.

The Joint Chiefs provided an exceptional reservoir of talent and dedication. Roosevelt relied heavily on Admiral Leahy's ability to summarize vast quantities of information and to set forth clearly the matters to be decided. The President had particular appreciation for the ability of Admiral King, who succeeded Admiral Stark as Chief of Naval Operations in March 1942, while remaining Chief of the U.S. Fleet. But Roosevelt also recognized that King's short temper and undiplomatic language created special problems. Another trusted adviser was General "Hap" Arnold, who was Chief of the Army Air Force and technically a subordinate of General Marshall. In the absence of legislation creating a separate air force, General Marshall tried to have Arnold treated as an equal to the other chiefs, so that he could present the point of view of the air arm. Indeed, Arnold was an active exponent of air power, although he recognized its limitations. On a personal level, Arnold gave all he had to the work of the Joint Chiefs, and his dedication and pleasant personality made him welcome in a variety of situations. He was especially effective in ironing out difficulties with the British by dealing with his opposite number in England, Sir Charles Portal. In addition, Marshall and Arnold had special access to Roosevelt by virtue of their responsibilities for operations and plans. This special channel was formalized by presidential order in February 1942.

As time went on, the President became more and more dependent on General Marshall, who was, in Leahy's words, "a tower of strength"[3] to Roosevelt. General Brooke also noted this dependence: "The President had no great military knowledge and was aware of that fact and consequently relied on Marshall and listened to Marshall's advice. Marshall never seemed to have any difficulties in countering any wildish plans which the President might put forward."[4] When the time came to choose the commander of the Allied forces that would launch the invasion of Western Europe, the President could not bear to think of being without Marshall's counsel. As a result, the coveted command went to Dwight D. Eisenhower. Marshall hid his disappointment and continued his selfless, dedicated service. But Roosevelt's dependence on Marshall meant also that he was increasingly influenced by the General's point of view, especially on the invasion of Western Europe and preparations for it. Marshall's and Roosevelt's conclusions about the second front and related operations eventually led to a number of other, similar decisions that were unpopular with Churchill. Even so, it was Churchill himself who later called Marshall "the true organiser of victory."[5] And Secretary of War Stimson wrote of Marshall: "His mind guided the grand strategy of our campaign. . . . His views guided Mr. Roosevelt throughout."[6]

Although he had no formal place in the military staff hierarchy, Harry Hopkins played an enormously important role in shaping Roosevelt's decisions. As the President's emissary, he moved on the national and international stage observing, listening, conveying advice and reporting to Roosevelt. Churchill, Secretary of War Stimson, and Marshall, among others, found Hopkins a vital link in bringing certain matters to the President's attention.

Marshall's and Leahy's ideas, plus Admiral King's pressure for more men and supplies for the Pacific theater, the desire to help the Russians to maintain pressure on the Germans, and Roosevelt's insistence on cooperation with the British, were major determinants of the Allied war strategy. As American industrial production increased, and as the German U-boat menace diminished, the British became increasingly dependent on the supplies and manpower of the United States. This dependence eventually forced Churchill and the British to go along with American strategic decisions. Indeed, in the last analysis it meant accepting Marshall's plans for winning the war. Some scholars, however, have argued that the strategy in Europe was actu-

3 William D. Leahy, *I Was There* (New York, 1950), p. 192.

4 Bryant, *Turn of the Tide*, p. 335.

5 Churchill to Field Marshal Sir Henry Maitland Wilson, March 31, 1945, quoted in Forrest C. Pogue, *George C. Marshall: Organizer of Victory 1943–1945* (New York, 1973), p. 585.

6 Stimson and Bundy, *On Active Service*, p. 662.

ally a blend of the most pronounced forms of the British and American views, with the balance tilted toward the British side. Others maintain that this argument is true only for the period before the summer of 1943.

The Pearl Harbor attack did not change America's longstanding strategy favoring the European theater, but the struggle in the Pacific gave a special urgency to winning the fight in Europe as soon as possible. Thus war material sent to Great Britain now had to be not only continued but increased. Britain, after all, was the logical jumping-off point for an invasion of Western Europe, and men, equipment, and supplies would have to be stockpiled there. But also, as much additional equipment and supplies as could be spared had to be sent to the Soviet Union to help the Russians and to keep the Germans occupied on their eastern front. These two related goals meant both eliminating the menace of the German U-boats in the North Atlantic and increasing the production of merchant shipping. Indeed, during much of the war the problem of shipping was the key to what the Allies could and could not do in the field of battle. As the war progressed, convoys traveling under naval escort were able to deliver much needed supplies and to cut down the shipping losses to submarines. And aggressive antisubmarine work by air and surface forces put the U-boats on the defensive. Eventually the Allies came to build more merchant ships than the enemy could destroy. Unfortunately, they could not uphold this record in other shipping categories, and throughout the war there was a shortage of landing craft.

In the Pacific the American strategy was to stop and roll back the Japanese long before the full weight of American power could be unleashed against them. The Americans also maintained faith in the latent fighting power of China and wanted to build up the Chinese army for future use against Japan. In any event, the Americans were able to stop the Japanese advance in 1942; and in August of that year they took the offensive with a landing at Guadalcanal. Thereafter the Navy in particular wanted to channel more men and resources to the Pacific in order to keep the Japanese off balance and continue the advance, even at the risk of withholding some support for Europe. This pressure, in turn, intensified the need for firm decisions on what was to be done in Europe and when.

Churchill, at once more visionary and more flexible in some ways than the American planners, saw the road to victory running through a series of grand strategic moves. First, the Allies had to stop the German and Japanese advances in the Atlantic, the Mediterranean, Africa, and the Indian Ocean. Second, when forces were sufficiently built up, they had to clear North Africa of Axis troops. Then, when North Africa was in Allied hands, the merchant ships in the Mediterranean could be released and war vessels could be used to threaten the southern shores of the European continent. Third, Italy would be knocked out of the war. If Turkey could be induced to enter the war, a supply route to the Soviet Union via the Black Sea would be opened, and further opportunities to harass the Germans in the Balkans would doubtless present themselves. Fourth, with the Mediterranean in Allied hands, additional men and resources could be sent to India and Southeast Asia for use against the Japanese, and British fleet units could also be employed in that theater. (Unlike the Americans, the British had no faith in the Chinese contribution to the war.) Meanwhile bombardment of Germany would continue. It was hoped that the bombing, plus pressure on the Axis flanks in the Mediterranean and perhaps Norway, would force the collapse of Germany. If an Allied invasion proved necessary, it would be mounted against a Germany worn down by a war of attrition. And once Germany was defeated the British and Americans would finish off Japan. For all their weighing of alternatives, the British, and especially Churchill, were reluctant to tie themselves too tightly to long-range plans. They wanted to have enough men, arms, aircraft, equipment, and supplies to exploit opportunities that might arise. But from the point of view of the American military planners, the problem with the British timetable was simply that it would take too long to win the war.

Late in March 1942 Secretary of War Stimson, General Marshall, General Eisenhower (then head of the War Plans Division of the War Department), and other officers worked out their own plan for the invasion of Europe in April 1943. This strategy called for forty-eight divisions, thirty of them American, to land in France between Le Havre and Boulogne. But the planners recognized the possibility that the Soviet Union might not be able to hold out until the spring of 1943. Accordingly, they planned for a possible emergency landing as early as the fall of 1942, although this would be no more than a limited action to seize and hold a beachhead until the major assault could be launched the following spring. But by forcing an air battle they might decimate the Luftwaffe. Roosevelt approved the plan, especially because it recognized the importance of giving prompt aid to the Russians. The President gave his formal assent on April 1, and at Harry Hopkins' suggestion Marshall and Hopkins flew to London to show the plan to Churchill.

The Prime Minister's initial reaction was favorable, but the more he thought about it the more cautious he became. An assault on France would be risky at best and might involve tremendous casualties. If the landing were not successful, the British would sustain losses they could not easily make up. Doubtless there would be political, military, and psychological repercussions to the attack. Churchill might be a gambler, but he was not willing to stake so much. Advising his superior, Brooke admitted the desirability of a frontal attack on Germany, but he pointed out that the shortage of landing craft and of shipping would make the attack very difficult in 1942 or even in 1943. And attempting an earlier landing ran the risk of major disaster. Finally, would not a small beachhead in France look ridiculous in comparison with the long Russian front? Churchill now began to ponder the possibility of launching a more limited and less risky attack on some weaker part of Axis-held Europe. Norway intrigued him as one possibility; others were North Africa and the Middle East.

Meanwhile Roosevelt asked Stalin to send Foreign Minister Vyacheslav Molotov to the United States to discuss a military operation that would relieve the German pressure on the Russians. En route to Washington, Molotov stopped off in London to confer with Churchill, and he found the Prime Minister vague about plans for the second front. Later, during his first night in Washington, Molotov found the President willing to talk about almost anything but the pending invasion. The next day, at Roosevelt's request, Molotov briefed the President, General Marshall, and Admiral King on the situation on the Russian front. He said that the Russians might not be able to stop the German drive in the Caucasus, and if that region fell the Axis war machine would be greatly strengthened. It was vital, therefore, that a second front be launched in 1942. Deeply impressed, Roosevelt authorized Molotov to tell Stalin that there would be a second front before the year was out, although General Marshall attempted to soften the promise by reminding the Russian envoy of the shortage of shipping. But Molotov insisted on a definite commitment, and he demanded to know what he could tell Stalin about the second front. Against Marshall's advice, Roosevelt promised a second front in 1942.

Churchill was extremely uneasy about this pledge to the Russians, doubting, as he did, that it could be kept. Even so, he did not mention his reservations to Molotov and instead added his own assurances that the front would be opened in 1942 or 1943. Molotov passed the news along to Stalin, and the Russians allegedly began to make plans in anticipation of the invasion.

While Churchill was meeting with Roosevelt in Washington in June 1942, news came of the surrender of the British garrison at Tobruk, Libya, to Axis forces under Field Marshal Erwin Rommel. Twenty-five thousand men had been captured, and Roosevelt asked what he could do to help. Churchill requested that the United States send all the new Sherman tanks it could spare to the British Eighth Army in Egypt. The President complied, even though this meant depriving American units of long-awaited new equipment. The disaster at Tobruk made Churchill even less willing to consider the possibility of a landing in

France in 1942. Instead he now suggested a strike at French North Africa. Marshall was opposed to this, but the President was already convinced of the advantages of such a campaign. From a political point of view the plan could be presented to the public as a tangible gain for the year 1942. So Roosevelt disregarded Marshall's advice and endorsed the North African invasion. The wisdom of this move was to be debated for years to come. General Eisenhower, who had a major role in drafting the plans for the European invasion in 1942 or 1943, eventually came around to the idea that it was better to have employed the troops in North Africa than to have had them remain idle until the second front in France could be mounted. Once the decision on North Africa was made, Churchill flew to Moscow to explain the plan to Stalin. At first Stalin was hostile to a landing anywhere but in France, but finally even he came to see advantages as well as risks in the operation.

The North African campaign began on November 8, 1942, and ended on May 13, 1943. Between January 14 and January 23, 1943, Churchill, Roosevelt, and their military advisers met at Casablanca to determine their strategy for the year. There they decided that when the campaign in Tunisia was won the island of Sicily would be attacked. Meanwhile, the battle against the German U-boats would be pressed, for if shipping losses could be held to a minimum, the commitments of supplies for the Soviet Union could be met. Also, the buildup of American air and ground units in Great Britain would continue, and high priority would be given to a combined Anglo-American bomber offensive against the Continent. In the Pacific the American forces were to advance toward the Philippines by way of the central and southwest Pacific routes, and additional supplies and aircraft would be sent to China. The reconquest of Burma (thereby opening the Burma Road to channel additional supplies to China) was tentatively scheduled for November 1943. All matters connected with China were to be handled by the United States, and all those with Turkey by the United Kingdom. At Casablanca Roosevelt and Churchill also tried to unify the French factions led by General Charles de Gaulle and General Henri Giraud. Finally, at the news conference held at the end of the Casablanca meetings Roosevelt announced that the Allies would pursue a policy of "unconditional surrender" toward their Axis enemies. This phrase proved to be an unfortunate choice of words, difficult to define and impossible or at least impractical to implement. Roosevelt soon backed away from any rigid interpretation of his fateful phrase, and in practice (except to some extent in the case of Germany) it was not applied against the Axis in the sense it was originally announced.

Late in May 1943 Roosevelt and Churchill met for a third time in

Washington with their military advisers. There they considered plans for the invasion of Sicily. The anti-U-boat campaign got additional attention, and support for China and Russia was stressed once more. The Allies decided that the French forces in North Africa should be prepared for active participation in the attacks on Axis-held Europe. The situation in the Pacific had improved greatly, and Roosevelt and Churchill agreed to take advantage of the new circumstances with unremitting pressure against Japan.

After the Washington meeting Marshall accompanied Churchill on a flight to Algiers where they conferred with Eisenhower on future operations. Here Marshall suggested that two planning groups be established. One would study the seizure of Corsica and Sardinia; the other a movement against the mainland of Italy. When the results of these studies were known it would be clear what the next target should be.

The invasion of Sicily came on July 10, and thirty-eight days later the island was in Allied hands. Churchill as well as the Americans now wanted to move on into Italy. Another conference between Churchill and Roosevelt was arranged for August 1943, this time in Quebec, and here plans for the invasion of Italy were approved. Mussolini had been deposed and arrested late in July, and Churchill particularly hoped that Italy, or at least a portion of it, could be seized quickly by the Allies. Earlier, in order to make use of surplus troops in the Mediterranean area, Marshall had been willing to consider such limited operations as the plans of the Combined Chiefs of Staff for seizing Corsica and Sardinia, making a diversionary landing in southern France in support of the main cross-channel operation, bombing central Europe from Italian bases, and sending supplies to guerrilla forces in the Balkans. But by the time of the Quebec meeting Marshall had reordered his priorities, and he was firm in wanting the cross-channel attack, now known as Operation Overlord, to take precedence. Actually, following the third Washington conference the previous May, an Anglo-American directive was issued to prepare an invasion plan with the target date of May 1, 1944. A planning group, headed by Lieutenant General Frederick E. Morgan, was established, and both Morgan and the group were known as the Chief of Staff to the Supreme Allied Commander, or COSSAC. Indeed, one of the main purposes of the Quebec meeting was to study the plans that had been drawn up by COSSAC. Marshall wanted to make sure that any involvement in the Mediterranean theater would not lead to a postponement of Overlord. Secretary of War Stimson and General Marshall stiffened the President's resolve to stick to the planned date of Overlord.

But at Quebec the date of Overlord was not an issue. Rather it was a question of whether the buildup for Overlord should have an "overriding" priority for supplies during 1943. The Joint Chiefs of Staff argued for this, but Roosevelt did not agree, and the subsequent decision avoided the use of the word.

By this time Marshall and even General Brooke thought that Churchill was damaging the Anglo-American alliance with his penchant for trying to reverse decisions and for continually offering alternatives to operations proposed. The Prime Minister still talked of a landing in Norway, of using Italy as a springboard for probes into the Balkans, and of bringing Turkey into the war—all matters that seemed to Marshall and Stimson to keep putting off the cross-channel attack. The postponement was not only damaging relations with the Soviet Union but also strengthening the hands of U.S. Navy and Army leaders who wanted to see a greater emphasis on the Pacific theater. As Brooke wrote in his diary: "The tragedy is that the Americans, whilst admiring him [Churchill] as a man, have little opinion of him as a strategist. They are intensely suspicious of him. All his alterations or amendments are likely to make them more suspicious than ever."[7] Brooke had to work hard to counteract unfavorable reactions by the Americans to Churchill's ideas, and Marshall and Stimson strove to offset the Prime Minister's influence on Roosevelt.

Prior to the conference Churchill offered to let Roosevelt name the supreme commander for Overlord. He thought that the President would choose Marshall, and indeed the General wanted the command as a fitting climax to his military career. Brooke also wanted the post, but Churchill gave the Chief of the Imperial General Staff the disappointing news while the men were still at Quebec. Actually, the President did not make his decision to name Eisenhower until later in the year.

As for the Pacific theater, proposed advances along routes in both the central and the southwest Pacific were approved. The movement to the central Pacific was to begin with the invasion of the Gilbert and Marshall islands. In Asia itself the Southeast Asia command was established, with Admiral Lord Louis Mountbatten as the supreme commander and General Joseph W. Stilwell as his deputy. China, of course, was not included in Mountbatten's command, and that country remained an area of American strategic responsibility. An offensive in northern Burma was scheduled to begin in February 1944.

One crucial agreement achieved at the Quebec conference concerned the exchange of information about atomic energy. It appears that Churchill had first raised the subject with Roosevelt as early as June 1942, while the two were at Hyde Park. At the time he had understood the President to be in favor of sharing equally the results of the research. But later, at Casablanca, Churchill complained that the infor-

---

[7] Bryant, *Triumph in the West*, p. 277.

mation exchange had ceased. Hopkins looked into the matter and found that the U.S. Army had taken partial charge of the research, with a consequent tightening up on the information exchange in the interest of security. Subsequently, British Foreign Secretary Anthony Eden brought up the matter during his discussions with Hopkins in Washington in March 1943, and Churchill mentioned it to Secretary of War Stimson during the latter's visit to England in July. Actually, all along Roosevelt's general position was that information on the military uses of atomic energy should not be given to anyone—not even an ally. But since the British had contributed to the work of developing that source of energy, the President agreed that they should share in information—for postwar industrial use. Churchill's reply was that since an atomic weapon might be developed during the war, the exchange of information fell within the general agreement on sharing secrets of research and invention. Finally, on August 19, 1943, Roosevelt and Churchill signed an agreement at Quebec providing for an exchange of atomic energy information, and a combined policy committee was established in Washington to expedite the collaboration and exchanges.

In spite of all the difficulties, personal and strategic, the plans laid at Quebec got off to a reasonably strong start. Allied landings at Salerno on September 9, 1943, marked the major invasion of Italy. The Italian government surrendered to the Allies, but Italy itself proved to be no easy conquest. The Germans rushed reinforcements to the area and soon the Allies were encountering stiff resistance to their movement up the boot. The Allies continued bombing German-held Europe, attempting to reduce German fighter aircraft strength as a necessary prelude to Operation Overlord. Meanwhile, the Allies were winning the battle in the Atlantic. American and British merchant ships were now larger than before the war, and convoys to the Soviet Union via the northern route could be resumed. Aided by supplies from the west, the advancing Russian armies opened a major offensive in the Kiev area early in November. Later that month American forces began the central Pacific offensive. The Italian, Atlantic, Russian, and Pacific offensives—these summarized the state of the war when Roosevelt and Churchill came together once again for a conference at Cairo on November 22. Joining them was Generalissimo Chiang Kai-shek, whose participation was to be limited to matters directly affecting China.

By the end of 1943 the strain was taking a toll on the planners in both patience and trust. The American and British military men traveled to Cairo with an attitude of mutual suspicion—each contingent thought that the other was acting in an underhanded way. The British had concluded that the correct strategy for Europe was to press on in Italy; to help induce the Balkan nations to break away from Germany by supplying the guerrilla forces there with arms and equipment; to bring Turkey into the war; and to postpone Operation Overlord for a few weeks. For the American service chiefs, in contrast, the situation was more a matter of sticking to previous agreements and plans for major operations.

Churchill was annoyed at Roosevelt for inviting Chiang Kai-shek to Cairo, and he was distressed at the further suggestion that the Russians be invited to send an officer to the Anglo-American military discussions. Churchill successfully resisted asking a Russian observer to Cairo, but he could do nothing about the Chinese leader. The Generalissimo was in Cairo when Roosevelt arrived; thus the Far East strategy was decided in advance of discussing the Anglo-American operations in Europe. This scheduling added to Churchill's sense of dissatisfaction.

At the Cairo conference Admiral Lord Louis Mountbatten presented his plans for the recovery of Burma. The Chinese were to send forces eastward from Yünnan province to support this operation, although Chiang agreed to cooperate only if the Allies agreed to launch an amphibious assault in the Bay of Bengal. Churchill felt that such an effort would interfere with his plans for projects in the Mediterranean and he refused to promise such extensive support. Roosevelt too was concerned that the promise Chiang required might interfere with Overlord. Still, he wanted to help the Chinese, and he attempted to mediate between Chiang and Churchill. In the end Chiang left Cairo with a promise from Roosevelt concerning the amphibious operation in the Bay of Bengal, and the United States agreed to equip ninety Chinese divisions—in the future.

When Churchill, Roosevelt, and their advisers turned to the European theater, the latent suspicions of both sides emerged. The Americans argued against dispersing forces any further in the Mediterranean. Churchill said that the British still supported Overlord, but they wanted a flexible strategy to take advantage of the opportunities they saw in the Mediterranean. But before final decisions could be reached, it was necessary for both sides to go to Teheran for a long-awaited and long-postponed meeting with Stalin.

More than eighteen months had passed since Roosevelt and Churchill had first promised the Soviet leader to establish a second front. The action had been postponed twice, and for a period the convoys carrying vital supplies to Russia had been suspended. But even without the assistance of a second front the Russians had stopped the Germans at Leningrad, Moscow, and Stalingrad, and they were now steadily pushing the enemy out of the Soviet Union. At the Teheran meeting Stalin was suspicious of his allies and of their attitudes toward his country. After listening to the President's review of the war and his comments on possible future operations, Stalin wanted to know when the invasion of France would take place—he insisted that the best way for the Western allies to get to Germany was through France, not Italy. Thus against Stalin too Churchill found himself defending the Italian campaign and the potential of the eastern Mediterranean. Roosevelt supported him on Italy but alternated between pressing for Overlord and acknowledging the merits of a thrust in Yugoslavia to link up with the Russians. The President tried rather desperately to convey to Stalin his friendship and trust as well as to dissipate the idea that the United States and Britain were "ganging up" on the Soviet Union. Some of these efforts did not sit well with Churchill. Soon it became apparent to Roosevelt too that while agreement might be reached with Stalin about strategy, there were political questions coming to the fore that could not be resolved. In the end Stalin got a promise that Overlord would be the main Anglo-American effort; that this invasion would be supported by another in southern France; and that both would get priority over all other operations. Thus Stalin helped to bring to a conclusion an effort begun by Stimson and Marshall in 1942. Roosevelt recognized the ironic circumstances, and after the Teheran conference he said to Stimson: "I have thus brought Overlord back to you safe and sound on the ways for accomplishment."[8] But Churchill had acquiesced in the situation, for in September 1943 he rallied to write Field Marshal Jan Christiaan Smuts, the Prime Minister of South Africa: "I hope you will realise that British loyalty to 'Overlord' is keystone to [the] arch of Anglo-American cooperation."[9]

Early in December Roosevelt and Churchill returned to Cairo for the second phase of their conference there. Stalin had already pledged that after the Germans were defeated the Soviet Union would help in the fight against Japan. Churchill argued that a Russian attack on Japan plus the gains being made in the central and southwest Pacific were reason enough for abandoning the proposed amphibious landing in the Bay of Bengal. But Roosevelt and his advisers disagreed: without the amphibious attack the Chinese might withdraw from the war, and Stalin might be unable or unwilling to act against Japan. In the end Roosevelt agreed to cancel the Bay of Bengal action, and even Admiral King went along reluctantly. Roosevelt may have won the battle against too many actions in Europe, but Churchill gained the same "victory" in the Asian theater of planning.

The decision to launch Overlord in May 1944 dominated strategic

---

[8] Stimson and Bundy, *On Active Service*, p. 443.
[9] Winston S. Churchill, *Closing the Ring* (Boston, 1951), p. 131.

thinking during the first half of that year. Roosevelt, Marshall, and Eisenhower had to resist Churchill's continued, strenuous efforts to cancel the invasion of southern France and substitute a drive from Italy into Austria. As always, he was reserving his options to exploit the enemy's weaknesses. The Allies kept the southern French invasion in the plans, but the date had to be shifted to August 1944.

During the six months preceding Overlord, political issues forced their way more and more into military planning. Long battles with de Gaulle made the President wary of setting up any kind of occupation duty that might keep Americans in France. Then, shortly before D Day in Normandy, he tried to trade the designated American "occupation zone" of Germany, in the southern part of that country, for the northern, industrial area slated for British control. But Churchill would not consider such a large-scale and late change in plans.

War was taking its toll on Roosevelt. At Teheran he became ill one evening at dinner and had to retire. By the early part of 1944 his hand trembled when he lit a cigarette. A medical examination revealed that he had an enlarged heart and suffered from hypertension. But no one told the President the seriousness of his condition; he was induced only to cut down on cigarettes, food, and daily work, to get lots of rest, and to take digitalis. Certainly, he looked worn and spent. Yet in this deteriorating condition he decided to go through the rigors of a presidential election and to attend two more international conferences.

The long-awaited invasion of Western Europe began on June 6. Churchill, who had questioned the timing of the operation so long, now wanted to attend the landing and watch it unfold from a cruiser. Fortunately for his safety, King George VI was able to stop him from doing this. But Churchill had his way later on, waving at the troops headed for the beaches of southern France.

Once the Allies were successfully ashore in Normandy and moving inland, a fresh controversy developed among the military men about how the advance to Germany should be conducted. Brooke and the British favored a major thrust to the northeast that would liberate the Low Countries, secure more ports for the landing of Allied supplies, overrun the German V-2 rocket installations, and capture Berlin. In effect, this strategy was intended to give the British and Canadian troops the opportunity for a victorious thrust, while the Americans were holding the Germans in check along a wide front. Not surprisingly, Generals Eisenhower, Bradley, and the Americans preferred a different approach, one that favored general advance along the entire front to bring all the troops into Germany and Austria at about the same time. Here again the American view prevailed. This was due in large measure to the fact that the balance of men and supplies had shifted sharply in favor of the Americans. Later both British General

Sir Bernard L. Montgomery and American General George S. Patton, Jr., argued that if their respective armies had been given ample supplies and encouragement at crucial (but different) times the war would have ended much sooner.

Churchill took a vital interest in the advance into Germany, but Roosevelt, ill, his powers waning, did not. He delegated military decisions to General Marshall, who in turn gave Eisenhower full authority. And generally the President could relax his military responsibility, because the war in Europe was being run the way the American military men wanted it. As the Americans saw the whole course of the war, they had been burned in the past by the political issues involved, both in North Africa and in the Italian campaign, as well as in the planning of Overlord. Finally, the political dimension was left aside, and decisions were being made on the basis of military considerations alone.

Roosevelt and Churchill met again in Quebec in September 1944 to determine the final strategic steps in the war. Germany was not yet defeated, but the end was near. Final arrangements were made about zones of occupation—Roosevelt was willing now to stick with the areas mapped earlier. Churchill enjoyed a minor strategic victory when the American Chiefs of Staff agreed to supply landing craft for British operations on the Istrian peninsula as a prelude to a drive on Vienna. He reciprocated the favor in good spirit, offering British naval and air force units for use against Japan; and the President accepted them. But Admiral King, who had no desire to use non-American units, said only that the use of British ships was being studied. Even with King's reluctance, a general atmosphere of cordiality and cooperation prevailed at this conference, in contrast to those that had preceded it.

The news from the Pacific was good in 1944. In June and July there were successful landings on Saipan, Tinian, and Guam in the Mariana Islands, and this rupture of Japan's inner ring of defense brought down the Tojo government. The Saipan landing also brought out the Japanese navy. At the first battle of the Philippine Sea the United States inflicted heavy damage on Japanese carrier-based planes. Late in July the President went to Pearl Harbor to hear Admiral Chester Nimitz and General MacArthur offer opposing arguments on landing ground forces on Formosa or on Leyte in the Philippines. He heard both men out and then decided to support MacArthur on the Leyte landing. Later, during the Quebec meeting, he received a copy of a message from Admiral William F. Halsey to Admiral Nimitz recommending that the invasion of Leyte be moved up from December 20 to October 20. Further information and support for the earlier date came from Admiral Nimitz and General MacArthur. Marshall conferred with his colleagues and sent back the President's approval of the change. This accelerated return to the Philippines helped to speed up the final stages of the Pacific war.

By the beginning of 1945, the Allies' military prospects were excellent, but political questions were subjecting the alliance to increasingly severe strain. In January Roosevelt and Churchill traveled to Yalta for what was to be their final conference with Stalin. Roosevelt's plan was to enlist Stalin's support for the war against Japan and for the United Nations organization he envisioned as the instrument for international cooperation in the postwar years. Stalin was suspicious of the organization and its procedures, but Roosevelt counted on resolving the difficulties with a face-to-face meeting. For four days the leaders covered routine matters, but on the fifth day Stalin finally brought up the subject of Russian participation in the Pacific war and his price for such a pledge—namely, the lower half of Sakhalin Island and the Kurile Islands. (Japan had taken the former from Russia in 1904 but had purchased the Kuriles under a treaty in 1875.) Roosevelt agreed to this exchange. Further, Stalin asked for and got Roosevelt's approval for the return of the lease on Port Arthur in China to the Soviet Union, the internationalization of the port of Dairen with recognition of the Russians' preeminent interests there, and the recognition of old czarist rights to the Manchurian railroads. (But Stalin agreed that China should retain full sovereignty in Manchuria and that the status quo in Outer Mongolia would be preserved.) Roosevelt's agreement on these points hinged partly on his hope of getting Chiang Kai-shek to agree to them, although in the end the Chinese were told of these arrangements—not consulted. The British also had little part in the arrangements, although Churchill signed the final conference statement on decisions. W. Averell Harriman, then U.S. ambassador to the Soviet Union, told Admiral Leahy about the Yalta arrangements; but so anxious was the President for Russian cooperation that even the Allied military men had little part in the agreements.

Roosevelt left Yalta in a rather optimistic mood, confident that he had achieved at least one of his major objectives—a firm commitment from Stalin to enter the war against Japan soon after Germany's final defeat. The President was especially pleased by this commitment since his advisers assured him that such Russian participation in the Pacific war would save thousands of American lives. But shortly after his return home, the President's optimism began to fade, and the last weeks of his life were partly taken up with increasingly bitter exchanges with Stalin over various military and political issues, and with at least one major disagreement with Churchill, also centering around a crucial military-political issue.

Even at Yalta, of course, the exchanges between Roosevelt, Churchill, and Stalin had not always been cordial, but their approaching victory over Nazi Germany seemed for the moment to cover over their more basic disagreements. But as the day of unconditional surrender drew nearer, old political suspicions came increasingly to the fore once more. Thus by late March the Russians were accusing the United States and Britain of conducing secret surrender negotiations with the Germans in Switzerland—of insisting on something less than the unconditional surrender of the German forces in the West, thus presumably allowing them to continue their last-ditch resistance to the Russians in the East.

Such unfounded charges—as well as the mounting crisis over Poland (of which the world also knew nothing at the time) —were a source of grave concern to Churchill. In late March, therefore, the Prime Minister made one last desperate effort to reorient Anglo-American strategy in Germany with a view to gaining what he regarded as important political objectives. Although the Big Three had previously agreed that Soviet troops would be the first to reach and occupy Vienna and Berlin, Churchill now sought a change of plans that might result in British and American forces being the first to reach the German capital. It soon became clear, however, that General Eisenhower—along with General Marshall—was opposed to such a scheme. When Eisenhower proceeded to communicate directly with Stalin and told him that he proposed to move ahead as originally planned—that is, cutting Germany in two and meeting the Russians in central Germany rather than heading for Berlin—Churchill exploded at Eisenhower's failure to consult his advisers, the Combined Chiefs of Staff, or his political superiors, and for what Churchill regarded as his lack of political judgment.

In the end Roosevelt and Marshall stood firmly behind Eisenhower's "decision to stop at the Elbe." Less than three weeks later, Roosevelt died suddenly, and it remained for succeeding generations to debate the wisdom of his military (and political) policies at Yalta and the strategic decisions of the last weeks of his life.

As a politician, Roosevelt liked to work in an unstructured and competitive environment in which he held all the strings and made all the final decisions. Despite his preference for frenetic activity, he liked to work regular hours, although as his illness progressed he put in shorter days. Certainly he did not like to plan too far ahead or to make decisions before he had to. But the demands of wartime leadership and the needs of the many nations and theaters of operation in his responsibility forced him to work within a military framework patterned after the British system. And the brute facts of limited supplies, shipping, and manpower ultimately forced him to think in terms of priorities and logistics. Yet he strove to do many things simultaneously, even though this meant keeping all parts of the war effort going at varying tempos in all directions. The sheer pitch of the President's operations was hard on him and his associates, but his methods did undoubtedly shorten the war, even though they meant that some things had to be done with slender resources. Remembering the excitement as well as the difficulty, Admiral Leahy later wrote a generous assessment of the wartime presidency: "One of the foundation stones of my admiration for Franklin Roosevelt was my respect for his unswerving determination to honor all pledges made by his government to the governments of other nations and at the same time, in the planning for postwar global adjustments, to permit liberated countries to select for themselves the form of government they desired."[10]

Part of Roosevelt's rather breathless success as a military leader stemmed from the easy and casual way he had with his Chiefs of Staff. He listened carefully to their recommendations, trusted them to do what they were explicitly ordered to do, did not argue, but at times overruled them.[1] They were good subordinates, but they had their worries, ranging from fears that the President was being cowed by Churchill or the Russians to anxieties that a whole campaign might be upset by some political gesture.[2] As the war wore on, Roosevelt's weakening physical condition made him more and more anxious to get the fighting over as soon as possible. Even so, when men, supplies, and equipment became more plentiful, a basic sense of caution restrained him, and he was not tempted to attempt more than was absolutely necessary. Always he tended to compartmentalize military and political affairs, and by 1944 political questions took more and more of his time. All of these—traits, preferences, and circumstances—affected his unquestioned great and warm personal friendship for Churchill. Gradually, Roosevelt's desire to win the war quickly and to give the Soviet Union the long-promised second front came to put him into opposition to some of Churchill's plans, particularly for the Mediterranean. The emergence of political questions also underscored his differences in policy and approach from the British as well as the Russians.

In quite a different and unique way, Winston Churchill was a superb leader of his nation in war. Possessed of an enormous amount

10 Leahy, I Was There, p. 268.

1 According to Kent Roberts Greenfield, Roosevelt overruled the Joint Chiefs of Staff on twenty-six occasions. See Kent Roberts Greenfield, American Strategy in World War II: A Reconsideration (Baltimore, 1963), pp. 56–84. For a criticism of this view see Forrest C. Pogue, "The Wartime Chiefs of Staff and the President" and the comments of other historians in United States Air Force Academy, Soldiers and Statesmen: Proceedings of the Fourth Military History Symposium (Washington, 1973), pp. 69–117.

2 For a quotation from Marshall on the political fears see Pogue, "The Wartime Chiefs of Staff and the President," Soldiers and Statesmen, p. 69.

of energy and an unquenchable curiosity about matters large and small, he had an electric, invigorating quality. His capacity for rich rhetoric enabled him to inspire countless thousands of people to bear great burdens cheerfully. In meetings and conferences he was a formidable contender in argument and enormously persuasive. He worked best in a definite, structured framework of government, although his well-known preference for working long hours was trying for his staff. Even so, the bright men with whom he surrounded himself, matching wits, found working for Churchill a fascinating experience.

Churchill regularly briefed and consulted his military advisers so that each knew the others' points of view. But such candor did not mean that decisions were easily reached. The Prime Minister argued, probed, cajoled, and extracted every item of information possible, along with the factual basis of any objection. His military men had to have well-thought-out, carefully reasoned answers to every question. More than any other man, General Brooke bore the brunt of arguments with the Prime Minister. Like his superior, Brooke liked to get things done quickly, but not at the sacrifice of thinking through the implications of a decision. He refused to be overwhelmed by Churchill's personality, and he did a tremendous job in pointing out the impracticality of some of the Prime Minister's ideas and in demonstrating the need for systematic planning. Of course, he shared most of the Prime Minister's ideas about the most desirable operations in particular situations.

Unlike Roosevelt, Churchill tended to think simultaneously in both military and political terms, and he liked to balance both long- and short-range goals. Sometimes he appeared unwilling to abide by joint decisions, and this tendency made the Americans suspicious that political considerations for the moment were uppermost in his mind. As a result the American military advisers tried to insulate the President against the Prime Minister's arguments. What began as military considerations often carried over into the political area as the war was being won; and in these sensitive areas the differences between the two leaders showed ever more clearly. But these were the quarrels of partners; the reality of the Atlantic alliance was never in doubt. Yet at a fundamental level the two men differed on the shape the postwar world should take. Churchill tended to think regionally and in terms of traditional power politics, while Roosevelt tended to think globally and in idealistic and futuristic terms.

How did those who worked closest with Churchill and Roosevelt view their capacity for wartime leadership? Lord Ismay thought of the Prime Minister as a man with the true instincts of a warrior: "He had far too much imagination to be fearless, but he was pre-eminently

brave."[3] The same thought struck Stalin, who at a Yalta dinner referred to Churchill as "the bravest governmental figure in the world."
Stalin added that he "knew few examples in history where the courage
of one man had been so important to the future history of the world."[4]
When Churchill left office in 1945, General Brooke noted in his
diary the departure of "the greatest war leader of our times, who
guided this country from the very brink of the abyss of destruction to
one of the most complete victories ever known in history."[5]

When Stalin was toasting the British and American leaders at Yalta,
he praised Roosevelt for the Lend-Lease Act. Stalin hailed Roosevelt
as "the chief forger of the instrument which had led to the mobilization of the world against Hitler."[6] The President's long and close
association with General Marshall had enormous implications for the
direction and tempo of the war. But so far as is known Marshall never
left any comment on Roosevelt as a wartime leader. He did, however,
give some insights. At the time of the loss of the Philippines he thought
the President showed courage. He did not let party or election concerns
influence the date of the North African landings, and he gave strong
support during the dark days of the Battle of the Bulge. On the other
hand, Marshall's superior, Secretary of War Stimson, recorded a number of rather critical comments about Roosevelt in the midst of war.
After the President's death, however, he summed up his contributions
to victory with this comment: "On the whole he has been a superb war
President—far more so than any other President of our history."[7] Admiral Leahy, the President's Chief of Staff, had nothing but praise for
Roosevelt: "It was fortunate for our country and particularly for our
Army, Navy, and Air Force, that we had in these critical years a
President with a superb knowledge of international affairs and an almost professional understanding of naval and military operations. I
believe history will record that he exercised greater skill in the direction of our global war effort than did his gallant and brilliant contemporary Winston Churchill."[8]

How has history dealt with the leadership of Roosevelt and Churchill? With the beginning of the cold war, Roosevelt's military and
political decisions in Europe during the final stages of the war came
under strong attack. Questions were raised about why the American
armies advanced in the central and southern part of Germany and let

3 Hastings Ismay, *The Memoirs of General Lord Ismay* (New York, 1960), p.
246.
4 Charles E. Bohlen, *Witness to History 1929–1969* (New York, 1973), p. 182.
5 Bryant, *Triumph in the West*, p. 482.
6 Bohlen, *Witness to History*, p. 182.
7 Stimson and Bundy, *On Active Service*, p. 666.
8 Leahy, *I Was There*, p. 95.

the Russian troops take Berlin. In the dark years immediately after the conflict's end it was easy to believe that if Great Britain had invaded the Balkans and moved northward to clear territory in advance of the Russian offensive, Eastern Europe might not have fallen under Communist control (to use the idiom of the time). This is one of the principal theses of Chester Wilmot's widely influential *The Struggle for Europe* (New York, 1952). This belief, coupled with all the discussion of what was and what was not done at Yalta, provided grist for the mill of political and scholarly argument. Within that context Churchill seemed to be right and Roosevelt terribly wrong in their respective awarenesses of the relationship of politics to military strategy.[9]

So too in the case of the Pacific. The argument here was that the atomic bomb made it unnecessary for the Soviet Union to enter the Pacific war. But Roosevelt insisted on the Russians' presence in the Far East, giving them access thereby to Manchuria, China, and Korea. Ultimately, according to this line of thought, Roosevelt's policy paved the way for the loss of China, the Korean War, and the instability of Asia down to the post-Vietnam years.

However, the publication of memoirs, critiques on strategy, and other studies of the war have put the Balkan and Western European aspects of the question in more accurate perspective. Also, in the case of the Pacific Roosevelt's motivations have become more understandable. For a while Churchill's own massive but incomplete writings stood as a deterrent to any critical study of his role in the war. But with the gradual appearance of official histories and documentary studies it has become easier to compare what Churchill wrote with the official record. The publication of this book, based on recently declassified telegrams between Roosevelt and Churchill, is a step in that process. Also, since Churchill's death critical appraisals of his life and work have appeared. Prominent among them is *Churchill Revised*, written by five British historians and published in 1969. In an analysis of Churchill in that volume Sir Basil Liddell Hart concluded that in World War I Churchill received too much blame and too little credit for his strategic contributions, but that in World War II he was overrated. "In brief," he says, Churchill's "dynamism was too strong for his statesmanship—and his strategy."[10]

[9] For some noteworthy examples see Samuel E. Morison, *Strategy and Compromise* (Boston, 1958); John Ehrman, *Grand Strategy* (London, 1956); J. R. M. Butler, *Grand Strategy* (London, 1957); Michael Howard, *The Mediterranean Strategy in the Second World War* (London, 1968); and Stetson Conn *et al., Command Decisions* (Washington, 1959), especially the chapters by Maurice Matloff and by Richard Leighton.

[10] A. J. P. Taylor *et al., Churchill Revised: A Critical Assessment* (New York, 1969), p. 225. On the whole, in their memoirs and retrospective commentaries, the

James MacGregor Burns, Roosevelt's leading biographer, compared the President with both Stalin and Churchill. In his view, both Stalin and Roosevelt were brilliant tacticians, masters of the art of timing, and superb in playing off adversaries against each other. But Stalin had a much greater ability than Roosevelt to link wartime strategic decisions to long-range security and to stick to them tenaciously.[11] Churchill, for Burns, had a longer but narrower view of the world than Roosevelt and no comprehension of the forces of unrest in Asia or Africa. Both the President and the Prime Minister were opportunistic and preferred to improvise their approach to grand strategy, but Churchill "lacked the comprehensive principles that gave at least a general direction and focus to Roosevelt's day-to-day decisions." Churchill's strategy "drew from intuition and insight rather than long-run purpose and settled goals." Also, the Prime Minister always favored the West in his strategic thinking. He "lacked the steadiness of direction, the comprehensiveness of outlook, the sense of proportion and relevance that mark the grand strategist."[12]

To Burns, Roosevelt the war leader was a divided person. One part of him was dominated by faith, ideals, and a distant vision of a better postwar world, while the other saw the realities of world politics and moved prudently, and with an eye to public opinion, toward narrow, short-run goals without losing any power or authority. The American people were also divided between a generous, idealistic outlook on the war and a strict, self-preservation stance. This "division in the war strategy of Franklin Roosevelt and in the moods and practices of the American people . . . informs all the lesser issues of the war. It was because Roosevelt acted both as a soldier bent on a military victory at

---

British military leadership has been far more critical of Churchill's conduct of the war than their American counterparts have been of Roosevelt's. See, for instance, Sir John Kennedy, *The Business of War* (New York, 1958), by the director of Military Operations of the British army staff 1940–1944. Roosevelt's military leadership also came in for criticism early in the war. Commenting on the President's reported refusal to establish a Joint Intelligence Committee with the British in mid-1941, the American military attaché in London recorded in his diary: "The President apparently could not see the idea, for he objected, saying that he had no man who was capable of doing the work. He cannot seem to understand that this is not a matter of personality so much as it is a matter of organization. It only confirms what I have always heard, which is that Roosevelt knows practically nothing, and cares less, about administration. We are going to pay a high price for this trait in terms of confusion, waste and misunderstanding in Washington. I suppose it is merely a continuation on a grander scale of what has been going on for the last eight years." James Leutze (ed.), *The London Journal of General Raymond E. Lee, 1940–1941* (Boston, 1971), pp. 300–301.

11 James MacGregor Burns, *Roosevelt: Soldier of Freedom* (New York, 1970), p. 551.

12 Burns, *Roosevelt: Soldier of Freedom*, p. 552.

a minimum cost to American lives and as an ideologue bent on achieving the Four Freedoms for peoples throughout the world that his grand strategy was flawed by contradictions that would poison American relations with Russia and with Asia."[13]

[13] Burns, *Roosevelt: Soldier of Freedom*, pp. vii, viii.

3. The Political and Diplomatic Relationship

IF THERE WERE substantial differences of opinion over Roosevelt's and Churchill's military policies, there was even greater controversy over their handling of political and diplomatic affairs. There was no moratorium on public discussion of the subject during the war, and no sooner was the ink dry on the German and Japanese surrenders than Anglo-American wartime diplomacy was subjected to a mounting barrage of criticism.

Most of this disagreement originated in the United States and was directed largely against President Roosevelt's foreign policy before and after Pearl Harbor. To be sure, British diplomacy also came in for a certain amount of criticism during the war. But like the Russians, the British were too preoccupied with the Nazi menace to pay more than cursory attention to Churchill's conduct of foreign policy, with the result that before V-E Day, there were only a handful of important parliamentary debates on British or Anglo-American diplomacy.

After the war, the British found themselves in such dire economic straits that there was little disposition to indulge in protracted debates or recriminations about recent British foreign policy. Such critical inquiries as appeared—like Sir Lewis Namier's brilliant studies[1] and G. M. Young's hostile authorized biography of Prime Minister Stanley Baldwin[2]—were largely concerned with the prewar era of appease-

1 Sir Lewis Namier, *Diplomatic Prelude 1936–1940* (London, 1948) , *Europe in Decay 1936–1940* (London, 1950) , and *In the Nazi Era* (New York, 1952) .
2 G. M. Young, *Stanley Baldwin* (London, 1952) .

[46]

ment, which had helped to destroy France in 1940 and had nearly cost Britain its life.

The attacks on Roosevelt's diplomacy, on the other hand, were many, and the last of them has yet to be heard. It must be remembered that by the summer of 1941 the United States was firmly committed to a policy of all-out aid to Great Britain "short of war," but there was no consensus about American entry into the war. Given the bitterness of the debate about American foreign policy in the months and years before Pearl Harbor,[3] it is not surprising that no sooner had the war come to an end than some of Roosevelt's political enemies began to charge him with major responsibility for the Japanese attack. Indeed, the aftermath of World War II soon proved to be so disturbingly different from what most Americans, whether liberals or conservatives, supporters or critics of the President, had expected that attacks on American wartime diplomacy were only to be expected.

The charges against Roosevelt's foreign policy were both grave and venomous, and they produced long and bitter—if rarely meaningful— debate. Some of Roosevelt's most vociferous critics, especially those on the right, charged that the President had deliberately led or even plotted to get the United States into World War II—a war in which, they believed, there was no compelling interest or reason to become involved.[4] Some of these critics also believed that Roosevelt's diplomacy played straight into Stalin's hands, that the President ought to have listened more carefully to Churchill's hardheaded advice about the menace of Russian communism. Ultimately, these critics charged, the postwar expansion of international communism, beginning in Eastern Europe, was the result of political misjudgments at the White House and the State Department.[5]

On the other hand, there were those observers on the political left, many of whom had long opposed American involvement in a new international conflict, who contended that President Roosevelt remained, to his last day, a devout believer in Soviet-American friend-

---

[3] See Manfred Jonas, *Isolationism in America 1935–1941* (Ithaca, N.Y., 1966) .

[4] "Our principles were right," the America First Committee insisted in its last statement issued after Pearl Harbor. "Had they been followed war could have been avoided." Quoted in Wayne S. Cole, *America First—The Battle Against Intervention 1940–1941* (Madison, Wis., 1953) , p. vii. By the early 1970s, after the United States had withdrawn its troops from Vietnam, it was less unfashionable than formerly to contend that the United States had no business becoming involved in World War II. See Bruce M. Russett, *No Clear and Present Danger—A Skeptical View of the United States Entry into World War II* (New York, 1972) .

[5] See, for instance, Hanson W. Baldwin, *Great Mistakes of the War* (New York, 1950) : "[F]undamentally the British evaluation was politico-military; we ignored the first part of that compound word" (p. 26) . See also Chester Wilmot, *The Struggle for Europe* (New York, 1952) , 714ff.

ship. As many of them saw it, such a friendship alone could have assured lasting peace in the world, but Roosevelt's sudden death and the unfortunate accession of an unprepared and otherwise ill-suited Vice President resulted in a rapid and unnecessary deterioration of U.S.-Soviet relations.[6] In recent years some American New Left historians have suggested that the United States fought the war largely to make the world safe for capitalism—to achieve a worldwide "open door" for American money, goods, and services.[7] In their view, despite all protestations of comradeship and fealty, the United States did not hesitate to use its growing economic power to achieve increasing economic influence within, if not over, the British Empire.[8]

There have been still other critics, including some of the President's former associates and diplomatic representatives—many of whom have given the President low marks for his wartime diplomacy[9]—who be-

[6] See, for instance, the views of the late Norman Thomas and of Robert M. Hutchins, most recently at the Pacem in Terris III convocation in Washington in October 1973. As one leading New Left historian has put it: "[The] possibility [of a *modus vivendi* with the Soviet Union] slowly slipped away as President Harry S. Truman reversed Roosevelt's tactic of accommodation. . . . Upon entering the White House, he did not seek to follow Roosevelt's tactic of adjustment and accommodation." Barton J. Bernstein, ed., *Politics and Policies of the Truman Administration* (Chicago, 1970) , pp. 17, 23. See also Athan Theoharis, "Roosevelt and Truman on Yalta: The Origins of the Cold War," *Political Science Quarterly,* 87 (June 1972) : "The opportunities for détente provided by Yalta were effectively subverted by the Truman administration" (p. 241) .

[7] "The United States' ultimate objective at the end of World War II was both to sustain and to reform world capitalism." Joyce Kolko and Gabriel Kolko, *The Limits of Power—The World and United States Foreign Policy 1945–1954* (New York, 1972) , p. 11. See also Gabriel Kolko, *The Politics of War—The World and United States Foreign Policy 1943–1945* (New York, 1968) ; Warren F. Kimball, "Lend Lease and the Open Door: The Temptation of British Opulence 1937–1942," *Political Science Quarterly,* 86 (June 1971) ; and Lloyd C. Gardner, Walter F. LaFeber, and Thomas J. McCormick, *Creation of the American Empire—U.S. Diplomatic History* (Chicago, 1973) , pp. 423ff.

[8] Kolko and Kolko, *Limits of Power,* pp. 6off. See also Robert Freeman Smith, "American Foreign Relations 1920–1942," in Barton J. Bernstein, ed., *Toward a New Past—Dissenting Essays in American History* (New York, 1968) : "The actual defense of the United States was one factor involved in the move to an 'all-out aid short of war' policy, but the restoration of the Open Door world order was of at least equal importance to the Roosevelt administration. . . . The British were in desperate straits in March 1941, but many United States officials seemed more concerned with squeezing concessions from them—as *quid pro quo* for Lend Lease aid—than with the war effort" (p. 251) .

[9] See, for instance, George F. Kennan, *Memoirs 1925–1950* (Boston, 1967), pp. 123, 164, 171–173, 214–215, 221. The late Charles E. Bohlen, who served as the President's interpreter at Teheran and Yalta, has written: "A deeper knowledge of history and certainly a better understanding of reactions of foreign peoples would have been

lieved, or seemed to suggest, that there was far too much political and diplomatic improvisation in Washington during the war, and that the lack of advance planning there and in London precipitated such problems as the series of dangerous Berlin crises which began in the spring of 1948.[10]

Now that the secret Roosevelt-Churchill correspondence is available in its entirety, it is possible to answer with reasonable certainty some of the most serious issues that have been raised, and to reach a more balanced assessment of Roosevelt's and Churchill's political and diplomatic leadership during the war.

No more serious charge has been brought against Roosevelt, and none has produced more bitter and extended debate, than the allegation implicitly made during the congressional hearings on Pearl Harbor in 1945–1946 that, as Harry Elmer Barnes wrote: "Roosevelt lied this country into the second World War."[1]—a statement echoed in *The New York Times* by Clare Boothe Luce as late as 1973.[2] Barnes also charged that "the full extent of [Roosevelt's] commitments to

---

useful to the President. . . . As far as the Soviets were concerned, I do not think Roosevelt had any real comprehension of the great gulf that separated the thinking of a Bolshevik from a non-Bolshevik, and particularly from an American. . . . [H]e did not understand . . . that Stalin's enmity was based on profound ideological convictions. The existence of a gap between the Soviet Union and the United States, a gap that could not be bridged, was never fully perceived by Franklin Roosevelt." *Witness to History*, pp. 210–211. Such criticism of Roosevelt as diplomat has not been limited to American observers and associates of the President. In *The Continuing Battle—Memoirs of a European 1936–1966* (Boston, 1972), the late Paul-Henri Spaak recalled with considerable bitterness his first meeting with Roosevelt at the White House in 1941: "I explained to him the food situation in occupied Belgium and exerted all my powers of persuasion to interest him in the fate of my compatriots. . . . When I had ended my plea, he declared coldly, without betraying the slightest sign of human warmth or compassion, that nothing could be done. This unfeeling answer was accompanied by comments which angered me, and this anger was all the harder to contain as I was forced to hide it. He declared that the trials through which Belgium was passing were not so tragic, that Germany had gone through much the same experience after the first World War and had yet produced a generation that was physically fit; the proof of this could be seen in the way the Germans were now fighting" (pp. 97–98) .

10 See Robert Murphy, *Diplomat Among Warriors* (New York, 1964) ; and the circumspect essays of Philip Mosely, *The Kremlin and World Politics* (New York, 1960) , esp. pt. 2.

1 Harry Elmer Barnes, *Perpetual War for Perpetual Peace* (Caldwell, Id., 1953), p. 652. That this revisionist school is by no means played out is indicated by James J. Martin, *American Liberalism and World Politics 1931–1941*, 2 vols. (New York, 1964) ; and by Kemp Tolley, "The Strange Mission of the *Lanikai*," *American Heritage*, 24 (October 1973) , and *The Cruise of the "Lanikai"* (Annapolis, 1973) .

2 "Democratic Strategy and Watergate," *The New York Times*, June 3, 1973.

Britain will not be known until the nearly two thousand secret communications between him and Prime Minister Churchill are revealed to scholars."[3]

The Roosevelt-Churchill correspondence lends no substance whatever to such charges. To begin with, during the first nine months of the war Roosevelt and Churchill exchanged relatively few messages. Although Roosevelt made no effort to disguise his personal sympathies for Britain and France, when in February 1940 he dispatched Undersecretary of State Sumner Welles on an extended fact-finding mission to Europe he carefully stipulated that "Mr. Welles will, of course, be authorized to make no proposals or commitments in the name of the Government of the United States."[4] There is every indication that, during his month-long mission to Berlin, London, Paris, and Rome, Welles adhered faithfully to the President's instructions.[5]

Nor did Roosevelt dispense with diplomatic circumspection when the German blitzkrieg in the West began on May 10, 1940. Five days after becoming Prime Minister, Churchill sent Roosevelt the first of many urgent appeals for military assistance—asking the President "to help us with everything short of actually engaging armed forces," beginning with "the loan of forty or fifty of your older destroyers," and adding for emphasis: "I trust you realise, Mr. President, that the voice and force of the United States may count for nothing if they are withheld too long." Roosevelt replied discreetly the following day that he was "giving every possible consideration to the suggestions made in your message." But in regard to the request for destroyers he told the Prime Minister: "As you know a step of that kind could not be taken except with the specific authorization of the Congress and I am not certain that it would be wise for that suggestion to be made at the moment."

Roosevelt proved himself even more circumspect when, at the height of the battle of France, on June 10, 1940, French Premier Paul Reynaud beseeched the President "to declare publicly that the United States will give the Allies aid and material support by all means 'short of an expeditionary force.' "[6] After waiting three days, Roosevelt replied that he was "moved very deeply" by Reynaud's message, adding that "this Government is doing everything in its power to make available to the Allied Governments the material they so

---

3 Barnes, *Perpetual War for Perpetual Peace*, p. 634.

4 U.S. Department of State, *Foreign Relations of the United States 1940*, 1 (Washington, 1959) : 4. Henceforth cited as *FR*.

5 Sir Llewellyn Woodward, *British Foreign Policy in the Second World War*, 1 (London, 1970) : 167ff.

6 *FR 1940*, 1: 246.

urgently require, and our efforts to do still more are being redoubled."[7] But when Churchill appealed to Roosevelt to publish his "magnificent message [which] may play a decisive part in turning the course of world history," Roosevelt answered that he was "unable to comply." He emphasized that his message to Reynaud "was in no sense intended to commit and did not commit this Government to military participation in support of the Allied Governments. You well know that there is no authority under our Constitution except in the Congress to make any commitment of this nature." The following day Reynaud resigned, and his successor, Marshal Henri Philippe Pétain, moved immediately to obtain an armistice with Germany.

Roosevelt has been much criticized for a remark made during his campaign speech in Boston on October 30, 1940: "And while I am talking to you mothers and fathers, I give you one more assurance. I have said this before, but I shall say it again and again and again: Your boys are not going to be sent into any foreign wars. . . . The purpose of our defense is defense."[8] But there is no evidence in the Roosevelt-Churchill correspondence to suggest that Roosevelt believed anything different, or that he was about to make any secret commitment to Churchill for American entry into the war. On the contrary, although Churchill's assessment of the military situation proved to have been overly optimistic, there is every reason to think that he meant what he said in his famous transatlantic broadcast of February 9, 1941: "Give us the tools and we will finish the job"[9]—without U.S. participation in the war.

During the year following the defeat of France, while Britain stood alone against the German onslaught, Churchill continued to request, and to receive, increasing amounts of military assistance from the United States, especially after the passage of the Lend-Lease bill in March 1941. In the bitter debates over that historic legislation, many of its opponents suggested that its enactment meant certain American entry into the war.[10] But nothing in the Roosevelt-Churchill corre-

7 FR 1940, 1: 248. See also John McVickar Haight, *American Aid to France 1938–1940* (New York, 1970).

8 Samuel I. Rosenman, ed., *The Public Papers and Addresses of Franklin D. Roosevelt*, vol. 9, *1940: War—and Aid to Democracies* (New York, 1941), p. 517. Henceforth cited as *PPR*.

9 Winston S. Churchill, *The Grand Alliance* (Boston, 1950), p. 128.

10 Cole, *America First*, pp. 44–46. Charles A. Lindbergh told the House Foreign Affairs Committee during the 1941 lend-lease hearings: "We are strong enough in this nation and in this hemisphere to maintain our own way of life regardless of . . . the attitude . . . on the other side. I do not believe we are strong enough to impose our way of life on Europe and on Asia." Quoted in Burns, *Roosevelt: Soldier of Freedom*, p. 46.

spondence suggests that the President and the Prime Minister viewed the legislation in such a light. In this connection, it is important to note that on May 3, 1941, following the disastrous British defeats in Greece and Crete, Churchill did indeed ask Roosevelt that the United States "immediately range itself with us as a belligerent power," only to have his request—the only one of its kind ever sent to Roosevelt— politely ignored.

As the German and Japanese menace continued to spread throughout Europe, Africa, and the Far East in the spring and summer of 1941, the United States appeared to draw slowly but steadily closer to war. America had long abandoned all pretense of neutrality. Germany and Japan had recognized and in effect accepted this position.[1] So also, although they later seemed to forget it, had most American isolationists, who knew perfectly well what information Congress had received and what actions it had approved. What was happening abroad and how America responded were clear for all the world to see. Roosevelt had made no secret commitments to Churchill in 1940 and would make none in 1941.

Indeed, it was Roosevelt's studied refusal even to consider Churchill's dramatic proposal of May 3, 1941, that made the Prime Minister all the more anxious to have a face-to-face meeting with the President. During the Atlantic conference at Argentia Bay, in August 1941, he hoped to obtain pledges for substantial American military and political commitments. Churchill was especially concerned about the deteriorating situation in the Far East, which had become even more serious since the Japanese takeover of southern Indochina in July 1941. But this hope was soon dashed. Roosevelt, who evidently regarded the fate of Indochina as a matter of great importance to the United States, had already responded to the Japanese takeover by freezing all Japanese assets in the United States.[2] But as Churchill was soon to learn, the President was not, for the moment at least, prepared to go beyond such action. Nor was he prepared to make substantive commitments on other fronts.

The most dramatic result of the first Roosevelt-Churchill meeting was, of course, the Atlantic Charter;[3] and there were isolationist critics

[1] See Andreas Hillgruber, *Hitlers Strategie—Politik und Kriegführung 1940–1941* (Frankfurt, 1965), pp. 401ff., 553ff.; James V. Compton, *The Swastika and the Eagle—Hitler, the United States, and the Origins of World War II* (Boston, 1967); Saul Friedlander, *Prelude to Downfall—Hitler and the United States 1939–1941* (New York, 1967); and Alton Frye, *Nazi Germany and the American Hemisphere 1933–1941* (New Haven, 1967).

[2] *PPR*, vol. 10, *1941: The Call to Battle Stations* (New York, 1950), no. 68.

[3] For the text of the Atlantic Charter, see *FR 1941*, 1 (Washington, 1958): 367–369.

of Roosevelt in the United States who viewed that declaration as further evidence of the President's determination to involve his country in the war as soon as possible.[4] Yet the available evidence, including the Roosevelt-Churchill correspondence, not only fails to support such charges but clearly refutes them.

Journeying to his first summit meeting with Churchill, Roosevelt was his usual paradoxical self. He wanted to demonstrate to friend and foe alike that the United States stood unshakably committed to the defense of Britain, and to reassure Churchill of continued and increasing military assistance "short of war." But as soon as the meeting got under way the President made it clear that he would enter into no military or political commitments "except as authorized under the terms of the Lend-Lease Act." To the Prime Minister's dismay, he proposed that he and Churchill issue identical statements to that effect in order to "make it impossible for extreme isolationist leaders in the United States to allege that every kind of secret agreement had been entered into during the course of these negotiations."[5]

Nor was Roosevelt disposed to issue further warnings to Japan at that time because he "felt very strongly that every effort should be made to prevent war with Japan."[6] As for Churchill's request that the President express support for an "effective international organization," Roosevelt refused "because of the suspicions and opposition that [such an agreement] on his part would create in the United States."[7] Indeed, Roosevelt wanted no concrete plans and no commitments at all.

To some extent, Roosevelt's reluctance to translate generalizations into policy stemmed from his historical mindedness. As the late Herbert Feis has noted, American policies during the war "were much colored by the recollections of the decision makers of past experiences or events."[8] Roosevelt, who had already informed Churchill on July 14, 1941, that he wanted no repetition of the secret agreements of World War I, hardly needed to remind the Prime Minister that he had no intention of repeating what he considered one of President Wilson's most egregious blunders. He therefore warmly welcomed the statement of the Permanent Undersecretary of State for Foreign

[4] So, for instance, Senator Robert A. Taft of Ohio in the *Washington Evening Star*, August 16, 1941.

[5] *FR 1941*, 1: 360.

[6] *FR 1941*, 1: 358.

[7] *FR 1941*, 1: 363.

[8] Herbert Feis, "Some Notes on Historical Record-Keeping, the Role of Historians, and the Influence of Historical Memories During the Era of the Second World War," in Francis L. Loewenheim, ed., *The Historian and the Diplomat—The Role of History and Historians in American Foreign Policy* (New York, 1967), p. 106.

Affairs, Sir Alexander Cadogan, that he would give "the most specific and positive assurance that the British had entered into no agreements and had made no commitments which had to do with frontiers or territorial adjustments with one possible exception"[9]—an unimportant one relating to Istria.

Although the intellectual and political significance of the Atlantic Charter, as well as its propaganda value, was incalculable, Roosevelt and Churchill neither signed the joint declaration nor made any specific plans to implement it.[10] This failure was not accidental. Even a year later Churchill remained wary of applying the Charter to specific situations. "We considered the wording of that famous document line by line together," he wrote anxiously to the President in August 1942, "and I should not be able, without mature considerations, to give it a wider interpretation. Its proposed application to Asia and Africa require much thought. . . . [I]n the Middle East the Arabs might claim by majority they could expel the Jews from Palestine, or at any time forbid all further immigration. I am strongly wedded to the Zionist policy, of which I was one of the authors. This is only one of the many unforeseen cases which will arise from new and further declarations." Roosevelt took the hint with little reluctance.

The Atlantic conference had been intended, in part at least, as a demonstration of continued Anglo-American solidarity, aimed at discouraging further German and Japanese aggression; but in this respect its mission soon proved a dismal failure. The Germans, while moving steadily closer to Leningrad, Moscow, and Kiev, intensified their ferocious submarine warfare in the Atlantic, posing an ever increasing threat to Britain's lifeline to the United States. In the Far East the Japanese poured additional reinforcements into Indochina and threatened further moves elsewhere in the South Pacific and Southeast Asia.

Roosevelt and Churchill found themselves in a dilemma. They knew, or thought they knew, what needed to be done to halt the spread of aggression, but Churchill lacked the means to do so and Roosevelt the domestic political support necessary to respond boldly to the Axis challenge. Roosevelt found himself, not for the first time

---

9 *FR 1941*, 1: 351–352.

10 When Roosevelt revealed this to the press on December 19, 1944, the disclosure understandably produced something of a sensation. "There isn't," said the President rather nonchalantly on that occasion, "any copy of the Atlantic Charter, so far as I know. I haven't got one. The British haven't got one. The nearest thing you will find is the radio operator on the *Augusta* and on the *Prince of Wales*. . . . It's one of the things that was agreed to on board ship, and there was no formal document. And the aides were directed to have the scribbled thing . . . sent off to the British government, and to the United States government, and released to the press. That is the Atlantic Charter." *Complete Presidential Press Conferences of Franklin D. Roosevelt* (New York, 1972), 11: 266–267. Henceforth cited as *PPC*.

during his presidency, in the anomalous position of warning his countrymen against the mounting dangers of aggression, without, at the same time, being prepared—militarily or politically—to check the mortal threat posed to America's principal ally and hence to the United States itself.[1]

In the weeks after Argentia Bay a mood of caution pervaded the Roosevelt-Churchill correspondence. Thus, while he continued his requests for American logistical support, Churchill carefully disavowed the need for "a large despatch of United States forces to Europe or Africa . . . in any period we can reasonably foresee in the future." And while Roosevelt proposed to ask Congress for authority to send American ships directly into British ports, he told Churchill, on November 7, that "after long conferences with congressional leaders, I have reached the conclusion that it would be disastrous to this legislation if one of our transports proceeding to or from Britain and in British water or British ports were to be sunk, when manned by U.S. Navy officers and men."

In September naval confrontation between Germany and the United States came into the open. On September 5 the U.S. destroyer *Greer* was attacked by a German submarine, and a month later the destroyers *Kearny* and *Robin Moor* were torpedoed, with the loss of 126 lives. Roosevelt bitterly denounced the German attacks: "From now on, if German . . . vessels of war enter these waters, the protection of which is necessary for American defense, they do so at their own peril."[2] The attacks on American warships ceased, but the sinkings of merchantmen bound for Great Britain continued to mount at an alarming rate, and Roosevelt and Churchill seemed powerless to reduce the toll.

The Atlantic remained Roosevelt's first concern in the early autumn of 1941; but the situation in the Far East continued to deteriorate, and Roosevelt and Churchill became increasingly concerned about it. In private, Roosevelt talked alternately tough and conciliatory with the Japanese negotiators, Kichisaburo Nomura and Saburo Kurusu, but neither tactic brought results. The Japanese strategy clearly was "talk and expand," and Roosevelt and Churchill were uncertain how to respond to Tokyo.[3]

On October 15 Roosevelt cabled Churchill prophetically: "The Jap

---

1 See Burns, *Roosevelt: Soldier of Freedom*, pp. 148ff.; and William L. Langer and S. Everett Gleason, *The Undeclared War 1940–1941* (New York, 1953), pp. 732ff. As late as October 1941 public opinion polls showed that between 75 and 80 percent of the population still strenuously opposed direct American intervention in the war.

2 *PPR*, vol. 10, no. 56.

3 Burns, *Roosevelt: Soldier of Freedom*, pp. 134ff., 193ff.; and Langer and Gleason, *Undeclared War*, pp. 842ff.

situation is definitely worse and I think they are headed north—however, in spite of this you and I have two months of respite in the Far East." On November 2 Churchill replied: "The firmer your attitude and ours, the less chance of their taking the plunge." A few days later, the President told Churchill that he favored continued military buildup but opposed "formalized verbal warning." On November 24 Roosevelt informed Churchill of the Japanese *modus vivendi* proposals—which were completely unacceptable to him—and the American counterproposals: "I am not very hopeful and we must all be prepared for . . . trouble, possibly soon."

Although neither Roosevelt nor Churchill was aware of it, the Japanese had already decided on war. Churchill, who was not in the habit of offering political advice to Roosevelt, opposed further concessions at the expense of China: "It is for you to handle this and we certainly do not want an additional war. . . . Our anxiety is about China. If they collapse our joint danger would enormously increase." Churchill, to be sure, preferred the United States as a full-fledged ally rather than as an unpredictable and distracted nonbelligerent, but he feared that an Asian war would further reduce American support to Britain. Up to the end he hoped that strong diplomatic language to Tokyo would suffice. On November 30 he told Roosevelt: "One important step remains unused in averting war between Japan and our two countries, namely a plain declaration, secret or public as may be thought best, that any further act of aggression by Japan will lead to the gravest consequences. I realise your constitutional difficulties, but it would be tragic if Japan drifted into war by encroachment without having before her fairly and squarely the dire character of a further aggressive step."

Churchill was mistaken. There is no evidence that any such warning would have made the slightest difference to the Japanese.[4] By November 30 Admiral Isoroku Yamamoto's fleet was heading toward Hawaii, and a week later—to Churchill's as to Roosevelt's dismay and surprise—the Japanese struck at Pearl Harbor.

If the success of the Pearl Harbor attack was largely the result of tactical surprise, the striking Japanese victories that soon followed—in Malaya, the Philippines, the Dutch East Indies, Thailand, Hong Kong, Guam, Midway, and Wake—came from years of political appeasement and military and naval unpreparedness. For nearly a year following Pearl Harbor Roosevelt and Churchill had to spend most of their energies trying to reverse the dire military situation in which Britain and the United States now found themselves.

---

4 See Nobutaka Ike, ed., *Japan's Decision for War: Records of the 1941 Policy Conferences* (Stanford, 1967) .

When Churchill arrived at the White House just before Christmas 1941 for the first of his wartime visits, military matters were uppermost in his mind. Roosevelt shared this concern, although the President also believed that it was time for another statement of political principles and objectives—of the anti-Axis coalition newly christened the United Nations.

Following a week of deliberations and intensive diplomatic activity, Roosevelt and Churchill agreed on the wording of what became known as the Declaration by the United Nations, and the document was formally signed by the United States, Great Britain, the Soviet Union, and China at the White House on New Year's Day. In the new declaration the four nations, joined later by nearly two dozen other governments, formally "subscribed to [the] common program of purposes and principles . . . known as the Atlantic Charter." They expressed their conviction that "complete victory over their enemies is essential to defend life, liberty, independence, and religious freedom and to preserve human rights and justice in their own lands as well as in other lands."[5] Stalin's support was obtained only after prolonged haggling over the term "freedom of religion," and the Free French were not invited to sign on the ground that they did not constitute a government.

The United Nations received the new declaration with enthusiasm, and for a time the fledgling alliance enjoyed something of a political honeymoon. Roosevelt and Churchill believed, or appeared to assume, that the Stalin regime was at last becoming less repressive or at least somewhat more responsive to international opinion. It seems not to have occurred either to the President or to the Prime Minister that Stalin's cooperativeness might be a passing phenomenon born of military necessity. Such guilelessness seems rather surprising not only for Churchill, whose anti-Communist credentials were of long standing, but for Roosevelt as well. The President had been deeply disappointed by the Russians' failure to live up to the terms of the 1933 recognition agreement; he disliked the Soviet ambassador in Washington, Constantine Oumansky; and he had been outraged by the Nazi-Soviet nonaggression pact of August 1939 and by the unprovoked Russian attack on Finland shortly after.[6] But Roosevelt and Churchill

5 *PPR*, vol. 11, *1942: Humanity on the Defensive* (New York, 1950), no. 1.

6 Burns, *Roosevelt: Soldier of Freedom*, pp. 102ff. "I think," said Roosevelt, "we should match every Soviet annoyance by a similar annoyance here against them." Donald G. Bishop, *The Roosevelt-Litvinov Agreements—The American View* (Syracuse, N.Y., 1965), p. 231. "More than twenty years ago," Roosevelt told the delegates to the pro-Soviet American Youth Congress in Washington in February 1940, "while most of you were very young children, I had the utmost sympathy for the Russian people. . . . I, with many of you, hoped that Russia would work out its own

found themselves in the same military boat as Stalin. They may also have taken Stalin's concurrence in the Declaration of the United Nations, with its specific endorsement of the Atlantic Charter, as an indication that the Soviet regime was undergoing one of its periodic transformations.

In any event, Stalin's apparently more cooperative new attitude soon proved deceptive. Even while Russian military fortunes were at their lowest, Stalin demanded of British Foreign Secretary Eden, who was visiting Moscow while Churchill prepared to go to Washington, that the British formally recognize the Soviet frontiers of June 1941, including Russian acquisitions in Poland, Rumania, Finland, and the Baltic States.[7]

Perhaps the most important aspect of the first Washington conference was the action that was not accomplished there. The United

---

problems, and that its government would eventually become a peace-loving, popular government with a free ballot, which would not interfere with the integrity of its neighbors. That hope is today either shattered or put away in storage against some better day. The Soviet Union, as everybody who has the courage to face the facts knows, is run by a dictatorship as absolute as any other dictatorship in the world. It has allied itself with another dictatorship, and it has invaded a neighbor so infinitesimally small that it could do no conceivable possible harm to the Soviet Union, a neighbor which seeks only to live at peace as a democracy, and a liberal, forward-looking democracy." *PPR*, vol. 9, p. 93. "It was," Charles E. Bohlen wrote later, "the first and, I believe, the only time [Roosevelt] had been booed and hissed by an audience as President of the United States." *The Transformation of American Foreign Policy* (New York, 1969), p. 63.

7 *The Memoirs of Anthony Eden, Earl of Avon*, vol. 2, *The Reckoning* (Boston, 1965), pp. 335ff. Henceforth cited as Eden, *Memoirs*. See also Woodward, *British Foreign Policy*, 2 (London, 1971): "At the time when Mr. Roosevelt suggested the term 'United Nations' . . . there were already signs, especially in the Russian attitude of aloofness and suspicion, that the problem of restoring political liberty, independence, and a sense of security to the states of Europe would not be solved merely by the defeat of Hitler" (p. 219). On December 20, while en route to Washington, Churchill had cabled that Great Britain would not make any agreement, "secret or public, direct or indirect," about postwar frontiers without consulting the United States and that "frontier questions . . . can only be resolved at the Peace Conference" (p. 235). Early in February 1942 a detailed report of the Anglo-Soviet discussions reached Assistant Secretary of State Adolf A. Berle, Jr., who recorded: "I see no reason why we should object to [the small countries of Eastern Europe] being within the orbit of Russia, provided we are assured that the U.S.S.R. would not use this power to subvert the governments, and set up a regime of terror and cruelty among the peoples—in other words, deal with the situation as they dealt with the Baltic countries. . . . This is, indeed, the chief distinction which exists between a power which seeks world domination and a power which does not." Beatrice Bishop Berle and Travis Beal Jacobs, eds., *Navigating the Rapids 1918–1971: From the Papers of Adolf A. Berle* (New York, 1973), p. 401. Henceforth cited as *Berle Papers*.

Nations Declaration expressed the President's strong desire to provide the new anti-Axis coalition with a political platform; but like the Atlantic Charter it suffered from Roosevelt's not infrequent failure to provide for machinery to translate his lofty rhetoric into political reality. This omission was all the more interesting when it is remembered that Roosevelt and Churchill established the Combined Chiefs of Staff, whose principal purpose was to develop and implement a future grand strategy for Britain and the United States.[8] That they established no political equivalent of the Combined Chiefs is not surprising considering the state of the war.[9] But they made no efforts in that direction even when the military tide had turned in their favor. This failure to plan ahead in politics and diplomacy was in a sense a continuation of prewar American and British policy; it also expressed Roosevelt's repeatedly stated feeling that the overriding purpose of the war was the total defeat of the Axis powers. The President worried that political and diplomatic issues would dissipate the energies and unity of the Grand Alliance.[10] Of course, even in the darkest days of the war, when virtually all their time and energy were devoted to military operations, politics and diplomacy were never entirely removed from Roosevelt's and Churchill's sphere of attention.

Thus early in 1942 Churchill gruffly dismissed any suggestion that he barter lend-lease assistance for a postwar abolition or relaxation of the imperial preference system, to which the United States had long objected. Not long after, he let Roosevelt know in no uncertain terms that Great Britain was not prepared to grant political autonomy to India while the war was in progress. In both instances, Roosevelt found it desirable not to press Churchill on his strongly held position.

As regards the political future of North Africa, where Anglo-American forces under General Eisenhower landed early in November 1942, Roosevelt and Churchill were as one—in their planlessness. The one point on which they readily agreed was that Charles de Gaulle was to be kept out of the operation and was not to be entrusted with any significant share of political authority and influence. It seems likely that both Roosevelt and Churchill were surprised by the public uproar

8 Ray S. Cline, *Washington Command Post—The Operations Division* (Washington, 1951), pp. 100–101.

9 A civil affairs committee was attached to the Combined Chiefs of Staff from the beginning, but its work remained largely technical and unconcerned with large political issues.

10 Stanley K. Hornbeck, State Department Advisor on Political Relations, was disturbed by this lack of long-range planning, as was Adolf Berle, to whom Roosevelt had remarked in June 1941: "I have not the slightest objection to your trying your hand at an outline of the post-war picture. But for Heaven's sake don't ever let the columnists hear of it." Burns, *Roosevelt: Soldier of Freedom*, p. 129. This was doubtless still Roosevelt's position six months later.

in Britain and the United States over the agreement appointing the Vichyite Admiral Jean François Darlan as political head of French North Africa under General Eisenhower—until Darlan's assassination a few weeks later. Apparently, though, Churchill was uneasy all along about the appointment, and later he repeatedly reminded Roosevelt of how he had steadfastly supported him on the "Darlan deal" in the face of bitter domestic opposition.

Roosevelt and Churchill seem not to have learned much from the awkward consequences of their lack of political planning in North Africa. When he journeyed to meet Churchill at Casablanca in January 1943, Roosevelt deliberately came unaccompanied by any senior members of the State Department. He announced his dramatic "unconditional surrender" policy at the close of this conference. This phrase may have been partly based on a State Department memorandum,[1] yet he kept Secretary of State Cordell Hull in the dark about his intentions in this regard,[2] and there is no evidence that he consulted either with Undersecretary Welles.

Even more difficult political problems confronted Roosevelt and Churchill in Italy. Once King Victor Emmanuel III had dismissed Mussolini (July 25, 1943) and Italy had surrendered the day British forces landed on the mainland (September 3, 1943), the question arose as to what sort of government Italy should now have. In North Africa Churchill had taken a stern anti-Fascist and anti-Nazi position. Now Roosevelt and Churchill agreed in principle that they would support any regime that could govern effectively and lend adequate support to the Allied war effort.

In practice, however, the two leaders soon found themselves in serious disagreement. The President, and American opinion generally, favored the prompt return of Count Carlo Sforza, the distinguished anti-Fascist exile, and the early abdication of Victor Emmanuel. Churchill, on the other hand, was highly suspicious of Sforza—as of some other moderate or liberal politicians—and was in no hurry to see the King replaced. The passage of time did nothing to moderate the differences between London and Washington, and when, late in 1944, Churchill vetoed for the second time the appointment of Sforza as Foreign Minister, the State Department, now headed by Edward R. Stettinius, Jr., issued a formal statement unmistakably disassociating itself from the British action.[3] Churchill's reply on December 6 was

1 Burns, *Roosevelt: Soldier of Freedom*, p. 323.

2 Cordell Hull, *The Memoirs of Cordell Hull*, 2 vols. (New York, 1948), 2: 1570. Henceforth cited as Hull, *Memoirs*.

3 In his statement of December 5, 1944, Stettinius "reaffirmed to both the British and Italian governments that we expect the Italians to work out their problems of

probably his angriest message to Roosevelt during the war: "I feel
. . . entitled to remind you that on every single occasion in the course
of this war I have loyally tried to support any statement to which you
were personally committed. . . . I do not remember anything that the
State Department has ever said about Russia or any other Allied state
comparable to this document with which Mr. Stettinius has inaugurated his assumption of office. I am sure such things have never been
said by the State Department about Russia even when very harsh
communications have been received and harsher deeds done."[4]

Roosevelt replied the same day: "I deplore any offense which the
press release . . . may have given you personally or any implication of
my lack of understanding for your responsibility before your country.
You must recognize, however, the untenable position in which we were
put. . . . While military operations continue, Italy is an area of
combined responsibility and our silence . . . made it appear that we
agreed with the action taken. . . . In the circumstances we had no
other choice than to make our own position clear." The letter did
little to soothe Churchill's bitter resentment. His veto on Sforza stuck,
and there were to be no closer nor more effective political consultations
between the President and the Prime Minister as a result of this highly
unpleasant affair.

One result of this failure was that in Greece, as in Italy, Roosevelt
and Churchill found themselves disagreeing over politics. As early as
1943 a State Department memorandum expressed concern that Britain
might seek to reimpose the exiled Greek monarch George II, and that,
if the United States failed to pay heed to widespread opposition in
Greece to such a move, the Greeks might turn for assistance to the
Soviet Union.[5] Curiously, at Cairo in November and December 1943
the roles were momentarily reversed, with Churchill seeking to persuade George II to abdicate,[6] and Roosevelt personally urging him to
stay on.[7]

By the end of 1944, however, the British were clearly seeking to
maintain the monarchy (if not George II himself), and they likewise
found it necessary to bring in a sizable number of troops to quell a
budding Communist-supported rebellion. As the war went on, it be-

---

government along democratic lines without influence from outside." Richard L.
Walker, *E. R. Stettinius, Jr.* (New York, 1965), p. 30.

[4] This was not new American policy in regard to Italy. As early as August 19,
1944, Secretary of State Hull had asked to be informed only about appointees to important posts in Italy. *FR 1944*, 3 (Washington, 1965) : 1145.

[5] *FR 1943*, 4 (Washington, 1964) : 126–127.

[6] Eden, *Memoirs*, 2: 498.

[7] U.S. Department of State, *The Conferences at Cairo and Tehran 1943* (Washington, 1961) , p. 844.

came clear that Churchill was increasingly concerned about the rise of political and social radicalism in liberated areas. This was true in Italy in 1944 and it soon became true in Greece as well.

In the United States, however, there was mounting opposition to Churchill's Greek policy, and Roosevelt found himself once more in the embarrassing position of having—privately at least—to disassociate himself from the Prime Minister's course of action. "As anxious as I am to be of the greatest help to you in this trying situation," Roosevelt wrote shortly after his reelection, "there are limitations imposed by the traditional policies of the United States and in part by the mounting adverse reaction of public opinion in this country. No one will understand better than yourself that I, both personally and as head of state, am necessarily responsive to the state of public feeling. It is for these reasons that it has not been possible for this Government to take a stand along with you in the present course of events." In this instance too Churchill remained unmoved by Roosevelt's remonstrance. The British succeeded in putting down the Communist revolt that Stalin himself found it desirable to disown, six weeks later, at the Yalta conference.[8]

Elsewhere in the Balkans, Roosevelt and Churchill found themselves alternately in agreement and disagreement. In Yugoslavia, Churchill early adopted a strong position in favor of Marshal Josip Broz Tito, head of the Communist guerrilla forces, and before long he persuaded Roosevelt to follow him.[9] Moreover, for reasons that are still obscure, but possibly related to Churchill's undoubted awareness of Great Britain's growing political weakness, in the summer and fall of 1944 Churchill moved openly toward a division of the Balkans into British and Russian spheres of influence. Roosevelt learned of British efforts in this direction by chance[10] and at once strongly protested. But

[8] U.S. Department of State, *The Conferences at Malta and Yalta 1945* (Washington, 1955), p. 782.

[9] For the curious circumstances surrounding Churchill's policy, see the informed account of Walter R. Roberts, *Tito, Mihailović, and the Allies 1941–1945* (New Brunswick, N.J., 1973).

[10] Woodward, *British Foreign Policy*, 3 (London, 1971): 115ff. This particular incident was one of Roosevelt's disconcerting excursions into personal diplomacy. Churchill first informed Roosevelt of the British plan on May 31; the President replied on June 10 generally deploring the British position. On June 11 Churchill came back with another forceful message, arguing that the spheres of influence would be in effect for only three months, after which the plan would be reviewed. Without consulting Secretary Hull or anyone else in the State Department, or even notifying them of his action, Roosevelt sent Churchill a message approving the limited proposal. The following day Hull sent the British Embassy a memorandum, previously approved by the President, arguing against the proposed Anglo-Russian agreement. And on June 22 Roosevelt sent Churchill another message, this time reverting to his original position and telling Churchill he was

Churchill insisted, probably correctly from his standpoint, that this was intended only as a temporary arrangement and refused to budge an inch. Indeed, in spite of Roosevelt's strong doubts and opposition, when Churchill visited Moscow in October 1944 he proposed to Stalin an arrangement for dividing political influence in each country according to a fixed percentage. Stalin readily agreed.[1] Roosevelt's reaction can easily be imagined.

Roosevelt and Churchill also faced the prospect of serious disagreement on a number of other postwar problems. For instance, the President staunchly denied Churchill's insinuation that the United States was "making sheep's eyes" at vital British oil reserves in the Middle East. He also disagreed sharply with the Prime Minister on U.S. postwar civil aviation policy, which sought to open up the British Empire and Commonwealth to American airlines. This disagreement came to a head late in 1944 during a conference on international civil aviation in Chicago, and despite Churchill's repeated pleas the President refused to modify the established American position. As if to rub salt into British wounds, early in 1945 the United States signed an air agreement with the Republic of Ireland without first consulting Great Britain. This again evoked Churchill's vigorous protest, but the American position remained unchanged.

These issues were trifling compared with a number of other political and diplomatic problems that confronted Roosevelt and Churchill in the last years of the war. The first of these concerned General de Gaulle, whose (to them) egotistical pretensions and policies angered Churchill and outraged Roosevelt. In June 1943 relations with de Gaulle hit bottom, and Roosevelt told Churchill: "I am fed up with de Gaulle. . . . I am absolutely convinced that he has been and is now injuring our war effort and that he is a very dangerous threat to us. I agree with you that he likes neither the British nor the Americans and that he would double-cross both of us at the first opportunity. I agree with you that the time has arrived when we must break with him. . . . We must divorce ourselves from de Gaulle . . . because he has proven to be unreliable, uncooperative, and disloyal to both our Governments."

However, there was no final break. But de Gaulle was kept completely in the dark about General Eisenhower's plans for the forthcoming invasion of Europe, and both before and after D Day de Gaulle was such an annoyance to the President and the Prime Minister that

---

disturbed that the British had taken the matter up with Washington only after they had presented it to the Russians. "Events," Hull wrote later, "fully justified the apprehensions we entertained over this Anglo-Russian arrangement, which duly entered into effect following the President's acquiescence." Hull, *Memoirs*, 2: 1453ff.

[1] Woodward, *British Foreign Policy*, 3: 150ff.

one wonders sometimes, on reading their secret correspondence, whether they regarded him as friend or foe. In the end it was Churchill who first recognized his—and the President's—longstanding misjudgment of the temperamental Frenchman. After D Day they discovered that de Gaulle enjoyed considerably more popular support in France than they had previously supposed, and by October 1944 Churchill had slowly won the reluctant Roosevelt to extend de facto recognition to de Gaulle's committee as the provisional government of France.

Anthony Eden, perhaps the most perspicacious Western participant in top-level wartime diplomacy,[2] wrote later that Roosevelt did not wish to see a strong postwar France.[3] Churchill, on the other hand, for compelling reasons of his own, as he made clear to the President, had a strong opposite desire. One of the overriding lessons of Atlantic history during the period between the wars, Churchill knew, was that Britain and the other European democracies no longer possessed sufficient strength to defend themselves against aggression without American support.[4] Churchill feared the withdrawal "not many years distant" of the American armies that had helped to liberate Europe from Hitler, and believed that "before five years are out there must be a French army to take on the main task of holding down Germany"—a French army at least partly equipped by the United States.

Roosevelt did nothing to ease Churchill's anxiety. "I am totally unwilling," he told Churchill in February 1944, "to police France and possibly Italy and the Balkans as well. After all, France is your baby and will take a lot of nursing in order to bring it to the point of walking alone. It would be very difficult for me to keep in France my military force or management for any length of time." Several weeks later Roosevelt returned to the subject: " 'Do please don't' ask me to keep any forces in France. I just cannot do it!"

Late in November 1944, after having been elected to an unprece-

---

[2] At Churchill's suggestion, Eden went to Washington in March 1943. See *FR 1943*, 3 (Washington, 1963): 13ff., 34–38. The Foreign Secretary "enjoyed . . . the exercise of the President's charm and the play of his lively mind . . . but . . . [Roosevelt] seemed to see himself disposing of the fate of so many lands, allied no less than enemy. He did all this with so much grace that it was not easy to dissect. Yet it was too like a conjurer, skilfully juggling with balls of dynamite, whose nature he failed to understand." Eden, *Memoirs*, 2: 433.

[3] Eden, *Memoirs*, 2: 541.

[4] This was clearly also one of the principal lessons of World War I. See Ernest R. May, *The World War and American Isolation 1914–1917* (Cambridge, Mass., 1959). For the years immediately preceding World War II, see Francis L. Loewenheim, "The Diffidence of Power—Some Notes and Reflections on the American Road to Munich," *Rice University Studies*, 58 (Fall 1972).

dented fourth term by a substantial majority, Roosevelt again dashed Churchill's hopes of equipping the postwar French army with American weapons: "I have at the present time no authority under which it would be possible for me to equip any postwar foreign army, and the prospect of getting such authority from the Congress is more than doubtful." At Yalta, six weeks later, Roosevelt told Churchill and Stalin that he "did not believe that American troops would stay in Europe much more than two years."[5] Stalin made no response to Roosevelt's statement, and one can only guess the apprehension with which Churchill heard the President's pronouncement. "Two years," Roosevelt repeated, "would be the limit." "I hope," Churchill remarked, "that would be according to circumstances."[6]

One principal reason for Churchill's concern about the withdrawal of American troops soon after the war was that by the end of 1944 relations with the Soviet Union were steadily deteriorating. At best—when his military situation was most precarious in 1941–1942—Stalin had been a demanding, grumbling, and secretive ally. As Soviet military fortunes improved, the future prospects of the Grand Alliance became increasingly doubtful.

The great symbol, if not the single most important source, of East-West disagreement was the fate of Poland. The Roosevelt-Churchill correspondence leaves little doubt of that. It also documents, perhaps, better than any other single source, how the cold war began in the last years of World War II.

In August 1939 Stalin and Hitler had agreed on a fourth partition of Poland, and a few weeks later carried out their infamous bargain. Even after Hitler attacked the Soviet Union, in June 1941, Russian relations with the Polish government-in-exile, based in London, were strained and unsatisfactory. In the darkest days of the war, in his conversations with Eden and other Western emissaries, Stalin left no doubt that he intended to retain the new Russian frontiers of June 22. In April 1943, the Germans discovered, near Katyn, what they claimed were the mass graves of thousands of Polish officers murdered by the Russians. The credibility of the Germans, themselves embarked on the unprecedented mass extermination of Jews and other racial enemies, was understandably not high. But when the Polish government in

---

5 *Conferences at Malta and Yalta*, p. 617. Roosevelt "went on to say that he felt that he could obtain support in Congress and throughout the country for any reasonable measures designed to safeguard the future peace, but he did not believe that this would extend to the maintenance of an appreciable American force in Europe." See also Ernest R. May, *"Lessons" of the Past—The Use and Misuse of History in American Foreign Policy* (New York, 1973) , p. 15.

6 *Conferences at Malta and Yalta*, p. 628.

London asked for an impartial investigation by the International Red Cross, the Russians were outraged and at once broke diplomatic relations with the London Poles.[7]

Much has been written in recent years about the coming of the cold war. Churchill is almost invariably described, especially by the American New Left, as a "premature cold warrior."[8] The Roosevelt-Churchill correspondence does not support this judgment. On the contrary, the Prime Minister strongly believed—as he told the London Poles early and often—that Poland would have to make territorial concessions to the Russians and get along with them. On the other hand, Roosevelt and Churchill were agreed—and so informed Stalin—that they could not possibly recognize a Soviet-created Polish government on Russian soil.

For better or worse, the President had long maintained that territorial questions should not be settled until the end of the war. At Teheran in December 1943 he departed from this principle and in agreement with Churchill in effect approved Stalin's proposals for Poland's postwar frontiers.[9] Actually, the Russians' long-range goals were at least suspected by some leading American diplomats. Soon after Teheran the late Charles E. Bohlen, the outstanding Soviet authority in Washington who served as Roosevelt's interpreter at Teheran, wrote: "[The] pattern of Soviet views concerning postwar Europe is sufficiently clear. . . . The result would be that the Soviet Union would be the only important military and political force on the continent of Europe. The rest of Europe would be reduced to military and political impotence."[10]

[7] See Kennan, *Memoirs*, 1: 200ff.; J. K. Zowadny, *Death in the Forest—The Story of the Katyn Forest Massacre* (South Bend, 1962) ; and Louis FitzGibbon, *Katyn—A Crime Without Parallel* (London, 1971) .

[8] See, for instance, Kolko, *Politics of War*, pp. 374ff. For a different New Left view of Churchill, see Lloyd C. Gardner, "From Liberation to Containment," in William Appleman Williams, ed., *From Colony to Empire: Essays in the History of American Foreign Relations* (New York, 1972) , pp. 343ff. See also Stephen E. Ambrose, *The Supreme Commander: The War Years of General Dwight D. Eisenhower* (New York, 1970) , pp. 645ff.

[9] *Conferences at Cairo and Tehran*, pp. 599–600, 604, 884–885, General Sikorski Historical Institute, *Documents on Polish-Soviet Relations, 1939–1945*, 2 (London, 1961) : 237; Stanislaw Mikolajczyk, *The Rape of Poland: Pattern of Soviet Aggression* (New York, 1948) and Lynn Ethridge Davis, *The Cold War Begins: Soviet-American Conflict over Eastern Europe* (Princeton, 1974) , pp. 94–96.

[10] Bohlen, *Witness to History*, p. 152. At a private meeting with Stalin in December Roosevelt indiscreetly told the Russian leader that he could not, publicly or secretly, agree to Russian demands in an election year. There were, Roosevelt said, in the United States from six to seven million Americans of Polish extraction, and as a practical man, he did not wish to lose their vote. Stalin replied that now that the President explained, he had understood. *Conferences at Cairo and Tehran*, p. 594.

But Bohlen's farsighted assessment seems not to have made a significant impression. By mid-1944 Stalin's attitude toward Poland became unmistakably clear. In August the Warsaw underground, responding to a signal from Soviet forces closing in on the city, rose up against the Germans. Roosevelt and Churchill expected Stalin to lend all possible aid to the Polish fighters. Stalin would do nothing of the kind, and when Roosevelt and Churchill sought permission for their planes to land at Russian-controlled airfields after dropping supplies to the Warsaw patriots, Stalin said no to that request as well.

Churchill was growing increasingly bitter. At the height of the Warsaw uprising he proposed to Roosevelt that they ask Stalin: "Why should [American planes from England] not land on the refuelling ground which has been assigned to us behind the Russian lines without enquiry as to what they have done on the way? We feel sure that if wounded British or American planes arrive behind the lines of your armies, they will be succoured with your usual consideration." In the event that Stalin would "not give any reply to this," Churchill went on to suggest, "I feel we ought to go and see what happens. I cannot conceive that he would maltreat or detain them."

Roosevelt replied that he did "not consider it advantageous to the long-range general war prospect . . . to join in the proposed message to U[ncle] J[oe]." But the President was also becoming increasingly concerned about relations with the Soviet Union. Soon after, at the second Quebec conference in September 1944, in a quite remarkable conversation with Archduke Otto of Austria, the President gave vent to his feelings about Stalin and the Russians: "Our main concern is how to keep the Communists out of Hungary and Austria." "It is evident," Otto's memorandum on the conversation with Roosevelt continued, "that the relationship between R[oosevelt] and the Russians is strained. . . . There was a general interest in keeping the Russians away as far as possible. . . . From all of R's remarks it is quite evident that he is afraid of the Communists and wants to do everything to contain Russia's power—naturally *short of war*."[1]

Whatever the President's private feelings about Stalin, from the summer of 1944 until his death in April 1945 his correspondence with Churchill was increasingly dominated by growing disagreements and problems with the Soviet Union. From the vantage point of the Roosevelt-Churchill correspondence, the Yalta conference can be seen as only a brief interruption in the downward course of East-West relations.

See also Edward J. Rozek, *Allied Wartime Diplomacy—A Pattern in Poland* (New York, 1958), pp. 159ff.; and Woodward, *British Foreign Policy*, 2: 651.

[1] U.S. Department of State, *The Conference at Quebec 1944* (Washington, 1972), pp. 367–368.

In his memoirs of World War II, Anthony Eden has written that "at Yalta the Russians had seemed relaxed and, so far as we could judge, friendly . . . [but] within a few weeks all this had changed."[2] The rapid deterioration of East-West relations after Yalta is set down at length in the Roosevelt-Churchill correspondence—it was probably its main theme in the last weeks of Roosevelt's life. But the correspondence also discloses that there had been a marked change long before Yalta. In mid-December 1944, for instance, Roosevelt (at once informing Churchill) told Stalin that "the United States Government stands unequivocally for a strong, free, independent, and democratic Poland" and asked him not to extend diplomatic recognition to the Communist regime at Lublin "before we meet, which I hope will be immediately after my inauguration on January 20."[3] But Stalin had no intention of waiting that long.

However, the Polish situation[4] was only one symptom of the rapidly deteriorating relations between the Soviet Union and the Western democracies. The increasingly troubled cables of W. Averell Harriman, Roosevelt's trusted ambassador in Moscow, bore witness to the growing difficulties.[5] All the same, Roosevelt declined to approve any systematic advance consultation with the British before Yalta, and he and Churchill arrived there as unprepared as they had at Teheran, fourteen months earlier.[6]

At Yalta Stalin agreed to "free and unfettered elections" in Poland and other liberated areas, and a good case can be made that the future

2 Eden, *Memoirs*, 2: 604.

3 See below, Doc. 487.

4 The central importance of the Polish issue was pointed up in a memorandum sent to Admiral Wilson Brown, the President's naval aide, by Lieutenant George M. Elsey, his assistant, on April 16, 1945, four days after the President's death: "Saturday afternoon, just before the services in the East Room, Admiral Leahy asked me if I had written any papers which would be of use to President Truman in learning the background of some of the current military-diplomatic questions. The Admiral said that there were two subjects which he believes the President should understand thoroughly at once: the Polish Question, and negotiations for surrender of German forces in Italy." (George M. Elsey Papers, Harry S Truman Library, Independence, Missouri.)

5 As early as September 9, 1944, Harriman had noted: "Now that the end of the war is in sight our relations with the Soviets have taken a startling turn evident during the last two months. They have held up our requests with complete indifference to our interests and have shown an unwillingness even to discuss pressing problems. . . . When it comes to the question of what we should do in dealing with the situation I am not going to propose any drastic action but a firm but friendly *quid pro quo* attitude. In some cases where it has been possible for us to show a firm hand we have been making definite progress." *Conference at Quebec 1944*, pp. 198–199. See also Martin Blumenson, *The Patton Papers, Vol. 2, 1940–1945* (Boston, 1974) , p. 583.

6 Eden, *Memoirs*, 2: 584, 592.

of Poland and other Russian-occupied areas would have been markedly different if Stalin had observed his Yalta promise.[7] On the other
hand, his failure to do so came as no surprise even to some of Roosevelt's most liberal associates, one of whom—Archibald MacLeish, then
Assistant Secretary of State for Public and Cultural Relations—referred at the time to the "wave of disillusionment which has distressed
us in the last several weeks"[8] and would surely grow if the American
people received the impression that "potentially totalitarian provisional governments were being installed in the liberated areas." "It
would be a blessing to the world," MacLeish added, "if we could walk
straight up on this occasion."[9]

It would indeed have been a blessing, but the fate of Eastern
Europe was a problem neither Roosevelt nor Churchill could face up
to for some weeks after Yalta, either in public or in their correspondence. Early in March Roosevelt told Churchill that he was "quite
correct in assuming that neither the Government nor the people of
this country will support participation in a fraud or a mere whitewash
of the Lublin government and the solution must be as we envisaged it
at Yalta." But he counseled against another direct approach to Stalin
until their ambassadors had had another chance at quiet diplomacy.
"I can assure you," Roosevelt told Churchill on March 11, in a statement that summed up perfectly their respective positions as regards
the Russians during the preceding year, "that our objectives are
identical. . . . The only difference I see is one of tactics."

7 "The map of Europe would look exactly the same as it does today if there had
never been a Yalta conference." Bohlen, *Witness to History*, p. 192, and *Transformation of American Foreign Policy*, p. 46.

8 The President could not have been unaware of the growing disillusionment mentioned by MacLeish. For in a memorandum to Roosevelt entitled "American Public
Opinion on Recent European Developments," dated December 30, 1944, Secretary of
State Edward R. Stettinius, Jr., referred to "increased public *confusion* and *disillusionment* [which] have developed as a result of: *Events in Europe . . . Lack of unity
. . . Doubts as to the effectiveness of U.S. diplomacy* vis-a-vis our Allies." Stettinius
added that, as regards Poland, "preponderant American opinion is *not* categorically
opposed to Russian acquisition of territory in pre-1939 Poland; it *is* opposed to Russian acquisition of Polish territory *without* Polish consent." (Edward R. Stettinius, Jr.,
Papers, Box 231, University of Virginia Library, Charlottesville, Virginia.) (Emphasis
in original.)

9 *Conferences at Malta and Yalta*, pp. 101–102; and John L. Gaddis, *The United
States and the Origins of the Cold War 1941–1947* (New York, 1972) , p. 159. According to Lisle A. Rose, the Declaration on Liberated Europe—in which Roosevelt,
Churchill, and Stalin specifically held out the promise of "free elections" and of
"processes which will enable the liberated people to . . . create democratic institutions of their own free choice"—was more or less meaningless as far as the United
States was concerned. The President "recognized the inherent weakness of the
Declaration and placed little faith in it as an effective expression of national diplomatic intent." *Dubious Victory: the United States and the End of World War II* in

The delay troubled Churchill deeply. On March 13 he told the President: "Poland has lost her frontier. Is she now to lose her freedom? . . . I do not wish to reveal a divergence between the British and the United States Governments, but it would certainly be necessary for me to make it clear that we were in presence of a great failure and an utter breakdown of what we settled at Yalta." Churchill was vexed and frustrated: "We can, of course, make no progress without your aid, and if we get out of step the doom of Poland is sealed." Roosevelt and Churchill addressed no further joint messages to Stalin as regards Poland for a week or two, but their self-restraint produced no moderation of Soviet policy. It is doubtful that additional joint protests would have had the slightest effect. The time for diplomatic protest was past.

The end of March marked something of a turning point in Roosevelt's outlook and policy, and while failing health undoubtedly thrust additional influence and authority into his subordinates' hands, the direction of American foreign policy remained his own. "I have," he wrote to Churchill on March 29, "likewise been watching with anxiety and concern the development of Soviet attitude since the Crimea conference." On April 3 Ambassador Harriman cabled Roosevelt from Moscow that if the United States did not begin to "stand firm . . . the Soviet Government will become increasingly convinced that they can force us to accept any of their decisions on all matters and it will be increasingly difficult to stop their aggressive policy." The following day Roosevelt sent Stalin his strongest and most indignant message,[10] and on April 6 he told Churchill: "We must not permit anybody to entertain a false impression that we are afraid. Our armies will in a very few days be in a position that will permit us to become 'tougher' than has heretofore appeared advantageous to the war effort." In less than a week, Roosevelt was dead, virtually his last message to Churchill affirming that "thus far our course is correct."

The world knew nothing of these historic messages, some of which did not come to light until 1972.[11] What passed through Roosevelt's mind in his last days must be deduced largely from his messages to Churchill. Unlike Churchill, who spoke frankly to Parliament about the growing confrontation with the Soviet Union, the President chose,

---

The Coming of the American Age, 1945–1946. (Kent, Ohio, 1973), pp. 30, 31. For a differing view see Davis, *The Cold War Begins,* pp. 199–201.

10 *FR 1945,* 3 (Washington, 1968) : 745–746.

11 Francis L. Loewenheim, "New Evidence Sheds Light on Beginning of Cold War," *The Houston Chronicle,* March 19, 1972, "Roosevelt and Stalin—A Revelation," *The New York Times,* March 27, 1972, and "A New Look at FDR and the Origins of the Cold War Era," *The Washington Sunday Star,* May 21, 1972.

regrettably, to say nothing in public.[12] There is no way of knowing what he and Churchill would have accomplished together had he lived longer. But the correspondence certainly indicates that in his last days Roosevelt stood together with Churchill as rarely before.

This is not the place to assess definitively Roosevelt and Churchill's relationship in those last months or, for that matter, even their collaboration earlier in the conflict. But from their secret correspondence it is possible to draw a number of conclusions about their political and diplomatic conduct of the war.

First, Roosevelt and Churchill apparently disagreed on political and diplomatic issues more frequently, and more intensely, than they did on substantive military questions.

Second, despite Churchill's strong interest and desire, Roosevelt never had any secret plans to take the United States into war in 1940–1941, nor did he make secret commitments to that effect.

Third, once the United States was in the war, Roosevelt and Churchill developed no coherent political strategy to match their highly successful grand military strategy. Indeed, they neglected almost entirely the ideological nature of the war. Despite frequent public references to them, the Atlantic Charter and (Roosevelt's) Four Freedoms remained little more than paper promises, which Roosevelt and Churchill made little effort to redeem.[1] Under the circumstances it was hardly surprising that their military triumphs were not matched by comparable political and diplomatic achievements and that aside from isolated efforts on Roosevelt's part the two leaders failed to discern how, once again, "war was becoming revolution"[2] in large parts of the world.

Fourth, despite Roosevelt's attempt to avoid Woodrow Wilson's mistakes during World War I, the President's determination to delay all substantive decisions about the conditions of peace until the Axis

12 At his press conference of March 13, 1945—the only time the subject came up there after Yalta—Roosevelt was asked: "Mr. President, do you feel that the recent developments in Rumania square with the Yalta declaration on liberated areas?" Roosevelt dismissed the subject with "Oh my God! Ask the State Department (laughter)." PPC, 12: 94. The unpublished wartime diary of Interior Secretary Harold L. Ickes, who was most interested in and usually well informed about American foreign policy during his twelve years in Roosevelt's cabinet, revealed that after Yalta the President's cabinet met only rarely, and Ickes for one had little or no idea of what had transpired there.

1 On February 23, 1945 Roosevelt said: "The Atlantic Charter is a beautiful idea. When it was drawn up, the situation was that England was about to lose the war. They needed hope, and it gave it to them." PPC, 12: 71–72.

2 We have borrowed the formulation from the title of the second volume of Allan Nevins, War for the Union (New York, 1960).

had been defeated—a strategy in which Churchill reluctantly concurred —proved to be a grave and costly miscalculation. Furthermore, while Churchill, in the last year of the war, was undoubtedly aware of Britain's growing weakness and sought to obtain not only substantial American economic aid but promises of political and military assistance, Roosevelt made it clear that "the Yanks were not staying."

Fifth, Roosevelt and Churchill did not anticipate and made no contingency plans for the possibility of renewed friction with the Soviet Union in 1944–1945 or for the coming of the cold war. The Roosevelt-Churchill correspondence is, or should be, unmistakable evidence that they remained faithful—if not farsighted—allies to each other and to the Russians to the end. Indeed, their letters demonstrate that far from deserving the "premature cold warrior" epithet, Churchill was prepared to go a long way toward satisfying the Soviet Union's interests in Poland and the Balkans.

Sixth, while Churchill relied on his Foreign Secretary and took care to consult on all vital matters with the War Cabinet even when he was out of the country, a very different situation existed in the United States. What Arthur Schlesinger, Jr., has called "the imperial presidency"[3] never flourished more vigorously—or dangerously—than in the wartime White House. Roosevelt excluded his Secretary of State from all but the last of his summit conferences; and he failed to keep State Department officials informed on many important issues. On at least one occasion, in October 1944, Roosevelt went so far as to ask Churchill to bypass the State Department (and the Foreign Office) on the highly sensitive issue of diplomatic recognition of the French provisional government. In these circumstances it was not surprising that only a portion of the Roosevelt-Churchill correspondence found its way into the files of the Department of State.[4] More important, lacking the

[3] Arthur M. Schlesinger, Jr., *The Imperial Presidency* (Boston, 1973). It should be added that Professor Schlesinger tends to make light of Roosevelt's contribution to the development of an over-powerful presidency.

[4] In his *Memoirs* 2: 1474 Secretary Hull wrote that Roosevelt "was, in general, accustomed to sending me the telegrams and messages he received from the Prime Minister on subjects involving foreign relations rather than military affairs." Nevertheless, when the Historical Division of the Department of State compiled the *Foreign Relations* volumes for the years 1941–1945, it was unable to locate copies of many of these telegrams and messages in its files and found it necessary to obtain copies of them from the Franklin D. Roosevelt Library at Hyde Park, which—it might be added—likewise found it impossible to locate a number of these documents. The mystery of what happened to the Churchill messages sent to Hull was resolved in a letter of September 7, 1962 to Professor Richard L. Walker from Rear Admiral William C. Mott, a former officer in the White House Map Room, the President's super-secret command post. "I used to take messages from Stalin or Churchill to the Secretary of State but he was not allowed to keep a copy and had to call in his ad-

diplomatic equivalent of a Marshall or an Eisenhower, and disdaining the expertise of his State Department specialists, Roosevelt came increasingly to depend on the diplomatically inexperienced Harry Hopkins, even though he remembered President Wilson's unfortunate experience with a favorite emissary and assured a concerned friend at the State Department in 1940 that he "planned to operate in the open . . . [and] there would be no 'Colonel House' business."[5] It should be added that, to their increasing concern and dismay, Roosevelt also continued to keep congressional leaders in the dark, leading Senator Arthur H. Vandenberg of Michigan to note in March 1944 that "none of us knows what President Roosevelt's commitments on our behalf have been at Quebec and Moscow and Teheran. . . . I do not see how we could endorse President Roosevelt's undisclosed international purposes."[6]

Seventh, for all their attention to a vast variety of important and unimportant problems in their correspondence, Roosevelt and Churchill displayed little interest in such fateful subjects as Nazi atrocities and the fate of the European Jews,[7] the development and uses of atomic weapons and power,[8] the future of China, the European

---

visers (like Sumner Welles) and have them read the messages in my presence." Walker, *Stettinius*, p. 14. According to a memorandum prepared by George M. Elsey, "The Map Room Files of President Franklin D. Roosevelt, 1941–1945," "[I]t was the President's wish to have in the Map Room the only complete file of the messages he exchanged with Churchill, Stalin, and Chaing Kai-shek, and for this reason messages from the Map Room were sent through Navy Department communications facilities and replies were received through the War Department. Thus neither Department has a complete file." (Elsey Papers, Truman Library)

5 Gaddis, *United States and the Origins of the Cold War*, p. 13.

6 Arthur H. Vandenberg, Jr., *The Private Papers of Senator Vandenberg* (Boston, 1952), p. 92.

7 The desperate plight of European Jews was evidently not a matter of great concern for the British government and apparently even less for Roosevelt. Thus when Anthony Eden met with the President and Secretary Hull at the White House on March 27, 1943, Hull pointed out that more than 60,000 Bulgarian Jews "are threatened with extinction unless we could get them out." Eden replied that, while the British were "ready to take about 60 thousand more Jews to Palestine . . . the whole problem of the Jews in Europe is very difficult and . . . we should move very cautiously about offering to take all Jews out of a country like Bulgaria. If we do that, then the Jews of the world will be wanting us to make similar offers to Poland and Germany. Hitler might well take us up on such an offer and there simply are not enough ships and means of transportation in the world to handle them." According to Harry Hopkins' memorandum of this conversation, Roosevelt said nothing whatever on the subject, and in effect nothing was done about it. *FR 1943*, 3: 38.

8 See Martin Sherwin, "The Atomic Bomb and the Origins of the Cold War: U.S. Atomic Energy Policy and Diplomacy 1941–1945," *American Historical Review*, 78 (October 1973).

resistance, the German opposition to Hitler, and the question of access to divided Berlin. This is not to suggest that Roosevelt was indifferent to the plight of the European Jews in the face of Auschwitz. But the fact remains that the subject of rescuing the European Jews had a rather low priority with him and his administration—and also with Churchill—until it was too late.

Eighth, contrary to the assertions of some American New Left historians, economic considerations did not bulk large in Roosevelt's relations and conduct of the war. It is true that, as early as the Atlantic conference, Undersecretary Welles, speaking for the President, told the British that the United States looked forward to—indeed definitely expected—a significant diminution of imperial preference after the war; and Roosevelt's and Churchill's subsequent disagreements over such matters as oil reserves in the Middle East and international air routes[9] were more than minor irritants. But there is no evidence that Roosevelt tried, so to speak, to throw his economic weight around,[10] or that Roosevelt and Churchill ever considered using economic power as a bargaining chip with the Russians. Roosevelt had little of Cordell Hull's passion for international economics—monetary questions, for instance, left him cold—and his correspondence with Churchill, who had no great interest in economic issues either, confirms that fact.

Ninth, Roosevelt and Churchill never really came to grips with the question of the future of the colonial empires. There is no doubt as to the President's anti-imperialist outlook—and there are a few examples of it in his correspondence with Churchill. But except for his messages on India in 1942, Roosevelt was reluctant to raise the subject directly with the Prime Minister,[1] who in turn defended as inviolate what he

[9] See *Berle Papers*, pp. 482ff.; and *FR 1944, 2* (Washington, 1967) : 355ff.

[10] See George C. Herring, Jr., "The United States and British Bankruptcy 1944–1945: Responsibilities Deferred," *Political Science Quarterly*, 86 (June, 1971) .

[1] Roosevelt and Churchill evidently had some rather unpleasant words about India at the second Quebec conference. According to a memorandum by Harry Dexter White, probably based on remarks by Treasury Secretary Henry Morgenthau, Jr., who was present, the subject came up at a dinner meeting of the President and the Prime Minister at the Citadel on September 13, 1944: "The conversation . . . got on to India and stayed on India for about hour. Churchill talked rather angrily at length about the difficulties the British were confronted with administering India and on the lack of understanding in the United States about the Indian problem. Churchill said, I will give the United States half of India to administer and we will take the other half and we will see who does better with each other's half. *Conference at Quebec 1944*, p. 327. In a memorandum for Secretary of State Stettinius dated January 1, 1945, Roosevelt wrote: "I still do not want to get mixed up in any Indochina decision. It is a matter for post-war. By the same token, I do not want to get mixed up in any military effort toward the liberation of Indochina from Japanese. You can tell Halifax that I made this very clear to Mr. Churchill. From both the

regarded as imperial institutions with characteristic zeal and vigor. Indeed, on the whole Roosevelt felt much less strongly, and took fewer hardline positions, on political problems than he did on the military issues that were uppermost in his mind.

Finally, it seems clear that Roosevelt and Churchill neglected the integral relationship of war, politics, and diplomacy. Anthony Eden, who probably understood that subject better than either the President or the Prime Minister, has written that "the Foreign Office . . . often warned of the clash of our short- and long-term interests. . . . Military needs . . . overpowered political forebodings."[2] The Roosevelt-Churchill correspondence confirms the justice of such doubts and warnings. It points up too Roosevelt's and Churchill's continued tendency to compartmentalize military, political, and diplomatic problems. The President and the Prime Minister were not reflective men, and despite their considerable experience during World War I and their desire to avoid repeating the mistakes of 1914–1918, their correspondence shows that they never took the time to assess their overall political and military situation and to examine, much less to plan how they might achieve particular objectives.

Granted that during the early years of World War II it would have been hard to foresee the rapid deterioration of East-West relations in 1944–1945, Roosevelt's and Churchill's conduct of the war as a political process was distinguished by a remarkable lack of foresight. Understandably preoccupied as they were with the military defeat of the Axis, they failed, for practical purposes, to discern that the war was not only a test of arms but a battle of ideas. As a conservative, Churchill had little interest in social forces and, except in a very limited way, in ideological combat. Roosevelt, though sensitive to domestic political currents, seemed indifferent to the tide of international politics and opinion.

Generally uninterested in postwar planning, both Roosevelt and Churchill seem to have been unaware of or indifferent to the kind of world that might emerge after the war. Neither seemed to have the slightest idea of the anti-imperialist tide that was soon to sweep the colonial world, and how it would reduce the power and role of the Western democracies in world affairs. Indeed, according to one of the President's close friends and advisers, Assistant Secretary of State Adolf A. Berle, Jr., toward the end of the war Roosevelt looked forward to turning away from world affairs and devoting the re-

---

military and civil point of view, action at this time is premature. F.D.R." (Stettinius Papers, Box 231, University of Virginia Library.) See also Gaddis Smith, *American Diplomacy During the Second World War, 1941–1945* (New York, 1965) , chap. 5.

2 Eden, *Memoirs*, 2: 533-534.

mainder of his fourth term to the unfinished business of domestic reform.[3] It should be added that Churchill went along with Roosevelt's deplorable tendency to mislead or keep the American people in the dark in an election year about the concessions he had secretly agreed to on the future of Poland. And the President, perhaps because of his waning physical if not mental powers,[4] seems not to have been concerned about what would happen if, at the close of the conflict, the American people became as disillusioned with the consequences of World War II as they had been after World War I.

It may well be that Roosevelt and Churchill simply made the best of a bad situation. In his *Russia and the West Under Lenin and Stalin*, George F. Kennan has pointed out that "the damage that had been done with the triumph of Bolshevism in Russia went deeper than people in the West supposed. By the mid-Thirties the Western democracies, whether they realized it or not, were on their own. There was no salvation from the East. . . . [By 1939] they were unable to defeat Hitler without accepting the aid of Russia; and for that aid there would then be a price—a bitter price—the full bitterness of which we of this generation are now being compelled to taste."[5] It may well have been true, that is to say, that by the outbreak of World War II the world balance of power—and the balance of ideas—had already shifted so greatly that the democracies, with the help of the Soviet Union, could win the war, but that they could not win the peace. And in that vast possibility lies the ultimate triumph and tragedy of Roosevelt and Churchill as revealed in their secret wartime correspondence.

[3] "He was planning and gathering himself for some kind of a tremendous mass attack on the internal economic plan of the United States." *Berle Papers*, p. 528.

[4] For a moving description of Roosevelt's declining physical powers, see Jim Bishop, *FDR's Last Year: April 1944–April 1945* (New York, 1974).

[5] George F. Kennan, *Russia and the West Under Lenin and Stalin* (Boston, 1961), p. 313.

PART I

September 1939 to October 1942

Introduction to Part I

"Today all of us are in the same boat. . . ."

ON September 1, 1939, Hitler's forces invaded Poland.
On September 3 Great Britain and France declared war on Germany, thus effectively turning the invasion into a world war.

On September 5 Franklin D. Roosevelt proclaimed American neutrality. But only six days later, in an extraordinary and virtually unprecedented move, the President of the neutral United States invited Winston Churchill, recently appointed First Lord of the Admiralty and thus a subordinate official of a foreign belligerent, to enter into direct correspondence with him.

Churchill took up the invitation and began to provide Roosevelt with explanations of British naval policy and actions, particularly with regard to the South Atlantic. At the same time, he sought to foster a feeling of trust and a sense of common purpose. Roosevelt at first replied only on rare occasions. In a memorandum to Secretary of State Cordell Hull he referred to a brief telegram of March 6, 1940, as "one of the few which I sent to Churchill when he was First Lord of the Admiralty," hastening to add that "[all] such messages obviously were related to naval matters."

In fact, very little of the friction that developed between the United States and Great Britain during the winter of 1939–1940 showed in the leaders' correspondence, in spite of their differences over such questions as the inspection of American merchant vessels, British interference with overseas mail, and the curtailment of agricultural imports from the United States. Sumner Welles' controversial peace mission to Rome, Berlin, Paris, and London, which the Undersecretary of State undertook at Roosevelt's request in February 1940, is not mentioned at all. Yet such messages as the President did send make it clear that he was by no means unaffected by the tone and contents of his communications from the First Lord of the Admiralty.

While Welles was on his tour of European capitals, concern over Hitler's next moves predominated in London, and even Churchill's part of the correspondence began to languish. On April 9, 1940, the German invasion of Norway and Denmark signaled the end of the so-called phony war—the lull in hostilities that had followed the conquest of Poland—and Churchill became occupied with matters of still more pressing concern. Further, Hitler's triumph in Norway led Prime Minister Neville Chamberlain to resign and opened the way for Churchill to form a coalition government. His accession to power on May 10 coincided with the invasion of the Low Countries and of France and thus presented him with problems of the most immediate urgency. But the new Prime Minister lost little time in reactivating his "American connection." His very first letter in his new post requested, among other things, the loan of American destroyers. It produced a response from Roosevelt which, though cautious and noncommittal, was undeniably sympathetic.

In June, when the fall of France became imminent, Churchill began a new flurry of correspondence, adding to his requests for ships and supplies a desperate plea for American diplomatic aid to prevent France from accepting surrender. He even suggested, for the first time, that the United States might enter the war. When France agreed to an armistice on June 22, the Roosevelt-Churchill correspondence was once more interrupted. But the Prime Minister continued to provide evidence of cooperation and good will by sending advance notice of the appointment of the Duke of Windsor as governor general of the Bahamas. He also offered to send to the United States a group of British scientists skilled in the installation of RDF (radar), the new British aircraft detection system.

Toward the end of July, however, various American organizations—including the so-called Century Group of prominent and influential interventionists and William Allen White's Committee to Defend America by Aiding the Allies—began publicly advocating greater aid to Britain, and Churchill resumed his campaign for American destroyers. The Prime Minister's anxieties were greatly increased by the onset of the blitz—the devastating bombing attacks on Great Britain designed to destroy British air strength by blasting airfields and key industries. The raids were widely regarded as a prelude to invasion.

While British pressure increased, the American response was slowed by the presidential election campaign. Partisan feeling in the United States was running high, making concerted action with Britain more difficult. Moreover, problems soon developed when the Americans insisted on formal contractual arrangements. The British were reluctant both to make unlimited territorial concessions and to give more than private assurances regarding the disposition of the British fleet in case of defeat. Despite this, the two powers reached broad agreement by September, though final details were not settled for another six months, on the "deal" which brought Britain not only fifty over-age American destroyers but also five B-17 bombers, 250,000 Enfield rifles, and 5 million rounds of .30-caliber ammunition. All this material was given in exchange for long-term leases to construct American bases in various British possessions in the Western Hemisphere. In large measure, the whole arrangement was made possible only because of the degree of trust and understanding that had already developed between Roosevelt and Churchill.

As soon as the destroyer deal was an accomplished fact and the American commitment to aid Great Britain was thereby clearly indicated, the correspondence turned to matters of global concern, and the Prime Minister began to involve Roosevelt in discussion of overall strategy. The two leaders discussed an attack on Dakar in French West Africa in order to prevent the establishment of a German submarine base there, the reopening of the Burma Road as a supply line for the Chinese armies of Generalissimo Chiang Kai-shek, the steps necessary to keep the French fleet stationed at Toulon out of Hitler's clutches, the threat posed by the pro-Axis posture of Spain's General Franco to the British naval base at Gibraltar, and other matters, even though these questions were presumably of minimal concern to a still neutral United States in the last three months of 1940. On December 7—a full year before Pearl Harbor—Churchill sent Roosevelt a fifteen-page report on "the prospects for 1941," adding for good measure a two-page statistical appendix on losses by enemy action of British, Allied, and neutral merchant tonnage for the period from June 2 to November 30. Frank and detailed, and couched in Churchill's most persuasive prose, the message stressed the "solid identity of interest between the British Empire and the United States," asked that America adopt a role of "constructive nonbelligerency," and pointed out that Britain was rapidly running out of money to pay for needed supplies, as required by the cash-and-carry provisions of the Neutrality Act of 1939. It was not, as the Prime Minister correctly pointed out, "an appeal for aid, but . . . a statement of the minimum action necessary to achieve our common purpose."

By this time, the President, who shared the sense of common purpose, had reached a similar conclusion. He told a press conference on December 17 that "quite aside from our historic and current interest in the survival of democracy in the world as a whole, it is equally important from a selfish point of view and of American defense that we should do everything possible to help the British Empire to defend itself." Roosevelt used the now famous analogy of lending a neighbor one's garden hose to help him put out a fire to explain how this purpose might best be accomplished. In a fireside chat on December 29 he asserted that "a nation can have peace with the Nazis only at the price of total surrender" and pledged that the United States would become "the great arsenal of democracy." At the same time, arrangements were made to invite British staff officers to come to the United States for talks with their American counterparts. Thus by the end of 1940 Roosevelt had committed the United States firmly to the principle of a "common cause," and this development is clearly reflected in his subsequent correspondence with Churchill. On January 10, 1941, the lend-lease bill, intended to formalize that commitment, was introduced in Congress as House Resolution 1776.

Churchill was careful to take no part in the public debate over lend-lease, and he did not raise the issue of aid in his letters to the President while the measure was under discussion. His public appeal of February 9, broadcast to the United States and containing the now famous "Give us the tools and we will finish the job," was prepared after consultation with Roosevelt's most trusted adviser, Harry Hopkins. Actually, the speech was designed primarily to still American fears of being asked to send an expeditionary force to Europe. Churchill's most important message to Roosevelt during this time dealt with the deteriorating situation in the Far East and warned of the danger of war with Japan "in the next few weeks or months."

The basis for future Anglo-American cooperation was broadened even before the final enactment of the lend-lease bill by the appointment of British Foreign Secretary Lord Halifax as ambassador to Washington, succeeding Lord Lothian, who died suddenly on December 12. Roosevelt also contributed to the future collaboration by sending Harry Hopkins to London in January 1941 and by ordering the preparation of ABC-1, the final report on the American-British staff conversations, which contained contingency plans for military cooperation with Great Britain "should the United States be compelled to resort to war."

After lend-lease became law on March 11, and American material assistance to Great Britain was thus assured, Churchill made new efforts to obtain diplomatic cooperation backed by military threat, particularly in relations with Greece, Yugoslavia, and France, all of which were under intense pressure from Germany. He and the President continued to disagree over dealings with the Vichy regime—Churchill refused to recognize that government and sought to treat it essentially as an enemy, while Roosevelt hoped to wean it away from

Germany by a carrot-and-stick policy which included the appointment of the highly respected Admiral William D. Leahy as ambassador. But by now the two men saw the world's problems in similar terms and opted for substantially similar solutions. At the same time, the President devoted himself to providing all-out aid to Britain short of war and proudly informed his counterpart in London of the progress he was making.

Churchill, though grateful for Roosevelt's efforts, was more pessimistic than the President with regard to their adequacy. In his telegram of May 3, 1941, he mentioned for the first time since June 1940 how much more effective U.S. military power would be "if the United States were immediately to range herself with us as a belligerent power." Roosevelt did not respond to this suggestion. The military situation had deteriorated steadily for the Allies. The Germans had entered North Africa in force in March, and Field Marshal Erwin Rommel's Afrika Korps had recaptured all of Cyrenaica by April 12. Yugoslavia was overrun by Hitler's forces by April 17, the Greek army surrendered to Germany on April 24, and German paratroopers launched an attack on Crete on May 20. In the face of such events, Roosevelt was prepared to stretch the meaning of "constructive non-belligerency" to its utmost limits, but as Harry Hopkins told Treasury Secretary Henry Morgenthau, Jr., he remained "loath to get into this war, and he would rather follow public opinion than lead it."

Roosevelt apparently hoped that public opinion would be turned toward intervention by the sudden flight of Hitler's deputy, Rudolf Hess, to Scotland on May 10, and he asked Churchill to have Hess questioned on Germany's plans concerning the Western Hemisphere. The Nazi official said only that "the Germans reckoned with American intervention and were not afraid of it," and that "America really wanted to inherit the British Empire." On the other hand, Churchill proposed a reply to an inquiry from Wendell Willkie, the Republican presidential candidate in 1940, in which he insisted that "no peace that is any use to you or which will liberate Europe can be obtained without American belligerence." The letter concluded: "How easy now—how hard a year hence will be the task." The President thought the reply would place him in "a most embarrassing situation" and asked the Prime Minister not to send it.

In his much heralded Pan American Day address of May 27—which, he assured Churchill, "goes farther than I thought was possible even two weeks ago"—Roosevelt in fact did no more than declare a state of unlimited national emergency, without clearly defining what that might mean. Psychologically, of course, this declaration was of some importance, and the concept of "all aid short of war" continued to be expanded thereafter.

By midsummer the path that Roosevelt was following was becoming progressively narrow. Public support for aid to Great Britain was based largely on the belief that such action would serve to keep the United States out of the war. Yet, increasingly, the President was being told by his closest advisers—among them Harry Hopkins, W. Averell Harriman, Secretary of War Henry L. Stimson, Secretary of the Treasury Henry Morgenthau, Jr., and Chief of Naval Operations Admiral Harold R. Stark—that this aid was inadequate for the task at hand and that he should prepare the country for the final plunge.

The long-expected German invasion of Russia, launched on June 22, 1941, added a further complication. Churchill had told the President on June 14 that "a vast German onslaught on the Russian frontier is imminent." He indicated his intention, in that event, to "give all encouragement and any help we can spare to the Russians, following the principle that Hitler is the foe we have to beat." "I trust," he concluded, "that a German-Russian conflict will not cause you any embarrassment." Roosevelt shared both Churchill's concerns and his intentions. But he was even more worried about American public reaction to a possible war on the side of the Soviet Union than he was about war on the side of Britain.

Moreover, time was now a crucial factor. Russia was generally expected to collapse within a matter of months, and such a development would strain the Allied situation enormously and thereby increase the direct danger to the United States. Further, Britain might be led out of desperation into postwar commitments that the United States would find difficult, if not impossible, to support. In an effort to resolve these problems, the President now sought a face-to-face meeting with Churchill.

Roosevelt had expressed interest in such a meeting as early as February 1940, and he told Hopkins in January 1941 that "a lot of this could be settled if Churchill and I could just sit down together for a while." Morgenthau's entry in his diaries for February 17 quotes Roosevelt: "I have just got to see Churchill myself in order to explain things to him." If the time for such a meeting was not then propitious, it now seemed possible and even more essential. Accordingly, Roosevelt sent Hopkins back to London on July 13, in part at least to arrange matters with the Prime Minister. The President's final instructions to his emissary read: "Economic or territorial deals—NO . . . no talk about war."

Though the President initially envisaged simply a personal meeting with Churchill, what ensued on August 9–12 off Argentia, Newfoundland, was in fact an informal international conference in which high-level military officials of both countries participated, along with the undersecretaries responsible for foreign policy, Sumner Welles and Sir

Alexander Cadogan. The mere fact of the meeting was of crucial importance in underlining the common interests of the two powers. The direct, personal contact established at this first meeting laid the basis for future cooperation and provided experience of great value for the subsequent wartime conferences. Moreover, the final statement of the conference, though it hardly deserves the grandiloquent title of Atlantic Charter, served to underscore the intention of the still neutral United States to cooperate fully with Great Britain not only in the prosecution of the war but also in the shaping of the postwar world and was both praised and condemned on these grounds by the American press. But the Atlantic conference did not actually change the relationship between Great Britain and the United States in any significant way, and when the correspondence between the two leaders resumed in September the tone of their letters was not markedly different than before.

New issues, of course, did arise. The two men discussed the feasibility of a supply route to Russia through Iran and of the United States transporting British troops to the Middle East. The President and the Prime Minister first mentioned formally the possible development of atomic weapons. By November the increasingly ominous developments in the Far East loomed ever larger in the correspondence.

Throughout 1941 Japan had extended its control over China and Indochina, thus posing a threat to the Dutch East Indies and Malaya. Having secured its northern border through a neutrality pact with the Soviet Union on April 13, Japan now saw only Great Britain and the United States as obstacles to further expansion. On July 26 Roosevelt froze all Japanese credits, and on August 17 he warned that any further policy of Japanese military domination of Asia would force the United States "to take immediately any and all steps necessary" to safeguard American interests. A week later Churchill announced that Britain would support the United States if negotiations with Japan failed.

The negotiations in fact made little or no progress in the late summer and early fall of 1941. When the relatively moderate Prince Fumimaro Konoye resigned as Prime Minister on October 17, to be replaced by the far more militant General Hideki Tojo, the prospects for a peaceful accommodation dimmed. On November 17 American ambassador Joseph C. Grew cabled from Tokyo that the Japanese might launch a sudden attack somewhere in the Pacific at any moment. Churchill had steadfastly hewed to the line that only firmness and determination, backed by the threat of force, could prevent Japan from going to war, and he continued to urge a "hard line" on Roosevelt. Late in 1941 he found a willing listener.

When the BBC reported the Japanese attack on Pearl Harbor of

December 7 on its Sunday night newscast, Churchill was in the company of U.S. ambassador John G. Winant and of the President's personal envoy Averell Harriman. He immediately telephoned Roosevelt for confirmation and then made plans to go to Washington. Without hesitation, he also drafted a British declaration of war against Japan. While the Prime Minister got ready to depart for his second meeting with Roosevelt, the cooperative ventures already under way were scarcely disturbed by the new and portentous turn of events.

Churchill met with Roosevelt in Washington between December 22, 1941, and January 14, 1942, discussing overall strategy, setting up various joint commands, and preparing the Declaration by the United Nations, the formal commitment of the Allied powers to the defeat of the Axis. He arrived back in London on February 17, and by March the exchange of views on matters of substance had again moved into high gear. Within a month communications were exchanged on such diverse subjects as the final settlement of the lend-lease arrangements, plans for an invasion of Madagascar, the criteria for future membership in the United Nations, the question of immediate Dominion status for India, the problem of accommodating within the Atlantic Charter Soviet annexations of the Baltic States and portions of Finland and Poland, and the simplification of the overall command structure. Churchill, profoundly affected by continuing reverses in the Far East and especially by the disastrous loss of Singapore on February 15, was for the time being more pessimistic than the President. He seemed more willing now to rely on American influence rather than Allied power in dealings with France, and he was more anxious even than Roosevelt to keep the Russians happy. Out of desperate concern over developments in Asia he even offered to postpone his cherished scheme for a North African invasion in favor of a highly dubious action calling for commando raids on Japanese-held islands from bases in California.

At the same time, Roosevelt seemed more sure of himself, more ready to contemplate grand strategy and to offer philosophical advice, and more optimistic that all would turn out well in the end. In his "Dear Winston" letter of March 18 he attempted to encourage Churchill by stressing their essential comradeship in words that conveyed almost equal parts of warmth and determination. This letter and the American plan for a cross-channel invasion doubtless helped to restore Churchill to his fighting self. (The idea of the invasion was first expressed in a memorandum of February 28 by Major General Dwight D. Eisenhower, then head of the War Plans Division of the War Department. Harry Hopkins and Army Chief of Staff George C. Marshall carried the memorandum to London on April 8.) In any event, by the middle of April the Prime Minister was confidently taking the lead in preparing for negotiations with the Russians and setting in motion the Madagascar invasion. He also began, politely but firmly, to dispute some of Roosevelt's priorities, particularly with regard to the allocation of American aircraft and to the American plan for a 1942 incursion in Europe designed to relieve pressure on the Soviet Union.

In May and early June the Americans won signal successes in the Pacific: they blunted the Japanese threat to Australia in the battle of Coral Sea and foiled Japan's attempt to capture Midway in what proved to be the turning point of the Pacific war. A successful round of negotiations with Russian Foreign Minister Vyacheslav Molotov in both London and Washington at almost the same time provided further encouragement, and Churchill soon decided to go to Washington for a third meeting with the President. Protocol between the two men had now been sufficiently relaxed to allow Roosevelt to inform his colleague that he would be at home in Hyde Park when Churchill arrived and to invite him to stop there before proceeding to Washington. The Prime Minister cheerfully complied with this invitation and arrived at the President's Dutchess County retreat on June 19.

For all their friendliness, Churchill was unsuccessful in trying to convince Roosevelt that all plans for a 1942 landing on the Continent should be abandoned and that, instead, the plan for a North African invasion should be revived. Not until Hopkins and Marshall went to London on July 16 was this question resolved. The agreement turned out to embody primarily Churchill's views, although this was not clear to the American negotiators until some time after they had returned from London. Despite Roosevelt's genuine concern about relieving pressure on the Russians—the only ally then engaged in large-scale fighting against the Germans—as soon as possible, he reluctantly gave up the idea of a 1942 cross-channel invasion when the British remained adamant in their opposition, and settled for the African venture on the condition that it be clearly an American operation. Roosevelt thus bowed to what was probably inevitable, against the advice of General Marshall, who steadfastly gave top priority to a direct attack on German-held Europe and therefore frequently clashed with Churchill, who believed such a course to be too risky. Roosevelt also began to weaken in his insistence that the British maintain and even increase the costly convoys bringing supplies to Russia by the northern route around Norway, accepting as valid the dubious claim that sufficient supplies could be provided to the Soviets via the Red Sea.

It was Churchill who went to see Stalin with the unpalatable news that there would be no second front in Europe in 1942 and that aid shipments would be at least temporarily curtailed. When these announcements produced some stormy conversations but no actual breakdown in relations, and when the major offensive the Germans had launched in Russia on July 2 ran into heroic resistance by the Red Army at the outskirts of Stalingrad, Roosevelt felt somewhat relieved. Both leaders then threw themselves into the planning for the North African invasion, code-named Torch, which was placed under the command of Dwight D. Eisenhower. Despite considerable differences at the outset, general agreement was reached on the overall plan by September 5, with both sides yielding some ground.

Committed at last to a major offensive action, which both Roosevelt and Churchill saw as the beginning of a happier phase of the war, the two men began to turn their eyes more resolutely toward the eventual victory. Anticipating an easy, perhaps even bloodless triumph in North Africa, they thought ahead to 1943, when more effective convoying techniques might allow an ever greater flow of American supplies to Britain, when an Anglo-American air force might be able to aid the Russians directly, and when plans for a direct attack on Hitler's "Fortress Europe" might come to fruition. When Churchill sent Roosevelt a new "wish list" on October 31, 1942, he by no means underestimated the problems that lay ahead, but he displayed at least a cautious optimism.

Indeed, by late 1942 the military situation looked more promising than ever before. In the Pacific the major Japanese effort to drive American marines off Guadalcanal had failed. In Russia Hitler's armies were reeling under the blows of counterattacks launched from Stalingrad, and in North Africa General Sir Bernard L. Montgomery's British forces had begun the final destruction of the Afrika Korps with the battle of El Alamein. On October 23 the Western Naval Task Force steamed out of Hampton Roads, Virginia, to take its place in the 850-ship armada that was soon to appear off Casablanca, Oran, and Algiers. The road to victory seemed, at last, to lie open ahead.

Messages and Notes

Doc. 1
ROOSEVELT TO CHURCHILL

September 11, 1939

My dear Churchill:

It is because you and I occupied similar positions in the World War[1] that I want you to know how glad I am that you are back again in the Admiralty. Your problems are, I realize, complicated by new factors but the essential is not very different. What I want you and the Prime Minister[2] to know is that I shall at all times welcome it if you will keep me in touch personally with anything you want me to know about. You can always send sealed letters through your pouch or my pouch.

I am glad you did the Marlboro [sic] volumes[3] before this thing started—and I much enjoyed reading them.

---

[1] Roosevelt served as Assistant Secretary of the Navy from 1913 to 1920, Churchill as First Lord of the Admiralty from 1911 to 1915.

[2] Neville Chamberlain became Prime Minister of Great Britain on May 28, 1937.

[3] The fourth and final volume of Churchill's *Marlborough—His Life and Times* had appeared in 1938.

Doc. 2
CHURCHILL TO ROOSEVELT

October 5, 1939

We quite understand natural desire of United States to keep belligerents out of their waters. We like the idea of a wide limit of say 300 miles within which no submarines of any belligerent country should act.[1] If America requests all belligerents to comply, we should immediately declare that we would respect your wishes. General questions of international law would of course remain unprejudiced. More difficulty arises about surface ships, because if a raider operates from or takes refuge in the American zone, we should have to be protected or allowed to protect ourselves. We have mentioned several other instances to Mr. Kennedy.[2] We do not mind how far south the prohibited zone goes, provided that it is effectively maintained.[3] We should have great difficulty in accepting a zone which was only policed by some weak neutral. But of course if the American Navy takes care of it, that is all right.

Thirdly, we are still not sure whether raider off Brazil is *Scheer* or *Hipper*, but widespread movements are being made by us to meet either case. The more American ships cruising along the South American coast the better, as you, sir, would no doubt hear what they saw or did not see. Raider might then find American waters rather crowded, or may anyhow prefer to go on to sort of trade route, where we are preparing.

We wish to help you in every way in keeping the war out of Americas.

[1] On October 3 the delegates of twenty-one American republics had met in Panama to set up a 300- to 600-mile-wide "security zone" around the Western Hemisphere within which no warlike acts were to be committed. German commerce raiders, including the *Admiral Scheer* and the *Admiral Graf Spee*, were operating within that zone, and the British soon set up "hunting groups" to track them down. See S. W. Roskill, *The War at Sea 1939–1945*, 1 (London, 1954): 70, 113–114.

[2] Joseph P. Kennedy, American ambassador to Great Britain.

[3] The policy of a specifically limited neutrality zone did not prove to be very effective, in part because of the limited American naval strength in the Atlantic. On October 9, 1939, Roosevelt instructed the Navy "to broadcast reports of sightings in plain English, a step that probably helped to persuade the German navy to keep its submarines and surface raiders out of the western North Atlantic during the early months of the war." Stetson Conn and Byron Fairchild, *The Framework of Hemisphere Defense* (Washington, 1960), p. 24.

Doc. 3
CHURCHILL TO ROOSEVELT

October 16, 1939

It is very odd that *Scheer* should have made no other prizes since September 30. As I told you we are taking some pains in looking for him. He may be anywhere by now. We have been hitting the U-boats hard with our new apparatus and on Friday 13th four including two of the largest and latest were destroyed. Sinking of *Royal Oak*[1] was a remarkable episode of which I will write you more fully.[2] It in no way affects the naval balance. Our accounts of Hitler's oil position make us feel he is up against time limits. This means that either he will make vehement attack on us for which we are prepared or that he is being held back by counsellors who see the red light. We propose to see what happens, feeling fairly confident that all will be well. We should be quite ready to tell you about our asdic methods[3] whenever you feel they would be of use to the United States Navy and are sure the secret will go no farther. They certainly are very remarkable in results and enable two destroyers to do the work that could not have been done by ten last time. We have not been at all impressed by the accuracy of the Germans' air bombing of our warships. They seem to have no effective bomb sights. I have not written as I promised because this and my former cable[4] give all my news.

[1] On October 14 a German submarine had sunk the British battleship *Royal Oak* while it was at anchor at the Home Fleet base at Scapa Flow in the Orkney Islands. See Roskill, *War at Sea*, 1: 73ff.

[2] "It is now known," the official historian of the Royal Navy during World War II wrote later, "that this operation was planned with great care by Admiral Dönitz, who was correctly informed of the weak state of the defences of the eastern entrances [of Scapa Flow]." Roskill, *War at Sea*, 1: 74.

[3] The asdic system, developed by and named after Britain's Antisubmarine Detection Investigation Committee, was later called sonar by the U.S. Navy.

[4] See above, Doc. 2.

Doc. 4
CHURCHILL TO ROOSEVELT

December 25, 1939

We have always conformed to undertaking not to use British submarines inside your zone and I am very sorry there seems to be trouble about recent incidents. We cannot always refrain from stopping enemy ships outside international three-mile limit when these may well be supply ships for U-boats or surface raiders, but instructions have been given only to arrest or fire upon them out of sight of United States shores.[1] As a result of action off Plate[2] whole South Atlantic is now clear and may perhaps continue clear of warlike operations. This must be a blessing to South American republics whose trade was hampered by activities of raider and whose ports were used for his supply ships and information centres. In fact we have rescued all this vast area from war disturbances. Earnestly hope this will be valued by South American states who may likely for long periods enjoy in practice not only three-hundred but three-thousand-mile limit. . . .

If we should break under load South American republics would soon have worse worries than the sound of one day's distant seaward cannonade. And you also, sir, in quite a short time would have more direct cares. I ask that full consideration should be given to strain upon us at this crucial period and best construction put upon action indispensable to end war shortly in right way. . . .

[1] See U.S. Department of State, *Foreign Relations of the United States 1939*, 5 (Washington, 1956) : 117–119. Henceforth cited as *FR*. On December 22 the British ambassador in Washington told Undersecretary of State Sumner Welles that "the British Government would agree to respect the neutral zone provided Germany agreed to respect it." The following day the signatories of the Panama pact issued a joint statement protesting recent British and German violations of the neutrality zone.

[2] On December 13 three British light cruisers had attacked the German raider *Admiral Graf Spee* in the Plate River estuary off Montevideo and chased her into the harbor. She was scuttled there by her commander on December 19. See Roskill, *War at Sea*, 1: 118ff.

Doc. 5
CHURCHILL TO ROOSEVELT

January 29, 1940

I gave orders last night that no American ship should, in any circumstances, be diverted into the combat zone round the British Islands declared by you. I trust this will be satisfactory.[1]

[1] Churchill was trying here to avoid ill will of the sort which British detention of U.S. merchant ships had produced in the United States during World War I. It was one of the very few decisions he made without proper consultation of the War Cabinet and was almost immediately modified.

Doc. 6
CHURCHILL TO ROOSEVELT

January 30, 1940

I trust that the information I gave you last night about the orders sent to British ships will not be made known until measures have been concerted which will remove appearance of discrimination. It has been pointed out to me that my signal to fleet can only be maintained if measures are taken to ensure in advance of their departure that United States ships carry no objectional [sic] cargo. Moreover, in exceptional cases it may be necessary to divert United States ships if we have definite ground for suspicion against them. It would be most helpful if some arrangement could be reached with Lothian[1] on these lines and meanwhile all publicity avoided.

[1] Lord Lothian (Philip Kerr), British ambassador in Washington since August 1939.

Doc. 7
ROOSEVELT TO CHURCHILL

February 1, 1940

My dear Churchill:
Ever so many thanks for that tremendously interesting account of the extraordinarily well-fought action of your three cruisers.[1] I am inclined to think that when we know more about the facts, it will turn out that the damage to the *Admiral Graf Spee* was greater than reported.[2]

At the time of dictating this, I think our conversation in regard to search and detention of American ships is working out satisfactorily— but I would not be frank unless I told you that there has been much public criticism here.[3] The general feeling is that the net benefit to your people and to France is hardly worth the definite annoyance caused to us. That is always found to be so in a nation which is 3,000 miles away from the fact of war.

[1] HMS *Ajax, Achilles,* and *Exeter,* which had fought the German pocket battle-ship *Admiral Graf Spee* at the battle of the River Plate off Montevideo on December 13, 1939; Churchill had sent Roosevelt a seven-page report on the action.

[2] This appears not to have been the case. See Roskill, *War at Sea,* 1: 118ff.

[3] See *FR 1940,* 2 (Washington, 1957): 6ff.

I wish much that I could talk things over with you in person—but I am grateful to you for keeping me in touch, as you do.

Always sincerely,

Doc. 8
CHURCHILL TO ROOSEVELT

May 15, 1940

Although I have changed my office,[1] I am sure you would not wish me to discontinue our intimate, private correspondence. As you are no doubt aware, the scene has darkened swiftly.[2] The enemy have a marked preponderance in the air,[3] and their new technique is making a deep impression upon the French.[4] I think myself the battle on land has only just begun, and I should like to see tanks engaged. Up to the present, Hitler is working with specialised units in tanks and air. The small countries are simply smashed up, one by one, like matchwood. We must expect, though it is not yet certain, that Mussolini will hurry in to share the loot of civilization. We expect to be attacked here ourselves, both from the air and by parachute and airborne troops in the near future, and are getting ready for them. If necessary, we shall continue the war alone and we are not afraid of that. But I trust you realise, Mr. President, that the voice and force of the United States may count for nothing if they are withheld too long. You may have a completely subjugated, Nazified Europe established with astounding swiftness, and the weight may be more than we can bear. All I ask now is that you should proclaim nonbelligerency, which would mean that you would help us with everything short of actually engaging armed forces. Immediate needs are: first of all, the loan of forty or fifty of your older destroyers to bridge the gap between what we have now

[1] Churchill had succeeded Neville Chamberlain as Prime Minister on May 10.

[2] The long-planned German attack on France, the Low Countries, and Luxembourg had begun early on the morning of May 10. By May 14 German forces had crossed the Meuse River and broken through at Sedan. For an account of the early days of the German offensive, see Winston S. Churchill, *Their Finest Hour* (Boston, 1949), chap. 2; and L. F. Ellis, *The War in France and Flanders 1939–1940* (London, 1953), chap. 3.

[3] On May 14 the German air force had carried out a terror raid, the first of its kind in the west, on Rotterdam, killing nearly 900 people and rendering nearly 80,000 homeless. The following morning the Dutch military forces capitulated.

[4] On May 14 French Premier Paul Reynaud had pleaded with the British government to send ten more fighter squadrons; he repeated his appeal the following morning. See J. R. M. Butler, *Grand Strategy*, vol. 2, *September 1939–June 1941* (London, 1957), pp. 183–184.

and the large new construction we put in hand at the beginning of the war. This time next year we shall have plenty. But if in the interval Italy comes in against us with another one hundred submarines, we may be strained to the breaking point. Secondly, we want several hundred of the latest types of aircraft, of which you are now getting delivery. These can be repaid by those now being constructed in the United States for us. Thirdly, anti-aircraft equipment and ammunition, of which again there will be plenty next year, if we are alive to see it. Fourthly, the fact that our ore supply is being compromised from Sweden, from North Africa, and perhaps from northern Spain makes it necessary to purchase steel in the United States. This also applies to other materials. We shall go on paying dollars for as long as we can, but I should like to feel reasonably sure that when we can pay no more, you will give us the stuff all the same. Fifthly, we have many reports of possible German parachute or airborne descents in Ireland. The visit of a United States squadron to Irish ports, which might well be prolonged, would be invaluable. Sixthly, I am looking to you to keep that Japanese dog quiet in the Pacific, using Singapore in any way convenient. The details of the material which we have in mind will be communicated to you separately.

Doc. 9
ROOSEVELT TO CHURCHILL

May 16, 1940

I have just received your message[1] and I am sure it is unnecessary for me to say that I am most happy to continue our private correspondence as we have in the past.

I am, of course, giving every possible consideration to the suggestions made in your message. I shall take up your specific proposals one by one.

First, with regard to the possible loan of forty or fifty of our older destroyers. As you know a step of that kind could not be taken except with the specific authorization of the Congress and I am not certain that it would be wise for that suggestion to be made to the Congress at this moment. Furthermore, it seems to me doubtful, from the standpoint of our own defense requirements, which must inevitably be linked with the defense requirements of this hemisphere and with our obligations in the Pacific, whether we could dispose even temporarily of these destroyers. Furthermore, even if we were able to take the step

1 See above, Doc. 8.

you suggest, it would be at least six or seven weeks at a minimum, as I see it, before these vessels could undertake active service under the British flag.

Second. We are now doing everything within our power to make it possible for the Allied Governments to obtain the latest types of aircraft in the United States.

Third. If Mr. Purvis[2] may receive immediate instructions to discuss the question of anti-aircraft equipment and ammunition with the appropriate authorities here in Washington, the most favorable consideration will be given to the request made in the light of our own defense needs and requirements.

Fourth. Mr. Purvis has already taken up with the appropriate authorities here the purchase of steel in the United States and I understand that satisfactory arrangements have been made.[3]

Fifth. I shall give further consideration to your suggestion with regard to the visit of the United States squadron to Irish ports.

Sixth. As you know, the American fleet is now concentrated at Hawaii, where it will remain at least for the time being.

I shall communicate with you again as soon as I feel able to make a final decision with regard to some of the other matters dealt with in your message and I hope you will feel free to communicate with me in this way at any time.

The best of luck to you.

[2] Arthur Purvis, a Canadian businessman, headed the Anglo-French Purchasing Board, which had been set up in Washington in December 1939 as a result of discussions at the second meeting of the Supreme War Council on September 22 of that year.

[3] For an account of British orders and purchases in the United States during the first year of the war, see Sir Keith Hancock and Margaret M. Gowing, *British War Economy* (London, 1949), chaps. 4, 9; M. M. Postan, *British War Production* (London, 1952), pp. 206–207, 227ff; H. Duncan Hall, *North American Supply* (London, 1955), chaps. 3–6; and H. Duncan Hall and C. C. Wrigley, *Studies of Overseas Supply* (London, 1956), chap. 2.

Doc. 10
CHURCHILL TO ROOSEVELT

May 18, 1940

Many thanks for your message[1] for which I am grateful. I do not need to tell you about the gravity of what has happened.[2] We are

[1] See above, Doc. 9.

[2] On May 17 German forces had occupied Brussels and the following day Antwerp had fallen to the enemy.

determined to persevere to the very end whatever the result of the great battle raging in France may be. We must expect in any case to be attacked here on the Dutch model[3] before very long and we hope to give a good account of ourselves. But if American assistance is to play any part it must be available.

[3] See above, Doc. 8, note 3.

Doc. 11
CHURCHILL TO ROOSEVELT

May 20, 1940

Lothian has reported his conversation with you. I understand your difficulties but I am very sorry about the destroyers. If they were here in six weeks they would play an invaluable part. The battle in France is full of danger to both sides. Though we have taken heavy toll of enemy in the air and are clawing down two or three to one of their planes, they have still a formidable numerical superiority. Our most vital need is therefore the delivery at the earliest possible date of the largest possible number of Curtis P-40 fighters now in course of delivery to your Army.

With regard to the closing part of your talk with Lothian, our intention is whatever happens to fight on to the end in this Island and, provided we can get the help for which we ask, we hope to run them very close in the air battles in view of individual superiority. Members of the present administration would likely go down during this process should it result adversely, but in no conceivable circumstances will we consent to surrender. If members of the present administration were finished and others came in to parley amid the ruins, you must not be blind to the fact that the sole remaining bargaining counter with Germany would be the fleet, and if this country was left by the United States to its fate no one would have the right to blame those then responsible if they made the best terms they could for the surviving inhabitants. Excuse me, Mr. President, putting this nightmare bluntly.[1] Evidently I could not answer for my successors who in utter despair and helplessness might well have to accommodate themselves to the German will. However, there is happily no need at present to dwell upon such ideas. Once more thanking you for your good will.

[1] Beginning on May 19, Churchill also arranged for copies of the daily telegrams on military operations, primarily compiled for the heads of the British Dominions, to be sent to Roosevelt for his private information. Butler, *Grand Strategy*, 2: 240.

Doc. 12
CHURCHILL TO ROOSEVELT

June 11, 1940[1]

We all listened to you last night and were fortified by the grand scope of your declaration.[2] Your statement that material aid of the United States will be given to the Allies in their struggle is a strong encouragement in a dark but not unhopeful hour. Everything must be done to keep France in the fight and to prevent any idea of the fall of Paris, should it occur, becoming the occasion of any kind of parley. The hope with which you inspired them may give them strength to persevere. [They should] continue to defend every yard of their soil and use full fighting force of their army. Hitler thus baffled of quick results will turn upon us and we are preparing ourselves to resist his fury and defend our Island. Having saved British Expeditionary Force[3] we do not lack troops at home and as soon as divisions can be equipped on much higher scale needed for Continental service they will be despatched to France. Our intention is to have a strong army fighting in France for campaign of 1941. I have already cabled you about aeroplanes including flying boats which are so needful to us in the impending struggle for the life of Great Britain.[4] But even more pressing is the need for destroyers. Italian outrage[5] makes it necessary for us to cope with much larger number of submarines which may

[1] No copy has been found in the files of the Roosevelt Library. See *FR 1940*, 3 (Washington, 1958) : 52.

[2] Churchill had listened to Roosevelt's University of Virginia commencement address of June 10 on shortwave radio. "Overwhelmingly," the President had declared, "we, as a nation—and this applies to all the other American nations—are concerned that military and naval victory for the gods of force and hate would endanger the institutions of democracy in the Western world, and that equally, therefore, the whole of our sympathies lies with those nations that are giving their life blood in combat against these forces. . . . In our American unity . . . we will extend to the opponents of force the material resources of this nation." See Samuel I. Rosenman, ed., *The Public Papers and Addresses of Franklin D. Roosevelt*, vol. 9, *War: And Aid to Democracies* (New York, 1941) , no. 58. Henceforth cited as *PPR*.

[3] In a naval operation of heroic proportions and enormous psychological significance, some 200,000 British and 130,000 French soldiers were evacuated from the beaches of Dunkirk between May 26 and June 4, despite constant harassment by German dive bombers. All their equipment was lost, however.

[4] See above, Doc. 11.

[5] Italy had declared war on France. Roosevelt remarked in his address: "On this tenth day of June, 1940, the hand that held the dagger has struck it into the back of its neighbor."

come out into the Atlantic and perhaps be based on Spanish ports. To this the only counter is destroyers. Nothing is so important as for us to have 30 or 40 old destroyers you have already had reconditioned. . . . Not a day should be lost. I send you my heartfelt thanks and those of my colleagues for all you are doing and seeking to do for what we may now indeed call a common cause.

Doc. 13
CHURCHILL TO ROOSEVELT

June 12, 1940

I spent last night and this morning at the French GQG,[1] where the situation was explained to me in the gravest terms by Generals Weygand[2] and Georges.[3] You have no doubt received full particulars from Mr. Bullitt.[4] The practical point is what will happen when and if the French front breaks, Paris is taken, and General Weygand reports formally to his Government that France can no longer continue what he calls "coordinated war." The aged Marshal Pétain[5] who was none too good in April and July 1918 is I fear ready to lend his name and prestige to a treaty of peace for France. Reynaud[6] on the other hand is for fighting on and he has a young General de Gaulle[7] who believes much can be done. Admiral Darlan[8] declares he will send the

[1] Grand Quartier Général (General Headquarters) .

[2] On May 19 Maxime Weygand had succeeded Maurice Gamelin as Chief of the General Staff and commander in chief of the French army.

[3] Joseph Georges was commander of the northeastern theater of operations and thus had operational control over the British Expeditionary Force on the western front.

[4] William C. Bullitt had been American ambassador to France since 1936. For his reports to the State Department on this subject, see *FR 1940*, 1 (Washington, 1959) : 217ff.; for his direct messages to Roosevelt, see Orville H. Bullitt, ed., *For the President: Personal and Secret* (Boston, 1972) , pp. 415ff.

[5] Marshall Henri Philippe Pétain, aged eighty-five, had entered the French Cabinet as Minister of State and Vice Premier on May 18 and led the peace forces in France.

[6] Paul Reynaud, who had succeeded Édouard Daladier as Premier on March 21, now also headed the Ministry of War and National Defense and favored continuing the war.

[7] Charles de Gaulle had been promoted to brigadier general on May 15 and was appointed Undersecretary of State for War and National Defense when Reynaud took over that ministry on June 6.

[8] Admiral Jean François Darlan, commander in chief of the French navy, became Minister of the Navy in the new Pétain government on June 16 but promised never to surrender the fleet to the Germans.

French fleet to Canada. It would be disastrous if the two big modern ships fell into bad hands. It seems to me that there must be many elements in France who will wish to continue the struggle either in France or in the French colonies or in both. This, therefore, is the moment for you to strengthen Reynaud the utmost you can and try to tip the balance in favour of the best and longest possible French resistance. I venture to put this point before you although I know you must understand it as well as I do.

Of course I made it clear to the French that we shall continue whatever happened and that we thought Hitler could not win the war or the mastery of the world until he had disposed of us, which has not been found easy in the past and which perhaps will not be found easy now. I made it clear to the French that we had good hopes of victory and anyhow had no doubts whatever of what our duty was. If there is anything you can say publicly or privately to the French now is the time.

Doc. 14
CHURCHILL TO ROOSEVELT

June 13, 1940

French have sent for me again, which means that crisis has arrived. Am just off. Anything you can say or do to help them now may make a difference.

We are also worried about Ireland. An American squadron at Berehaven[1] would do no end of good I am sure.

[1] A port in the Irish Republic (Eire).

Doc. 15
CHURCHILL TO ROOSEVELT

June 14, 1940[1]

Ambassador Kennedy will have told you about the British meeting today with the French at Tours of which I showed him our record.[2] I

[1] This telegram was sent through Ambassador Kennedy to the State Department. No copy has been found in the files of the Roosevelt Library. See *FR 1940*, 1: 250–251.

[2] For Kennedy's report, see *FR 1940*, 1: 248–249. Kennedy wrote that "Reynaud had told Churchill that [General] Weygand was insisting on an armistice; the

cannot exaggerate its critical character. They were very nearly gone. Weygand had advocated an armistice while he still had enough troops to prevent France from lapsing into anarchy. Reynaud asked us whether in view of the sacrifice and sufferings of France we would release her from the obligation about not making a separate peace. Although the fact that we have unavoidably been largely out of this terrible battle weighed with us, I did not hesitate in the name of the British Government to refuse consent to an armistice or separate peace. I urged that this issue should not be discussed until a further appeal has been made by Reynaud to you and the United States, which I undertook to second. Agreement was reached on this and a much better mood prevailed for the moment with Reynaud and his ministers.

Reynaud felt strongly that it would be beyond his power to encourage his people to fight on without hope of ultimate victory, and that hope could only be kindled by American intervention up to the extreme limit open to you. As he put it, they wanted to see light at the end of the tunnel.

While we were flying back here your magnificent message was sent and Ambassador Kennedy brought it to me on my arrival.[3] The British Cabinet was profoundly impressed and desire me to express their gratitude for it, but, Mr. President, I must tell you that it seems to me absolutely vital that this message should be published tomorrow, June 14,[4] in order that it may play the decisive part in turning the course of world history.[5] It will I am sure decide the French to deny

---

French Army could not fight any longer. . . . [I]t was only a matter of hours but that the Army would refuse to fight. . . . [I]t seems to me that for the record it really got down to Reynaud saying that unless the United States declared war on Germany and came in France was not going to fight."

3 A reference to Roosevelt's message to Reynaud of June 13: "As I have already stated to you and to Mr. Churchill, this Government is doing everything in its power to make available to the Allied Governments the material they so urgently require, and our efforts to do still more are being redoubled." *FR 1940*, 1: 248. Reading this message to the War Cabinet, Churchill commented that "the President could hardly urge the French to continue to struggle, and to undergo further torture, if he did not intend to support them." Some members of the War Cabinet were evidently more skeptical. "It was generally felt, although the implications of the message might be clear to the Anglo-Saxon mind, they might appear in a rather different light to the French, who would be looking for something more definite." Roger Parkinson, *Blood, Toil, Tears, and Sweat—The War History from Dunkirk to Alamein* (New York, 1973), p. 32.

4 Churchill dictated this telegram before midnight on June 13.

5 In fact, both Hull and Roosevelt absolutely refused to have this message published. When it was first cabled to Paris at 1 P.M. on June 13, Hull stated that "when this message is delivered it must be made entirely clear that this message is personal and private and not for publication." At 10 that evening Roosevelt sent a

Hitler a patched-up peace with France. He needs this peace in order to destroy us and take a long step forward to world mastery. All the far-reaching plans, strategic, economic, political, and moral, which your message expounds may be stillborn if the French cut out now. Therefore I urge that the message should be published now. We realise fully that the moment Hitler finds he cannot dictate a Nazi peace in Paris he will turn his fury on to us. We shall do our best to withstand it and if we succeed wide new doors are opened upon the future and all will come out even at the end of the day.

---

message to Ambassador Kennedy reemphasizing that "my message to Reynaud is not to be published under any circumstances. It was in no sense intended to commit and does not commit this Government to the slightest military activities in support of the Allies. . . . There is of course no authority except in Congress to make any commitment of this nature. . . . If there is any possibility of misunderstanding please insist that Churchill at once convey this statement to the appropriate French officials." *FR 1940*, 1: 250. When the War Cabinet met at 12:30 P.M. on June 14 Churchill laid before them Roosevelt's definite refusal.

Doc. 16
ROOSEVELT TO CHURCHILL

June 14, 1940[1]

I am very much impressed by your message,[2] and I am grateful to you for giving me so frankly the account of the meeting at Tours yesterday.

The magnificent courage and determination shown by the British and French Governments and by the British and French soldiers have never been exceeded.

You realize, as I hope Prime Minister Reynaud realizes, that we are doing our utmost in the United States to furnish all of the matériel and supplies which can possibly be released to the Allied Governments. At the same time, I believe you will likewise realize that, while our efforts will be exerted towards making available an ever increasing amount of matériel and supplies, a certain amount of time must pass before our efforts in this sense can be successful to the full extent desired.

As I asked Ambassador Kennedy last night to inform you, my message of yesterday's date addressed to the French Prime Minister was

[1] This message was sent through the State Department. No copy has been found in the FDR Library. See *FR 1940*, 1: 254–255.

[2] See above, Doc. 15.

in no sense intended to commit and did not commit this Government to military participation in support of the Allied Governments. You well know that there is of course no authority under our Constitution except in the Congress to make any commitment of this nature.[3] As Ambassador Kennedy also informed you, when I sent the message I had very much in mind the question of the French fleet and its disposition for future use. I regret that I am unable to agree to your request that my message be published,[4] since I believe it to be imperative that there be avoided any possible misunderstanding with regard to the facts set forth above.

I have asked the Congress as a first step to appropriate fifty million dollars for the immediate furnishing of food and clothing to civilian refugees in France, and the Senate yesterday unanimously approved this recommendation.[5]

I appreciate fully the significance and weight of the considerations set forth in your message.

As naval people you and I fully appreciate the vital strength of the fleet in being, and command of the seas means in the long run the saving of democracy and the recovery of those suffering temporary reverses.

It seems logical to assume that in any war if an armistice is asked for, it becomes almost impossible thereafter to avoid inclusion of a fleet in the terms discussed, especially if such fleet is still under the control of the government seeking the armistice. On the other hand, if a general seeks an armistice for his land forces, he does not control or include the disposition of naval forces.

3 See above, Doc. 15, note 5. For Ambassador Kennedy's own strongly anti-interventionist position during this period, see David E. Koskoff, *Joseph P. Kennedy: A Life and Times* (Englewood Cliffs, N.J., 1974), pp. 239ff.

4 In a phone conversation with Churchill on the morning of June 14 Kennedy, basing himself on Roosevelt's specific instructions of the preceding day, "explained again clearly that there was no authority in the United States Government except in Congress to make any commitment regarding war." Shortly after, Kennedy reported to Roosevelt that "Churchill was terribly disappointed as he had counted on publication of this message to put a little stiffening into the French backbone." Churchill was afraid that Roosevelt's refusal to allow the message to be published and his subsequent explanation that his principal concern was the disposition of the French fleet "would merely dampen what fires remained." *FR 1940*, 1: 251–252.

5 See *PPR*, vol. 9, no. 60. In the Emergency Relief Appropriation Act of 1941, signed by Roosevelt on June 26, Congress appropriated $50 million for refugee relief.

Doc. 17
CHURCHILL TO ROOSEVELT

June 15, 1940

. . . I understand all your difficulties with American public opinion and Congress, but events are moving downward[1] at a pace where they will pass beyond the control of American public opinion when at last it is ripened.[2] Have you considered what offers Hitler may choose to make to France? He may say "Surrender the fleet intact and I will leave you Alsace Lorraine," or alternatively "If you do not give me your ships I will destroy your towns." I am personally convinced that America will in the end go to all lengths, but this moment is supremely critical for France. A declaration that the United States will, if necessary, enter the war might save France. Failing that in a few days French resistance may have crumbled and we shall be left alone.

Although the present government and I personally would never fail to send the fleet across the Atlantic if resistance was beaten down here, a point may be reached in the struggle where the present ministers no longer have control of affairs and when very easy terms could be obtained for the British Islands by their becoming a vassal state of the Hitler empire. A pro-German government would certainly be called into being to make peace and might present to a shattered or a starving nation an almost irresistible case for entire submission to the Nazi will. The fate of the British fleet as I have already mentioned to you would be decisive on the future of the United States because if it were joined to the fleets of Japan, France, and Italy and the great resources of German industry, overwhelming sea power would be in Hitler's hands. He might, of course, use it with a merciful moderation. On the other hand he might not. This revolution in sea power might happen very quickly and certainly long before the United States would be able

[1] On May 20 the Germans had captured Amiens and Abbeville, and the Belgian army surrendered on May 28. On June 5 the "battle of France" began. On June 10 Italy declared war on France. On June 14 German troops entered Paris. See Winston S. Churchill, *The Gathering Storm* (Boston, 1948), chaps. 3–4; and Butler, *Grand Strategy*, 2: 189ff., 209ff.

[2] Churchill was beginning to be leary of American public opinion. On June 28 he told Ambassador Lothian: "Too much attention should not be paid to eddies of United States opinion. Only force of events can govern them. Up till April they were so sure the Allies would win that they did not think help necessary. Now they are so sure we shall lose that they do not think it possible." Churchill, *The Gathering Storm*, p. 228.

to prepare against it. If we go down you may have a United States of Europe under the Nazi command far more numerous, far stronger, far better armed than the new [world].

I know well, Mr. President, that your eye will already have searched these depths but I feel I have the right to place on record the vital manner in which American interests are at stake in our battle and that of France. . . .

The seizure of the channel ports by the enemy has provided him both with convenient bases and stepping-off ground for descents on our coast. This means that our east coast and channel ports will become much more open to attack and in consequence more shipping will have to be concentrated on west coast ports. This will enable the enemy to concentrate their submarine attacks on this more limited area, the shipping lanes of which will have to carry the heavy concentration of shipping.

This alone is a serious enough problem at a time when we know that the enemy intend to carry out the bitter and concentrated attack on our trade routes, but added to our difficulties is the fact that Italy's entry into the war has brought into the seas another 100 submarines many of which may be added to those already in the German U-boat fleet, which at a conservative estimate numbers 55.

The changed strategical situation brought about by the possession by the enemy of the whole coast of Europe from Norway to the channel has faced us with a prospect of invasion which has more hopes of success than we had ever conceived possible. While we must concentrate our destroyers on protecting the vital trade, we must also dispose our naval forces to meet this threat.

If this invasion does take place, it will almost certainly be in the form of dispersed landings from a large number of small craft and the only effective counter to such a move is to maintain numerous and effective destroyer patrols.

To meet this double threat we have only the 68 destroyers mentioned above. Only 10 small-type new construction destroyers are due to complete in next four months.

The position becomes still worse when we have to contemplate diverting further destroyer forces to the Mediterranean as we may be forced to do when the sea war there is intensified.

We are now faced with the imminent collapse of French resistance and if this occurs the successful defence of this Island will be the only hope of averting the collapse of civilisation as we define it.

We must ask therefore as a matter of life or death to be reinforced with these destroyers. We will carry out the struggle whatever the odds

but it may well be beyond our resources unless we receive every reinforcement and particularly do we need this reinforcement on the sea.[3]

[3] After reading Churchill's message, Secretary of the Treasury Henry Morgenthau,
Jr., informed the President in a confidential memorandum of June 18 that "unless
we do something to give the English additional destroyers, it seems to me it is
absolutely hopeless to expect them to keep going."

Doc. 18
CHURCHILL TO ROOSEVELT

June 15, 1940

Since sending you my message this afternoon[1] I have heard that
Monsieur Reynaud, in a telegram which he has just sent to you, has
practically said that the decision of France to continue the war from
overseas depends on your being able to assure the French Government
that the United States of America will come into the war at a very
early date.

When I sent you my message just now I did not know that Monsieur
Reynaud had stated the dilemma in these terms, but I am afraid there
is no getting away from the fact that this is the choice before us now.

Indeed, the British Ambassador in Bordeaux tells me that if your
reply does not contain the assurance asked for, the French will very
quickly ask for an armistice, and I much doubt whether it will be
possible in that event for us to keep the French fleet out of German
hands.

When I speak of the United States entering the war I am, of course,
not thinking in terms of an expeditionary force, which I know is out of
the question. What I have in mind is the tremendous moral effect that
such an American decision would produce not merely in France but
also in all the democratic countries of the world and in the opposite
sense of the German and Italian peoples.[2]

[1] See above, Doc. 17.

[2] The replacement of Reynaud by Pétain on June 16 made the surrender of
France certain and rendered moot Churchill's plea, to which Roosevelt could not
have responded positively in any event.

Doc. 19
CHURCHILL TO ROOSEVELT

July 31, 1940

It is some time since I ventured to cable personally to you, and many things both good and bad have happened in between.[1] It has now become most urgent for you to let us have the destroyers, motor boats, and flying boats for which we have asked. The Germans have the whole French coastline from which to launch U-boats, dive-bomber attacks upon our trade and food, and in addition we must be constantly prepared to repel by sea action threatened invasion in the narrow waters, and also to deal with breakouts from Norway towards Ireland, Iceland, Shetlands, and Faroes. Besides this we have to keep control of the exit from the Mediterranean, and if possible the command of that island sea itself, and thus to prevent the war spreading seriously into Africa.

We have a large construction of destroyers and anti-U-boat craft coming forward, but the next three or four months open the gap of which I have previously told you. Latterly, the air attack on our shores has become injurious. . . . We could not keep up the present rate of casualties for long, and if we cannot get a substantial reinforcement, the whole fate of the war may be decided by this minor and easily remediable factor.

This is a frank account of our present situation and I am confident, now that you know exactly how we stand, that you will leave nothing undone to ensure that 50 or 60 of your oldest destroyers are sent to me at once. I can fit them very quickly with asdics and use them against U-boats on the western approaches and so keep the more modern and better-gunned craft for the narrow seas against invasion.

Mr. President, with great respect I must tell you that in the long history of the world, this is a thing to do now. Large construction is

1 Between May 27 and June 4 the British had withdrawn their ground forces (around 335,000 in number) from the Continent, mostly by way of Dunkirk, and on June 22 France had agreed to a humiliating armistice with Germany. On July 3 a British naval squadron attacked the French fleet anchored at Mers-el-Kebir, near Oran, to keep it from falling into German hands. The incident resulted in the death of nearly 1,300 Frenchmen. The French battle cruiser *Strasbourg* escaped to Toulon, but the *Dunkerque* went aground, and two other battleships were blown up or disabled. On July 8 the battleship *Richelieu*, anchored at Dakar, was seriously damaged by a British air torpedo. See Churchill, *The Gathering Storm*, chap. 5; Ellis, *War In France and Flanders*, chaps. 14–21; and Butler, *Grand Strategy*, 2: 202ff., 209ff.

coming to me in 1941, but the crisis will be reached long before 1941. I know you will do all in your power but I feel entitled and bound to put the gravity and urgency of the position before you.

If the destroyers were given, the motor boats and flying boats, which would be invaluable, could surely come in behind them.[2]

[2] On the following day Roosevelt received a memorandum from the Century Group—an organization of prominent American interventionists—which urged that destroyers be supplied to Britain in return for a guarantee that the Royal Navy would, in the event of a German invasion of England, operate from Canadian or American bases, and for immediate naval and air concessions in British possessions in the Western Hemisphere. This idea was agreed to in principle at a Cabinet meeting on August 2 and was made the subject of public debate by August 6. For an analysis of the role of the Century Group, see Mark Lincoln Chadwin, *The Hawks of World War II* (Chapel Hill, N.C., 1968), esp. chap. 4.

Doc. 20
ROOSEVELT TO CHURCHILL

August 13, 1940[1]

. . . It is my belief that it may be possible to furnish to the British Government as immediate assistance at least fifty destroyers, the motor torpedo boats heretofore referred to, and, insofar as airplanes are concerned, five planes each of the categories mentioned, the latter to be furnished for war-testing purposes. Such assistance, as I am sure you will understand, would only be furnished if the American people and the Congress frankly recognized that in return therefor the national defense and security of the United States would be enhanced. For that reason it would be necessary, in the event that it proves possible to. release the matériel above mentioned, that the British Government find itself able and willing to take the following steps:

1. Assurance on the part of the Prime Minister that in the event that the waters of Great Britain become untenable for British ships of war, the latter would not be turned over to the Germans or sunk but would be sent to other parts of the Empire for continued defense of the Empire.

2. An agreement on the part of Great Britain that the British Government would authorize the use of Newfoundland, Bermuda, the Bahamas, Jamaica, St. Lucia, Trinidad, and British Guiana as naval and air bases by the United States in the event of an

[1] This message has not been found in the files of the Roosevelt Library. It is printed in William L. Langer and S. Everett Gleason, *The Challenge to Isolation, 1937–1940* (New York, 1952), pp. 758–759.

attack on the American hemisphere by any non-American nation; and in the meantime the United States to have the right to establish such bases and to use them for training and exercise purposes with the understanding that the land necessary for the above could be acquired by the United States through purchase or through ninety-nine-year lease.

With the agreement suggested in point 2 above, I feel confident that specific details need not be considered at this time and that such questions as the exact locations of the land which the United States might desire to purchase or lease could be readily determined upon subsequently through friendly negotiation between the two Governments. . . .

Doc. 21
CHURCHILL TO ROOSEVELT

August 15, 1940

I need not tell you how cheered I am by your message[1] or how grateful I feel for your untiring efforts to give us all possible help. You will, I am sure, send us everything you can, for you know well that the worth of every destroyer that you can spare to us is measured in rubies. But we also need the motor torpedo boats which you mentioned and as many flying boats and rifles as you can let us have. We have a million men waiting for rifles.

The moral value of this fresh aid from your Government and people at this critical time will be very great and widely felt.

We can meet both the points you consider necessary to help you with Congress and with others concerned, but I am sure that you will not misunderstand me if I say that our willingness to do so must be conditional on our being assured that there will be no delay in letting us have the ships and flying boats. As regards an assurance about the British fleet, I am, of course, ready to reiterate to you what I told Parliament on June 4th.[2] We intend to fight this out here to the end

[1] See above, Doc. 20.
[2] For the text of Churchill's address, see *Parliamentary Debates*, Commons, 5th ser. (1909–) , vol. 361, cols. 787–796. Concluding that address, Churchill told the House of Commons: "Even though large tracts of Europe and many old and famous States have fallen or may fall into the grip of the Gestapo and all the odious apparatus of Nazi rule, we shall not flag or fail. We shall go on to the end. . . . We shall fight on the beaches, we shall fight on the landing grounds, we shall fight in the fields and in the streets, we shall fight in the hills; we shall never surrender, and

and none of us would ever buy peace by surrendering or scuttling the fleet. But in any use you may make of this repeated assurance you will please bear in mind the disastrous effect from our point of view and perhaps also from yours of allowing any impression to grow that we regard the conquest of the British Islands and its naval bases as any other than an impossible contingency. The spirit of our people is splendid. Never have they been so determined. Their confidence in the issue has been enormously and legitimately strengthened by the severe air fighting of the past week.

As regards naval and air bases, I readily agree to your proposal for 99-year leases which is easier for us than the method of purchase. I have no doubt that, once the principle is agreed between us, the details can be adjusted and we can discuss them at leisure. It will be necessary for us to consult the Governments of Newfoundland and Canada about the Newfoundland base in which Canada has an interest. We are at once proceeding to seek their consent.

Once again, Mr. President, let me thank you for your help and encouragement which means so much to us.

---

even if, which I do not for a moment believe, this Island or a large part of it were subjugated and starving, then our Empire beyond the seas, armed and guarded by the British Fleet, would carry on the struggle, until, in God's good time, the new world, with all its power and might, steps forth to the rescue and liberation of the old."

Doc. 22
CHURCHILL TO ROOSEVELT

August 22, 1940[1]

I am most grateful for all you are doing on our behalf. I had not contemplated anything in the nature of a contract, bargain, or sale between us. It is the fact that we had decided in Cabinet to offer you naval and air facilities off the Atlantic coast quite independently of destroyers or any other aid.[2] Our view is that we are two friends in danger helping each other as far as we can. We should therefore like to give you the facilities mentioned without stipulating for any return and even if tomorrow you found it too difficult to transfer the destroyers, et cetera, our offer still remains open because we think it is in the general good.

[1] No copy has been found in the FDR Library. This message was transmitted by Ambassador Kennedy to the State Department. *FR 1940*, 3: 68–69.

[2] The idea of a unilateral British offer had first been placed before the War Cabinet on July 29. See Parkinson, *Blood, Toil, Tears, and Sweat*, p. 82.

I see difficulties and even risks in the exchange of letters now suggested[3] or in admitting in any way that the munitions which you send us are a payment for the facilities. Once this idea is accepted people will contrast on each side what is given and received. The money value of the armaments would be computed and set against the facilities and some would think one thing about it and some another.

Moreover, Mr. President, as you well know each island or location is a case by itself. If, for instance, there were only one harbor or site, how is it to be divided and its advantages shared? In such a case we should like to make you an offer of what we think is best for both rather than to embark upon a close-cut argument as to what ought to be delivered in return for value received.

What we want is that you shall feel safe on your Atlantic seaboard so far as any facilities in possessions of ours can make you safe and naturally if you put in money and make large developments you must have the effective security of a long lease. Therefore I would rather rest at this moment upon the general declaration made by me in the House of Commons yesterday,[4] both on this point and as regards the future of the fleet. Then if you will set out in greater detail what you want we will at once tell you what we can do and thereafter the necessary arrangements, technical and legal, can be worked out by our experts. Meanwhile we are quite content to trust entirely to your judgement and sentiments of the people of the United States about any aid in munitions, et cetera, you feel able to give us. But this would be entirely a separate spontaneous act on the part of the United States arising out of their view of world struggle and how their own interests stand in relation to it and the causes it involves.

Although the air attack has slackened in the last few days and our strength is growing in many ways I do not think that bad man has yet struck his full blow. We are having considerable losses in merchant ships on the northwestern approaches, now our only channel of regular communication with the oceans, and your 50 destroyers if they came along at once would be a precious help.

3 This exchange had apparently been proposed, on August 19, by Undersecretary of State Welles. See Parkinson, *Blood, Toil, Tears, and Sweat,* p. 97.

4 On August 20 Churchill told the House of Commons: "[S]ome months ago we came to the conclusion that the interests of the United States and of the British Empire both required that the United States should have facilities for the naval and air defence of the Western hemisphere against the attack of a Nazi power. . . . [W]e had therefore decided spontaneously, and without being asked or offered any inducement, to inform the Government of the United States that we would be glad to place such defence facilities at their disposal in our transatlantic possessions for their greater security." *Parliamentary Debates,* Commons, 5th ser., vol. 364, col. 1170.

Doc. 23
CHURCHILL TO ROOSEVELT

August 25, 1940

I fully understand legal and constitutional difficulties which make you wish for a contract,[1] embodied in letters, but I venture to put before you the difficulties and even dangers which I foresee in this procedure.

For the sake of precise list of instrumentalities mentioned, which in our sore need we greatly desire, we are asked to pay undefined concessions in all islands and places mentioned from Newfoundland to British Guiana "as may be required in the judgement of the United States." Suppose that we could not agree to all your experts asked for, should we not be exposed to a charge of breaking our contract, for which we had already received value? Your commitment is definite, ours unlimited.[2] Much though we need destroyers, we should not wish to have them at the risk of a misunderstanding with the United States, or indeed any serious argument. If the matter is to be represented as a contract, both sides must be defined with far more precision on our side than has hitherto been possible. But this might easily take some time. As I have several times pointed out, we need destroyers chiefly to bridge the gap between now and the arrival of our new construction, which I set on foot on the outbreak of the war. This construction is very considerable. For instance, we shall receive by the end of February new destroyers and new medium destroyers 20. Corvettes, which are a handy type of submarine-hunter, adapted to ocean work 60. Motor torpedo boats 37. MAS boats 25.[3] Fairmiles, a wooden antisubmarine patrol boat 104. 72 ft. motor launches 29. An even greater inflow will arrive in the following 6 months. It is just in the gap from September to February inclusive, while this new crop is coming in and working up, that your fifty destroyers would be invaluable. With them we could minimize the shipping losses in northwestern approaches, and also take a stronger line against Mussolini in the Mediterranean.

[1] To make the "deal" more acceptable in America, Roosevelt wanted a formal British agreement to the quid pro quo suggested in his message of August 13 (Doc. 20 above). Since in formal terms the United States received far more than it gave, Churchill preferred to look on the transaction as two unrelated gifts.
[2] This sentence is garbled in the original text, but the meaning given here is clearly indicated.
[3] MAS boats were Motor Antisubmarine boats used in convoy operations in coastal waters.

Therefore time is all-important. We should not, however, be justified in the circumstances if we gave a blank cheque on the whole of our transatlantic possessions merely to bridge this gap, through which anyhow we hope to make our way, though with added risk and suffering. This I am sure you will see puts forth our difficulties plainly.

Would not following procedure be acceptable?

I would offer at once certain fairly well-defined facilities which will show you the kind of gift we have in mind and your experts could then discuss these or any variants of them with ours, we remaining the final judge of what we can give. All this we will do free, trusting entirely to the generosity and good will of the American people as to whether they on their part would like to do something for us. But anyhow it is the settled policy of His Majesty's Government to offer you and make available to you when desired solid and effective means of protecting your Atlantic seaboard. I have already asked the Admiralty and Air Ministry to draw up in outline what we are prepared to offer, leaving your experts to suggest alternatives. I propose to send you this outline in two or three days and to publish in due course. In this way there can be no possible dispute and the American people will feel more warmly towards us because they will see that we are playing the game by the world's cause and that their safety and interests are dear to us.

If your law or your Admiral require that any help you may choose to give us must be presented as a quid pro quo,[4] I do not see why the British Government have to come into that at all.

Could you not say that you did not feel able to accept this fine offer which we make unless the United States matched it in some way and that therefore Admiral would be able to link the one with the other?

I am so very grateful to you for all the trouble you have been taking and I am so sorry to add to your burden knowing what a good friend you have been to us.

[4] American legislation stipulated that war materiel could be sold or transferred to foreign powers only if the chief of staff concerned—in this case the Chief of Naval Operations—certified that it was not needed by U.S. forces.

Doc. 24
CHURCHILL TO ROOSEVELT

August 27, 1940

Lord Lothian has cabled me outline of facilities you have in mind. Our naval and air experts studying question from your point of view had reached practically the same conclusions except that in addition they thought that Antigua might be useful as a base for flying boats. To this also you would be very welcome. Our settled policy is to make the United States safe on their Atlantic seaboard beyond a peradventure, to quote a phrase you may remember.[1]

We are quite ready to make you a positive offer on these lines forthwith. There would of course have to be an immediate conference on details but for reasons which I set out in my last telegram[2] we do not like the idea of an arbiter should any difference arise because we feel that as donor we must remain the final judges of what the gift is to consist of within the general framework of the faciiities which will have been promised and always on the understanding that we shall do our best to meet the United States' wishes. . . .

If you felt able after our offer had been made to let us have instrumentalities which have been mentioned, or anything else you think proper, this could be expressed as an act not in payment or consideration for but in recognition of what we had done for the security of the United States.

Mr. President, this business has become especially urgent in view of recent menace which Mussolini is showing to Greece. If our business is put through on bilateral lines and in the highest spirit of good will, it might even now save that small historic country from invasion and conquest. Even the next forty-eight hours are important.

[1] In his note to Germany of October 14, 1918, President Woodrow Wilson had written: "It is indispensable that the Governments associated against Germany should know beyond a peradventure with whom they are dealing." *FR 1918*, Supplement 1 (Washington, 1933) : 359.

[2] See above, Doc. 23.

Doc. 25
ROOSEVELT TO CHURCHILL

September 23, 1940

As soon as your message[1] was received from Lord Lothian arrangements were undertaken for the release of the 250,000 Enfield rifles to the Purchasing Commission. I am informed that the rifles are already under way to New York for shipment.

[1] Not printed.

Doc. 26
CHURCHILL TO ROOSEVELT

September 24, 1940

I was encouraged by your reception of information conveyed by Lord Lothian about Dakar.[1] It would be against our joint interests if strong German submarine and aircraft base were established there. It looks as if there might be a stiff fight. Perhaps not, but anyhow orders have been given to ram it through. We should be delighted if you would send some American warships to Monrovia [or] Freetown, and I hope by that time to have Dakar ready for your call. But what really matters now is that you should put it across [to] the French Government that a war declaration would be very bad indeed for them in all that concerns United States. If Vichy declare war that is same thing as Germany, and Vichy possessions in Western Hemisphere must be considered potentially German possessions. Many thanks also for your hint about invasion. We are all ready for them. I am very glad to hear about rifles.

[1] The British had considered destroying the base at Dakar in French West Africa (Senegal) as early as July. Between August 5 and August 27 the Cabinet approved plans involving the use of British ships and marines as well as Free French and Polish troops in an effort to seize the port. The expedition arrived off Dakar on September 23, but its mission proved impossible and it was recalled two days later. See Churchill, *Their Finest Hour,* book two, chap. 9.

Doc. 27
CHURCHILL TO ROOSEVELT

October 4, 1940

After prolonged consideration of all the issues involved we today decided to let the Burma Road be reopened when the three months' period expires on October 17.[1] Foreign Secretary[2] and I will announce

[1] On July 11 the Japanese had demanded the closing of the track linking Burma and western China through the mountains of Yünnan, which was almost the only supply route open to Chiang Kai-shek. When it became apparent that a refusal would receive no more than diplomatic support in Washington, the British had complied, agreeing to a three-month closing on July 17. See *FR 1940,* 4 (Washington, 1955): 152, 156–157, 160; and J. R. M. Butler, *Lord Lothian (Philip Kerr) 1882–1940* (London and New York, 1960), pp. 301–303.

[2] Lord Halifax (Edward Frederick Lindley Wood), British Foreign Secretary since February 1938.

this to Parliament on Tuesday 8th. I shall say that our hopes for a just settlement being reached [between] Japan and China have not borne fruit and that the Three Power Pact revives the Anti-Comintern Pact of 1939[3] and that it has a clear pointer against the United States. I know how difficult it is for you to say anything which would commit the United States to any hypothetical course of action in the Pacific. But I venture to ask whether at this time a simple action might not speak louder than words. Would it not be possible for you to send an American squadron, the bigger the better, to pay a friendly visit to Singapore? There they would be welcome in a perfectly normal and rightful way. If desired, occasion might be taken of such a visit for a technical discussion of naval and military problems in those and Philippine waters and the Dutch might be invited to join. Anything in this direction would have a marked deterrent effect upon a Japanese declaration of war upon us over the Burma Road opening. I should be very grateful if you would consider action along these lines as it might play an important part in preventing the spreading of the war. . . .

3 The Tripartite Pact of September 27, 1940, was a mutual aid treaty among Italy, Germany, and Japan which seemed directly aimed at forestalling U.S. intervention in the Far East. The so-called Anti-Comintern Pact, calling for joint opposition to international communism, was concluded between Japan and Germany, not in 1939 but on November 25, 1936. Italy adhered to the agreement almost immediately and Spain followed on April 7, 1939. Although Hitler succeeded in widening this largely ceremonial arrangement into a military alliance with Italy on May 22, 1939, Japan refused to ally itself more closely with Germany until the signing of the Tripartite Pact.

Doc. 28
CHURCHILL TO ROOSEVELT

October 21, 1940

We hear rumours from various sources that the Vichy government are preparing their ships and colonial troops to aid the Germans against us. I do not myself believe these reports, but if the French fleet at Toulon were turned over to Germany it would be a very heavy blow. It would certainly be a wise precaution, Mr. President, if you would speak in the strongest terms to the French Ambassador[1] emphasising the disapprobation with which the United States would view such a betrayal of the cause of democracy and freedom. They will pay great heed in Vichy to such a warning. . . .

1 Gaston Henry-Haye.

Doc. 29
ROOSEVELT TO CHURCHILL

October 24, 1940

I have had conveyed to the French Ambassador a personal message from me to the following effect for immediate communication to his Government.

In the opinion of the United States Government the fact that the French Government alleges that it is under duress and consequently cannot act except to a very limited degree as a free agent is in no sense to be considered as justifying any course on the part of the French Government which would provide assistance to Germany and her allies in their war against the British Empire. The fact that a government is a prisoner of war of another power does not justify such a prisoner in serving its conqueror in operations against its former ally.

The Government of the United States received from the Pétain government during the first days it held office the most solemn assurances that the French fleet would not be surrendered. If the French Government now permits the Germans to use the French fleet in hostile operations against the British fleet, such action would constitute a flagrant and deliberate breach of faith with the United States Government.

I further stated that any agreement entered into between France and Germany which partook of the character above mentioned would most definitely wreck the traditional friendship between the French and American peoples, would permanently remove any chance that this Government would be disposed to give any assistance to the French people in their distress, and would create a wave of bitter indignation against France on the part of American public opinion.

I finally stated that if France pursued such a policy as that above outlined, the United States would make no effort when the appropriate time came to exercise its influence to ensure to France the retention of her overseas possessions.

I was glad to receive your message[1] and happy to know that the former American destroyers will soon be in action. I fully realize what a need you have at the present moment for small craft. I trust that things may steadily improve for you from now on.

[1] Not printed.

Doc. 30
CHURCHILL TO ROOSEVELT

October 27, 1940

We have not yet heard what Vichy has agreed to.[1]

If, however, they have betrayed warships and African and other colonial harbours to Hitler, our already heavy task will be grievously aggravated. If Oran and Bizerte become German-Italian submarine bases, our hopes of stopping or impeding the reinforcement of the hostile army now attacking Egypt will be destroyed, and the heaviest form of German-organised Italian attack must be expected. The situation in the western Mediterranean will also be gravely worsened. If Dakar is betrayed, very great dangers will arise in the Atlantic unless we are able to rectify the position, which will not be easy.

On the other hand, the announcement of Vichy's terms may lead to much desired revolt in the French Empire, which we should have to aid and foster with further drains upon our slowly expanding resources.

Either way, therefore, immense exertions will be required from us in the Mediterranean during the next year.

We are endeavouring to assemble a very large army in the Middle East, and the movement of troops thither from all parts of the Empire, especially from the mother country, has for some months past been unceasing. The campaign which will develop there certainly in the new year, and which may involve Turkey and Greece, makes demands upon our shipping and munitions output and resources which are enormous and beyond our power without your help to supply to a degree which would ensure victory.

All the time we have to provide for the defence of the Island against invasion which is fully mounted and for which sixty of the best German divisions and superior air forces stand ready.

Lastly, the U-boat and air attacks upon our only remaining lifeline, the northwestern approach, will be repelled only by the strongest concentration of our flotillas.

You will see, therefore, Mr. President, how very great are our problems and dangers. We feel, however, confident of our ability, if we are

[1] Vice Premier Pierre Laval and Marshal Pétain had met with Hitler at Montoire on October 22 and 24 respectively. Although they had agreed in principle to Franco-German cooperation, they had made no specific commitments. The relevant German documents make this quite clear. See U.S. Department of State, *Documents on German Foreign Policy 1918–1945*, ser. D, vol. 9 (Washington, 1960), no. 207.

given the necessary supplies, to carry on the war to a successful conclusion, and anyhow we are going to try our best.

You will, however, allow me to impress upon you the extreme urgency of accelerating delivery of the programme of aircraft and other munitions which has already been laid before you by Layton[2] and Purvis. So far as aircraft is concerned, would it be possible to speed up deliveries of existing orders so that the numbers coming to our support next year will be considerably increased? Furthermore, can new orders for expanded programme also be placed so promptly that deliveries may come out in the middle of 1941?

The equipment of our armies, both for home defence and overseas, is progressing, but we depend upon American deliveries to complete our existing programme which will certainly be delayed and impeded by the bombing of factories and disturbances of work.

A memorandum on the technical details is being furnished you through the proper channels, and having placed all the facts before you I feel confident that everything humanly possible will be done. The world cause is in your hands.

2 Sir Walter Thomas Layton, director general of programs for the British Ministry of Supply from 1940 to 1942.

Doc. 31
CHURCHILL TO ROOSEVELT

November 6, 1940[1]

I did not think it right for me as a foreigner to express any opinion upon American politics while the election was on but now I feel that you will not mind my saying that I prayed for your success and that I am truly thankful for it.[2] This does not mean that I seek or wish for anything more than the full, fair, and free play of your mind upon the world issues now at stake in which our two nations have to discharge their respective duties.

We are entering upon a sombre phase of what must evidently be a

1 The original of this message has not been found. Churchill, however, sent it for a second time on November 8, 1944. Churchill wrote later: "Curiously enough, I never received any answer to this telegram. It may well have been engulfed in the vast mass of congratulatory messages which were swept aside by urgent work." Churchill, *Gathering Storm,* p. 554.

2 Roosevelt was elected to a third term on November 5, defeating Wendell Willkie by nearly 5 million votes. The Democrats retained substantial majorities in both houses of Congress.

protracted and broadening war, and I look forward to being able to interchange my thoughts with you in all that confidence and good will which has grown up between us since I went to the Admiralty at the outbreak.

Things are afoot which will be remembered as long as the English language is spoken in any quarter of the globe, and in expressing the comfort I feel that the people of the United States have once again cast these great burdens upon you I must avow my sure faith that the lights by which we steer will bring us all safely to anchor.

Doc. 32
CHURCHILL TO ROOSEVELT

November 10, 1940

We have been much disturbed by reports of intention of French Government to bring the *Jean-Bart* and the *Richelieu*[1] to the Mediterranean for completion. It is difficult to exaggerate the potential danger if this were to happen, and so open the way for these ships to fall under German control. We should feel bound to do our best to prevent it. . . .

It would be most helpful if you felt able to give a further warning at Vichy on this matter, for if things went wrong it might well prove an extreme danger for us both.

[1] Reports had reached Churchill that the Germans were pressing the French to move the two new battleships from Casablanca and Dakar to ports within German control. Although the reports were true, Pétain had no intention of complying with this request.

Doc. 33
ROOSEVELT TO CHURCHILL

November 13, 1940

I have received your message with regard to the possible transfer by the French Government of the *Jean-Bart* and *Richelieu* to the Mediterranean for completion. Instructions have been sent immediately to the American Chargé d'Affaires[1] in Vichy to obtain a confirmation or

[1] H. Freeman Matthews, the first secretary of the American legation, served at the time as chargé d'affaires.

a denial of this report and to point out that it is of vital interest to the Government of the United States that these vessels remain in stations where they will not be exposed to control or seizure by powers which might employ them to ends in conflict with the interests of the United States in the future of the French fleet.[2]

If the report is confirmed, the Chargé d'Affaires has been instructed to convey to Marshal Pétain an expression of the grave concern of this Government and to point out that the Government of the United States, mindful of the community of interests which has existed for more than a century between France and the United States, believes that if it is necessary, for purposes of reconditioning or repairs, to move the units in question the French authorities will not transfer the *Jean-Bart* and *Richelieu* to places where they would be subject to a control inconsistent not only with the best interests of France but with the ultimate interests of the United States as well.

It will also be made clear, should the report be confirmed, that such a step on the part of the French Government would inevitably seriously prejudice Franco-American relations.

For your personal information only, I am letting the French Government know that this Government would be prepared to buy these two ships if they will dispose of them to us. I will let you know the result.

2 See *FR 1940*, 2: 485–486.

Doc. 34
CHURCHILL TO ROOSEVELT

November 23, 1940

Our accounts show that the situation in Spain is deteriorating and that the peninsula is not far from the starvation point. An offer by you to dole out food month by month so long as they keep out of the war might be decisive. Small things do not count now and this is a time for very plain talk to them. The occupation by Germany of both sides of the Straits would be a grievous addition to our naval strain, already severe.[1] The Germans would soon have batteries working by radio

1 Although the danger that General Francisco Franco might join the war on the side of the Axis was in fact diminishing, the Spanish dictator had given Hitler renewed assurances of support at a meeting in Hendaye on October 23. Moreover, the Spanish, in violation of British rights, had assumed administrative control of the international zone of Tangier on November 4. The British concern over the situation was therefore not unfounded. See *Documents on German Foreign Policy*, ser. D, vol. 9, nos. 220, 236.

direction finding, which would close the Straits both by night and day. With a major campaign developing in the eastern Mediterranean and need of reinforcement and supply of our armies there all round the Cape we could not contemplate any military action on the mainland at or near the Straits. The Rock of Gibraltar will stand a long siege but what is the good of that if we cannot use the harbour or pass the Straits? Once in Morocco the Germans will work south, and U-boats and aircraft will soon be operating from Casablanca and Dakar. I need not, Mr. President, enlarge upon the trouble this will cause to us or [the] approach of trouble to the Western Hemisphere. We must gain as much time as possible.

Doc. 35
CHURCHILL TO ROOSEVELT

December 7, 1940

As we reach the end of this year I feel that you will expect me to lay before you the prospects for 1941.[1] I do so strongly and confidently because it seems to me that the vast majority of American citizens have recorded their conviction that the safety of the United States as well as the future of our two democracies and the kind of civilisation for which they stand are bound up with the survival and independence of the British Commonwealth of Nations. Only thus can those bastions of sea power, upon which the control of the Atlantic and the Indian Oceans depends, be preserved in faithful and friendly hands. The control of the Pacific by the United States Navy and of the Atlantic by the British Navy is indispensable to the security of the trade routes of both our countries and the surest means to preventing the war from reaching the shores of the United States.

There is another aspect. It takes between three and four years to convert the industries of a modern state to war purposes. Saturation point is reached when the maximum industrial effort that can be spared from civilian needs has been applied to war production. Germany certainly reached this point by the end of 1939. We in the British Empire are now only about halfway through the second year. The United States, I should suppose, was by no means so far advanced as we. Moreover, I understand that immense programmes of naval,

---

[1] "This letter," Churchill emphasized in his memoirs, "was one of the most important I ever wrote." For the background and effect of the letter, see Churchill, *Their Finest Hour*, pp. 554ff.; and Warren F. Kimball, *The Most Unsordid Act: Lend-Lease, 1939–1941* (Baltimore, 1969), pp. 111ff.

military, and air defence are now on foot in the United States, to complete which certainly two years are needed. It is our British duty in the common interest as also for our own survival to hold the front and grapple with Nazi power until the preparations of the United States are complete. Victory may come before the two years are out; but we have no right to count upon it to the extent of relaxing any effort that is humanly possible. Therefore I submit with very great respect for your good and friendly consideration that there is a solid identity of interest between the British Empire and the United States while these conditions last. . . .

[W]e must try to use the year 1941 to build up such a supply of weapons, particularly aircraft, both by increased output at home in spite of bombardment and through oceanborne supplies, as will lay the foundation of victory. In view of the difficulty and magnitude of this task, as outlined by all the facts I have set forth to which many others could be added, I feel entitled, nay bound, to lay before you the various ways in which the United States could give supreme and decisive help to what is, in certain aspects, the common cause.

The prime need is to check or limit the loss of tonnage on the Atlantic approaches to our Islands. This may be achieved both by increasing the naval forces which cope with attacks and by adding to the number of merchant ships on which we depend. For the first purpose there would seem to be the following alternatives:

(1) The reassertion by the United States of the doctrine of the freedom of the seas from illegal and barbarous warfare in accordance with the decisions reached after the late Great War, and as freely accepted and defined by Germany in 1935.[2] From this, the United States ships should be free to trade with countries against which there is not an effective legal blockade.

(2) It would, I suggest, follow that protection should be given to this lawful trading by United States forces, i.e., escorting battleships, cruisers, destroyers, and air flotillas. . . .

(3) Failing the above, the gift, loan, or supply of a large number of American vessels of war, above all destroyers already in the Atlantic, is indispensable to the maintenance of the Atlantic route. Further, could not United States naval forces extend their sea control over the American side of the Atlantic, so as to prevent molestation by enemy vessels of the approaches to the new line of naval and air bases which the United States is establishing in British islands in the Western Hemisphere? The strength of the United States naval forces is such that the assistance in the Atlantic that they could afford us, as described above, would not jeopardise control over the Pacific.

[2] No explanation of this allusion has been found. The Anglo-German naval agreement of June 1935 contained no reference to this subject.

(4) We should also then need the good offices of the United States, and the whole influence of its Government continually exerted, to procure for Great Britain the necessary facilities upon the southern and western shores of Eire for our flotillas, and still more important, for our aircraft, working westward into the Atlantic. . . .

The object of the foregoing measures is to reduce to manageable proportions the present destructive losses at sea. In addition it is indispensable that the merchant tonnage available for supplying Great Britain, and for the waging of the war by Great Britain with all vigour, should be substantially increased beyond the one and a quarter million tons per annum which is the utmost we can now build. The convoy system, the detours, the zigzags, the great distances from which we now have to bring our imports, and the congestion of our western harbours have reduced by about one-third the value of our existing tonnage. To ensure final victory, not less than three million tons of additional merchant shipbuilding capacity will be required. Only the United States can supply this need. . . .

Moreover we look to the industrial energy of the Republic for a reinforcement of our domestic capacity to manufacture combat aircraft. Without that reinforcement reaching us in a substantial measure, we shall not achieve the massive preponderance in the air on which we must rely to loosen and disintegrate the German grip on Europe. . . .

May I invite you then, Mr. President, to give earnest consideration to an immediate order on joint account for a further 2,000 combat aircraft a month? Of these aircraft I would submit that the highest possible proportion should be heavy bombers, the weapon on which above all others we depend to shatter the foundations of German military power. . . .

You have also received information about the needs of our armies. In the munitions sphere, in spite of enemy bombing, we are making steady progress. Without your continued assistance in the supply of machine tools and in the further release from stock of certain articles we could not hope to equip as many as 50 divisions in 1941. I am grateful for the arrangements already practically completed for your aid in the equipment of the army which we have already planned and for the provision of American-type weapons for an additional 10 divisions in time for the campaign of 1942. But when the tide of dictatorship begins to recede, many countries, trying to regain their freedom, may be asking for arms, and there is no source to which they can look except to the factories of the United States. I must therefore also urge the importance of expanding to the utmost American productive capacity for small arms, artillery, and tanks. . . .

Last of all I come to the question of finance. The more rapid and abundant the flow of munitions and ships which you are able to send us, the sooner will our dollar credits be exhausted. They are already as you know very heavily drawn upon by payments we have made to date. Indeed as you know orders already placed or under negotiation, including expenditure settled or pending for creating munitions factories in the United States, many times exceed the total exchange resources remaining at the disposal of Great Britain. The moment approaches when we shall no longer be able to pay cash for shipping and other supplies. While we will do our utmost and shrink from no proper sacrifice to make payments across the exchange, I believe that you will agree that it would be wrong in principle and mutually disadvantageous in effect if, at the height of this struggle, Great Britain were to be divested of all saleable assets so that after victory was won with our blood, civilisation saved, and time gained for the United States to be fully armed against all eventualities, we should stand stripped to the bone. Such a course would not be in the moral or economic interests of either of our countries.[3] . . .

Moreover I do not believe the Government and people of the United States would find it in accordance with the principles which guide them to confine the help which they have so generously promised only to such munitions of war and commodities as could be immediately paid for. You may be assured that we shall prove ourselves ready to suffer and sacrifice to the utmost for the Cause, and that we glory in being its champion. The rest we leave with confidence to you and to your people, being sure that ways and means will be found which future generations on both sides of the Atlantic will approve and admire.

If, as I believe, you are convinced, Mr. President, that the defeat of the Nazi and Fascist tyranny is a matter of high consequence to the people of the United States and to the Western Hemisphere, you will regard this letter not as an appeal for aid, but as a statement of the minimum action necessary to the achievement of our common purpose.[4]

3 Roosevelt had not been wholly unprepared for this particular approach. Arriving in New York on November 23, Ambassador Lothian had told the press: "Well, boys, Britain's broke; it's your money we want." The remark reportedly annoyed Roosevelt and, according to Lothian's biographer, earned him "a mild rebuke from home." Butler, *Lord Lothian*, p. 307.

4 The immediate consequence of Churchill's letter was the development of the lend-lease program, which Roosevelt discussed publicly for the first time on December 17: "Now what I am trying to do is [to] . . . get rid of the silly, foolish, old dollar sign." *PPR*, vol. 9, no. 149. Roosevelt's fireside chat of December 29 included the famous phrase "We must be the great arsenal of democracy." *PPR*, 9: 643. "In this speech for the first time," Samuel I. Rosenman, the President's counsel and the editor of his public papers, wrote later, "Roosevelt presented a long-range plan

of action for the United States. Up to now the help had been piecemeal, on an emergency, *ad hoc* basis. But he was now no longer a President whose term was about to expire, as he was when France fell in June 1940. He had just been elected for four more years, and he was now in a position to lay long-term plans. I could not help but notice the difference that that fact made in the attitude and spirit with which he handled the job of helping the Allies." Two days after the President's address, on New Year's Eve, Churchill sent Roosevelt a warm message of thanks. "We cannot tell what lies before us," he wrote, "but with this trumpet-call we march forward heartened and fortified and with the confidence which you have expressed that in the end all will be well for the English speaking peoples and those who share their ideals." Roosevelt incorporated the lend-lease idea in his annual message to Congress on January 6, 1941, the same address in which he also set forth his Four Freedoms—"freedom of speech and expression," "freedom of every person to worship God in his own way—everywhere in the world," "freedom from want," and "freedom from fear." *PPR*, 9: 668–669, 672.

Doc. 36
CHURCHILL TO ROOSEVELT

December 13, 1940

I am sure you will be pleased about our victory in Libya.[1] This coupled with his Albanian reverses may go hard with Mussolini if we make good use of our success. The full results of the battle are not yet to hand but if Italy can be broken our affairs will be more hopeful than they were four or five months ago.

North Atlantic transport remains the prime anxiety. Undoubtedly Hitler will augment his U-boat and air attack on shipping and operate ever farther into the ocean.[2] Now that we are denied the use of Irish ports and airfields our difficulties strain our flotillas to the utmost limit. We have so far only been able to bring a very few of your fifty destroyers into action on account of the many defects which they naturally develop when exposed to Atlantic weather after having been laid up so long. I am arranging to have a very full technical account prepared of renovations and improvements that have to be made in the older classes of destroyers to fit them for the present task, and this may be of use to you in regard to your own older flotillas.

[1] On December 6 General Sir Archibald Wavell had launched an offensive aimed at driving the Italians out of Egypt. His victory at Sidi Barani on December 11, was followed by the invasion of Libya, which resulted in the virtual elimination of the Italian army as a serious factor in North African operations and led to the dispatch of the German Afrika Korps under Field Marshal Erwin Rommel.

[2] "The only thing that ever really frightened me during the war," Churchill confessed later, "was the U-boat peril. . . . The losses inflicted on our merchant shipping became most grave during the twelve months from July '40 to July '41. . . ." Churchill, *Their Finest Hour*, pp. 598–599.

In the meanwhile we are so hard pressed at sea that we cannot undertake to carry any longer the 400,000 tons of feeding stuffs and fertilisers which we have hitherto convoyed to Eire through all the attacks of the enemy. We need this tonnage for our own supply and we do not need the food which Eire has been sending us. We must now concentrate on essentials and the Cabinet propose to let de Valera[3] know that we cannot go on supplying him under present conditions. He will, of course, have plenty of food for his people but they will not have the prosperous trading they are making now. I am sorry about this but we must think of our own self-preservation and use for vital purposes our own tonnage brought in through so many perils. Perhaps this may loosen things up and make him more ready to consider common interests. I should like to know quite privately what your reactions would be if and when we are forced to concentrate our own tonnage upon the supply of Great Britain. We also do not feel able in present circumstances to continue the heavy subsidies we have hitherto been paying to the Irish agricultural producers. You will realise also that our merchant seamen as well as public opinion generally take it much amiss that we should have to carry Irish supplies through air and U-boat attacks and subsidise them handsomely when de Valera is quite content to sit happy and see us strangled.

[3] Eamon de Valera was Prime Minister of Ireland from 1932 to 1948.

Doc. 37
ROOSEVELT TO CHURCHILL

January 20, 1941

Dear Churchill:

Wendell Willkie[1] will give you this—he is truly helping to keep politics out over here.

I think this applies to you people as it does to us:

> "Sail on, Oh Ship of State!
> Sail on, Oh Union strong and great.
> Humanity with all its fears
> With all the hope of future years
> Is hanging breathless on thy fate."[2]

As ever yours,

[1] Wendell Willkie, the Republican presidential candidate in 1940, was by now an outspoken advocate of all-out aid to Britain. His visit to Britain was undertaken on his own initiative.

[2] On January 28 Churchill wrote Roosevelt: "I received Willkie yesterday and was deeply moved by the verse of Longfellow's which you had quoted. I shall have it

framed as a souvenir of these tremendous days, and as a mark of our friendly relations, which have been built up telegraphically, but also telepathically under all the stresses." Winston S. Churchill, *The Grand Alliance* (Boston, 1950) , pp. 25–26.

Doc. 38
CHURCHILL TO ROOSEVELT

January 21, 1941

You probably know that Lord Halifax[1] will arrive at Annapolis in our new battleship HMS *King George V*.[2] She cannot, of course, stay more than twenty-four hours. I do not know whether you would be interested to see her. We should be proud to show her to you or to any of your high naval authorities, if you could arrange this. She is due at the entrance to Chesapeake Bay at seven A.M. January 24th. If you will communicate to me any suggestion or wishes, we will do our best to meet them.

[1] Lord Lothian died suddenly on December 12 and was succeeded as British ambassador in Washington by Lord Halifax, then British Foreign Secretary.

[2] The new British battleship also carried representatives of the British Chiefs of Staff, who had been invited to meet with their American counterparts. By the time they submitted their final report (ABC-1) on March 29, 1941, they had defined their purpose as determining "the best methods by which the armed forces of the United States and the British Commonwealth . . . could defeat Germany and the Powers allied with her, should the United States be compelled to resort to war." The full text of this report appears in U.S. Congress, *Hearings Before the Joint Committee on the Investigation of the Pearl Harbor Attack*, 79th Cong., 1st sess. (Washington, 1946) , 15: 1485–1550.

Doc. 39
ROOSEVELT TO CHURCHILL

January 22, 1941

Delighted ship is coming to Annapolis. If I can manage it I will go there Friday afternoon and meet Halifax off the harbor. Destroyer will meet her off Cape and act as escort. Would greatly appreciate it if two of our admirals and an aide could go up bay on her.[1] Many thanks.

[1] The *King George V* arrived in Chesapeake Bay on January 24, but due to inclement weather Roosevelt abandoned his earlier plan to inspect the new British battleship. Instead he circled the *George V* in his own yacht, *Potomac*, and there received Lord Halifax. As the latter has written: "After a good dinner, the President drove us to the Embassy in Washington, to sleep our first night in the United

States." Lord Halifax, *Fullness of Days* (New York, 1957), p. 245. As Halifax's biographer put it: "There was considerable meaning in this gesture of the President. With that sense of timing which he could at times so brilliantly exhibit he intended to certify to the world in a manner at once dramatic and unmistakable his sympathy with the cause of embattled Britain. . . . Halifax never forgot this moment of kinship and welcome." The Earl of Birkenhead, *Halifax* (London, 1965), p. 474.

Doc. 40
CHURCHILL TO ROOSEVELT

February 15, 1941

Many drifting straws seem to indicate Japanese intention to make war on us or do something that would force us to make war on them in the next few weeks or months.[1] I am not myself convinced that this is not a war of nerves designed to cover Japanese encroachments in Siam and Indochina. However, I think I ought to let you know that the weight of the Japanese navy, if thrown against us, would confront us with situations beyond the scope of our naval resources. I do not myself think that the Japanese would be likely to send large military expedition necessary to lay siege to Singapore. The Japanese would no doubt occupy whatever strategic points and oil fields in Dutch East Indies and thereabouts that they covet and thus get into a far better position for a full-scale attack on Singapore later on. They would also raid Australian and New Zealand ports and coasts causing deep anxiety in those Dominions which have already sent all their best-trained fighting men to the Middle East. But the attack which I fear the most would be by raiders including possibly battle cruiser upon our trade routes and communications across the Pacific and Indian Oceans. We could by courting disaster elsewhere send a few strong ships into these vast waters, but all trade would have to go into convoy and escorts would be few and far between. Not only would this be a most grievous additional restriction and derangement of our whole war economy, but it would bring altogether to an end all reinforcements of the armies we had planned to build up in the Middle East from Australasian and Indian resources. Any threat of a major invasion of Australia or New Zealand would of course force us to withdraw our fleet from the eastern Mediterranean with disastrous military

[1] "Various reports were laid before me," Churchill wrote after the war, "which certainly gave the impression that [the Japanese Embassy and colony in London] had received news from home which required them to pack up. . . . This agitation . . . made me feel that a sudden act of war upon us by Japan might be imminent." Churchill, *Grand Alliance*, pp. 177–178.

possibilities there, the certainty that Turkey would have to make some accommodation, and reopen German trade and oil supplies from the Black Sea. You will therefore see, Mr. President, the awful enfeeblement of our war effort that would result merely from the sending out by Japan of her battle cruiser and her twelve eight-inch gun cruisers into the Eastern oceans, and still more from any serious invasion threat against the two Australasian democracies in the southern Pacific.

Some believe that Japan in her present mood would not hesitate to court an attempt to wage war both against Great Britain and the United States. Personally, I think the odds are definitely against that, but no one can tell. Everything that you can do to inspire the Japanese with fear of a double war may avert the danger. If however they come in against us and we are alone, the grave character of the consequences cannot easily be overstated.

Doc. 41
ROOSEVELT TO CHURCHILL

February 25, 1941

I have been very much concerned at the delay in reaching an agreement in respect to the naval and air bases.[1] At your request I was glad to reconsider the question of the place in which the negotiations were to take place and in view of the considerations advanced by you to send a delegation to London. This delegation has now been in London over a month and a satisfactory agreement has not yet been reached. Indeed the negotiations appear to be deadlocked on a number of points of considerable importance.

In connection with request for appropriations to construct these bases, our War and Navy Departments will be questioned by congressional committee within the next week. They will be asked detailed questions in regard to the status of these bases and the provisions of the leases. On the basis of the present situation, inability to give satisfactory answers would probably lead to still more questions. Already adverse discussion has developed in Congress and in the press, in regard to the conditions under which we are acquiring these bases.

[1] Although the "destroyer deal" had been officially concluded on September 2, 1940, and nine American destroyers sent immediately thereafter, the details of the British quid pro quo were worked out only in March 1941. See Churchill, *Their Finest Hour*, pp. 398ff.; Cordell Hull, *The Memoirs of Cordell Hull* (New York, 1948), vol. 2, chap. 60; and Langer and Gleason, *Challenge to Isolation*, chap. 12.

It seems to me imperative, in all these circumstances, that a satisfactory agreement in respect to the bases be completed without further delay. Such an agreement would provide effective answers to questions which may otherwise prove to be embarrassing in the working out of many of the important immediate problems we have before us. I do hope that you will be able to urge your people to expedite the decisions our negotiators are now awaiting.

Doc. 42
ROOSEVELT TO CHURCHILL

March 8, 1941

Notwithstanding some delay the ultimate passage by vote of sixty to thirty-one is highly satisfactory.[1] Final concurrent action by the House followed by my signature should take place Tuesday evening.[2] Confidentially I hope to send estimate for new orders and purchases under the bill to the House on Wednesday. Best of luck.

1 Roosevelt sent this personal note within hours of the passage of the Lend-Lease Act by the Senate.

2 As Roosevelt predicted, on March 11 the House of Representatives approved certain Senate amendments by a vote of 317 to 1. Roosevelt signed the bill the same day, and, as he noted later, "within a few minutes thereafter, army and navy war materials were speeding on their way to Great Britain and Greece." *PPR*, vol. 9, no. 152.

Doc. 43
CHURCHILL TO ROOSEVELT

March 9, 1941

Our blessings from the whole British Empire go out to you and the American nation for this very present help in time of trouble.[1]

1 Churchill later described the Lend-Lease Act to Parliament as "the most unsordid act in the history of any nation." Churchill, *Their Finest Hour*, p. 569.

Doc. 44
CHURCHILL TO ROOSEVELT

March 10, 1941

I have been working steadily about the bases on turning the mountains back into molehills, but even so, the molehills remain to be
disposed of. I hope to send you a cable on Monday leaving very little
that is not cleared away. Please lend a hand with the shovel if you can.
Remember it is the inflexible policy of His Majesty's Government,
with or without any reciprocal consideration, to make sure that the
United States has full, effective military security both in war and in
necessary peacetime preparations for war in these Islands and areas.
Give us the best chance you can to bring the local people along, for
after all these Islands are their only home, and I want them to be your
friends as well as ours.

Doc. 45
CHURCHILL TO ROOSEVELT
March 10, 1941

I must now tell you what we have resolved about Greece.[1] Although
it was no doubt tempting to push on from Benghazi to Tripoli,[2] and
we may still use considerable forces in this direction, we have felt it
our duty to stand with the Greeks who have declared to us their
resolve, even alone, to resist the German invader. Our Generals

[1] Italy had invaded Greece on October 28, 1940, and the Greek President, General
John Metaxas, had at once appealed for British aid. Although some aid was forthcoming, the British lacked the resources necessary for really effective assistance. The
imminence of a German invasion of Greece (it actually came on April 6, 1941) gave
the whole matter renewed urgency. For the official Greek viewpoint, see *The Battle
of Greece* (Government White Paper), English trans. (Athens, 1949). See also
Churchill, *Grand Alliance*, pp. 220ff.

[2] This decision, originally made on January 21, was reaffirmed on February 11
even though all of Cyrenaica (including Benghazi) had been captured by February
9 and the Italian Tenth Army had been totally cut off. In the process, the British
captured 130,000 prisoners, 400 tanks, and nearly 1,300 guns at the cost of less than
2,000 casualties. "It was a fantastic and slightly unbelievable victory at a time when
the British public and the British Army badly needed one." Fred Majdalany, *The
Battle of El Alamein—Fortress in the Sand* (Philadelphia, 1965), p. 10.

Wavell[3] and Dill,[4] who have accompanied Mr. Eden[5] to Cairo, after heart-searching discussion with us, believe that we have a good fighting chance. We are therefore sending the greater part of the Army of the Nile to Greece, and are reinforcing to the utmost possible in the air. Smuts[6] is sending South Africans to the Delta. Mr. President, you can judge these hazards for yourself. At this juncture the action of Yugoslavia is cardinal. No country ever had such a military chance. If they will fall on the Italian rear in Albania there is no measuring what might happen in a few weeks.[7] The whole situation might be transformed, and the action of Turkey also decided in our favour. One has the feeling that Russia, though actuated mainly by fear, might at least give some reassurance to Turkey about not pressing her in the Caucasus or turning against her in the Black Sea. I need scarcely say that concerted influence of your Ambassadors in Turkey, Russia, and above all in Yugoslavia would be of enormous value at the moment, and indeed might possibly turn the scales.

In this connection I must thank you for the magnificent work done by Donovan[8] in his prolonged tour of the Balkans and the Middle East. He has carried with him throughout an animating, heart-warming flame.

[3] Sir Archibald Wavell, commander in chief of British forces in the Middle East.

[4] Sir John Dill, Chief of the Imperial General Staff.

[5] Anthony Eden, Churchill's coordinator in the Middle East, had succeeded Lord Halifax as Foreign Secretary in January.

[6] Jan Christiaan Smuts, Prime Minister of the Union of South Africa since 1939.

[7] For an account of Yugoslav policy, see J. B. Hoptner, *Yugoslavia in Crisis 1931–1941* (New York, 1962), chaps. 8–9.

[8] William J. Donovan, a political opponent but close personal friend of the President, had been in southeastern Europe since December 1940, ostensibly as unofficial observer for Secretary of the Navy Frank Knox but actually as Roosevelt's personal envoy. He had conferred frequently with British commanders and diplomats in the Mediterranean and the Balkans. From January 23 to 25 Donovan had been in Belgrade, conferring with Yugoslavia's Prince Paul and various political and military leaders. See Corey Ford, *Donovan of OSS* (Boston, 1970), pp. 98ff.

Doc. 46
CHURCHILL TO ROOSEVELT

March 12, 1941

Admiral Darlan's declaration and threat make me wonder whether it would not be best for you to intervene as a friend of both sides and try to bring about a working agreement.[1] We do not wish to push things to extremes, and we naturally should be most reluctant in a thing like this to act against your judgement after you have weighed all the pros and cons. We fear very much prolongation of the war and its miseries which would result from breakdown of blockade of Germany, and there are immense difficulties in preventing Germany from profiting directly or indirectly from anything imported into unoccupied France. Dealing with Darlan is dealing with Germany, for he will not be allowed to agree to anything they know about which does not suit their book. Also there is the danger of rationing spreading to occupied France, Belgium, Holland, and Norway. Perhaps however you might be able to devise a scheme under which supervision would limit leakage and might also give you a number of agents in favourable positions in unoccupied France and in French Africa. It would be easier for you to talk to Vichy, with whom you are in regular diplomatic relations, than for us to negotiate via Madrid or by making speeches on broadcast. Besides this, Darlan has old scores to pay out against us in the dire action we were forced to take against his ships.[2]

Would you therefore consider coming forward on the basis of how shocked you were at the idea of fighting breaking out between France and Great Britain, which would only help the common foe? Then you might be able to procure Vichy assent to a scheme allowing a ration of wheat to go through, month by month, to unoccupied France and something for French Africa as long as other things were satisfactory.[3] These other things might form the subject of a secret arrangement of which the Germans will not know, by which German infiltration into Morocco and French African ports would be limited to the bare armistice terms, and by which an increasing number of French warships would gradually be moving from Toulon to Casablanca or Dakar. . . .

The bases question has, I think, been tidied up, and I hope to bring

---

[1] The outspokenly anti-British Darlan had become French Minister of Foreign Affairs on February 9, 1941. In a statement to American correspondents at Vichy he had publicly threatened to use the French fleet to prevent further British interference with the importation of food and other supplies to occupied France.

[2] On July 3, 1940, the British had destroyed three French battleships and a destroyer at Mers-el-Kebir, near Oran, and had seized a number of lesser warships anchored at Plymouth and Portsmouth. On July 8 they had attacked and damaged the battleship *Richelieu* at Dakar.

[3] Churchill in effect was attempting to undercut the so-called Murphy-Weygand agreement of February 26, under which the United States agreed to supply North Africa's economic needs, provided the supplies were consumed there, their distribution supervised by American control officers, and payments made out of French funds frozen in the United States. In return, he held out the possibility that at least some food shipments would be allowed into France itself, as Roosevelt had requested in a message of December 30, 1940. See *FR 1941*, 2 (Washington, 1959): 107ff., 241ff., 269ff.; and Robert Murphy, *Diplomat Among Warriors* (New York, 1964), chap. 6.

an agreed document before the Cabinet tomorrow, Thursday afternoon. Will you let me know when you would like the announcement to be made? Does it matter if it comes on morrow of passing lease-lend bill?

Doc. 47
CHURCHILL TO ROOSEVELT

March 19, 1941

On March 8th the German battle cruisers *Scharnhorst* and *Gneisenau* approached one of our convoys north of Cape de Verde Island[1] but on seeing our battleship escort retreated. On the morning of the 15th our shipping which was returning independently to America was attacked by them at a point about five hundred miles southeast of Newfoundland where owing to fog on the Great Banks the shipping is at this season compelled to concentrate. Several ships were sunk by gunfire.[2] . . .

It would be a very great help if some American warships and aircraft could cruise about in this area as they have a perfect right to do without any prejudice to neutrality. Their mere presence might be decisive as the enemy would fear that they might report what they saw and we could then despatch an adequate force to try to engage them. The more ships that go out to cruise and the sooner they go the greater advantage.

I will report any further enemy moves of which we become aware.

1 The Cape Verde Islands.

2 According to the official historian of British naval operations, between January 23 and March 22 the *Scharnhorst* and *Gneisenau* "not only sank or captured twenty-two ships of 115,622 tons but also, for a time, completely dislocated our Atlantic convoy cycles, with serious consequences to our vital imports. Their depredations forced the wide dispersal of our already strained naval resources." Roskill, *War at Sea*, 1: 379.

Doc. 48
CHURCHILL TO ROOSEVELT

March 27, 1941

I hope you will agree that in the present situation we are bound to do all we can to help and encourage the elements prepared to resist

German penetration.[1] If new government shows readiness to share in Greek heroic resistance, we propose to recognise it at once as the Government of Yugoslavia, and extend to it in the fullest possible measure the aid which we are already giving to Greece. We should encourage the Yugoslavians to roll up the Italians in Albania which would produce result of prime importance and give them a good packet of arms. I trust that you will take similar line and will sustain the new government with promise of America's powerful support and backing.

[1] Despite strong British pressures to the contrary, Yugoslavia had succumbed to Hitler's demands and adhered to the Tripartite Pact on March 25. Two days later a coup engineered by General Dušan Simović replaced the regent, Prince Paul, with the young King Peter and brought a new government willing to resist the Germans. Roosevelt in fact sent congratulations to the new king on March 28, and the State Department arranged for lend-lease aid for the purpose of repelling aggression. See *FR 1941*, 2: 944, 969. This meant nothing to the Germans. Early on Sunday morning April 6 they attacked Yugoslavia, beginning with an air strike against Belgrade that killed 17,000 Yugoslavs, and within twelve days they had occupied the country.

Doc. 49
ROOSEVELT TO CHURCHILL

March 29, 1941

I have today made allotments for substantial quantities of food and for immediate purchase [of] fifty-four hundred airplanes, four hundred thousand Thompson submachine guns, thirty-four hundred Universal carriers, and substantial quantities of other miscellaneous military equipment. I have also authorized fifty-five hundred Oerlikon guns and ammunition for them, sixty patrol bombing planes, and one hundred eighty Navy fighting planes. These actions will be followed in the near future as soon as I have had opportunity to confer with your representatives and their opposites in our Government. You can be sure these matters will be prosecuted vigorously here.

Doc. 50
ROOSEVELT TO CHURCHILL

April 2, 1941

I have this morning allotted funds for the building of 58 additional shipping ways and 200 additional ships. I have also made complete arrangements for repairs to merchant ships and for your larger friends.

Doc. 51
ROOSEVELT TO CHURCHILL

April 11, 1941

We propose immediately to take the following steps in relation to the security of the Western Hemisphere, which steps will favorably affect your shipping problem. It is important for domestic political reasons which you will readily understand that this action be taken by us unilaterally and not after diplomatic conversations between you and us. Therefore before taking this unilateral action I want to tell you about the proposal.

This Government proposes to extend the present so-called security zone and patrol areas which have been in effect since very early in the war to a line covering all North Atlantic waters west of about west longitude 25 degrees.[1] We propose to utilize aircraft and naval vessels working from Greenland, Newfoundland, Nova Scotia, the United States, Bermuda, and West Indies, with possible later extension to Brazil if this can be arranged. We will want in great secrecy notification of movement of convoys so our patrol units can seek out any ships or planes of aggressor nations operating west of the new line of the security zone. We will immediately make public to you position [of] aggressor ships or planes when located in our patrol area west of west longitude 25 degrees.

We propose to refuel our ships at sea where advisable. We suggest your longer shipping hauls move as much as possible west of new line up to latitude of the northwest approaches.

We have declared Red Sea area no longer a combat zone.[2] We

1 The extension of the patrol area to the twenty-fifth meridian, in the words of Secretary of War Henry L. Stimson, "midway between the westernmost bulge of Africa and the easternmost bulge of Brazil," was more than the British had requested and stretched the concept "Western Hemisphere" considerably. (Henry L. Stimson Diary, Sterling Library, Yale University, New Haven, Connecticut [April 10, 1941]. Henceforth cited as Stimson Diary.) On April 9 the United States had acquired the right to establish bases in Greenland by agreement with the Danish ambassador to the United States, Henrik de Kauffmann. As a result, most of Greenland was now included in the American security zone. See *FR 1940*, 2: 343ff.; and *FR 1941*, 2: 35ff.

2 The President's proclamation of April 10, 1941, removed the Red Sea region from the list of combat areas forbidden to American shipping since June 1940. This action in effect allowed the United States to supply British forces in Egypt directly, as had been urged for about a month by W. Averell Harriman, then the President's special representative, with the rank of minister, in Great Britain, in charge of facilitating lend-lease assistance to the British Empire.

propose sending all types of goods in unarmed American flagships to Egypt or any other nonbelligerent port via Red Sea or Persian Gulf. We think we can work out sending wheat and other goods in American ships to Greenland or Iceland through the next six months.

We hope to make available for direct haul to England a large amount of your present shipping which is now utilized for other purposes. We expect to make use of Danish ships very soon and Italian ships in about two months.[3]

I believe advisable that when this new policy is adopted here no statement be issued on your end. It is not certain I would make specific announcement. I may decide to issue necessary naval operations orders and let time bring out the existence of the new patrol area.

[3] Congress in fact authorized the President to requisition already seized Axis and Danish vessels for government use in June.

Doc. 52
ROOSEVELT TO CHURCHILL

May 1, 1941

. . . Our patrol is already on way to take positions assigned, and I think liaison work between the two naval services is being established satisfactorily.

In regard to yours of April 29,[1] my thought in regard to eastern Mediterranean is:

(A) You have done not only heroic but very useful work in Greece, and the territorial loss is more than compensated for by necessity for enormous German concentration and resulting enormous German losses in men and materials.[2]

(B) . . . I am satisfied that both here and in Britain public opinion is growing to realize that even if you have to withdraw further in the eastern Mediterranean, you will not allow any great debacle or

[1] Not printed.

[2] On April 6 German forces had attacked Greece, and more than 53,000 Australian and New Zealand troops were rushed to its defense. The Germans, however, overcame determined Allied resistance and by April 27 had occupied Athens. The British imperial forces were withdrawn to Egypt and to Crete. There they were joined by the surviving Greek units, which immediately became Hitler's next objective. He attacked the combined Allied forces on May 20. The delays Hitler suffered in Yugoslavia and Greece, however, required repeated postponement of his planned attack on the Soviet Union, thus weakening the chances of his campaign against Russia.

surrender, and that in the last analysis the naval control of the Indian Ocean and the Atlantic Ocean will in time win the war.

(C) In regard to Turkey, I fear there is little we can do except to stiffen them morally and leave it to you to send such equipment to them as you can spare from American shipments going to the Red Sea.

(D) I think of the Syrian problem[3] as almost identical with the French problem in North Africa. I do not think there is any chance of persuading Vichy to break with the Germans, if the latter violate Syria or North Africa. I wish you would let me have your views on the following policy, which I would be glad to introduce:

(1) Recognize that Vichy is in a German cage and still issues orders to Weygand,[4] Syria, and Indochina.

(2) That because Vichy has already ordered French colonies to resist British occupation, Vichy can and ought to issue orders to colonies equally to resist German occupation.

(3) United States can as quid pro quo for such orders send two more children's food ships to Marseilles and offer to send oil and perhaps some ammunition and other munition to Weygand on west coast of Morocco, this being conditioned, of course, on agreement of Weygand to resist German occupation. . . .

(E) If Germany crosses Straits of Gibraltar with land forces, she can probably eventually occupy Tunis, Algiers, and Morocco down to Casablanca, but it is of utmost importance to keep Germans out of the Moroccan ports as long as possible, including Port of Sisnes[5] in Río de Oro. We think it almost impossible for Germans to reach Dakar over land, especially with what is left of French army and navy concentrated there.

(F) Personally, I am not downcast by more spread of Germany to additional large territories. There is little of raw materials in all of them put together—not enough to maintain nor compensate for huge occupation forces. The exception is oil in Mosul[6] and Iraq and I

3 The reverses in Yugoslavia and Greece raised British anxieties about the eastern Mediterranean. The possibility that the Germans might launch air attacks on the Suez Canal and the Abadan oil refineries from bases in Syria was of special concern, particularly after the pro-German coup in Iraq in early April. In talks on May 5 and 6, Admiral Darlan agreed to permit the Germans to use the Syrian airfields.

4 Weygand was now French delegate general in North Africa.

5 Geography was not Roosevelt's strong point. The reference is probably to Villa Cisneros.

6 Roosevelt was also confused about the location of the oil fields. There are none at Mosul.

assume production there could be practically destroyed by you in event of necessity.

Keep up the good work.

Doc. 53
CHURCHILL TO ROOSEVELT

May 3, 1941

. . . We must not be too sure that the consequences of the loss of Egypt and the Middle East would not be grave. It would seriously increase the hazards of the Atlantic and Pacific and could hardly fail to prolong the war with all the suffering and military dangers that this would entail. We shall fight on whatever happens, but please remember that the attitude of Spain, Vichy, Turkey, and Japan may be finally determined by the outcome of the struggle in this theater of war. I cannot take the view that the loss of Egypt and the Middle East would be a mere preliminary to the successful maintenance of a prolonged oceanic war. If all Europe, the greater part of Asia, and Africa became, either by conquest or agreement under duress, a part of the Axis system, a war maintained by the British Isles, the United States, Canada, and Australia against this mighty agglomeration would be a hard, long, and bleak proposition. Therefore, if you cannot take more advanced positions now or very soon, the vast balances may be tilted heavily to our disadvantage. Mr. President, I am sure that you will not misunderstand me if I speak to you exactly what is in my mind. The one decisive counterweight I can see to balance the growing pessimism in Turkey, the Near East, and Spain would be if the United States were immediately to range herself with us as a belligerent power.[1] If

---

[1] In a cable of April 10 to Alexander W. Weddell, the U.S. ambassador in Spain, Secretary of State Cordell Hull declared: "At this crucial period in the struggle against totalitarian world aggression . . . the Government and people of the United States have made it abundantly clear that we do not intend to stand on the sidelines, but that on the contrary, we do intend to play our part in resisting the forces of aggression. . . . The President relies upon you to make clear the scope of our national effort and determination to resist aggression to the civil and military leaders of the Government and of public opinion in Spain. . . . We are convinced that a continuous, forceful presentation of our position and of the scope of our national effort to resist aggression at this time will have a salutary effect upon official and public opinion in countries such as Spain which have not yet been drawn directly into the conflict, and will help greatly to counteract the cumulative effect of totalitarian propaganda." FR 1941, 2: 880ff. Similar telegrams went to the heads of U.S. diplomatic missions in Portugal, Finland, Sweden, Italy, and Rumania.

this were possible I have little doubt that we could hold the situation in the Mediterranean until the weight of your munitions gained the day.

Doc. 54
ROOSEVELT TO CHURCHILL

May 3, 1941

In my message of May 1[1] I did not intend to minimize in any degree the gravity of the situation, particularly as regards the Mediterranean. I am well aware of its great strategic importance and I share your anxiety in regard to it. . . .

I have issued instructions that supplies insofar as they are available here are to be rushed to the Middle East at the earliest possible moment. Thirty ships are now being mobilized to go within the next three weeks to the Middle East. I want to emphasize we intend to continue the supplies and to get the ships to carry them until there is a final decision in the Mediterranean. I know of your determination to win on that front and we shall do everything that we possibly can to help you do it.

My previous message merely meant to indicate that should the Mediterranean prove in the last analysis to be an impossible battleground[,] that I do not feel that such fact alone would mean the defeat of our mutual interests. I say this because I believe the outcome of this struggle is going to be decided in the Atlantic and unless Hitler can win there he cannot win anywhere in the world in the end. . . .

Our patrols are pushing farther out into the Atlantic.[2] I have just added all of our heavy units of the Coast Guard to the Navy for the purpose of implementing that patrol.[3] Other steps to strengthen that patrol will be taken soon.

With this message goes my warm personal regards to you.

1 See above, Doc. 52.

2 For details of the operation of the Atlantic patrols, see Samuel Eliot Morison, *History of United States Naval Operations in World War II*, 1 (Boston, 1947) : 51, 56ff., 62ff.; and Roskill, *War at Sea*, 1: 454ff.

3 The Coast Guard's role is explained in Malcolm F. Willoughby, *The U.S. Coast Guard in World War II* (Annapolis, 1957) , chap. 7, pp. 192–193.

Doc. 55
CHURCHILL TO ROOSEVELT

May 10, 1941

I expect you are now acquainted with the splendid offer which General Arnold[1] made to us of one-third of the rapidly expanding capacity for pilot training in the United States to be filled with pupils from here. We have made active preparations and the first 550 young men are now ready to leave as training was to have begun early next month. A second batch of 550 will follow quickly on their heels. I now understand there are legal difficulties. I hope, Mr. President, that these are not serious as it would be very disappointing to us and would upset our arrangements if there were now to be delay. General Arnold's offer was an unexpected and very welcome addition to our training facilities. Such ready-made capacity of aircraft, airfields, and instructors all in balance we could not obtain to the same extent and in the same time by any other means. It will greatly accelerate our effort in the air.[2]

[1] Henry H. ("Hap") ·Arnold, American Deputy Chief of Staff for Air.

[2] As was the case with the naval services in the spring and summer of 1941, there was now increasingly close cooperation between the U.S. Army Air Force and the Royal Air Force. In May 1941, for instance, "the War Department established the Special Observer Group in London, and through its reports and those of occasional special missions the Air Corps was constantly informed of the latest material developments in England." James Lee Cate and E. Kathleen Williams, "The Air Corps Prepares for War 1939–1941," in Wesley Frank Craven and James Lee Cate, eds., *The Army Air Forces in World War II*, 1 (Chicago, 1948) : 109, 577ff.

Doc. 56
ROOSEVELT TO CHURCHILL

May 11, 1941

All plans discussed with you by Arnold for training pilots have been approved here. There are no legal difficulties in the way and the training can begin promptly. We are rushing six additional small aircraft carriers for you. First three should be available in three or four months.

Doc. 57
ROOSEVELT TO CHURCHILL

May 29, 1941

In spite of the best reports of the organization now handling flight delivery of combat aircraft from this country to England, I am advised that substantial numbers of these planes are accumulating in the country and that this condition is apt to grow worse as production reaches an accelerated rate over the next few months. In our common interest and in order to relieve the situation as much as possible, I am prepared to direct the Army and Navy to assume full responsibility for the transfer of American-built aircraft from factory to the point of ultimate takeoff and to supply maintenance and servicing facilities along the way and at the ultimate staging field. . . .

For example, the American Army said Navy could deliver planes at Botwood, Newfoundland, ready and serviced for the RAF to take them over and fly them across. Later and depending on developments we might be able to deliver them to your people in Iceland.

Doc. 58
CHURCHILL TO ROOSEVELT

May 29, 1941

We cordially welcome your taking over Iceland at the earliest possible moment,[1] and will hold ourselves and all our resources there at your disposal as may be found convenient. It would liberate a British division for defence against invasion of the Middle East. It would enable us to concentrate our flying boats now there on northwestern approaches. If it could be done in the next three weeks or less, or even begun, it would have a moral effect even beyond its military importance. You have only to say the word and our staffs can get to work at once.

At any time now Hitler may obtain air bases in southern Spain or in North Africa, Spanish or French, from which he can make Gibraltar

[1] In an effort to forestall a possible German takeover, Iceland had terminated its connection with the Danish crown on May 17. Roosevelt's decision to send American marines there was reached on June 5.

harbour unuseable by our fleet. The moment this happens, for we are sure it is going to happen, we shall send our expeditions, which have long been prepared and are waiting beside their ships, to occupy the Grand Canary, the Cape Verde Islands, and one of the Azores. The code names for these three expeditions will be cabled in a separate message. . . .

We should welcome collaboration with an American token force, before, during, or after occupation of Atlantic islands and if you wish would turn them over to you as a matter of mutual war convenience.[2]

We should naturally welcome United States occupation of Dakar, and would afford all facilities in our power.

[2] The President had in fact already directed the Army and Navy on May 28 to prepare a joint expeditionary force for the purpose of occupying the Azores, should that be required to prevent hostile belligerent forces from gaining control of the islands. For details of this and the Iceland occupation, see Maurice Matloff and Edwin M. Snell, *Strategic Planning for Coalition Warfare* (Washington, 1953), pp. 49ff.

Doc. 59
CHURCHILL TO ROOSEVELT

June 3, 1941

I am finding it necessary to build up a much stronger organization of the rearward services in the Middle East to sustain the large forces now gathering in and about the Nile Valley[1] and an important mission is going out by air, comprising high military and civilian experts. We must consider the formation of a well-equipped base, either at Port Sudan (as your son suggested)[2] or/and at Massawa near which lies the town of Asmara with its fine buildings, in order to arrange for the reception of American materials which you are sending to us in increasing quantities. American tanks and American aircraft

[1] This message followed shortly after the arrival in Washington of a special emissary from Cairo, Brigadier J. M. Whiteley, who brought with him "a list of the stores which would have to be supplied in the next three months if Suez was to be saved. . . . This novel and unorthodox procedure was designed to dramatize the situation and to convince the Americans . . . that, if [the requirements] were met, Egypt could and would be held." Although current Washington opinion was skeptical on this subject, and although the "Whiteley list" was a long one, most of the supplies the British asked for were on their way to Suez before the end of the summer. Hall and Wrigley, *Overseas Supply*, pp. 24–25.

[2] Captain Elliott Roosevelt, the President's son, was then in England on a military mission.

require a good sprinkling of American civilian volunteer personnel to instruct us in their use and help keep them serviceable. I should be grateful if you would allow Averell Harriman[3] to go out with the mission as independent observer, taking with him one or two of his own assistants. He would then be able to advise upon the best measures to be taken to ensure the most efficient use of all that you are sending. He is quite willing to go; indeed, he would like it. The trip might take him six weeks but it would be well worth it.

[3] Harriman had been in London since March 1, as a special representative of the President with the rank of minister.

Doc. 60
CHURCHILL TO ROOSEVELT

June 7, 1941

We enter Syria in some force tomorrow morning in order to prevent further German penetration. Success depends largely upon attitude of local French troops. De Gaulle's Free French outfit will be prominent but not in the van. He is issuing a proclamation to the Arabs offering in the name of France complete independence and opportunity to form either three or one or three-in-one free Arab states. Relations of these states with France will be fixed by treaty, safeguarding established interest somewhat on the Anglo-Egyptian model. General Catroux[1] is not to be called High Commissioner but French Delegate and Plenipotentiary.

I cannot tell how Vichy will react to what may happen. I do not, myself, think they will do much worse than they are now doing, but of course they may retaliate on Gibraltar or Freetown. I should be most grateful if you would keep your pressure upon them. We have no political interests at all in Syria, except to win the war.[2]

Thank you so much for letting Harriman go to the Middle East.[3]

[1] Georges Catroux had been governor general of Indochina at the time of the French surrender and had then joined de Gaulle's Free French forces in London.

[2] Australian, Indian, and Free French forces entered Syria on June 8. Reinforced by British troops, and after some hard fighting, they overcame the defending Vichy army, which surrendered on July 12. "The successful campaign in Syria," Churchill wrote later, "greatly improved our strategical position in the Middle East." Churchill, *Grand Alliance*, p. 331.

[3] Roosevelt permitted Harriman to go on this trip with "the same opportunities for inspection that he would have commanded if he were a member of the British War Cabinet." Robert E. Sherwood, *Roosevelt and Hopkins* (New York, 1948), pp.

He is seeing your son tomorrow before leaving, and I shall see him myself, I hope, at luncheon Monday.

311–313. But the President turned down Churchill's request, dated June 8, to have an American representative attend a meeting of Allied and Dominion representatives on June 12.

Doc. 61
CHURCHILL TO ROOSEVELT

June 11, 1941

I am looking forward to welcoming your son here. I have been told that he has a plan to take over, equip, and defend an air base at Bathurst in Gambia as a staging and servicing point for heavy United States bombers to be flown across the Atlantic to the Middle East. His idea is that United States of America should lease base, and install naval, military, and air defences. Bombers would be flown from United States of America via Pernambuco to be serviced [at] Bathurst, then flown on by American ferry pilot organisation to Egypt. Bathurst base [would be] all American. We are wholeheartedly in favour of this proposal and would be prepared to give you a lease at Bathurst on similar terms to those already given for bases in the western Atlantic.[1] I had intended to postpone putting this proposal to you until I had talked it over with your son, but he has been delayed and the matter is so urgent that I wanted to put it to you at once. If the proposal commends itself to you in principle, our staffs over here could work out the details.

[1] Bathurst became a terminal point for the bomber ferrying operations which Pan American Airways carried out under U.S. government contract after August 12. See Craven and Cate, *Army Air Forces*, 1: 320ff.

Doc. 62
ROOSEVELT TO CHURCHILL

June 17, 1941

Army is studying possible ferry from Natal with idea that African landing places might be three in number—Bathurst, Freetown, and Liberia. I see no reason for any United States lease, but if the plan works out we would deliver the planes either in Natal or on African coast. Also, we would undertake the building of any necessary servicing facilities. I feel there should be three possible landing places because of proximity of Bathurst to Dakar. When your Air Vice Marshal[1] arrives our people will immediately confer with him. I find a feeling here that up to recently there has been a good deal of delay in delivery between Takoradi and lower Egypt, chiefly through difficulty in servicing the small hopping stones on the way across the Continent. Please let me know how you regard the working out of this problem.

I have a distinct feeling in my bones that things are looking up with you and with us. After freezing the German and Italian assets on Saturday, I closed the German consulates and agencies yesterday, and the reaction here is, I should say, 90% favorable.

1 Arthur T. Harris, who had been Britain's Deputy Air Chief of Staff and was on his way to Washington as the Royal Air Force member of the British military mission.

Doc. 63
CHURCHILL TO ROOSEVELT

June 26, 1941

I am concerned at the result which may follow from British and American tank design for the future proceeding on independent lines. Already the M-3 American medium tank is being produced in three types to American, British, and Canadian orders. These types although basically identical vary in several respects particularly as regards main armament. You have retained the seventy-five mm gun whereas we and the Canadians are going for the six pdr gun with seventy-five mm and two pdr weapons as interim steps.

It is obvious that nothing must be done to disturb production now in hand here or in North America. We want all the tanks we can get as soon as possible.[1]

At the same time I am impressed with the importance of strengthening the liaison between the United States of America and the British and I suggest we should evolve machinery which will ensure that

1 On the history of British tank procurement in the United States and the standardization of designs in 1940–1941, see Hall and Wrigley, *Overseas Supply:* "No supplies were more eagerly awaited from America than medium tanks, on which, more than on any other single factor, it seemed that the issue of the North African war would turn" (p. 27). Tanks, as the official British historians have pointed out, "were an even more striking example of British dependence on American supplies. . . . [O]ver the whole period from July 1940 to the end of the war Britain received about thirty per cent of all the American tanks produced" (p. 10).

future designs in each class of tank are as similar as possible, thus eliminating unnecessary maintenance difficulties.

At the present moment tank design in the States is controlled by the United States Ordnance Board while in England it is controlled by our Tank Board.

I would strongly suggest for your consideration that a joint Anglo-American Tank Board[2] should be set up in America to include Canadian as well as British representation for the purpose of controlling and coordinating tank design and production as regards new types. . . .

I think there is already ample evidence that we can learn a lot from your technicians on the mechanical side while we can possibly give you valuable advice obtained by newly bought experience as to the fighting requirements.

If you agree I would suggest that the detailed composition of the board and your representation on our board here might be discussed by your representatives with the British Army Staff and British Supply Council.

[2] The proposed tank board was presumably modeled after the Anglo-American Tank Commission, established during World War I. See Constance McLaughlin Green, Harry C. Thomson, and Peter C. Roots, *The Ordnance Department—Planning Munitions for War* (Washington, 1955) , p. 189.

Doc. 64
ROOSEVELT TO CHURCHILL

July 10, 1941

I have given consideration to your recent cable[1] relative to a joint Anglo-American Tank Board. We have had here for some months a joint British-American Tank Board[2] which we think has done some very good work in coordinating designs and production. It may be that it should have some additional members on it but I think it would be very unwise to create a new board in the light of the good start we have already made.[3]

[1] See above, Doc. 63.

[2] The board had been in existence for longer than that. In the draft for this reply prepared on July 8 Secretary of War Stimson referred to "its success last summer and autumn in coordinating British and American designs, including the establishment of the turret in our tanks." Hall and Wrigley, *Overseas Supply*, pp. 102–103.

[3] Roosevelt proved to be a very good prophet. "On no other type of matériel," wrote the official historians of U.S. munitions design and production, "was collabora-

I have taken steps to get our tank production very substantially increased and will let you know soon the new estimates.

---

tion with the British so extensive and carefully organized as on tanks, tank guns, and tank accessories." Green, Thomson, and Roots, *Ordnance Department*, pp. 268–269.

Doc. 65
ROOSEVELT TO CHURCHILL

July 12, 1941

We have had a thorough review of our whole tank situation here during the last few days and I can now give you the following results.

We plan to increase our peak production of our medium tank from 600 to 1,000 a month reaching that goal by April 1, 1942. We will build 600 medium tanks more than we had planned prior to January 1. We will increase our light tank production by 150 per month so that we will have 900 more light tanks prior to January 1 than we had planned. Assuming these schedules are maintained, and I believe they will be, it means that we can give you 800 to 1,000 medium tanks prior to January 1. I will send you in a few days the exact scheduling of these.

We can also as of August 1 start training 500 of your Tank Corps men in this country if you think that would be helpful. Will you let me know about this soon so that we can make our plans immediately?

Doc. 66
ROOSEVELT TO CHURCHILL

July 14, 1941

I know you will not mind my mentioning to you a matter which is not in any way serious at this time but which might cause unpleasant repercussions over here later on. I refer to rumors which of course are nothing more nor less than rumors regarding trades or deals which the British Government is alleged to be making with some of the occupied nations. As for example the crazy story that you have promised to set up Yugoslavia again as it formerly existed and the other story that you had promised Trieste to Yugoslavia.[1]

1 Early in March 1941 the Allies sought desperately to persuade Yugoslavia to resist the Germans. Foreign Secretary Eden met in Athens with Ronald Ian Camp-

In certain racial groups in this country there is of course enthusiastic approval for such promises in relation to postwar commitments, but on the other hand there is dissension and argument among other groups such as the Czechs and Slovaks and among the Walloons and Flemish.

You will of course remember that back in early 1919 there was serious trouble over actual and alleged promises to the Italians and to others.[2]

It seems to me that it is much too early for any of us to make any commitments for the very good reason that both Britain and the United States want assurance of future peace by disarming all trouble-makers and secondly by considering the possibility of reviving small states in the interest of harmony even if this has to be accomplished through plebiscite methods.

---

bell, the British ambassador to Yugoslavia, and authorized Campbell to tell Prince Paul that Britain would support Greece with air and ground forces as strongly and as rapidly as possible. Campbell was also instructed to say that the British government was studying "with sympathy" the case for the revision of the Istrian frontier with Italy and was "disposed to think that this case could be established and advocated by them at the Peace Conference." The Cabinet formally approved this step on March 3. Sir Llewellyn Woodward, *British Foreign Policy in the Second World War,* 1 (London, 1970) : 52. Word of the British offer evidently reached the State Department, and on July 8 Assistant Secretary of State Adolf A. Berle, Jr., sent Roosevelt a memorandum: "It is now evident that preliminary commitments for the postwar settlement of Europe are being made, chiefly in London. Perhaps you are being kept informed of these. I am not clear that the State Department is being kept informed of all of them by the parties. . . . You will recall that at Versailles President Wilson was seriously handicapped by commitments made to which he was not a party and of which he was not always informed. I have suggested to Sumner [Welles] that we enter a general caveat, indicating that we could not be bound by any commitments to which we had not definitely assented. . . ." Beatrice Bishop Berle and Travis Beal Jacobs, eds., *Navigating the Rapids 1918–1971: From the Papers of Adolf A. Berle* (New York, 1973) , p. 372. Henceforth cited as *Berle Papers.* On July 11 Berle entered in his diary: "I have been working a little on the British peace commitments—if they really are peace commitments. Some of them we know are. One of them, the alleged turning over of Trieste to Yugoslavia, has already been denied. Yesterday . . . I sent a memorandum to the President. I understand that the President wrote a message to Churchill last night in the general sense that the United States could not be bound by any commitments to which they were not a party." *Berle Papers,* pp. 372–373.

2 When the Paris peace settlement came before the United States Senate for its advice and consent in 1919, Senator Henry Cabot Lodge of Massachusetts, chairman of the Committee on Foreign Relations, invited spokesmen for various disaffected nationality groups—including Italian- and Irish-Americans—to vent their bitter opposition to the Paris treaty's provisions regarding their homelands, thus contributing materially to the eventual defeat of the treaty and the League of Nations. See Thomas A. Bailey, *Woodrow Wilson and the Great Betrayal* (New York, 1945) , pp. 81–82.

The plebiscite was on the whole one of the few successful outcomes of the Versailles Treaty and it may be possible for us to extend the idea by suggesting in some cases preliminary plebiscites to be followed a good deal later on by second or even third plebiscites. For example, none of us know at the present time whether it is advisable in the interest of quiet conditions to keep the Croats away from the throats of the Serbs and vice versa.

I am inclined to think that an overall statement on your part would be useful at this time, making it clear that no postwar peace commitments as to territories, populations, or economies have been given. I could then back up your statement in very strong terms.[3]

[3] According to the authoritative (unpublished) account of Captain Tracy B. Kittridge, "United States–British Naval Cooperation 1939–1942," the British had flatly rejected any efforts to link the ABC-1 agreement (the contingency plans should the United States enter the war), with a commitment "that the United States and United Kingdom furnish each other . . . full texts and particulars of any treaties, secret or otherwise, . . . which may affect . . . the peace terms to be agreed upon after the cessation of hostilities." Theodore A. Wilson, *The First Summit— Roosevelt and Churchill at Placentia Bay 1941* (Boston, 1969), p. 184.

Doc. 67
CHURCHILL TO ROOSEVELT

July 25, 1941

. . . I am much interested in your suggestion that men for our Tank Corps should be trained in the United States.[1] We are examining it here and will let you know our views as soon as possible.

We have been considering here our war plans, not only for the fighting of 1942 but also for 1943. After providing for the security of essential bases it is necessary to plan on the largest scale the forces needed for victory. In broad outline, we must aim first at intensifying the blockade and propaganda. Then, we must subject Germany and Italy to a ceaseless and ever growing air bombardment. These measures may themselves produce an internal convulsion or collapse. But plans ought also to be made for coming to the aid of the conquered populations by landing armies of liberation when opportunity is ripe. For this purpose it will be necessary, not only to have great numbers of tanks but also of vessels capable of carrying them and landing them direct onto beaches. It ought not to be difficult for you to make the necessary adaptation in some of the vast numbers of merchant vessels you are building so as to fit them for tank-landing fast ships.

[1] See above, Doc. 65.

If you agree with this broad conception of bringing Germany to her knees, we should not lose a moment in:

(A) Framing an agreed estimate as to our joint requirements of the primary weapons of war: e.g., aircraft, tanks, etc.

(B) Therefore, considering how these requirements are to be met by our joint production.

Meanwhile I suggest that our combined staffs in London should set to work as soon as possible on (A) and that thereafter our technical experts should proceed with (B).

Doc. 68
CHURCHILL TO ROOSEVELT

July 25, 1941

Cabinet has approved my leaving. Am arranging if convenient to you to sail August 4th,[1] meeting you some time 8th–9th–10th. Actual secret rendezvous need not be settled till later. Admiralty will propose details through usual channels.

Am bringing First Sea Lord Admiral Pound,[2] CIGS[3] Dill, and Vice Chief of Air Staff Freeman.[4] Am looking forward enormously to our talks, which may be of service to the future.

[1] Churchill left Scapa Flow aboard the *Prince of Wales* on August 5 and rendezvoused with the USS *Augusta,* carrying Roosevelt, off Newfoundland on August 9.

[2] Admiral of the Fleet Sir Dudley Pound.

[3] Chief of the Imperial General Staff.

[4] Air Vice Marshal Sir Wilfrid Freeman.

Doc. 69
CHURCHILL TO ROOSEVELT

July 27, 1941

Suggest Averell[1] comes back Tuesday by air and I bring Harry[2] with me. It will do him good.

Policy Middle East and air generally seem to require discussion.

[1] W. Averell Harriman.

[2] Harry L. Hopkins, the President's special assistant, had flown on to Moscow the previous day and was not expected back in London before August 3.

Presume you wish me to bring Dill and Air Chief and necessary small staff.

Looking forward keenly to this event. Kindest regards.

Doc. 70
CHURCHILL TO ROOSEVELT

August 5, 1941

Harry returning dead beat from Russia but is lively again now. We shall get him in fine trim on voyage. We are just off. It is 27 years ago today that the Huns began their last war. We all must make good job of it this time. Twice ought to be enough. Look forward so much to our meeting. Kindest regards.

THE ATLANTIC CONFERENCE
AUGUST 1941

[The first wartime conference between Roosevelt and Churchill took place on August 9–12, 1941, on board the U.S. heavy cruiser *Augusta* and the British battleship *Prince of Wales,* anchored at Placentia Bay off Newfoundland. Churchill brought with him his Chiefs of Staff, General Dill and Admiral Pound; his Air Vice Marshal Sir Wilfrid Freeman; the Permanent Undersecretary of State for Foreign Affairs, Sir Alexander Cadogan; his scientific adviser, Lord Cherwell; the Assistant Secretary to the War Cabinet, L. C. Hollis; his principal private secretary, J. M. Martin; his flag commander, R. W. Thompson; and a number of service staff officers. Roosevelt's party included his military chiefs—Admiral Ernest J. King, commander in chief of the Atlantic Fleet; Admiral Harold R. Stark, Chief of Naval Operations; General George C. Marshall, Army Chief of Staff; and General Henry H. Arnold, Deputy Chief of Staff for Air—as well as Undersecretary of State Sumner Welles, W. Averell Harriman, and Harry Hopkins.

Roosevelt, Churchill, and their advisers reviewed at length the principal problems confronting them in Europe, Africa, and the Far East. During their first meeting, at dinner on the *Augusta* on the evening of August 9, Churchill emphasized the need for more ships, planes, and tanks. He asked that the United States extend its convoy

operations into the North Atlantic and that a stiff message be sent to
the Japanese, warning them against further expansion in the southwest
Pacific, a problem that deeply concerned him. Although the conference
had been weeks in the making, Roosevelt and his advisers seemed ill
prepared for specific discussions and concrete decisions. As General
Marshall's authorized biographer has written: "Murky was the word
for the American position. More interested in covering the Allied situation in a broad sweep than in detailed examination of possible Anglo-
American collaboration, the President paid little attention to the issues
that harassed his service advisers." For their part, the British contended
that Nazi Germany would be defeated without a landing on the Continent, and that continued blockading, heavy bombing, and skilled
propaganda would destroy the Germans' will to fight. Even if an
invasion became unavoidable, there would be no need for large numbers of ground troops. Marshall, for one, strongly disagreed with this
position. Roosevelt and Churchill listened with special interest to
Hopkins' report on his recent trip to Russia and agreed to send a joint
message to Stalin proposing an early high-level meeting in Moscow to
ascertain "the needs and demands of your and our armed services," and
meanwhile assuring Stalin that "we shall continue to send you supplies
and more tanks as rapidly as possible." Roosevelt, on the other hand,
declined to accept Churchill's argument for an inflexible American
position vis-à-vis Japan, promising only that he would see the Japanese
ambassador, Admiral Kichisaburo Nomura, immediately upon his return to Washington.

The most striking result of the first Roosevelt-Churchill conference
was the Atlantic Charter, a joint Anglo-American declaration of principles modeled on Wilson's Fourteen Points and Roosevelt's Four
Freedoms. The document was especially desired by Roosevelt and after
being drafted, at Churchill's suggestion, by Sir Alexander Cadogan, was
revised by Roosevelt, Churchill, Cadogan, and Sumner Welles. In the
joint declaration—a preamble and eight points—the two countries
pledged to seek no territorial or other aggrandizement, denounced
territorial changes "that do not accord with the freely expressed wishes
of the people concerned," affirmed "the right of all people to choose
the form of government under which they will live," favored "the fullest collaboration between all nations in the economic field," supported
("with due respect for their existing obligations") equal access to trade
and raw materials for all nations, and looked toward a peace in which
"all men in all the lands may live out their lives in freedom from fear
and want."

The Atlantic Charter was not formally signed. It was, as Robert
Sherwood wrote later, "merely mimeographed and released. Neverthe-

less, its effect was cosmic and historic." It turned up, the historian of the first Roosevelt-Churchill summit has noted, "like a copper penny throughout the war—alternately embarrassing and pleasing its designers." Roosevelt seems to have come away from the meeting well pleased, and Churchill cabled his Lord Privy Seal: "I am sure I have established warm and deep personal relations with our great friend." Therein, perhaps, lay the greatest significance of the conference. Even so, after returning to London Churchill wrote plaintively to Hopkins that throughout the Cabinet and informed circles there was "a wave of depression . . . about [the] President's many assurances and no closer to war, etc."]

Doc. 71
CHURCHILL TO ROOSEVELT

September 1, 1941

The good results which have been so smoothly obtained in Persia puts [sic] us in touch with the Russians[1] and we propose to double or at least greatly improve the railway from the Persian Gulf to the Caspian, thus opening a sure route by which long-term supplies can reach the Russian reserve positions in the Volga basin. Besides this there is the importance of encouraging Turkey to stand as a solid block against German passage to Syria and Palestine. In view of both these important objectives I wish to reinforce the Middle East armies with two regular British divisions, 40,000 men, in addition to the

[1] On August 17 an Anglo-Russian note had been presented to the Iranian government demanding the ouster of the German colony in that country. Despite a show of agreement, the Iranians "hedged their compliance with so many conditions and qualifications as to make the whole unacceptable." J. M. A. Gwyer and J. R. M. Butler, *Grand Strategy*, vol. 3, pt. 1, *June 1941–August 1942* (London, 1964), p. 188. British and Russian forces therefore entered Iran on August 25. Effective Iranian resistance ceased by August 28. Under the terms of the armistice, specified parts of the country were to be occupied by British and Russian troops, the German colony was to be expelled, and transit rights were to be granted for British and Russian troops and matériel. This was not, however, the end of the affair. The Iranian government was unwilling, or unable, to carry out promptly the provisions of the armistice. On September 15, therefore, British and Russian troops began to move on Teheran. By late October—when the Anglo-Russian demands had been fully complied with—their troops withdrew from Teheran to the originally specified areas of occupation, leaving behind a small force to guard key railway points. In January 1942 an agreement was signed governing the relations of the three countries for the duration of the war. Gwyer and Butler, *Grand Strategy*, 3 (pt. 1): 189–191.

150,000 drafts and units which we are carrying ourselves between now and Christmas. We cannot, however, manage to find the whole of the shipping by ourselves. Would it be possible for you to lend us twelve United States liners and twenty United States cargo ships manned by American crews from early October till February? These would come carrying cargo to United Kingdom ports under any flag arrangement convenient. If they could arrive here early in October, we would send them forward as additions to our October and November convoys to the Middle East.

I know, Mr. President, from our talks that this will be difficult to do, but there is a great need for more British troops in the Middle East and it will be an enormous advantage if we can hold Turkey and sustain Russia, and by so doing bar further advance eastward by Hitler. It is quite true that the loan of these liners would hamper any large despatch of United States forces to Europe or Africa, but as you know I have never asked for this in any period we can reasonably foresee in the near future.

It is for you to say what you would require in replacements of ships sunk by enemy action. Hitherto we have lost hardly anything in our well-guarded troop convoys. I am sure this would be a wise and practical step to take at the present juncture and I shall be very grateful if you can make it possible.

Doc. 72
ROOSEVELT TO CHURCHILL

September 5, 1941

I am sure we can help with your project to reinforce the Middle East army.[1]

At any rate I can now assure you that we can provide transports for 20,000 men. These ships will be United States Navy transports manned by Navy crews. Our Neutrality Act permits public ships of the Navy to go to any port.

Maritime Commission is arranging to place ten or twelve additional ships in the North Atlantic run between American ports and Great Britain so that you could release ten or twelve of your cargo ships for carrying cargo to the Middle East. . . .

For your private and very confidential information I am planning to make a radio address Monday night relative to the attack on our

[1] See above, Doc. 71.

destroyer[2] and to make perfectly clear the action we intend to take in the Atlantic.

[2] On September 4 a German submarine fired two torpedoes at the USS *Greer*, 175 miles southwest of Iceland. The *Greer* had been trailing the submarine and broadcasting its location for three and a half hours when the submarine suddenly attacked. Fortunately, the torpedoes missed their target. Even so, the incident caused something of a sensation in the United States. In his fireside chat of September 11 Roosevelt said: "To be ultimately successful in world mastery, Hitler knows that he must get control of the seas. . . . This attack on the *Greer* was no localized military operation in the North Atlantic. . . . This was one determined step toward creating a permanent world system based on force, on terror, and on murder. . . . Our patrolling vessels and planes will protect all merchant ships . . . engaged in commerce in our defensive waters. . . . From now on, if German or Italian vessels of war enter the waters, the protection of which is necessary for American defense, they do so at their own peril." *PPR*, vol. 10, *1941: The Call to Battle Stations* (New York, 1950), no. 88. Under orders issued to the Atlantic Fleet on September 13, American warships could henceforth escort convoys of any nationality and destroy German or Italian naval, land, or air forces which they might encounter.

Doc. 73
ROOSEVELT TO CHURCHILL

September 17, 1941

I held a preliminary conference on tank production this morning. Present production schedule is coming along very well and goes up each month until it reaches 1,400 a month in May 1942. I am making every effort to accelerate this rate but more important I am going to develop a program which I hope will double this monthly capacity and get our full tank capacity up to a minimum of 2,500 a month and a maximum of 3,000 a month.[1] As soon as I can hold a further conference with the Army on Monday or Tuesday of next week I will cable the exact numbers of tanks which can be exported from this country each month beginning September 1, 1941, through June 1942. The number will be substantial and I think not a discouraging one from the point of view of our two missions going to Moscow.[2]

[1] "In the midst of this concerted drive to speed production President Roosevelt dropped a bombshell in mid-September. At a White House conference . . . the President reviewed current military production plans. When he came to the schedule calling for production of 1,000 medium tanks and 400 light tanks per month, the President paused, placed a cigarette in his famous long holder, lit it, and then calmly issued this short directive: 'Double it!' " Harry C. Thomson and Linda Mayo, *The Ordnance Department—Procurement and Supply* (Washington, 1960), p. 232.

[2] Roosevelt's plans to extend lend-lease assistance to the Soviet Union led to the dispatch late in September of a supply mission to Moscow headed by W. Averell

You have undoubtedly been advised by the Admiralty that the transport plan has been completed.

Harriman and to a promise to furnish the Soviet Union with $1 billion in military assistance by June 30, 1942. Congress gave at least tacit approval to the President's policy by rejecting, on October 7, an amendment barring such assistance. On November 7 Roosevelt officially declared the defense of the Soviet Union to be vital to that of the United States and the Soviet Union therefore eligible for lend-lease assistance. See Raymond H. Dawson, *The Decision to Aid Russia 1941—Foreign Policy and Domestic Politics* (Chapel Hill, N.C., 1959), chaps. 6–10; Marvin D. Bernstein and Francis L. Loewenheim, "Aid to Russia—The First Year," in Harold Stein, ed., *American Civil-Military Decisions* (Montgomery, Ala., 1963), pp. 112ff.; and George C. Herring, Jr., *Aid to Russia 1941–1946: Strategy, Diplomacy, The Origins of the Cold War* (New York, 1973).

Doc. 74
CHURCHILL TO ROOSEVELT

September 22, 1941

Your cheering cable[1] about tanks arrived when we were feeling very blue about all we have to give up to Russia. The prospect of nearly doubling the previous figures encouraged everyone. The missions[2] have started in great good will and friendship. Kindest regards.

[1] See above, Doc. 73.
[2] At an Anglo-American supply conference held in London on September 15–18, the British had expressed concern over a "drain" of supplies to Russia. The American and British missions, led by W. Averell Harriman and Lord Beaverbrook, Minister of Supply, left for Moscow on September 22. See Stein, *Civil-Military Decisions*, pp. 116–117.

Doc. 75
ROOSEVELT TO CHURCHILL

September 30, 1941

I have cabled our mission in Moscow today that we can make available from July 1, 1942, to January 1, 1943, 1,200 tanks a month for England and Russia combined; from January 1, 1943, to July 1, 1943, 2,000 tanks a month. I told our mission to make a commitment to Russia of 400 tanks a month beginning July 1 in addition to those already promised and advised them after consultation with your representatives to increase the amount still further if that seemed desirable.

We are making commitment to the Russians over and above the commitments made to July 1 of 3,600 combat planes between July 1, 1942, and July 1, 1943.[1]

We are going to put the production of tanks to well over 2,500 a month. This large increase in tanks is due to our doubling our whole tank production.

[1] "The spirit of the American officials sent to Moscow was one disposed 'to give and give and give, with no expectation of any return' save that of keeping Russia steadfastly in the fight against Hitler." Dawson, *Decision to Aid Russia*, p. 251. The first protocol was signed in Moscow on October 1. See Sherwood, *Roosevelt and Hopkins*, pp. 387ff.

Doc. 76
ROOSEVELT TO CHURCHILL

October 7, 1941

At this very late date I deeply regret necessity of reopening with you what had been agreed on in regard to American flag Navy-operated transports going to England for proposed troop movement to Near East.[1]

I do so with utmost confidence that you will sympathetically consider the problem and my frank statement of it.

I have determined to send a message to Congress in the immediate future recommending sweeping amendments to our Neutrality Act. I am convinced that the Act is seriously crippling our means of helping you.[2] I want not only to arm all of our ships but I want to get the authority from Congress to send American flagships directly into

[1] See above, Doc. 72.

[2] Sections 2, 3, and 6 of the Neutrality Act of 1939, which prohibited American ships from sailing in proclaimed combat zones and forbade the arming of American merchantmen, now seemed highly imprudent restrictions on proclaimed American policy. Submitting his proposals to Congress on October 9, Roosevelt declared that "we have known what victory for the aggressors would mean to us. . . . We know that we could not defend ourselves in Long Island Sound or in San Francisco Bay. That would be too late. It is the American policy to defend ourselves wherever such defense becomes necessary under the complex condition of modern warfare. . . . We will not let Hitler prescribe the waters of the world on which our ships may travel. The American flag is not going to be driven from the seas either by his submarines, his airplanes, or his threats." *PPR*, vol. 10, no. 94. Following bitter debate, the legislation was approved by Congress—in the Senate by a vote of 50 to 37, in the House by only 212 to 194—and was signed by the President on November 17.

British ports. After long conferences with congressional leaders, I have reached the conclusion that it would be disastrous to this legislation if one of our transports proceeding to or from Britain, and in British waters of British port, were to be sunk, when manned by U.S. Navy officers and men. Such an event might jeopardize our lend-lease and other aid.

I appreciate to the full your dilemma of rearranging plans for transfer of men to Near East.

I have given careful study to other means of accomplishing same ultimate objective.

As a first alternative, I suggest you send here, or transfer from your ships under repair here, enough officers and men to man our six transports. This would take a total of about 3,000 officers and men. These ships would then sail from Canadian ports under British flag and with British crews under lend-lease arrangements.

The second alternative would be for U.S. to continue manning these six transports, send them to Halifax, you to send the troops to board transports in Halifax. We would then transport the expedition through Western Hemisphere waters and hence to Near East destination. We believe, if considered advisable by Navy Department and Admiralty, we could escort this fast convoy all the way.

I feel that one of the two foregoing alternatives is necessary in order not to jeopardize the legislation to eliminate the restrictions under which we are now operating, or to break down growing public sentiment for policy of additional aid and cause this sentiment to reverse itself. Of the two alternatives offered, I prefer the first, namely you using your crews to man transports.

I have directed Admiral Stark[3] to acquaint Admiral Little[4] with the foregoing.

[3] Harold R. Stark, U.S. Chief of Naval Operations.
[4] Sir Charles Little, the naval member of the British joint staff mission in Washington.

Doc. 77
CHURCHILL TO ROOSEVELT

October 9, 1941

Fully understand situation which can quite well be coped with here.[1] We definitely prefer your second alternative of sending our

[1] See above, Doc. 76.

troops to Halifax for transshipment and onward passage to Near East in United States escorts so far as needful. This plan lessens greatly dislocation of complex escort programmes and delay in subsequent convoys.[2] Furthermore your valuable fast ships would not run any appreciable risk from U-boat attack by having to run in and out of the danger zones. If you agree our experts can make a firm programme whereby nine British liners arrive at Halifax with 20,800 men comprising the Eighteenth Division and start transshipment to your transports on November 7.

[2] The allusion is to the British plan designed to achieve a decisive victory over the German Afrika Korps in the western Sahara and having conquered Tripoli, in Churchill's words, "to descend upon Sicily, and thus open up the only possible 'Second Front' in Europe within our power, while we were alone in the West." Churchill, *Grand Alliance*, p. 540. Meanwhile Churchill was concerned about transporting "four divisions of our best troops" from the United Kingdom to the Near East. See also Churchill's message to Roosevelt of October 20, 1941. Churchill, *Grand Alliance*, pp. 544–548.

Doc. 78
ROOSEVELT TO CHURCHILL

October 11, 1941

It appears desirable that we should soon correspond or converse concerning the subject which is under study by your Maud Committee, and by Dr. Bush's organization in this country,[1] in order that any extended efforts may be coordinated or even jointly conducted. I suggest, for identification, that we refer to this subject as Mayson.

I send this message by Mr. Hovde,[2] head of the London office of our

[1] Maud was the cover name for a committee of scientists headed by Sir George Thomson which had been investigating the possibilities of producing a "uranium bomb" since April 1940. Vannevar Bush was director of the Office of Scientific Research and Development. An optimistic Maud report of July 15 had led Bush to press for greater efforts to develop atomic weapons. The most immediate results were the establishment of a "top policy group" consisting of Vice President Henry A. Wallace, Army Chief of Staff General George C. Marshall, Secretary Stimson, Harvard President Dr. James Bryant Conant, and Bush, and the sending of this letter. For the American side of these developments, see Henry D. Smyth, *Atomic Energy for Military Purposes* (Princeton, N.J., 1945); for the British side, see Margaret Gowing, *Britain and Atomic Energy 1939–1945* (London, 1964), esp. chaps. 2–4.
[2] Frederick L. Hovde headed the London mission of the Office of Scientific Research and Development. Though Churchill did not express his "readiness to collaborate" until December, he at once permitted Hovde to discuss these matters

scientific organization, as he can, if necessary, identify the subject more explicitly, or answer your questions concerning the form of organization by which it is now being handled in this country.

---

both with the Home Secretary, Sir John Anderson, and with his personal assistant for scientific affairs, Lord Cherwell.

Doc. 79
ROOSEVELT TO CHURCHILL

October 15, 1941

Dear Winston:

Mountbatten[1] has been really useful to our Navy people and he will tell you of his visit to the fleet in Hawaii. The Jap situation is definitely worse and I think they are headed north—however in spite of this you and I have two months of respite in the Far East.[2]

Dicky will tell you of a possibility for your people to study—to be used only if Pétain goes and Weygand plays with us.[3]

I wish I could see you again!

As ever yours,

[1] Admiral Lord Louis Mountbatten (Dicky) had been in the United States since August 19 supervising the repair of the British aircraft carrier *Illustrious* in the Norfolk navy yard. He had paid a visit to Pearl Harbor and was returning to England to become "adviser for combined operations."

[2] The belief that Japan would move against Russia, thus reducing its pressure on Southeast Asia for the time being, was widely held in Washington at the time and was not seriously affected by the resignation of Prince Fumumaro Konoye as Prime Minister on October 16 and his replacement, two days later, by General Hideki Tojo, who also assumed the positions of Minister of War and Home Minister. In mid-October the President sent the State Department the text of a message he proposed to send to Emperor Hirohito of Japan, the last sentence of which declared: "If . . . Japan were to start new wars north or south of here, the United States, in accordance with her policy of peace, would be very much concerned and would try to prevent any extension of such condition of war." *FR 1941*, 4 (Washington, 1956): 514. However, the idea of a presidential message to Hirohito was, for the time being, abandoned.

[3] Roosevelt continued to be much enamored of the idea of seizing Dakar or launching a "preventive occupation" of North Africa, but the Army General Staff was strongly opposed to the idea and Secretary Stimson had warned against "getting bogged down on a sidetrack which was not in the direct line of our strategical route towards victory." Stimson Diary, October 8, 1941. There was, moreover, no reason to believe that General Maxime Weygand, who commanded the Vichy French forces in North Africa, would countenance such an American scheme.

Doc. 80
CHURCHILL TO ROOSEVELT

November 2, 1941

As your naval people have already been informed, we are sending that big ship you inspected[1] into the Indian Ocean as part of the squadron we are forming there. This ought to serve as a deterrent on Japan. There is nothing like having something that can catch and kill anything. I am very glad we can spare her at this juncture as it is more than we thought we could do some time ago. The firmer your attitude and ours, the less chance of their taking the plunge.[2]

I am grieved at the loss of life you have suffered with *Reuben James.*[3] I salute the land of unending challenge!

[1] HMS *Prince of Wales,* which had carried Churchill and his party to the Atlantic conference in August 1941.

[2] On October 20 Churchill had written Roosevelt: "I still think . . . that the stronger the action of the United States toward Japan, the greater the chance of preserving peace." Churchill, *Grand Alliance,* p. 547. On November 5 he was even more explicit: "What we need now is a deterrent of the most general and formidable character. . . . No independent action by ourselves will deter Japan because we are so tied up elsewhere. But of course we will stand with you and do our utmost to back you in whatever course you choose." Churchill, *Grand Alliance,* p. 592.

[3] On October 31 a German submarine had sunk the American destroyer *Reuben James,* killing 155 crewmen, including all the ship's officers. The sinking of the destroyer, the first U.S. naval vessel lost in World War II, "was a deliberate act in the undeclared state of war that existed between the United States and Germany." Morison, *History of U.S. Naval Operations,* 1: 94.

Doc. 81
ROOSEVELT TO CHURCHILL

November 7, 1941

We have very much in mind the situation to which Chiang Kai-shek's appeal is addressed.[1] While we feel that it would be a serious

[1] Fearful of a successful Japanese attack from Indochina that would overrun Kunming and cut the Burma Road, Generalissimo Chiang Kai-shek cabled Churchill (repeating his message to Roosevelt) early in November: "China has reached the most critical phase of her war of resistance. . . . If the Japanese can break our front here we shall be cut off from you, and the whole structure of your own air and naval coordination with America and the Netherland East Indies will be seriously threatened in new ways and from a new direction." *FR 1941,* 5 (Washington, 1956): 749.

error to underestimate the gravity of the threat inherent in that situation, we doubt whether preparations for a Japanese land campaign against Kunming have advanced to a point which would warrant an advance by the Japanese against Yünnan in the immediate future. In the meantime we shall do what we can to increase and expedite lend-lease aid to China and to facilitate the building up of the American volunteer air force, both in personnel and in equipment. We have noted that you would be prepared to send pilots and some planes to China.

We feel that measures such as the foregoing and those which you have in mind along the lines we are taking, together with continuing efforts to strengthen our defenses in the Philippine Islands, paralleled by similar efforts by you in the Singapore area, will tend to increase Japan's hesitation, whereas in Japan's present mood new, formalized verbal warning or remonstrances might have, with at least even chance, an opposite effect.

This whole problem will have our continuing and earnest attention, study, and effort.

I shall probably not *repeat* not make express reply to Chiang Kai-shek before the first of next week.[2] Please keep within the confidence of your close official circle what I have said above.

2 Roosevelt replied to Chiang Kai-shek that "we are subjected at present, as you know, to demands from many quarters and in many connections. . . . Nevertheless, I shall do my utmost toward achieving expedition of increasing amounts of material for your use." *FR 1941*, 5: 758–760.

Doc. 82
ROOSEVELT TO CHURCHILL

November 24, 1941

On November 20 the Japanese Ambassador communicated to us proposals for a *modus vivendi*.[1] He has represented that the conclusion of such a *modus vivendi* might give the Japanese Government

1 On November 6 the Imperial Conference had approved a last effort to negotiate with the United States on the basis of two proposals, designated as Plan A and Plan B. Three weeks were to be allowed for their discussion, after which military action was to follow immediately if no agreement was reached. Plan A had been presented to Hull by Ambassador Kichisaburo Nomura on November 7 and was rejected by November 15. Plan B, for a stopgap agreement, here called *modus vivendi*, was presented by Nomura and the new special envoy, Saburo Kurusu, on November 20. See William L. Langer and S. Everett Gleason, *The Undeclared War, 1940–1941* (New York, 1953), chaps. 26–27.

opportunity to develop public sentiment in Japan in support of a liberal and comprehensive program of peace covering the Pacific area and that the domestic political situation in Japan was so acute as to render urgent some relief such as was envisaged in the proposal. The proposal calls for a commitment on the part of Japan to transfer to northern Indochina all the Japanese forces now stationed in southern Indochina pending the restoration of peace between Japan and China or the establishment of general peace in the Pacific area when Japan would withdraw all its troops from Indochina; commitments on the part of the United States to supply Japan a required quantity of petroleum products and to refrain from measures prejudicial to Japan's efforts to restore peace with China; and mutual commitments to make no armed advancement in the southeastern Asiatic and southern Pacific areas (the formula offered would apparently not exclude advancement into China from Indochina), to cooperate toward obtaining goods required by either in the Netherlands East Indies, and to restore commercial relations to those prevailing prior to the adoption of freezing measures.

This Government proposes to inform the Japanese Government that in the opinion of this Government the Japanese proposals contain features not in harmony with the fundamental principles which underlie the proposed general settlement and to which each Government has declared that it is committed. It is also proposed to offer to the Japanese Government an alternative proposal[2] for a *modus vivendi* which will contain mutual pledges of peaceful intent; a reciprocal undertaking not to make armed advancement into areas which would include northeastern Asia and the northern Pacific area, southeast Asia, and the southern Pacific area; an undertaking by Japan to withdraw its forces from southern French Indochina, not to replace those forces, to limit those in northern Indochina to the number there on July 26, 1941, which number shall not be subject to replacement and shall not in any case exceed 25,000, and not to send additional forces to Indochina. This Government would undertake to modify its freezing orders to the extent to permit exports from the United States to Japan of bunker and ship supplies, food products, and pharmaceuticals with certain qualifications, raw cotton up to $600,000 monthly, petroleum on a monthly basis for civilian needs, the proportionate amount to be exported from this country to be determined after consultation with the British and Dutch Governments. The United States would permit imports in general, provided that raw silk constitute at least two-thirds in value of such imports. The proceeds of such imports would be available for the purchase of the

2 For the draft text of the American counterproposal, see *FR 1941*, 4: 661–664.

designated exports from the United States and for the payment of interest and principal of Japanese obligations within the United States. This Government would undertake to approach the British, Dutch, and Australian Governments on the question of their taking similar economic measures. Provision is made that the *modus vivendi* shall remain in force for three months with the understanding that at the instance of either party the two parties shall confer to determine whether the prospects of reaching a peaceful settlement covering the entire Pacific area warrant extension of the *modus vivendi*.

This seems to me a fair proposition for the Japanese but its acceptance or rejection is really a matter of internal Japanese politics. I am not very hopeful and we must all be prepared for that trouble, possibly soon.[3]

---

[3] On November 24 Admiral Stark, who was well informed about the latest diplomatic developments, told Admirals Husband E. Kimmel and Thomas C. Hart, the U.S. commanders at Pearl Harbor and at Manila: "Chances of favorable outcome of negotiations with Japan very doubtful. This situation coupled with statements of Japanese Government and movements of their naval and military forces indicate in our opinion that a surprise aggressive movement in any direction including attack on Philippines or Guam is a possibility." U.S. Congress, *Hearings on Pearl Harbor Attack*, 79th Cong., 1st sess., 4: 1571.

Doc. 83
CHURCHILL TO ROOSEVELT

November 26, 1941

Your message about Japan received tonight.[1] Also full accounts from Lord Halifax of discussions and your counterproject to Japan on which Foreign Secretary[2] has sent some comments. Of course, it is for you to handle this business and we certainly do not want an additional war.[3] There is only one point that disquiets us. What about

---

[1] See above, Doc. 82.

[2] Anthony Eden.

[3] Churchill's lukewarm response was probably the ultimate factor in Washington's decision not to proceed with its *modus vivendi* proposal. It should be noted, however, that Australia and the Netherlands, both of which had been consulted as regards the *modus vivendi*, had expressed serious reservations, and that Canada, which was not consulted, complained bitterly at this exclusion. See *FR 1941*, 4: 655, 667. In any event, on November 26 Secretary of State Hull handed the Japanese a ten-point long-range plan—based largely on a memorandum submitted on November 17 by Harry Dexter White, special assistant to Treasury Secretary Morgenthau—which was almost certainly unacceptable to Japan. Langer and Gleason, *Undeclared War*, pp. 875–876. For the text of the White memorandum, as presented to Secretary Hull, see *FR 1941*, 4: 606–613.

Chiang Kai-shek? Is he not having a very thin diet? Our anxiety is about China. If they collapse our joint dangers would enormously increase. We are sure that the regard of the United States for the Chinese cause will govern your action.[4] We feel that the Japanese are most unsure of themselves.[5]

[4] Chiang Kai-shek, not surprisingly, was also strongly opposed to any American compromise with Japan. In a message to Secretary Hull on November 25 the Generalissimo said: "We . . . only request the United States Government to be uncompromising, and announce that if the withdrawal of Japanese armies is not settled, the question of relaxing of the embargo or freezing could not be considered. . . . The certain collapse of our resistance will be an unparalleled catastrophe to the world, and I do not indeed know how history in future will record this episode." *FR 1941*, 4: 660–661.

[5] For the Japanese behind-the-scenes debate on war and peace, see Langer and Gleason, *Undeclared War*, pp. 902ff.; and Robert J. C. Butow, *Tojo and the Coming of the War* (Princeton, N.J., 1961).

Doc. 84
CHURCHILL TO ROOSEVELT

November 30, 1941

It seems to me that one important method remains unused in averting war between Japan and our two countries, namely a plain declaration, secret or public as may be thought best, that any further act of aggression by Japan will lead immediately to the gravest consequences. I realise your constitutional difficulties but it would be tragic if Japan drifted into war by encroachment without having before her fairly and squarely the dire character of a further aggressive step. I beg you to consider whether, at the moment which you judge right which may be very near, you should not say that "any further Japanese aggression would compel you to place the gravest issues before Congress" or words to that effect.[1] We would, of course, make a similar declaration or share in a joint declaration, and in any case arrangements are being made to synchronise our action with yours.[2] Forgive me, my dear

[1] Roosevelt ruled out such a warning for the time being and contented himself with inquiring of the Japanese, on December 2, why they maintained larger forces in Indochina than was permitted under their agreement with Vichy. He pointed out the threat posed to neighboring states and asked for clarification of Japanese intentions. Japan's evasive reply was received by Hull on December 5.

[2] For the text of President Roosevelt's last message to Emperor Hirohito, dated December 6, 1941, see *FR Japan 1931–1941*, 2 (Washington, 1942): 784, 786. The message was delivered to the Japanese Foreign Minister early the following morning, and copies were immediately transmitted to Churchill and Chiang Kai-shek. In his

friend, for presuming to press such a course upon you, but I am convinced that it might make all the difference and prevent a melancholy extension of the war.

---

message Roosevelt emphasized the continued movement of large numbers of Japanese military, naval, and air forces into southern Indochina, adding that "it is only reasonable that the people of the Philippines, of the hundreds of Islands of the East Indies, of Malaya, and of Thailand itself are asking themselves whether these forces of Japan are preparing or intending to make attack in one or more of these many directions. . . . It is clear that a continuation of such a situation is unthinkable. . . . Thus a withdrawal of the Japanese forces from Indo-China would result in the assurance of peace throughout the whole of the South Pacific area."

A draft for an even stronger British warning to Japan reached Washington, ironically, on December 7. It threatened "appropriate measures" should the Japanese move against the Netherlands East Indies, Malaya, or Thailand and concluded: "Should hostilities unfortunately result, the responsibility will rest with Japan." FDR Library, President's Secretary's File: Great Britain. Roosevelt was by this time prepared to send such a warning on December 9, with British and Dutch ones to follow within twenty-four hours. For two views of British-American interplay on the eve of Pearl Harbor, see Woodward, *British Foreign Policy* (abridged ed., London, 1962), pp. 174ff.; and Raymond A. Esthus, "President Roosevelt's Commitment to Britain to Intervene in a Pacific War," *Mississippi Valley Historical Review,* 50 (June 1963) : 28–38; and Woodward, *British Foreign Policy,* vol. 2, chap. 24.

Doc. 85
ROOSEVELT TO CHURCHILL

December, 8 1941 (7:30 A.M.)

I think it best on account of psychology here that Britain's declaration of war be withheld until after my speech at 12:30 Washington time. I am asking for declaration. Any time after would be wholly satisfactory.

Delighted to know of message to de Valera.[1]

[1] Churchill's message to Prime Minister Eamon de Valera, designed to wean Ireland away from a neutrality beneficial to Germany, had declared: "Now is your chance. Now or never! A nation once again! I am very ready to meet you at any time." *FR 1941,* 4: 732. De Valera was not moved by the appeal.

Doc. 86
ROOSEVELT TO CHURCHILL

December 8, 1941 (3 P.M.)

The Senate passed the all-out declaration of war eighty-two to nothing, and the House has passed it three hundred eighty-eight to one.[1] Today all of us are in the same boat with you and the people of the Empire and it is a ship which will not and cannot be sunk.

[1] The lone opposing vote was cast by Representative Jeannette Rankin of Montana, who had also voted against American entry into World War I and who, ironically, had only returned to the House of Representatives in March 1941. By the time Roosevelt's message reached Churchill, the Prime Minister was already addressing the House of Commons. The British declaration of war, dispatched by the Foreign Office to the British ambassador in Tokyo at 5 P.M. on December 8, 1941, was based, in the words of the formal declaration, on the fact that "Japanese forces without previous warning either in the form of a declaration of war or in the form of an ultimatum with a conditional declaration of war had attempted a landing on the coast of Malaya and bombed Singapore and Hong Kong." *FR 1941*, 4: 733, 735.

Doc. 87
CHURCHILL TO ROOSEVELT

December 9, 1941[1]

I am grateful for your telegram on December 8.[2] Now that we are, as you say, "in the same boat," would it not be wise for us to have another conference? We could review the whole war plan in the light of reality and new facts, as well as the problems of production and distribution. I feel that all these matters, some of which are causing me concern, can best be settled on the highest executive level. It would also be a very great pleasure to me to meet you again, and the sooner the better.

I could, if desired, start from here in a day or two, and come by warship to Baltimore or Annapolis. Voyage would take about eight days, and I would arrange to stay a week, so that everything important could be settled between us. I would bring Pound, Portal,[3] Dill,[4] and Beaverbrook,[5] with necessary staffs.

Please let me know at earliest what you feel about this.[6]

[1] No copy of this telegram has been found in the files of the Roosevelt Library. The above text is printed in Churchill, *Grand Alliance*, p. 609.

[2] See above, Doc. 86.

[3] Air Chief Marshal Sir Charles Portal, Chief of the Royal Air Force.

[4] Dill had resigned as Chief of the Imperial General Staff in November and had been replaced by General Sir Alan Brooke. Churchill subsequently appointed Dill to head the British military mission in Washington.

[5] Lord Beaverbrook (William Maxwell Aitken), Minister of Supply.

[6] Among his colleagues Churchill was somewhat less restrained. When, according to General Sir Alan Brooke's biographer, at a Chiefs of Staff meeting on December 8 "someone continued to advocate the same cautious approach to America that had seemed politic when her intentions were in doubt, [Churchill] answered with a

wicked leer in his eye: 'Oh! That is the way we talked to her while we were wooing her; now that she is in the harem, we talk to her quite differently!' " Arthur Bryant, *The Turn of the Tide* (Garden City, N.Y., 1957) , p. 225.

Doc. 88
CHURCHILL TO ROOSEVELT

December 10, 1941

We do not think there is any serious danger about return journey.[1] There is, however, great danger in our not having a full discussion on the highest level about the extreme gravity of the naval position as well as upon all the production and allocation issues involved. I am quite ready to meet you at Bermuda or to fly from Bermuda to Washington.[2] I feel it would be disastrous to wait for another month before we settled common action in face of new adverse situation particularly in Pacific.[3] I had hoped to start tomorrow night, but will postpone my sailing till I have received rendezvous from you. I never felt so sure about the final victory, but only concerted action will achieve it. Kindest regards.

[1] According to the editors of the official American documents on the first Washington conference: "There was apparently a telegram (no copy of which has been found) from Roosevelt to Churchill on December 9, in which Roosevelt expressed fears about Churchill's safety on the return journey to the British Isles." U.S. Department of State, *The Conferences at Washington 1941–1942 and Casablanca 1943* (Washington, 1968) , p. 7.

[2] As it turned out, the meeting was set for December 22, and Churchill and his party sailed for Hampton Roads, Virginia, on the battleship *Duke of York* on December 14.

[3] The Japanese attack on Pearl Harbor was accompanied by naval and air attacks on British Malaya, Indochina, Thailand, Singapore, Guam, Hong Kong, Wake, and the Philippines, where the Japanese staged a highly successful raid on the U.S. Air Force base at Clark Field, removing "at one stroke the greatest single obstacle to [the Japanese] advance southward." Louis Morton, *The Fall of the Philippines* (Washington, 1953) , p. 90. By dawn of Pearl Harbor day (December 8 west of the international date line) Japanese forces had occupied Shanghai and entered the leased territory of Hong Kong. On December 8 Japanese troops invaded Thailand from Indochina and the following day occupied Bangkok without firing a shot. "Nothing could have been less accurate," the official historian of the U.S. Navy wrote later, "than the prewar assumption of Allied planners that the Japanese would be able to strike only one objective at a time." Morison, *History of U.S. Naval Operations,* 3 (Boston, 1948) : 90. On December 10 Japanese aircraft sank the British battleship *Prince of Wales* and the battle cruiser *Repulse,* thus disposing of the only Allied capital ships in the Pacific west of Hawaii. "The Allies lost face throughout the Orient and began to lose confidence in themselves." Morison, *History of U.S. Naval Operations,* 3: 190. See also Roskill, *War at Sea,* vol. 1, chap. 26.

Doc. 89
ROOSEVELT TO CHURCHILL

December 10, 1941

Delighted to have you here at White House. Impossible for me to leave country during intensive mobilization and clarification [of] naval action in Pacific.

I know you will bear in mind that the production and allocation problems can and will be worked out with complete understanding and accord. We shall have to use allotted planes for about three weeks but hope to resume schedule of shipments to you and Russia by January 1st. Practically all other lend-lease articles are continuing to be shipped. Details of production and allocation can be handled at long range.

Naval situation and other matters of strategy require discussion.[1]

My one reservation is great personal risk to you—believe this should be given most careful consideration, for the Empire needs you at the helm and we need you there too.

The news is bad[2] but will be better.

Warm regards.

[1] For American and British advance planning for the forthcoming Roosevelt-Churchill meeting, see *Conferences at Washington and Casablanca*, pp. 9ff., and Churchill, *Grand Alliance*, chap. 14.

[2] "It means," wrote General Brooke on the night the *Prince of Wales* and *Repulse* went down, "that from Africa eastwards to America through the Indian Ocean and Pacific we have lost command of the sea." Bryant, *Turn of the Tide*, p. 226.

Doc. 90
CHURCHILL TO ROOSEVELT

December 12, 1941

We feel it necessary to divert Eighteenth Division now rounding the Cape in your transports to Bombay to reinforce army we are forming against Japanese invasion of Burma and Malaya. I hope you will allow your ships to take them there instead of to Suez.[1] Route is both shorter and safer.

[1] The Eighteenth Division had been brought to Halifax, Nova Scotia, early in November for transshipment. See above, Docs. 71, 72, 76, and 77. Roosevelt's initial response to this request was written in the margin: "I think OK. Check Army & Navy. . . . Expedite." The Army and Navy agreed at once, and the convoy was rerouted as requested.

Our previous telegrams.[2] Thank you so much. Hope rendezvous will be about 21st. I am enormously relieved at turn world events have taken.

[2] See above, Docs. 87, 88, and 89.

Doc. 91
ROOSEVELT TO CHURCHILL

December 12, 1941

Thanks so much for your message.[1] I am in entire agreement and orders have already been issued for the diversion of the convoy, as requested.

[1] See above, Doc. 90.

THE FIRST WASHINGTON CONFERENCE
DECEMBER 1941–JANUARY 1942

[The first Washington conference, known as Arcadia, lasted from December 22, 1941, to January 14, 1942. Churchill, accompanied by most of his military chiefs, including Admiral Pound, General Dill, and Air Marshal Portal, as well as Minister of Supply Lord Beaverbrook and Ambassador Harriman, arrived off Hampton Roads, Virginia, after an eight-day voyage on board the new battleship *Duke of York*. Churchill was flown to Washington, where he was greeted by President Roosevelt. For nearly three weeks Churchill stayed at the White House. As he remembered later: "[Roosevelt and I] saw each other for several hours every day, and lunched always together, with Harry Hopkins as a third. We talked of nothing but business, and reached a great measure of agreement on many points, both large and small. Dinner was a more social occasion, but equally intimate and friendly. The President punctiliously made the preliminary cocktails himself, and I wheeled him in his chair from the drawing-room to the lift as a mark of respect, and thinking also of Sir Walter Raleigh spreading his cloak before Queen Elizabeth. I formed a very strong affection, which grew with our years of comradeship, for this formidable politician who had imposed his will for nearly ten years upon the American scene, and whose heart seemed to respond to many of the impulses that stirred my own. As we both, by need or habit, were forced to do much of our work in bed, he visited me in my room whenever he felt inclined, and encouraged me to do the same to him."

The conference led to agreements on a wide range of issues, although some of these agreements were reached only after vigorous, not to say stormy, discussions. The United States affirmed its adherence to a Germany-first strategy and agreed in principle to the plans Churchill and his military advisers had drafted during their Atlantic crossing. ("Reviewing these documents," Churchill concluded after the war, "it will be seen that they bear a very close resemblance to what was actually done by Britain and the United States during the campaigns of 1942 and 1943.") The plans called for the replacement of British forces by American troops in Northern Ireland, American participation in an invasion of North Africa (a project then called Gymnast and planned for as early as March 1942), and the dispatch of U.S. bomber squadrons to bases in the British Isles. The British in turn agreed to strengthen their military and naval forces in the Pacific.

Perhaps the most difficult moment of the conference came on Christmas morning, when General Marshall and his staff learned that, at a private meeting with Churchill and his advisers the previous evening, Roosevelt had agreed to turn over to the British certain American reinforcements destined for the Philippines if it proved impossible to reach the beleaguered American forces there. Believing this to be a British scheme to write off the Philippines in favor of Singapore—and dismayed to find that Roosevelt had made the agreement with Churchill without consulting his own military chiefs—Marshall, Arnold, and Brigadier General Eisenhower (a member of the Operations Division of the War Department since mid-December 1941) rushed over to Secretary Stimson's office to protest Roosevelt's action. "This astonishing paper made me extremely angry," Stimson noted in his diary, "and, as I went home for lunch and thought it over again, my anger grew until I finally called up Hopkins . . . and . . . said if that [paper] was persisted in, the President would have to take my resignation." A few hours later Roosevelt summoned his advisers—Generals Marshall and Arnold, Admirals King and Stark, Navy Secretary Knox, and Harry Hopkins—to the White House and declared nonchalantly that "a paper had been going around which was nonsense and which entirely misrepresented a conference [with] Churchill." As Stimson saw it, "this incident [showed] the danger of talking too freely in international matters without the President carefully having his military and naval advisers present"; Hopkins informed Stimson that "he had told the President that he should be more careful about the formality of his discussions with Churchill."

Among the Arcadia conference's major accomplishments were the establishment of a unified American-British-Dutch-Australian command (ABDA) in the Far East headed by General Sir Archibald Wavell, the creation of a Combined Chiefs of Staff headquartered in Washington with Sir John Dill as head of the British joint staff mission, and a notable increase in American production goals to meet the demands of an enormously wider war. Finally, the conference produced the Declaration by the United Nations, signed on New Year's Day by Roosevelt, Churchill, Chinese Foreign Minister T. V. Soong, and Soviet ambassador Maxim Litvinov. The statement reaffirmed the principles set forth in the Atlantic Charter and pledged each signatory (and the other twenty-two states that soon signed) to make no separate peace with the enemy and to employ its full resources until victory had been won, "complete victory . . . [being] essential to defend life, liberty, and religious freedom, and to preserve human rights and justice in their own lands as well as in other lands."

On the evening of January 15 Churchill and his party left Washington by train for Norfolk. Roosevelt and Hopkins saw them off, and the latter recorded: "On the way back, the President made it perfectly clear that he too was very pleased with the meetings. There was no question but that he grew genuinely to like Churchill and I am sure Churchill equally liked the President."]

Doc. 92
ROOSEVELT TO CHURCHILL

February 4, 1942

I have asked the State Department through Halifax and Winant[1] to express to the British Government my strong hope that it promptly agree to the present draft of interim lend-lease agreement and I now ask your personal help in bringing this about.[2]

I understand your need of maintaining unity at home in the great task of winning the war. I know you also understand how essential it is that we maintain unity of purpose between our two Governments and

[1] John G. Winant had succeeded Joseph P. Kennedy as American ambassador to Great Britain in January 1941. He took up his duties on March 18.

[2] The British—including Churchill himself during his recent visit to Washington—had registered strong objection to Article 7 of the proposed mutual aid agreement. The article dealt with the terms of the eventual lend-lease settlement and postwar economic relations, and it seemed to them to undermine the system of imperial preference established by the Ottawa Agreements of 1932. The system conferred special benefits on Britain and the Dominions as regards direct trade between them. For that very reason, it was highly objectionable to Secretary Hull and other leading members of the State Department.

peoples in this and equally important in the unfinished tasks that will follow it.

I am convinced that further delay in concluding this agreement will be harmful to your interests and ours. I am likewise convinced that the present draft is not only fair and equitable but it meets the apprehension which some of your colleagues have felt and which Halifax has brought to our attention.

No one knows better than I how busy you are. I should not add this matter to the long list of your worries if after giving it much personal attention I were not convinced that a failure to sign this agreement would do much mischief.

Doc. 93
CHURCHILL TO ROOSEVELT

No. 25[1]   February 7, 1942

. . . Although the French nation increasingly centers its hopes on the United States, the Vichy attitude described by you and manifesting itself in many ways is rotten. They have certainly been helping Rommel[2] with supplies.[3] I see that Vichy does not like the Miquelon-St. Pierre communiqué and that Darlan threatens to retaliate by pushing American observers out of Morocco. It seems to me vital that Donovan's activities of which you told me should have full play and that American observers should in no circumstances be withdrawn.[4]

1 At the conclusion of this message Churchill suggested consecutive numbering of future messages. He began with 25 and urged Roosevelt to begin with 100; most subsequent messages were numbered in these two series.

2 Field Marshal Erwin Rommel, commander of the German Afrika Korps.

3 From Vichy, U.S. ambassador William D. Leahy cabled the State Department along the same lines on February 6, 1942. *FR 1942*, 2 (Washington, 1962): 126–127.

4 On December 24, 1941, despite strong American objections, Free French naval forces had ousted the Vichy garrisons and assumed control of Miquelon and St. Pierre, two small fishing islands off Newfoundland. See Douglas G. Anglin, *The St. Pierre and Miquelon Affair of 1941* (Toronto, 1966). In a plebiscite held on Christmas Day, 98 percent of the islands' population voted to "rally to free France." In the communiqué, drafted by Churchill while visiting Washington, the United States and Great Britain declared that the islands should be demilitarized and governed by their consultative assembly, with assistance from Canadian and American officials. *FR 1942*, 2: 403–404. The Free French occupation of the islands produced considerable bad feeling not only between de Gaulle and Washington, which at one time considered sending a battleship to evict the small Gaullist forces, but between Washington and London, which did not share Secretary Hull's—and also the President's—hostility to the Free French movement. For an account of the

Otherwise what becomes of Gymnast[5] and its variants? You hold the master key in Martinique where there are reputed to be twenty French ships, forty-five hundred seamen many of whom would join Free French, fifty millions of gold from the *Émile Bertin*, and one hundred American fighter planes which, contrary to previous reports, are said to have been kept in good condition.[6]

I hope nothing will be done to give guarantees for the nonoccupation of Madagascar and Réunion. The Japanese might well turn up at the former one of these fine days, and Vichy will offer no more resistance to them there than in French Indochina. A Japanese air, submarine, and/or cruiser base at Diego Suarez would paralyse our whole convoy route both to the Middle and to the Far East. We have therefore for some time had plans to establish ourselves at Diego Suarez by an expedition either from the Nile or from South Africa.[7] At present action is indefinitely postponed as our hands are too full, but I do not want them tied. Of course we will let you know before any action is resolved.

I am delighted Magnet[8] is going forward. . . .

Your telegram about lease-lend. I found Cabinet at its second meeting on this subject even more resolved against trading the principle of imperial preference as consideration for lease-lend. I have always been opposed or lukewarm to imperial preference, but the issue did not turn on the fiscal aspect. This might well form part of a traffic or economic discussion, the latter of which we are ready to begin at once. The great majority of the Cabinet felt that if we bartered the principle of imperial preference for the sake of lease-lend we should have accepted an intervention in the domestic affairs of the British Empire, and that this would lead to dangerous debates in Parliament as well as to a further outbreak of the German propaganda of the kind you read to me on the second night of my visit about the United States breaking up the British Empire and reducing us to the level of territory of the Union. We should only play into the enemy's hands if we gave the slightest colour to all this nonsense. On the other hand we are all for sweeping away trade barriers and it is quite likely that we shall

---

American intelligence operation in Morocco, headed by Colonel William J. Donovan, see Murphy, *Diplomat Among Warriors*, pp. 89ff.

5 Code name for the planned invasion of North Africa.

6 At Martinique in the West Indies were a number of French warships, including the aircraft carrier *Béarn*; 106 American warplanes, which had been dispatched to France in June 1940; and $245 million in gold bullion, which had been moved from Canada. Various suggestions that the United States occupy the island soon appeared in the American press, but ultimately only diplomatic means were used to keep the island—and its contents—out of German hands.

7 See below, Docs. 107, 108, and 112.

8 Code name for the sending of American troops to Northern Ireland.

be willing to go further than Congress in this direction. Our whole aim is to work with you in constructing a free, fertile economic policy for the postwar world. I hope most earnestly therefore that you will make allowances for all these difficulties and try to help forward the suggestions being made by us through the Foreign Office and State Department. . . .

Doc. 94
ROOSEVELT TO CHURCHILL

No. 105   February 11, 1942

In regard to the proposed exchange of notes relating to Article 7 of the interim lend-lease agreement, referred to in your message No. 25,[1] I want to make it perfectly clear to you that it is the furthest thing from my mind that we are attempting in any way to ask you to trade the principle of imperial preference as a consideration for lend-lease.

Furthermore, I understand something of the nice relationships your Constitution requires of your home government in dealing with the Dominions. Obviously the Dominions must not only be consulted but I assume you must have their approval on any affirmative changes in existing arrangements which might be developed in the broad discussions which you and I both contemplate.

It seems to me the proposed note leaves a clear implication that empire preference and, say, agreements between ourselves and the Philippines are excluded before we sit down at the table.

All I am urging is an understanding with you that we are going to have a bold, forthright, and comprehensive discussion looking forward to the construction of what you so aptly call "a free, fertile economic policy for the postwar world." It seems perfectly clear to me that nothing should now be excluded from those discussions. None of us knows how those discussions will turn out, although, as I told you when you were here last, I have great confidence that we can organize a different kind of world where men shall really be free economically as well as politically.

The idea of attaching notes to this interim agreement would seem to me to give an impression to our enemies that we were overly cautious. I believe the peoples not only of our two countries but the peoples of all the world will be heartened to know that we are going to try together and with them for the organization of a democratic postwar

1 See above, Doc. 93.

world and I gladly accept your intimation that we might get going at once with our economic discussions.

What seems to be bothering the Cabinet is the thought that we want a commitment in advance that empire preference will be abolished. We are asking for no such commitment, and I can say that Article 7 does not contain any such commitment. I realize that that would be a commitment which your Government could not give now if it wanted to; and I am very sure that I could not, on my part, make any commitment relative to a vital revision of our tariff policy. I am equally sure that both of us are going to face in this realistic world adjustments looking forward to your "free and fertile economic policy for the postwar world," and that things which neither of us now dreams of will be subjects of the most serious consideration in the not too distant future. So nothing should be excluded from the discussions.

Can we not, therefore, avoid the exchange of notes which, as I have said, seems to dilute our statement of purpose with cautious reservations, and sign the agreement on the assurances which I here give in reference to the matter that seems to be the stumbling block?[2]

I feel very strongly that this would demonstrate to the world the unity of the American and British people.

In regard to coming to a meeting of minds with you at an early date, I only need to say to you that there are very important considerations here which make an early understanding desirable.

In saying this, I want again to tell you that I am not unmindful of your problem. We have tried to approach the whole matter of lend-lease in a manner that will not lead us into the terrible pitfalls of the last war.

[2] The mutual aid agreement, including the much disputed Article 7—by which the signatories agreed to the principle of multilateral trade and no discrimination, to be attained "in the light of governing economic conditions"—was signed on February 23, 1942.

Doc. 95
CHURCHILL TO ROOSEVELT

No. 28   February 12, 1942

Reference your 105.[1] I am deeply grateful to you for all you say, which entirely meets my difficulties. We shall agree through Foreign Office forthwith subject to clearing matter finally with Dominions to document without the need of formal interchange of letters. Of course

[1] See above, Doc. 94.

when I am asked I shall state my view of the public document from my own standpoint in terms which will lie within your assurances. I do not intend to quote you. . . .

Scharnhorst and *Gneisenau* are beating their way up channel and have run the batteries at Dover. We are out after them with everything we have.[2]

A fierce battle is raging at Singapore and orders have been given to fight it out.[3]

[2] The two German battle cruisers, along with the cruiser *Prinz Eugen*, had escaped from Brest through the blockade on February 11 and, though damaged, were heading for Norway. See Roskill, *War at Sea*, 2: 149ff.

[3] On the night of February 8–9, Japanese forces had succeeded in crossing the 800-yard Johore Strait to the island of Singapore.

Doc. 96
ROOSEVELT TO CHURCHILL

No. 106   February 18, 1942

I realize how the fall of Singapore has affected you and the British people.[1] It gives the well-known back-seat drivers a field day but no matter how serious our setbacks have been, and I do not for a moment underrate them, we must constantly look forward to the next moves that need to be made to hit the enemy.

I hope you will be of good heart in these trying weeks because I am very sure that you have the great confidence of the masses of the British people.[2] I want you to know that I think of you often and I know you will not hesitate to ask me if there is anything you think I can do.

When I speak on the radio next Monday evening I shall say a word about those people who treat the episode in the channel as a defeat. I

[1] Singapore had surrendered to Japan on February 15, with more than 85,000 British, Australian, and Indian troops taken prisoner. See S. Woodburn Kirby, *Singapore—The Chain of Disaster* (New York, 1971), and *The War Against Japan*, vol. 1, *The Loss of Singapore* (London, 1957), chap. 24.

[2] At the beginning of a three-day debate in the House of Commons, on January 27, Churchill had confronted his critics, public and private: "It is because things have gone badly and worse is to come that I demand a Vote of Confidence." He received it—by a vote of 464 to 1—followed by a cable from Roosevelt noting that "there was also one vote in opposition to us" (a reference to Congresswoman Jeannette Rankin's vote against a declaration of war against Japan). The President added: "It is fun to be in the same decade with you." Sherwood, *Roosevelt and Hopkins*, p. 494. Roosevelt had just passed his sixtieth birthday.

am more and more convinced that the location of all the German ships in Germany[3] makes our joint North Atlantic naval problem more simple.

I have been giving a good deal of thought during the last few days to the Far East. It seems to me that we must at all costs maintain our two flanks—the right based in Australia and New Zealand and the left in Burma, India, and China.

It seems to me that the United States is able because of our geographical position to reinforce the right flank much better than you can and I think that the United States should take the primary responsibility for that immediate reinforcement and maintenance, using Australia as the main base.

While the defense of Java looks difficult, I believe we both should fight hard for it but we must plan for the more southerly permanent base to strike back from. This will include some of the islands further north, such as New Caledonia and Fiji.

Britain is better prepared to reinforce Burma and India and I visualize that you would take responsibility for that theater. We would supplement you in any way we could, just as you would supplement our efforts on the right flank.

The United States should continue to move our supplies, principally aircraft, through into China because I think it is important that we have an effective offensive operation from there. Let me know what you think of this.

Because of the possibility of the loss of most of the ABDA area active operations will move fairly rapidly into the Burma area on the west and the ANZAC area on the east.[4] This would cause reconsiderations of the ABDA commands and the shifting of personnel.

I have not heard how Chiang Kai-shek is getting on but I am under the impression that his visit will be useful.[5]

Do let me hear from you.

---

[3] Roosevelt was mistaken in his belief that the French ships that had escaped from Brest were headed for German-controlled ports. See *PPR*, vol. 11, *1942: Humanity on the Defensive* (New York, 1950), no. 23.

[4] The American-British-Dutch-Australian command (ABDA) under General Sir Archibald Wavell had originally included the entire Far East. The Japanese attacks on the Asian mainland, however, taxed Wavell's resources to the utmost and suggested almost at once the desirability of carving out a separate Australian-New Zealand command (ANZAC) for the area between Australia and the mainland.

[5] Chiang visited India and Burma in February and March.

Doc. 97
CHURCHILL TO ROOSEVELT

No. 30   February 19, 1942

I am most deeply grateful to you for your warm-hearted telegram No. 106.[1] The pressure here has never been dangerous and I have used it to effect wholesome changes and accessions. You may take it everything is now solid.[2]

I am grieved about Max,[3] but he really does need two or three months in sunshine for his asthma and I know you will realise what friends we are and how helpful his driving power will be when he has recovered his health.

I do not like these days of personal stress and I have found it difficult to keep my eye on the ball. We are however in the fullest accord in all main things, and I will teleprint you more at large over the weekend. Democracy has to prove that it can provide a granite foundation for war against tyranny. I am looking forward to your rubbing it in about the easement in the Atlantic by the German flight from Brest, but of course we cannot dwell too much upon the damage they sustained. Every good wish and very many thanks.

[1] See above, Doc. 96.

[2] Churchill had just completed a substantial reconstruction of the War Cabinet, with Clement Attlee, Lord Privy Seal, becoming Deputy Prime Minister and Secretary of State for Dominion Affairs; Oliver Lyttelton succeeding Lord Beaverbrook, Minister of Supply, as first Minister of Production; and Sir Stafford Cripps, ambassador to Russia, becoming Lord Privy Seal and leader of the House of Commons.

[3] Lord Beaverbrook had resigned as Minister of Supply because of poor health, but according to his authorized biographer "support for Soviet Russia was the real cause of his resignation." A. J. P. Taylor, *Beaverbrook* (New York, 1972), p. 520.

Doc. 98
ROOSEVELT TO CHURCHILL

No. 107   February 20, 1942

I hope you can persuade Australian Government to allow proposed temporary diversion of their leading Australian division to Burma. I think this is of utmost importance. Tell them I am speeding addi-

tional troops as well as planes to Australia and that my estimate of the
situation there is highly optimistic and by no means dark.[1] Harry is
seeing Casey[2] at once.

[1] Earlier on February 20 Churchill had cabled Roosevelt that "the only troops
who can reach Rangoon in time to stop the enemy and enable other reinforcements
to arrive are the leading Australian division," but that the Australian government
had "refused point blank" to permit it to go. He asked Roosevelt for a message he
could pass on to Australian Prime Minister John Curtin. See Lionel Wigmore, *The
Japanese Thrust: Australia in the War of 1939–1945,* 1, *Army,* vol. 4 (Canberra,
1957) , p. 450.
[2] Harry Hopkins' conversation with Richard G. Casey, the Australian ambassador
in Washington, led Casey to inform Prime Minister Curtin on February 21 that the
United States had decided to send the Forty-first Division to Australia and that it
would sail early in March.

Doc. 99
CHURCHILL TO ROOSEVELT

No. 33   February 27, 1942

I believe that a number of foreign individuals, organisations, or
groups have recently told the United States Government, and in some
cases they have told us as well, of their wish to accede to the United
Nations Declaration as "appropriate authorities" within the terms of
the statement issued by the United States Government on January 6.
You will remember that this statement was devised for the Free
French. Applications have been received, among others, from Otto
Strasser's Free German movement, the Basque and Catalan émigré
movements, King Zog, and the Latvian Minister at Washington.[1]
Halifax has told the State Department that the acceptance of statements of accession by these groups would be embarrassing to us and I
understand that there is not in fact any question of such accessions
being accepted. We may, however, shortly have to consider approaches
from more welcome candidates such as Persia and Ethiopia and possibly Iraq and Saudi Arabia as well as the Free French. My feeling is
that it should be left to the country desiring to join to take the initia-

[1] Otto Strasser, once a leader of the left wing of the Nazi party, had broken with
Hitler in 1930 and emigrated in 1933. In 1942 he was residing in Canada and his
"movement" existed largely on paper. The small Basque and Catalan émigré movements sought the independence of their respective provinces from Spain. King Zog of
Albania had been deposed when his country was overrun by Italy in April 1939. The
Latvian ambassador in Washington represented the government that had been
overthrown when his country was incorporated into the Soviet Union in June
1940.

tive but that we should welcome adherence of these particular countries. I am most anxious that you and we should keep in step and that no accession should be accepted without previous consultation between the two of us. As I understand that you are dealing personally with this question, I put my views directly to you. Each particular case which arises can of course be discussed through the usual channels.

Doc. 100
ROOSEVELT TO CHURCHILL

No. 112   March 3, 1942

The views outlined in your telegram No. 33[1] on the adherences to the United Nations Declaration very closely coincide with mine.

I believe we should without question accept the adherence of the French National Committee[2] in London, whenever submitted, but that we should consult as to the action to be taken on requests for further adherences from governments with which we are still in official communication.

We might then determine at what moment we should bring the Soviet Government, and other governments of the United Nations which may be directly concerned, into these consultations.

As for "free groups" representing the populations of occupied countries, and other organizations, I have no intention of taking any action without full consultation with you.

[1] See above, Doc. 99.
[2] The French National Committee was the Free French organization in London headed by General Charles de Gaulle.

Doc. 101
CHURCHILL TO ROOSEVELT

No. 34   March 4, 1942

We are earnestly considering whether a declaration of Dominion status[1] after the war, carrying with it if desired the right to secede,

[1] Churchill was referring to India, where the political situation had become increasingly critical after the fall of Singapore and the Japanese advance in Burma. Roosevelt had told Churchill in December 1941 that he favored termination of India's colonial status. "I reacted so strongly and at such length," Churchill wrote

should be made at this critical juncture. We must not on any account break with the Moslems who represent a hundred million people and the main army elements on which we must rely for the immediate fighting. We have also to consider our duty towards thirty to forty million untouchables and our treaties with the princely states of India, perhaps eighty millions. Naturally we do not want to throw India into chaos on the eve of invasion.

Meanwhile, I send you in my immediately following telegram[2] two representative messages I have received and a summary of a memorandum by the Military Secretary, India Office.

I will keep you informed.

---

later about their conversation, "that he never raised it verbally again." Winston S. Churchill, *The Hinge of Fate* (Boston, 1950), p. 209. Nevertheless, Roosevelt instructed Harriman to raise the question in London in February, and on February 25 he wrote (but did not send) a long letter along the lines of his earlier conversation. For the development of American opinion on India and official policy early in 1942, see Gary R. Hess, *America Encounters India 1941–1947* (Baltimore, 1971).

2 Not printed.

Doc. 102
CHURCHILL TO ROOSEVELT

No. 37   March 4, 1942

When I reflect how I have longed and prayed for the entry of the United States into the war, I find it difficult to realise how gravely our British affairs have deteriorated by what has happened since December 7. We have suffered the greatest disaster in our history at Singapore, and other misfortunes will come thick and fast upon us. Your great power will only become effective gradually because of the vast distances and the shortage of ships. It is not easy to assign limits to the Japanese aggression. All can be retrieved in 1943 or 1944. But meanwhile there are very hard forfeits to pay. The whole of the Levant-Caspian front now depends entirely upon the success of the Russian armies. The attack which the Germans will deliver upon Russia in the spring will I fear be most formidable. The danger to Malta grows constantly and large reinforcements are reaching Rommel in Tripoli en route for Cyrenaica.[1] . . .

1 In a report to Hitler on February 13 Grand Admiral Erich Raeder, Commander in Chief of the German Navy, had argued that now was "a golden opportunity" for an attack on Egypt and the Suez Canal, since "except for Singapore, the British position is at present weakest in the North Africa–Suez area." On February 25 German naval officers had pointed out that "a successful operation in the near

You will realise what has happened to the army we had hoped to gather on the Levant-Caspian front, and how it has nearly all been drawn off to India and Australia, and you will see at once what our plight will be should the Russian defence of the Caucasus be beaten down. It would certainly be a great help if you could offer New Zealand the support of an American division as an alternative to their recalling their own New Zealand division, now stationed in Palestine. This also applies to the last Australian division in the Middle East. One sympathises with the natural anxiety of Australia and New Zealand when their best troops are out of the country, but shipping will be saved and safety gained by the American reinforcement of Australia and New Zealand rather than by a move across the oceans of these divisions from the Middle East. I am quite ready to accept a considerable delay in Magnet to facilitate your additional help to Australia. . . .

I am entirely with you about the need for Gymnast, but the check which Auchinleck[2] has received and the shipping stringency seem to impose obstinate and long delays. . . .

Permit me to refer to the theme I opened to you when we were together. Japan is spreading itself over a very large number of vulnerable points or trying to link them together by air and sea protection. The enemy are becoming ever more widely spread and we know this is causing anxiety in Tokyo. Nothing can be done on a large scale except by long preparation of the technical and tactical apparatus. When you told me about your intention to form commando forces on a large scale on the California shore I felt you had the key. Once several good outfits are prepared, any one of which can attack a Japanese-held base or island and beat the life out of the garrison, all their islands will become hostages to fortune. Even this year, 1942, some severe examples might be made causing great perturbation and drawing further upon Japanese resources to strengthen other points.

---

future against the main artery of the British Empire . . . would prove of vital importance to the war as a whole. Sea communications would be established with Japan and Anglo-American operations dealt a serious blow." J. M. A. Gwyer and J. R. M. Butler, *Grand Strategy*, vol. 3, pt. 2, *June 1941–August 1942* (London, 1964) , p. 443. Rommel, on the other hand, was bitterly critical of the failure of Hitler and the German high command to send him additional reinforcements, not realizing, in his own words, that "a few more divisions for my army, with supplies for them guaranteed, would have sufficed to bring about the complete defeat of the entire British forces in the Near East." B. H. Liddell Hart, ed., *The Rommel Papers* (New York, 1953) , p. 191.

2 Sir Claude Auchinleck had succeeded General Wavell as commander in chief of British forces in the Middle East in July 1941. Rommel's Afrika Korps had retaken Benghazi on January 21 and forced the British back to within forty miles of Tobruk by February 7, thus ruling out a North African invasion for the time being.

But surely if plans were set on foot now for the preparation of the ships, landing craft, aircraft, expeditionary divisions, etc., all along the California shore for a serious attack upon the Japanese in 1943 this would be a solid policy for us to follow. Moreover, the strength of the United States is such that the whole of this Western party could be developed on your Pacific coast without prejudice to the plans against Hitler across the Atlantic we have talked of together. For a long time to come it seems your difficulty will be to bring your forces into action and that the shipping shortages will be the stranglehold.

Doc. 103
CHURCHILL TO ROOSEVELT

No. 40   March 7, 1942

The increasing gravity of the war has led me to feel that the principles of the Atlantic Charter ought not to be construed so as to deny Russia the frontiers she occupied when Germany attacked her.[1] This was the basis on which Russia acceded to the Charter, and I expect that a severe process of liquidating hostile elements in the Baltic States, etc., was employed by the Russians when they took these regions at the beginning of the war.[2] I hope therefore that you will be able to give us a free hand to sign the treaty which Stalin desires as soon as possible.[3] Everything portends an immense renewal of the German invasion of Russia in the spring and there is very little we can do to help the only country that is heavily engaged with the German armies.

With regard to your conversation with the staffs about my long

[1] Article 3 of the Atlantic Charter provided for "the right of all peoples to choose the form of government under which they will live" and asserted that "sovereign rights and self-government [should be] restored to those who have been forcibly deprived of them."

[2] "When the Germans launched their attack on Russia in 1941, the Communists evacuated the Baltic States too hastily to destroy all evidence of their terror tactics. Documents came to light relating to mass executions and deportations, and many photographs of mass graves were taken, a good many of which I have seen. The evidence is irrefutable, and all testifies to a horror system so terrible it is difficult to believe that it could exist in the twentieth century." John Alexander Swetterham, *The Tragedy of the Baltic States* (New York, 1954), p. 72.

[3] Since Foreign Secretary Eden's visit to Moscow in December 1941, the Russians had been pressing for a treaty with Great Britain which would guarantee them the Polish, Finnish, and Baltic territories they had acquired prior to the German attack. See *The Memoirs of Anthony Eden, Earl of Avon*, vol. 2, *The Reckoning* (Boston, 1965), pp. 335ff. Henceforth cited as Eden, *Memoirs*. Roosevelt, at least at this time, was adamantly opposed to such an agreement.

telegram,[4] I should like to tell you, for yourself alone, that I am by no means excluding an effort from here to take the weight off Russia once Hitler is definitely committed to the attack. I do not want to discuss this with the combined staffs at all at the present time. I hope it can remain secret between us.

I am keeping you informed about India so that you may see the difficulties I have to face. The weight of the war is very heavy now and I must expect it to get steadily worse for some time to come.

4 See above, Doc. 102.

Doc. 104
ROOSEVELT TO CHURCHILL

No. 113   March 7, 1942

We have been in constant conference since receipt of your message of March 4th[1] to ensure that nothing is left unexplored which can in any way improve our present prospects. We recognize fully the magnitude of the problems confronting you in the Indian Ocean and are equally concerned over those which confront us in the Pacific, particularly since the United States assumes a heavy responsibility regarding measures for the defense of Australia, New Zealand, and the guarding of their sea approaches. You, on the other hand, will recognize the difficulties under which we labor in deploying and maintaining, in unprepared and distant positions, the considerable forces which will be required to meet this critical situation. I know that you will also appreciate that success in holding this region depends largely upon the adequacy of shipping, and the availability of munitions and aircraft for arming Dominion forces. The magnitude of the effort which may be put forth by the U.S. in the southwest Pacific has a direct relation to the magnitude of the air offensive which the U.S. will be able to undertake from United Kingdom bases.

The U.S. is now operating a large part of the Pacific Fleet in the ANZAC region,[2] for the defense of Australia and New Zealand, for preserving a base area for a future decisive offensive against Japan, and for containing Japanese naval and air forces in the Pacific. Pro-

1 See above, Doc. 102.

2 For all practical purposes, the original American-British-Dutch-Australian command (ABDA) had now been split. This left the area between Australia and the Asian mainland (ANZAC) without formal command but operationally under American jurisdiction. It had already been agreed that General Douglas MacArthur would take over that command whenever he could leave the Philippines. See Gwyer and Butler, *Grand Strategy*, 3 (pt. 1) : 381–383.

vided their bases in the west of Australia can be kept secure, U.S. submarines will continue to operate in the ABDA area against Japanese supply lines and against naval forces that exit to the Indian Ocean.

While Japan is indeed extending herself over a large area, it must be admitted that the deployment has been skillfully executed and continues to be effective. The energy of the Japanese attack is still very powerful. It is only through a greater energy, skill, and determination that Japan can be halted before she attains a dominating position from which it would prove most difficult to eject her. The U.S. agrees that the Pacific situation is now very grave and, if it is to be stabilized, requires an immediate, concerted, and vigorous effort by the United States, Australia, and New Zealand. To establish the many defended bases now planned and to transport to them their garrisons, together with enough amphibious troops for even minor offensives, requires the movement there of some of our amphibious forces, and the use of all our combat-loaded transports which are not urgently needed at home for elementary training of additional amphibious formations. The loan to the British of transports for further troop movements to India requires the use of combat transports for carrying U.S. garrisons to positions in the Pacific, and thus seriously reduces present possibilities of offensive action in other regions.

We concur in your estimate of the importance of the Indian and Middle East areas and agree that reinforcements are required. We also agree that the Australian and New Zealand divisions now in that region should remain. The 41st Division is leaving the United States by the 18th of this month, reaching Australia about April 10th. As a replacement for Australian and New Zealand divisions allotted to the Middle East and India, the United States is prepared to dispatch two additional divisions: one to Australia and one to New Zealand. . . .

The U.S. can furnish shipping to move 2 divisions (40,000 men) with their equipment from the U.K. to the Middle East and India. The first convoy consisting of all the U.S. shipping and the *Aquitania* can depart for U.K. about April 26 and the remainder about May 6. The supplying of these ships is contingent upon acceptance of the following during the period they are so used:

(a) Gymnast cannot be undertaken.
(b) Movements of U.S. troops to the British Isles will be limited to those which these ships can take from the U.S.
(c) Direct movements to Iceland (C) cannot be made.
(d) Eleven cargo ships must be withdrawn from sailings for Burma and Red Sea during April and May. These ships are engaged in transportation of lend-lease material to China and the Middle East.

(e) American contribution to an air offensive against Germany in 1942 would be somewhat curtailed and any American contribution to land operations on the continent of Europe in 1942 will be materially reduced. . . .

The deployment of the American air forces, which, at this stage, must be regarded as wholly tentative, including Army and shore-based naval aviation, will be in accordance with the following strategic concept: offense against Germany using maximum forces; defense of the general area Alaska, Hawaii, Australia, using necessary forces in support of the United States Navy in that area and in maintaining essential sea communications in all U.S. areas; defense of North and South America using essential forces. . . .

In confiding thus fully and personally to you the details of our military arrangements I do not mean that they should be withheld from your close military advisers. I request, however, that further circulation be drastically reduced.

I am sending you a personal suggestion on Sunday in regard to simplification of area responsibilities.

This may be a critical period but remember always it is not as bad as some you have so well survived before.

Doc. 105
ROOSEVELT TO CHURCHILL

No. 115   March 9, 1942

I telegraphed you Saturday night[1] in accordance with general recommendations of combined staffs as you doubtless recognized from the context. I want to send you this purely personal view so that you may know how my thoughts are developing relative to organization.[2]

I am concerned by the complexity of the present operational command setup to which is added equal complexity in the political setup.

When all is considered the overwhelming contribution of all the United Nations, with the exception of Russia, and to lesser extent China, comes and will increasingly come from the resources of Britain and the United States. Ever since our January meetings the excellent arrangements of that period have largely become obsolescent in relation to the whole southwest Pacific area.

I wish therefore that you would consider the following operational simplification.

1 See above, Doc. 104.
2 For the background of this message, including Roosevelt's message to Churchill of February 18, see Matloff and Snell, *Strategic Planning*, pp. 165ff.

The whole of the operational responsibility for the Pacific area will rest on the United States. . . .

The Supreme Command in this area will be American. Local operating command on the continent of Australia will be in charge of an Australian. Local operating command in New Zealand will be under a New Zealander. Local operating command in Dutch Indies would be given to a Dutchman if later on an offensive can regain that area from the Japanese. . . .

The middle area extending from Singapore to and including India and the Indian Ocean, Persian Gulf, Red Sea, Libya, and the Mediterranean would fall directly under British responsibility. All operational matters in this area would be decided by you. . . .

The third area would include the protection of the waters of the North and South Atlantic and would also include definite plans for establishment of a new front on the European continent. This would be the joint responsibility of Britain and the United States. . . .

It is intended of course to carry through all possible aid to Russia. . . .

The grand strategy of actual operations in the three areas would remain as they are today the subject of study and decisions by the combined staffs both here and in London, and the joint committees on shipping, on raw materials, and on munitions would continue to function as they do now—all subject to our joint approval.

I wish you would think this over. It appeals to me because of the simplification it offers under existing operational difficulties. Incidentally I am inclined to think that the Australians, New Zealanders. Dutch, and Chinese would rather welcome it.[3]

Best of luck

[3] In a long telegram dated March 17 Churchill approved in principle what a leading British historian has described as Roosevelt's "majestic concept." Churchill suggested, however, that the naval commands for the Pacific and Middle East areas be coordinated, that there be two Pacific war councils, one sitting in London and one in Washington, and that a more important role be assigned Australian, New Zealand, Dutch, and Chinese officers. See Gwyer and Butler, *Grand Strategy*, 3 (pt. 2): 473–474.

Doc. 106
ROOSEVELT TO CHURCHILL

No. 116 (Purely Personal)   March 10, 1942

I have given much thought to the problem of India and I am grateful that you have kept me in touch with it.[1]

[1] See above, Docs. 101 and 103.

As you can well realize, I have felt much diffidence in making any suggestions, and it is a subject which, of course, all of you good people know far more about than I do.

I have tried to approach the problem from the point of view of history and with a hope that the injection of a new thought to be used in India might be of assistance to you.

That is why I go back to the inception of the Government of the United States. During the Revolution, from 1775 to 1783, the British colonies set themselves up as thirteen states, each one under a different form of government, although each one assumed individual sovereignty. While the war lasted there was great confusion between these separate sovereignties, and the only two connecting links were the Continental Congress (a body of ill-defined powers and large inefficiencies) and second the Continental Army, which was rather badly maintained by the thirteen states. In 1783, at the end of the war, it was clear that the new responsibilities of the thirteen sovereignties could not be welded into a federal union because the experiment was still in the making and any effort to arrive at a final framework would have come to naught.

Therefore, the thirteen sovereignties joined in the Articles of Confederation, an obvious stopgap government, to remain in effect only until such time as experience and trial and error could bring about a permanent union. The thirteen sovereignties, from 1783 to 1789, proved, through lack of a federal power, that they would soon fly apart into separate nations. In 1787 a Constitutional Convention was held with only twenty-five or thirty active participants, representing all of the states. They met, not as a Parliament, but as a small group of sincere patriots, with the sole objective of establishing a federal government. The discussion was recorded but the meetings were not held before an audience. The present Constitution of the United States resulted and soon received the assent of two-thirds of the states.[2]

It is merely a thought of mine to suggest the setting up of what might be called a temporary government in India, headed by a small representative group, covering different castes, occupations, religions, and geographies—this group to be recognized as a temporary Dominion government. It would, of course, represent existing governments of the British Provinces and would also represent the Council of Princes.[3]

[2] Printing Roosevelt's letter in his memoirs, Churchill the historian found it irresistible to add a footnote at this point: "Actually, Rhode Island was not represented and the Constitution became effective upon the ratification of nine states." Churchill, *Hinge of Fate*, pp. 212–214.

[3] Roosevelt presumably meant the Chamber of Princes, a consultative body consisting of 108 princes sitting in their own right and 12 more representing 127 other

But my principal thought is that it would be charged with setting up a body to consider a more permanent government for the whole country—this consideration to be extended over a period of five or six years or at least until a year after the end of the war.

I suppose that this central temporary governing group, speaking for the new Dominion, would have certain executive and administrative powers over public services, such as finances, railways, telegraphs, and other things which we call public services.

Perhaps the analogy of some such method to the travails and problems of the United States from 1783 to 1789 might give a new slant in India itself, and it might cause the people there to forget hard feelings, to become more loyal to the British Empire, and to stress the danger of Japanese domination, together with the advantage of peaceful evolution as against chaotic revolution.

Such a move is strictly in line with the world changes of the past half-century and with the democratic processes of all who are fighting Nazism.

I hope that whatever you do the move will be made from London and that there should be no criticism in India that it is being made grudgingly or by compulsion.[4]

For the love of Heaven don't bring me into this, though I do want to be of help.[5] It is, strictly speaking, none of my business,[6] except insofar as it is a part and parcel of the successful fight that you and I are making.

---

autonomous Indian states, which had been established by Royal Proclamation in February 1921.

[4] The same day, although before Roosevelt's message was received in London, Churchill informed the Viceroy of India, Lord Linlithgow, that he would announce to Parliament the following day his decision to send Sir Stafford Cripps, the Lord Privy Seal, on a special mission to present "our united policy . . . which is our utmost limit"—a declaration the essence of which was that "the British Government undertook solemnly to grant full independence to India if demanded by a Constitutional Assembly after the war." Churchill, *Hinge of Fate*, p. 215. Lord Halifax communicated the plan to Undersecretary of State Sumner Welles, for transmittal to the President, on March 28, the day before it was made public.

[5] On March 9, as a concrete expression of his desire to be helpful, Roosevelt had appointed Louis Johnson as head of a new U.S. economic mission to India and as U.S. commissioner in Delhi. On March 24 Roosevelt named Johnson his personal representative to the government of India. For a brief account of the Johnson mission, a rather unhappy affair, see Hess, *America Encounters India*, pp. 47ff.

[6] This, as Robert Sherwood wrote after the war, was probably "the only part of that cable with which Churchill agreed. . . . [India] was indeed one subject on which the normal broad-minded, good-humored, give-and-take attitude which prevailed between the two statesmen was stopped cold." Sherwood, *Roosevelt and Hopkins*, p. 512.

Doc. 107
CHURCHILL TO ROOSEVELT

No. 44   March 14, 1942

We have decided to do Bonus,[1] and as it is quite impossible to weaken our eastern fleet we shall have to use the whole of Force H[2] now at Gibraltar. This will leave the western exit of the Mediterranean uncovered, which is most undesirable. Would it be possible for you to send say two battleships, an aircraft carrier, some cruisers and destroyers, from the Atlantic, to take the place of Force H temporarily? . . . It is most unlikely that French retaliation, if any, for Bonus would take the form of attacking United States ships by air. Moral effect of United States ships at Gibraltar would, in itself, be highly beneficial on both sides of the Straits. Operation Bonus cannot go forward unless you are able to do this. On the other hand, there are the greatest dangers in leaving Bonus to become a Japanese base.[3] . .

[1] Code name for the projected capture of Madagascar. A more limited plan was adopted by the British War Cabinet on March 14. It called only for the seizure of the naval base at Diego Suarez at the northern end of the island and was carried out on May 5–7. The remainder of Madagascar was not occupied until September.

[2] Code name for the British naval forces normally stationed at Gibraltar (also Force Hypo) .

[3] According to Major General S. Woodward Kirby the Japanese never considered occupying Madagascar, but at the end of February the U.S. Chiefs of Staff had "also stressed the desirability of denying the enemy the use of Diego Suarez." Roskill, *War at Sea*, 2: 185–186. For graphic accounts of Operation Bonus, see Kirby, *War Against Japan*, vol. 2 (London, 1958) , chap. 8; and Roskill, *War at Sea*, 2: 187ff.

Doc. 108
ROOSEVELT TO CHURCHILL

No. 119   March 16, 1942

Prefer to meet request contained in your dispatch number 44[1] regarding Ironclad[2] as to temporary replacement of Force Hypo by

[1] See above, Doc. 107.

[2] New code name for the modified plan to occupy northern Madagascar.

sending detachment to join Home Fleet equivalent in strength to force detached therefrom to replace Force Hypo.

Our ships now being made ready with view to early departure.

Doc. 109
CHURCHILL TO ROOSEVELT

No. 47   March 17, 1942

Your No. 121.[1] We are delighted MacArthur has arrived in Australia and that he has been appointed Supreme Commander with general acclamation.[2] . . .

[1] Not printed.

[2] General Douglas MacArthur had arrived that day, and his appointment as supreme commander of the southwest Pacific area was warmly applauded by Prime Ministers John Curtin of Australia and Peter Fraser of New Zealand. On April 9 the Japanese completed their conquest of the Bataan peninsula, and Corregidor, the last American foothold in the Philippines, fell on May 6.

Doc. 110
ROOSEVELT TO CHURCHILL

March 18, 1942

Dear Winston:

I am sure you know that I have been thinking a lot about your troubles during the past month. We might as well admit the difficult military side of the problems; and you have the additional burdens which your delightful unwritten Constitution puts your form of government into in war times just as much as in peacetime.[1] Seriously, the American written Constitution, with its four-year term, saves the unfortunate person at the top a vast number of headaches.

Next in order is that delightful god, which we worship in common, called "The Freedom of the Press." Neither one of us is much plagued by the news stories which, on the whole, are not so bad. But literally we are both menaced by the so-called interpretative comment by a

[1] Some of the Prime Minister's critics were already planning a second effort to challenge Churchill's leadership by bringing a motion of censure in the House of Commons. The motion was formally tabled on June 25, and it was defeated on July 2 by a vote of 475 to 25. See Churchill, *Hinge of Fate*, chap. 23.

handful or two of gentlemen who cannot get politics out of their heads in the worst crisis, who have little background and less knowledge, and who undertake to lead public opinion on that basis.

My own press—the worst of it—the McCormack-Patterson people, the Hearst papers, and the Scripps-Howard chain—are persistently magnifying relatively unimportant domestic matters and subtly suggesting that the American role is to defend Hawaii, our east and west coasts, do the turtle act, and wait until somebody attacks our home shores. Curiously enough these survivors of isolationism are not attacking me personally except to reiterate that I am dreadfully over-burdened, or that I am my own strategist, operating without benefit of military or naval advice. It is the same old story. You are familiar with it.[2]

Here is a thought from this amateur strategist. There is no use giving a single further thought to Singapore or the Dutch Indies. They are gone. Australia must be held and, as I telegraphed you,[3] we are willing to undertake that. India must be held and you must do that; but, frankly, I do not worry so much about that problem as many others do. The Japanese may land on the seacoast west of Burma. They may bombard Calcutta. But I do not visualize that they can get enough troops to make more than a few dents on the borders—and I think you can hold Ceylon. I hope you can get more submarines out there—more valuable than an inferior surface fleet.

I hope you will definitely reinforce the Near East more greatly than at present. You must hold Egypt, the Canal, Syria, Iran, and the route to the Caucasus.

Finally, I expect to send you in a few days a more definite plan for a joint attack in Europe itself.[4]

2 Churchill's concern over the conduct of the British press was best expressed in his memorandum to the Minister of Information, Brendan Bracken, on March 22. Churchill, *Hinge of Fate*, p. 849.

3 See above, Docs. 104 and 105.

4 An American plan was then nearing completion for a cross-channel invasion to begin on April 1, 1943, including provisions for an "emergency" invasion in September or October 1942, should such an operation prove necessary to save the Russians from imminent defeat. First formulated in the February 28 memorandum of Major General Dwight D. Eisenhower, the plan was based on a concept discussed by the Army and Navy early in 1941—namely, that a large ground force would be needed in Western Europe to overthrow Hitler. After some initial resistance this scheme received the enthusiastic support of the President. See Matloff and Snell, *Strategic Planning*, pp. 177ff.; and G. A. Harrison, *Cross-Channel Attack* (Washington, 1951), chap. 1. In December 1941 Eisenhower had come to Washington to take over the Pacific and Far East section of the War Department's War Plans Division. He was made head of the War Plans Division on February 16, 1942, remaining in charge after it was redesignated Operations Division on March 23.

By the time you get this you will have been advised of my talk with Litvinov,[5] and I expect a reply from Stalin shortly. I know you will not mind my being brutally frank when I tell you that I think I can personally handle Stalin better than either your Foreign Office or my State Department. Stalin hates the guts of all your top people. He thinks he likes me better, and I hope he will continue to do so.

My Navy has been definitely slack in preparing for this submarine war off our coast.[6] As I need not tell you, most naval officers have declined in the past to think in terms of any vessel of less than two thousand tons. You learned the lesson two years ago. We still have to learn it. By May first I expect to get a pretty good coastal patrol working from Newfoundland to Florida and through the West Indies. I have begged, borrowed, and stolen every vessel of every description over eighty feet long—and I have made this a separate command with the responsibility in Admiral Andrews.[7]

I know you will keep up your optimism and your grand driving force, but I know you will not mind if I tell you that you ought to take a leaf out of my notebook. Once a month I go to Hyde Park for four days, crawl into a hole, and pull the hole in after me. I am called on the telephone only if something of really great importance occurs. I wish you would try it, and I wish you would lay a few bricks or paint another picture.

Give my warm regards to Mrs. Churchill. I wish much that my wife and I could see her.

As ever yours,

[5] Roosevelt had told Maxim Litvinov, the Soviet ambassador in Washington, that he strenuously opposed guaranteeing Russia's border as of June 22, 1941. See *FR 1942*, 3 (Washington, 1961) : 494ff.

[6] See Morison, *History of U.S. Naval Operations*, vol. 1, chap. 6, esp. pp. 125ff. "Such protection," wrote Admiral Morison, "as the Navy could furnish to shipping, during this blitz, was pitifully inadequate" (p. 131) .

[7] Vice Admiral Adolphus Andrews, commander of the Eastern Sea Frontier. See Morison, *History of U.S. Naval Operations*, 1: 208.

Doc. 111
ROOSEVELT TO CHURCHILL

No. 126   March 22, 1942

We have been keeping Halifax informed of the progress of our attempts to obtain from Vichy definite commitments to supplement the assurances already given that it will not afford military aid either direct or indirect to the Axis and that its colonial territories in North Africa and the Western Hemisphere will not be available as bases for the Germans. The terms of the French replies have been communicated to you.[1]

Under these circumstances, I am considering whether as part of the United Nations' effort we cannot fulfill a useful role by resuming the program of limited economic assistance to North Africa and by sending further Red Cross aid to children in France to help keep the French people in line.[2] The success of recent bombing operations such as at Renault factories and the realization which that must have brought to the French people that they are still in the war are a way of thwarting the collaborationists.[3] It seems to me that it would be useful to supplement this by another method. At a time when the United Nations are preparing to meet the enemy by force before it can occupy various areas it seems to me important that we should take advantage of the possibility that we can hold the Axis off from other areas by using such psychological and economic weapons as are available.

Should France go over it would mean, of course, that the Iberian peninsula as well is lost to us. We are obtaining for our common cause vital military and strategic information by the presence of our observers in North Africa and from our missions in France itself. In order

1 The Vichy government had repeatedly stated that it would resist any invasion or use of French territory by the Free French, Germans, British, or Americans. See, for instance, Marshal Pétain's message to President Roosevelt of February 16, Ambassador Leahy's note to Roosevelt of February 21, and especially the Vichy government's note of February 25 reaffirming "once again its will to abstain from any action . . . which would not be in conformity with the position of neutrality in which it has been placed since June 1940 and which it intends to maintain." *FR 1942*, 2: 132–134, 140. But see also Leahy's doubts about an "escape clause" in the Vichy government's messages of February 25 and March 14 "that can be used when necessary." *FR 1942*, 2: 149–151.

2 In a memorandum to the State Department on March 3, 1942, the French Embassy had declared: "If, indeed, the United States wishes one day to have again the support and friendship of a nation whose qualities and geo-political situation remain important, it is essential that its children at least do not perish, while its youth is imprisoned and its aged population becomes more feeble every day. The American Government, by alleviating the sufferings of the children, would gain the immediate gratitude of hundreds of thousands of French families." *FR 1942*, 2: 260–261.

3 On the night of March 3 RAF bombers staged a highly destructive raid on the Renault auto works in the northern Paris suburbs, killing 500 and injuring 1,200, mostly civilians. Ambassador Leahy learned from visitors to the plant that "the attack had been accurate and effective and that production by the factory which was contributing to the Nazi war effort would be stopped for an indefinite time." *FR 1942*, 2: 82–88. The raid led to an outbreak of anti-British sentiment in occupied and unoccupied France.

that this remaining bridgehead to Europe may be held as long as it serves our purpose it is necessary that our position there be reinforced from time to time through limited economic aid, thereby not abandoning the field entirely to the Germans.

I am therefore proposing to resume this economic effort at such a moment as may appear expedient and wanted to let you know beforehand of this step, which I am convinced may prove of immense importance to the aims of the United Nations.

Doc. 112
CHURCHILL TO ROOSEVELT

No. 59   March 27, 1942

Your 126.[1] I asked the Foreign Office to send you a note on the details of your project which I hope may be considered. We do not mind your sending very limited quantities of supplies to French North Africa provided the American observers can penetrate the country freely especially if you could get compensating advantages in securing the control of strategic materials now going to Germany.[2] We value your contacts with Vichy and it is well worth paying a certain price but please—

Nothing must interfere with Operation Ironclad to which we are now committed and no assurances offered by the French about defending their empire like they did Indochina should be accepted by the United States in such a way as to enable them to complain of a breach of faith. . . .

It would be a great help if we could give the impression by dropping leaflets at the moment of attack that the expedition was Anglo-American. Please consider whether you can let us do this or anything like it.[3]

---

[1] See above, Doc. 111.

[2] At a conference on the North African supply program held at the State Department on March 19, the British representative "recognized and so stated the importance of maintaining, for political and military reasons, relations with the French Government which would permit American observers and control officers to remain not only in France but, which was more important, in North Africa as well." *FR 1942*, 2: 273.

[3] Roosevelt repeatedly refused this request. On April 3, for instance, he cabled Churchill that it would be "unwise to identify the expedition in the manner indicated by your telegram." The President added that the United States was "the only nation that can intervene with any hope of success with Vichy and it seems to

me extremely important that we are able to do this without the complications that might arise by the dropping of leaflets or other informal methods in connection with your operation." Churchill, *Hinge of Fate,* p. 230.

Doc. 113
CHURCHILL TO ROOSEVELT

No. 61   March 31, 1942

Air attack on Malta is very heavy.[1] There are now in Sicily about four hundred German and two hundred Italian fighters and bombers. Malta can only now muster twenty or thirty serviceable fighters. We keep feeding Malta with Spitfires in packets of sixteen loosed from *Eagle* carrier from about 600 miles west of Malta.

This has worked a good many times quite well but *Eagle* is now laid up for a month by defects in her steering gear. . . .

Would you be willing to allow your carrier *Wasp* to do one of these trips provided details are satisfactorily agreed between the naval staffs? With her broad lifts, capacity, and length, we estimate that *Wasp* could take fifty or more Spitfires. Unless it were necessary for her to fuel, *Wasp* could proceed through the Straits at night without calling at Gibraltar until on the return journey as the Spitfires would be embarked in the Clyde.[2] . . .

1 See Roskill, *War at Sea,* 2: 57ff.; and Morison, *History of U.S. Naval Operations,* vol. 1, chap. 8. Axis planes dropped not quite 1,000 tons of bombs on Malta in February, 2,170 tons in March, and 6,278 tons in April. "The interrelation between Malta and the Desert operation," Churchill wrote later, "was never so plain as in 1942, and the heroic defense of the island in that year formed the keystone of the prolonged struggle for the maintenance of our position in Egypt and the Middle East." Churchill, *Hinge of Fate,* p. 295. By late March Hitler had decided that an operation to capture Malta should precede a new assault on Tobruk, but the planned attack on Malta was repeatedly postponed. See Gwyer and Butler, *Grand Strategy,* 3 (pt. 2) : 445.

2 Roosevelt speedily agreed to the use of the *Wasp,* which made three invaluable trips to Malta during the next two months. (The siege and blockade of Malta lasted until late July.) "But for the courage and resources of individual Maltese, the island would probably have fallen; ay, and would certainly have fallen but for the assistance afforded by the USS *Wasp.*" Morison, *History of U.S. Naval Operations,* 1: 197.

Doc. 114
ROOSEVELT TO CHURCHILL

No. 129   April 1, 1942

As I have completed survey of the immediate and long-range problems of the military situations facing the United Nations, I have come to certain conclusions which are so vital that I want you to know the whole picture and to ask your approval.[1] The whole of it is so dependent on complete cooperation by the United Kingdom and United States that Harry and Marshall[2] will leave for London in a few days to present first of all to you the salient points. It is a plan which I hope Russia will greet with enthusiasm and, on word from you when you have seen Harry and Marshall, I propose to ask Stalin to send two special representatives to see me at once.

I think it will work out in full accord with trend of public opinion here and in Britain. And, finally, I would like to be able to label it the plan of the United Nations.

[1] The reference is to the American plan for a cross-channel invasion. See above, Doc. 110, esp. note 4.

[2] Hopkins and General George C. Marshall, U.S. Army Chief of Staff.

Doc. 115
CHURCHILL TO ROOSEVELT

No. 62   April 1, 1942

Delighted by your letter of March 18 just received.[1] I am so grateful for all your thoughts about my affairs, and personal kindness. Our position here has always been quite solid, but naturally with nothing but disaster to show for one's work people were restive in Parliament and the press. I find it very difficult to get over Singapore but I hope we shall redeem it ere long. . . .

I am looking forward to receiving your plan. We are working very hard here, not only at plans but at preparations. . . .

All now depends upon the vast Russo-German struggle. It looks as if the heavy German offensive may not break until after the middle of May or even the beginning of June. We are doing all we can to help

[1] See above, Doc. 110.

and also to take the weight off. We shall have to fight every convoy through to Murmansk.[2] Stalin is pleased with our deliveries. They are due to go up fifty percent after June and it will be very difficult to do this in view of the new war and also of shipping. Only the weather is holding us back from continuous heavy bombing attack on Germany. Our new methods are most successful. Essen, Cologne, and above all Lübeck were all on the Coventry scale.[3] I am sure it is most important to keep this up all through the summer, blasting Hitler from behind while he is grappling with the Bear. Everything that you can send to weight our attack will be of the utmost value. At Malta also we are containing, with much hard fighting, nearly six hundred German and Italian planes. I am wondering whether these will move to the south Russian front in the near future. There are many rumours of an airborne attack on Malta, possibly this month.

Having heard from Stalin that he was expecting the Germans would use gas on him, I have assured him that we shall treat any such outrage as if directed upon us, and will retaliate without limit. This we are in a good position to do.[4] I propose at his desire to announce this toward the end of the present month and we are using the interval to work up our own precautions. Please let all the above be absolutely between ourselves. . . .

My wife and I both send our kindest regards to you and Mrs. Roosevelt. Perhaps when the weather gets better I may propose myself for a weekend with you and flip over. We have so much to settle that would go easily in talk.

2 Before Japan entered the war, lend-lease supplies had reached Russia through its Pacific port of Vladivostok. The only routes now open, however, were the ones through the Persian Gulf (where land transport posed a problem) and around the northern coast of Norway to Murmansk and Archangel. The latter route was extremely hazardous. See below, Docs. 126 and 127.

3 For an account of the massive British air attacks, see Sir Charles Webster and Noble Frankland, *The Strategic Air Offensive Against Germany 1939–1945*, vol. 1, *Preparation* (London, 1961), pp. 389ff. The attack on Lübeck, on March 28, carried out by 234 aircraft of the Bomber Command, was the first test of the Air Staff's conclusion, the previous autumn, that "saturation incendiary tactics were likely to prove far more destructive than the conventional high-explosive attacks." Subsequent photographic reconnaissance showed that almost half the city had been destroyed, most of it by fire. The German attack on Coventry on the night of November 14–15, 1940, was mounted by 437 aircraft, which dropped 450 tons of bombs and 127 parachute mines, killing 380 people and seriously injuring about 800 others. Denis Richards, *Royal Air Force 1939–1945*, vol. 1, *The Fight at Odds* (London, 1953), p. 211.

4 In mid-March Soviet ambassador Ivan Maisky told Churchill that there was some evidence the Germans might decide to use gas warfare during the forthcoming spring offensive. On March 20 Churchill cabled Stalin that "His Majesty's Government will treat any use of this weapon of poison gas against Russia exactly as if it was directed against ourselves." Churchill, *Hinge of Fate*, p. 329.

Doc. 116
ROOSEVELT TO CHURCHILL

April 3, 1942[1]

Dear Winston,

What Harry and Geo. Marshall will tell you all about has my heart and *mind* in it. Your people and mine demand the establishment of a front to draw off pressure on the Russians, and these peoples are wise enough to see that the Russians are today killing more Germans and destroying more equipment than you and I put together. Even if full success is not attained, the *big* objective will be.

Go to it! Syria and Egypt will be made more secure, even if the Germans find out about our plans.

Best of luck. Make Harry go to bed early, and let him obey Dr. Fulton, USN,[2] whom I am sending with him as supernurse with full authority.

As ever,

[1] No copy of this message has been found in the files of the Roosevelt Library. The above text appears in Churchill, *Hinge of Fate*, p. 314.

[2] Commander James R. Fulton, U.S. Navy. Hopkins had suffered from cancer in 1937, and a large portion of his stomach was removed then. While the cancer did not recur, the operation produced nutritional maladjustments, and Hopkins required almost constant medical care thereafter. In the fall of 1939, his doctors had given him only four more weeks to live. See Sherwood, *Roosevelt and Hopkins*, pp. 112–114, 118–122.

Doc. 117
ROOSEVELT TO CHURCHILL

No. 132   April 11, 1942

I most earnestly hope that you may find it possible to postpone Cripps'[1] departure from India until one more final effort has been made to prevent a breakdown in the negotiations.

I am sorry to say that I cannot agree with the point of view set forth in your message to me[2] that public opinion in the United States believes that the negotiations have failed on broad general issues. The

[1] Sir Stafford Cripps, the Lord Privy Seal, had been in India since March 22 in a vain effort to work out with Hindu leaders an acceptable formula for the future status of India.

[2] Not printed.

general impression here is quite the contrary. The feeling on the contrary is almost universally held that the deadlock has been caused by the unwillingness of the British Government to concede to the Indians the right of self-government, notwithstanding the willingness of the Indians to entrust technical military and naval defense control to the competent British authorities. American public opinion cannot understand why, if the British Government is willing to permit the component parts of India to secede from the British Empire after the war, it is not willing to permit them to enjoy what is tantamount to self-government during the war.[3]

I feel I must place this issue before you very frankly and I know you will understand my reasons for so doing. If the present negotiations are allowed to collapse because of the issues as presented to the American people and India should subsequently be successfully invaded by Japan with attendant serious military or naval defeats for our side, the prejudicial reaction on American public opinion can hardly be over-estimated.

Consequently, would it not be possible for you to have Cripps postpone his departure on the ground that you personally have sent him instructions to make a final effort to find a common ground of understanding? . . .

If you made such an effort and Cripps were then still unable to find an agreement, you would at least on that issue have public opinion in the United States satisfied that a real offer and a fair offer had been made by the British Government to the people of India and that the responsibility for such failure must clearly be placed upon the Indian people and not upon the British Government.

3 For American public response to the Cripps mission, see Hess, *America Encounters India*, pp. 44ff., which concludes that "the Cripps offer met with almost unanimously favorable response in America. In general it was hailed as proof of the sincerity of Britain's promises and as an offer of reasonable compromise which the National Congress should accept. . . . With the State Department, the Cripps offer [also] met with unequivocal praise."

Doc. 118
ROOSEVELT TO CHURCHILL

No. 68   April 12, 1942

I have read with earnest attention your masterly document about future of the war and the great operations proposed.[1] I am in entire

1 For the full text of Roosevelt's proposal, usually referred to as the Marshall Memorandum (though it was largely the work of Eisenhower and his staff), see Gwyer and Butler, *Grand Strategy*, 3 (pt. 2) : app. 3.

agreement in principle with all you propose, and so are the Chiefs of Staff. We must of course meet day-to-day emergencies in the East and Far East while preparing for the main stroke. All the details are being rapidly examined and preparations where action is clear have already begun. The whole matter will be discussed on evening of Tuesday, the 14th, by Defence Committee, to which Harry and Marshall are coming,[2] and I have no doubt that I shall be able to send you our complete agreement.

I may say that I thought the proposals made for an interim operation in certain contingencies this year met the difficulties and uncertainties in an absolutely sound manner. If, as our experts believe, we can carry this whole plan through successfully, it will be one of the grand events in all the history of war.

About 3 A.M. this morning, the 12th, when contrary to your instructions Harry and I were still talking, the text of your message to me about India came through from London.[3] I could not decide such a matter without convening the Cabinet which was not physically possible till Monday. Meanwhile Cripps had already left and all the explanations had been published by both sides. In these circumstances, Harry undertook to telephone to you explaining the position, but owing to atmospherics he could not get through. He is going to telephone you this afternoon and also cable you a report.

You know the weight which I attach to everything you say to me, but I did not feel I could take responsibility for the defence of India if everything has again to be thrown into the melting pot at this critical juncture. That I am sure would be the view of Cabinet and of Parliament. As your telegram was addressed to Former Naval Person[4] I am keeping it as purely private, and I do not propose to bring it before the Cabinet officially unless you tell me you wish this done. Anything like a serious difference between you and me would break my heart and surely deeply injure both our countries at the height of this terrible struggle.[5]

---

[2] Hopkins and Marshall had carried the invasion proposal to London on April 8. For a discussion of their activities there, see Sherwood, *Roosevelt and Hopkins,* chap. 23; Forrest C. Pogue, *George C. Marshall: Ordeal and Hope, 1939–1943* (New York, 1966), pp. 308ff.; Bryant, *Turn of the Tide,* chap. 7; Matloff and Snell, *Strategic Planning,* 187ff.; and Gwyer and Butler, *Grand Strategy,* 3 (pt. 2) : 572ff.

[3] See above, Doc. 117.

[4] Churchill had used this transparent "code name" for himself frequently in addressing messages to Roosevelt. Roosevelt almost certainly did not intend the message to be private.

[5] In his memoirs, Churchill's comment on Roosevelt's latter proposal was considerably less polite: "I was thankful that events had already made such an act of madness impossible. The human race cannot make progress without idealism, but

idealism at other people's expense and without regard to the consequences of ruin and slaughter which fall upon millions of humble homes cannot be considered as its highest or noblest form." Churchill, *Hinge of Fate*, p. 219.

Doc. 119
CHURCHILL TO ROOSEVELT

No. 134   April 16, 1942

Your Secret No. 69.[1] . . . I fully appreciate the present lack of Naval butter to cover the bread but I hope you will agree with me that because of operational differences between the two services there is a grave question as to whether a main fleet concentration should be made in Ceylon area with mixed forces.

Partly because of this and partly because of my feeling that for the next few weeks it is more important to prevent Japanese landing anywhere in India or Ceylon that we are inclined to give greater consideration to temporary replacement of your Home Fleet units[2] rather than mixing units in Indian Ocean.

It is my personal thought that your fleet in Indian Ocean can well be safeguarded during next few weeks without fighting major engagement, in the meantime building up land based plane units to stop Japanese transports. I hope you will let me know your thought in regard to the Air Force measures indicated above.[3] We could put them into effect at once.

1 Not printed. Reacting to serious losses inflicted on the British fleet off Ceylon by Japanese planes on April 6–9, Churchill suggested augmenting that fleet with American ships in order to ward off an expected Japanese amphibious attack on Ceylon or South India. See Kirby, *War Against Japan*, vol. 2, chap. 8.

2 Roosevelt feared that in the event of an allied naval buildup, the Japanese would either renew their direct attacks on the fleet—with disastrous results—or else land somewhere beyond its range of operations, perhaps near Calcutta. One American battleship was eventually sent to the Home Fleet, and three British battleships as well as three aircraft carriers sailed for India. The invasion never materialized.

3 Roosevelt had passed on a suggestion originating with the U.S. Air Force that the USS *Ranger* be used to ferry land aircraft to India for use against Japanese transports. Only in June, however, did the *Ranger* begin this operation with sixty-eight P–40 fighters. They were carried to the west coast of Africa from where they were flown across to India. Nine lost their way over the desert and crashed. See Craven and Cate, eds., *The Army Air Forces in World War II*, 2: 340.

Doc. 120
ROOSEVELT TO CHURCHILL

(Personal)   April 16, 1942

Dear Winston:

I do not want to add to our troubles but we know each other so well that I think you ought to see the enclosed copy of a letter from one of our best newspapermen in regard to the Burma situation.[1]

I have never liked Burma or the Burmese! And you people must have had a terrible time with them for the last fifty years. Thank the Lord you have HE-SAW, WE-SAW, YOU-SAW under lock and key.[2] I wish you could put the whole bunch of them into a frying pan with a wall around it and let them stew in their own juice.

As ever yours,

[1] A confidential letter from Chicago *Daily News* correspondent Leland Stowe which strongly suggested that Burmese leaders were negotiating with the Japanese had been forwarded to Roosevelt by Secretary of the Navy Frank Knox, the publisher of the *Daily News*.

[2] U Saw was Premier of Burma in 1941. Late that year he traveled to London to persuade the British government to grant Burma full self-government effective at the end of the war, but the request was refused. On his way back to Burma he stopped over at Lisbon, where he contacted Japanese representatives. Passing through Palestine shortly after, on January 19, 1942, he was arrested by the British and detained in Uganda for the duration of the war.

Doc. 121
CHURCHILL TO ROOSEVELT

No. 70   April 17, 1942

Your envoys will take back with them a full note of our memorable meeting last Tuesday[1] and a detailed commentary on your proposals by our Chiefs of Staff. I think, however, that you would wish to have at once a short account of the conclusions which were reached.

We wholeheartedly agree with your conception of concentration against the main enemy, and we cordially accept your plan with one

[1] For the British military's memorandum on the meeting with Hopkins and Marshall, see Churchill, *Hinge of Fate*, pp. 317-320.

broad qualification. As you will see from my 69 of the 15th of April,[2] it is essential that we should prevent a junction of the Japanese and the Germans. Consequently, a proportion of our combined resources must, for the moment, be set aside to halt the Japanese advance.[3] This point was fully discussed at the meeting, and Marshall felt confident that we could together provide what was necessary for the Indian Ocean and other theatres, and yet go right ahead with your main project.

The campaign of 1943 is straightforward, and we are starting joint plans and preparations at once. We may, however, feel compelled to act this year. Your plan visualised this, but put mid-September as the earliest date. Things may easily come to a head before then. Marshall explained that you had been reluctant to press for an enterprise that was fraught with such grave risks and dire consequences until you could make a substantial air contribution; but he left us in no doubt that if it were found necessary to act earlier, you, Mr. President, would earnestly wish to throw in every available scrap of human and material resources. We are proceeding with plans and preparations on that basis. Broadly speaking, our agreed programme is a crescendo of activity on the Continent, starting with an ever increasing air offensive both by night and day, and more frequent and larger-scale raids, in which United States troops will take part.

I agree with the suggestion in your telegram No. 129 of second April[4] that you should ask Stalin to send two special representatives to see you at once about your plans. It will in any case be impossible to conceal the vast preparations that will be necessary, but with the whole coast of Europe, from the North Cape to Bayonne, open to us, we should contrive to deceive the enemy as to the weight, timing, method, and the direction of our attacks. It is indeed for consideration whether it would not be right to make a public announcement that our two nations are resolved to march forward into Europe together in

[2] Not printed.

[3] This point had been recognized by General Eisenhower in a memorandum of February 28, which stated: "Oversimplification of the Japanese problem, because our primary objective lies elsewhere, is likely to discount the enormous advantages that will accrue to our enemies through conquest of India, the domination of the Indian Ocean, the severing of all lines of British communication to the Near and Middle East, and the physical junction of our two principal enemies." Matloff and Snell, *Strategic Planning,* pp. 157–158. The British military situation in the Far East was then extremely critical. On April 5, for instance, Japanese aircraft had bombed Colombo, on April 6 the coast of India, and on April 9 Trincomale, in the Indian Ocean, sinking a light aircraft carrier and two heavy cruisers. "We are not," said the Combined Chiefs of Staff, "far off the last ditch so far as Japan is concerned." Gwyer and Butler, *Grand Strategy,* 3 (pt. 2) : 575.

[4] See above, Doc. 114. (Roosevelt's 129 was sent April 1.)

a noble brotherhood of arms on a great crusade for the liberation of the tormented peoples.[5] I will cable you further on this last point.

[5] The radiant optimism of Churchill's message was, as developments were soon to prove, not fully justified. Marshall informed General Joseph T. McNarney, Deputy Chief of Staff of the U.S. Army, on April 12 that "virtually everyone agrees with us in principle" but "many if not most" had "reservations regarding this or that." Pogue, *Marshall: Ordeal and Hope*, p. 318. According to General Sir Alan Brooke's biographer, the Chief of the Imperial General Staff and his colleagues had not "committed themselves to a cross-channel operation in 1942 or even in 1943, but merely to the desirability of launching one if, and only if, conditions at the time made its success seem probable. Bryant, *Turn of the Tide*, p. 287. Churchill's failure, and that of his associates, to make his reservations explicitly clear was to create considerable difficulty later. As his Chief of Staff Sir Hastings Ismay recalled: "Our American friends went happily homewards under the mistaken impression that we had committed ourselves to [a cross-channel operation]. . . . For, when we had to tell them after the most thorough study . . . that we were absolutely opposed to it, they felt that we had broken faith with them." *Memoirs of General Lord Ismay* (New York, 1960), p. 250.

Doc. 122
CHURCHILL TO ROOSEVELT

No. 74   April 20, 1942

Will you kindly consider whether you should not now make an offer to Pétain and/or Darlan of British and American support if they will carry the French fleet to Africa?[1] Should you favour such a policy I will cable you exactly what we could put in on invitation to Morocco unopposed, and at what dates. It seems to me they ought to be offered blessings as well as cursings.

[1] Churchill's suggestion was prompted by the appointment of Pierre Laval, the leading pro-German collaborator at Vichy, as head of the French government on April 18.

Doc. 123
ROOSEVELT TO CHURCHILL

No. 138   April 21, 1942

Replying to your number 74,[1] believe wiser to let situation jell a little before making the approach you suggest. This business must be watched with the greatest care. I will cable you again about it in the near future.

[1] See above, Doc. 122.

Doc. 124
ROOSEVELT TO CHURCHILL

No. 139   April 22, 1942

Replying to your number 70,[1] I am delighted with the agreement which was reached between you and your military advisers and Marshall and Hopkins. They have reported to me of the unanimity of opinion relative to the proposal which they carried with them and I appreciate ever so much your personal message confirming this.

I believe that this move will be very disheartening to Hitler and may well be the wedge by which his downfall will be accomplished. I am very heartened at the prospect and you can be sure that our Army will approach the matter with great enthusiasm and vigor.

I would like to think over a bit the question of a public announcement. I will let you know my feeling about this soon. . . .

I have a cordial message from Stalin telling me that he is sending Molotov[2] and a general to visit me.[3] I am suggesting that they come here first before going to England. Will you let me know if you have any other view about this? I am quite pleased about the Stalin message.

While our mutual difficulties are many I am frank to say that I feel better about the war than at any time in the past two years.

I want to thank you for your cordial reception of Marshall and Hopkins.

[1] See above, Doc. 121.
[2] Vyacheslav M. Molotov, Soviet Foreign Minister.
[3] For Stalin's message of April 20, see Ministry of Foreign Affairs of the U.S.S.R., *Correspondence Between the Chairman of the Council of Ministers of the U.S.S.R. and the Presidents of the U.S.A. and the Prime Ministers of Great Britain During the Great Patriotic War of 1941–1945* (New York, 1958), vol. 2, no. 18. Henceforth cited as *Stalin's Correspondence*.

Doc. 125
CHURCHILL TO ROOSEVELT

No. 78   April 24, 1942

With regard to what you say in your telegram number 139[1] about Molotov's journeyings, I have had message from Stalin[2] saying he is

[1] See above, Doc. 124.
[2] *Stalin's Correspondence*, vol. 1, no. 40.

sending M here to discuss certain divergences in draft texts of our agreement,[3] which he wants settled as soon as possible. He may even be already on his way. You will understand that I cannot now suggest to him a change in the order of his visits. If and when, therefore, Molotov bears down upon us, I propose to agree to a discussion of our drafts and would hope to clear main difficulties out of the way. But I will suggest to him that he should then go on to Washington and see you before anything is finally signed.

[3] The proposed twenty-year Anglo-Soviet treaty of alliance.

Doc. 126
ROOSEVELT TO CHURCHILL

No. 141   April 26, 1942

I have seen your cable to Harry this morning relative to the shipments to Russia.[1] I am greatly disturbed by this because I fear not only the political repercussions in Russia but even more the fact that our supplies will not reach them promptly. We have made such a tremendous effort to get our supplies going that to have them blocked except for most compelling reasons seems to me a serious mistake. . . .

I do hope particularly that you can review again the size of the immediate convoys so that the stuff now backed up in Iceland can get through[2] and I hope that in any conversations that Eden may have with the Russian Ambassador[3] they be confined to telling him the difficulties and urging their cooperation in bringing the convoys in rather than any firm statement about the limit to the number of ships that can be convoyed.

I can and will make some immediate adjustments at this end but I very much prefer that we do not seek at this time any new understanding with Russia about the amount of our supplies in view of the impending assault on their armies. It seems to me that any word reaching Stalin at this time that our supplies were stopping for any reason would have a most unfortunate effect.

[1] In response to an urgent telegram from Hopkins requesting additional and larger convoys, Churchill had sent an evasive reply on April 26. Churchill, *Hinge of Fate*, p. 258.

[2] For the problems of the Arctic convoys in the early spring of 1942, see Churchill, *Hinge of Fate*, chap. 25; and Roskill, *War at Sea*, 2: 119ff.

[3] Ivan Maisky, Soviet ambassador to Great Britain.

Doc. 127
CHURCHILL TO ROOSEVELT

No. 80   April 28, 1942

Your No. 141.[1] . . . Voyage of each of these convoys now entails major fleet operation. With the best will in the world cycle of convoys cannot be more than 3 in 2 months. One convoy (PQ 15),[2] limited to 25 merchant ships, has just sailed. In view of what you tell me we are ready to consider, in the light of the experience gained in this convoy, whether the number of merchant ships in future convoys can be increased to as many as 35. Convoy should reach north Russia ports in about 10 days' time. Meanwhile we are arranging for 35 merchant ships to be loaded for the next convoy (PQ 16), due to leave Iceland (C) on the 17th May. But 35 is the absolute maximum number which it is safe to risk without further experience of the scale of enemy attack.[3] . . .

[1] See above, Doc. 126.

[2] Convoy routes were given double-letter designations, with F or S sometimes being added as a third letter to indicate fast or slow convoys. The P Q route was from home, i.e. Great Britain, to northern Russia. "Q P" was used for the return route. Numbering was consecutive for convoys using the particular route.

[3] Churchill persisted in dispatching the convoys to the Soviet Union in the face of grave doubts expressed by his naval chiefs. Admiral Sir John Tovey, commander in chief of the Home Fleet, for instance, believed that "unless the [German] airfields in north Norway could be neutralised, or some cover obtained from darkness, the convoys should be stopped." On May 18 the First Sea Lord, Sir Dudley Pound, wrote to Admiral Ernest J. King, who had succeeded Admiral Stark as U.S. Chief of Naval Operations on March 26, 1942, that "the whole thing is a most unsound operation with the dice loaded against us in every direction." Admiral King sympathetically agreed. Roskill, *War at Sea*, 2: 130.

Doc. 128
CHURCHILL TO ROOSEVELT

No. 81   April 28, 1942

We have given further thought to Ironclad, and we feel that, in order to reduce to a minimum the risk of warlike reaction by Vichy, it is essential that you should come in fully behind us immediately the operation has taken place.

What we would ask is that in addition: (1) to authorising leaflets as proposed in my telegram No. 59,[1] you should (2) if possible send a token United States detachment to join the occupying forces as soon as possible; (3) in any event inform the Vichy government immediately the operation has taken place that the operation has your approval and support; and (4) immediately make public that such a communication has been made [to] Vichy. . . .

1 See above, Doc. 112.

Doc. 129
ROOSEVELT TO CHURCHILL

No. 142   April 28, 1942

Your number 81.[1] . . . I fully approve your third and fourth suggestions and will get this to the French Ambassador[2] on the morning of zero day and will add that if for the defeat of the Axis powers it is desirable that American troops or ships use Ironclad in the common cause of the civilized peoples, we shall not hesitate to do so at any time.[3]

1 See above, Doc. 128.

2 Gaston Henry-Haye, Vichy French ambassador to the United States.

3 In a radio address the same evening Roosevelt approved measures "to prevent the use of French territory in any part of the world by the Axis powers." *PPR*, 11: 228. While Roosevelt refused publicly to involve the United States directly with the Madagascar attack, on May 4 the State Department instructed the U.S. chargé d'affaires at Vichy, S. Pinckney Tuck, to inform the French government that the United States "gave its full approval and support" to the British position, and that "if it becomes necessary or desirable for American troops or ships to use Madagascar in the common cause, the United States will not hesitate to do so at an early time." *FR 1942*, 2: 698.

Doc. 130
CHURCHILL TO ROOSEVELT

No. 82   April 29, 1942

. . . I have had a telegram from Curtin[1] saying that General MacArthur has asked him to request me "to divert to Australia the 2nd British Infantry Division which will be rounding the Cape during the

1 John Curtin, Prime Minister of Australia.

latter part of April and the beginning of May, and also the Armoured Division which is to round the Cape 1 month later." The diversion, he says, "would be of a temporary nature, and these forces would remain in Australia only until such time as the 9th Australian Imperial Force Division and the remainder of the 6th Division are returned." I should not be able to send these forces to Australia unless it is definitely invaded by 8 or 10 Japanese divisions. They are all urgently needed in India. I fear this is a prelude to the recall of the Australian 9th Division.

General MacArthur also asks for a British aircraft carrier, pointing out that it is wasteful to operate an unbalanced naval force. He further requests an additional allocation of shipping on the Australian-American run, stating that the present amount of 250,000 tons is quite inadequate to complete requisite defence strength apart from offensive action.

I should be glad to know whether these requirements have been approved by you or the Washington Pacific Defence Council, and whether General MacArthur has any authority from the United States for taking such a line. We are quite unable to meet these new demands which are nonetheless a cause of concern when put forward on General MacArthur's authority.[2]

[2] For the background of this request see Matloff and Snell, *Strategic Planning*, pp. 212ff.; Dudley McCarthy, *South-West Pacific Area—First Year: Kokoda to Wau* (Canberra, 1959) , pp. 23–24, 118–119; and Louis Morton, *The War in the Pacific— Strategy and Command: The First Two Years* (Washington, 1962) , pp. 220–221.

Doc. 131
ROOSEVELT TO CHURCHILL

No. 144   April 30, 1942

. . . It seems probable to me that the request made upon you by Mr. Curtin[1] for two divisions and for additional marine assistance was made upon his own responsibility although probably based upon conversations with General MacArthur. The directive under which General MacArthur holds his command provides that the United States Chiefs of Staff will constitute the executive agency through which orders are to be passed to him, and we had assumed that any request of his for reinforcement would be directed here. . . .

We will instruct General MacArthur, immediately, that his future

[1] See above, Doc. 130.

requests for reinforcements, except for routine supply which should follow accustomed channels, will be processed to the United States Chiefs of Staff.[2] Where your forces are concerned, we will then communicate with the British Chiefs of Staff. With this arrangement definitely prescribed and understood, you will know that any request reaching you from Mr. Curtin is made upon his own responsibility. If you think it advisable I will express the hope to Mr. Curtin that he will not ask the return of any of his troops from the Near East.

[2] Roosevelt cabled MacArthur: "I see no reason why you should not continue discussion of military matters with Australian Prime Minister, but I hope you will try to have him treat them as confidential matters and not use them for public messages or for appeal to Churchill and me." Matloff and Snell, *Strategic Planning*, p. 214.

Doc. 132
ROOSEVELT TO CHURCHILL

No. 147   May 19, 1942

I have been giving a great deal of thought to the allocation of combat aircraft manufactured here. It is my clear conviction that except for a reasonable number in the British Isles all reserve planes should be removed from a reserve status which is in fact an inactive status in order to strengthen maximum and continuous air impact on the enemy.

I am sure you will understand our great desire to make the most effective contribution to our combined war effort in every appropriate theater to the limit of our growing capacity. I am confident that our respective air forces can adapt themselves in essential cooperation with our respective ground and sea forces whenever and wherever the common cause can be advanced. Today it is evident that under current arrangements the U.S. is going to have increasingly trained air personnel in excess of combat planes in sight for them to use. We are therefore anxious that every appropriate American-made aircraft be manned and fought by our own crews. Existing schedules of aircraft allocations do not permit us to do this.

Not only are present conditions different from those existing at the time of the lend-lease arrangements of last year but they are different from those arrived at in the so-called Arnold-Portal agreement[1] of the

[1] The agreement between General Arnold and Air Chief Marshal Portal on January 13, 1942, continued the lend-lease policy of diverting a large part of American bomber production to build up the Royal Air Force. For details of this

days immediately following our entry into the war. One example of this difference of situation is the current position of Australia and New Zealand now and as of five months ago.

My thought is that the Combined Chiefs of Staff, with your approval and mine, would determine the strength of aircraft to be maintained in the respective theaters of war. I think the maximum number of planes possible should be maintained in combat and the minimum number consistent with security be held in reserve and in operational training units, and that American pilots and crews be assigned to man American-made planes far more greatly than at present on the combat fronts. . . .

---

agreement and the revisions proposed by Roosevelt, see Craven and Cate, *Army Air Forces,* vol. 1, chaps. 7, 16; and Sir John Slessor, *The Central Blue* (New York, 1957) , p. 405.

Doc. 133
CHURCHILL TO ROOSEVELT

No. 88   May 20, 1942

Your No. 147.[1] We understand and respect the generous impulse which inspires the United States Air Force to engage American lives in the conflict at the earliest moment. God knows we have no right to claim undue priority in the ranks of honour. Let us each do our utmost. So may it be to the end.

The sole objective must be the maximum air impact on the enemy, month by month. We have both of us to find together the highest fulfilment of this irrespective of whether British or United States pilots man the aircraft.

For this purpose a common expansion plan is necessary, and a ruthless scrutiny of reserves, discrepancies, or anything clogging the pipelines. Please send Arnold and Towers[2] at the earliest possible moment. We shall lay everything before them. Portal will return with them and if necessary I will come myself.

I ought to tell you however that as we understand it, General Arnold's proposals for revision of the allocations of American aircraft to the Royal Air Force mean the loss of nearly 5,000 aeroplanes to us this year. The effect would be to reduce by over 100 squadrons (nearly 2,000 first-line aeroplanes) the force which we had planned to have in

[1] See above, Doc. 132.
[2] Rear Admiral John H. Towers, director of the Bureau of Aeronautics.

action by the spring of 1943. Dependent on your expected deliveries we have already taken into service and are now training pilots, crews, and mechanics for this plan, and ancillary equipment of all kinds will be available for it. Indeed, we have in active theatres of war awaiting aeroplanes at this moment about 30 squadrons, some of them veteran units which have lost their equipment in action.

I hope, Mr. President, you will not take any final decision without considering how these hundred squadrons are to be replaced by American units on the various battlefronts by the dates expected. Without your assurance on these points the whole structure of our plans would collapse, and an entirely new view of the war would have to be taken.[3]

---

[3] Sir John Slessor, who had negotiated the first Anglo-American allocation agreement in 1941, remembered later: "The Arnold-Portal Agreement worked smoothly to begin with. . . . Then in April it began to appear that Washington was weakening on it, and the horrid rumor arose that it was the President's policy that American aircraft should be manned only by American crews." Slessor, *Central Blue*, p. 405.

Doc. 134
CHURCHILL TO ROOSEVELT

No. 89   May 27, 1942

We have done very good work this and last week with Molotov, and as Winant will no doubt have informed you we have completely transformed the treaty proposals.[1] They are now in my judgement free from the objections we both entertained[2] and are entirely compatible with our Atlantic Charter. The treaty was signed yesterday afternoon with great cordiality on both sides.[3]

Molotov is a statesman and has a freedom of action very different from what you and I saw with Litvinov. I am very sure you will be

---

[1] Soviet Foreign Minister Molotov had arrived in London on May 20. The Anglo-Soviet treaty signed on May 26 made no mention of boundaries and was simply a twenty-year mutual assistance pact. See above, Docs. 103, 110, and 125.

[2] For British objections to earlier Russian proposals, see Eden, *Memoirs*, 2: 378ff.; and Churchill, *Hinge of Fate*, pp. 326ff. For American objections, see *FR 1942*, 3: 504ff., 539–542, 558. On the other hand, both Ambassador Halifax and Sir Stafford Cripps favored acceptance of the Russian proposal on frontiers. *FR 1942*, 3: 513, 531.

[3] The treaty was announced in Parliament on June 11 and ratifications were exchanged in Moscow on July 4.

able to reach good understandings with him.[4] Please let me know your impressions. . . .

I must express my gratitude for your allocation of 70 tankers to build up United Kingdom stocks of oil. Without this help our stocks would have fallen to a dangerous level by the end of this year. This action is the more generous considering recent heavy American tanker losses and the sacrifices involved in releasing so many ships.

[4] Molotov did not arrive in Washington until May 29.

Doc. 135
ROOSEVELT TO CHURCHILL

No. 149   May 27, 1942

We are expecting the visitor tonight[1] but will not discuss Bolero[2] until Thursday. Can you let me have quickly a short summary of what you and he said to each other about Bolero? It would help me to know.[3]

[1] Molotov.
[2] Code name for the cross-channel invasion buildup.
[3] Churchill complied with Roosevelt's request by sending lengthy notes on his conversations with Molotov.

Doc. 136
ROOSEVELT TO CHURCHILL

No. 152   May 31, 1942

. . . Molotov's visit is, I think, a real success because we have got on a personal footing of candor and as good friendship as can be acquired through an interpreter.[1] His departure will be delayed two or three days more.

He has made very clear his real anxiety as to the next four or five months, and I think this is sincere and not put forward to force our hand. I have a very strong feeling that the Russian position is precarious and may grow steadily worse during the coming weeks.

[1] For Roosevelt's meetings with Molotov in Washington from May 29 to June 1, which covered a wide variety of military and political problems, see FR 1942, 3: 566ff.

Therefore, I am more than ever anxious that Bolero proceed to definite action beginning in 1942.[2] We all realize that because of weather conditions the operation cannot be delayed until the end of the year.

After talking with our staff, I believe German air forces cannot be defeated or indeed brought to battle to an extent which will bring them off the Russian front until we have made a landing. I have great confidence in the ability of our joint air forces to gain complete control of the channel and enough of the land for appropriate bridgeheads to be covered. This will result in either: (a) pulling German air force away from the Russian front, with effort to destroy it on our part, or (b) if German air force fails to come out, the ground troops operation can be increased with objective of establishing permanent positions.

United staffs are now working on proposal to increase shipping for use in Bolero by cutting out a large portion of materials for Russia, other than munitions which can be used in battle this year.[3] This ought not to diminish supplies of munitions like planes, tanks, guns, ammunition, which Russians could use in combat this summer. I think we can cut further on Murmansk-Archangel convoys and send more ready-to-use munitions via Basra.[4] This should make your Home Fleet task easier, particularly destroyers.

I will telegraph you when Molotov leaves, and I am especially anxious that he carry back some real results of his mission and that he will give a favorable account to Stalin. I am inclined to think that at present all the Russians are a bit down in the mouth.

But the important thing is that we may be and probably are faced with real trouble on the Russian front and must make our plans to meet it.

[2] Roosevelt's own draft of this message mentioned August as the proposed invasion date. The final version was redrafted by Hopkins. Sherwood, *Roosevelt and Hopkins*, pp. 569–570.

[3] At his last conversation with Molotov, on June 1, Roosevelt proposed that the "Soviet Government consider reducing its lease-lend requirements from 4,100,000 to 2,000,000 tons. This reduction would release a large number of ships . . . and thus speed up the establishment of [a second] front." Hopkins emphasized that "everything that the Red Army could use in actual fighting would still go forward." *FR 1942*, 3: 582.

[4] Roosevelt's view that Russia could now be effectively supplied through the Persian Gulf was unfounded. Neither the port facilities at Basra, Iraq, nor the road and rail lines from there to Russia were capable of handling greatly expanded traffic until well into 1943. See Richard M. Leighton and Robert W. Coakley, *Global Logistics and Strategy 1940–1943* (Washington, 1955), chaps. 20–21. See also T. H. Vail Motter, *The Persian Corridor and Aid to Russia* (Washington, 1952), pp. 149ff.

Doc. 137
ROOSEVELT TO CHURCHILL

No. 155   June 6, 1942

I delivered to Molotov our joint protocol of supplies from July 1, 1942, to June 30, 1943. I amended the general statement somewhat but in no important degree. A copy of the protocol and of the preliminary statement has been given to the appropriate British representatives here.

I was greatly pleased with the visit. He warmed up far more than I expected and I am sure that he has a far better understanding of the situation here than when he arrived.

I confess that I view with great concern the Russian front and am going to wire you in a day or two a specific proposal which I have in mind.[1]

The business in the Pacific is going well and I am sure we are inflicting some very severe losses on the Jap fleet.[2] The outcome, however, is still indecisive but we should know more before the day is over. I am sure our aircraft are giving very good account of themselves.[3] I will keep you informed.

[1] The specific proposal was to ferry bombers to Russia via Alaska and Siberia, to which the Russians agreed on June 8. See *FR 1942*, 3: 590–591.

[2] The U.S. Navy scored its first major victory in the Pacific in the battle of Midway on June 4–7, which proved to be the turning point of the Pacific war. See Morison, *History of U.S. Naval Operations*, vol. 4 (Boston, 1949), chaps. 6–8. Admiral Yamamoto's ambitious plan, which Japanese generals had long resisted, called for an initial blow at the western Aleutians followed by the main attack on Midway, which had as its ultimate goal the destruction of what remained of the U.S. Pacific Fleet. A week before Yamamoto's fleet began to move into position, however, American cryptoanalysts—in possession of the top-secret Japanese code—discovered the ultimate Japanese objectives. As a result, as the Japanese neared Midway disaster befell them from waiting U.S. aircraft, some carrier-based, some shore-based. All four aircraft carriers in Yamamoto's fleet were sunk, while the United States lost only the already damaged carrier *Yorktown*. As Admiral King summed it up after the war: "The Battle of Midway was the first decisive defeat suffered by the Japanese Navy in 350 years. Furthermore, it put an end to the long period of Japanese offensive action and restored the balance of naval power in the Pacific." Ernest J. King and Walter Muir Whitehill, *Fleet Admiral King* (New York, 1952), p. 380.

[3] Like the battle of the Coral Sea early in May, which marked the first serious setback the Japanese had suffered since Pearl Harbor, the battle of Midway was largely a confrontation between American aircraft and Japanese ships and aircraft.

Doc. 138
CHURCHILL TO ROOSEVELT

No. 101   June 13, 1942

. . . I had a long talk with Mountbatten[1] last night, and in view of the impossibility of dealing by correspondence with all the many difficult points outstanding, I feel it is my duty to come to see you. I shall hold myself ready to start as weather serves from Thursday 18th onwards and will advise you later. . . .

Please let plan be secret till we arrive.

This is the moment for me to send you my heartiest congratulations on the grand American victories in the Pacific which have very decidedly altered the balance of the naval war. All good wishes to you and friends.

[1] Admiral Mountbatten, the Chief of Combined Operations, had just returned from Washington, where he had gone to present to Roosevelt and Hopkins the British case against an invasion of Europe in 1942. Mountbatten reported that the President's interest in a North African invasion was reviving. While in Washington, Mountbatten also discussed Churchill's ubiquitous plan for an invasion of Norway, an idea which the latter had outlined to his Chief of Staff, General Ismay, on May 1, and which General Brooke believed "offered no strategic prospects of any kind." Bryant, *Turn of the Tide*, p. 302. For Mountbatten's summary of his meeting with Roosevelt and Hopkins, see Sherwood, *Roosevelt and Hopkins*, pp. 582–583.

Doc. 139
ROOSEVELT TO CHURCHILL

No. 158   June 13, 1942

I find I must be in Hyde Park 19th, 20th, and 21st.

If you land any time before noon of Sunday the 21st come to Hyde Park and we can leave for Washington that night getting to White House Monday morning.

The set of books has just come and I am thrilled.[1]

[1] Churchill had sent Roosevelt a set of his "complete works."

THE SECOND WASHINGTON CONFERENCE
JUNE 1942

[Churchill, accompanied by a few of his top military chiefs, including Generals Brooke and Ismay, flew from Scotland to Washington on the evening of June 17. On the morning of June 19 the Prime Minister flew on to Hyde Park, where he conferred that day and the next with the President. Then, on June 21, Roosevelt and Churchill traveled together to Washington. The second Washington conference was largely concerned with urgent military problems, including the possible development of an atomic weapon. (Shortly after Churchill's visit, Roosevelt ordered work begun on the atomic bomb.)

Although Churchill had told Roosevelt that he regarded "the continued heavy sinkings at sea [as] our greatest and most immediate danger," the principal subjects of discussion at this conference were future Allied grand strategy and the sudden and dramatic deterioration of the situation in North Africa, where Rommel, on June 21, had captured Tobruk (which had managed to hold out against the German offensive in April 1941), together with 33,000 men and a large store of weapons and supplies. Roosevelt at once offered to reinforce the sadly depleted British and imperial forces with 300 of the latest-model Sherman tanks and 100 self-propelled howitzers, a generous offer which Churchill accepted with alacrity and gratitude.

As regards future strategy, the conference was rather less productive. While Secretary of War Stimson had cautioned the President against what he called Churchill's "wildest kind of diversionary debauch," the Prime Minister now put it to Roosevelt that "we hold strongly to the view that there should be no substantial landing in France this year unless we are going to stay." And if, Churchill continued, "no plan can be made in which any responsible authority has good confidence," it was time to take another look at Gymnast, the proposed invasion of French North Africa. Both Marshall and Stimson, however, considered Gymnast a poor substitute for Bolero, the proposed plan for an invasion of Western Europe, and so did the Combined Chiefs of Staff. In any event, no ultimate conclusion on Anglo-American strategy was reached, although the conference's final decision, as incorporated in a secret memorandum of General Ismay, was a disguised victory for the British position: "If . . . detailed examination shows that despite all efforts, success [of the proposed invasion of France] is improbable, we must be ready with an alternative." General Marshall recorded that "the result of the conference . . . was that we managed to preserve the basic plan for Bolero," but the end result of the face-saving compromise, as Marshall foresaw, was that the adoption of Gymnast would kill any invasion of the European continent, even in 1943.

On June 23–24 Churchill, Brooke, and Ismay, together with Marshall and Stimson, made an inspection trip to Fort Jackson, South Carolina, where they witnessed the training of the rapidly growing U.S. Army, which greatly impressed the Prime Minister. On the following day he and his party flew home from Baltimore.]

Doc. 140
CHURCHILL TO ROOSEVELT

No. 107   July 8, 1942

No responsible British general, admiral, or air marshal is prepared to recommend Sledgehammer[1] as a practicable operation in 1942. The Chiefs of the Staff have reported: "The conditions which would make Sledgehammer a sound, sensible enterprise are very unlikely to occur." They are now sending their paper to your Chiefs of Staff. . . .

In the event of a lodgement being effected and maintained it would have to be nourished and the bomber effort on Germany would have to be greatly curtailed. All our energies would be involved in defending the bridgehead. The possibility of mounting a large-scale operation in 1943 would be marred if not ruined. All our resources would be absorbed piecemeal on the very narrow front which alone is open. It may therefore be said that premature action in 1942 while probably ending in disaster would decisively injure the prospect of well-organised large-scale action in 1943.

I am sure myself that Gymnast is by far the best chance for effective relief to the Russian front in 1942. This has all along been in harmony with your ideas. In fact it is your commanding idea. Here is the true second front of 1942. I have consulted Cabinet and Defence Committee and we all agree. Here is the safest and most fruitful stroke that can be delivered this autumn.[2] . . .

---

[1] Code name for the invasion of the Continent in 1942, designed to relieve pressure on the Russians.

[2] Churchill wished to continue Bolero and even suggested that General Marshall be appointed commander but quickly added: "I hope, Mr. President, you will make sure that appointment of a United States commander over Bolero 1943 does not prejudice operations of immediate consequence such as Gymnast." (Churchill to Roosevelt, July 8, 1942. Not printed.)

Doc. 141
CHURCHILL TO ROOSEVELT

No. 113   July 14, 1942

Only four ships have reached Archangel with four or five more precariously in the ice off Novaya Zemlya out of the 33 included in convoy PQ 17. If a half had got through we should have persevered, but with only about a quarter arriving the operation is not good enough. For instance out of nearly 600 tanks in PQ 17 little over 100 have arrived and nearly 500 are lost.[1] This cannot help anybody except the enemy. The Admiralty cannot see what better protection can be devised, nor can they hazard battleships east of Bear Island.[2] Stark[3] agrees with Admiralty view and that all possible was done by us last time. *Washington* has already been withdrawn for her task in the Pacific.

We therefore advise against running PQ 18 which must start 18th at latest. If it were composed only of our merchant ships we should certainly not send them, but no fewer than 22 are your own American ships. We should therefore like to know how you feel about it.

Future prospects of supplying Russia by this northern route are bad.[4] Murmansk has been largely burnt out and there are several signs of an impending German attack upon it. By the time that perpetual daylight gives place to the dark period, Archangel will be frozen. Some additional supplies may be passed over the Basra route. This is being pressed, but it will not amount to much. Thus Russia is confronted at this anxious moment with a virtual cutting off of the northern sea communications. We wait your answer before explaining things to Stalin. The message which it is proposed to send to him, if you agree that the convoy is not to go, is being sent to you later today.[5] Meanwhile the convoy is continuing to load and assemble.

Allied shipping losses in the seven days ending July 13th including the Russian convoy were reported at not far short of 400,000 tons for

1 For the disastrous history of convoy PQ 17, see Roskill, *War at Sea*, 2: 136ff.

2 Bear Island lies near the twentieth meridian, 350 miles north of Norway.

3 Admiral Harold R. Stark, former U.S. Chief of Naval Operations, had been sent by Roosevelt to London in March as his representative on naval matters.

4 "These Russian convoys," Admiral Pound, the First Sea Lord, wrote to Admiral King on May 18, 1942, "are becoming a regular millstone around our necks, and cause a steady attrition in both cruisers and destroyers." Roskill, *War at Sea*, 2: 115.

5 See below, Doc. 143, note 2.

this week, a rate unexampled in either this war or the last, and if maintained evidently beyond all existing replacement plans.

Doc. 142
CHURCHILL TO ROOSEVELT

No. 114   July 14, 1942

I am most anxious for you to know where I stand myself at the present time. I have found no one who regards Sledgehammer as possible. I should like to see you do Gymnast as soon as possible, and that we in concert with the Russians should try for Jupiter.[1] Meanwhile all preparations for Roundup[2] in 1943 should proceed at full blast, thus holding the maximum enemy forces opposite England. All this seems to me as clear as noonday.

[1] Code name for a proposed Allied landing in Norway.
[2] Code name used at that time for the full invasion of France.

Doc. 143
ROOSEVELT TO CHURCHILL

No. 166   July 15, 1942

After consultation with King[1] I must reluctantly agree to the position which the Admiralty has taken regarding the Russian convoy to the north and I think your message to Stalin is a good one.[2] I assume you will send it at once.

[1] Admiral Ernest J. King had succeeded Admiral Stark as Chief of Naval Operations on March 26, 1942.
[2] Churchill's message to Stalin declared that "to attempt to run the next convoy, PQ 18, would bring no benefit to you and would only involve a dead loss to the common cause." Churchill further informed Stalin that "my naval advisers tell me that if they had the handling of the German surface, submarine, and air forces in present circumstances, they would guarantee to complete destruction of any convoy to north Russia." At the same time he promised Stalin substantially increased assistance by way of the Persian Gulf. To that message the Russian leader replied that "according to our naval experts, the arguments of British naval experts . . . are untenable," adding that "the Soviet Government cannot tolerate the second front in Europe being postponed till 1943." *Stalin's Correspondence*, vol. 1, nos. 56, 57.

In the meantime we must omit nothing that will increase the traffic through Persia.[3]

A suggestion has been made that American railway men take over the operation of the railroad. Have you any opinion about this? They are first class at this sort of thing.

[3] See Motter, *Persian Corridor*, chap. 10.

Doc. 144
ROOSEVELT TO CHURCHILL

No. 167   July 15, 1942

Marshall, King, and Hopkins leaving for London at once.[1] They will discuss all implications of your several cables to me. I will send you personal cable in a day or two.

[1] In his instructions to Marshall, King, and Hopkins, dated July 16, Roosevelt declared: "The military and strategic changes have been so great since Mr. Churchill's visit to Washington that it becomes necessary to reach immediate agreement on joint operational plans between the British and ourselves along two lines: (a) Definitive plans for the balance of 1942. (b) Tentative plans for the year 1943. . . . If Sledgehammer is finally and definitely out of the picture, I want you to consider the world situation as it exists at that time, and determine upon another place for U.S. troops to fight in 1942. . . . I hope for total agreement within one week of your arrival." Matloff and Snell, *Strategic Planning*, pp. 276–278. Churchill described the President's message as "the most massive and masterly document on war policy that I ever saw from his hand." Churchill, *Hinge of Fate*, p. 441.

Doc. 145
CHURCHILL TO ROOSEVELT

No. 123   July 27, 1942

I was sure you would be as pleased as I am, indeed as we are all here, at the results of this strenuous week. Besides reaching agreement on action, relations of cordial intimacy and comradeship have been cemented between our high officers.[1] I doubt if success would have been achieved without Harry's invaluable aid.

[1] For accounts of the Marshall-King-Hopkins mission, see Sherwood, *Roosevelt and Hopkins*, pp. 606ff.; Churchill, *Hinge of Fate*, pp. 441ff.; Bryant, *Turn of the Tide*, pp. 341ff.; Gwyer and Butler, *Grand Strategy*, 3 (pt. 2): 632ff.; and Pogue, *Marshall: Ordeal and Hope*, pp. 342ff.

We must establish a second front this year and attack at the earliest moment. As I see it this second front consists of a main body holding the enemy pinned opposite Sledgehammer and a wide flanking movement called Torch (hitherto called Gymnast). Now that everything is decided we can, as you say, go full steam ahead.[2] All depends on secrecy and speed and on having a regular schedule of political and military action. Every hour counts and I agree with you that October 30th is the latest date which should be accepted.

Secrecy can only be maintained by deception. For this purpose I am running Jupiter and we must also work up Sledgehammer with the utmost vigour. These will cover all movements in the United Kingdom. When your troops start for Torch everyone except the secret circles should believe they are going to Suez or Basra, thus explaining tropical kit. The Canadian army here will be fitted for Arctic service. Thus we shall be able to keep the enemy in doubt till the last moment. . . .

We were disappointed at not breaking Rommel's front last week though heavy losses were inflicted upon him in bitter fighting. We have far heavier reinforcements approaching and far better communications than he has and marked superiority in the air. The Eighth British Armoured and Forty-fourth British Infantry Divisions are now landed; and the Fifty-first British Infantry arrives in three weeks besides at least forty or fifty thousand replacements flowing in steadily. The Shermans should arrive early in September and we hope to bring them into action during that month. Thus I feel confident we can defend Egypt and I trust Auchinleck may destroy this man where he now stands.[3] I am delighted to have the United States Armoured Division and hope it may follow the Fifty-sixth which lands early in October.

If Auchinleck beats Rommel we shall have about seven divisions which can either be directed to follow up a victory in the western desert into Acrobat[4] or, should the Russian southern front give way, to the Levant-Caspian theatre.

I still feel that in spite of all other demands upon us we ought to try to place twenty, thirty, or even forty air squadrons on the Russian

[2] The results of the London discussions represented, not unexpectedly, a defeat for the American position, with the substitution of Torch for Sledgehammer, which Roosevelt agreed to against the advice of both Marshall and King.

[3] Despite his striking victory at Tobruk, Rommel had reached the high tide of his power. Thereafter he was twice defeated at El Alamein (first by Auchinleck in July and then by General Sir Bernard Montgomery in October 1942). The second and decisive defeat came shortly after the Allied landings in French North Africa.

[4] Code name for the advance on Tripoli.

southern flank, thus helping them to hold the barrier formed by the Caspian, the Caucasus Mountains, and a Turkey confirmed in neutrality. It also seems necessary to have something solid to offer Stalin. Whatever happens however nothing must interfere with Torch or weaken Auchinleck before he has won.[5]

[5] See above, Docs. 148 and 156.

Doc. 146
ROOSEVELT TO CHURCHILL

No. 170   July 27, 1942

The three musketeers arrived safely this afternoon and the wedding is still scheduled.[1]

I am, of course, very happy in the result and especially in the successful meetings of minds.

I cannot help feeling that the past week represented a turning point in the whole war and that now we are on our way shoulder to shoulder.

I agree with you that secrecy and speed are vital and I hope the October date can be advanced.

I will talk with Marshall in regard to scale of supplies and equipment in terms of tonnage and in terms of the U.K. importations of food and raw materials.

Also I will do my best to get the air squadron on the Russian southern flank. I fully agree that this should be done.

[1] Marshall, King, and Hopkins had just returned from London. Hopkins was married to Louise Macy on July 30, in the Oval Room of the White House. Roosevelt acted as best man.

Doc. 147
CHURCHILL TO ROOSEVELT

No. 124   July 29, 1942

I do not propose to embark on an argument, but Stalin will no doubt expect some account of our recent conversations here on the second front. Subject to what you may feel, I propose to refer Stalin to the *aide-mémoire* explaining our attitude handed to Molotov here just before he left for Moscow, which I showed you,[1] and to say that it still represents our general position, but that we have agreed with you on certain action, although at present stage nothing can be said about time and place.

We might also say that we hope to resume convoys in September, if Russians can provide necessary air force to deny German surface ships use of Barents Sea, and that if the battle in Egypt goes well we should be able to make a firm offer of air support on the Russian southern flank.

What are your views?

In the meanwhile we are explaining to Maisky[2] in detail nature of problems of Russian convoys and latest position about bombing attacks on Germany and plans for commando raids.

[1] In that *aide-mémoire* Churchill declared: "We are making preparations for a landing on the Continent in August or September 1942. . . . It is impossible to say in advance whether the situation will be such as to make this operation feasible when the time comes. We can therefore give no promise in the matter, but provided that it appears sound and sensible we shall not hesitate to put our plans into effect." Churchill, *Hinge of Fate*, p. 342.

[2] Ivan Maisky's tendentious *Memoirs of a Soviet Ambassador—The War 1939–1945* (New York, 1968) , pp. 295–296, makes no reference to this part of the conversation.

Doc. 148
ROOSEVELT TO CHURCHILL

No. 171   July 29, 1942

I agree with you that your reply to Stalin must be handled with great care. We have got always to bear in mind the personality of our ally and the very difficult and dangerous situation that confronts him. No one can be expected to approach the war from a world point of view whose country has been invaded. I think we should try to put ourselves in his place.

I think he should be told, in the first place, quite specifically that we have determined upon a course of action in 1942. I think that without advising him of the precise nature of our proposed operations the fact that they are going to be made should be told him without any qualification.

While I think that you should not raise any false hopes in Stalin relative to the northern convoy, nevertheless I agree with you that we should run one if there is any possibility of success, in spite of the great risk involved.[1]

I am still hopeful that we can put air power directly on the Russian front and I am discussing that matter here. I believe it would be unwise to promise this air power only on conditions that the battle in Egypt goes well. Russia's need is urgent and immediate.[2] I have a feeling it would mean a great deal to the Russian army and the Russian people if they knew some of our air force was fighting with them in a very direct manner.[3]

While we may believe that the present and proposed use of our combined air forces is strategically the best, nevertheless I feel that Stalin does not agree with this. Stalin, I imagine, is in no mood to engage in a theoretical strategical discussion and I am sure that other than our major operation the enterprise that would suit him the best is direct air support on the southern end of his front.

[1] In his message to Stalin of July 30 Churchill declared: "We are making preliminary arrangements for another effort to run a large convoy through to Archangel the first week of September." The Prime Minister offered ("if you invite me") to meet with Stalin "in Astrakhan, the Caucasus, or some similar convenient meeting place," adding that "I could then tell you plans we have made with President Roosevelt for offensive action in 1942." Churchill, *Hinge of Fate*, pp. 453–454.

[2] Following their initial summer campaign in the Crimea, climaxed by the capture of Sevastopol on July 1, the Germans had begun their main offensive in the east, aimed at the control of southern Russia (the Caucasus oil fields and the Black Sea). Despite some indecisiveness and differences of opinion between Hitler and his generals, German forces had rapidly scored a number of significant victories. On July 7, for instance, the Germans entered Voronezh (which they never, however, fully controlled). On July 15 they captured Boguchar and Millerova, and by July 27 they had occupied Rostov and crossed the Don River at that point.

[3] In his memoirs General Arnold recalled that about mid-April 1942 President Roosevelt talked to him about stationing American planes and crews in the Soviet Union for shuttlebombing raids against Germany. "I assured the President," Arnold recalled, "that I should like nothing better than shuttlebombing between England and Italy to Russia, hitting targets in eastern Germany en route. I told him I would start the ball rolling at once. However, as in all cases where cooperation with the Russians was desired, much time was lost in endless discussions and delays before we could actually start operations." Henry H. Arnold, *Global Mission* (New York, 1949), pp. 306–307.

Doc. 149
ROOSEVELT TO CHURCHILL

No. 172   July 29, 1942

I have today received a long and urgent message from Chiang Kai-shek. He asks me to regard this message as strictly confidential, but in view of its nature I naturally wish to inform you immediately of its contents.[1] . . .

I shall have to give a reply to Chiang Kai-shek in the near future and I shall be grateful if you will let me have as soon as possible your thoughts and any suggestions you may wish to offer with regard to the nature of the reply I should make to him.[2]

[1] Chiang told Roosevelt that "the Indian situation has reached an extremely critical stage. . . . If India should start a movement against Britain or against the United States, this will cause a deterioration in the Indian situation from which the Axis powers will surely reap benefit." He went on to urge Roosevelt, in strong language, to pressure Britain into granting immediate independence to India. This message was not Chiang's first foray into Indian affairs. In February 1942, for instance, Chiang and his wife had visited India to rally Indian opposition against Japan, pleading fervently that "real political power" be promptly transferred to India. See Dorothy Norman, ed., *Nehru—The First Sixty Years*, 2 (New York, 1965) : 75.

[2] For the background of Roosevelt's message, see James MacGregor Burns, *Roosevelt: Soldier of Freedom* (New York, 1970), pp. 238ff.

Doc. 150
CHURCHILL TO ROOSEVELT

No. 125   July 31, 1942

Your No. 172.[1] We do not agree with Chiang Kai-shek's estimate of the Indian situation. The Congress party in no way represents India and is strongly opposed by over ninety million Mohammedans, forty million untouchables, and the Indian states comprising some ninety millions, to whom we are bound by treaty. Congress represents mainly the intelligentsia of nonfighting Hindu elements, and can neither defend India nor raise revolt. The military classes on whom everything depends are thoroughly loyal; in fact over a million have volunteered for the army and the numbers recently volunteering greatly exceed all previous records. Their loyalty would be gravely impaired by handing over the Government of India to Congress control. The reckless declarations of Congress have moreover given rise to widespread misgiving, even among its own rank and file.

The Government of India have no doubt of their ability to maintain order and carry on government with efficiency and secure India's maximum contribution to the war effort whatever Congress may say or

[1] See above, Doc. 149.

even do, provided of course that their authority is not undermined. His Majesty's Government here have no intention of making any offer beyond the sweeping proposals which Sir Stafford Cripps carried to India and in fact could not do so without creating grave internal trouble in India. So far as I am concerned, I could not accept responsibility for making further proposals at this stage. We have however only today in Parliament made clear that while the specific proposals suggested by Cripps failed to secure agreement we stand firmly by broad intention of our offer which is that India should have the fullest opportunity at the earliest possible moment after the war to attain to complete self-government under constitutional arrangements of her own devising.[2] I earnestly hope therefore, Mr. President, that you will do your best to dissuade Chiang Kai-shek from his completely misinformed activities, and will lend no countenance to putting pressure upon His Majesty's Government.

[2] On July 30, 1942, L. S. Amery, Secretary of State for India and Burma, told the House of Commons that "His Majesty's Government stand firmly by the broad intention of their offer," adding that "the present demand of Congress completely ignores this far-reaching offer and would, if conceded, bring about a complete and abrupt dislocation of the vast and complicated machinery of government. . . . [M]en of good-will everywhere must refuse to envisage such a catastrophic development in one of the most vital theatres of war." *Parliamentary Debates*, Commons, 5th ser., vol. 381, col. 674.

Doc. 151
CHURCHILL TO ROOSEVELT

No. 126A

August 4, 1942

I should greatly like to have your aid and countenance in my talks with Joe.[1] Would you be able to let Averell come with me? I feel that things would be easier if we all seemed to be together. I have a somewhat raw job. Kindly duplicate your reply to London.

Am keeping my immediate movements vague.

[1] This is the first such reference to Stalin in the correspondence, but by no means the last. Churchill had gone to Cairo on August 3 and reorganized the entire Middle East command while there. He left for the Soviet Union on August 11.

Doc. 152
ROOSEVELT TO CHURCHILL

No. 173   August 5, 1942

I am asking Harriman to leave at earliest possible moment for Moscow.[1] I think your idea is sound and I am telling Stalin Harriman will be at his and your disposal to help in any way.[2]

[1] At first Roosevelt did not want Harriman to go to Moscow. Harriman had telegraphed the President on August 4 proposing that he join Churchill in Moscow because "your sending me along would indicate to our host our agreement on military and political matters and show your extreme personal interest at this critical moment. Also my personal report to you might be of particular value." Roosevelt replied that he hesitated to have Harriman proceed because "I do not want anyone anywhere to have the slightest suspicion that you are acting as an observer." However, after receiving Churchill's cable of August 4 (see above, Doc. 151), Roosevelt changed his mind and the following day authorized Harriman to proceed to Moscow as soon as possible. *FR 1942, 3:* 616, note 10.

[2] On August 5 Roosevelt cabled Stalin: "I have asked Harriman to go to Moscow to be at your call and that of your visitor [Churchill] to render any help which he may possibly give." *Stalin's Correspondence,* vol. 2, no. 33.

Doc. 153
ROOSEVELT TO CHURCHILL

No. 174   August 6, 1942

The proposal of the British Chiefs of Staff dated August 6th that General Eisenhower[1] be designated as Commander in Chief for the Torch operation is acceptable to me and to the United States Chiefs of Staff. The formal directive for General Eisenhower's guidance submitted by the British Chiefs of Staff is being studied and will be reported upon shortly. Meanwhile General Eisenhower should have your authority to proceed with the development of his staff and planning.

[1] Churchill had first met Eisenhower, at that time head of the War Plans Division of the War Department, during his visit to Washington in June 1942. Late in June Eisenhower had moved to London as Commanding General, U.S. Army, European Theater of Operations, and on July 26 General Marshall had personally informed Eisenhower that he had been chosen to lead the Allied invasion of French North Africa.

Doc. 154
CHURCHILL TO ROOSEVELT

No. 127   August 8, 1942

You will no doubt have seen the cables sent by the British Chiefs of Staff London to the Combined Chiefs of Staff Washington about accelerating the date of Torch. I am sure that nothing is more vital than this, and that superhuman efforts should be made. Every day counts. I have already telegraphed to London welcoming the appointment of General Eisenhower as Allied Commander in Chief for Torch and the British Chiefs are cooperating with him to the full.

I also wish to endorse the suggestion of the Admiralty about some United States submarines working from Gibraltar.

I have been busy here with a reorganisation of the High Command which was necessary. I am detaching Iraq and Persia from the Middle East command and transferring General Auchinleck there. Alexander[1] will succeed him as Commander in Chief. General Gott[2] who was to have been appointed to command Eighth Army under Alexander was killed yesterday. I propose to appoint General Montgomery[3] in his place. This will promote the utmost concentration upon the battle. A victory here might have a decisive effect upon the attitude of the French towards Torch.

All these changes are of the utmost secrecy and no announcement will be made until the command has been definitely transferred. Pray therefore let this be for yourself alone.

I am giving my own personal attention in detail on the spot to the reception and utilisation of the Shermans[4] and 105s[5] for which we are eagerly waiting. I am visiting the units tomorrow that are to receive these weapons.

Averell has just arrived, and we shall be off soon on our further quest. I will keep you informed.

1 General Sir Harold Alexander, commander in chief in Burma.
2 General W. H. E. Gott, commander of the 13th Corps in North Africa.
3 General Sir Bernard L. Montgomery, head of the Southeastern Command in England.
4 An American medium tank.
5 The 105-mm howitzer cannon.

Doc. 155
CHURCHILL TO ROOSEVELT

No. 128   August 9, 1942

I hope you will let me see beforehand the text of any message you are thinking of sending me upon the anniversary of the Atlantic Charter on August 14. We considered the wording of that famous document line by line together and I should not be able, without mature consideration, to give it a wider interpretation than was agreed between us at the time. Its proposed application to Asia and Africa requires much thought. Great embarrassment would be caused to the defence of India at the present time by such a statement as the Office of War Information has been forecasting.[1] Here in the Middle East the Arabs might claim by majority they could expel the Jews from Palestine, or at any time forbid all further immigration. I am strongly wedded to the Zionist policy, of which I was one of the authors. This is only one of the many unforeseen cases which will arise from new and further declarations.

Would it not be sufficient to dwell on the progress made in this memorable year, to the growth of the United Nations, to the continued magnificent resistance of Russia to aggression, to the success of the arms of the United States in the Pacific, and to the growth of our combined air power? Finally we could reaffirm our principles and point to the hope of a happier world after some preliminary intervening unpleasantness had been satisfactorily got over. I am sure you will consider my difficulties with the kindness you always show to me.

[1] In its broadcasts, the Office of War Information had stressed the commitment of the Atlantic Charter signatories to the principle of self-determination for all peoples.

Doc. 156
CHURCHILL TO ROOSEVELT

No. 129   August 13, 1942

. . . I began conference with Stalin at Kremlin at seven P.M.[1] This lasted nearly four hours. There were present only Stalin, Molotov,

[1] This message was in fact a copy of Churchill's simultaneous report to the War Cabinet. For a detailed account of Churchill's activities see Woodward, *British Foreign Policy*, vol. 2, chap. 17.

Voroshilov,[2] myself, Harriman, and our Ambassador[3] with interpreter. The first two hours were bleak and sombre. I explained at length, with maps and arguments, why we would not do Sledgehammer. He said that he did not agree with our reasons. He argued the other way and everyone was pretty glum. Finally he said that he did not accept our view but we had the right to decide. In this discussion I had, of course, explained Roundup, which he passed over too lightly because it was remote and there were great difficulties in landing anywhere outside fighter cover. However, the figures of American arrivals in U.K. and our own proposed expeditionary force were told as solid facts.

We then passed on to the ruthless bombing of Germany, which gave general satisfaction. Monsieur Stalin emphasised the importance of striking at the morale of the German population, and I made it clear that this was one of our leading military objectives. He said he attached the greatest importance to bombing and that he knew raids were having a tremendous effect in Germany. After this prolonged discussion, it seemed that all we were going to do was no Sledgehammer, no Roundup, and pay our way by bombing Germany. I thought it was best to get the worst over first. I did not try to relieve it, and I asked specially that there should be the plainest speaking between friends and comrades in peril. However courtesy and dignity prevailed.

This was the moment in the battle when I brought Torch into action. As I told the whole story Stalin became intensely interested. His first question was what would happen in Spain and Vichy France. A little later on he remarked that the operation was militarily right but he had political doubts about the effect on France. He asked particularly the timing, and I said not later than October 30th, but the President and all of us were trying to pull it forward to October 7th. This seemed a great relief to the three Russians. At this point Monsieur Stalin said, according to the interpreter, "May God prosper this undertaking."

This marked the turning point in our conversation. He then began to raise various political objections fearing that the Anglo-American seizure of Torch regions would be misunderstood in France. What were we doing about de Gaulle? I said if he were thought helpful he would be used, but at present we thought the American flag was a far better chance of an easy entry. Harriman backed this very strongly by referring to reports by American agents all over Torch territories on

2 Marshal Kliment Voroshilov, vice president of the Soviet Council of People's Commissars and a member of the State Committee of Defense.

3 Sir Archibald Clark Kerr, British ambassador to the Soviet Union.

which the President relies, and also Admiral Leahy's opinion.[4] Presently Monsieur Stalin epitomised four main reasons for Torch. First. It would hit Rommel in the back. Second. It would overawe Spain. Third. It would produce fighting between Germans and Frenchmen in France and, fourth, it would expose Italy to the whole brunt of the war. This statement pleased me greatly as showing his swift and complete mastery of a problem hitherto novel. I added, of course, the fifth reason, namely shortening of the sea route through the Mediterranean. He was concerned to know whether we were able to pass through the Straits of Gibraltar. I also told him the changes of command in Egypt and our determination to fight a decisive battle there in late August or September. Finally, it was clear that they all liked Torch though Molotov asked whether it could not be in September.

I then proceeded to open the prospect of our placing an Anglo-American air force on the southern flank of the Russian armies to defend the Caspian and the Caucasian [sic] Mountains and generally to fight in this theatre. I did not, however, go into details, as of course we had to win our battle in Egypt first and I had not the President's plans for the American contribution. If Stalin liked the idea we would set to work in detail upon it. He replied that they would be most grateful for this aid, but that the details of location, etc., would require study. As you know, I am very keen on this project because it will bring about more hard fighting between the Anglo-American air power and the Huns, all of which aids the gaining of mastery in the air under more fertile conditions than looking for trouble over the Pas de Calais.

Thus all ended cordially, and I expect I shall establish a solid and sincere relationship with this man and convince him of our ardent desire, shared by the President, to get into battle heavily and speedily to the best advantage. About the Russians, he said only that the Germans had produced more tanks and power than had been expected, that the news from the south was not good, and that the Russians had started divisions as at Rzhev, which was making progress.

I must tell you what a help Harriman was in this extremely serious, tense, and at one time critical discussion. He came in heavily in the name of the President in everything about Torch, and his presence throughout was invaluable.[5] . . .

[4] Admiral William D. Leahy, U.S. ambassador to Vichy France.
[5] Harriman later reported to Roosevelt on the meeting: "Under all the circumstances I believe the discussion could not have been developed better nor the conclusion more satisfactory. . . . The Prime Minister was at his best and could not have handled the discussion with greater brilliance." FR 1942, 3: 618–620.

Doc. 157
ROOSEVELT TO CHURCHILL

No. 179   August 14, 1942

I am made very happy by Mr. Stalin's cordiality and understanding of our difficult problems. I wish I could be with you both, for that would make the party complete. Give him my warm regards and keep me in touch.

Doc. 158
CHURCHILL TO ROOSEVELT

No. 131   August 15, 1942

. . . [W]e all repaired to the Kremlin at eleven P.M. and were received only by Stalin and Molotov with the interpreter. Then began a most unpleasant discussion. Stalin handed me the enclosed document to which see also my reply.[1] When it was translated I said I would answer it in writing and that he must understand we have made up our minds upon the course to be pursued and that reproaches were vain. Thereafter we argued for about two hours, during which he said many disagreeable things, especially about our being too much afraid of fighting the Germans, and if we tried it like the Russians we should find it not so bad, that we had broken our promise about Sledgehammer, that we had failed in delivering the supplies promised to Russia and only sent remnants after we had taken all we needed for ourselves. Apparently these complaints were addressed as much to the United States as to Britain.[2]

[1] In his *aide-mémoire* to Churchill and Harriman, dated August 13, Stalin asserted: "As is well known, the organization of a second front in Europe was predecided during the sojourn of Molotov in London, and it found expression in the agreed Anglo-Soviet communiqué on the 12th June last." The Soviet leader went on to reject all the arguments against Sledgehammer that Churchill had presented and, in closing, noted that "Mr. Harriman . . . fully supported Mr. Prime Minister." *FR 1942*, 3: 621–622. In his reply of August 14 Churchill declared categorically: "No promise has been broken by Great Britain or the United States." Churchill, *Hinge of Fate*, pp. 491–492. And in a letter to Stalin, likewise dated August 14, Harriman asserted: "I must reaffirm [Churchill's] statement that no promise has been broken regarding the second front." *FR 1942*, 3: 622.

[2] In his telegram to Roosevelt, sent from Moscow at 8:15 P.M. on August 14 and received in Washington at 12:35 A.M. on August 15, Harriman noted that "the technique used by Stalin last night resembled closely that used with Beaverbrook

I repulsed all his contentions squarely but without taunts of any kind. I suppose he is not used to being contradicted repeatedly but he did not become at all angry or even animated. On one occasion I said, "I pardon that remark only on account of the bravery of the Russian troops." Finally he said we could carry it no further. He must accept our decision and abruptly invited us to dinner at eight o'clock tonight.

Accepted the invitation [but] said I would leave by plane at dawn the next morning, i.e., fifteenth. Joe seemed somewhat concerned at this and asked could I not stay longer. I said certainly, if there was any good to be done, and that I would wait one more day anyhow. I then exclaimed there was no ring of comradeship in his attitude. I had travelled far to establish good working relations. We had done our utmost to help Russia and would continue to do so. We had been left entirely alone for a year against Germany and Italy. Now that the three great nations were allied, victory was certain provided we did not fall apart, and so forth. I was somewhat animated in this passage and before it could be translated he made the remark that he liked the temperament or spirit of my utterance. Thereafter the talk began again in a somewhat less tense atmosphere.

He plunged into a long discussion of two Russian trench mortar-firing rockets which he declared were devastating in their effects and which he offered to demonstrate to our experts if they could wait. He said he would let us have all information about them, but should there not be something in return. Should there not be an agreement to exchange information of inventions. I said that we would give them everything without any bargaining except only those devices which, if carried in aeroplanes over the enemy lines and shot down, would make our bombing of Germany more difficult. He accepted this. He also agreed that his military authorities should meet our generals and this was arranged for three o'clock this afternoon.[3] . . . All this part of the

and myself in our second meeting last year. I cannot believe there is cause for concern and I confidentially expect a clearcut understanding before the Prime Minister leaves." *FR 1942*, 3: 622. General Brooke, who also attended the meeting, was considerably less hopeful. "Winston," he recorded in his diary, "appealed to sentiments in Stalin which do not, I think, exist. Altogether, I felt we were not gaining much ground. Personally, I feel our policy with the Russians has been wrong from the very start. . . . We have bowed and scraped to them, done all we could for them, and never asked them for a single fact or figure concerning their production, strength, dispositions, etc. As a result, they despise us and have no use for us except for what they can get out of us." Bryant, *Turn of the Tide*, p. 373.

[3] This meeting with three Russian generals, including Marshals Voroshilov and B. M. Shaposhnikov, the Russian Chief of Staff, proved quite unproductive. "As they," Brooke put it in his diary, "have not got the vaguest conception of the conditions prevailing in France or England, nor any real idea of the implications of amphibious operations, it was a hopeless task from the start." Bryant, *Turn of the Tide*, p. 378.

talk was easier, but when Harriman asked about the plans for bringing American aircraft across Siberia, to which the Russians have only
recently consented after long American pressing, he replied, curtly,
"Wars are not won with plans." Harriman backed me up throughout
and we neither of us yielded an inch nor spoke a bitter word. . . .

It is my considered opinion that in his heart so far as he has one
Stalin knows we are right and that six divisions on Sledgehammer
would do him no good this year. Moreover I am certain that his sure-
footed and quick military judgement makes him a strong supporter of
Torch. I think it not impossible that he will make amends. In that
hope I persevere. Anyhow I am sure it was better to have it out this
way than any other. There was never at any time the slightest suggestion of their not fighting on and I think myself that Stalin has good
confidence that he will win. . . .

Doc. 159
CHURCHILL TO ROOSEVELT

No. 132   August 16, 1942

. . . Any consoling or heartening message you feel like sending to
Stalin secretly would be helpful.[1] You will have seen my full accounts.
I do not know what I should have done without Averell.

[1] In a cable of August 19 Roosevelt informed Stalin that over 1,000 tanks were
leaving the United States for Russia that month, in addition to other strategic
materials, including aircraft. The President concluded: "The fact that the Soviet
Union is bearing the brunt of the fighting and losses during the year 1942 is well
understood by the United States and I may state that we greatly admire the
magnificent resistance which your country has exhibited. We are coming as quickly
and as strongly to your assistance as we possibly can and I hope you will believe me
when I tell you this." *FR 1942*, 3: 626.

Doc. 160
CHURCHILL TO ROOSEVELT

No. 133   August 17, 1942

Reference my telegram number 131.[1] . . . When I said good-bye to
Stalin he said that any differences that existed were only of method. I

[1] See above, Doc. 158.

said we would try to remove even those differences by deeds. After a cordial handshake I then took my departure and got some way down the crowded room but he hurried after me and accompanied me an immense distance through corridors and staircases to the front door where we again shook hands.[2]

Perhaps in my account to you of the Thursday night meeting I took too gloomy a view. I feel I must make full allowance for the really grievous disappointment which they feel here that we can do nothing more to help them in their immense struggle. In the upshot they have swallowed this bitter pill. Everything for us now turns on hastening Torch and defeating Rommel. . . .

[2] On August 18 Harriman, who had left Moscow with Churchill and his party, cabled Roosevelt from Teheran: "The last meeting of the Prime Minister with Stalin when they met alone made deep and favorable impression on Prime Minister." *FR 1942*, 3: 625.

Doc. 161
CHURCHILL TO ROOSEVELT

No. 136   August 26, 1942

I am concentrating my main thought upon Torch from now on, and you may trust me to do my utmost to make your great strategic conception a decisive success. It seems to me from talks I have had with Eisenhower, Clark,[1] and our own people here that the best and indeed the only way to put this job through is to fix a date for the party and make everything conform to that, rather than saying it will start when everything is ready. It would be an immense help if you and I were to give Eisenhower a directive something like this: "You will start Torch on October 14, attacking with such troops as are available and at such places as you deem fit." This will alter the whole character of the preparations. Eisenhower will really have the power he should have as the Allied Commander in Chief. Endless objections, misgivings, and well-meant improvements will fall back into their proper places, and action will emerge from what will otherwise be almost unending hemmings and hawings. I think Eisenhower would like this, and it would anyhow give him a chance which he has not now got.

As I see this operation it is primarily political in its foundations.

[1] General Mark W. Clark, Eisenhower's deputy, commanded U.S. troops stationed in Britain.

The first victory we have to win is to avoid a battle. The second, if we cannot avoid it, to win it. In order to give us the best chances of the first victory we must (a) present the maximum appearance of overwhelming strength at the moment of the first attack, and (b) attack at as many places as possible. This is an absolutely different kind of operation from the Dieppe business[2] or any variants of Sledgehammer. There we were up against German efficiency and the steel-bound, fortified coasts of France. In Torch we have to face at the worst weak, divided opposition and an enormous choice of striking points at which to land. Risks and difficulties will be doubled by delay and will far outstrip increase of our forces. Careful planning in every detail, safety first in every calculation, far-seeing provisions for a long-term campaign to meet every conceivable adverse contingency, however admirable in theory, will ruin the enterprise in fact. Anything later than the date I have mentioned enormously increases the danger of leakage and forestalment.

In order to lighten the burden of responsibility on the military commanders I am of opinion that you and I should lay down the political data and take this risk upon ourselves. In my view it would be reasonable to assume (a) that Spain will not go to war with Britain and the United States on account of Torch; (b) that it will be at least two months before the Germans can force their way through Spain or procure some accommodation from her; (c) that the French resistance in North Africa will be largely token resistance, capable of being overcome by the suddenness and scale of the attack, and that thereafter the North African French may actively help us under their own commanders; (d) that Vichy will not declare war on the United States and Great Britain; (e) that Hitler will put extreme pressure on Vichy, but that in October he will not have the forces available to overrun unoccupied France while at the same time we keep him pinned in the Pas de Calais, etc. All these data may prove erroneous. In which case

2 Nearly 5,000 Canadian troops and commandos and some 50 U.S. rangers, supported by a small naval force that included eight destroyers, had carried out a raid—"a reconnaissance in force"—on Dieppe in Normandy on August 19. See C. P. Stacey, *Official History of the Canadian Army in the Second World War*, vol. 1, *Six Years of War—The Army in Canada, Britain, and the Pacific* (Ottawa, 1957), chaps. 11–12, esp. pp. 397ff.; and Gwyer and Butler, *Grand Strategy*, 3 (pt. 2): 638ff. Although the Canadian forces in particular suffered extremely heavy losses—with nearly 3,400 men killed, wounded, missing, or taken prisoner—the Dieppe raid, an official British historian concluded, "increased the nervousness from which Hitler had long suffered with regard to the northern and western coasts of his empire. . . . [I]t is probable that the Germans' success in repelling the Dieppe raid influenced their strategy, which proved fatal in 1944, of attempting to hold an attempt at invasion on the beaches instead of relying on a mobile reserve." Gwyer and Butler, *Grand Strategy*, 3 (pt. 2): 641, 643.

we shall have to settle down to hard slugging. For this we have always been prepared, but a bold, audacious bid for a bloodless victory at the outset may win a very great prize. Personally I am prepared to take any amount of responsibility for running the political risks and being proved wrong about the political assumptions. . . .

Doc. 162
CHURCHILL TO ROOSEVELT

No. 139   August 27, 1942

We are all profoundly disconcerted by the memorandum sent us by the United States Joint Chiefs of Staff on the twenty-fifth instant about Torch.[1] It seems to me that the whole pith of the operation will be lost if we do not take take Algiers as well as Oran on the first day. In Algiers we have the best chance of a friendly reception and even if we got nothing except Algeria a most important strategic success would have been gained. General Eisenhower with our cordial support was in fact planning landings at Philippeville and Bône for day three. . . .

An operation limited to Oran and Casablanca would not give the impression of strength and of widespread simultaneous attack on which we rely for the favourable effect on the French in North Africa. We are all convinced that Algiers is the key to the whole operation.

[1] For the background of this plan, see Matloff and Snell, *Strategic Planning*, pp. 286ff.; George F. Howe, *Northwest Africa—Seizing the Initiative in the West* (Washington, 1957) , pp. 25ff.; Pogue, *Marshall: Ordeal and Hope*, pp. 402ff.; and Michael Howard, *Grand Strategy*, vol. 4, *August 1942–September 1943* (London, 1972) , pp. 117ff. See also I. S. O. Playfair and C. J. C. Molony, *The Mediterranean and the Middle East*, vol. 4, *The Destruction of the Axis Forces in Africa* (London, 1966) , chap. 5. As Professor Howard, the official historian of British grand strategy for this period of the war, noted: "The position was now somewhat ironical. Only a month earlier it had been the Americans who had been urging that all risks should be taken in order to launch Operation 'Sledgehammer,' and the British who had taken counsel of their fears. Now it was the British who, to secure a major objective, were prepared to run what seemed to their Allies to be inordinate risks. . . . It was clear that this deadlock, like that over 'Sledgehammer,' would have to be resolved on a higher level. . . . [Churchill's message of August 27] opened an exchange in which the two civilian leaders, guided by their military advisers, were amicably and intelligently to work out an agreed programme in a fashion which will long remain a model of how Allies should discuss and resolve their differences." Howard, *Grand Strategy,* 4: 127–128.

General Anderson,[2] to whom this task has been assigned by Eisenhower, is confident of his ability to occupy Algiers. The occupation of Algeria and the movement towards Tunis and Bizerte is an indispensable part of the attack on Italy which is the best chance of enlisting French cooperation and one of the main objects of our future campaign.

We are all agreed about Oran and of course we should like to see Casablanca occupied as well, but if it came to choosing between Algiers and Casablanca it cannot be doubted that the former is incomparably the more hopeful and fruitful objective. . . .

A complete change in the plans such as the memorandum suggests would of course be fatal to the date and thus possibly to the whole plan. In October Hitler will not have the power to move into Spain or into unoccupied France. In November and with every week that passes this power to bring pressure upon Vichy and Madrid governments increases rapidly.

I hope, Mr. President, you will bear in mind the language I have held to Stalin supported by Harriman with your full approval. If Torch collapses or is cut down as is now proposed, I should feel my position painfully affected. For all these reasons I most earnestly beg that the memorandum may be reconsidered and that the American Allied Commander in Chief may be permitted to go forward with the plans he has made, upon which we are all now working night and day.[3] The staffs are communicating similar views to their American colleagues.

2 Major General K. A. N. Anderson, commander of the British First Army for Torch.

3 According to General Brooke's biographer, "for a few days the American War Department's view was so strongly maintained that the Prime Minister had thoughts of another visit to Washington, and a plane was kept in permanent readiness to carry him and [the Chief of the Imperial General Staff] there." Bryant, *Turn of the Tide*, p. 402.

Doc. 163
ROOSEVELT TO CHURCHILL

No. 180   August 30, 1942

I have considered carefully your numbers 136[1] and 139[2] in reference to the Torch operation. It is my earnest desire to start the attack at the

1 See above, Doc. 161.
2 See above, Doc. 162.

earliest possible moment.[3] Time is of the essence and we are speeding up preparations vigorously.

I feel very strongly that the initial attacks must be made by an exclusively American ground force supported by your naval and transport and air units. The operation should be undertaken on the assumption that the French will offer less resistance to us than they will to the British.

I would even go so far as to say I am reasonably sure a simultaneous landing by British and Americans would result in full resistance by all French in Africa whereas an initial American landing without British ground forces offers a real chance that there would be no French resistance or only a token resistance.

I need a week if possible after we land to consolidate the position for both of us by securing the nonresistance of the French. I sincerely hope I can get this.

Then your force can come in to the eastward. I realize full well that your landing must be made before the enemy can get there. It is our belief that German air and parachute troops cannot get to Algiers or Tunis in any large force for at least two weeks after initial attack. Meanwhile your troops would be ashore we hope without much opposition and would be moving eastward.

As to the place of the landings it seems to me that we must have a sure and permanent base on the northwest coast of Africa because a single line of communication through the Straits is far too hazardous in the light of our limited joint resources.

I propose therefore that: (a) American troops land simultaneously near Casablanca and near Oran; (b) that they seek to establish road and rail communication with each other back of the mountains. The distance is little more than 300 miles. This gives to the enterprise a supply base in Morocco which is outside the Straits and can be used to reinforce and supply the operations in Algiers and Tunis.

The real problem seems to be that there is not enough cover and combat loadings for more than two landings. I realize it would be far better to have three with you handling the one to the eastward a week after we get in. To this end I think we should reexamine our resources

---

[3] Sensing increasing public concern and impatience, Roosevelt was extremely anxious to commence an important U.S. military operation before the congressional midterm elections, to be held on November 3, 1942. General Marshall later recalled: "When I went in to see Roosevelt and told him about [planning for] Torch, he held up his hands in an attitude of prayer and said 'Please make it before Election Day.' However, when I found we had to have more time and it came afterward, he never said a word. He was very courageous. Steve Early, Roosevelt's press secretary, who was told only an hour before the attack, blew up about it because it came after the election." Pogue, *Marshall: Ordeal and Hope,* p. 402.

and strip everything to the bone to make the third landing possible. We can give up the Russian convoy temporarily at that time and risk or hold up other merchant shipping. It is essential, of course, that all ships now assigned to Eisenhower for his two landings remain intact. Hence the eastward landing must be made on ships not now available to Torch. I will explore this at our end. Can we not get an answer on this within forty-eight hours or less?

I want to emphasize however that under any circumstances one of our landings must be on the Atlantic.

The directive to the Commander in Chief of the operation[4] should prescribe that the attack should be launched at the earliest practicable date. The date should be consistent with the preparation necessary for an operation with a fair chance of success and accordingly it should be determined by the Commander in Chief, but in no event later than October 30th. I still would hope for October 14th.

[4] General Eisenhower.

Doc. 164
CHURCHILL TO ROOSEVELT

No. 142   September 1, 1942

We have carefully considered your number 180.[1] The Chiefs of Staff have also talked things over with Eisenhower. We could not contest your wish if you so desire it to take upon the United States the whole burden, political and military, of the landings. Like you I assign immense importance to the political aspect. I do not know what information you have of the mood and temper of Vichy and North Africa,[2] but of course if you can get ashore at the necessary points

[1] See above, Doc. 163.

[2] Despite continued heavy German political pressure and covert intervention in Vichy affairs, that government attempted, apparently, to pursue a policy of genuine neutrality. On May 18 the U.S. chargé d'affaires at Vichy, S. Pinckney Tuck, had cabled the State Department that he was "still of the belief—heartily endorse Admiral Leahy's opinion—that a continuance of diplomatic relations is for various reasons desirable provided of course [Vichy] refrains from lending military assistance to our enemies." On August 31, Tuck reported, on the basis of information from a reliable source, that although Pierre Laval, the head of the Vichy government, had been receptive to a German proposal for a Franco-German agreement "for the defense of French North and West Africa," Admiral Paul Auphon, the French Navy Minister, "took the stand that such a pact exposed France to the danger of inviting an Anglo-Saxon attack on Africa" and reportedly threatened to resign if

without fighting or only token resistance, that is the best of all. We cannot tell what are the chances of this.

I hope however that you have considered the following points: (a) Will not British participation be disclosed by the assembly of British small craft and aircraft at Gibraltar for some time beforehand? (b) Would it not be disclosed at the time of landing whatever flag we wear? (c) Would not initial fighting necessarily be between French and British aircraft and French batteries and British ships? (d) If the approach and landing take place in the dark as is indispensable to surprise, how will the Americans be distinguished from British? In the night all cats are grey. (e) What happens if, as I am assured is four to one probable, surf prevents disembarkation on Atlantic beaches?

Moreover if, contrary to your hopes, the landings are stubbornly opposed and even held up, we shall not be able to give you the follow-up help for some considerable time because all our assault vessels would have been used for your troops and our reinforcements would be embarked in vessels which can only enter by captured harbours. Thus if the political bloodless victory, for which I agree with you there is a good chance, should be amiss, a military disaster of very great consequence will supervene. We could have stormed Dakar in September 1940 if we had not been cluttered up with preliminary conciliatory processes. It is that hard experience that makes our military experts rely so much upon the simplicity of force. Will you have enough American-trained and -equipped forces to do this all by yourselves, or at any rate to impress the enemy by the appearance of ample strength?

This sudden abandonment of the plan on which we have hitherto been working will certainly cause grievous delay. General Eisenhower says that October 30th will be the very earliest date. I myself think that it may well mean the middle of November. Orders were given to suspend loadings yesterday in order that, if necessary, all should be recast. I fear the substitution of November for October will open up a whole new set of dangers far greater than those which must anyhow be faced.

Finally, in spite of the difficulties it seems to us vital that Algiers should be occupied simultaneously with Casablanca and Oran. Here is the most friendly and hopeful spot where the political reaction would be most decisive throughout North Africa. To give up Algiers for the sake of the doubtfully practicable landing at Casablanca seems to us a very serious decision. If it led to the Germans forestalling us not only

such an agreement was concluded. This threat, according to Tuck's source, had led Laval "for the moment [to] put aside the idea of such a joint defensive pact." *FR 1942*, 2: 186, 194.

in Tunis but in Algeria, the results on balance would be lamentable throughout the Mediterranean. . . .

Doc. 165
ROOSEVELT TO CHURCHILL

No. 182   September 2, 1942

Your message No. 142[1] has been received and given careful consideration. Your willingness to cooperate by agreeing that all initial landings will be made by U.S. ground forces is appreciated. It is true that British participation in the form of naval and air support will be disclosed to the defenders early in the operation. However, I do not believe that this will have quite the same effect that British forces making the first beach landing would have. . . .

In view of your urgent desire that Algiers should be occupied simultaneously with Casablanca and Oran, we offer the following solution:

Simultaneous landings at Casablanca, Oran, and Algiers with assault and immediate follow-up troops generally as follows:

A. Casablanca (U.S. troops): 34,000 in the assault and 24,000 in the immediate follow-up to land at a port,

B. Oran (U.S. troops): 25,000 in the assault and 20,000 in the immediate follow-up to land at a port,

C. Algiers (U.S. and British troops): In the beach landing 10,000 U.S. troops followed within an hour by British troops to make the landing secure, the follow-up to be determined by the CINC.[2] This follow-up to land at a port in noncombat-loaded ships. . . .

If the operation is to be executed along the lines indicated, namely simultaneous landings at Casablanca, Oran, and Algiers, all the remaining requirements must be furnished from British sources. As we see it, this would mean in general that it will be necessary for you to furnish:

(A) All shipping (including combat loaders) required for the Oran and Algiers forces except the U.S. shipping now in the U.K. earmarked for Torch,

(B) The additional troops required for the Algiers assault and follow-up forces, and

---

1 See above, Doc. 164.
2 The Commander-in-Chief, i.e., General Eisenhower.

(C) The naval forces required for the entire operation less the U.S. naval force indicated above.

In order that I may continue with vigorous preparations for the execution of Torch at the earliest practicable date please confirm by cable that the United Kingdom will provide the troop lift, troops, naval forces, and shipping noted herein as necessary.

I reiterate the belief expressed in my No. 180[3] that the Commander in Chief should be directed to execute the operation at the earliest practicable date and that this date should be fixed by him. I am convinced of the absolute necessity for an early decision. I feel that the operation, as outlined herein, is as far as I can go toward meeting your views, and seems to me to be a practical solution which retains the Algiers operation and is sufficiently strong to be a good risk throughout.

Our latest and best information from North Africa is as follows:

(A) An American expedition led in all three phases by American officers will meet little resistance from the French army in Africa. On the other hand, a British-commanded attack in any phase or with de Gaullist cooperation would meet with determined resistance.

(B) Maintenance of the French civil government is essential to friendly relations, and I have several experienced civilians who would be persona-grata to accompany the landings and be charged with getting French civil cooperation.

(C) I am willing to risk explanation of British troops in Algiers by telling the French that they are not intended to remain in French territory but that their object is primarily to march into Axis-held Tripoli from the rear.

Because of this information I consider it vital that sole responsibility be placed with Americans for relations with French military and civil authorities in Africa.

As you and I decided long ago, we were to handle the French in North Africa, while you were to handle the situation in Spain.[4]

[3] See above, Doc. 163.
[4] See Howard, *Grand Strategy*, vol. 4, chap. 9.

Doc. 166
CHURCHILL TO ROOSEVELT

No. 143   September 3, 1942

Your 182.[1] We have spent the day looking into physical possibilities. Accepting your general outlines we think that a working plan can be

[1] See above, Doc. 165.

made on the basis that the emphasis is shifted somewhat, namely reducing Casablanca by ten or twelve thousand (making up deficiency in the follow-ups) . These troops with their combat-loaded ships would give sufficient strength inside, while making the entire assault American. This evens up the three landings and gives the essential appearance of strength at all vital points. Without such a transference there is no hope of Algiers on account of shortage of combat loaders and landing craft. We all think this would be a great blemish to the plan. . . .

Delay due to change already extends three weeks. Free French have got inkling and are leaky.[2] Every day saved is precious. We have therefore already ordered work to go forward on these lines but of course the decision rests with you.

[2] According to General Mark W. Clark, de Gaulle already "knew something was in the wind" at the time Marshall, King, and Hopkins visited London in mid-July. Mark W. Clark, *Calculated Risk* (New York, 1950) , p. 36. In his war memoirs de Gaulle wrote: "By the end of July I foresaw what would happen. . . . I left [London] on August 5, having first seen Mr. Churchill and Mr. Eden whose somewhat embarrassed remarks confirmed my feeling that they were going to be party to an enterprise incompatible with the agreement which had bound us since June 1940." Charles de Gaulle, *The Complete War Memoirs*, 3 vols. (New York, 1964) , vol. 2, *Unity 1942–1944*, pp. 13–14.

Doc. 167
ROOSEVELT TO CHURCHILL

No. 183   September 4, 1942

Replying to your 143,[1] we are getting very close together. I am willing to reduce the Casablanca force by the number of combat loaders capable of carrying a force of one regimental combat team, approximately 5,000 men. Since a similar reduction was made in original Oran assault force this releases a total of British and U.S. combat loaders for some 10,000 men for use at Algiers. The combat-loaded force of American troops can be used as the nucleus on which to complete that force. I am sure that the additional troops can be found in the U.K. . . .

[1] See above, Doc. 166.

Doc. 168
CHURCHILL TO ROOSEVELT

No. 144   September 5, 1942

Your number 183.[1] We agree to the military layout as you propose
it. We have plenty of troops highly trained for landing. If convenient,
they can wear your uniform. They will be proud to do so. Shipping
will be all right. . . .

1 See above, Doc. 167.

Doc. 169
CHURCHILL TO ROOSEVELT

No. 148   September 14, 1942

. . . I am hoping to receive your wishes about the Anglo-American
air force on the Russian southern flank. I am not without hopes of a
favourable decision in Egypt in the next few weeks.[1] Unless we can
offer Stalin something definite for say December, we shall not get the
full facilities we need for preparing airfields, etc., thereabouts. Moreover if we are able to make a firm offer, albeit contingent on favourable events in Egypt, it would be possible at the same time to ask for
some favours for the Poles. Stalin has given us sixty thousand Poles
with thirty thousand dependents out of which two and a half divisions
are being made, but no provision has been made for recruitment of
further Poles, officers and men, to keep these forces going. Of these

1 Rommel had begun his long-awaited attack on General Montgomery's Eighth
Army at Alam El Halfa on the night of August 31, but his limited fuel supplies
forced him to withdraw on September 1. According to Montgomery, the withdrawal
was subsequently described by one of Rommel's staff officers as "the turning point of
the desert war, and the first of a long series of defeats on every front which
foreshadowed the defeat of Germany." Montgomery recalled: "I think officers and
men knew in their hearts that if we lost Alam Halfa we would probably have lost
Egypt." *The Memoirs of Field Marshal the Viscount Montgomery* (Cleveland,
1958), pp. 101, 106. Henceforth cited as Montgomery, *Memoirs*. On September 14
General Montgomery issued his own battle plan: "to trap the enemy in his present
area and destroy him there." Howard, *Grand Strategy*, 4: 63. Operation Lightfoot,
known as the battle of El Alamein, which was to end with Rommel's disastrous rout,
commenced on the night of October 23.

there are great numbers in various sorry plights throughout Russia.[2] I thought we might help two birds with one piece of sugar. . . .

In the whole of Torch, military and political, I consider myself your lieutenant asking only to put my viewpoint plainly before you. We shall have a wireless station of overriding power available by zero, so that if you dictate your appeals to France and other propaganda material to gramophone records beforehand, these can be blared out over everything during the performance. The British will come in only as and when you judge expedient. This is an American enterprise in which we are your helpmates.

I agree with you that de Gaulle will be an irritant and his movement must be kept out.[3] We do not yet know what the local generals will do or whether perhaps you are going to bring Giraud[4] to the scene. At your leisure please let me know your ideas. . . .

[2] During the spring and summer of 1942 the Russians had released to the British some of the Polish prisoners they had taken in September 1939, sending them out through Iran. The Polish government-in-exile, however, regarded the number of prisoners thus freed as insufficient. In the course of a conversation with Lieutenant General Wladyslaw Anders, Polish army commander in the Soviet Union, in Cairo on August 22, 1942, Churchill said he "thought it possible that the Russians were averse to letting the Polish officers go, for fear of the stories that they might spread of the treatment they had received." Anders declared: "There was no justness or honour in Russia, and there was not a single man in that country whose word could be trusted." Churchill "pointed out how dangerous such language would be if it were spoken in public. No good could come of antagonising the Russians." General Sikorski Historical Institute, *Documents on Polish-Soviet Relations 1939–1945*, vol. 1, *1939–1943* (London, 1961), no. 259.

[3] This position had been adopted by the U.S. military chiefs some months earlier. Although he left the fact unrecorded in his memoirs, de Gaulle had met with Marshall, King, Eisenhower, and Brigadier General Walter Bedell Smith during the London visit in July 1942. According to General Clark, who was also present, de Gaulle wished to see Marshall "to get some information about the Allied war plans," but Marshall, like the British, feared that such highly secret information might well find its way into enemy hands. Accordingly, after Admiral King had ordered champagne in honor of the occasion—de Gaulle declined to drink—Marshall and King made "polite and complimentary but non-committal remarks." De Gaulle then exclaimed: "Dites-moi, qu'est ce que vous penser faire pour le deuxième front?" When Marshall and King made equally "non-committal replies," de Gaulle declared that he would not take up "any more of your time," and "after a cool handshake, he marched out with his aide behind him." Clark, *Calculated Risk*, pp. 36–37.

[4] General Henri Giraud had escaped from a German prison camp in April and was then living on the Riviera. American intelligence representatives had already contacted him and thought was being given to using him in North Africa, in preference to either de Gaulle or Admiral Darlan.

Doc. 170
ROOSEVELT TO CHURCHILL

No. 187   September 16, 1942

It is pleasing to be reassured by your message of September 15th[1] that on your side effort is concentrated on preparations for the earliest practicable date. We are late making the same effort. I agree fully and consider it essential that de Gaulle be kept out of the picture and be permitted to have no *repeat* no information whatever regardless of how irritated and irritating he may become. What would you think of our asking him to come to Washington about November 10? He might advertise this unduly but on the other hand it might tend to soften his attitude after a certain event takes place.

It is my present intention to prepare a radio statement for both the Continental and colonial French to be made as late as possible prior to the landing.

It appears advisable for you to accomplish the propaganda and preventative effort in Spain.

In regard to the Persian railway, the combined planners have not yet completed their study.[2] I am pushing them.

The proposed Anglo-American air force on Russia's southern flank is now under consideration by the War Department. It is expected that the War Department will recommend the following possibility:

As soon as the situation in Egypt permits, Great Britain to divert a balanced combat air force from Egypt to the Caucasus, the U.S. to replace these British units by fulfilling commitments to Egypt on dates previously agreed upon. The U.S. to provide after November first one group of transport planes to operate in support of the Caucasus force.[3]

All of the above is tentative pending completion of the study.

I am distressed by your news of the PQ convoy.[4]

1 Churchill's message, dated September 14 but received in Washington September 15, is printed as Doc. 169 above.

2 The Combined Chiefs of Staff formulated a specific directive on September 22. See Matloff and Snell, *Strategic Planning*, p. 337; and Howard, *Grand Strategy*, 4: 45–46.

3 The President ultimately rejected this War Department proposal and, despite the advice of both Marshall and Arnold, opted for greater American participation. See below, Doc. 176. See also Matloff and Snell, *Strategic Planning*, pp. 329ff.

4 See above, Doc. 127, note 2. In a portion of his message No. 148 of September 14, Churchill had informed Roosevelt that twelve of the ships in PQ 18 had been sunk by torpedo bombers, with at least two more days remaining before they could get

out of the danger zone. He raised the possibility that PQ 19 might have to be cancelled, and Stalin so informed.

Doc. 171
CHURCHILL TO ROOSEVELT

No. 150   September 16, 1942

The results of the first operations by your flying fortresses have been most encouraging.[1] General Spaatz[2] has wisely been feeling his way and they have not struck very deep.[3] But we may hope that when they are available in sufficient numbers they will be able, with the help of their escorting fighters, to carry the air war into Germany by day on a heavy scale. This would be a development of the highest importance. . . .

I hope you may consider it wise to build up General Spaatz's strength. We are following with admiration your fight in the Solomons.[4] We must make Torch a success. But I am sure we should be missing great opportunities if we did not concentrate every available fortress and long-range escort fighter as quickly as possible for the attack on our primary enemy.

[1] U.S. B-17 bombers (flying fortresses) went into action for the first time on August 17, 1942, in an attack on the important Sotteville marshaling yards at Rouen, an attack their commander described the following day as "far exceed[ing] in accuracy any previous high-altitude bombing in the European theater by German or Allied aircraft." Arthur B. Ferguson, "Rouen-Sotteville No. 1, 17 August 1942," in Craven and Cate, *Army Air Forces*, 1: 663. For an account of the mounting Allied bombing offensive after that date, see Arthur B. Ferguson, "Origins of the Combined Bomber Offensive," in Craven and Cate, *Army Air Forces*, 2 (Chicago, 1949); 216ff.

[2] Major General Carl Spaatz, commander of the Eighth Air Force, stationed in the British Isles.

[3] The British continued to have some doubts concerning the ultimate effectiveness of the B-17 bombers. Air Chief Marshal Portal told Sir Archibald Sinclair, Minister of State for Air, on September 27 that a force of 3,000 heavy and medium bombers "able to pick off small targets with precision in any part of Germany by day would enable us to win the war," but he did not believe American bombers would ever be able to achieve "such accuracy." In a personal message to Harry Hopkins on October 16 Churchill declared that "the very accurate results so far achieved in the daylight bombing of France . . . does not give our experts the same confidence as yours in the power of the day bomber to operate far into Germany." Webster and Frankland, *Strategic Air Offensive*, 1: 358, 360.

[4] On August 7 U.S. marines had landed on Guadalcanal in the Solomon Islands in the first major effort by American ground forces to dislodge the Japanese from areas they had conquered. Bitter fighting continued for months, with the outcome very much in doubt. The Japanese didn't evacuate the island until February 1943. See John Miller, Jr., *Guadalcanal: The First Offensive* (Washington, 1949).

Doc. 172
CHURCHILL TO ROOSEVELT

No. 151   September 22, 1942

. . . General Eisenhower announced that the final date for Torch would be Nov. 8. Everything is being worked to this.

We now know that PQ 18 carried 27 ships safely to Archangel and 13 are sunk.[1] For PQ 19 forty ships are already loaded but it is impossible to send this convoy without throwing back the date of Torch by three weeks. We all regard any delay in Torch as inadmissible.[2]

The time has therefore come to tell Stalin, first that there will be no PQ 19 and secondly we cannot run any more PQs till the end of the year, that is, January. This is a formidable moment in Anglo-American-Soviet relations and you and I must be united in any statement made about convoys.

We are solemnly pledged to the supply of Russia and the most grave consequences might follow from failure to make good. For 1943 there may be two choices. First to run from January onwards Arctic convoys under the present conditions of danger, waste, and effort, observing that we used 77 warships for PQ 18 and think ourselves fortunate to have lost no more than one-third of the merchant ships.

Secondly, the operation called Jupiter.[3] It is more than doubtful

[1] For the fate of convoy PQ 18, see Roskill, *War at Sea*, 2: 28off. The losses, however, were by no means one-sided. For instance, forty German aircraft were shot down and three submarines sunk while attacking the convoy. Moreover, as the official British historian relates, "though the Admiralty could not possibly have realized it at the time, we now know that the success achieved in the passage of PQ 18 and QP 14 [a return convoy that left Archangel on September 13] was, in a way, decisive. Never again did the enemy deploy such great air strength in the north." By the time the next Arctic convoys sailed, the North African landings forced Hitler "to send south his entire heavy bomber and torpedo striking forces of Ju. 88s and He. 111s . . . and because the African landings drew the Luftwaffe south more British and American tanks, vehicles, and aircraft were before long helping the Russians in their great counter-offensive on the eastern front." Roskill, *War at Sea*, 2: 288.

[2] On September 21 Churchill had told the War Cabinet: "If we decided to send a further PQ convoy before Operation 'Torch,' this would mean Operation 'Torch' would have to be delayed until either 24 or 28 November," and he believed that such delay would "court disaster." Parkinson, *Blood, Toil, Tears, and Sweat—The War History from Dunkirk to Alamein*, p. 466.

[3] The proposed invasion of northern Norway had been discussed at a meeting of the British Chiefs of Staff, attended by Churchill and Eisenhower, on the morning of September 21.

whether the developments of Torch will leave shipping and escort resources sufficient for Jupiter unless you can help at any rate with the latter. We must however also know what importance Stalin would attach to the operation and what contribution he would make to it. See the account of my last conversation with him where I mentioned two divisions and he offered three.[4] Our estimate here is that larger numbers would be required and I repeat the shipping problem is unsolved and is anyhow dependent on Torch developments.

It seems to me that simply to tell him now that no more PQs till 1943 is a great danger, and I therefore wish to open staff conversations on Jupiter under all necessary reserves. . . .

I gained the impression at the conference[5] that Roundup was not only delayed or impinged upon by Torch but was to be regarded as definitely off for 1943. This will be another tremendous blow for Stalin. Already Maisky is asking questions about the spring offensive. . . .

If Torch proves hard and costly and if we have to fight French and Germans and perhaps Spaniards, there could of course be no question of Jupiter. We British would require to reinforce Torch from Great Britain. Thus it is all the more necessary that we receive the fullest flow of American divisions and air forces to the United Kingdom.

But there is a more favourable assumption to which personally I incline, namely that by the end of November the United States with French assistance will be masters of French North Africa and that the British expedition will be striking from Torch at Tripoli. General Alexander will attack in sufficient time to influence Torch favourably should he be successful. His operation is called Lightfoot. If all goes well on both operations we might control the whole North African shore by the end of the year, thus saving some of the masses of shipping now rounding the Cape. This is our first great prize.

It would then be open to us to decide on the next move. If the Russian need were sufficiently grave and their demands imperative we might decide to do Jupiter instead of attacking the underbelly of the Axis by Sardinia, Sicily, and even possibly Italy. We ought to have the option open which entails not only paper staff studies but all such preparations as do not hamper our immediate agreed actions.

To sum up, my persisting anxiety is Russia, and I do not see how we can reconcile it with our consciences or with our interests to have no more PQs till 1943, no offer to make joint plans for Jupiter, and no signs of a spring, summer, or even autumn offensive in Europe. I should be most grateful for your counsel on all this. We wish urgently

4 See above, Doc. 160.
5 The conference of the British Chiefs of Staff on September 21.

to send the telegram (of which copy follows separately) to Stalin,[6] and hope that you will back it up as strongly and as soon as you can."

[6] In his telegram Churchill proposed to tell Stalin about Operation Torch, explaining that "we are trying to find means of sending you supplies by the northern route during the rest of 1942." He added that "we intend to resume the full flow of supplies from January 1943" and invited Stalin to discuss further "the possibility of carrying out Operation 'Jupiter' during this winter." Churchill, *Hinge of Fate*, p. 572. In the meantime, Churchill sent Stalin an urgent message warning of a German naval attack in the Caspian Sea: "I have got the . . . information from the same source that I used to warn you of the impending attack on Russia a year and a half ago. I believe this source to be absolutely trustworthy. Pray let this be for your own eye." Churchill added that he was all the more anxious therefore to reinforce "your air force in the Caspian and Caucasian theatre by twenty British and American squadrons." *Stalin's Correspondence*, vol. 1, no. 74.

[7] On September 27 Roosevelt, then on a two-week military inspection trip to the South, the Southwest, and the Far West, replied that he realized "the realities of the situation require us to give up P Q 19." Agreeing that this was "a tough blow for the Russians," Roosevelt added: "I believe that 'Torch' should not be delayed a single day. We are going to put everything in that enterprise, and I have great hope for it." Churchill, *Hinge of Fate*, p. 573.

Doc. 173
ROOSEVELT TO CHURCHILL

No. 189   October 5, 1942

I have gone over carefully your message number 154,[1] which is the proposed message to Stalin. I feel very strongly that we should make a firm commitment to put an air force in the Caucasus and that that operation should not be contingent on any other.

The Russian front is today our greatest reliance[2] and we simply must find a direct manner in which to help them other than our diminishing supplies. We shall, on our part, undertake to replace in

[1] Not printed. On September 22 Churchill had proposed to inform Stalin of the date of Torch, to pledge resumption of a full flow of supplies in January 1943, and to offer to send a mission to Moscow to discuss the invasion of Norway. Roosevelt had already sent an evasive but essentially negative reply on September 22, and Churchill's message was never sent to Stalin.

[2] The Germans had launched their great offensive against Stalingrad on August 22 and succeeded in entering the city by September 14. A week later Soviet forces counterattacked from the northeast and on October 1 from the southeast. Nevertheless, on October 3 Stalin cabled Churchill: "I must inform you that our position in the Stalingrad area has changed for the worse since the early days of September," adding that "we could forgo for a while our request for tanks and guns, if Britain and U.S.A. together could supply us with 800 fighters a month." *Stalin's Correspondence*, vol. 1, no. 75.

the Middle East all of our own planes which are transferred and assist you in every way possible with your own air problems in the Middle East.

Insofar as PQ 19 is concerned, I feel most strongly that we should not tell Stalin that the convoy will not sail. . . .

Please let me know when you send message to Stalin and I will immediately send him a similar message, but I am certain both our messages should be so phrased as to leave a good taste in his mouth.[3]

[3] Churchill's message to Stalin of October 8 reflected Roosevelt's advice. Churchill informed Stalin of the plan, duly carried out, "to send you supplies by the northern route by means of ships sailed independently instead of in escorted convoys. . . . Ten of ours are preparing in addition to what Americans will do." Churchill, *Hinge of Fate*, pp. 579–580. Of the thirteen ships that actually sailed to northern Russia between October and December 1942, four were sunk, three were turned back, one was wrecked, and five arrived safely. Roskill, *War at Sea*, 2: 289. Roosevelt sent his own message to Stalin on October 8, emphasizing his efforts "to move as rapidly as possible to place an air force under your strategic command in the Caucasus" and concluding: "The gallant defense of Stalingrad has thrilled everyone in America and we are confident of its success." *FR 1942*, 3: 731–732. Stalin's laconic reply to Churchill read in full: "I received your message of October 9. Thank you." Churchill, *Hinge of Fate*, pp. 580. Stalin apparently made no reply at all to Roosevelt's message.

Doc. 174

ROOSEVELT TO CHURCHILL

No. 190   October 6, 1942

Winant tells me that the Chicago *Tribune* has applied to Bracken[1] for license to publish a daily paper in England primarily for the use of our troops. Earnestly hope that this application will not be approved.

The fact is that it should be turned down on the ground that the Chicago *Tribune* prints lies and deliberate misrepresentations in lieu of news.

Application can be rejected if you agree on the ground that the United States Government proposes to print a daily paper through an agency approved by you or a daily paper published by our Army or the troops themselves, such as "The Stars and Stripes" in Paris in 1918. I do not believe, therefore, that the application should be turned down on the lack of paper.

You will readily see that I do not trust the Chicago *Tribune* further than you can throw a bull by the tail but I do think we need a paper of our own for the soldiers in England.

[1] Brendan Bracken, British Minister of Information.

Doc. 175
CHURCHILL TO ROOSEVELT

No. 161   October 7, 1942

Your 190.[1] Bracken tells me that when he heard of the Chicago *Tribune*'s proposal he told some of the American correspondents that the Ministry of Information would not allow McCormick[2] to publish any paper in England on the ground that the Chicago *Tribune* had done everything in its power to injure the cause of the United Nations. No official application for facilities has yet been made. When it is McCormick will be told that no opportunity will be given to him to reproduce in England the lies and misrepresentations which are the staple of the Chicago *Tribune*'s editorial policy.

Bracken told Eisenhower yesterday that every possible facility will be given to the American Army if it will produce a daily paper for the American troops.

[1] See above, Doc. 174.
[2] Colonel Robert R. McCormick, publisher of the Chicago *Tribune*.

Doc. 176
CHURCHILL TO ROOSEVELT

No. 172   October 24, 1942

You have seen my message to Stalin which I sent you for your concurrence and despatched on the 8 October (our series message No. 167).[1] There is also the telegram you sent him quoted in your No. 193 to me.

On the same day that I sent my long telegram I sent a short one to him imparting a piece of secret news. On the 13 October I received the somewhat cryptic answer "thank you." Otherwise I have had no response.

We asked our Ambassador[2] to which telegram the "thank you" referred. Molotov's private secretary though repeatedly pressed has given an evasive answer. But Maisky has now indicated in response to an indirect enquiry that he regards Stalin's reply as referring to the

[1] The messages referred to in this document are not printed; but see Doc. 172, note 6, and Doc. 173, note 3, which also concern the "secret news."
[2] Sir Archibald Clark Kerr.

longer message. Have you had any answer to your message quoted in your 193?

Meanwhile fourteen days have passed and no progress has been made in the necessary arrangements with the Russians for choosing landing grounds, etc., to enable our twenty squadrons to take station on the Russian southern flank in January. Nor have we received any comment from Moscow on the other parts of the message affecting the hundred and fifty plus equivalent spare parts of fifty Spitfires offered by us, all mounting cannon guns.[3]

Lastly, we are sending both of us our ships in the dark period of October by the Arctic route hoping to get a good many through to Murmansk or Archangel. Yet this effort on our part entails a considerable Russian movement of aircraft and submarines to help these brave ships in.

As you see I have received nothing but this cryptic "thank you." Baffling as all this is we are persevering because of the splendid fighting of the Russian armies.[4] I wonder whether anything has occurred inside the Soviet animal to make it impossible for Stalin to give an effective reply. It may be that the Russian army has acquired a new footing in the Soviet machine. All this chatter about Hess[5] may be another symptom. I am frankly perplexed and would be grateful for your thoughts at the earliest moment because time is passing.

[3] On September 26, at a Kremlin dinner for Wendell Willkie, then on an information-gathering journey, Stalin, according to Colonel Philip R. Faymonville, the U.S. lend-lease representative in the Soviet Union, "expressed great dissatisfaction over Lend-Lease shipments of older types of munitions from the United States and United Kingdom in place of newer types which he said are needed on Russian front. Stalin especially angry that United Kingdom is shipping Hurricane-type planes instead of Spitfires and that United States is shipping P-40s instead of Aircobras desired." *FR 1942*, 3: 725–726.

[4] The battle of Stalingrad was then at its height, and Soviet historians later described the fortnight after October 14 as "the period of the bitterest fighting of the whole battle." Earl F. Ziemke, *Stalingrad to Berlin* (Washington, 1968), p. 46.

[5] On October 15 Molotov had publicly demanded that an international tribunal immediately try as a war criminal Hitler's deputy, Rudolf Hess, who was in British custody after flying to Scotland on May 10, 1941. See James Douglas Hamilton, *Motive for a Mission—The Story Behind Hess's Flight to Britain* (London, 1971).

Doc. 177
ROOSEVELT TO CHURCHILL

No. 198   October 24, 1942

I have been canvassing this morning the possibilities of increasing our escort vessels and merchant ships for 1943 and I am convinced that by making some readjustments we can build at least seventy more escort vessels than we now plan in 1943 and something more than two million additional dead-weight tons of merchant ships which would enable us to transport before the end of 1943 more than 500,000 additional soldiers abroad with their equipment and maintain them. I have felt for a long time that our airplane program was dragging here and I took the bull by the horns the other day and told them they had to build 100,000 combat planes in 1943. Since that time I have held numerous conferences about it and have agreed this morning to reduce it to eighty-two thousand combat planes actually delivered in 1943, and it is not merely a goal to shoot at.[1] The types of course must be decided by the military with appropriate conferences with you. I will talk to Lyttelton[2] about this when he gets here. I have no additional news about Guadalcanal but you of course know that we are hard pressed there.

I am sure you are keeping my wife's official business[3] to the minimum. I would appreciate it if you would let me know occasionally how things are going with her. Harry and I are going off for a quiet weekend. All good luck in the Libyan desert.[4]

[1] On October 29 Roosevelt instructed Donald M. Nelson, chairman of the War Production Board, to give "highest priority" to the 107,000-plane objective and "whatever preference is needed to insure its accomplishment." Craven and Cate, *Army Air Forces*, 2: 291.

[2] Oliver Lyttelton had succeeded Lord Beaverbrook, Minister of Supply, as First Minister of Production on February 14.

[3] Eleanor Roosevelt was in England from October 21 to November 17, at the invitation of Queen Elizabeth. She investigated the war work being done by British women and visited American troops.

[4] The British Eighth Army, under General Montgomery, had begun its massive assault on Rommel's forces at El Alamein the previous day. In a message to his troops, Montgomery declared: "The battle which is now about to begin will be one of the decisive battles of history. It will be the turning point of the war." Montgomery approvingly cites that judgment on page 126 of his *Memoirs*.

Doc. 178
CHURCHILL TO ROOSEVELT

No. 174   October 26, 1942

I hear that you would prefer to omit from the British message to the Spanish Government a reference to the participation of British forces in Torch.[1]

[1] President Roosevelt's message to General Franco, delivered by Carlton J. H. Hayes, the U.S. ambassador to Spain, on the morning of November 7, 1942, made no

I am satisfied that it is important to inform both the Spanish and Portuguese Governments of British participation, if only to remove any suspicions about the object of our own concentrations at Gibraltar and to lend force to the assurances we are giving to them. The considerations which apply to the handling of the French do not necessarily apply to that of the Spaniards and Portuguese, for which you agreed that we should be primarily responsible.

There will be no question of our publishing the full text of our declarations to Spain and Portugal on zero day. All that we should make public would be the substance, omitting any passages such as those about British participation which would not be in accord with the general line we are both taking in public in the first stage of the operation.

We should of course say to both Spaniards and Portuguese that what we tell them about our share in the operation is for their strictly confidential information.

---

reference to British participation in the operation, and Sir Samuel Hoare, the British ambassador, delivered to the Spanish Foreign Minister, Count Jordana, a separate statement from his government. Carlton J. H. Hayes, *Wartime Mission in Spain, 1942–1945* (New York, 1956), p. 88. Interestingly enough, as Churchill cabled Roosevelt on November 5, the Prime Minister proposed to tell de Gaulle the day before the landings "that the reason I have not mentioned 'Torch' to him is that it is a United States enterprise and a United States secret." Churchill, *Hinge of Fate,* p. 605.

Doc. 179
ROOSEVELT TO CHURCHILL

No. 202   October 27, 1942

I am not unduly disturbed about our respective responses or lack of responses from Moscow.[1] I have decided they do not use speech for the same purposes that we do.

I had not heard of any difficulty at our end about arrangements for landing fields on the Russian southern flank but I shall explore that from my end at once.[2]

I feel very sure the Russians are going to hold this winter and that we should proceed vigorously with our plans both to supply them and

1 See above, Doc. 176.

2 See Herring, *Aid to Russia,* p. 72; and Richard C. Lukas, *Eagles East: The Army Air Forces and the Soviet Union* (Tallahassee, Fla., 1970), pp. 109ff. Roosevelt continued to press, for instance, for the prompt implementation of Operation Velvet—the establishment of an Anglo-American bombing force, under Russian command, in the Caucasus.

to set up an air force to fight with them.[3] I want us to be able to say to Mr. Stalin that we have carried out our obligations one hundred percent.[4]

[3] The Russians proved notoriously difficult when it came to accepting the planes Roosevelt was making every effort to send them. As General Arnold informed Marshall on October 30: "[The Russians'] attitude toward our aircraft is one of tolerant acceptance. At no time have they shown any enthusiasm regarding performance or other characteristics." He added later: "In other words, they were not really so anxious to get the airplanes as the senior officers of the Russian Government would have our President and our Secretary of War believe." Arnold, *Global Mission*, p. 387.

[4] Roosevelt persisted in his efforts to speed lend-lease shipments to the Soviet Union even in the face of vicious *Pravda* cartoons charging the British with cowardice and collaboration with the Nazis, and of Stalin's letter to Henry Cassidy, Moscow correspondent of the Associated Press, published on the front page of *Pravda* on October 5, declaring that "in comparison with the assistance which the Soviet Union, drawing off the main forces of the German Fascist troops, is rendering to its Allies, the assistance from the Allies to the Soviet Union is meanwhile of little effect." *FR 1942*, 3: 461.

Doc. 180
CHURCHILL TO ROOSEVELT

October 31, 1942

My dear Mr. President,

Oliver Lyttelton will talk to your officers about production in its various aspects as they affect the layout we now have to make on what are our last remaining reserves of manpower; but I hope you will let him discuss with you some of the major points governing our joint action in the war.

First of all, I put the U-boat menace. This, I am sure, is our worst danger. It is horrible to me that we should be budgeting jointly for a balance of shipping on the basis of 700,000 tons a month loss. True, it is not yet as bad as that. But the spectacle of all these splendid ships being built, sent to sea crammed with priceless food and munitions, and being sunk—three or four every day—torments me day and night. Not only does this attack cripple our war energies and threaten our life, but it arbitrarily limits the might of the United States coming into the struggle. The oceans, which were your shield, threaten to become your cage. . . .

Therefore I submit to you for your good judgement the maximum allocation of steel for merchant shipbuilding, and then out of that the maximum construction of escort vessels which engine capacity will allow. From the important measures which you have lately taken, I am sure your mind is moving in exactly the same direction.

We must ask for a fair share of the merchant shipping and of the escort vessels. All our labour and capacity is engaged in the war effort. We have had to sacrifice 100,000 tons of merchant shipbuilding in order to get more corvettes, and we cannot hope to produce more than 1,100,000 British gross tons of new merchant ships in the calendar year 1943. We have lost enormously in ships used in the common interest, and we trust to you to give us a fair and just assignment of your new vast construction to sail under our own flag. . . .

We have been so well treated by you in tanker tonnage, that it is with diffidence that I mention the figure of 1,000,000 tons additional, which is what we need in 1943.

Mr. President, I cannot cut the food consumption here below its present level. We need to import 27,000,000 tons for our food and war effort in 1943. More than three-quarters of our immense marine is engaged in war transport of one kind or another. We are asking for 2,500,000 dead-weight nontanker tonnage to be assigned to us from the beginning of 1943 from your new construction. Our stocks are running down with dangerous rapidity. Any further inroads upon them, except for some great emergency, would be highly improvident. These Islands are the assembly base for the war against Hitler; many of your troops will be here; and we must have a margin in case of a renewed blitz on the Mersey and the Clyde, or exceptional concentration of U-boats on the Atlantic routes. Rather than cut any further on the food of the people, I should be forced to reduce our general contribution to the overseas war effort. . . .

I have not yet heard from you in reply to that part of my long telegram about Russia which dealt with the need to place more American divisions in this country, and to go forward with Bolero for a retarded Roundup.[1] I had hoped to have, even on the new layout, seven or eight United States divisions in these Islands by April, and we are still making preparations on a very large scale for the reception of a great American army. I recognise that shipping is the limiting factor. Practically only the two Queens[2] are running now. I trust however you will allow your officers to discuss with ours the whole process of moving continuously divisions at the fastest rate into these Islands, and thus make us both able to push our forces outwards where needed,

1 See above, Doc. 172.
2 The giant Cunard liners *Queen Elizabeth* and *Queen Mary* were first pressed into war service in May 1941 to bring troops from Australia to Suez. Beginning in the summer of 1942, they ferried troops from New York to Britain and from there to Suez. Each ship could carry as many as 15,000 men.

as well as making the forward-striking base safe, and holding the enemy pinned on the French shore.

Lastly, I come to the air. Oliver Lyttelton is also thoroughly informed about this, and I have already communicated with Harry on the subject. An ever increasing weight of bomb discharge upon Germany and Italy must be our unrelenting aim. In our view, night bombing has already yielded results which justify it being backed by the United States, at any rate as a follow-up to your day bombing. But also the anti-U-boat war will require many long-range flying boats and aircraft. So far as fighters are concerned, our opinion is that the latest British Spitfires and the improved American Mustang will hold the leadership in 1943.

Lyttelton is fully authorised to discusss all the above matters with you, and he is in full possession of our views.[3] He will be with you during tremendous days, about which I shall be telegraphing to you pretty constantly. I pray that this great American enterprise, in which I am your lieutenant and in which we have the honour to play an important part, may be crowned by the success it deserves. So far, all promises well.

I hope also to report to you about the battle in Egypt, which is now entering upon a more important phase.

Believe me,

—Always your most sincere friend,

Winston S. Churchill

[3] On Roosevelt's copy of this letter Hopkins noted that the President had added a note in longhand to the one sent to Churchill which read substantially as follows: "I would like to reserve final decision on the matter of transport planes. The Russians have asked us for 500 and I think we should give them some." For Roosevelt's full reply see below, Doc. 189.

November 1942
to
December 1943

Introduction to Part II

"Our enterprises have prospered beyond our hopes and we must not neglect the good gifts of fortune. . . ."

ON November 8, 1942, Allied forces launched Operation Torch, landing on the coasts of Algeria and Morocco in French North Africa. There was heavy fighting with the Vichy French defenders before the Allies worked out an agreement with the French Vice-Premier, Admiral Jean François Darlan, who was in Algiers, for the French forces to end their resistance. By the morning of November 11 this had been accomplished.

In reaction to the invasion, the government of Vichy France broke off diplomatic relations with the United States. In turn, Hitler responded to Darlan's ceasefire by ordering German troops to march into the previously unoccupied areas controlled by the Vichy regime in France.

The arrangements approved by General Dwight D. Eisenhower, commander of the Allied forces, called for Admiral Darlan to act as the head of the French government in North Africa, subject to Eisenhower's supervision. General Henri Giraud, a Free French officer, was to be commander in chief of the French armed forces in North Africa. Many in the United States and Great Britain condemned this "deal" on the grounds that the Allies should have nothing to do with officials who had collaborated with the enemy. But Eisenhower defended his action on the ground that it saved Allied lives and time, and Roosevelt supported Eisenhower. The President explained the circumstances to Churchill for the benefit of the British critics, and in a press conference Roosevelt tried to put a good face on the arrangement.

The Darlan affair prompted Roosevelt to appoint Robert D. Murphy,

[267]

the former American minister to Vichy France and consul general at Algiers, as his personal political adviser, attached to Eisenhower's headquarters. After some discussion, Churchill appointed Harold Macmillan to act in a similar capacity for him at Eisenhower's headquarters.

All these decisions were made without the cooperation of General Charles de Gaulle, recognized by the British as the leader of the Free French forces, who refused to have anything to do with Darlan. Darlan was assassinated by a young Frenchman on December 24, 1942, and de Gaulle felt he could cooperate with Giraud in North Africa. Giraud restored representative government in French North Africa and then proceeded to suppress Vichy organizations there. When Giraud began arresting former officers of the Vichy regime, Roosevelt and Churchill were obliged to register a strong protest, since such measures were contrary to the armistice agreement. Eisenhower also warned the French that no retaliations would be tolerated. The whole Darlan affair and its aftermath were distasteful to Eisenhower and to Army Chief of Staff General George C. Marshall, and the experience seems to have reinforced their view that future political decisions ought be left to the politicians.

Relations between Churchill and de Gaulle had been thorny from the beginning, and with the entry of the United States into North Africa American officials found that they also had to deal with a proud and difficult man. Roosevelt distrusted de Gaulle and opposed any action that might prejudge the leadership of France after it had been liberated. Yet Roosevelt and Churchill both recognized the necessity of working for military goals with de Gaulle and the French Committee of National Liberation, although Roosevelt wanted to have the relationship carefully defined. Churchill was under heavy pressure to recognize the French committee as a government-in-exile, but Roosevelt held off such action. Not until after the invasion of France had begun did the United States recognize the committee as the de facto government of France, temporarily in charge of liberated areas—but even then de Gaulle's committee was under Eisenhower's military supervision.

Operation Torch was one of a series of climactic actions during 1942 and 1943 that marked a change in the fortunes of the Allied powers. Early in 1942 they had not been able to stop the Japanese conquest of the Philippines, Singapore, Burma, the Dutch East Indies, and the islands of Wake and Guam. In March, 1942, the Japanese captured Lae and Salamaua in New Guinea and soon moved against Port Moresby in preparation for an invasion of Australia. Then, in May, came the American naval victory at the battle of the Coral Sea, which effectively halted the Japanese threat to Australia. A month later American airmen beat back a Japanese naval force intent on taking Midway Island and moving against Hawaii. Their victory at Midway is generally regarded as a turning point in the Pacific war. After Midway, American and Australian troops were able to begin the work of driving the Japanese from New Guinea. On August 7, U.S. marines landed on Guadalcanal and other islands in the Solomons group. By the following February Guadalcanal was secure, and the long process of seizing successive strategic points in Japanese-held areas of the Pacific could begin. By the end of 1943 the situation in the southwest Pacific was favorable enough to permit the start of new offensive operations in the central Pacific.

The spring and summer of 1942 were disastrous for the Soviet Union. The Russians were forced to yield Sevastopol in the Crimea to the advancing German armies in July. An Allied convoy carrying war supplies to the Soviet Union by way of the Barents Sea was subjected to a devastating attack by German submarines, and in consequence the British suspended convoys to the Soviet Union by way of this northern route. Efforts were made to send supplies through the Persian Gulf to Iran and overland to the Soviet Union, but the amounts delivered were disappointingly small.

Even on the Russian front, the closing months of 1942 saw a turning of the tide. In late August, the German Sixth Army, commanded by General Friedrich Paulus, launched an all-out attack on Stalingrad, "the keystone on the Volga." After months of fighting, in which most of Stalingrad was destroyed, Russian troops finally surrounded the German forces, and by February 2 Paulus (now a field marshal) along with 24 generals and about 90,000 troops had surrendered to the Russians. Stalingrad has rightly been described as one of the great turning points of the war; as a result of the disastrous German defeat the myth of Hitler's military genius suffered irreparable damage.

In the United Kingdom news broadcasts told the British people of the steady retirement of their Eighth Army across North Africa under heavy pressure from the German and Italian forces under Field Marshal Erwin Rommel. Tobruk fell in June 1942. By August the Eighth Army was in a defensive position at El Alamein, where it prepared to stop Rommel's drive into Egypt. General Sir Bernard L. Montgomery arrived from the United Kingdom to take command of the Eighth Army under the overall direction of General Sir Harold Alexander, commander in chief of the British Middle East forces. Bolstered by reinforcements of American tanks and equipment, the Eighth Army stemmed Rommel's advance at El Alamein. Then, on October 23, 1942, the British launched a counteroffensive. A few days after the American landings in North Africa the Eighth Army reached Libya. Pressing on, the British recaptured Tobruk and continued moving westward toward the American forces.

By the beginning of the new year, the Allied forces were solidly established in North Africa and the American forces took the offensive against Axis troops in Tunisia. In mid-February 1943 the Americans suffered a defeat at the hands of General Rommel at Kasserine Pass, but under a new commander, they soon rallied and resumed their advance. American, British, and Free French forces in Tunisia, under the immediate command of Generals Montgomery and Omar Bradley, pressed in on the Axis troops and forced their surrender on May 13, 1943. North Africa was free of the enemy at last.

Even before that final victory in Africa had been won, the Combined Chiefs of Staff sought a decision on the next Anglo-American target. The North African campaign had been essentially a British idea. General Marshall and other American military planners had supported the project somewhat reluctantly because they believed that it would delay the cross-channel attack on the continent. For their part, the British feared that an invasion of Western Europe would be costly in lives, and they much preferred a strategy of wearing down the Germans and probing and exploiting their possible weak spots. While they were committed to a Europe-first strategy, the Americans recognized that the strategic plans advocated by the British would delay the defeat of Japan, and in the meantime Japan's hold over the vast reaches of the Pacific would be strengthened. Now that some gains had been made and some territory recovered they wanted to press on. When definite plans for Europe had been worked out, the Americans believed, men and matériel could be made available for use in the Pacific. Churchill, on the other hand, favored plans that were flexible enough to take advantage of unforeseen opportunities. He was particularly interested in further campaigns in the Mediterranean, where one goal was to induce Turkey to join the war against the Axis. Like the Americans, Stalin wanted a second Allied front in Western Europe as soon as possible so that some of the tremendous German pressure on the Soviet armies would be reduced.

Roosevelt and Churchill decided to meet at Casablanca in January 1943 to discuss future plans. The President and the Prime Minister invited Stalin to join them there or at some other location, but the Russian leader felt unable to relinquish the direction of his armies even for a short period of time. At Casablanca, the Americans and British debated and bargained long and hard. Churchill knew exactly what he wanted; Roosevelt was less certain. It was agreed that the next Anglo-American target in Europe should be Sicily, but also that the bomber offensive against German-occupied Europe should be greatly intensified. In the Far Eastern theater, the Allied advance was to continue through the central and southwest Pacific toward the Philippines, and the United States air forces were to be built up in the China-Burma-India area in preparation for the recapture of Burma.

At Casablanca Roosevelt and Churchill also decided to give top priority to the security of communications by sea. They recognized that the shortage of shipping hampered all their operations, and that attacks by German submarines in the Atlantic were cutting into their already limited number of vessels. Indeed, between March and November 1942 shipping losses had reached a dangerous new high, and Churchill and Roosevelt and their staffs recognized that overcoming the U-boat menace was a matter of paramount importance. Following Casablanca, the Allies stepped up their anti-submarine activity: merchant vessels continued to travel in convoy under a naval escort, while an improved type of British radar system was installed in bombers that patrolled the seas. From bases in the North and South Atlantic, the United Kingdom, Iceland, and the Caribbean, aircraft and naval vessels sought out the U-boats. On the basis of their treaty of 1373, the British were able to obtain from neutral Portugal the right to use the Azores as a base for additional anti-submarine activity.

As a result of all these measures, the destruction of enemy submarines increased and shipping losses declined correspondingly. Nevertheless, when Churchill sought to publish news of the Allied anti-submarine victories, Roosevelt objected on the ground that such information would give the public a false sense that victory was just around the corner. Having seen that the announcement of earlier Allied victories had tended to slow down war production, the President did not wish to do anything to encourage such a tendency. In any event, by the middle of 1943, it was apparent that the German U-boat menace had been largely eliminated.

While Allied military fortunes showed slow but significant improvement throughout 1943, Anglo-American relations with the Soviet Union were undergoing increasing strain as result of growing differences over Poland. In discussions about post-war frontiers, the Russians made it clear that they intended to retain the portions of eastern Poland they had seized in the summer of 1939 following the signing of the Nazi-Soviet pact and the German invasion from the West. The Polish government-in-exile in London, on the other hand, felt strongly that it neither could nor should accept any such arrangement. Polish leaders had the sympathy of the United States and Britain, but neither Roosevelt nor Churchill was prepared to press very hard for the Poles. Given the relatively small size of the Allied campaign in North Africa, and the delays in bringing it to a victorious conclusion, compared with the huge Soviet forces engaging the Germans on the Eastern front,

Roosevelt did not feel himself in a position to make demands on Stalin. Also, he believed that frontier questions should generally be left to be dealt with at the end of the war. Churchill and the British government believed that strong statements by the Polish government-in-exile were neither helpful for winning the war nor for planning the peace. Eventually, the Russians began to support a Communist-dominated Polish Committee of National Liberation, an organization prepared to do Moscow's bidding.

The problem of Poland came to a head in April 1943 when the German government announced that its forces had discovered the graves of thousands of Polish officers who had surrendered to the Russians in 1939. The Polish government-in-exile asked the International Red Cross to investigate the matter and instructed its ambassador at Moscow to seek an answer to the German allegations from the Soviet government. The latter responded by breaking off diplomatic relations with the Polish government-in-exile, charging that no unbiased investigation was possible in Nazi-held territory. The British and Americans tried to repair this breach in the alliance, but Stalin refused to reverse his action. At the Moscow conference of foreign ministers, in October 1943, the United States and Britain tried again to resolve the troubled boundary question, but neither the Polish government in London nor the Soviet Union would accept the other's position. In the end, therefore, the American and British governments advised the Poles to accept the unalterable Soviet position. The Polish government refused to do so, and the bitter dispute continued for another year and a half.

During the final days of the Tunisian campaign, Roosevelt, Churchill, and the Combined Chiefs of Staff assembled for another meeting in Washington. At this conference, code-named Trident (May 12–25, 1943), the President and the Prime Minister reconsidered their grand strategy in the light of recent United Nations victories in North Africa and Russia. The most important decision to come out of this meeting was their agreement that a cross-channel attack on Western Europe, now code-named Overlord, was set for May 1, 1944. In addition, Roosevelt and Churchill discussed their future plans for the Mediterranean where Churchill sought unsuccessfully to obtain American agreement for an attack on the Italian mainland once Sicily had been conquered. Priorities were set for other operations and activities in the Balkans, Burma, and the central Pacific.

Operation Husky, the invasion of Sicily by the armies of Generals Montgomery and Patton under the supreme command of General Eisenhower, began on July 10, 1943. Weeks of heavy fighting followed, but organized enemy resistance ceased on August 16, with the remnants of the German forces withdrawing to Italy. About the same time,

Roosevelt, Churchill, and the Combined Chiefs of Staff met again, this time at Quebec in a conference code-named Quadrant (August 14-24, 1943). This was a time of great expectations. On July 25 King Victor Emmanuel III had dismissed Mussolini and had appointed Marshal Pietro Badoglio to head a new Italian government. Badoglio's representatives promptly asked the United Nations for an armistice, and the Combined Chiefs of Staff responded by directing General Eisenhower to send representatives to Lisbon to sign the formal instrument of surrender. The signing of the military terms accordingly took place on September 3, 1943.

During their Quebec meeting, Roosevelt and Churchill reaffirmed May 1, 1944 as the target date for Operation Overlord and agreed on detailed plans for the bombing offensive to precede it. Churchill was still not fully reconciled to the need for a major operation in Western Europe and favored instead further ventures in the Mediterranean area. But in the Pacific the British accepted the American arguments for a two-pronged offensive from the southwest and central Pacific, the latter to begin with an early attack on the Gilbert and Marshall island groups. As for Southeast Asia, Admiral Lord Louis Mountbatten was appointed supreme commander in that theater, with General Joseph W. Stilwell as his deputy. Roosevelt and Churchill agreed also that China was to be an area of American strategic responsibility and that Stilwell was to be accountable to Generalissimo Chiang Kai-shek. A major Allied offensive in northern Burma was to begin in February 1944.

During the Quebec conference, the President and the Prime Minister also approved final plans for the invasion of Italy, and, shortly after the end of the conference, on September 3, British troops landed on the toe of the Italian boot at Reggio di Calabria. The same day, Badoglio signed an armistice agreement to become effective on September 9. News of the armistice was broadcast to the American troops as they were under way for their landing at Salerno the same day.

Originally the Allies hoped to seize the entire area extending from the toe of the boot to a line running from Rome across the middle of the Italian peninsula. Indeed, Churchill was convinced that the overthrow of the Mussolini regime would allow the Allies to make speedy progress in Italy. But Hitler moved rapidly to deprive the Allies of any advantage from the armistice. Additional German troops were rushed into Italy, and instead of a rapid march on Rome the Allies encountered bitter German resistance at Salerno and elsewhere in the south of Italy.

Nevertheless, the British and Americans were able to form a line across the peninsula, and by October, they had seized the airfields at Foggia, thereby obtaining bases for bomber attacks on southern Germany, Austria, and Rumania. But the fighting south of Naples proved to be so costly and time-consuming that the Allies began studying possible ways to land behind the German lines. On November 25 the Fifth Army's plan for an amphibious landing at Anzio was approved, and the attack was scheduled to take place in January 1944.

Meanwhile, the Americans and British began to run into political complications in Italy. Although Victor Emmanuel had long permitted Mussolini to rule virtually unchecked, and Marshal Badoglio had been one of the top commanders in Mussolini's rape of Abyssinia, for the time being the Allies allowed the king to keep his throne and Badoglio to administer the areas liberated by Allied troops. Not surprisingly, this "collaboration" with former Fascists, and their royal protector, produced an outpouring of criticism both in the United States and Britain. Especially critical were those elements who had disapproved of the arrangements with Admiral Darlan and other pro-Vichyites in North Africa. Roosevelt and Churchill were much annoyed by such criticism, and they also began to disagree between themselves concerning the Italian political factions most deserving of their support.

Although Roosevelt and Churchill were largely preoccupied with Italian affairs, the forces of the United Nations were continuing to record new victories on battlefronts throughout the world. By early September, Soviet troops had recaptured Kharkov, Stalino, and the industrial region of the Donbas, and in the Pacific the Allies recovered from the Japanese territory in New Guinea, Bougainville, Makin, Tarawa, and New Britain. In mid-October the new Italian government formally declared war on Germany.

While most of the Roosevelt-Churchill correspondence at this time was taken up with strategic or other military matters, the two were also confronted with a variety of other problems. The President and the Prime Minister had to deal with such difficult and heartrending problems as Jewish refugees, Nazi atrocities, and the hungry civilians in German-occupied territories. They were concerned with a number of complicated disputes, such as the intense rivalry between competing guerrilla factions in Greece and Yugoslavia. Also, alarming reports reached them of the Germans' intense activity in building long-range rockets. The President was particularly concerned about what he believed were unduly revealing news stories in *The New York Times,* the *Chicago Sun,* and the *Washington Post.*

By the autumn of 1943, it was clear that the time had come for another summit meeting, and the President and the Prime Minister made still another attempt to persuade Stalin to join them. Chiang Kai-shek was also to be invited. This meeting was not easy to arrange since the Soviet Union and Japan were not at war, and Stalin therefore declined to participate in a conference with Chiang Kai-shek. In the end, it was agreed that Roosevelt and Churchill would meet with

Stalin at Teheran, at a conference code-named Eureka, and that before and after that meeting Roosevelt and Churchill would confer at Cairo, at a meeting code-named Sextant, in which Chiang Kai-shek would participate.

At their first meeting at Cairo, November 22–26, 1943, the President and the Prime Minister held inconclusive talks on the forthcoming invasion of western Europe and the possible expansion of operations in the Mediterranean. But the bulk of their discussions concerned possible operations in the China-Burma-India theater. Churchill was very skeptical of the value of a campaign designed to reopen the Burma Road to increase the flow of supplies to China. He believed that even if this operation proved successful, the buildup of China would come too late to be of substantial assistance in ending the war with Japan. Further, he considered that the resources necessary for operations in northern Burma and for an amphibious operation against the Andaman Islands in the Indian Ocean would be better employed in the Mediterranean, and he wanted to have forces available to strike at Sumatra and possibly retake Singapore and Hong Kong.

On the other hand, the President and the American Chiefs of Staff looked upon China as potentially an important base for long-range air attacks on Japan. The Burma campaign would be a necessary prelude to the more effective participation of China in the war. In the end, a plan for such a campaign was formally discussed, and Chiang Kai-shek agreed to commit his forces in Yünnan province and to assist in the reconquest of Burma.

After four days at Cairo, Roosevelt and Churchill flew to Teheran, where they met with Stalin from November 28 to December 2, 1943. They began with a look at their military situation. After the Big Three had surveyed the principal battle fronts and listened to Churchill's vigorous views on possible operations in Italy, the eastern Mediterranean, and the Balkans, Stalin suggested that a better use of troops prior to Overlord would be an invasion of southern France. Further, he insisted that the British and Americans settle on the details of Overlord and determine its date and commander. If there were a landing in southern France about the same time as that in Normandy, Stalin declared that he could plan simultaneous attacks on the German forces in Russia. He also promised that the Soviet Union would join the war against Japan after the defeat of Germany. Subsequently, the Combined Chiefs of Staff agreed on a plan whereby Overlord would be launched in May 1944, and a second landing in southern France, code-named Anvil, would take place at the same time on as large a scale as possible. Roosevelt and Churchill approved these plans and then returned to Cairo to discuss other matters in the light of the Teheran decisions.

During the second phase of the Cairo conference, held December 3–7, 1943, the President found himself in the position of having to alter some of his earlier plans for that meeting. Now that Stalin had pledged that the Soviet Union would enter the war against Japan after Hitler was defeated, there seemed to be less immediate need to build up China as a base for the closing phase of the war against Japan. Furthermore, it was clear that the projected landing in southern France (Operation Anvil) would absorb ships, landing craft, men, and supplies previously earmarked for operations in Burma, and Roosevelt, therefore, acceded to Churchill's request that the amphibious assault in the Bay of Bengal be canceled. The Combined Chiefs of Staff thereupon asked Admiral Lord Louis Mountbatten to suggest an alternative operation, but it was decided that no major amphibious venture could be undertaken. Finally, because of Roosevelt's insistence that something be done to encourage China to stay in the war, the Combined Chiefs of Staff promised to increase the number of aircraft and the flow of supplies over the Himalaya Mountains into China.

If the conferences at Cairo and Teheran were generally most successful from a military planning point of view, they were considerably less so from a political standpoint. At Teheran, Roosevelt and Churchill had in effect begun to accept Stalin's ideas for altering the postwar frontiers of Poland without the approval of the Polish government-in-exile—indeed against the Poles' dogged opposition. Their acquiescence may have led Stalin to believe that the President and the Prime Minister would, sooner or later, also agree to further plans he might have for Poland and other neighboring states. At the Cairo meeting, Chiang Kai-shek, whose country had borne the brunt of Japanese aggression since 1931, came away with little more than paper promises of future military assistance.

Yet the conferences at Cairo and Teheran marked more than a diplomatic watershed. Since November 1942 the Anglo-American collaboration had grown from a small offensive in North Africa to victories there and in Sicily and to a slow but steady advance in Italy. The German submarine menace had been largely overcome. Ships and escort vessels were coming off the ways in great numbers. The Japanese had been stopped in the Pacific and were being pushed back more rapidly than had been anticipated. Soviet troops had halted the German advance and were now driving Hitler's armies steadily westward. Allied air power was inflicting heavy damage on Germany—the Royal Air Force by night and the U.S. Army Air Force by day. Finally, Britain and the United States were now building up enormous numbers of men and ships and immense quantities of supplies for their invasion of France in 1944.

But despite these advances, Anglo-American collaboration was showing signs of increasing strain. In 1942 the President overruled General Marshall's position on North Africa, and a year later he had to give way to Churchill's stand on amphibious operations in Burma. At the same time, the American military planners had enlisted the aid of the President in standing firm against any more campaigns in the eastern Mediterranean. They had also managed to retain sufficient manpower and supplies to keep their Pacific offensive going. Roosevelt had offended Churchill by his independent efforts to deal with Chiang Kai-shek and Stalin. But the President was concerned about the political implications of Churchill's strategy, and he was anxious to present the United States as being independent of British influence. But for the President and the American Joint Chiefs of Staff, the most important results of what has been called "a year of conferences" were, first, that there was now at last an agreed date for the invasion of western Europe, and, second, that Stalin had promised eventually to enter the Pacific war.

Messages and Notes

Doc. 181
ROOSEVELT TO CHURCHILL

No. 210   November 11, 1942

I am very happy with the latest news of your splendid campaign in Egypt, and of the success that has attended our joint landing in West and North Africa.

This brings up the additional steps that should be taken when and if the south shore of the Mediterranean is cleared and under our control.

It is hoped that you with your Chiefs of Staff in London and I with the combined staff here may make a survey of the possibilities including forward movements directed against Sardinia, Sicily, Italy, Greece, and other Balkan areas and including the possibility of obtaining Turkish support for an attack through the Black Sea against Germany's flank.

In regard to de Gaulle, I have hitherto enjoyed a quiet satisfaction in leaving him in your hands—apparently I have now acquired a similar problem in brother Giraud.[1]

I wholly agree that we must prevent rivalry between the French émigré factions and I have no objection to a de Gaulle emissary visit-

1 General Henri Giraud had arrived in Algeria on November 9. See above, Doc. 169, note 4. See also Brian Crozier, *De Gaulle: The Warrior* (New York, 1973), pp. 196–197.

ing Kingpin[2] in Algiers. We must remember that there is also a cat fight in progress between Kingpin and Darlan,[3] each claiming full military command of French forces in North and West Africa.

The principal thought to be driven home to all three of these prima donnas is that the situation is today solely in the military field and that any decision by any one of them, or by all of them, is subject to review and approval of Eisenhower.

Also I think it would be well to find out before de Gaulle's man leaves for Africa just what his instructions are.[4]

[2] Code name for General Giraud.

[3] Admiral Jean François Darlan, Vice Premier of Vichy France at this time.

[4] On December 1 General de Gaulle asked Eisenhower, the Allied commander in North Africa, to receive at Algiers General François d'Astier de la Vigerie, who was appointed by de Gaulle as his liaison with French leaders in North Africa. Eisenhower agreed, and d'Astier arrived in Algiers on December 20.

Doc. 182
CHURCHILL TO ROOSEVELT

No. 090[1]   November 15, 1942

General Eisenhower's number 527 on political arrangements in French North Africa.[2]

We cannot say that our doubts or anxieties are removed by what is proposed or that the solution will be permanent or healthy. Nevertheless, in view of the dominating importance of speed and of the fact that the Allied Commander in Chief's opinion is so strongly and ably expressed that it is endorsed by our officers including Admiral Cunningham[3] who were with him on the spot, we feel we have no choice but to accept General Eisenhower's arrangements for maintaining local and interim equilibrium and for securing the vital positions in Tunis.

We feel sure you will consult us on the long-term steps, pursuing always the aim of uniting all Frenchmen who will fight Hitler.

Great care must be taken that we are not double-crossed. There were

[1] This message was a radiogram received by the War Department Code Center. The number is apparently theirs, not Churchill's.

[2] Eisenhower argued that since Darlan bore much of the prestige of Marshall Henri Philippe Pétain, head of the Vichy government, a workable ceasefire could be brought about only by an agreement between Admiral Darlan and General Giraud. See Alfred D. Chandler, Jr., et al. eds., The Papers of Dwight David Eisenhower: The War Years (Baltimore and London, 1970), 2: 707–711. Hereafter cited as PDDE.

[3] Admiral Sir Andrew Brown Cunningham, commander in chief of the British fleet in the Mediterranean.

some disquieting evidences in our magics[4] two days ago. On the other hand we have these men in our power and should be vigilant lest they escape from us.

We do not see any need to publish the press release contained in General Eisenhower's number 544 or anything like it at present, pending further developments in Tunis and Dakar, and hope our views may be met.

[4] Intercepted cable messages.

Doc. 183
ROOSEVELT TO CHURCHILL

No. 214 November 17, 1942

I have accepted General Eisenhower's political arrangements made for the time being in northern and western Africa.

I thoroughly understand and approve the feeling in the United States and Great Britain and among all the other United Nations that in view of the history of the past two years no permanent arrangement should be made with Admiral Darlan.[1] People in the United Nations likewise would never understand the recognition of a reconstituting of the Vichy government in France or in any French territory.

We are opposed to Frenchmen who support Hitler and the Axis. No one in our Army has any authority to discuss the future government of France and the French Empire.

The future French government will be established—not by any individual in metropolitan France or overseas—but by the French people themselves after they have been set free by the victory of the United Nations.

[1] The basic story of the arrangement with Darlan is set forth in William L. Langer, *Our Vichy Gamble* (New York, 1947), pp. 344–381. This is supplemented by Dwight D. Eisenhower, *Crusade in Europe* (Garden City, N.Y., 1948), pp. 104–114; Winston S. Churchill, *The Hinge of Fate* (Boston, 1950), pp. 610–647; Robert E. Sherwood, *Roosevelt and Hopkins* (New York, 1948), pp. 648–655; Cordell Hull, *The Memoirs of Cordell Hull* (New York, 1948), 2: 1196–1200 (henceforth cited as Hull, *Memoirs*); Robert Murphy, *Diplomat Among Warriors* (Garden City, N.Y., 1964), pp. 127–143; and George F. Howe, *Northwest Africa—Seizing the Initiative in the West* (Washington, 1957), pp. 269–271. Eisenhower's correspondence on the subject is printed in *PDDE*, 2: 689–692, 696–697, 705–710. For American diplomatic documents, see U.S. Department of State, *Foreign Relations of the United States 1942*, 2 (Washington, 1962): 429–501. Henceforth cited as *FR*. For the British side, see Sir Llewellyn Woodward, *British Foreign Policy in the Second World War*, 2 (London, 1971): 360–385; and I. S. O. Playfair and C. J. C. Molony, *The Mediteranean and the Middle East*, vol. 4, *The Destruction of the Axis Forces in Africa* (London, 1966), chap. 6.

The present temporary arrangement in North and West Africa is only a temporary expedient, justified solely by the stress of battle.

The present temporary arrangement has accomplished two military objectives. The first was to save American and British lives on the one hand, and French lives on the other hand.

The second was the vital factor of time. The temporary arrangement has made it possible to avoid a "mopping up" period in Algiers and Morocco which might have taken a month or two to consummate. Such a period would have delayed the concentration for the attack from the west on Tunis, and we hope on Tripoli.

Every day of delay in the current operation would have enabled the Germans and Italians to build up a strong resistance, to dig in and make a huge operation on our part essential before we could win. Here again, many more lives will be saved under the present speedy offensive than if we had had to delay it for a month or more.

It will also be noted that French troops, under the command of General Giraud, have already been in action against the enemy in Tunisia, fighting by the side of American and British soldiers for the liberation of their country.

Admiral Darlan's proclamation assisted in making a "mopping up" period unnecessary. Temporary arrangements made with Admiral Darlan apply, without exception, to the current local situation only.

I have requested the liberation of all persons in northern Africa who had been imprisoned because they opposed the efforts of the Nazis to dominate the world, and I have asked for the abrogation of all laws and decrees inspired by the Nazi Governments or Nazi ideologists. Reports indicate that the French of North Africa are subordinating all political questions to the formation of a common front against the common enemy.[2]

2 Churchill subsequently requested and received permission to read this telegram at a secret session of Parliament.

Doc. 184
ROOSEVELT TO CHURCHILL

No. 218   November 19, 1942

Replying to your message No. 196 of November 18[1] I am in complete agreement that every effort should be made to send another convoy to Russia at the earliest possible date.

1 Not printed. Churchill requested twelve U.S. destroyers for use in supporting a convoy to northern Russia.

It is noted that you can make available escort vessels for the close escort and some for the covering and striking forces but you feel that twelve additional destroyers are necessary for adequate protection.

You are familiar with the necessity of our radical reduction of escort forces even to retaining in the Atlantic destroyers urgently required in the Pacific in order to provide escort vessels for Torch.[2]

The movement of essential follow-up convoys from America to Africa is contingent upon availability of escort vessels and the Torch operation must be adequately supported.

Destroyer losses and damage to destroyers in recent naval operations in the Pacific have been so serious as to necessitate an immediate return of the destroyers borrowed from the Pacific for Torch.

This will leave in the Atlantic only minimum requirements for follow-up convoys to Africa and makes it impossible for us to provide the destroyers for the Russian convoy suggested in your message number 196. I wish I could send you a more favorable answer.

2 Code name for the Allied landing in North Africa.

Doc. 185
ROOSEVELT TO CHURCHILL

No. 219   November 19, 1942

I told the press yesterday in confidence an old orthodox church proverb used in the Balkans that appears applicable to our present Darlan-de Gaulle problem. QUOTE. My children, it is permitted you in time of grave danger to walk with the devil until you have crossed the bridge. UNQUOTE.[1]

In regard to North Africa and possibly additional future areas, I think you and I might give some consideration to the idea of appointing one Britisher and one American to whom would be given authority not to administer civil functions but to hold a veto power over French civil administrators, and to direct them in rare instances to follow out certain policies. For example, I sent word to Eisenhower that all political prisoners in North and West Africa must be released. If Darlan fails to carry out this directive, Eisenhower must at once exercise his authority as Supreme Commander and take independent action in the matter.

1 A few weeks later Secretary of War Henry L. Stimson provided Roosevelt with a new analogy for the Darlan situation. In the Bible story Joshua sent spies to Jericho, where they made a pact with the harlot Rahab which Joshua ratified. Roosevelt laughed with delight at the story. See Henry L. Stimson and McGeorge Bundy, *On Active Service in Peace and War* (New York, 1948), p. 545.

Doc. 186
CHURCHILL TO ROOSEVELT

No. 202   November 20, 1942

One of the most potent weapons for hunting the U-boat and protecting our convoys is the long-range aircraft fitted with ASV equipment.[1]

The German U-boats have recently been fitted with a device enabling them to listen to our one and one-half metre ASV equipment and thus dive to safety before our aircraft can appear on the scene. As the result our day patrols in the bay have become largely ineffective in bad weather and our night patrols, with searchlight aircraft, have been rendered almost entirely useless. Sightings of U-boats have accordingly declined very sharply from 120 in September to 57 in October. No improvement can be expected until aircraft fitted with a type of ASV to which they cannot at present listen called "Centimetre ASV" become available.

One of the main objects of patrolling the bay is to attack U-boats in transit to and from the American Atlantic seaboard. This region is doubly urgent now so many American Torch convoys pass in the vicinity.

We can deal with the inner zone of the Bay of Biscay by modifying and diverting to our Wellingtons[2] a form of Centimetre ASV which has been developed as a target location device for our heavy bombers.

A more difficult situation arises in the outer zone of the bay where aircraft of longer range fitted with Centimetre ASV are essential.

The very heavy sinkings in mid-Atlantic have forced us to convert our own Liberators[3] for work in this area. This leaves us with no

[1] See above, Doc. 3, note 3. Air to Surface Vessel radar developed by the Royal Navy which enabled planes to detect surface vessels at sea. The 1½ meter type in use at this time was replaced by a new 10 centimeter ASV in March 1943.

[2] Wellingtons were two-engine, low-wing bombers built by Vickers Armstrong Ltd. before and during World War II. They were becoming obsolete for use in the bombardment of Germany and were diverted to the Coastal Command's work of hunting U-boats.

[3] Liberator was the British name for the American B-24 four-engine bomber. It had a distinctive twin-tail construction and a range of about 2,850 miles. For the role of aircraft in the battle against the U-boats, see Wesley Frank Craven and James Lea Cate, eds., *The Army Air Forces in World War II*, 2 (Chicago, 1949) : 392–411; Sir Charles Webster and Noble Frankland, *The Strategic Air Offensive Against Germany 1939–1945*, vol. 2, pt. 4 (London, 1961) , pp. 97–98, 286–287; S. W. Roskill, *The War at Sea 1939–1945*, 2 (London, 1956) : 77–90, 351–353, and 3 (London,

aircraft with adequate range for the outer zone of the bay, unless we make a further diversion from the small force of long-range bombers responsible for the air offensive against Germany. Even if this diversion were made, a considerable time would necessarily elapse before the essential equipment could be modified and installed.

I am most reluctant to reduce the weight of bombs we are able to drop on Germany as I believe it is of great importance that this offensive should be maintained and developed to the utmost of our ability throughout the winter months. I would, therefore, ask you, Mr. President, to consider the immediate allocation of some 30 Liberators with Centimetre ASV equipment from the supplies which I understand are now available in the United States. These aircraft would be put to work immediately, in an area where they would make a direct contribution to the American war effort.

1960): 15–34, 37–55; Samuel Eliot Morison, *The Battle of the Atlantic* (Boston, 1950), pp. 139–142, 152–154, 237–251, and *The Atlantic Battle Won* (Boston, 1956), pp. 88–107 in *History of United States Naval Operations in World War II;* and Sir John Slessor, *The Central Blue* (London, 1956), pp. 464–538. A recent critical study is Anthony Verrier, *The Bomber Offensive* (New York, 1969), pp. 116–120.

Doc. 187
CHURCHILL TO ROOSEVELT

No. 211   November 24, 1942

We have had a letter from General Hartle[1] stating that under directive from the United States War Department "any construction in excess of the requirements for a force of 427,000 must be accomplished entirely by your own labour and with your own materials and that lend-lease materials cannot be furnished in these instances." This has caused us very great concern, not so much from the standpoint of lend-lease but on grounds of grand strategy. We have been preparing under Bolero[2] for 1,100,000 men, and this is the first intimation we have had that this target is to be abandoned. We had no knowledge that you had decided to abandon forever Roundup,[3] and all our preparations were proceeding on a broad front under Bolero.

[1] Major General Russell P. Hartle, deputy commander of U.S. forces in the European theater of operations.

[2] Code name for the cross-channel invasion buildup.

[3] Code name for an earlier cross-channel plan calling for the full invasion of France in 1943.

It seems to me that it would be a most grievous decision to abandon Roundup. Torch is no substitute for Roundup and only engages 13 divisions as against the 48 contemplated for Roundup. All my talks with Stalin in Averell's[4] presence were on the basis of a postponed Roundup. But never was it suggested that we should attempt no second front in Europe in 1943 or even 1944.

Surely, Mister President, this matter requires most profound consideration. I was deeply impressed with all General Marshall's[5] arguments that only by Roundup could the main forces be thrown into France and the Low Countries and only in this area could the main strength of the British metropolitan and United States overseas air forces be brought into action. One of the arguments we used against Sledgehammer[6] was that it would eat up in 1942 the seed corn needed for the much larger Roundup in 1943. No doubt we have all been sanguine of our shipping resources, but that is a matter which time can correct. Only by the building up of a Roundup force here as rapidly and regularly as other urgent demands on shipping allow can we have the means of coming to grips with the main strength of the enemy and liberating the European nations. It may well be that, try as we will, our strength will not reach the necessary levels in 1943. But if so it becomes all the more important to make sure we do not miss 1944.

Even in 1943 a chance may come. Should Stalin's offensive reach Rostov on the Don, which is his aim, a first-class disaster may overtake the German southern armies. Our Mediterranean operations following on Torch may drive Italy out of the war. Widespread demoralisation may set in among the Germans, and we must be ready to profit by any opportunity which offers.

I do beg of you, Mister President, to let me know what has happened. At present we are completely puzzled by this information and the manner in which it has reached us. It seems to me absolutely necessary either that General Marshall and Admiral King[7] with Harry[8] should come over here or that I should come with my people to you.

4 W. Averell Harriman, then the American lend-lease expediter in London.

5 General George C. Marshall, U.S. Army Chief of Staff. For Marshall's views on the impact of Torch on Roundup, see Forrest C. Pogue, *George C. Marshall: Ordeal and Hope 1939–1943* (New York, 1966), pp. 399–400.

6 Code name for an emergency plan to invade the Continent in 1942 if required by developments on the Russian front.

7 Admiral Ernest J. King, U.S. Chief of Naval Operations.

8 Harry L. Hopkins, special assistant to the President.

Doc. 188
ROOSEVELT TO CHURCHILL

No. 222   November 25, 1942

In reply to your 211.[1] We of course have no intention of abandoning Roundup. No one can possibly know now whether or not we may have the opportunity to strike across the channel in 1943 and if the opportunity comes we must obviously grasp it. However the determination as to the size of the force which we should have in Bolero in 1943 is a matter which should require our joint strategic considerations. It is my present thought that we should build up as rapidly as present active operations permit a growing striking force in the U.K. to be used quickly in event of German collapse or a very large force later if Germany remains intact and assumes a defensive position.

The conclusions of the Combined Chiefs of Staff at the meeting last summer in London indicated that the mounting of Torch necessarily postponed the assembling of the required forces in the United Kingdom. In view of our requirements for the initiation and maintenance of Torch our studies indicated that we could not send forces and matériel to the United Kingdom at this time in excess of that stated by General Hartle. Until we have provided adequately against the possible reactions from Spanish Morocco, and are clear as to the situation in Tunisia, North Africa must naturally take precedence. We are far more heavily engaged in the southwest Pacific than I anticipated a few months ago.[2] Nevertheless, we shall continue with Bolero as rapidly as our shipping and other resources permit. I believe that as soon as we have knocked the Germans out of Tunisia, and have secured the danger against any real threat from Spain, that we should proceed with a military strategical conference between Great Britain, Russia, and the United States. I am hoping that our military position in Africa will be such that a conference might be held in a month or six weeks. Our own Combined Chiefs of Staff will, I believe, have a recommendation for us within a few days as to what the next steps should be, but I feel very strongly that we have got to sit down at the

---

[1] See above, Doc. 187.

[2] The naval battle of Guadalcanal took place during the night of November 12–13. The Japanese force was turned back but the United States sustained heavy losses, with two cruisers and four destroyers sunk. Another night battle took place on November 14–15 in which the Japanese were again turned back and their troops on the island virtually isolated. In this fight the United States lost three destroyers, and two other warships were damaged.

table with the Russians. My notion would be a conference in Cairo or Moscow: that each of us would be represented by a small group meeting very secretly: that the conclusions of the conference would of course be approved by the three of us. I would probably send Marshall to head up our group but I presume that all services should be represented. I think it would be wise to keep the numbers down to three from each of us.

I have given Oliver[3] some private messages to you which I do not wish to put on the cables and he will be returning I believe next Monday. I hope that all of his problems will have been substantially resolved.

Will you let me know as soon as you can what you think of my proposal?[4]

3 Oliver Lyttelton, British Minister of Production, visited the United States in November in an effort to adjust British and American production schedules for the coming year. For the most private of the messages carried back by Lyttelton, see below, Doc. 189.

4 Churchill replied on November 25 that he had learned there was to be no change in the general plan of Roundup or Bolero, and that General Hartle's letter referred "only to the rate at which accommodation should be provided for the buildup. I am very glad this misunderstanding has been cleared away and that we are as ever in closest agreement."

Doc. 189
ROOSEVELT TO CHURCHILL

November 30, 1942

I presume that we shall never satisfy ourselves as to the relative need of merchant ships versus escort vessels. In this case I believe we should try to have our cake and eat it too.

At any rate we are moving aggressively here to increase both of these programs and have given them the highest priority for matériel and machine tools.[1]

As far as merchant shipping is concerned, we have, after reexamination of our steel plate problem and other facilities, determined to increase it to 18,800,000 dead-weight tons in 1943. I intend to raise this to 20 million tons if after reexamination by our people it should prove possible.

Of one thing I think you can be sure, that we will build in this country a minimum of 18,800,000 tons of merchant shipping of all

1 Churchill had raised these issues and the others discussed in this message in a letter dated October 31, which Lyttelton had carried to Washington. See above, Doc. 180.

kinds. Your offices here will keep you informed of the types of ships that are being built and, naturally, I would welcome your judgment in regard to this, because it is very important that we have a proper balance between tankers, cargo vessels, and transports.

I agree that this is the time for me to reply to you concerning the very urgent requirements of the British shipping program in 1943.

I have had the 27 million ton figure of imports to the British Isles examined rather hurriedly here by our own people and they are satisfied that this figure is substantially correct.

Our joint war effort requires that this pipeline of matériel and food to Britain be maintained, that the moving of this tonnage at reasonably even levels is a matter of primary importance. I recognize it as such.

I am well aware of the concern with which your Government faces the serious net losses in tonnage to your merchant fleet. It is a net loss which persists and I think we must face the fact that it may well continue through all of next year. I, therefore, want to give you the assurance that from our expanding fleet you may depend on the tonnage necessary to meet your import program.

Accordingly, I am instructing our Shipping Administration to allocate through the machinery of the Combined Shipping Adjustment Board enough dry cargo tonnage out of the surplus shipbuilding to meet your imports, the supply and maintenance of your armed forces, and other services essential to maintaining the war effort of the British Commonwealth, to the extent that they cannot be transported by the fleet under British control.

I have been given to understand by our combined shipping people that an average of nearly 300,000 tons each month of carrying capacity will have to be used to supplement the tonnage already engaged on behalf of the British war effort. Because of the commitments already made, the allocation of ships during the next three months must of necessity be less than the average for the whole period.

We may hope for a substantial reduction in this if we can make our way through the Mediterranean. Furthermore, I think that you and I should insist that every possible economy is exercised by our shipping and military authorities.

You will, I am sure, agree that emergencies may develop which may require me to divert for our own military purposes tonnage which it is now contemplated will be utilized for imports to Great Britain. There will, no doubt, be other cases in which we shall wish jointly to confer relative to vital military uses of merchant tonnage.

I want you to know that any important diversions of tonnage will be made only with my personal approval, because I am fully cognizant of the fact that your Government may feel that decisions might be made to divert tonnage in contravention of the policy which I am laying down in this letter.

The allocation of tonnage month by month must be worked out by the Combined Shipping Adjustment Board. And hence I confine myself to the above statement of policy. I wish to give you the definite assurance, subject to the qualifications I have indicated, that your requirements will be met.

We have increased our escort program recently by 70 for 1943, so that we should turn out 336 escort vessels during the next calendar year. I am asking Admiral King to confer with your representative here and make arrangements about the distribution of these ships.

The problem of getting our troops to England is a serious one. I recognize that there must be a minimum joint force there, well equipped and prepared to meet any eventuality.

While Roundup seems more and more difficult, I do not think it should be taken off the boards by any means. We never can tell when the opportunity may come for us to strike across the channel and if that opportunity comes we must be ready to take it. Obviously, however, the success of our joint enterprise in North Africa requires us to review the movement of our troops during the next few months. We need to come to an early decision as to what our next steps are going to be and upon that decision must rest the determination of the number of American divisions that should be in England. We have this whole matter very much in mind here and our Chiefs of Staff have it under constant consideration.

As you know, we have recently agreed upon a program of 82,000 combat planes. There have been misgivings in some quarters about the size of this program. I have none. We simply must get a complete domination of the air next year, even though other important things give way.

One thing is sure, that the aircraft must be brought to bear on the enemy at the earliest possible moment and, if there are competent British and Russian crews to fight these planes and you can get at the enemy quicker and just as effectively as we can, then I have no hesitancy in saying that you and the Russians should have the planes you need.

We must give consideration to the shipping difficulties that are met when we send our U.S. air forces great distances. We have heavy commitments in the southwest Pacific. We are rapidly assuming similar commitments in North Africa, and the bombing of Germany and Italy, whether from England or Russia, must be an unrelenting and constant business.

There have been many conferences taking place here between our respective representatives regarding the distribution of aircraft. I am in accord with the agreement that has been reached. Oliver will tell you of this. A detailed memorandum of the agreement will follow in a few days. Oliver has impressed upon me the necessity of making an early decision regarding the distribution of our combined aircraft production. I think the decisions that we have come to regarding aircraft are of the highest importance.

I am told that there is a substantial meeting of minds between your representatives and ours relative to the medium tank. I must confess that I think we are both underrating the need for these medium tanks. It is quite possible that the Russians may again press for large increases in medium tanks and I have a feeling that we are cutting our pattern pretty thin. I am asking General Marshall to explore this once more. I should think it would be no great strain on our production to get a few more thousand medium tanks in 1943.

I understand that some of your ground force requirements have not yet been discussed with my officers. These are being considered. Every effort will be made to include your essential requirements in our Army supply program and I have asked to have a report of these further discussions submitted to me as early as possible.

I also recognize that your own production for Navy, Army, and Air, and for the minimum needs of the civilian population, requires an assured flow of materials, machine tools, components, and complementary items from America. These supplies, unless unforeseen circumstances intervene, will be maintained.

In conclusion, I want you to feel that this letter, together with the agreements that Oliver is taking home with him, gives you the assurances that you need in planning your own production, and that you may regard them as a firm base upon which to make the allocations of your remaining reserves of manpower.

Doc. 190
ROOSEVELT TO CHURCHILL

No. 224   December 2, 1942

I have been giving a good deal of thought to our proposed joint conference with the Russians and I agree with you that the only satisfactory way of coming to the vital strategic conclusions the military situation requires, is for you and me to meet personally with Stalin. My thought would be that each of us would be accompanied by a very small staff made up of our top Army, Air, and Navy Chiefs of Staff. I should bring Harry and Averell but no State Department representative although I believe we should arrive at tentative procedures to be adopted in event of a German collapse. I should like to see the conference held about January fifteenth or soon thereafter. Tunis and Bizerte should have been cleared up and Rommel's[1] army liquidated before the conference. As to the place. Iceland or Alaska are impossible for me at this time of year and I believe equally so for Stalin. I should prefer a secure place south of Algiers or in or near Khartoum. I don't like mosquitoes. I think the conference should be very secret and that the press should be excluded. I would question the advisability of Marshall and the others going to England prior to the conference because I do not want to give Stalin the impression that we are settling everything between ourselves before we meet him.

I think that you and I understand each other so well that prior conferences between us are unnecessary and when the time comes we can work things out from day to day. Our military people will also be in close cooperation at all times from now on.

I think that this conference may well result in knocking out Germany sooner than we anticipated. As you know Stalin has already agreed to a purely military conference to be held in Moscow and I have today sent him a message urging him to meet you and me. I believe he will accept.[2]

I prefer a comfortable oasis to the raft at Tilsit.[3]

[1] Field Marshal Erwin Rommel, commander of the German Afrika Korps.

[2] Stalin replied to Churchill and Roosevelt on December 7 that the winter campaign operations, including those in the Stalingrad area, made it impossible for him to leave the Soviet Union. See below, Doc. 197.

[3] Napoleon I and Alexander I of Russia met in 1807 on a barge on the Niemen River in East Prussia for discussions preliminary to the signing of the Treaty of Tilsit. For a detailed account of the preliminaries of the Casablanca meeting see U.S. Department of State, *The Conferences at Washington 1941–1942 and Casablanca 1943* (Washington, 1968), pp. 488–520.

Doc. 191
ROOSEVELT TO CHURCHILL

December 7, 1942

I deeply appreciate your message.[1] Much has happened since the treacherous attack in the Pacific one year ago today. For months, most

[1] Not printed. In a letter of December 7 Churchill recalled that both the British and the Americans had been attacked by Japan a year ago. He added that the people of the British Commonwealth looked forward to the day when their strength could be added to that of the Dutch and Chinese for the final destruction of Japan.

of the news was bad despite heroic resistance of Chinese, Dutch, British Commonwealth, and American forces. The injuries that all of us have suffered at the hands of Japan are indeed grievous. A partial retribution in kind has been meted out to the Japanese forces during the last seven months. This is only the beginning. We will continue to strike them, with ever increasing force. I welcome your statement and join with you in the resolution that Japan's aggressive power must be utterly destroyed. In no other way can we be certain that their infamous aggression will not be repeated.[2]

[2] Attached to this message, which was drafted in the State Department, was a White House memorandum stating that Mr. George Willmot Renchard in the office of the Secretary of State had called to say that the State, War, and Navy Departments felt that it was unwise to give the Churchill-Roosevelt messages to the press on the grounds that "the less emphasis put on this anniversary the better."

Doc. 192
ROOSEVELT TO CHURCHILL

No. 231   December 8, 1942

The following is a close paraphrase of the message I sent to Stalin today:

"It was with deep disappointment that I learned that you felt that you could not get away for a meeting with me in January. Many matters of great import should be discussed between us. They appertain not only to vital strategic decisions, but likewise to matters we should discuss in a tentative way respecting emergency policies which we should be prepared with, if and when conditions in Germany permit.

"Included also would be other matters relating to future policies in North Africa and the Far East, which matters cannot be discussed by our military people alone.

"The necessity for your presence near the fighting front, and your strenuous situation which exists now and in the immediate future, is fully realized by me.

"Therefore I wish to offer a suggestion that a tentative date be set for a meeting in North Africa about the first of March."[1]

[1] Roosevelt cabled Churchill that same day: "For the sake of the record, I am sending another telegram which follows in my next number, as I think we should continue to make every effort for the African meeting and put the responsibility for declining up to our friend."

Doc. 193
CHURCHILL TO ROOSEVELT

No. 227   December 9, 1942

I have been disturbed by reports received during the last few days from North Africa about conditions in French Morocco and Algeria. These reports, which come from independent and reliable sources, all paint the same picture of the results which follow from our inability in existing circumstances to exercise a proper control over the local French authorities in internal administrative matters. You are, I am sure, fully aware of this state of affairs, but I think it my duty to let you know the position as it appears in the light of our own reports.

These reports show that the SOL[1] and kindred Fascist organisations continue their activities and victimise our former French sympathisers some of whom have not yet been released from prison. The first reaction of these organisations to the Allied landing was rightly one of fear but it seems that they have now taken courage to regroup themselves and continue their activities. Well-known German sympathisers who had been ousted have been reinstated. Not only have our enemies been thus encouraged but our friends have been correspondingly confused and cast down. There have been cases of French soldiers being punished for desertion because they tried to support the Allied forces during the landing.

There is an almost complete absence of control on the Franco-Spanish frontier. The result of this is that undesirables of all sorts, including Axis agents, cross the frontier in both directions, carrying information to the enemy and preparing trouble for us throughout North Africa. Unless proper control is instituted soon our military operations may be endangered and we may witness sabotage in North Africa on a large scale and other incidents of a serious nature which may culminate in risings in various parts of North Africa. There is no Allied control of postal and telegraph censorship and therefore nothing to stop enemy agents from writing and telegraphing information to Europe. One informant for example states that certain Germanophile Spanish consuls in the French zone send full reports about the military situation by telephone and telegraph to the Spanish High Commissioner at Tetuán.

Veiled anti-Allied propaganda continues in the press and on the radio and positive enemy propaganda increases daily.

1 The Service d'Ordre Légionnaire, a Vichy veterans' organization.

In short, elements hostile to the United Nations are being consolidated within the administration and conditions are being created which will make North Africa a favourable resort for Axis troublemakers. If we were to suffer serious setbacks in Tunisia the Axis may be relied upon to exploit the situation to the full and there is no knowing what difficulties we may then encounter even at the hand of those Frenchmen who now appear to be cooperating with us.

It occurs to me that there is one step which we might usefully take and that is to see that such good friends of ours as Generals Bethouard[2] and Mast[3] are appointed to high military commands in Morocco. Mast is at present serving as Giraud's liaison officer at Allied headquarters while Bethouard has been sent to Gibraltar to perform nonexistent liaison duties. It is a pity that men like these, who took such grave risks on our behalf, should not be in active employment. Bethouard, who commanded a division at Casablanca, would be particularly useful in Morocco where a man of his stamp seems to be badly needed.

All of this reinforces the need for immediate political and administrative help for Eisenhower. As you know we are very ready to give any assistance in our power.

[2] Brigadier General Marie Émile Bethouard was a French divisional commander at Casablanca who was in sympathy with the Allies. A few hours before the American landings he and a few like-minded officers took over the headquarters in Rabat but failed to stop the French opposition to the Allied invasion.

[3] Brigadier General Charles Mast, General Giraud's representative in Algiers, collaborated with the Allies in the North African landings.

Doc. 194
ROOSEVELT TO CHURCHILL

December 11, 1942

I have not had an answer to my second invitation[1] to our Uncle Joe[2] but, on the assumption that he will again decline, I think that in spite of it you and I should get together, as there are things which can be definitely determined only by you and me in conference with our staff people. I am sure that both of us want to avoid the delays which attended the determination on Torch last July.

On the grounds of vile climate and icing on the wings, Iceland must be definitely out for both of us.

[1] See above, Doc. 192.
[2] The reference is to Stalin (U.J.) .

England must be out for me for political reasons.

There will be a commotion in this country if it is discovered that I have flown across any old seas. Therefore, Bermuda would be just as much out for me as Africa. However, on condition that I can get away in absolute secrecy and have my trip kept secret until I am back, I have just about made up my mind to go along with the African idea—on the theory that public opinion here will gasp but be satisfied when they hear about it after it is over.

One mitigating circumstance would be the knowledge that I had seen our military leaders in North and West Africa, and that is why I think it would be best if we could meet somewhere in that neighborhood instead of Khartoum. Incidentally, I could actually see some of our troops.

Incidentally also, it would do me personally an enormous amount of good to get out of the political atmosphere of Washington for a couple of weeks.

My thought is, therefore, that if the time suits your plans we could meet back of Algiers or back of Casablanca about January fifteenth. That would mean that I would leave about January eleventh, and pray for good weather. My route would be either from here to Trinidad and thence to Dakar and thence north—or from here to Natal, Brazil, and cross to Liberia or Freetown and north from there.

In view of Stalin's absence, I think you and I need no foreign affairs people with us—for our work will be essentially military. Perhaps your three top men and my three top men could meet at the same place four or five days in advance of our arrival and have plans in fairly good tentative shape by the time we get there. I asked General Smith,[3] who left here four or five days ago, to check up confidentially on some possible tourist oasis as far from any city or large population as possible. One of the dictionaries says "an oasis is never wholly dry." Good old dictionary!

Here is an alternate plan in case Uncle Joe says he will meet us about March first:

I would suggest that your staff people and mine should meet with the Russian staff people somewhere in Africa, or even as far as Baghdad, and come to certain recommendations which would at least get the preliminaries of new moves started. The three of us could, when we meet, close up the loose ends and also take up some of the postwar matters.

3 Major General Walter Bedell Smith, Eisenhower's Chief of Staff.

Doc. 195
ROOSEVELT TO CHURCHILL

No. 235   December 16, 1942

Referring to your 273 of December 11,[1] I will appoint Mr. Murphy[2] personal representative of the President on General Eisenhower's staff with the rank of minister.

Harold Macmillan[3] will be entirely acceptable in the same status if approved by Eisenhower.

[1] Not printed. The number is an error in transmission for a telegram that would have been numbered between 230 and 234; the "273" was subsequently crossed out on the White House copy.

[2] Robert D. Murphy was U.S. consul general at Algiers. In view of the importance of his coming assignment, the Combined Chiefs of Staff recommended that he be given a higher rank in the foreign service. The President therefore appointed him as his personal representative to French North Africa with the rank of minister. For the background of his appointment, see his *Diplomat Among Warriors*, chaps. 5–12, and p. 164.

[3] Harold Macmillan was a member of the House of Commons. In the Churchill government he served as parliamentary secretary to the Minister of Supply and in the same capacity in the Colonial Office before accepting the assignment to Eisenhower's headquarters in North Africa. For Roosevelt's initial ideas on the purpose of these appointments, see above, Doc. 185.

Doc. 196
CHURCHILL TO ROOSEVELT

No. 234   December 17, 1942

With reference to my immediately preceding telegram,[1] the following are the measures proposed for arresting the decline of the U.K. oil stocks.

(A) To institute direct tanker convoys every twenty days between the Dutch West Indies and the United Kingdom, by which we should hope to improve our imports by one hundred thousand tons a month.
(B) To find the escorts for these convoys by a further opening of the cycle of the transatlantic convoys from eight to ten days, which will enable four groups of escort vessels to be released.

By the opening of the transatlantic cycle to ten days, it will be possible to operate these convoys with eight groups of escorts by ac-

[1] Not printed.

cepting a shorter period of layover between voyages and it is proposed that the eight British-manned groups should be employed on this duty. The four groups released would therefore consist of the American group and three Canadian-manned groups which it is proposed should be temporarily transferred to the escort of Torch buildup convoys. This would enable four long-endurance groups to be released which would provide three groups of increased strength for the D.W.I.-to-U.K. tanker convoys. It is necessary to have groups of increased strength for these convoys as we hope to include an escort aircraft carrier in the escort of these convoys.

The effect on our nontanker import programme of opening the transatlantic cycle is serious in view of the acute shortage of shipping in the early part of next year. It is estimated it will result in a loss of thirty thousand tons a month using the shipping we have at present available. It is hoped however when more escorts become available in the summer of 1943 that it will be possible to restore the cycle to eight days.

The effect of the above measures on the U.K. oil situation combined with the loading of tankers from the U.S. Navy pool at New York will, it is estimated, do little more than arrest the decline of our stocks and it is therefore necessary to consider measures to build up our stock position. . . .

The only ways that can be suggested of effecting any substantial improvement in our stock position are: (A) By direct shipment of oil from the Gulf or Dutch West Indies to the U.K. using fast, independently sailed U.S. tankers. This is the quickest way of building up the stocks in this country. (B) Increasing the supplies of oil in the New York Navy pool for on-carriage to the U.K., thus enabling more tankers of convoy speed to be employed on the shortest voyage from New York to the United Kingdom. (C) To meet the oil requirements, both civil and military, of the Torch area by direct shipment from the United States or Dutch West Indies, preferably by fast United States tankers. (D) The tankers referred to in (C) above to be allowed to proceed to discharge ports in the Mediterranean.

Doc. 197
ROOSEVELT TO CHURCHILL

No. 238   December 17, 1942

I have received the following from Stalin:

QUOTE. I too must express my deep regret that it is impossible for me to leave the Soviet Union either in the near future or even at the beginning of March. Front business absolutely prevents it, demanding my constant presence near our troops.

So far I do not know what exactly are the problems which you, Mr. President, and Mr. Churchill intended to discuss at our joint conference. I wonder whether it would not be possible to discuss these problems by way of correspondence between us, as long as there is no chance of arranging our meeting? I admit that there will be no disagreement between us.

Allow me also to express my confidence that the time is not being lost and that the promises about the opening of a second front in Europe given by you, Mr. President, and by Mr. Churchill in regard of 1942, and in any case in regard of the spring of 1943, will be fulfilled, and that a second front in Europe will be actually opened by the joint forces of Great Britain and the United States of America in the spring of the next year.

In view of all sorts of rumors about the attitude of the Union of Soviet Socialist Republics toward the use made of Darlan and of other men like him, it may not be unnecessary for me to tell you that, in my opinion, as well as in that of my colleagues, Eisenhower's policy with regard to Darlan, Boisson,[1] Giraud, and others is perfectly correct. I think it a great achievement that you succeeded in bringing Darlan and others into the waterway of the Allies fighting Hitler. Some time ago I made this known also to Mr. Churchill. UNQUOTE.[2]

When you receive the letter[3] I sent you by courier please send me your answer yes or no.

[1] Pierre Boisson, Vichy governor general of French West Africa.
[2] Stalin's message is published in Ministry of Foreign Affairs of the U.S.S.R., *Correspondence Between the Chairman of the Council of Ministers of the U.S.S.R. and the Presidents of the U.S.A. and the Prime Ministers of Great Britain During the Great Patriotic War of 1941–1945* (New York, 1958), vol. 2, no. 58. Henceforth cited as *Stalin's Correspondence*.
[3] Not printed.

Doc. 198
CHURCHILL TO ROOSEVELT

No. 235

December 18, 1942

This bears out what I have said and shows how absolutely necessary it is for us to have a plan which we can put to him fairly and squarely.[1]

[1] See Stalin's message to Roosevelt passed along to Churchill on Dec. 17, Doc. 197.

It is bound to be a joint plan, and I can do nothing until I hear from you.[2]

2 Roosevelt had asked Churchill on December 8 for his opinion on having military officials from the United Kingdom, the Soviet Union, and the United States meet in Algiers, Khartoum, or some other suitable location and discuss the major moves for the coming summer. Their recommendations would be taken up in the three capitals before final approval. Churchill answered on December 12 that conversations among military officials without parallel meetings by the heads of state would accomplish little. The only question the Russians were likely to ask was whether there would be a second front in 1943, and no answer could be given until Roosevelt and Churchill and their staffs met and talked things over. For Roosevelt's reply, see below, Doc. 200. See *Conferences at Washington and Casablanca*, pp. 498–500.

Doc. 199
ROOSEVELT TO CHURCHILL

No. 239   December 18, 1942

Your 233[1] and 234.[2] I am most anxious that every practicable measure may be taken to assure adequate petroleum supply to United Kingdom. The problem continues to have the constant attention of authorities here. Assuming average two notional cargoes[3] per day from New York pool beginning January 1, 1943, plus two additional notional cargoes per day from Caribbean and U.S. Gulf, shipments would amount to approximately 1,250,000 tons per month or 15,000,000 tons per year, thus leveling off if not increasing your inventories in view of possibility of your offtakes being somewhat reduced if movements direct to Torch area are later found practicable. This development seems reasonably assured under present plans without giving effect to convoy and escort changes suggested in your 234[4]. Navy Department studying your proposal alterations, upon which reply will be made promptly, but time is required to consider possible effect upon all other convoy and escort responsibilities. Any immediate interruption or diversion of our limited carrying and escorting facilities at this time would entail new procedures with consequent loss of efficiency.

As of December 3, U.K. reported stock positions very substantially better by comparison than those of other combatant areas. For example, no Pacific base, including Australia, had over ten weeks' supply

1 Not printed.
2 See above, Doc. 196.
3 Theoretical, not actual, cargoes.
4 See above, Doc. 196.

of 100 octane gasoline against at least 27 weeks' supply U.K. Similarly these bases did not have over 12 weeks' supply fuel oil, and this in Nouméa only, as against 21 weeks' supply in U.K. Atlantic bases including West Indies, Greenland, Newfoundland had average of 100 octane gasoline and fuel oil of eight and four weeks' supply respectively compared to above U.K. figures. While everything possible will be done to prevent further shrinkage of U.K. inventories and in fact build these stocks to safer levels, I am confident you agree that the importance of inventories in other areas must be considered and facilities so distributed as to prevent actual shortage in any important area.

Supply petroleum products to North Africa for civil administration also dependent upon availability [of] tankers and escorts. Present arrangements for regular convoys [in] that area do not make any provision for such tankers. When and if French tankers and French escort vessels are made available, a more accurate estimate as to petroleum relief for North Africa will be possible.

The two special convoys, one slow and one fast, scheduled to depart from Netherlands West Indies early January should relieve the situation to the extent of at least one million barrels, the resulting deliveries being of course applied against total requirements Allied services Torch area.

DOC. 200
ROOSEVELT TO CHURCHILL

No. 242   December 21, 1942

Following is the substance of letter which courier has for you:[1]
QUOTE. In spite of Stalin's inability to meet with us I think we should plan a meeting at once with our respective military staffs. I should like to meet in Africa about January fifteenth. There is I believe a satisfactory and safe place just north of Casablanca. It might be wise for some of our military men to precede us by a few days to clear the ground. I should think if we could have four or five days together we could clear up all of our business.

Will you let me know what you think of this? UNQUOTE.[2]

[1] For the text of Roosevelt's letter, see *Conferences at Washington and Casablanca*, p. 498.

[2] Churchill replied on December 21: "Yes, certainly; the sooner the better. I am greatly relieved. It is the only thing to do. All arrangements here will be made on the basis that it is a staff meeting only. Suggested code name Symbol." *Conferences at Washington and Casablanca*, p. 501.

Doc. 201
ROOSEVELT TO CHURCHILL

No. 243

December 22, 1942

I have agreed to send certain relief into Norway to be furnished by the American Red Cross to the Swedish Red Cross and by that organization used in Norway for the feeding and clothing of children.[1] The food would be put in their mouths in the centers of populations where it is most needed and would not be obtainable by the enemy.

However a trial would be made in one locality to determine its practicability and safety before any further food is sent in.

Apparently your Government does not agree to this suggestion. I hope that either this plan or an equally good one can be put through as the internal situation in Norway is heartrending. A few extra calories for the children might save a lot of lives.[2]

[1] Former President Herbert Hoover had long been interested in plans to feed children in occupied areas, and these proposals had been studied in the State Department. Secretary of State Cordell Hull was opposed to them because of the shortage of shipping and the American commitments to Great Britain. At Hull's request, the British agreed that neither party would undertake any new relief effort without the consent of the other. Subsequently Roosevelt became interested in the plight of Norwegian children and sent a memorandum to Undersecretary of State Sumner Welles asking about sending food packages and clothing to Norway. Welles replied on December 12, 1942, that the American Red Cross was prepared to furnish the Swedish Red Cross with bulk shipments of food which would be distributed to children at schools and feeding centers in Norway; in this way no food would fall into the hands of the Germans. Children's clothing could also be furnished. When asked for their consent to these plans, the British declined. Later, however, they reported having conversations with the Norwegian government-in-exile in London to the effect that the Norwegians would be satisfied with a clandestine relief operation. Welles therefore suggested that the President take the matter up directly with Churchill.

[2] For Churchill's reply, see below, Doc. 207.

Doc. 202
CHURCHILL TO ROOSEVELT

No. 239   December 23, 1942

Your No. two four one.[1] The differences between our systems of
government make it impossible to achieve exact similarity. For instance, by minister I meant political minister and you think diplomatic minister. Again Murphy is the personal representative of you as
head of the state. I could not make any similar appointment of a
diplomatic character. The best I can do is to send Macmillan out as
"His Majesty's Government's political representative at General
Eisenhower's headquarters," reporting to me direct, and enjoying
exact equality of rank with Murphy. Will this suit you?

In your No. 219 of November 20[2] you seemed to contemplate the
two political representatives being capable of relieving Eisenhower of
large part of his political burdens and that real power should be vested
in them jointly of course to the ultimate military control of the Commander in Chief. I think this is most urgently necessary as from all I
hear the tangles of local French politics and their world implications
force themselves into the first place in the military mind and might
well become detrimental to operations.[3]

[1] Not printed. On December 19 Roosevelt cabled that he understood Macmillan
was to have the same status as Murphy—that is, as a political member on Eisenhower's staff—and that he hoped Churchill would make the promotion. For the background of Macmillan's appointment as minister resident at Allied Headquarters in
Northwest Africa, see his *The Blast of War, 1939–1945* (London, 1967), pp. 215ff.

[2] See above, Doc. 185 (actually, received on December 20).

[3] For Roosevelt's reply, see below, Doc. 205.

Doc. 203
ROOSEVELT TO CHURCHILL

No. 245   December 26, 1942

In consideration of unsettled condition in North Africa caused by
assassination of Admiral Darlan,[1] I believe that arrival of Macmillan
in Africa should be postponed until situation is stabilized.

[1] Admiral Darlan was assassinated in Algiers on Christmas Eve. Roosevelt instructed Eisenhower to put General Giraud provisionally in charge of French civil
and military authorities. See Peter Tompkins, *The Murder of Admiral Darlan: A
Study in Conspiracy* (New York, 1965).

I think it would be best for de Gaulle to postpone visit here. This will give Symbol[2] a chance to clear situation first.

2 Code name for the coming conference at Casablanca.

Doc. 204
CHURCHILL TO ROOSEVELT

No. 244   December 28, 1942

I had some long talks yesterday with Generals de Gaulle and d'Astier,[1] the latter just returned from Algiers. De Gaulle holds it of first importance to create a strong, united, national French authority. He is anxious to meet Giraud, in whom he sees the commander who will lead the French troops to the liberation of France after North Africa has been cleared. He considers that Giraud is more suited for military than for political functions. He is quite ready to work with Noguès[2] but apparently less so with Boisson,[3] though I cannot think he would be obstinate about it. I must say I strongly favour a meeting between de Gaulle and Giraud as soon as possible, before rivalries crystallise.

1 General d'Astier had gone to North Africa as an observer for the French Committee of National Liberation. When he first arrived there Darlan's men attempted to arrest him. But after d'Astier argued that he should be allowed to confer with all followers of de Gaulle in North Africa, Eisenhower saw that he talked to Darlan and then sent him back to England.
2 General Auguste Paul Noguès, Vichy resident governor of French Morocco.
3 General Pierre Boisson, Governor General of French West Africa.

Doc. 205
ROOSEVELT TO CHURCHILL

No. 247   December 29, 1942

The designation of Macmillan as QUOTE minister resident at Allied headquarters UNQUOTE is satisfactory to me period. It is my understanding that General Eisenhower will continue to have full veto power over all civil officials in the area of operations when in his (Eisenhower's) opinion such veto is advantageous to military operations or prospects.

Doc. 206
ROOSEVELT TO CHURCHILL

No. 248   December 31, 1942

Arrangements for Symbol satisfactory. Our Chiefs of Staff will arrive twelfth and I will follow two days later so that we could all meet together on fifteenth. I believe our staffs can cover the ground in a two-day preliminary conference. The prospect pleases me.

Doc. 207
CHURCHILL TO ROOSEVELT

No. 250   January 1, 1943

Your telegram number 243.[1]
About two months ago Mr. Hull[2] asked for an assurance, which we gladly gave, that the British Government was in agreement with the United States Government that the blockade of enemy territory should be vigorously maintained. This is our policy, as agreed with your Government. The single exception is Greece, where alone of all Allied countries the enemy allowed wholesale starvation conditions to develop. We have resisted extremely strong pressure from the Belgian Government and others to depart from it. To abandon the principle that the enemy is responsible for the territories he has conquered will lead very quickly to our having the whole lot on our backs, a burden far beyond our strength.

Conditions in Belgium are worse than in Norway and in our judgement it would not be right to make a concession to Norway and not to Belgium. It would be impossible, too, to dispute the claims of other Allied governments who would certainly press violently for equal privileges.

In our view the plan you propose might therefore have the eventual effect of reversing our whole joint food blockade policy, and this, I am sure you will agree, we should not contemplate.

As you are no doubt aware, we have already agreed with your authorities upon a secret scheme, which while distinct from ordinary

1 See above, Doc. 201.
2 Cordell Hull, U.S. Secretary of State.

relief, will help our Norwegian friends without dangerous repercussions. This scheme, which has been welcomed by the Norwegian Government, provides for the despatch in the Gothenburg [Göteborg] traffic of limited quantities of supplies disguised as Swedish imports, to be distributed in Norway through secret channels. If it is put into operation it will bring material aid to our friends, although it is of course vital that none but the Norwegian officials directly concerned should know of it.

We are also anxious to proceed with plans for the evacuation of Norwegian, Belgian, and other children to Sweden and Switzerland respectively, where they could be maintained by extra imports through the blockade.

I should be grateful for an expression of your views.

Doc. 208
ROOSEVELT TO CHURCHILL

No. 250   January 1, 1943

In reply to your 249[1] I feel very strongly that we have a military occupation in North Africa and as such our Commanding General has complete charge of all matters civil as well as military. We must not let any of our French friends forget this for a moment. By the same token I don't want any of them to think that we are going to recognize anyone or any committee or group as representing the French Government or the French Empire. The people of France will settle their own affairs after we have won this war. Until then we can deal with local Frenchmen on a local basis wherever our armies occupy former French territory. And if these local officials won't play ball we will have to replace them.

I agree that Eisenhower has had to spend too much time on political affairs but Marshall has sent him very explicit instructions on this point.[2] I don't know whether Eisenhower can hold Giraud in line with another Frenchman running the civil affairs but I shall find out.

1 Not printed. Churchill was concerned that the Allied commander in chief be supreme in all civil and military matters without any prejudice to the postwar government of France. In a recent broadcast to the French people, de Gaulle had claimed to be uncontested leader of the resistance movement.

2 On December 22, 1942, General Marshall wrote to Eisenhower: "I think you should delegate your international diplomatic problems to your subordinates and give your complete attention to the battle of Tunisia and the protection of the Straits of Gibraltar." Harry L. Coles and Albert K. Weinberg, *Civil Affairs: Soldiers Become Governors* (Washington, 1964), p. 47; and Pogue, *Marshall: Ordeal and Hope,* p. 423.

Why doesn't de Gaulle go to war? Why doesn't he start north by west
half west from Brazzaville?[3] It would take him a long time to get to
the Oasis of Somewhere.

A happy new year to you and yours.

[3] The river port of Brazzaville was the capital of the Middle Congo Territory and
of French Equatorial Africa, now the Republic of the Congo. By the end of 1942 de
Gaulle had control of the French forces there.

Doc. 209
ROOSEVELT TO CHURCHILL

No. 251   January 2, 1943

Referring further to your 233[1] and 234.[2] As result of studies in
Navy Department it has been found that the following can be accomplished: Lengthen cycle in North Atlantic convoys to ten days and
deliver average of two notional tanker cargoes daily by that route.
This will release four Canadian escort groups for assignment to U.K.
for replacement of long-legged escorts for duty with Aruba—U.K.
tanker convoys which should deliver an additional two notional
cargoes daily. Total of above deliveries supplemented from time to
time by spare tankers as found available should be about fifteen
million tons annually. Consider independently routed tankers inadvisable at this time. U.S. cannot agree to delivery of more than above
amount to U.K. and even this not practicable except as considered
with problem of Torch supply which in our opinion must be combined responsibility. Can furnish fast tankers to inaugurate supply
[in] that area but escorts must be combined and provided equally by
U.S. and U.K. Fast tankers will not proceed beyond Gibraltar or
Casablanca. Further deliveries into Mediterranean to be made by U.K.
tankers. Above most economical use of Allied tankers for delivery of
requirements of oil for U.K. and Torch. If the foregoing meets your
approval I suggest that further details be worked out between the
Admiralty and the Navy Department.

[1] Not printed.
[2] See above, Doc. 196.

THE CASABLANCA CONFERENCE
JANUARY 1943

[Churchill arrived at Casablanca by air on January 13, 1943, and
went to the large hotel in the suburb of Anfa, where his meeting with

Roosevelt was to take place. The President arrived by air the following afternoon and promptly asked to see Churchill. Drinks and talks followed in the President's quarters, and later that evening Roosevelt gave a dinner for the Prime Minister and his military advisers.

In the course of the dinner both the President and the Prime Minister expressed a strong desire to visit the front lines. But the Combined Chiefs of Staff were determined that Roosevelt and Churchill not expose themselves to unnecessary danger. Finally the President called upon the heads of the British and American air staffs—Air Chief Marshal Sir Charles Portal and General Henry H. Arnold—to determine the places where the two leaders might go. Portal and Arnold arranged for the President and Prime Minister to see front-line troops, but not in a combat zone.

The following morning the President held a conference in his bedroom attended by Hopkins, Harriman, Marshall, King, Arnold, and Brigadier General John R. Deane, at which the President was informed of the state of the discussions with the British on future operations in Europe and in China. In the afternoon Roosevelt met with General Eisenhower and Robert D. Murphy, the special representative of the President on Eisenhower's staff. Churchill brought General Sir Harold Alexander, commander of the British Middle East forces, Air Chief Marshal Sir Arthur Tedder, and his Chief of Staff Sir Hastings Ismay to meet the President at his villa late in the afternoon. Churchill could not resist the temptation to point out that the meeting was being held on ground recently liberated by British and American troops, and that it had been captured as result of a campaign vigorously opposed by the President's military advisers. Roosevelt regarded his trip also as an opportunity to visit American troops in a combat zone—the first American President since Lincoln to do so.

While the landings in North Africa were still in progress, Churchill had talked about invading Sicily next, and the British military staffs still favored attacking either Sicily or Sardinia as a prelude to the invasion of Italy. The Americans had virtually given up hope of any cross-channel attack in 1943 but did not want to get entangled in the Mediterranean in the meantime. Churchill was not so pessimistic. For a while it appeared that North Africa and Sicily might be captured and that the ships and landing craft could be returned to England in time to attack France during the summer of 1943. But Hitler's decision to reinforce the German troops in North Africa, together with poor transportation facilities and bad weather, forced a drastic revision of the Allied timetable. At Casablanca Roosevelt became convinced of the value of taking Sicily. The American Chiefs of Staff had concluded that only limited Mediterranean operations were feasible that year and that Sicily was the best target.

The Combined Chiefs of Staff met fifteen times at Casablanca and held three meetings with Churchill and Roosevelt. Out of all this came agreement on the following points: (1) the campaign against German submarines in the Atlantic would have first priority; (2) American forces in Great Britain would be built up as rapidly as possible; (3) the aerial bombardment of Germany would be intensified, including daylight attacks by American bombers operating from Great Britain; (4) an effort would be made to bring Turkey into the war on the Allied side; (5) a joint staff would be appointed to start planning a cross-channel attack for 1943; and (6) as soon as Tunisia was cleared of Axis troops the island of Sicily would be attacked in an effort to take some of the German weight off the Soviet Union. This last point was challenged by the British Joint Planning Committee, which argued that Sardinia could be taken three months earlier than Sicily. When the time came for a final decision, Churchill stood firm for an attack on Sicily and a June or July invasion date, and Roosevelt agreed with him.

There was little discussion of political or diplomatic matters at Casablanca. But soon after, on his way back to London from Turkey, where he had flown from North Africa, Churchill sent Roosevelt a long memorandum entitled "Morning Thoughts—Note on Postwar Security," one of Churchill's most important messages on postwar policy. In it the Prime Minister discussed the practicalities of the postwar world as he saw them—reparations, aid, resistance to aggression, and the role of the United States. The President made no direct reply (although he gave a copy of the memorandum to Secretary Hull).

During their visit to North Africa the President and the Prime Minister took time to dine with the Sultan of Morocco, to whom Roosevelt made some infelicitous remarks about postwar independence that Churchill reportedly much resented. The President also met with the French resident general at Rabat and made some remarks that certainly seem ill-chosen, considering that the Nazi death factories at Auschwitz, Buchenwald, and elsewhere were going full blast. According to a memorandum of conversation prepared by his naval aide, Captain John L. McCrae, Roosevelt maintained that "the number of Jews engaged in the practice of the professions (law, medicine, etc.) should be definitely limited to the percentage that the Jewish population in North Africa bears to the whole of the North African population. . . . [T]his plan would further eliminate the specific and understandable complaints which the Germans bore towards the Jews in Germany, namely, that while they represented a small part of the population, over fifty percent of the lawyers, doctors, schoolteachers, college professors, etc., in Germany were Jews."

On the last day of the Casablanca conference Roosevelt and Churchill met with the press to describe in general terms the results of their deliberations. Much to Churchill's surprise, Roosevelt publicly announced that the Allies would demand the "unconditional surrender" of their Axis enemies. The phrase, as well as its meaning and effect, was to be the subject of increased discussion in coming years and especially as the war entered its final victorious phase.

General de Gaulle had been persuaded to come to Casablanca to meet with Roosevelt and Churchill, who also held separate talks with General Giraud, and at the press conference the two Frenchmen were induced to shake hands for the benefit of photographers. Roosevelt and Churchill were hopeful that the meeting would mark the beginning of a closer collaboration between the two French leaders. But the "shotgun marriage" had a permanence only on film. De Gaulle considered himself the only leader of Free France, and eventually Giraud acknowledged this claim.

Roosevelt and Churchill regarded Casablanca as a great success. "I think," said Roosevelt at their closing press conference, "that the studies during the past week or ten days are unprecedented in history. Both the Prime Minister and I think back to the days of the first world war when conferences between the French and British and ourselves very rarely lasted more than a few hours or a couple of days. . . . Furthermore, these conferences have discussed, I think for the first time in history, the whole global picture. It isn't just one front, just one ocean, or one continent—it is literally the whole world; and that is why the Prime Minister and I feel that the conference is unique in the fact that it has this global aspect."

Churchill was even more euphoric: "Well, one thing I should like to say, and . . . I think I can say it with full confidence—nothing that may occur in this war will ever come between me and the President. . . . I hope you gentlemen [of the press] . . . will be able to build up to our people all over the world a good and encouraging story . . . of the unity, thoroughness, and integrity of the political chiefs . . . make them feel that there is some reason behind all that is being done. Even when there is some delay there is design and purpose and, as the President has said, the unconquerable will to pursue this quality until we have procured the unconditional surrender of the criminal forces who plunged the world into storm and ruin."]

Doc. 210
CHURCHILL TO ROOSEVELT

February 2, 1943[1]

Morning Thoughts
Note on Postwar Security

When United Nations led by three great powers, Great Britain, United States, and U.S.S.R., have received unconditional surrender of Germany and Italy, Great Britain and United States will turn their full force against Japan in order to punish effectively that greedy and ambitious nation for its treacherous assaults and outrages and to procure likewise from Japan unconditional surrender.

In this, although no treaty arrangement has been made, it seems probable that Great Britain and United States will be joined by Russia.

The peace conference of the victorious powers will probably assemble in Europe while final stages of war against Japan are still in progress. At this conference the defeated aggressor countries will receive directions of victors. Object of these directions will be to prevent as effectively as possible renewal of acts of aggression of the kinds which have caused these two terrible wars in Europe in one generation. For this purpose and so far as possible total disarmament of guilty nations will be enforced. On the other hand no attempt will be made to destroy their peoples or to prevent them gaining their living and leading a decent life in spite of all the crimes they have committed.

It is recognised that it is not possible to make the vanquished pay for war as was tried last time, and consequently task of rebuilding ruined and starving Europe will demand from conquerors a period of exertion scarcely less severe than that of the war. Russia particularly

[1] After the Casablanca conference Churchill and his military advisers flew to Adana on the Turkish-Syrian border, where the Prime Minister was to confer with President Ismet Inönü and Foreign Minister M. Numen Menemencioglu of Turkey while the British military staff talked to the head of the Turkish army. For maximum security, the conferences were to take place on a special train. Churchill and his party landed at Adana on January 30 and boarded the train, where they spent two days. This document was written by Churchill on the morning of January 31, and on February 2, he sent a copy to Lord Halifax, the British ambassador at Washington, for delivery to Roosevelt. Subsequently, on February 10, Halifax sent a note to the President saying that the document represented Churchill's personal views and that the Prime Minister had not had time to consult the Cabinet about its contents.

which has suffered such a horrible devastation will be aided in every possible way in her work of restoring the economic life of her people. It seems probable that economic reconstruction and rehabilitation will occupy full energies of all countries for a good many years in view of their previous experiences and lessons they have learned.

Russia has signed a treaty with Great Britain on basis of Atlantic Charter binding both nations mutually to aid each other. The duration of this treaty is twenty years. By it and by Atlantic Charter the two nations renounce all idea of territorial gains. Russians no doubt interpret this as giving them right to claim, subject to their agreement with Poland, their frontier of June 1941 before they were attacked by Germany.

It is the intention of chiefs of the United Nations to create a world organisation for the preservation of peace based upon the conceptions of freedom and justice and the revival of prosperity. As a part of this organisation an instrument of European government will be established which will embody the spirit but not be subject to the weakness of former League of Nations. The units forming this body will not be the great nations of Europe and Asia Minor only. Need for a Scandinavian bloc, Danubian bloc, and a Balkan bloc appears to be obvious. A similar instrument will be formed in the Far East with different membership and the whole will be held together by the fact that victorious powers as yet continue fully armed, especially in the air, while imposing complete disarmament upon the guilty. None can predict with certainty that the victors will never quarrel amongst themselves, or that the United States may not once again retire from Europe, but after the experiences which all have gone through, and their sufferings and the certainty that a third struggle will destroy all that is left of culture, wealth, and civilisation of mankind and reduce us to the level almost of wild beasts, the most intense effort will be made by the leading powers to prolong their honourable association and by sacrifice and self-restraint to win for themselves a glorious name in human annals. Great Britain will certainly do her utmost to organise a coalition of resistance to any act of aggression committed by any power; it is believed that the United States will cooperate with her and even possibly take the lead of the world, on account of her numbers and strength, in the good work of preventing such tendencies to aggression before they break into open war.

The highest security for Turkey in postwar world will be found by her taking her place as a victorious belligerent and ally at the side of Great Britain, the United States, and Russia. In this way a start will be made in all friendliness and confidence, and a new instrument will grow around the good will and comradeship of those who have been in the field together, with powerful armies.

Turkey may be drawn into war either by being attacked in the despairing convulsions of a still very powerful Nazi power, or because her interests require her to intervene to help prevent total anarchy in the Balkans, and also because the sentiments of modern Turkey are in harmony with the large and generous conceptions embodied in the Atlantic Charter, which are going to be fought for and defended by new generations of men.

We must therefore consider the case of Turkey becoming a belligerent. The military and technical side is under examination by Marshal Chakmak,[2] Generals Brooke,[3] Alexander,[4] Wilson,[5] and other high technical authorities. The political aspect is no less important. It would be wrong for Turkey to enter the war unless herself attacked, if that only led her to a disaster, and her ally Britain has never asked and will never ask her to do so under such conditions. On the other hand if the general offensive strength of Turkey is raised by the measures now being taken, and also by the increasing weakness of Nazi Germany, or by their withdrawal to a greater distance, or by the great divisions taking place in Bulgaria, or by the bitter quarrel between the Rumanians and the Hungarians over Transylvania, or through the internal resistance to German and Italian tyranny shown by Yugoslavia and Greece: for any or all of these reasons and causes, Turkey should play a part and win her place in the council of victors.

In the first instance it is possible that the military situation might be such that Turkey would feel justified in taking the same extended view of neutrality or nonbelligerency as characterised the attitude of the United States of America towards Great Britain before the United States of America was drawn into the war. In this connexion the destruction of Rumanian oil fields by air attacks by British and American aircraft operating from Turkish airfields, or refuelling there, would have far-reaching consequences and might in view of the oil scarcity in Germany appreciably shorten the struggle. In the same way also the availability of air bases or refuelling points in Turkey would be of great assistance to Great Britain in her necessary attack on the Dodecanese, and later upon Crete, for which in any case, whether we get help or not, General Wilson has been directed to prepare during the present year. There is also the immensely important question of opening the Straits to Allied and then closing [them] to Axis traffic. The case contemplated in this paragraph is one in which Turkey would

---

[2] Field Marshal Feuzi Chakmak, Chief of Staff of the Turkish army.

[3] General Sir Alan Brooke, Chief of the Imperial General Staff.

[4] General Sir Harold Alexander, commander in chief of British forces in the Middle East.

[5] General Sir Henry Maitland Wilson, commander of the British Ninth Army in Syria.

have departed from strictly impartial neutrality and definitely have taken sides with the United Nations without however engaging her armies offensively against Germany or Bulgaria; and those nations would put up with this action on the part of Turkey because they would not wish to excite her to more active hostility.

However, we cannot survey this field without facing the possibility of Turkey becoming a full belligerent and of her armies advancing into the Balkans side by side with the Russians on the one hand in the north and the British to the southward. In the event of Turkey becoming thus directly involved either offensively or through being attacked in consequence of her attitude, she would receive the utmost aid from all her allies and in addition it would be right for her before incurring additional risks to seek precise guarantees as to her territorial rights after the war. Great Britain would be willing to give these guarantees in a treaty at any time quite independently of any other power. She is also willing to join with Russia in giving such guarantees and it is believed that Russia would be willing to make a treaty to cover the case of Turkey becoming a full belligerent either independently or in conjunction with Great Britain. It seems certain to Mr. Churchill that President Roosevelt would gladly associate himself with such treaties and that the whole weight of the United States would be used in peace settlement to that end. At the same time one must not ignore the difficulties which United States Constitution interposes against prolonged European commitments. These treaties and assurances would naturally fall within the ambit of the world instrument to protect all countries from wrongdoing which it is our main intention and inflexible resolve to create, should God give us the power and lay this high duty upon us.

Doc. 211
CHURCHILL TO ROOSEVELT

No. 261   February 8, 1943

I propose to give the House of Commons some account of our joint affairs on Thursday 11th at noon BST.[1]

I have received from General Alexander a message saying that the directive I gave him on August 18th has been fully accomplished, as the enemy have been driven out of Egypt, Cyrenaica, and Tripolitania (see my immediately following telegram).[2] Moreover the advance

1 British Standard Time (same as Greenwich Mean Time).
2 Not printed.

forces of the Desert Army are already advancing into Tunisia. This therefore is the moment when the Eighth Army should come under the command of General Eisenhower. I propose to announce this, as it should certainly come from this end. I therefore propose to you that Alexander's and Tedder's appointments[3] should be released to synchronise with my statement in Parliament. If you agree, the best arrangements for synchronising can be made between the press officers concerned. I hope however that no advance information about the Eighth Army will get out before I tell Parliament.

I have just returned from Algiers where I had very satisfactory talks with Eisenhower, Smith, Giraud, Murphy, and others.[4] I hope you will approve of the amended drafts of the document conferring a certain additional status and power upon Giraud.[5] I had not seen it beforehand although my name was mentioned. Murphy and Macmillan arrived at a complete agreement which Giraud very readily accepted.

I have been travelling almost continuously since I saw you last and will send you a further report in a few days. I am sending you a separate message about your proposed amendments to my telegram to Joe.[6] At first sight they seem to be admirable. Every good wish to you, Harry, and all friends.

[3] General Alexander was named commander of the Eighteenth Army Group, which included the British Fifth and Eighth Armies, and deputy commander of Allied forces in French North Africa. Air Chief Marshal Sir Arthur W. Tedder was appointed commander in chief of the newly constituted Mediterranean Air Command, a move designed to provide unified control over all Allied forces in the Middle East, North Africa, and Malta. The appointments were announced on February 17. Both men were under General Eisenhower's overall command.

[4] After the Casablanca conference Churchill flew to Turkey for talks with Turkish leaders, then on to Cyprus, Cairo, Tripoli, and Algiers before returning to London.

[5] The British and American staffs pondered the political future of French nationals and territory. Finally, on May 28, they produced a document guaranteeing aid to Giraud and the French National Committee under de Gaulle to unify all Frenchmen fighting the Germans. See Woodward, *British Foreign Policy*, 2: 417–420.

[6] See below, Doc. 213.

Doc. 212
ROOSEVELT TO CHURCHILL

No. 257   February 8, 1943

Your 261 of February 8.[1] I am in agreement to your announcing on February 11 the placing of your Eighth Army under the command of

[1] See above, Doc. 211.

General Eisenhower and the appointment of Alexander as deputy under Eisenhower, and also the appointment of Tedder.

It is my opinion that cooperation by French forces will be best if the American Supreme Command in North Africa is stressed, and I consider it inadvisable to release and thereby make available to the enemy any information whatever as to the details of the duties of Alexander or Tedder.

It is recommended that British and American press officers in London send me draft of proposed press release and London time of release in order that the news may be given to the press of both countries simultaneously.

I am so glad you are safely back. You have accomplished marvels.

Doc. 213
CHURCHILL TO ROOSEVELT

No. 263   February 10, 1943

I send you the message I have sent to Joe as amended in accordance with your wishes. "Prime Minister Churchill to Premier Stalin most secret and personal.

"Your message of 30 January.[1] I have now consulted the President and the matter has been referred to the staffs on both sides of the ocean. I am authorised to reply for us both as follows: (A) There are a quarter of a million Germans and Italians in eastern Tunisia. We hope to destroy or expel these during April, if not earlier. (B) When this is accomplished, we intend in July, or earlier if possible, to seize Sicily with the object of clearing the Mediterranean, promoting an Italian collapse with the consequent effect on Greece and Yugoslavia, and wearing down the German air force: this is to be closely followed by an operation in the eastern Mediterranean, probably against the

---

[1] Stalin cabled on January 30: "Your friendly joint message reached me on January 27. Thank you for informing me of the Casablanca decisions about the operations to be undertaken by the U.S. and British armed forces in the first nine months of 1943. Assuming that your decisions on Germany are designed to defeat her by opening a second front in Europe in 1943, I should be grateful if you would inform me of the concrete operations planned and of their timing.

"As to the Soviet Union, I can assure you that the Soviet armed forces will do all in their power to continue the offensive against Germany and her allies on the Soviet-German front. We expect to finish our winter campaign, circumstances permitting, in the first half of February. Our troops are tired, they are in need of rest, and they will hardly be able to carry on the offensive beyond that period." *Stalin's Correspondence*, vol. 2, no. 71.

Dodecanese.[2] (C) This operation will involve all the shipping and landing craft we can get together in the Mediterranean and all the troops we can have trained in assault landing in time, and will be of the order of 300,000 or 400,000 men. We shall press any advantage to the utmost once ports of entry and landing bases have been established. (D) We are also pushing preparations to the limit of our resources for a cross-channel operation in August, in which both British and United States units would participate. Here again, shipping and assault landing craft will be limiting factors. If the operation is delayed by weather or other reasons, it will be prepared with stronger forces for September. The timing of this attack must of course be dependent upon the condition of German defensive possibilities across the channel at that time.[3] (E) Both the operations will be supported by very large United States and British air forces, and that across the channel by the whole metropolitan air force of Great Britain. Together these operations strain to the very utmost the shipping resources of Great Britain and the United States.[4] (F) The President and I have enjoined upon our Combined Chiefs of Staff the need for the utmost speed and for reinforcing the attacks to the extreme limit that is humanly and physically possible."

I send you also a telegram I have had from him about Turkey, and the consequential message I have sent to Inönü[5] after a long talk with Maisky[6] who urged it. Perhaps you can emphasise it through your channels. I hope we may be more successful in making this marriage than the other.[7] "Premier Stalin to Premier Churchill personal and secret.

"I received your messages concerning the Turkish question on the 2nd and 3rd February.[8] Many thanks for information on your talks with the leading Turkish personalities in Adana.

"In connexion with your suggestion that the Turks would reciprocate any friendly gesture from the Soviet Union I would like to mention that we have already made a number of statements, the friendly character of which is well known to the British Government, some

2 Roosevelt was responsible for adding the phraseology in (B).

3 The wording of (D) follows the suggestions sent by Roosevelt to Churchill in a message of February 5.

4 Items (A) through (E), except as amended above, were in a message sent by Churchill to Roosevelt on February 3.

5 Ismet Inönü, President of Turkey since 1938.

6 Ivan Maisky, Soviet ambassador to Great Britain.

7 The reference is to the attempt to bring de Gaulle and Giraud together.

8 For the text of Churchill's message of February 2, see Churchill, *Hinge of Fate*, pp. 713–715. The Prime Minister reported that while he had not asked or received any pledge from the Turks to enter the war, he believed that they would do so before the end of the year.

months before the Soviet-German war as well as after its beginning. However the Turks did not react to our steps. Apparently they were afraid to incur the wrath of the Germans. I am afraid that a similar reception will be accorded to the gesture suggested by you.

"The international position of Turkey remains very delicate. On the one hand Turkey has the Treaty of Neutrality and Friendship with the U.S.S.R. and the Treaty of Mutual Assistance Against Aggression with Great Britain—on the other hand she has the Treaty of Friendship with Germany signed 3 days before the German attack against the U.S.S.R. It is not clear to me how in the present circumstances Turkey thinks to combine her obligations vis-à-vis the U.S.S.R. and Great Britain with her obligations vis-à-vis Germany. Still if Turkey wishes to make her relations with the U.S.S.R. more friendly and intimate let her say so. In this case the Soviet Union would be willing to meet Turkey halfway.

"Of course I have no objection against you making a statement that I was kept informed on the Anglo-Turkish meeting although I cannot say that the information was very full.

"I wish the First and the Eighth Armies as well as the American troops in North Africa every success in the coming offensive and a speedy expulsion of the German-Italian forces from the African soil.

"Let me thank you for your friendly congratulations on the surrender of the Field Marshal Paulus[9] and on the successful annihilation of the encircled enemy troops near Stalingrad."

"Prime Minister to Monsieur Saragoglu[10] for President Inönü personal and secret.

"I told Premier Stalin about our talks, and have described to him the Turkish desire for closer understanding with the Soviet Union.

"In reply Premier Stalin has recalled a number of statements of a friendly character towards Turkey which have been made by the Soviet Government in recent years. Nonetheless Monsieur Stalin tells me that if it is the wish of Turkey to make her relations with the U.S.S.R. more friendly and intimate, then the Soviet Government is willing to meet the Turkish Government halfway and would welcome any suggestions that the Turkish Government could make to improve relations between the 2 countries.

"In these conditions it seems to me of first importance that you should carefully consider the nature of the arrangements which would best contribute to the growth of confidence between Turkey and the Soviet Union. If you feel able to formulate these I feel sure that

9 Field Marshal Friedrich Paulus, Commander in Chief of the German Sixth Army, captured at Stalingrad.
10 Sukru Saragoglu, the Turkish Prime Minister.

Premier Stalin would be ready to give them close and sympathetic examination. You will know that my good offices are always available to promote the successful outcome of any negotiations between our Turkish and Soviet allies.

"I feel most strongly that this is a very fine opportunity. I cannot conceal my desire for a warm renewal of friendship between Russia and Turkey similar to that achieved by Mustapha Kemal.[11] Thus Turkey while increasing her own defences would stand between two victorious friends. In all this I am thinking not only of the war, but of the postwar period. Tell me if there is anything I can do."

Your number 257.[12] I will act in the way you wish but I cannot guarantee that there will be no criticism. I have received the attached note from Brendan Bracken[13] who is in close touch with the British and American press here.

"I am having quite a lot of trouble in persuading some of the newspapers not to criticise the American handling of the North African campaign. If General Eisenhower's appointment as Supreme Commander is stressed and General Alexander's and Air Vice Marshal Tedder's respective functions are left vaguely undefined, I think we must expect a [spate?] of criticism from the British press. In this respect I have no doubt that the press would be reflecting the general feeling in the country and there would be far too many people who would honestly feel that British commanders and troops had been unfairly ignored for the sake of some move in international politics.

"The British Government is accustomed to criticism and is not likely to be unduly ruffled. But the Americans will very much resent the almost inevitable resulting criticism of General Eisenhower's appointment or any comparison between his military qualifications and those possessed by General Alexander. I think it is important therefore that the public should be told that General Eisenhower is Generalissimo, that Alexander is commanding the forces of the United Nations fighting in Tunis, that Tedder is commanding the air forces."

I shall utter the most solemn warning against controversy in these matters and every effort will be made by Bracken behind the scenes. Please do the like on your side to help your faithful partner. The Russian successes seem to me to be opening altogether a new situation. My hearty congratulations on Guadalcanal.[14]

---

[11] Mustapha Kemal Pasha, an ardent Turkish nationalist and President of Turkey from 1923 to 1928, had made a treaty with the Soviet Union by which Turkey gave back to Russia the port of Batum on the Black Sea.

[12] See above, Doc. 212.

[13] British Minister of Information.

[14] Organized Japanese resistance on Guadalcanal had ended on February 9.

Doc. 214
CHURCHILL TO ROOSEVELT

No. 271   March 4, 1943

So far we have sent no answer to Stalin's telegram of Feb. 16th which was addressed to both of us.[1] We think it important here that we should keep together. I have therefore drafted the following. Perhaps you will let me know what you and your advisers think about it. Draft telegram begins:

"Most secret. Jointly from President Roosevelt and Prime Minister Churchill to Premier Stalin. Personal and most secret.

"1. We thank you for your full statement of the 16th Feb.

"2. In spite of the delay in clearing the Axis out of North Africa, plans and preparations are being pressed forward to carry out operation Husky[2] (which is the new code word, see our immediately following telegram)[3] in June.

"3. We are also preparing plans for operations in the eastern Mediterranean, such as (a) the capture of Crete and/or the Dodecanese, and (b) a landing in Greece. The time of these operations is largely governed by the result of Husky and the availability of the necessary assault shipping and landing craft. The assistance of Turkey would of course be of immense value.

"4. The Anglo-American attempt to get Tunis and Bizerte at a run was abandoned in December because of the strength of the enemy, the impending rainy season, the already sodden character of the ground, and the fact that the communications stretched 500 miles from Algiers and 160 miles from Bône through bad roads and a week of travelling over single-track French railways. It was only possible to get supplies up to the Army by sea on a small scale owing to the strength of enemy air and submarine attack. Thus it was not possible to accumulate the petrol or other supplies in the forward areas. Indeed, it was only just possible to nourish the troops already there. The same was true of the air, and improvised airfields became quagmires. When we stopped attacking there were about 40,000 Germans in Tunisia apart from Italians and from Rommel who was still in Tripoli. The German force

---

1 Stalin cabled that the postponement from February to April for completing the campaign in Tunisia was undesirable and that the launching of a second front in Europe, now scheduled for August or September, should be moved up to spring or early summer. See *Stalin's Correspondence*, vol. 2, no. 75.

2 Code name for the invasion of Sicily.

3 Not printed.

in north Tunisia is now more than double that figure, and they are rushing over every man they can in transport aircraft and destroyers. We suffered some sharp local reverses towards the end of last month but the position has now been restored.[4] We hope that the delays caused by this setback will be repaired by the earlier advance of Montgomery's[5] army which should have 6 divisions (say 200,000 men) operating from Tripoli with sufficient supplies against the Mareth position[6] by March 19th or perhaps a little earlier. In the northern sector of Tunisia, however, the ground is still too wet for major operations.

"5. We thought that you would like to know these details of the story although it is on a small scale compared with the tremendous operations over which you are presiding.

"6. Our staffs estimate that about half the number of divisions which were sent to the Soviet-German front from France and Low Countries since last November have already been replaced mainly by divisions from Russia and Germany, and partly by new divisions formed in France. They estimate that at the present time there are 30 German divisions in France and the Low Countries.

"7. The bomber offensive from the United Kingdom has been going steadily forward. During February over 10,000 tons of bombs were dropped on Germany and on German-occupied territory. Our staffs estimate that out of a German first-line strength of 4,500 aircraft, 1,850 are now on the Russian front, the remainder being held opposite us on the western and Mediterranean fronts.

"8. With regard to an attack across the channel, it is our earnest wish that our troops should be in the general battle in Europe which you are fighting with such astounding prowess. But you should know that our shipping situation is very serious at the moment. In order to sustain the operations in North Africa, the Pacific, and India, and to carry supplies to Russia, the import programme into the United Kingdom has been cut to the bone, and we have eaten, and are eating, deeply into reserves. It would be impossible to provide the shipping to bring back any of the forces now in North Africa in time for operations across the channel this year. However we are doing all that we can to concentrate a strong American land and air force in the United Kingdom. Here again we are crippled for lack of shipping. In case the enemy should weaken sufficiently we are preparing to strike earlier than August, and plans are kept alive from week to week. If he does

[4] The reference is to the Allied defeat at the battle of Kasserine Pass, February 14–22, 1943. The Allies recovered the pass on February 25.

[5] General Sir Bernard L. Montgomery, commander of the British Eighth Army in North Africa.

[6] The German defensive line in Tunisia.

not weaken, a premature attack with insufficient forces would merely lead to a bloody repulse and a great triumph for the enemy."[7]

[7] Roosevelt responded on March 5, when he forwarded a copy of his message to Stalin of February 22 pointing out that the United States was doing all that it could for the war effort. See *Stalin's Correspondence*, vol. 2, no. 76. In his message to Churchill the President added: "In view of my reply to Mr. Stalin it does not seem advisable that your message be considered a joint message from both of us."

Doc. 215
CHURCHILL TO ROOSEVELT

March 18, 1943

[Text of message received from Marshal Stalin, March 18, 1943:]

"I have received your reply to my message of February 16th.[1]

"It is evident from this reply that Anglo-American operations in North Africa have not only not been expedited but on the contrary they have been postponed to the end of April. Even this date is not quite definite. Thus at height of our fighting against Hitler's forces, i.e., in February–March, the weight of Anglo-American offensive in North Africa has not only (not?) increased but there has been no development of offensive at all and time limit for operations set by yourself was extended. Meanwhile Germany succeeded in transferring 36 divisions (including 6 armoured divisions) from west against Soviet troops. It is easy to see what difficulties this created for Soviet armies and how position of Germans on Soviet-German front was alleviated.

"Fully realising importance of Husky I must however point out it cannot replace second front in France. Still I welcome by all means contemplated acceleration of this operation.

"Now as before I see main task in hastening of second front in France. As you remember you admitted possibility of such a front already in 1942 and in any case not later than in the spring of 1943. There were serious reasons for possibility admittedly. Naturally enough I underlined in my previous message necessity of the blow from the west not later than in the spring or in the early summer of this year.

"The Soviet troops spent whole winter in tense fighting which continues even now. Hitler is carrying out important measures with a view to replenishing and increasing his army for spring and summer operations against U.S.S.R. In these circumstances it is (words unde-

[1] See above, Doc. 214.

cypherable) important that blow from the west should not be put off and that it should be struck in the spring or in early summer.

"I recognise difficulties of Anglo-American operations in Europe. Notwithstanding all that I deem it my duty to warn you in the strongest possible manner how dangerous would be from the viewpoint of our common cause further delay in opening second front in France. This is the reason why uncertainty of your statements concerning contemplated Anglo-American offensive across channel arouses grave anxiety in me about which I feel I cannot be silent."

Doc. 216
CHURCHILL TO ROOSEVELT

March 24, 1943

I am extremely anxious about shipping situation. The British Chiefs of Staff have been examining position in relation to requirements of military operations and analysis which they have sent to Washington shows, after allowing for our minimum import programme, there will not be sufficient shipping to implement in full the decisions taken at Casablanca. The commanders of various operations have been told that they must cut their requirements to the bone. For Husky the mounting of British share cannot be made without an increase of 14 ships over and above shipping already allocated to the Middle East in April. Provision of these ships by you is therefore an urgent and immediate necessity. Also the British Chiefs of Staff see little prospect of Anakim,[1] much less Bolero, unless from now onwards a good deal more shipping than is now in sight can be provided for Indian and United Kingdom theatres.

As to United Kingdom programme, I realise that the United States are making great efforts to find the necessary tonnage for our imports in accordance with terms of your letter to me.[2] The imports during early part of this year have been at such a low rate that even with increasing allocations already notified for forward months, it is going to be extremely difficult to make up the leeway.

I need not go into details of all this as I have asked Eden to explain the situation and its extreme gravity more fully.[3]

[1] Code name for the plan to recapture Burma.
[2] Not printed.
[3] Foreign Secretary Anthony Eden presented this message to Roosevelt during his visit to Washington. Roosevelt replied to Churchill on April 1: "Anthony will give you my thoughts in regard to Anakim. The quid pro quo is threefold. First, greater

air support for China air operations against the Japanese shipping and home islands. Second, more general shipping leeway during next six months. Third, opportunity definitely to mount Bolero for a later date. I have not consulted the combined staff on this as I want your personal slant first."

Doc. 217
ROOSEVELT TO CHURCHILL

No. 265   March 28, 1943

Referring to your proposed message to Stalin delivered by Mr. Eden, I agree with you.[1] I have after serious consideration further concluded that we are not justified in wasting available tonnage by keeping the present Russian convoy (JW 54)[2] loaded, and that it is advisable to give Stalin the inevitable bad news now. It is suggested that your proposed message be amended as follows:

"1. The Germans have concentrated at Narvik a powerful battle fleet consisting of *Tirpitz, Scharnhorst, Lützow,* one six-inch cruiser, and eight destroyers. Thus danger to Russian convoys which I described in my message to you of July 17th last year has been revived in even more menacing form. I told you then that we did not think it right to risk our Home Fleet in Barents Sea where it could be brought under attack of German shore-based aircraft and U-boats, without adequate protection against either; and I explained that if one or two of our most modern battleships were to be lost or even seriously damaged while *Tirpitz* and other large units of the German battle fleet remained in action, the whole command of the Atlantic would be jeopardized with dire consequences to our common cause.

"2. President Roosevelt and I have therefore decided with the greatest reluctance that it is impossible to provide adequate protection for the next Russian convoy and that without such protection there is not the slightest chance of any of the ships reaching you in the face of the known German preparations for their destruction. Orders have therefore been issued that sailing of March convoy is to be postponed.

"3. It is a great disappointment to President Roosevelt and myself that it should be necessary to postpone March convoy. Had it not been

1 Eden was in Washington from March 15 to March 31. Churchill's proposed message informed Stalin that the March convoy to northern Russia would have to be postponed because the German battle fleet was concentrated at Narvik, Norway.

2 The convoys to Murmansk, originally designated PQ (see above, Docs. 126, 127, 141 and 143), were redesignated JW in December 1942, when their route was changed to eliminate the stop at Reykjavik, Iceland. See Morison, *Battle of the Atlantic,* in *History of the United States Naval Operations in World War II,* p. 365ff.

for German concentration it had been our firm intention to send you a convoy of 30 ships each in March and again early May. At the same time we feel it only right to let you know at once that it will not be possible to continue convoys by northern route after early May, since from that time onward every single escort vessel will be required to support our offensive operations in the Mediterranean leaving only a minimum to safeguard our lifeline in the Atlantic. In the latter we have had grievous and almost unprecedented losses during the last three weeks. Assuming Husky goes well we should hope to resume the convoys in early September provided disposition of German main units permits and that the situation in North Atlantic is such as to enable us to provide the necessary escorts and covering force.

"4. We are doing our utmost to increase the flow of supplies by southern route. The monthly figure has been more than doubled in the last six months. We have reason to hope that increase will progress and that figures for August will reach 240,000 tons. If this is achieved, the monthly delivery will have increased eightfold in 12 months. Furthermore the United States will materially increase shipments via Vladivostok.[3] This will in some way offset both your disappointment and ours at the interruption to northern convoys."

When you send this or similar message to Stalin would you like to have me send confirming or supporting message? Let me have text of your final message.

[3] Shipments to Vladivostok had begun in 1941, but since the distance to that port from American West Coast ports was much greater than that from East Coast ports to Archangel and Murmansk, the Pacific city was not much used before the fall of 1942. Even then, the Pacific route and the Persian Gulf route never made up for the postponement of the northern convoys. See George C. Herring, Jr., *Aid to Russia 1941–1946: Strategy, Diplomacy, the Origins of the Cold War* (New York and London, 1973), pp. 43, 70, 72–73, 97; and Robert Huhn Jones, *The Roads to Russia: United States Lend-Lease to the Soviet Union* (Norman, Okla., 1969), pp. 84, 89, 107, 113, 119, 122–124, 134, 154–155, 163, 209–210, 213–214.

Doc. 218
ROOSEVELT TO CHURCHILL

No. 270   April 11, 1943

Our staffs now urgently at work on what to do after Husky. I think there are two or three good alternatives but until our respective staffs give us their views I see no advantage of immediate conferences with Marshall and Harry. It is quite possible, and I hope probable, that we can reach agreement quickly about our post-Husky operations. At the moment we have the Tunisian business to clean up and that may take longer than we think. Should that be unduly delayed that, in itself, might well unfavorably affect Husky and if Rommel's army should escape in any substantial force to Husky land[1] that would make it doubly difficult.

I think the situation in Tunisia will clarify within a week so that it would be possible for us to make a pretty good guess as to when the enemy will be out of Africa.

As I think I told you at Casablanca we should continue every preparation for Husky but that you and I should hold ourselves ready to consider one or more alternatives up to June 1. Conditions may greatly change by that time. Our preparations for Husky should not be slowed down one iota but 95% of these operations would be equally valuable for some other point. If that should seem best.

We pretty much scraped the bottom to get the first twenty cargo ships for Anakim and that whole business of the combined use of our merchant fleet needs the closest watching or we will find ourselves conducting operations without adequate cargo shipping. I have been having an examination made here of a modified Anakim and will let you know later my thoughts on that.[2]

I am planning to leave early in the week for a two weeks' tour of Army and Navy bases. This trip will be off the record, hence I do not wish it known in England. I have good communications, however, and you can get in touch with me quickly. Harry will remain here.

I have been very pleased with the recent successful bombings of Germany and we must give them an ever increasing dose.[3] We are making special efforts here to get our big bomber units in England built up as rapidly as possible. I don't believe the Germans like that medicine and the Italians will like it less.

Give my congratulations to Portal[4] and Harris.[5]

Anthony's[6] visit cleared up many things here and I think it was altogether useful.

---

1 Sicily.

2 On May 3, General Marshall notified General Joseph W. Stilwell, commander of the U.S. forces in Southeast Asia, of President Roosevelt's decision to undertake a major air effort in China along with preparations for the recapture of Burma in a modified version of Operation Anakim.

3 After the Casablanca conference the bombardment of targets in Germany had begun with the U.S. Eighth Air Force's attack on Wilhelmshaven on January 27. U.S. bombers struck Wilhelmshaven again on February 26. Then came attacks on Hamm on March 4 and Vegesack on March 18. On April 17 the Eighth Air Force launched its largest mission up to that time when 107 planes bombed Bremen.

4 Air Chief Marshal Sir Charles Portal, Chief of the British Air Staff.

5 Air Chief Marshal Sir Arthur Harris, chief of the RAF Bomber Command.

6 Foreign Secretary Eden.

Doc. 219
CHURCHILL TO ROOSEVELT

No. 283   April 15, 1943

Your number 271.[1] I hope that paragraph 3 of my number 282[2] made it perfectly clear that I contemplated Husky as our joint enterprise on terms of perfect equality, with our usual intimacy and confidence, and with no question of a "senior partner."

This expression only applied to the actual executive work to be done by the Military Governor who would receive his directive from you and me in complete agreement. In the executive and administrative sphere there ought not to be two voices but only one voice which will say what you and I have agreed. General Alexander would be directing the military operations under the Supreme Commander and he would delegate the powers of Military Governor to a British officer mutually agreeable to us both.

I entirely agree with you that the utmost advantage should be taken of American ties with Italy and that at least half of the officers of the Allied military government should be American and, further, if in [a particular] case or district it is found that American preeminence is more useful to the common cause, this should at once be arranged. The 2 flags should always be displayed together and we should present a united and unbreakable front in all directions. All the above is of course without prejudice to the United States being supreme throughout the whole of French North Africa and my continuing to be your lieutenant there. I hope I have given satisfaction.

[1] Not printed. In that message, dated April 13, Roosevelt approved the appointment of General Alexander as Allied military governor in Sicily but added: "In view of friendly feelings toward America entertained by a great number of the citizens of Italy and in consideration of the large number of citizens of the United States who are of Italian descent it is my opinion that our military problem will be made less difficult by giving to the Allied military government as much of an American character as is practicable." The President emphasized that this military government "should be presented to the world as a definitely joint Allied control" and that there should be no "senior partner." FR 1943, 2 (Washington, 1964): 327.

[2] Not printed. Churchill wrote: "I hope that you may feel in view of the fact that the Force Commander under the supreme direction of General Eisenhower will be British we should be senior partner in the military administration of enemy occupied territory in that area." But he went on to say that the appointment of a British military governor with a joint Anglo-American staff "would of course in no way affect decisions on major policy being taken as usual by agreement between our two Governments [or] if convenient by personal correspondence between you and me." FR 1943, 2: 326.

I am ready to study with you the outlines of a directive foreseeing and forecasting as far as possible our policy towards (a) conquered districts and (b) peace overtures. These latter may come upon us swiftly and suddenly and we must be ready for them. I have on this subject at present only 2 thoughts. First, we cannot treat with Mussolini and, secondly, we should be immense gainers by getting Italy out of the war as soon as possible.

Your number 272[3] has just arrived. There must be a pause while the armies are regrouping in the north [and] while Montgomery is dragging up his customary battery, but I hope for great events before April is out. I continue to have very agreeable correspondence with Joe who has taken the convoy blow extremely well. He is very pleased that we should attempt to send the British and American aircraft quotas to him through Africa or the Mediterranean. I am trying to arrange this through Averell and will communicate with Harry. I trust your inspection tour will be as pleasant as it will be memorable.

Let me take this opportunity of thanking you for all your kindness and hospitality to Anthony. He has greatly enjoyed his visit and everyone here has acclaimed it.

[3] Not printed.

Doc. 220
CHURCHILL TO ROOSEVELT

No. 285   April 25, 1943

I repeat to you herewith the reply I have just received to my telegram which I forwarded to you in my number 284.[1] I shall be glad of your views.

Begins: "Premier Stalin to Premier Churchill personal and most secret. Kremlin April 25th.

"I received your message concerning the Polish affairs. Many thanks for your interest in the matter. I would like, however, to point out that

[1] Not printed. Churchill sent the texts of two messages he sent to Stalin in reply to the latter's message of April 21 on Poland. In the first Churchill said that the British would oppose any investigation of the Katyn Forest massacre by the International Red Cross or any other group acting under the authority of the Germans. He urged Stalin not to interrupt relations with the Polish government-in-exile. In the second message, dated April 25, Churchill noted that the Polish government's appeal to the Red Cross came after several inquiries about the missing Polish officers had been made to the Soviet government and that the Poles had nothing to do with the Germans' making a propaganda issue of their request. The Prime Minister again asked Stalin not to break off relations. FR 1943, 3 (Washington, 1965) : 393-395.

the interruption of relations with the Polish Government is already decided and today V. M. Molotov[2] delivered a note to this effect. Such action was demanded by my colleagues as the Polish official press is ceaselessly pursuing and even daily expanding its campaign hostile to the U.S.S.R. I was obliged also to take into account the public opinion of the Soviet Union which is deeply indignant at the ingratitude and treachery of the Polish Government.

"With regard to the publication of the Soviet document concerning the interruption of relations with the Polish Government, I am sorry to say that such publication cannot be avoided."[3]

[2] Vyacheslav M. Molotov, Peoples' Commissar for Foreign Affairs, the Soviet Foreign Minister.

[3] For further information on the British side of the dealings with Stalin, see Woodward, *British Foreign Policy*, 2: 618–662; and Churchill, *Hinge of Fate*, pp. 757–761.

Doc. 221
CHURCHILL TO ROOSEVELT

No. 288   April 26, 1943

Your number 274.[1]

I like your telegram to Stalin very much and will read it to the Cabinet today. We must work together to heal this breach. So far it has been Goebbels' show.[2]

[1] Not printed. Roosevelt sent Churchill the text of his message to Stalin of April 26, in which he denied that the Polish government-in-exile had "in any way whatsoever collaborated with the Nazi gangsters" and reminded Stalin that there were several million Americans of Polish ancestry in the United States, all of them anti-Nazi. He urged Stalin not to sever diplomatic relations with the Polish government in London. See *FR 1943*, 3: 395–396; and *Stalin's Correspondence*, vol. 2, no. 81.

[2] The reference is to the use made by the German Minister of Propaganda, Joseph Goebbels, of the Polish request that the International Red Cross investigate the Katyn Forest massacre.

Doc. 222
CHURCHILL TO ROOSEVELT

No. 289   April 28, 1943

The Poles are issuing tonight the communiqué in my immediately following.[1] You will see that we have persuaded them to shift the

[1] Not printed. For the text see General Sikorski Historical Institute, *Documents on Polish-Soviet Relations, 1930–1945*, vol. 1 (London, 1961), no. 318.

argument from the dead to the living and from the past to the future. I have therefore sent the following message to Stalin feeling sure it will be in accordance with your views. Anything that you can put in now will be most helpful. Message begins:

"Eden and I have pointed out to the Polish Government that no resumption of friendly or working relations with Soviet Russia is possible while they make charges of an insulting character against the Soviet Government and thus seem to countenance the atrocious Nazi propaganda. Still more would it be impossible for any of us to tolerate enquiries by the International Red Cross held under Nazi auspices and dominated by Nazi terrorism. I am glad to tell you that they have accepted our view and that they want to work loyally with you. Their request now is to have the dependents of the Polish army in Persia and the fighting Poles in the Soviet Union sent to join the Poles you have already allowed to go to Persia. This is surely a matter which admits of patient discussion. We think the request is reasonable if made in the right way and at the right time and I am pretty sure the President thinks so too. We hope earnestly that, remembering the difficulties in which we have all been plunged by the brutal Nazi aggression, you will consider this matter in a spirit of magnanimity.

"The Cabinet here is determined to have proper discipline in the Polish press in Great Britain. Even miserable rags attacking Sikorski[2] can say things which the German broadcast repeats open-mouthed to the world to our joint detriment. This must be stopped and it will be stopped.

"So far this business has been Goebbels' greatest triumph. It has now been suggested that the U.S.S.R. will set up a left-wing Polish government on Russian soil and deal only with them. We could not recognise such a government and would continue our relations with Sikorski who is far the most helpful man you or we are likely to find for the purposes of the common cause. I expect this will also be the American view.

"My own feeling is that they have had a shock and that after whatever interval is thought convenient, the relationship established on July 30th, 1941,[3] should be restored. No one will hate this more than Hitler and what he hates most is wise for us to do.

"We owe it to our armies now engaged, and presently to be more heavily engaged, to maintain good conditions behind the fronts. I and

[2] General Wladyslaw Sikorski, head of the Polish government-in-exile in London.
[3] The Polish-Soviet pact of July 30, 1941, was a treaty of friendship and collaboration. It provided for the annulment of the Russo-German partition pact of September 28, 1939, but did not restore Poland's prewar eastern frontier. Cf. Woodward, *British Foreign Policy*, 2: 612ff. For text see General Sikorski Historical Institute, *Documents on Polish-Soviet Relations*, vol. 1, no. 106.

my colleagues look steadily to the ever closer cooperation and understanding of the U.S.S.R., the U.S.A., and the British Commonwealth
and Empire, not only in the deepening war struggle but after the
war. What other hope can there be than this for the tortured world?"
Message ends.

The Foreign Office are sending a fuller statement through our
Ambassador in Moscow[4] setting out our formal and official view and
dwelling more in detail on the Polish grievances and on the dangers to
the United Nations which would follow from their being incessantly
aired all over the world. Ambassador Winant[5] is being kept fully
informed.[6]

[4] Sir Archibald Clark Kerr, British ambassador to the Soviet Union.

[5] John G. Winant, U.S. ambassador to Great Britain.

[6] For the American reaction to the developing Polish-Russian problems, see *FR
1943*, 3: 314–402.

Doc. 223
ROOSEVELT TO CHURCHILL

No. 275   May 2, 1943

I am really delighted you are coming.[1] I agree most heartily that we
have some important business to settle at once; the sooner the better.
Marshall and King have postponed their Pacific trip. I want you of
course to stay here with me.

[1] For the background of the third Washington conference, see U.S. Department of
State, *The Conferences at Washington and Quebec 1943* (Washington, 1970), pp.
1–17.

Doc. 224
CHURCHILL TO ROOSEVELT

No. 293A   May 10, 1943

Admiralty have now routed us a somewhat longer course and we
shall probably be several hours late. I should like to go by train to
Washington and will arrive there during the afternoon. I shall be
delighted to come to Hyde Park for the weekend, and I daresay we
may have better news from North Africa than we did at the time of
Tobruk in June.[1] Look forward to seeing you.

[1] Churchill had been visiting Roosevelt on June 21, 1942, when news came of the
fall of Tobruk.

THE THIRD WASHINGTON CONFERENCE
MAY 1943

[Churchill and Roosevelt met on short notice in Washington from May 12 to May 25, 1943, to reconsider Anglo-American strategy in the light of the Axis defeat in Tunisia, the Japanese occupation of two Aleutian islands, and the surrender of the German Sixth Army at Stalingrad. Churchill and his top military advisers, as well as Lord Beaverbrook, then Lord Privy Seal, crossed the Atlantic on the *Queen Mary* together with several thousand German and Italian prisoners of war who had been captured in North Africa and were being sent to camps in the United States. Harry Hopkins was on hand at Staten Island to greet Churchill and his party and to accompany them to Washington.

The President insisted that Churchill stay at the White House rather than at the British Embassy, and the Prime Minister agreed. This time the American Chiefs of Staff were prepared to make a unified presentation to their British colleagues. They met with the President the day before Churchill arrived, and there was general agreement that their principal goal should be to obtain a firm commitment from the British for a cross-channel attack as soon as possible. This achieved, all-out preparations could then begin for an invasion of Europe in the spring of 1944.

The Prime Minister and the Combined Chiefs of Staff met with Roosevelt in his study on May 12. Churchill argued that the major Anglo-American effort for the remainder of 1943 should be to knock Italy out of the war. This would have the psychological effect of eliminating one-third of the Axis, of forcing the withdrawal of Italian troops from the Near East, and of inducing Turkey to consider aligning itself with the Allies. As for a cross-channel attack, Churchill declared that adequate preparations could not be made in time for the spring of 1944 unless Germany collapsed in the meantime. Rather than keep a large number of troops idle for that length of time, the Prime Minister sought a commitment to invade Italy. On the Pacific front Churchill promised that British ground and naval forces would be deployed against the Japanese once Germany was defeated. He believed that, in the meantime, every practical effort should be made to keep the beleaguered Chinese in the war.

Roosevelt emphasized that the most important goal, as he saw it, was the defeat of Nazi Germany and that all efforts should be concentrated toward that end. He was therefore opposed to an attack on the Italian mainland, although he would agree to the seizure of Sicily and

Sardinia. At Churchill's insistence, however, Roosevelt agreed to have his military chiefs study the feasibility of an attack on Germany by way of Bulgaria, Rumania, and Turkey. Since he and Churchill were in accord on the importance of keeping China in the war, the President wanted to start moving large amounts of military supplies into China by air as soon as possible.

Roosevelt and Churchill further agreed to seek the Portuguese government's consent to Anglo-American use of the Azores as a naval and air base in the campaign against German submarines, which were continuing to inflict heavy losses on Allied shipping in the Atlantic. In addition, the Azores would serve as a base for ferrying aircraft from the United States to the United Kingdom and to North Africa, and this shorter route would save millions of gallons of high-octane gasoline. The atmosphere of the meeting was greatly buoyed by the news that all Axis resistance in Tunisia had come to an end that day with the capture of about 160,000 enemy prisoners and a considerable amount of military equipment.

Prior to the third Washington conference, there was an extended exchange between Roosevelt, Hopkins, Churchill, and their respective scientific advisers concerning the sharing of highly sensitive atomic energy information between the two countries. But the President and the Prime Minister seem not to have discussed the subject, certainly not at length or in any detail, during Churchill's stay.

On May 14 the Combined Chiefs of Staff held another meeting with Roosevelt and Churchill to discuss ways and means of helping China. In addition to the airlifting of supplies, the Americans (like the Chinese) wanted a land route opened through Burma. The British, on the other hand, set forth the considerable difficulties involved in establishing an overland route.

On the weekend of May 15 the President invited Churchill to Shangri-la, his retreat in the Catoctin Mountains of Maryland. (The retreat was renamed Camp David by President Eisenhower ten years later.) Driving through the town of Frederick, Maryland, Churchill noted signs advertising a local product—Barbara Fritchie candy. Roosevelt explained that it was named for a local woman of supposed Civil War fame about whom John Greenleaf Whittier had written a poem. The President could recall only two lines of the work, whereupon Churchill recited the entire poem from memory. The Prime Minister also noted road signs showing the direction and distance to Gettysburg and, speaking as one with a longstanding interest in the American Civil War, expressed his delight at finding himself on ground associated with one of the decisive battles of that war.

After a refreshing weekend in the Maryland countryside, the President and the Prime Minister returned to Washington for further conferences. On May 23 the Combined Chiefs of Staff presented to Roosevelt and Churchill an ambitious list of proposed operations for 1943–1944. These included a cross-channel attack on France in May 1944, intensification of the combined bombing offensive against Germany, an attack on Sicily and a general commitment to knock Italy out of the war, an air campaign to destroy the Rumanian oil fields at Ploesti, occupation of the Azores, the airlifting of supplies to China from India at a level of 10,000 tons a month, elimination of the Japanese foothold in the Aleutians, and seizure of the Marshall, Caroline, and other islands in the Solomons, as well as the Bismarck archipelago and New Guinea. Churchill contended that the capture of Rangoon and Bangkok and the reopening of the Burma Road were not feasible in the light of existing circumstances, but he continued to press for the seizure of northern Sumatra as a base for subsequent attacks on Malaya, Singapore, and Thailand. Roosevelt insisted that China had to be kept in the war and that its army had to be built up.

The following day Churchill rejected the final report of the Combined Chiefs of Staff on the ground that it contained no definite recommendation for an attack on the Italian mainland once Sicily had been occupied. He argued again for an invasion of Italy and for possible thrusts into Yugoslavia and Greece. The American military chiefs, on the other hand, believed that such Mediterranean operations would tend to dilute and postpone the buildup of men and supplies needed for an invasion of Europe. They were prepared to consider the seizure of Sardinia but nothing more. Churchill declared that this approach would keep a large number of troops idle for nearly a year. Given the magnitude of the Russian war effort, such a pause in Anglo-American operations could not be justified. Finally, Churchill gave way and agreed in principle that a cross-channel invasion should be launched by May 1, 1944, with an earlier plan—an emergency crossing code-named Sledgehammer—to remain as a standby in case of sudden need on the Russian front.

Churchill's arguments against the cross-channel attack did not sway the President, who was unwilling to press his military advisers to accept the Prime Minister's position. Hopkins told Churchill that if he wished to change the President's mind, he would have to spend at least another week in Washington, and even then there was no assurance that he could convince Roosevelt. Since such an extension of his visit was out of the question, Churchill asked Roosevelt to permit General Marshall to accompany him to North Africa for a meeting with the Allied commanders there, and Roosevelt agreed. Later, at the North African meeting, the military leaders decided to postpone a final decision about an Italian invasion until the results of the capture of Sicily could be evaluated.

Despite his busy round of conferences in Washington, Churchill found time to have lunch at the British Embassy with Vice President Henry A. Wallace, Secretary of War Stimson, Interior Secretary Harold Ickes, Undersecretary of State Welles, and Senator Tom Connally of Texas, chairman of the Foreign Relations Committee. In the course of a general talk about a postwar settlement, he took the occasion to argue for a closer association of the United States and the British Commonwealth; it was in this speech that he suggested "there might even be a common form of citizenship, under which citizens of the United States and of the British Commonwealth might enjoy voting privileges after residential qualification and be eligible for public office in the territories of the other, subject of course to the laws and institutions there prevailing."

Although he had finally been persuaded to agree to a May 1944 invasion of Western Europe, and had been unable to persuade Roosevelt as regards a number of his own military objectives, Churchill seemed well pleased with the work of the third Washington conference. As at the end of the Casablanca talks five months earlier, he and the President held a joint press conference. Churchill was again in an expansive and optimistic mood: "I am very much more satisfied than I was when I was here last [June 18, 1942]. . . . [F]rom every point of view we must regard the last ten or eleven months as examples of highly successful war—a perfectly indisputable turning of the tide."]

Doc. 225
CHURCHILL TO ROOSEVELT

No. 298   May 31, 1943

Please accept my warmest thanks to you and Mrs. Roosevelt for your great kindness and charming hospitality to me during my visit. I carry away the most pleasant memories and also I am certain that our discussions have averted many difficulties and will grip and focus our whole effort in the next few months.

I am staying here or hereabouts for the next week and Anthony joins me tomorrow.[1] The weather is lovely and the conditions most agreeable. I have had very good talks with Eisenhower and our people and yesterday had a first preliminary meeting. It looks as if complete

[1] After the Washington conference Churchill and his staff, accompanied by General Marshall, flew to Gibraltar and then to Algiers, where this message was written. Churchill telegraphed Eden on May 29 asking him to come to Algiers. See Churchill, *Hinge of Fate*, pp. 810–816.

agreement will be reached when we resume the conference on Monday.

The bride arrives here noon today.[2] I thought Anthony would make a better best man than I. I am therefore reserving for myself the part of heavy father. General Georges[3] whom I flew out of France is here and makes a very good impression. I think there is a chance of his being included in the new council.[4] It seems essential to make the composition of this council such that it can restrain any individual who pushes personal pretensions which are harmful to the cause. Murphy and Macmillan work hand in hand together, in the closest accord. I will keep you fully informed of any developments while I am here.

Once more a thousand thanks. You know how I value your friendship. Kindest regards to all.

2 The reference is to Charles de Gaulle. Churchill and Eden were still trying to bring about a union between de Gaulle and Giraud. At the Washington conference Churchill saw that the Americans still harbored suspicion of de Gaulle, and he cabled Eden asking whether British political support for the French leader should not be ended. Eden replied that the French Committee of National Liberation would collapse without de Gaulle. Also de Gaulle and Giraud were finally at the point of uniting their respective factions. See Woodward, *British Foreign Policy*, 2: 424–442; and *The Memoirs of Anthony Eden, Earl of Avon*, vol. 2, *The Reckoning* (Boston, 1965), pp. 447–452. Henceforth cited as Eden, *Memoirs*.

3 General Alphonse Georges was working with Giraud. Eden called him "a reactionary old defeatist." Eden, *Memoirs*, 2: 450.

4 Roosevelt and Churchill believed that de Gaulle was trying to fill the French National Committee with a majority of his own supporters by enlarging its membership. After prolonged negotiations a new National Committee of seven members was established, with de Gaulle and Giraud as co-presidents. The committee was to be the central authority with power over French forces and territory, until a provisional government could be established in liberated France. See Woodward, *British Foreign Policy*, 2: 424–442; Winston S. Churchill, *Closing the Ring* (Boston, 1952), pp. 172–173; *Conferences at Washington and Quebec*, pp. 191–192, 320–324; *FR 1943*, 2: 129–130; Murphy, *Diplomat Among Warriors*, pp. 177–180; and Macmillan, *The Blast of War*, pp. 263–295.

Doc. 226
ROOSEVELT TO CHURCHILL

No. 277 June 3, 1943

I know that you will agree with me that we may expect the followers of the Mikado to seize upon any hint we may let fall about weapons, method, or tactics used by us in successful antisubmarine warfare. It would be difficult to foretell the serious consequences of premature publication of our scientific development. We may be sure it will cost us many submarines and many lives. It seems to me that within the past month too much has been published both in the United States and in England and that serious harm will result if we do not check further disclosures. Can we not agree on a submarine statement to be issued jointly on the tenth day of each calendar month and take steps to prevent any other public statements about submarine warfare except carefully censored versions of individual combat?[1]

1 Churchill replied on June 4 that he was not aware of any serious leaks, but he agreed to the idea of a joint monthly statement setting forth in general terms the progress of the campaign against the U-boats.

Doc. 227
CHURCHILL TO ROOSEVELT

No. 296   June 5, 1943

General Marshall has himself prepared the following version of the approved decisions of the Combined Chiefs of Staff to be sent to Russia.[1] CIGS[2] and I agree with every word of it, and strongly hope that it can be sent to Stalin as the statement by the Chief of the United States Staff, concurred in by the CIGS, and that it has our (President and Prime Minister's) joint approval. If you agree, will you kindly implement without further reference to me. Message begins: "Draft of message from the President and the Prime Minister to Premier Stalin.

"In general, the overall strategy agreed upon is based upon the following decisions: (A) To give first priority to the control of the submarine menace and the security of our overseas lines of communication. (B) Next in priority, to employ every practicable means to support Russia. (C) To prepare the ground for the active or passive participation of Turkey in the war on the side of the Allies. (D) To maintain an unremitting pressure against Japan for the purpose of

1 At the end of the third Washington conference Roosevelt and Churchill prepared and emended several drafts of what they wanted to report to Stalin about their proceedings. When they were unable to reach an agreement, Churchill offered to take the drafts away with him and to send back a final version for the President's approval. On the plane to Algiers Churchill tried to do this, but, hitting a snag, he turned the material over to General Marshall, who in two hours completed a draft of which neither the President nor the Prime Minister changed a word. See Churchill, *Hinge of Fate*, pp. 811–813.

2 Chief of the Imperial General Staff, General Sir Alan Brooke.

continually reducing her military power. (E) To undertake such measures as may be practicable to maintain China as an effective ally and as a base for operations. (F) To prepare the French forces in Africa for active participation in the assaults on Axis Europe.

"With reference to (A) above regarding submarines, the immediate results of the recent deployment of long-range aircraft with new equipment and special attack groups of naval vessels give great encouragement, better than one enemy submarine a day having been destroyed since May 1st. If such a rate of destruction can be maintained it will greatly conserve, therefore increase, available shipping and will exert a powerful influence on the morale of the German submarine armada.

"With reference to the support of Russia, agreement was reached as follows: (A) To intensify the present air offensive against the Axis powers in Europe. This for the purpose of smashing German industry, destroying German fighter aircraft, and breaking the morale of the German people. The rapid development of this air offensive is indicated by the events of the past 3 weeks in France, Germany and Italy, Sicily and Sardinia, and by the growth of the United States heavy bomber force in England from some 350 planes in March to approximately 700 today with a schedule calling for 900 June 30, 1,150 September 30, and 2,500 April 1st. The British bomber force will be constantly increasing. (B) In the Mediterranean the decision was taken to eliminate Italy from the war as quickly as possible. General Eisenhower has been directed to prepare to launch offensives immediately following the successful completion of Husky (the assault on Sicily) for the purpose of precipitating the collapse of Italy and thus facilitating our air offensive against eastern and southern Germany as well as continuing the attrition of German fighter aircraft and developing a heavy threat against German control in the Balkans. General Eisenhower may use for the Mediterranean operations all those forces now available in that area except for 3 British and 4 American divisions which are to participate in concentration in England, next to be referred to. (C) It was decided that the resumption of the concentration of ground forces in England could now be undertaken with Africa securely in our hands and that while plans are being continuously kept up to date by a joint U.S.-British staff in England to take instant advantage of a sudden weakness in France or Norway, the concentration of forces and landing equipment in the British Isles should proceed at a rate to permit a full-scale invasion of the Continent to be launched at the peak of the great air offensive in the spring of 1944. Incidentally, the unavoidable absorption of large landing craft in the Mediterranean, the southwest Pacific, and the Aleutian

Islands[3] has been our most serious limiting factor regarding operations out of England.

"We have found that the undertakings listed utilise our full resources. We believe that these operations will heavily engage the enemy in the air and will force a dispersion of his troops on the ground to meet both actual attacks and heavy threats of attack which can readily be converted into successful operations whenever signs of Axis weakness become apparent."[4]

[3] U.S. forces had recaptured Attu Island in the Aleutians after a campaign between the landing on May 11 and the end of organized resistance on May 30. In the Pacific a landing had been made on Russell Island in the Solomons group on February 21.

[4] See *Stalin's Correspondence*, vol. 2, no. 90.

Doc. 228
CHURCHILL TO ROOSEVELT

No. 300   June 6, 1943

Your telegram through Eisenhower of June 5th.[1]

We had the whole French Committee to luncheon on Friday and everybody seemed most friendly. General Georges, whom I got out of France a month ago and who is a personal friend of mine, is a great support to Giraud. If de Gaulle should prove violent or unreasonable, he will be in a minority of 5 to 2 and possibly completely isolated. The Committee is therefore a body with collective authority with which in my opinion we can safely work.

I consider that the formation of this Committee brings to an end my official connexion with de Gaulle as leader of the Fighting French which was set out in the letters exchanged with him in 1940 and certain other documents of later date, and I propose insofar as is necessary to transfer these relationships, financial and otherwise, to the Committee as a whole. While I consider the Committee is a safe depository for arms and supplies, I feel that we should see how they conduct their business and themselves before deciding what degree of recognition we should give them as representing France. Macmillan and Murphy are working in the closest accord and will keep Eisen-

[1] Not printed. In that message Roosevelt emphasized Anglo-American unity in North Africa: "Eisenhower can be used on what you and I want." The President complained that de Gaulle got better publicity than either he or Churchill, adding: "Best of luck in getting rid of our mutual headache."

hower, with whom the supreme and ultimate power rests, fully informed.

I was not aware that there was any question of Boisson being dismissed from his post.[2] I should be strongly opposed to it. To make doubly sure I am telling Macmillan to associate himself with your instructions to Murphy. I expect however he has already done so.

I agree with you that the publicity is most one-sided. This is due to the press correspondents, most of whom have a de Gaullist bias. I will consult with Anthony about what can be done to correct this. I cannot however help feeling fairly confident that things will work better now. Please note that my Godefroy has come to heel before your Robert.[3]

I am very glad that I went to North Africa and, above all, that you sent Marshall with me. He was a tower of strength and sagacity. The concord and confidence of Eisenhower's headquarters and the ardour and conviction of the commanders actually charged with the operations was most bracing. I was nearly hung up by weather at Gibraltar but at the last moment a good report came in and we nipped through safely and comfortably. I should have liked to stay another week as the weather was delicious and the bathing was doing me no end of good.

Every good wish to you and all.

2 De Gaulle wanted to remove Pierre Boisson as governor general of French West Africa, but the Americans feared that this might increase de Gaulle's influence.

3 Admiral René Emile Godefroy had been reluctant to bring French naval vessels, demilitarized at Alexandria, to the Allied cause if they might fall to de Gaulle. In May 1943 he joined his squadron with the naval forces of France in North Africa. The reference to "your Robert" is to Robert Murphy, Roosevelt's personal representative in North Africa.

Doc. 229
CHURCHILL TO ROOSEVELT

No. 303   June 10, 1943

I send you in my immediately following[1] a note which has been prepared here about procedure in Husky land. It seems to me that there is a certain amount of heavy weather being made unnecessarily about two points which will settle themselves quite simply if left to Eisenhower and to the people on the spot.

First, about Macmillan. He is my personal representative just as Murphy is yours. Both get along perfectly well with Eisenhower and with each other in all matters relating to the Torch area. I cannot see

1 Not printed.

why exactly the same relationship should not continue in the Husky period and should not apply to the wider areas which may be brought under our joint control. Orders and formal correspondence would go through the combined staffs, but it is necessary that the heads of governments should have early and intimate information about what happens in the civil and political sphere. All this is working quite smoothly and easily at the present time, and all that is necessary is a ruling from you and me that the present relationship of our representatives to the Supreme Commander will cover the new acquisitions of territory and will not be altered thereby. I certainly left under the impression that this would be quite agreeable to Eisenhower.

The second point is about the degree of British and American control and administration which should be imposed upon any newly conquered regions. It would certainly seem wise to make them run themselves as much as possible. Prominent or malignant Fascists should be removed and we must be ready to supply trustworthy administrators in their place, insofar as these cannot be found for our purposes from the local population. It would, I feel sure, be a mistake to flood out all these places with many hundreds of British and American Gauleiters,[1] however well trained or well meaning they may be.

However, it is quite impossible to foresee in advance what the local conditions or temper of the people in the conquered regions will be. It should surely be left to the Supreme Commander to propose to our two Governments what British and American officers he wants and the degree of their infusion into the local life. My own feelings are that he would want to interfere as little as possible and make things run themselves, subject to the paramount interests of the armies and of the operations.

[1] The Germans had extended their system of administrative districts to the areas they annexed and had appointed German district leaders (Gauleiter), many of whom had acquired unsavory reputations long before 1943.

Doc. 230
CHURCHILL TO ROOSEVELT

No. 309   June 12, 1943

The castigation we have both received from Uncle Joe under date of June 11th[1] was naturally to be expected in view of the inevitable

[1] After learning from the report on the Washington conference that the second front in Europe was being put off until the spring of 1944, Stalin cabled: "Need I

course of events governing our decisions. In my opinion the best answer will be to knock Italy out of the war and let him feel the relief which will come to him thereby. I quite understand their vexation, though they cannot understand the facts that dominate our action. Any answer I may make will be entirely good-tempered and I will show it to you first.

The last paragraph, about his not participating or "any attempt to consider together etc." is the limit in view of the efforts we have made to bring about a tripartite conference.[2] All this makes me anxious to know anything you care to tell me about your letter sent to him by Mr. Davies and the answer which has been received from him.[3]

I will of course come anywhere you wish to a rendezvous and I am practising every day with my pistol to make head against the mosquitoes. Nevertheless, I once again beg you to consider Scapa Flow, which is safe, secret, and quite agreeable in July and August. If you could come there in a battleship I do not think it would be difficult for him to join us. Every kind of convenient arrangement could be made for you in Scotland, should you wish to go there. Of course, I should try to lure you farther south, but you would remain as usual master of the situation. The King, who has now safely arrived in Torch area,[4] is very keen on your coming and will, of course, welcome you either secretly or publicly as you may decide. At any rate, it seems to me that this is the moment to make such a suggestion to U.J. If you have any better idea, pray share it with me. He ought I think at least to have an offer.

---

speak of the dishearteningly negative impression that this fresh postponement of the second front and the withholding from our Army, which has sacrificed so much, of the anticipated substantial support by the Anglo-American armies, will produce in the Soviet Union—both among the people and in the Army?" *Stalin's Correspondence,* 2: 92.

2 Stalin wrote here that the Soviet government "cannot align itself with this decision, which, moreover, was adopted without its participation and without any attempt at a joint discussion of this highly important matter and which may gravely affect the subsequent course of the war."

3 Roosevelt had sent Joseph E. Davies, former U.S. ambassador to the Soviet Union, to Moscow in May to assure Stalin and Molotov that their differences with the Western allies could be resolved. Stalin was skeptical but was about to agree to a personal meeting with the President when he learned that Churchill wanted to be included as well, and then he dropped the idea. The letters Churchill mentions are Roosevelt's request for a meeting, possibly in the Bering Straits, and Stalin's reply that such a meeting might be possible in July or August. See U.S. Department of State, *The Conferences at Cairo and Tehran 1943* (Washington, 1961), pp. 3–4, 6–7.

4 King George VI of England arrived in Algiers on July 4, 1943.

Doc. 231
CHURCHILL TO ROOSEVELT

No. 310   June 13, 1943

This is what I propose to send to Joe. I should be very glad to know what you think of it before it goes. You will no doubt send your own message, which I should also like to see.[1] Begins:

"I have received a copy of your telegram of about June 11 to the President. I quite understand your disappointment but I am sure we are doing not only the right thing but the only thing that is physically possible in the circumstances. It would be no help to Russia if we throw away a hundred thousand men in a disastrous cross-channel attack such as would, in my opinion, certainly occur if we tried under present conditions and with forces too weak to exploit any success that might be gained at very heavy cost. In my view and that of all my expert military advisers, we should, even if we got ashore, be driven into the sea, as the Germans have forces already in France superior to any we could put there this year, and can reinforce far more quickly across the main lateral railways of Europe than we could do over the beaches or through any of the destroyed channel ports we might seize. I cannot see how a great British defeat and slaughter would aid the Soviet armies. It might, however, cause the utmost ill feeling here if it were thought it had been incurred against the advice of our military experts and under pressure from you. You will remember that I have always made it clear in my telegrams to you that I would never authorise any cross-channel attack which I believed would lead only to useless massacre.

"The best way for us to help you is by winning battles and not by losing them. If we can knock Italy out of the war this year, as is my earnest and sober hope, we shall draw far more Germans off your front than by any other means open. The great attack which is now not far off will absorb the capacities of every port under our control in the Mediterranean, from Gibraltar to Port Said inclusive. If Italy should be forced out of the war, the Germans will have to occupy the Riviera front, make a new front either on the Alps or the Po, and above all provide for the replacement of the numerous Italian divisions now in the Balkans. The moment for inviting Turkish participation in the war, active or passive, will then arrive. The bombing of the Rumanian

---

[1] Roosevelt did send a message to Stalin on June 20 agreeing with Churchill. See *Stalin's Correspondence*, vol. 2, no. 95.

oil fields can be carried through on a decisive scale. Already we are holding in the west or south of Europe the larger part of the German air force, and our superiority will increase continually.

"We are also ruining a large part of the cities and munitions centres of Germany. If the favourable trend of the anti-U-boat warfare in the last few months continues, it will quicken and increase the movement of United States forces to Europe, which is being pressed to the full limit of the available shipping. No one has paid more tributes than I have to the immense contribution of the Soviet Government to the common victory, and I thank you also for the recognition which you have lately given to the exertions of your two Western allies. It is my firm belief that we shall confront you before the end of the year with results which will give you substantial relief and satisfaction.

"I have never asked you for detailed information about the strength and dispositions of the Russian armies because you have been and are still bearing the brunt on land. I should, however, be glad to have your appreciation of the situation and immediate prospects on the Russian front and whether you think a German attack is imminent. We are already again at the middle of June and no attack has been launched. Surely this is a favourable factor. Our information about German intentions is conflicting. On the balance I think Hitler will attack you again, probably in the Kursk Salient, and that he will cut his losses in Italy. On the other hand, our intelligence reports show that the Japanese are urging him not to make a third attack on Russia but to turn his forces against the United States and Great Britain.

"At the end of your message you complain that Russia has not been consulted in our recent decisions. I fully understand the reasons which prevented you from meeting the President and me at Khartoum, whither we would have gone in January, and I am sure you were right not to relinquish even for a week the direction of your immense and victorious campaign. Nevertheless, the need and advantages of a meeting are very great. I can only say that I will go at any risk to any place that you and the President may agree upon. I personally believe that Scapa Flow, our main naval harbour in the north of Scotland, would be the most convenient, the safest, and, if desired, the most secret. I have again suggested this to the President. If you could come there by air at any time in the summer you may be sure that every arrangement would be made to suit your wishes, and you would have a most hearty welcome from your British and American comrades."

Doc. 232
ROOSEVELT TO CHURCHILL

No. 286   June 14, 1943

Replying to your 303[1] and 304[2] of 10 June 1943, I am in agreement that the present equal status of Macmillan and Murphy should continue unchanged in the Husky and post-Husky periods and that they should continue to communicate to the heads of their respective Governments early and intimate information regarding the civil and political sphere, informing the Supreme Commander in each instance.

I am also in agreement that in territory occupied by our combined forces in the future the Supreme Commander should during the period of occupation inform our two Governments what British and American officials he wants and the purposes for which he desires to use them in the local administration and that no other civil officials than those requested by the Supreme Commander should be sent to his area.

[1] See above, Doc. 229.
[2] Not printed.

Doc. 233
ROOSEVELT TO CHURCHILL

No. 288   June 17, 1943

I am fed up with de Gaulle, and the secret personal and political machinations of that Committee in the last few days indicate that there is no possibility of our working with de Gaulle.[1] If these were peace times it wouldn't make so much difference but I am absolutely convinced that he has been and is now injuring our war effort and

[1] On June 7 de Gaulle had maneuvered General Giraud into enlarging the French National Committee from seven to fourteen persons; Giraud later said that he did not understand the significance of his actions. Murphy reported that the enlargement now assured de Gaulle a position of supremacy on the committee, since a majority of the new members supported de Gaulle. Further, de Gaulle refused to name Giraud supreme commander of the French forces. See Churchill, *Closing the Ring*, pp. 174–175; Murphy, *Diplomat Among Warriors*, pp. 180–183; and *FR 1943*, 3: 149–153.

that he is a very dangerous threat to us. I agree with you that he likes neither the British nor the Americans and that he would double-cross both of us at the first opportunity. I agree with you that the time has arrived when we must break with him. It is an intolerable situation. I think the important thing is that we act together and my thinking regarding the whole matter runs about as follows:

We must divorce ourselves from de Gaulle because, first, he has proven to be unreliable, uncooperative, and disloyal to both our Governments. Second, he has more recently been interested far more in political machinations than he has in the prosecution of the war and these machinations have been carried on without our knowledge and to the detriment of our military interests. One result of this scheming on the part of de Gaulle has been that Eisenhower has had to give half his time to a purely local political situation which de Gaulle has accentuated. The war is so urgent and our military operations so serious and fraught with danger that we cannot have them menaced any longer by de Gaulle.

Our two countries have solemnly pledged that they will liberate the French Republic and, when we drive the Germans out, return that country to the control of the sovereign French people. This pledge we renew.

All of the above can be put by us in language which will be mutually agreeable. Above all I am anxious that the break be made on a basis and for reasons which are identical with both our Governments. There are plenty of emotional and dissident people throughout the world who will try to separate England and the United States in this matter and we must stand shoulder to shoulder, identically and simultaneously through this miserable mess. My affirmative thought is that we should go ahead and encourage the creation of a committee of Frenchmen made up of people who really want to fight the war and are not thinking too much about politics. I am sure we can find such a group. During the formation period we can continue to deal with the military authorities as in the past.

The first step in any event should be the deferment of any meeting of the French Committee in North Africa until later. In the meantime you can well suggest your views as to how you will approach and deal with the de Gaulle situation most effectively from the standpoint of later public opinion, also anything this Government might say concurrently with any public utterance you may make. Will you communicate with Macmillan to cooperate with Eisenhower in postponing any further meeting of the French Committee in North Africa?

I am anxious to have your thoughts on this as soon as possible.

Doc. 234
CHURCHILL TO ROOSEVELT

No. 316   June 18, 1943

Your No. 288.[1]

1. It is imperative that the French army in northwest Africa should be in loyal and trustworthy hands especially on the eve of the great operations which impend. I agree with you that no confidence can be placed in de Gaulle's friendship for the Allies, and I could not myself be responsible to the British nation whose armies have been placed under Eisenhower's command in North Africa if our base and lines of communication were disturbed or endangered through the existence of a French army under potentially hostile control and not properly subordinated to the Supreme Commander. I am glad therefore to learn the clear instructions you have given General Eisenhower not to "permit de Gaulle to direct himself or to control through partisans of any committee the African French army, either in the field of supplies, training, or operations."

2. I am not in favour at this moment of breaking up the Committee of 7 or forbidding it to meet. I should prefer that General Eisenhower should take your instructions as his directive, and that Murphy and Macmillan should work towards its fulfilment by whatever means they find most appropriate. HM Government will associate themselves with this policy.

3. The Committee will then be confronted with a choice of either accepting our decision by a majority or definite opposition to the two rescuing powers. If as I deem probable they accept the decision by a majority, it will be for de Gaulle to decide whether he and other dissentients will submit or resign. If de Gaulle resigns he will put himself in the wrong with public opinion and the necessary measures must be taken to prevent him from creating a disturbance. If he submits we shall probably have further trouble in the future, but this will be better than our sweeping away a Committee on which many hopes are founded among the United Nations as well as in France. We should prescribe the conditions essential for the safety of our forces and place the onus on de Gaulle. At any rate it would be wise to try this first.

4. I have already notified Massigli[2] through Macmillan that no

---

1 See above, Doc. 233.
2 René Massigli, Free French Minister of Foreign Affairs.

further payments will be made from British funds to the French National Committee in London and that any further payments will only be made to the new Committee of 7 acting by a majority. I have received from Macmillan the following paraphrased message. Begins:

"I take the right interpretation of your wishes to be full support of General Eisenhower in order to ensure that Giraud remains in effective command of French forces. This must include measures to ensure that reorganisation of personnel and appointments only take place with his concurrence. If this can be achieved while French unity is preserved, and de Gaulle remains on the Committee, well and good. Failing this our first requirement must be military security." Ends.

5. In view of the situation that has now developed "the measures to secure that any reorganisation of personnel and appointments should have his (Giraud's) concurrence" would not be satisfied by any division of military control between Giraud as Commander in Chief and de Gaulle as Minister of Defence. This last office should be put in the hands of General Georges or some other officer equally acceptable to the rescuing powers.

Doc. 235
ROOSEVELT TO CHURCHILL

No. 297   June 28, 1943

Your 328.[1] I did not suggest to U.J. that we meet alone but he told Davies that he assumed (a) that we would meet alone and (b) that he agreed that we should not bring staffs to what would be a preliminary meeting.[2]

He intimated that he would bring only a total of four or five people and on this assumption I would propose to take only Hopkins and Harriman.

There are certain advantages in such a preliminary meeting which I know you will appreciate. First, that without staffs there will be no military collisions in regard to demands for an immediate Roundup. Second, that he will not think that we are demanding a Russian offensive this summer if the Germans do not attack. Third, that in my opinion he will be more frank in giving his views on the offensive

---

[1] Not printed. Churchill cabled on June 25 that he knew of the President's desire to meet with Stalin in Alaska. He argued that a meeting of all three powers was necessary, because Axis propagandists would make much of any meeting from which the British were excluded. See *Conferences at Cairo and Tehran*, pp. 10–11.

[2] See above, Doc. 230, note 3.

against Japan now and later. Fourth, that he would also be more frank in regard to China. Fifth, that he would be more frank in regard to the Balkan States, Finland, and Poland.

I want to explore his thinking as fully as possible concerning Russia's postwar hopes and ambitions. I would want to cover much the same field with him as did Eden for you a year ago.

What would you think of coming over soon afterwards and that you and I with staffs should meet in the Citadel in Quebec? I am sure the Canadian Government would turn it over to us and it is a thoroughly comfortable spot, with thoroughly adequate accommodations there and at the Hotel Frontenac. It is far better than Washington at that time of year.

While U.J. gave no definite dates he suggested the end of July or early August. This is wholly tentative and I do not expect to hear anything further until about the fifteenth of July.

If he confirms this, I would be back about August fifteenth. I would have to be in Washington for a week but could easily get to some place in eastern Canada by the twenty-fifth of August.

Of course, you and I are completely frank in matters of this kind and I agree with you that later in the autumn we should most definitely have a full dress meeting with the Russians. That is why I think of a visit with Stalin as a preparatory talk on what you rightly call a lower level. Finally I gather from Davies the Kremlin people do not at all like the idea of U.J. flying across Finland, Sweden, Norway, and the North Sea to Scapa [Flow], especially at this time of year when there is practically no darkness.

I have the idea that your conception is the right one from the short point of view, but mine is the right one from the long point of view. I wish there were no distances.

Doc. 236
CHURCHILL TO ROOSEVELT

No. 336   June 29, 1943

I have now received your 297[1] and I repeat what I said in my 334[2] that if you and Uncle J can fix a meeting together I should no longer

1 See above, Doc. 235.

2 Not printed. Churchill enclosed an unpleasant message from Stalin on the second front, which he thought would have a bearing on the President's proposal to meet with the Soviet leader. But Churchill added that if Roosevelt could get Stalin to come to a meeting he would no longer try to prevent it. See *Conferences at Cairo and Tehran*, p. 12.

deprecate it. On the contrary in view of his attitude I think it important that this contact should be established.

I should be very glad to arrange for a meeting between us and our staffs about the end of August in Quebec which I am sure Mackenzie King[3] would welcome. Later on I will put the point to him.

Many thanks for your very full message.

[3] William Lyon Mackenzie King, Canadian Prime Minister and Secretary of State for External Affairs.

Doc. 237
ROOSEVELT TO CHURCHILL

No. 298   June 30, 1943

Regarding our messages on Supreme Command for Southeast Asia, I should like to ask your consideration of the following plan which appears to be in general accord with your ideas. The one point in which this plan differs from that set forth in your number 332, June 28th,[1] lies in the method of integration of the Chinese effort.

General Stilwell,[2] I feel, should be appointed Deputy Supreme Commander. His function as deputy would be to command, under the Supreme Commander, all ground and air forces at present under him in the Southeast Asia theater and such additional U.S. and Chinese forces as may in the future be made available. Furthermore he must continue to have certain direct responsibilities to the Generalissimo.[3] Upon his relationship with the Generalissimo will depend the positive action by the Chinese in operations against Burma. To secure this cooperation, Stilwell should have under his immediate control the tangible means to give effect to his requests, including the command of all those U.S. forces which have been deployed for the purpose of making effective the U.S. aid to China.

The deployment of the 10th Air Force in India, as has been previously mentioned,[4] was for the purpose of supporting China. Its offensive operations now and in the future against strategic targets in

1 Not printed. Churchill proposed that a new Southeast Asia command be established south of China, including the Indo-Chinese peninsula, part of Sumatra, and part of Australia. All troops operating within the boundaries, including the Chinese, should be under the supreme Allied commander.

2 General Joseph W. Stilwell, commander of U.S. air and ground forces in Southeast Asia.

3 Chiang Kai-shek.

4 The U.S. Tenth Air Force, with headquarters in New Delhi, began transporting supplies from India to Burma in March, 1942.

Burma and Thailand and in support of Chinese troops in the Assam-North Burma area, its operations in defense of the India-China air line, and its situation as a strategic air reserve for the 14th Air Force are all bound up with our program of increasing aid to China. As regards the 14th Air Force, I am of the opinion that the Generalissimo would raise serious objection to subjecting Chennault's[5] operations into Burma under any direct Supreme Command in India other than that provided by the channels already in existence.

I agree with your boundary for the Southeast Asia theater. Admiral Sir Andrew B. Cunningham would be especially acceptable as Supreme Commander. Air Marshal Tedder is also favorably considered. In view of the established United States policy of aid to China, however, the more appropriate command relationship would be for the Supreme Commander to report to the Combined Chiefs of Staff. I could agree, therefore, only to this command relationship following the Eisenhower pattern, with the British Chiefs of Staff designated as the agency for the Combined Chiefs of Staff charged with the issue of instructions to the Supreme Commander.

A British Allied naval commander, RAF commander, and a British Army commander all would be selected by you.

I believe that the above plan will permit us to integrate the Chinese potential with operations against Burma from India.

[5] Major General Claire ·L. Chennault, commander of the U.S. Fourteenth Air Force, operating in China.

Doc. 238
CHURCHILL TO ROOSEVELT

No. 342   July 3, 1943

1. We have given earnest consideration to the plan set out in your number 298.[1] The Chiefs of Staff had contemplated that General Stilwell (a) should be appointed Deputy Supreme Commander: (b) should continue to have his direct responsibilities to the Generalissimo: (c) should be given the responsibility for the operation of the air route to China, and for the defence of its Indian terminal, having an American Air Commander in Chief under him for this purpose: (d) should control the discipline and administration of all American forces in the Southeast Asia command.

2. The Chiefs of Staff feel that, having regard to the above responsible and multifarious duties and to the fact that (b) may necessitate frequent visits to China, it would be very difficult for General Stilwell

1 See above, Doc. 237.

to exercise *executive* command over a part of the land forces and a part of the operational air force. Nevertheless, we will certainly try what you suggest. We can always make adjustments afterwards in the light of experience.

3. On the question of command relationship, we still think that the MacArthur pattern[2] is more appropriate to this theatre and I hope that you will be able to agree to it, subject to the modification that the allocation of American and British resources of all kinds between the China theatre and the Southeast Asia command will be controlled by the Combined Chiefs of Staff.

4. I am sending you a separate telegram about a Supreme Commander.[3]

2 In the "Eisenhower pattern" all forces were unified under a single supreme commander; in the "MacArthur pattern" there was no comparable single chief.

3 Not printed. Admiral Mountbatten was named supreme commander in the Southeast Asia command on August 24, 1943.

Doc. 239
ROOSEVELT TO CHURCHILL

No. 308   July 8, 1943

This refers to your 339, June 30, 1943,[1] regarding provision for refugees in North Africa.

I will set out the elements of the problem as I understand them:

1. There are at present an estimated five or six thousand stateless or enemy-nationality refugees in Spain to be moved, largely of the Jewish race.

2. I am asking Generals Eisenhower and Giraud to designate Mogador or some other place in French North Africa as a place of temporary residence for these refugees and others who may be able to escape from Axis territory into Spain. They have already agreed in principle to the establishment of such a place of temporary residence.

3. I will arrange for the transportation of these refugees by land from Spain to the selected port in Portugal for their embarkation.

4. You will arrange for their sea transportation from Portugal to a port in North Africa.

5. I will request the American military authorities to make avail-

1 Not printed. Churchill wrote that refugees, especially Jews, needed more assistance, and supported establishing a small camp in North Africa. "Our immediate facilities for helping the victims of Hitler's Anti-Jewish drive are so limited at present," he wrote, "that the opening of the small camp proposed for the purpose. of removing some of them to safety seems all the more incumbent on us. . . ."

able cots and tents in sufficient number to meet the emergency needs of the refugees arriving at the temporary place of residence.

6. I will also arrange that preparations will be begun immediately for a temporary reception center of more substantial character where the refugees can be housed and cared for until subsequent arrangements are made for their disposition which should be at the earliest possible moment.

7. The costs of the refugees' transportation from Spain and their maintenance in the place of temporary residence until such time as a more permanent settlement is agreed upon will be borne equally by our two Governments.

8. The work of administration for the refugees at the temporary place of residence will be the responsibility of the Office of Foreign Relief and Rehabilitation Operations under Governor Lehman,[2] with representatives of your Government cooperating and assisting.

9. I am in complete accord with the thought of the French military authorities in that area that both for political and military reasons it is evential to transfer the refugees, after their arrival at the temporary place of residence, to a place of more permanent settlement for the duration. In this connection the Department of State has just been informed by your Embassy here in response to conversations Lord Halifax[3] has had with Mr. Myron Taylor[4] that certain places, among them Tripolitania, Cyrenaica, and Madagascar, are under active discussion and it appears not impossible that sites may be available there for the refugees. It is also my understanding that a limited number of the refugees may be admitted into Palestine.

10. The subsequent transportation of the refugees from the temporary place of residence to places of more permanent settlement and their continued care thereafter would be provided under the auspices and jurisdiction of the Executive Committee of the Intergovernmental Committee[5] the costs thereof to be underwritten jointly by the British and American Governments.

[2] Herbert H. Lehman, former governor of New York State, had been appointed head of the United Nations Relief and Rehabilitation Administration.

[3] British ambassador to the United States.

[4] Myron C. Taylor, President Roosevelt's personal representative at the Vatican.

[5] The Intergovernmental Committee on Political Refugees had been created in July 1938 at an international conference on the refugee crisis at Evian-les-Bains, France. Representatives of 32 nations attended the Evian conference, which had come about at the suggestion of President Roosevelt. The IGC was primarily involved in futile negotiations with the German government in an effort to facilitate the emigration of Jews. It was kept alive, at Roosevelt's insistence, after war had broken out and gained new prominence after the Bermuda conference in April 1943. That conference also launched the North African camp project for refugees evacuated from Spain. See Henry L. Feingold, *The Politics of Rescue* (New Brunswick, N.J., 1970), esp. chaps. 2 and 7.

I trust that you will let me know at the earliest convenient moment that we are in complete accord when I shall issue the necessary directives to complement those which you will issue.[6]

[6] On July 16, 1943 the State Department telegraphed Robert Murphy at Algiers, informing him of the President's agreement with Churchill's proposal, and instructing him "to ask General Eisenhower and the French North African authorities to designate a place in French North Africa as a place of temporary residence for those refugees of enemy nationality or stateless at present in Spain whose numbers are still estimated to be around six thousand at present." The Department's message continued: "To avoid the implication that the United States is conducting a concentration camp for these refugees it is contemplated that they should be given some freedom of movement and that those who are qualified to help meet the labor shortage in French North Africa should be granted permits to work temporarily while awaiting transfer elsewhere." The telegram was approved "O. K. F. D. R."

Doc. 240
ROOSEVELT TO CHURCHILL

No. 311   July 9, 1943

In reply to your No. 342, July 3rd.[1] Our agreement in maintaining American deployment in the Southeast Asia theater under Stilwell's command should assist us in resolving the problem of securing Chinese coordination.

As to the relationship of the Supreme Commander of the Southeast Asia theater following the MacArthur rather than the Eisenhower pattern,[2] practical consideration of the entire deployment against Japan brings me to the conclusion our solution should be the Eisenhower pattern.

Planned operations in the Southeast Asia theater must be more closely integrated with our efforts in the entire Pacific theater as the tempo of the war in the Pacific is stepped up. I can foresee that centralization in Washington will eventually be required not only to effect coordination but also to furnish the control necessary to prevent undue lag in massing of our means to defeat Japan after Germany's collapse.

To center in London on the one hand the major operational planning and strategic control of the Southeast Asia command and direct from Washington on the other the war in the Pacific would materially weaken our combined efforts against Japan.

1 See above, Doc. 238.
2 See above, Doc. 238, note 2.

Another consideration we cannot overlook. The Generalissimo has no representation on our combined staffs. Through the Pacific War Council, also in Washington, where he is represented by Dr. Soong,[3] we might be able to enhance our chances of securing cooperation from the Generalissimo.

[3] Dr. T. V. Soong, Chinese Minister of Foreign Affairs.

Doc. 241
CHURCHILL TO ROOSEVELT

No. 363   July 14, 1943

I was wrong when I said 5 U-boats in 24 hours.[1] It is 7 in 36. In these circumstances I suggest we release at a concerted moment the following. Begins:

"The President of the United States and the Prime Minister of Great Britain announce that in the 36 hours ending noon July 13th 7 U-boats were destroyed in the Mediterranean and in the Atlantic by British and American naval and air forces. This is the record killing of U-boats ever yet achieved in so short a time, and is therefore made the subject of a special announcement under the new system of monthly statements on the anti-U-boat war."

[1] In a message of July 13, Churchill claimed that a world record had been set with the destruction of five U-boats by Anglo-American forces in twenty-four hours. For a table of German U-boat losses from June 1, 1943, to May 31, 1944, see Roskill, *War at Sea*, 3 (pt. 1) : 365–372.

Doc. 242
ROOSEVELT TO CHURCHILL

No. 317   July 15, 1943

I assume that the special release you suggest in your No. 363[1] is based on the idea that the news will tend to discourage the Axis, particularly Italy, at this most opportune time, and that it will raise the enthusiasm and morale of the associated powers. While I concur of course in the first idea, nevertheless I feel that any possible advantages

[1] See above, Doc. 241.

would be more than offset by any pronouncement such as this which would intensify the now unfortunate feeling in this country that victory is in sight. The wave of optimism that has followed recent successes and our latest release on the antisubmarine situation is definitely slowing down production. We cannot afford to further inflate this costly public disregard of the realities of the situation, and therefore I doubt the wisdom at this time of giving the cat another canary to swallow.[2]

2 After receiving this message, Churchill referred to destroyed submarines as canaries.

Doc. 243
CHURCHILL TO ROOSEVELT

No. 366   July 16, 1943

I like very much the plan of our meeting in Canada and think the Heights of Abraham most attractive.[1] We think it most important to have the meeting earlier than September 1. The combined staffs at Washington agreed to meet again at the end of July or the beginning of August. We could come with our outfit by the same method as last time arriving at the very spot between the 12th and 15th of August. If this is agreeable to you, I will open the matter to Mackenzie King in the greatest secrecy.

Events in Husky are moving so fast and the degeneration of Italian resistance is so marked that decisions about the Toe, Ball, and Heel, which were regarded as a part of Husky, will almost certainly have to be taken before we meet. We shall, however, need to meet together to settle the larger issues which the brilliant victories of our forces are thrusting upon us about Italy as a whole. Mid-August will only just be in time for this work. This, also, will be the time to check up intimately upon de Gaulle, U.J., and other equally agreeable topics. I hope, therefore, that you will be able to give me this date.

1 For documents on the planning of the Quebec conference, see *Conferences at Washington and Quebec*, pp. 391-414.

Doc. 244
ROOSEVELT TO CHURCHILL

No. 324   July 25, 1943

By coincidence I was again at Shangri-la this afternoon when the news from Rome came, but this time it seems to be true.[1] If any overtures come we must be certain of the use of all Italian territory and transportation against the Germans in the north and against the whole Balkan peninsula, as well as use of airfields of all kinds. It is my thought that we should come as close as possible to unconditional surrender followed by good treatment of the Italian populace. But I think also that the head devil should be surrendered together with his chief partners in crime. In no event should our officers in the field fix on any general terms without your approval and mine. Let me have your thoughts.

[1] On July 25, two weeks after the Allied invasion of Sicily, King Victor Emmanuel III dismissed Mussolini and announced the establishment of a new government. See below, Doc. 246. See also Sir Ivone Kirkpatrick, *Mussolini—Study of a Demagogue* (New York, 1964), pp. 503ff. and chap. 20.

Doc. 245
CHURCHILL TO ROOSEVELT

No. 382   July 25, 1943

Changes announced in Italy probably portend peace proposals. Let us consult together so as to take joint action. The present stage may only be transition. But anyhow, Hitler will feel very lonely when Mussolini is down and out.[1] No one can be quite sure this may not go farther.

[1] For Hitler's response to Mussolini's dismissal, see F. W. Deakin, *The Brutal Friendship—Mussolini, Hitler and the Fall of Italian Fascism* (New York, 1963), pp. 489ff.

Doc. 246
ROOSEVELT TO CHURCHILL

No. 331   July 30, 1943

Your message No. 383 dated 26 July 1943[1] expresses generally my thoughts of today on prospects and methods of handling the Italian situation with which we are now confronted.

In the following draft I have suggested for consideration certain minor changes, the reasons for which if they are not obvious we can discuss at our next meeting.

It seems highly probable that the fall of Mussolini will involve the overthrow of the Fascist regime and that the new government of the King[2] and Badoglio[3] will seek to negotiate a separate arrangement with the Allies for an armistice. Should this prove to be the case it will be necessary for us to make up our minds first of all upon what we want and secondly upon the measures and conditions required to gain it for us.

At this moment above all others our thoughts must be concentrated upon the supreme aim, namely the destruction of Hitler and Hitlerism.[4] Every military advantage arising out of the surrender of Italy (should that occur) must be sought for this purpose.

The first of these is the control of all Italian territory and transportation against the Germans in the north and against the whole Balkan peninsula[5] as well as the use of airfields of all kinds. This must include the surrender to our garrisons of Sardinia, the Dodecanese, and Corfu as well as of all the naval and air bases in the Italian mainland as soon as they can be taken over.

Secondly and of equal importance the immediate surrender to the Allies of the Italian fleet, or at least its effective demobilization and the disarmament of the Italian air and ground forces to whatever extent we find needful and useful. The surrender of the fleet will

1 Not printed. Churchill urged Roosevelt to consider favorably any anti-Fascist Italian government that could lead effectively. He sent the President "Thoughts on the Fall of Mussolini by the Prime Minister and Minister of Defence." See FR 1943, 2: 332–335.

2 King Victor Emmanuel III of Italy.

3 Marshal Pietro Badoglio.

4 The President eliminated Churchill's phrase "and next Germany" after "Hitlerism."

5 In Churchill's draft, he put "against the whole Balkan peninsula" in quotes.

liberate powerful British naval forces for service in the Indian Ocean against Japan and will be most agreeable to the United States.

Also of equal consequence the immediate surrender or withdrawal to Italy of all Italian forces[6] wherever they may be outside of Italy proper.

Another objective of the highest importance about which there will be passionate feeling in this country and Britain is the immediate liberation of all United Nations[7] prisoners of war in Italian hands and the prevention which can in the first instance only be by the Italians of their being transported northwards to Germany. We regard it as a matter of honor and humanity to get our own flesh and blood back as soon as possible and spare them the measureless horrors of incarceration in Germany during the final stages of the war.

The fate of the German troops in Italy and particularly of those south of Rome will probably lead to fighting between the Germans and the Italian army and population.[8]

When we see how this process goes we can take a further view about action to be taken north of Rome. We should however try to get possession at the earliest moment of a safe and friendly area on which we can base the whole forward air attack upon south and central Germany and of points[9] on both the west coast and east coast railways of Italy as far north as we dare. This is a time to dare.

In our struggle with Hitler and the German army we cannot afford to deny ourselves any assistance that will kill Germans. The fury of the Italian population may now be turned against the German intruders who have as they will feel brought these miseries upon Italy and then come so scantily and grudgingly to her aid. We should stimulate this process in order that the new, liberated anti-Fascist Italy shall afford us at the earliest moment a safe and friendly area on which we can base the whole forward air attack upon south and central Germany.

This air attack is a new advantage of the first order as it brings the whole of the Mediterranean air forces into action from a direction which turns the entire line of air defenses in the west and which furthermore exposes all those centers of war production which have been increasingly developed to escape air attack from Great Britain. It

---

[6] The President eliminated Churchill's enumeration of Corsica, the Riviera, Yugoslavia, Albania, and Greece.

[7] Roosevelt substituted "United Nations" for "British."

[8] Churchill's draft included three sentences demanding the surrender of any Italian government and discussing the possibility that German troops would move northward in spite of the Italian forces. He urged that the Allies assist the Italians in forcing the German troops south of Rome to surrender.

[9] The President added the words beginning with "possession" and eliminated "and" from the beginning of the last sentence.

will become urgent in the highest degree to get agents, commandos, and supplies by sea across the Adriatic into Greece, Albania, and Yugoslavia. It must be remembered that there are fifteen German divisions in the Balkan peninsula of which ten are mobile. Nevertheless once we have control of the Italian peninsula and of the Adriatic and the Italian armies in the Balkans withdraw or lay down their arms it is by no means unlikely that the Hun will be forced to withdraw northwards to the line of the Sava and Danube, thus liberating Greece and other tortured countries.

We cannot yet measure the effects of Mussolini's fall and of Italian capitulation upon Bulgaria, Rumania, and Hungary. They may be profound. In connection with this situation the collapse of Italy should fix the moment for putting the strongest pressure on Turkey to act in accordance with the spirit of the alliance and in this Britain and the United States should if possible be joined or at least supported by Russia.[10] I believe that in any important negotiations affecting the Balkans the concurrence of Russia should be obtained if practicable.

It is my opinion that an effort to seize the "head devil" in the early future would prejudice our primary objective which is to get Italy out of the war. We can endeavor to secure the person of the "head devil" and his assistants in due time,[11] and to then determine their individual degrees of guilt for which "the punishment should fit the crime."

[10] Churchill's version of the paragraph ended here.

[11] Here Churchill speculated on Mussolini's fate and raised the issue of punishment for war criminals.

Doc. 247
ROOSEVELT TO CHURCHILL

No. 334   July 30, 1943

There are some contentious people here who are getting ready to make a row if we seem to recognize the House of Savoy[1] or Badoglio. They are the same element which made such a fuss over North Africa.[2]

I told the press today that we have to treat with any person or persons in Italy who can best give us first disarmament and second assurance against chaos, and I think also that you and I after an

[1] The royal family of Italy, headed by King Victor Emmanuel III.

[2] Opponents of the Darlan "deal." See James MacGregor Burns, *Roosevelt: Soldier of Freedom*, pp. 384–385, 391–394, 422, 548, 608.

armistice comes could say something about self-determination in Italy at the proper time.

Doc. 248
CHURCHILL TO ROOSEVELT

No. 403   August 4, 1943

Your number 342.[1] War Cabinet have now given most careful consideration to proposals to make Rome an open city on the conditions specified. We are sure that the effect on public opinion here would be most unfortunate. What will the Russians say? It would be taken as a proof that we were going to make a patched-up peace with the King and Badoglio and had abandoned the principle of unconditional surrender. It would be taken all over the world and throughout Italy as a success for the new Italian government who would have rescued Rome from all further danger. No doubt their greatest hope is to have Italy recognised as a neutral area, and Rome would seem to be a first instalment. Considering that Badoglio, according to all our information and especially the most secret, is giving repeated assurances to Germany and Japan that they mean to carry on the war and be faithful to their engagements, and that they are even repeating this kind of statement on the radio, we do not think they should be given the slightest encouragement. Although in the interval it would be convenient to secure the conditions proposed for Rome, this advantage in our opinion is far outweighed by the political misunderstanding which would arise among our own people and the stimulus given to a hostile Italian government.

We hope that in a few months Rome will be in our hands, and we shall need to use its facilities for the northward advance. If Rome has been declared an open city by us, it will be practically impossible for us to take away its status when we want to use it and its communications and airfields. The British Chiefs of Staff say these "open city" conditions, applied to us, would paralyse the whole further campaign: and certainly the Germans would threaten Rome with bombardment if they were altered or broken. We think this a great danger.

[1] Not printed. Roosevelt cabled on August 3: "I think we would be in a difficult position if we were to turn down the plea to make Rome an open city. I have just received from Washington [the President was then at Birch Island, Ontario] the proposed conditions and given my approval in principle but I think we must be very sure of the inspection if the terms are accepted by Italy." For details on this question, see *Conferences at Washington and Quebec*, pp. 527–531, 549–572, 594–598. On August 14 the Italian government officially declared Rome an open city.

In these circumstances would it not be better for us to talk the matter over when we meet? In the interest of putting the maximum political and military pressure on the Italian people and Government as well as for strictly military reasons we are most reluctant to interrupt such bombing of the marshalling yards, etc., as Eisenhower evidently thought desirable: but if you so desire, it must be postponed until you and I have met.[2]

Your number 343.[3] On this ground also I am so glad that we are going to meet. Pressure is growing from all quarters in this country, from the Dominions, particularly from Canada, and from several of the United Nations governments with which we are in touch to "recognise" the French National Committee. Macmillan reports that he and Murphy are agreed in favouring this and that extreme bitterness and resentment will be caused among all classes of Frenchmen by continued refusal. In accordance with your wishes however we shall take no step pending our meeting to which I am keenly looking forward for reasons far removed from all this tiresome business.

[2] At the Quebec conference two weeks later Secretary of State Hull told Foreign Secretary Eden that the United States had made no commitment on the open city proposal and intended to make none. See *Conferences at Washington and Quebec*, pp. 1054–1091, 1161–1176; and *FR 1943*, 2: 910–953. On December 15, 1943, the Combined Chiefs of Staff issued an order to General Eisenhower that Vatican City was to be treated as neutral territory. Allied troops were instructed to avoid the Vatican's churches and other buildings outside the city, since they were recognized under the Lateran Treaty as having diplomatic immunity.

[3] Not printed. On August 3 Roosevelt cabled: "I earnestly hope that nothing will be done in the matter of recognition of the Committee of National Liberation until we have an opportunity to talk it over together."

Doc. 249
CHURCHILL TO ROOSEVELT

No. 408   August 11, 1943

Following is draft referred to in my immediately preceding telegram.[1] Begins:

"During July the U-boats have obtained very poor results for their widespread effort against Allied shipping. The steady flow of transatlantic supplies on the greatest scale has continued unmolested, and such sinkings as have taken place in distant areas have had but an insignificant effect on the conduct of the war by the Allies. In fact,

[1] Not printed.

July is probably our most successful month because the imports have been high, shipping losses moderate, and U-boat sinkings heavy.

"Before the descent upon Sicily an armada of warships, troop transports, supply ships, and landing craft proceeded through Atlantic and Mediterranean waters with scarcely any interference from U-boats. Large reinforcements have also been landed on that island. Over 2,500 vessels were involved in these operations and the losses are only about 80,000 tons. On the other hand, the U-boats which attempted to interfere with these operations suffered severe losses.

"Our offensive operations against Axis submarines continue to progress most favourably in all areas. And during May, June, and July we have sunk at sea a total of over 90 U-boats, which represents an average loss of nearly 1 U-boat a day over the period.

"The decline in the effectiveness of the U-boats is illustrated by the following figures. In the first 6 months of 1943 the number of ships sunk per U-boat operating was only half that in the last 6 months of 1942 and only a quarter that in the first half of 1942.

"The tonnage of shipping in the service of the United Nations continues to show a considerable net increase. During 1943 new ships completed by the Allies exceed all sinkings from all causes upwards of 3,000,000 tons.

"In spite of this very favourable progress in the battle against the U-boats, it must be remembered that the enemy still has large U-boat reserves, completed and under construction. It is necessary therefore to prepare for intensification of the battle both at sea and in the shipyards and to use our shipping with utmost economy to strengthen and speed the general offensive of the United Nations. Continued success can only be expected if there is no relaxation of effort."[2]

2 The White House press release of August 14, issued in the names of Roosevelt and Churchill, followed very closely the wording of Churchill's draft. For the final text, see *Conferences at Washington and Quebec*, pp. 833–834. For an overview of the campaign against the U-boats, see Churchill, *Closing the Ring*, pp. 10–15; Morison, *Atlantic Battle Won* in *History of United States Naval Operations in World War II*, pp. 85–248; and Roskill, *War at Sea*, 3 (pt. 1) : 15–55, 245–282.

Doc. 250
CHURCHILL TO ROOSEVELT

No. 410   August 11, 1943

Following is text referred to in para 3 of my number 409.[1] Begins:
"I have just returned from the front and already had time to

1 Not printed. The message quoted here is from Stalin.

become familiar with the message of British Government dated 7 August.

"I agree that a meeting of the heads of three governments is absolutely desirable. Such a meeting must be realised at the first opportunity, having arranged with the President the place and time of this meeting.

"At the same time, I ought to say that in the existing situation on the Soviet-German front, I, to my regret, have no opportunity to absent myself and to leave the front even for one week. Although recently we have had several successes on the front, an extreme strain on the strength and exceptional watchfulness are required in regard to the new possible actions of the enemy from the Soviet troops and from the Soviet command just now. In connexion with this, I have to visit the troops on that or other parts of our front more often than usual. In the circumstances, at the present time I am not able to visit Scapa Flow or any other distant point for a meeting with you and the President.

"Nevertheless, in order not to postpone an examination of the questions which interest our countries, it would be expedient to organise a meeting of the responsible representatives of our states and we might come to an understanding in the nearest future concerning the place and date of such a meeting.

"Moreover, it is necessary beforehand to agree on the scope of the questions to be discussed and the drafts of the proposals which have to be accepted. The meetings will hardly give any tangible result without that.

"Taking this opportunity I congratulate the British Government and the Anglo-American troops on the occasion of their most successful operations in Sicily which have already caused the downfall of Mussolini and the breakup of his gang."

For reply see my immediately following telegram.[2]

2 See below, Doc. 251.

Doc. 251
CHURCHILL TO ROOSEVELT

No. 411   August 12, 1943

Following is reply being sent to message in my number 410[1] referred to in para 3 of my number 409.[2] Begins:

"Prime Minister to Marshal Stalin. Most secret and personal.

1 See above, Doc. 250.
2 Not printed.

"Your telegram of August 9 gives me the opportunity to offer you my heartfelt congratulations on the recent most important victories gained by the Russian armies at Orel and Byelgorod opening the way to your further advances towards Bryansk and Kharkov. The defeats of the German army on this front are milestones to our final victory.

"I have arrived at the Citadel, Quebec, and start this afternoon to meet the President at his private home. Meanwhile, the staffs will be in conference here and the President and I will join them at the end of the week. I will show the President your telegram about meeting of our responsible representatives in the near future which certainly seems desirable. I quite understand you cannot leave the front at this critical period when you are actually directing the victorious movement of your armies.

"Thank you for your congratulations on our Sicilian success, which we shall endeavour to exploit to the full without prejudice to Overlord.[3] Certainly our affairs are much better in every quarter than when we met at Moscow exactly a year ago.

"I am sending you a small stereoscopic machine with a large number of photograph slides of the damage done by our bombing to German cities. They give one a much more vivid impression than anything that can be gained from photographs. I hope you will find half an hour in which to look at them. This we know for certain, eighty percent of the houses in Hamburg are down. It is only now a question of a short time before the nights lengthen and even greater destruction will be laid upon Berlin. This subject only to weather. This will be continued for several nights and days and will be the heaviest ever known.

"Finally in the U-boat war we have in the months of May, June, and July destroyed U-boats at the rate almost of one a day, while our losses have been far less than we planned for. Our net gain in new tonnage is very great. All this will facilitate the establishment of the large-scale Anglo-American fronts against the Germans which I agree with you are indispensable to the shortening of the war."

[3] New code name for the cross-channel attack, now scheduled for the spring of 1944.

Doc. 252
CHURCHILL TO ROOSEVELT

No. 413   August 16, 1943

First of all, the Governor General[1] will meet you at a wayside station outside Quebec. Mackenize King and I will also be there. The

[1] The Earl of Athlone, governor general of Canada.

Governor General will drive you to the Citadel where a guard of honour will be paraded, and he would like to have a small reception immediately on your arrival where about forty principal persons could be presented to you. This can be cut out if you feel it would be tiring. In the evening, the Governor General will give a dinner in the Citadel to your personal party and mine to which Mackenzie King, the High Commissioner,[2] and one or two others will be asked—in all about twenty. I hope this will be agreeable to you. Anthony and Brendan[3] will be there if they arrive in time.[4]

2 Malcolm MacDonald, British high commissioner in Canada.
3 Anthony Eden and Brendan Bracken.
4 Roosevelt replied on August 16: "Delighted with arrangements. Things are progressing everywhere." See "The President's Log," in *Conferences at Washington and Quebec*, pp. 837–840.

THE FIRST QUEBEC CONFERENCE
AUGUST, 1943

[Churchill, accompanied by his top military advisers, as well as his wife and daughter Mary, traveled to Canada on the *Queen Mary*. Despite wartime censorship, word of his arrival had spread in advance, and a large and enthusiastic crowd was on hand when the Prime Minister's party landed at Halifax and boarded a train for Quebec, where they arrived on August 11.

The following day Churchill and his daughter set out for Hyde Park, where they stayed with the Roosevelts for several days before returning to Quebec. Churchill found the American summer heat oppressive. Unable to sleep, one night he found cool breezes and serenity by sitting on a bluff overlooking the Hudson River until dawn. Roosevelt left Hyde Park for a last-minute conference with some of his advisors in Washington, arriving in Quebec on September 17.

At Hyde Park Churchill had prepared a statement on British strategic policy including future operations in Burma and the Indian Ocean. In Europe Churchill felt that the capture of Sicily and the recent fall of Mussolini made the invasion of Italy a natural follow-up. By seizing the moment, the Allies might be able to push north as far as Leghorn and Ancona by November. The surrender of Italy and the Italian fleet would weaken the Axis hold on the Mediterranean. This, in turn, would make it possible to transport additional forces through the Suez Canal to India, where they would be available for service in Southeast Asia. Finally, the improved situation in the Mediterranean would facilitate the supplying of resistance groups in Savoy, the French Alps, and the Balkans.

Before Roosevelt left Washington, he learned from Churchill the encouraging news that Italy had begun to make peace overtures. At a meeting with the Combined Chiefs of Staff on August 19 Churchill repeated his previous argument for a campaign in Sumatra, but the President doubted its value and the project was dropped. For his part, Roosevelt was determined to launch a combined American, British, and Chinese offensive in Burma in order to open up a land route over which supplies could be sent directly to China, thereby bringing that embattled country more actively into the war against Japan. The two agreed on naming Admiral Lord Louis Mountbatten supreme Allied commander for the Southeast Asia theater, with General Joseph Stilwell, who commanded the American ground and air forces in Southeast Asia as well as the Chinese troops in Burma, as his deputy. No final decision on Burma was reached at the conference.

The most important result of the first Quebec conference was the blueprint for the cross-channel attack, now renamed Overlord. In ratifying this plan, Roosevelt and Churchill agreed that it was to constitute the major Anglo-American effort against the European Axis. Originally, the President and the Prime Minister had agreed that a British officer should be in charge of the invasion of Europe. Indeed, Churchill had already decided that General Sir Alan Brooke should have the post and Brooke had been so informed. Since it became increasingly obvious, however, that the United States would furnish the bulk of the forces for the operation, it was only fitting that they should be commanded by an American general. At Hyde Park Churchill suggested to Roosevelt that he appoint an American to command Overlord. The President agreed but postponed a final decision until the end of the year.

Roosevelt and Churchill also gave final approval to plans for the forthcoming invasion of Italy, but with the specific provision that only troops already allocated to this operation were to be used. As regards the Pacific war, the President and the Prime Minister agreed that the thrusts toward Japan should continue both along the southwest and central Pacific routes. Finally, they signed an agreement providing for the exchange of atomic energy information and set up a combined policy committee to expedite collaboration in this field.

The first Quebec conference ended on August 24, and most of the participants rapidly dispersed. Roosevelt returned to Washington, and Churchill traveled to the Lake of the Snows, about seventy-five miles from Quebec, where he spent some time fishing before returning to the conference city for a radio address. On September 1 he left for Washington and again took up residence at the White House, arriving there the same day as news of the Italian acceptance of the Allied surrender terms.

Churchill remained in Washington for most of the next twelve days, conferring with American leaders and closely following developments in Italy. On September 9 the President and the Prime Minister had another meeting at the White House to discuss the implications of the Italian situation. For the occasion, Churchill prepared a statement declaring that if the Italian fleet fell into Allied hands as a result of the Italian surrender, a British naval squadron in the Mediterranean could be released for service in the Pacific. Italy was to be encouraged to join the war against Nazi Germany, with the Italian navy operating under British or American control.

In Italy itself Churchill hoped that, following a successful landing at Salerno—the dramatic battle for which plans were under way during his stay in Washington—the Allies would speedily advance northward until they reached the main German defense lines. If this occurred, Churchill hoped, it would open up the possibility of seizing one or more ports on the Dalmatian coast through which supplies could be funneled to the anti-Nazi guerrillas operating in the Balkans. Furthermore, Free French units could occupy Corsica while the British seized the island of Rhodes, a favorite Churchill objective. The result of all this, Churchill believed, would be that anti-German sentiment would increase considerably in Hungary, Rumania, and Bulgaria and that Turkey might finally be induced to enter the war on the Allied side. Since Churchill's statement, however, amounted to a negation of what had only recently been agreed upon at Quebec—namely, that the Italian campaign should be conducted with limited forces in order to concentrate on preparations for Overlord—it received a cool reception from the President and his military chiefs, and no final action was taken on the proposal.

On September 10 Roosevelt departed Washington for Hyde Park, leaving Churchill behind at the White House. The President told the Prime Minister to treat the residence as his own home and to call any conference he wished. Churchill availed himself of the privilege on September 11 by convening another meeting with the U.S. Chiefs of Staff as well as Harry Hopkins, W. Averell Harriman, and Admiral William D. Leahy, who represented the President. The meeting dealt mostly with recent developments in Italy, but no additional decisions were reached.

On September 12 Churchill left Washington for Halifax, stopping off at Hyde Park to say good-bye to the President. En route to Canada, Churchill sent Roosevelt one of his most cordial messages: "You know how I treasure the friendship with which you have honoured me and how profoundly I feel that we might together do something really fine and lasting for our two countries and, through them, for the future of all."]

Doc. 253
ROOSEVELT TO CHURCHILL

No. 351   September 19, 1943

Delighted you are all safely home, and I hope you had a smooth run.[1] All is quiet here. Congress has been here for a week and it is still quiet.[2] My best to all three of you.

[1] Churchill, his wife, and daughter arrived back in Great Britain on September 19.

[2] See Burns, *Roosevelt: Soldier of Freedom*, pp. 426–429. Roosevelt was concerned among other things about the debate on the Fulbright and Connally Resolutions which called for United States participation in the "establishment and maintenance of international authority with power to prevent aggression and to preserve the peace of the world." With the fight over the League of Nations still clearly in his mind, he was determined that congressional planning for a successor to the League be gradual, unemotional, and wholly bipartisan. The House passed the Fulbright Resolution by a large majority on September 21, and the Senate the Connally Resolution on November 5. See Hull, *Memoirs*, 2: 1218–1263, 1314; H. Bradford Westerfield, *Foreign Policy and Party Politics: Pearl Harbor to Korea* (New Haven, 1955), pp. 155–159. *Congressional Record*, 78th Congress, 1st Session, 89: 7729 (September 21, 1943) and 9222 (November 5, 1943).

Doc. 254
ROOSEVELT TO CHURCHILL

No. 373   October 4, 1943

On the front page of the Washington *Post*, dated Saturday morning, October 2, there appeared a story headlined as follows: "Stalin Said to Have Rejected London as Meeting Place."

The article stated in substance that Russia had politely rejected a proposal made by me personally to change the location of the three-power conference from Moscow to London because the health of the Secretary of State, Cordell Hull, made the longer journey undesirable. In order to appear in this edition of the newspaper, the story had to be released actually many hours before I had personally received Stalin's reply stating that he did not care to change the location.

This article, written by Frederick Kuh and copyrighted by the Chicago *Sun*, appeared under a London dateline. Since the Chicago *Sun* is a highly reputable paper and friendly to this administration it seems reasonable to conclude that the dateline was not faked and so the story did in fact originate in London. To my mind the mere fact that this story got into the newspapers in the first place indicates a dangerous leak somewhere and, furthermore, indicates a bad mistake on the part of some censor for passing the story for publication as he must have in this case.

Don't you think perhaps it would be beneficial to us both if this leak could be run down and so avoid another one in the future when there is more at stake?

Doc. 255
CHURCHILL TO ROOSEVELT

No. 437   October 5, 1943

The text of the telegram referred to in my 436[1] is as follows:

"Prime Minister to Marshal Stalin. Personal and most secret. For your eye alone, Sept. 25, 1943.

"I have been pondering about our meeting of heads of governments at Teheran.[2] Good arrangements must be made for security in this somewhat loosely controlled area. Accordingly, I suggest for your consideration that I make preparations at Cairo[3] in regard to accommodation, security, etc., which are bound to be noticed in spite of all praiseworthy efforts to keep them secret. Then perhaps only two or three days before our meeting we should throw a British and a Russian brigade around a suitable area in Teheran including the airfield and keep an absolute cordon till we have finished our talks. We would not tell the Persian Government nor make any arrange-

---

[1] Not printed.

[2] This city was Churchill's suggestion, although no agreement had yet been reached on a site for a meeting. Stalin cabled Roosevelt and Churchill on September 12 that he would have no objection to Teheran.

[3] Mustafa an-Nahas Pasha, the prime minister of Egypt, first mentioned Cairo as a Big Three meeting site in an interview in the London *Evening News*. Stalin opposed the idea because the Soviet Union had no representation in Egypt. When the President decided to include Chiang Kai-shek, he settled on Cairo as a convenient place to meet the Chinese leader after meeting with Stalin at Teheran. See *Conferences at Cairo and Tehran*, pp. 3–107.

ments for our accommodation until this moment comes. We should of course have to control absolutely all outgoing messages. Thus we shall have an effective blind for the world press and also for any unpleasant people who might not be as fond of us as they ought.

"I suggest also that in all future correspondence on this subject we use the expression 'Cairo 3' instead of Teheran which should be buried and also that the code name for the operation should be Eureka which I believe is Ancient Greek. If you have other ideas let me know and we can then put them to the President. I have not said anything to him about this aspect yet."

Doc. 256
CHURCHILL TO ROOSEVELT

No. 438   October 7, 1943

I am much concerned about the situation developing in the eastern Mediterranean. On the collapse of Italy we pushed small detachments from Egypt into several of the Greek islands especially Kos which has a landing ground and Leros which is a fortified Italian naval base with powerful permanent batteries.[1] We ran this risk in the hope that the Italian garrisons which welcomed us would take part in the defence. This hope appears vain and Kos has already fallen except for some of our troops fighting in the mountains. Leros may well share its fate. Our enterprises against Rhodes have not yet succeeded.[2]

I believe it will be found that the Italian and Balkan peninsulas are militarily and politically united and that really it is one theatre with which we have to deal. It may indeed not be possible to conduct a

[1] Beginning on September 15, the British landed a battalion of troops on the islands of Kos, Leros, and Samos, plus smaller garrisons on some of the other Greek islands. The Germans began air raids against Kos on September 18, and on October 3 German parachutists overwhelmed the British garrison.

[2] The British wanted to attack Rhodes about October 20, and thereby hold Leros and then retake Kos. To do this they needed three landing ship tanks, a few military transport ships, a hospital ship, naval escorts, bombarding vessels, and air transportation for a battalion of paratroopers. Churchill asked Eisenhower to allocate these forces on the grounds that Rhodes was the key to both the Aegean Sea and the eastern Mediterranean and that the Germans should not be allowed to consolidate there. Initially, Eisenhower's response was encouraging, but the increasing demands of the Italian campaign led to postponements of other operations. Churchill then took his case to the President. See PDDE, 3 (Baltimore, 1970): 1460–1461; and Churchill, Closing the Ring, pp. 203–211.

successful Italian campaign ignoring what happens in the Aegean. The Germans evidently attach the utmost importance to this eastern sphere and have not hesitated to divert a large part of their straitened air force to maintain themselves there. They have to apprehend desertion by Hungary and Rumania and a violent schism in Bulgaria. At any moment Turkey may lean her weight against them. We can all see how adverse to the enemy are the conditions in Greece and Yugoslavia. When we remember what brilliant results have followed from the political reactions in Italy induced by our military efforts, should we not be short-sighted to ignore the possibility of a similar and even greater landslide in some or all of the countries I have mentioned? If we were able to provoke such reactions and profit by them our joint task in Italy would be greatly lightened.

I have never wished to send an army into the Balkans but only by agents, supplies, and commandos to stimulate the intense guerrilla [activity] prevailing there. This may yield results measureless in their consequence at very small cost to main operations. What I ask for is the capture of Rhodes and the other islands of the Dodecanese. The movement northward of our Middle Eastern air forces and their establishment in these islands and possibly on the Turkish shore which last might well be obtained would force a diversion on the enemy far greater than that required of us. It would also offer the opportunity of engaging the enemy's waning air power and wearing it down in a new region. This air power is all one and the more continually it can be fought the better.

Rhodes is the key to all this. I do not feel the present plan of taking it is good enough. It will require and is worth at least up to a first-class division which can of course be replaced by static troops once the place is ours. Leros which for the moment we hold so precariously is an important naval fortress and once we are ensconced in this area air and light naval forces would have a most fruitful part to play. The policy should certainly not be pursued unless done with vigour and celerity requiring the best troops and adequate means. In this way the diversion from the main theatre would only be temporary while the results may well be of profound and lasting importance.

I beg you to consider this and not let it be brushed aside and all these possibilities lost to us in the critical months that lie ahead. Even if landing craft and assault ships on the scale of a division were withheld from the buildup of Overlord for a few weeks without altering the zero date it would be worthwhile. I feel we may easily throw away an immense but fleeting opportunity. If you think well would you very kindly let General Marshall see this telegram before any decision is taken by the Combined Chiefs of Staff?

Doc. 257
ROOSEVELT TO CHURCHILL

No. 379   October 7, 1943

Reference your 438.[1]
I do not want to force on Eisenhower diversions which limit the
prospects for the early successful development of the Italian operations
to a secure line north of Rome. I am opposed to any diversion which
will in Eisenhower's opinion jeopardize the security of his current
situation in Italy, the buildup of which is exceedingly slow considering
the well-known characteristics of his opponent who enjoys a marked
superiority in ground troops and panzer divisions.

It is my opinion that no diversion of forces or equipment should
prejudice Overlord as planned.

The American Chiefs of Staff agree.

I am transmitting a copy of this message to Eisenhower.

[1] See above, Doc. 256.

Doc. 258
ROOSEVELT TO CHURCHILL

No. 381   October 8, 1943

I have received your numbers 441[1] and 443[2] and given careful
personal consideration to the points you make. I have given careful
thought to them and so has the staff. I am concerned about the possibility of our armies suffering a reverse by the action of an enemy with
superior forces except by air, under a commander of proved audacity

[1] Not printed. Churchill wrote on October 8 that the failure to take Rhodes
would be a strategic blunder. The troops needed for the job could be sent and
returned to Italy before the main forces there reached the Germans' main line. He
was willing to go to Eisenhower's headquarters with his Chiefs of Staff if Roosevelt
would send General Marshall or a personal representative to discuss the matter at a
meeting. See Churchill, *Closing the Ring*, pp. 212–213.

[2] Not printed. Later on the same day Churchill wrote that landing craft he could
use for the Rhodes operation were starting for England as a preparation for
Overlord. Since the major offensive was nearly six months away, he pleaded again
for a delay of six weeks in sending them out from the Mediterranean; the delay
would not affect their future use. See Churchill, *Closing the Ring*, p. 213.

and resourcefulness. This applies especially to the absolute safety to the line we hope to gain in Italy.

With a full understanding of your difficulties in the eastern Mediterranean, my thought in sending No. 379[3] was that no diversion of force from Italy should be made that would jeopardize the security of the Allied armies in Italy, and that no action toward any minor objective should prejudice the success of Overlord.

We have almost all the facts now at our disposal on which to judge the commitments probably involved in the Rhodes operation. As I see it, it is not merely the capture of Rhodes but it must mean of necessity, and it must be apparent to the Germans, that we intend to go further. Otherwise Rhodes will be under the guns of both Kos and Crete.

I was in accord with obtaining whatever hold we could in the Dodecanese without heavy commitments, but the present picture involves not only a well-organized, determined operation, but a necessary follow-through. This in turn involves the necessity of drawing for the means, largely shipping and air, not ground troops, from some other source which inevitably must be Italy, Overlord, or possibly Mountbatten's amphibious operation.[4] The problem then is, are we now to enter into a Balkan campaign starting with the southern tip, or is there more to be gained, and with security, by pushing rapidly to the agreed-upon position north of Rome? It appears to me that a greater Allied threat against the Balkans is implied in this than by a necessarily precarious amphibious operation against Rhodes with a lack evident to the enemy of the necessary means for the follow-through. Strategically, if we get the Aegean islands, I ask myself where do we go from there and vice versa where would the Germans go if for some time they retain possession of the islands.

As to the meeting you propose for Sunday in Africa,[5] this would be in effect another meeting of the Combined Chiefs of Staff necessarily only involving a partial representation and in which I cannot participate. Frankly I am not in sympathy with this procedure under the circumstances. It seems to me the issue under discussion can best be adjusted by us through our CCS setup in better perspective than by the method you propose. We have most of the facts and will soon have the results of the conference scheduled for tomorrow in Tunis.[6]

[3] See above, Doc. 257.

[4] Admiral Lord Louis Mountbatten was in charge of the Southeast Asia command. See above, Doc. 238, note 3.

[5] At Eisenhower's headquarters in Tunis.

[6] Churchill wrote to Roosevelt on October 9 that Eisenhower was interpreting the President's message of October 8 as an order, which closed the subject. Roosevelt duly cabled Eisenhower that there should be a "full, free, patient, and unprejudiced consideration" of the whole Rhodes question at the meeting. See Churchill, *Closing the Ring*, pp. 216–217.

Doc. 259
CHURCHILL TO ROOSEVELT

No. 449   October 10, 1943

Many thanks for your number 383.[1] I have now read General Eisenhower's report of the meeting.[2] The German intention to reinforce immediately the south of Italy and to fight a battle before Rome is what General Eisenhower rightly calls "a drastic change within the last forty-eight hours." We have always trusted this kind of evidence and I therefore agree that we must now look forward to very heavy fighting before Rome is reached instead of merely pushing back rear guards. I therefore agree with the conclusions of the conference that we cannot count on any comparative lull in which Rhodes might be taken and that we must concentrate all important forces available on the battle, leaving the question of Rhodes, etc., to be reconsidered as General Eisenhower suggests after the winter line north of Rome has been successfully occupied.

I have now to face the situation in the Aegean. Even if we had decided to attack Rhodes on the 23rd Leros might well have fallen before that date. I have asked Eden to examine with General Wilson and Admiral Cunningham whether with resources still belonging to the Middle East anything can be done to regain Kos on the basis that Turkey lets us use the landing grounds close by. If nothing can be worked out on these lines and unless we have luck tonight or tomorrow night in destroying one of the assaulting convoys, the fate of Leros is sealed.

I propose, therefore, to tell General Wilson that he is free, if he judges the position hopeless, to order the garrison to evacuate by night taking with them all Italian officers and as many other Italians as possible and destroying the guns and defences. The Italians cannot be relied upon to fight and we have only twelve hundred men, quite insufficient to man even a small portion of the necessary batteries, let alone the perimeter. Internment in Turkey is not strict and may not last long: or they may get out along the Turkish coast.

---

1 Not printed. See above, Doc. 258, note 6.

2 Eisenhower reported to Churchill on October 9 that the commanders in chief in the Mediterranean and Middle East had met to discuss the situation in the Aegean. Meanwhile the Germans, instead of fighting only a delaying action in Italy, were sending in reinforcements. All at the meeting agreed that the "current situation in Italy, aggravated by drastic changes of the last forty-eight hours," did not permit the diversion of strength necessary for the Rhodes operation. See *PDDE*, 3: 1494–1498.

I will not waste words in explaining how painful this decision is to me.[3]

I am repeating this telegram to General Eisenhower.

[3] For Churchill's account of this incident, see his *Closing the Ring*, pp. 215–225.

Doc. 260
CHURCHILL TO ROOSEVELT

No. 453   October 12, 1943

Would you very kindly consider whether something like the following might not be issued over our three signatures?[1]

"Great Britain, the United States, and the Soviet Union (in whatever order is thought convenient, we being quite ready to be last) have received from many quarters evidence of the atrocities, massacres, and cold-blooded mass executions which are being perpetrated by the Hitlerite forces in the many countries they have overrun and from which they are now being steadily expelled. The brutalities of the Nazi domination are no new thing, and all peoples or territories in their grip have suffered from the worst forms of government by terror. What is new is that many of these territories are now being redeemed by the advancing armies of the liberating powers and that, in their desperation, the recoiling Hitlerites and Huns are redoubling their ruthless cruelties.

"Accordingly the aforesaid three Allied powers, speaking in the interest of the thirty-two United Nations, hereby solemnly declare, and give full warning of their declaration, as follows:

" 'At the time of the granting of any armistice to any government which may be set up in Germany, those German officers and men and members of the Nazi party who have been responsible for or have taken a consenting part in the above atrocities, massacres, and executions will be sent back to the countries in which their abominable deeds were done in order that they may be judged and punished according to the laws of these liberated countries and the free governments which will be erected therein. Lists will be compiled in all possible detail from all these countries, having regard especially to the invaded parts of Russia, to Poland and Czechoslovakia, to Yugoslavia,

[1] Churchill maintained that he intended this declaration to serve as a basis for a discussion of war criminals at the forthcoming Big Three meeting at Teheran. See Churchill, *Closing the Ring*, pp. 296–298. The Prime Minister sent a copy to Stalin, and another copy went, via the State Department, to Secretary of State Hull, who was in Moscow for the foreign ministers' conference.

Greece, including Crete and other islands, to Norway, Denmark, the Netherlands, Belgium, Luxembourg, France, and Italy. Thus Germans who take part in the wholesale shootings of Italian officers or in the execution of French, Dutch, Belgian, or Norwegian hostages, or of Cretan peasants, or who have shared in the slaughters inflicted on the people of Poland or in the territories of the Soviet Republic which are now being swept clear of the enemy, will know that they will be brought back, regardless of expense, to the scene of their crimes and judged on the spot by the peoples whom they have outraged. Let those who have hitherto not imbrued their hands with innocent blood beware lest they join the ranks of the guilty, for most assuredly the three Allied powers will pursue them to the uttermost ends of the earth and will deliver them to their accusers in order that justice may be done.'

"The above declaration is without prejudice to the case of the major criminals, whose offences have no particular geographical localisation. Signed Roosevelt-Stalin-Churchill."[2]

If this, or something like this (and I am not particular about the wording) , were put over our three signatures, it would I believe make some of these villains shy of being mixed up in butcheries now that they know they are going to be beat. We know, for instance, that our threats of reprisals about Poland have brought about a mitigation of the severities being inflicted on the people there. There is no doubt that the use of the terror weapon by the enemy imposes an additional burden on our armies. Lots of Germans may develop moral scruples if they know they are going to be brought back and judged in the country, and perhaps in the very place, where their cruel deeds were done. I strongly commend to you the principle of the localisation of judgement as likely to exert a deterrent effect on enemy terrorism. The British Cabinet endorse this principle and policy.

2 With a few changes in wording this document was later endorsed and accepted. For the establishment of the United Nations Commission for the Investigation of War Crimes, see *FR 1943*, 1 (Washington, 1963) : 402–438.

Doc. 261
CHURCHILL TO ROOSEVELT

No. 455   October 13, 1943

Your telegram 373 of October 4th.[1]
An investigation has been made into this leakage. Your telegram

1 See above, Doc. 254.

containing Stalin's reply was dated October 2nd and reached me on that day. Kuh's cable was filed on evening of October 1st. Although the Soviet Embassy here are not generally so promptly and fully informed by Moscow, these facts suggest that they were on this occasion told the terms of Stalin's reply before that reply reached you and that they gave its contents to Kuh.

The censor who passed Kuh's cable made an error of judgement and has been reproved. He was influenced by the statement in Kuh's cable that its contents came from "trustworthy American sources." This may have been a device to disguise its real origin.

Kuh's messages frequently show him to be in possession of information to which he is not entitled. He often causes us trouble. We are trying to track down his sources. Any help your people can give would be welcome.[2]

[2] On October 14 the President drafted a message to the Prime Minister: "Thank you very much for your number 455. We will also keep an eye on him. . . . I agree with you that you and I must do all that we can to prevent the growth of friction between our press and our people. You have probably noted the general annoyance expressed throughout our press at what they consider repeated instances of publishing information in London that is withheld by agreement in the United States. The most recent instances are: First, the premature disclosure in London of Italy's determination to declare war against Germany and also action of British censorship in passing dispatch originating in London signed by Reston of *New York Times*. Reston's cable arrived in New York at 7:19 P.M. Eastern War Time, October 12th. Text of this cable available in British censorship files also discloses prematurely our agreement to recognize Italy as co-belligerent.

"Secondly, the distribution from London of photograph of you and me in automobile made at Hyde Park Sunday, September 14. I am informed that this picture was made by Captain Horton, under pledge previously given to U.S. Secret Service that no picture made by him at Hyde Park would be published. Publication of this picture in *one group of* American newspapers most embarrassing because American cameramen were not permitted in grounds at Hyde Park and no authorized disclosure of our presence at Hyde Park had been made for publication.

"I know you would want me to tell you frankly that such incidents not only endanger national security but arouse antagonisms in the Press which do not contribute to Anglo-American cooperation and good will."

The message was never sent. The next day, Hopkins wired Brendan Bracken: ". . . The publication of this picture has caused a hell of a row here and the President feels that something must be done to stop this sort of business. It adds to the antagonism already developing against Great Britain because every newspaper that gets beat with this kind of picture promptly thinks of some way to take a crack at Britain.

"This, coming on top of the premature disclosure in London of Italy's determination to declare war against Germany, and the action of British censorship in passing dispatch originating in London signed by Reston of *New York Times*. . . . Text of cable available in British censorship files also discloses prematurely our agreement to recognize Italy as co-belligerent.

"There are just too many of this type of thing happening in London and I think you should give this business your most serious personal attention and do not, for a minute, underrate the effect these are having over here on Anglo-American relations. I am putting it mildly when I say the highest circles are irritated with these things. "Why, in God's name, when we have a tough war to fight, do we have to cope with these unnecessary leaks, premature and otherwise?"

Doc. 262
ROOSEVELT TO CHURCHILL

No. 388   October 14, 1943

I have finally sent the following telegram to U.J. and I think your idea is an excellent one. St. Peter sometimes had real inspirations. I like the idea of three tabernacles.[1] We can add one later for your old friend Chiang.

QUOTE. The problem of my going to the place you suggested[2] is becoming so acute that I feel I should tell you frankly that, for constitutional reasons, I cannot take the risk. The Congress will be in session. New laws and resolutions must be acted on by me after their receipt and must be returned to the Congress physically before ten days have elapsed. None of this can be done by radio or cable. The place you mentioned is too far to be sure that the requirements are fulfilled. The possibility of delay in getting over the mountain—first, eastbound and then westbound—is insurmountable. We know from experience that planes in either direction are often held up for three or four days.

I do not think that any one of us will need legation facilities, as each of us can have adequate personal and technical staffs. I venture, therefore, to make some other suggestions and I hope you will consider them or suggest any other place where I can be assured of meeting my constitutional obligations.

In many ways Cairo is attractive, and I understand there is a hotel and some villas out near the Pyramids which could be completely segregated.

[1] In a message of October 14 Churchill suggested a new site for the forthcoming Big Three conference that would mean an easier journey for the President than going from Teheran to Cairo. The place, later identified as Habbaniya, Iraq, was in the desert, and they could meet there in comfort and security. In the meantime the President was referred to St. Matthew, chapter 17, verse 4. The White House Map Room staff looked up the reference and typed the following quotation on the Churchill telegram: "Then answered Peter, and said unto Jesus, Lord it is good for us to be here: if thou wilt, let us make here three tabernacles; one for thee, and one for Moses, and one for Elias."
[2] Teheran.

Asmara, the former Italian capital of Eritrea, is said to have excellent buildings and a landing field—good at all times.

Then there is the possibility of meeting at some port in the eastern Mediterranean, each one of us to have a ship. If this idea attracts you we could easily place a fine ship entirely at your disposal for you and your party so that you would be completely independent of us and, at the same time, be in constant contact with your own war front.

Another suggestion is in the neighborhood of Baghdad where we could have three comfortable camps with adequate Russian, British, and American guards. This last idea seems worth considering.

In any event, I think the press should be entirely banished, and the whole place surrounded by a cordon so that we would not be disturbed in any way.

What would you think of November twentieth or November twenty-fifth as the date of the meeting?

I am placing a very great importance on the personal and intimate conversations which you and Churchill and I will have, for on them the hope of the future world will greatly depend.

Your continuing initiative along your whole front heartens all of us. UNQUOTE.[3]

3 See *Stalin's Correspondence*, 2: 127.

Doc. 263
ROOSEVELT TO CHURCHILL

No. 389   October 16, 1943

I am disturbed about the buildup of our air facilities at Assam. The determination of the supplies that go over the railroad from Calcutta to Assam is under British control.[1]

The amount of tonnage flown over the mountains to Chennault's air force has been very disappointing to me.[2] Chennault's air force

1 On October 4 General Marshall sent Roosevelt a memorandum on the tonnages carried "over the hump" from India to China since April. In his final paragraph Marshall said: "The British control every rail movement between Calcutta and Assam and they make the final decision as to what will and will not move. This undoubtedly has affected the movement of necessary supplies to improve airports and will continue to affect movements over the hump in the future." In reply the President sent Marshall a copy of his cable to Churchill and asked him to tell Lieutenant General Brehon B. Somervell, head of the Services of Supply, to give the matter his special attention.

2 According to Marshall's figures, the tonnage had gone up every month since April, and from then to September 21 a total of 18,261 tons had been lifted.

cannot operate without the supplies and his striking force is the one specific contribution that can be made in China proper by us during the next few months.

Our own transport planes have been disappointing.

I wish you would take a personal part in this business because I am a bit apprehensive that without new project in Burma our air force in China will be forgotten and I think that is a great mistake.[3]

3 For Churchill's reply, see below, Doc. 266. See also Churchill, *Closing the Ring*, pp. 559–560.

Doc. 264
CHURCHILL TO ROOSEVELT

No. 459   October 16, 1943

Please see my No. 429[1] about Russian convoys. I have now received the immediately following telegram from Uncle Joe[2] which I think you will feel is not exactly all one might hope for from a gentleman for whose sake we are to make an inconvenient, extreme, and costly exertion. I have sent the following suggested answer to Anthony for him to handle as he thinks best.

I think or at least I hope this message came from the machine rather than from Stalin as it took 12 days to prepare. The Soviet machine is quite convinced it can get everything by bullying and I am sure it is a matter of some importance to show that this is not necessarily always true.

1 Not printed. Convoys to the Soviet Union by the northern route had been suspended in April 1943 because of the great strain they imposed on the available destroyers, and because the German fleet was concentrated in Norwegian waters. On September 21 Soviet Foreign Minister Molotov asked Clark Kerr, the British ambassador at Moscow, for a resumption of the convoys, pointing out that for three months the Soviet Union's armies had been engaged in a large offensive but were operating with less than one-third of the previous year's supplies. Shipments through the Persian Gulf were not enough to make up for the loss of cargo through the northern route. Now that the anti-U-boat campaign in the North Atlantic had forced the German submarines into more southerly waters and the Italian fleet was in Allied hands, the Soviet Union wanted the convoys to be resumed. The British government began working toward this goal, and the project became more feasible when Churchill learned that a British midget submarine had torpedoed the German battleship *Tirpitz* in Norway and that the pocket battleship *Lützow* had gone to the Baltic. See Churchill, *Closing the Ring*, pp. 256–263; and Roskill, *War at Sea*, 3 (pt. 1) : 76–89.

2 See below, Doc. 265.

I entirely agree with the telegram you have sent to Uncle Joe about Eureka.[3] Let me know what he replies.

Please also see Saint Mark 9 verses 5 and 6 especially sixth verse.[4]

[3] See above, Doc. 262. The site for the meeting with Stalin (code-named Eureka) had not yet been selected.

[4] The Map Room staff at the White House typed the following quotation on the cable:

"5. And Peter answered and said to Jesus, Master, it is good for us to be here: and let us make three tabernacles; one for thee, and one for Moses, and one for Elias.

"6. For he wist not what to say; for they were sore afraid."

Doc. 265
CHURCHILL TO ROOSEVELT

No. 460   October 16, 1943

My No. 459.[1] Following is telegram received from Uncle Joe. Begins:

"Premier Stalin to Premier Churchill.

"1. I received your message of Oct 1st[2] informing me of the intention to send four convoys to the Soviet Union by the northern route in November, December, January, and February. However, this communication loses its value by your statement that this intention to send northern convoys to the U.S.S.R. is neither an obligation nor an agreement, but only a statement which, as it may be understood, is one the British side can at any moment renounce regardless of any influence it may have on the Soviet armies at the front. I must say that I cannot agree with such a posing of the question. Supplies from the British Government to the U.S.S.R., armaments, and other military goods cannot be considered otherwise than as an obligation which, by special agreement between our countries, the British Government undertook in respect of the U.S.S.R., which bears on its shoulders, already for the third year, the enormous burden of struggle with the common enemy of the Allies—Hitlerite Germany.

"It is also impossible to disregard the fact that the northern route is the shortest way which permits delivery of armaments supplied by the Allies within the shortest period to the Soviet-German front, and the realisation of the plan of supplies to the U.S.S.R. in appropriate volume is impossible without an adequate use of this way. As I already

[1] See above, Doc. 264.

[2] Churchill advised Stalin on October 1 that the convoys on the northern route would be resumed. He also asked Stalin to smooth out some of the difficulties facing British servicemen stationed in northern Russia.

wrote to you earlier, and as experience has shown, delivery of armaments and military supplies to the U.S.S.R. through Persian ports
cannot compensate in any way for those supplies which were not
delivered owing to the absence of delivery of (such?) equipment and
materials by the northern route.[3] (These), as it can be well understood, were taken into account when planning the supplies for the
Soviet armies. By the way, for some reason or other, there was a very
considerable decrease in the delivery of military goods sent by the
northern route this year in comparison with those received last year:
and this makes it impossible to fulfil the established plan of military
supplies and is in contradiction to the corresponding Anglo-Soviet
protocol for military supplies. Therefore, at the present time, when the
forces of the Soviet Union are strained to the utmost to secure the
needs of the front in the interests of success of the struggle against the
main forces of our common enemy, it would be inadmissible to have
the supplies of the Soviet armies depend on the arbitrary judgement of
the British side. It is impossible to consider this posing of the question
to be other than a refusal of the British Government to fulfil the
obligations it undertook, and as a kind of threat addressed to the
U.S.S.R.

"2. Concerning your mention of controversial points allegedly contained in the statement of M. Molotov, I have to say that I do not find
any foundation for such a remark.[4] I consider the principle of reciprocity and equality proposed by the Soviet side for settlement of the
visa question in respect of personnel of the military missions to be a
correct and indeed a just one. The reference to the difference in the
functions of the British and Soviet military missions to exclude the
usage of that principle, and that the numbers of the staff of the British
military mission must be determined by the British Government only,
I consider to be unconvincing. It has already been made clear in detail
in the previous *aide-mémoires* of the People's Commissariat for Foreign Affairs on this question.

"3. I do not see the necessity for increasing the number of British
servicemen in the north of the U.S.S.R. since the great majority of
British servicemen who are already there are not adequately employed,
and for many months have been doomed to idleness, as has already
been pointed out several times by the Soviet side. For example, it can
be mentioned that owing to its nonnecessity, the question of the
liquidation of the 126th British Port Base in Archangel was put for-

[3] The Persian Gulf operations had not reached their target capacity of 200,000
tons a month until September. See Herring, *Aid to Russia*, pp. 72–73, 97.

[4] According to Churchill, Molotov had asked the British government to restrict
British servicemen in northern Russia to the number of the Soviet Union's military
and trade delegation people in the United Kingdom.

ward several times, and only now the British side have agreed to liquidate it. There are also regrettable facts of the inadmissible behaviour of individual British servicemen who attempted, in several cases, to recruit, by bribery, certain Soviet citizens for intelligence purposes. Such instances, offensive to Soviet citizens, naturally gave rise to incidents which led to undesirable complications.[5]

"4. Concerning your mention of formalities and certain restrictions existing in northern ports, it is necessary to have in view that such formalities and restrictions are unavoidable in zones near and at the front, if one does not forget the war situation which exists in the U.S.S.R. I may add that this applies equally to the British and other foreigners as well as to Soviet citizens. Nevertheless, the Soviet authorities granted many privileges in this respect to the British servicemen and seamen, about which the British Embassy was informed as long ago as last March. Thus, your mention of many formalities and restrictions is based on inaccurate information.[6]

"Concerning the question of censorship and prosecution of British servicemen, I have no objection if the censorship of private mail for British personnel in northern ports would be made by the British authorities themselves on condition of reciprocity, and also if cases of small violations committed by British servicemen which did not involve court procedure would be given to the consideration of the appropriate military authorities."[7]

[5] Churchill said that 170 Navy men needed to be relieved from duty in North Russia but that the Soviet Union had not given them visas. He had also requested visas for a small medical unit scheduled to go to Archangel, but they had not been issued. The discipline problems were the result of the harsh conditions under which the men were serving.

[6] The restrictions included the need for passes between two British shore stations, the lack of stores, mail, or luggage facilities free from Soviet officials' surveillance, the censorship of mail, and no ship-to-ship contact between British vessels except in a Russian boat and with Soviet officials examining documents.

[7] Churchill called these "modest requests," but they were not answered for nearly two weeks. See Churchill, *Closing the Ring*, pp. 263–266.

Doc. 266
CHURCHILL TO ROOSEVELT

No. 465   October 19, 1943

Your number 389.[1] Though the Quadrant[2] decision that operations in Upper Burma should be given priority will inevitably result in a

[1] See above, Doc. 263.
[2] Code name for the conference at Quebec in August 1943.

moderate decrease in the air lift to China, I agree that there must be ceaseless effort to build up your air force there and on the air route.

Our joint staffs have recently considered this problem and as a result have informed Generals Stilwell and Auchinleck[3] of their anxiety that the reduction in lift to China should not be greater than is necessary to implement the Quadrant decision, and have instructed them to submit an agreed recommendation as to the minimum air lift that should be maintained to support the 14th Air Force in China and the Yünnan advance.[4]

I feel that this is not a matter which can be examined in detail either in Washington or London, and that we should await the report from Stilwell and Auchinleck before taking further action.

Latest figures show an increase in September from 4,380 tons in August to 6,740 tons.

I grieve to say that Wingate[5] is down with typhoid fever. All his work and plans are being vigorously pressed forward and I have every hope that he will resume his duties early in December.

[3] General Sir Claude J. E. Auchinleck had become commander in chief of the British forces in India on June 20, 1943.

[4] Chinese army forces in China's Yünnan province were to cooperate in the liberation of Burma.

[5] Brigadier General Orde C. Wingate, who had developed the use of long-range penetration groups behind the Japanese lines in Burma, had come to the Quebec conference with Churchill. See Christopher Sykes, *Orde Wingate* (Cleveland and New York, 1959) and Derek Tulloch, *Wingate in Peace and War* (London, 1972).

Doc. 267
ROOSEVELT TO CHURCHILL

No. 393   October 22, 1943

The chaotic condition developing in the Balkans causes me concern.[1] I am sure you are also worried. In both Yugoslavia and Greece the guerrilla forces appear to be engaged largely in fighting each other

[1] For documents on the concern of the United States about the disunity among Yugoslav resistance forces, see *FR 1943*, 2: 962–1022. The British side is set forth in Woodward, *British Foreign Policy*, 3 (London, 1971): 278–335. The activities of the Office of Strategic Services in Yugoslavia are described in R. Harris Smith, *OSS: The Secret History of America's First Central Intelligence Agency* (Berkeley, Cal., 1972), pp. 129–162. A recent study is Walter R. Roberts, *Tito, Mihailović, and the Allies 1941–1945* (New Brunswick, N.J., 1973).

The British side of the Greek problem is set forth in Woodward, *British Foreign Policy*, 3: 278–335. American documents pertaining to the situation are in *FR 1943*, 4 (Washington, 1964): 124–154.

and not the Germans. If these forces could be united and directed toward a common end they would be very effective. In the present confused condition the only hope I see for immediate favorable action is the presence of an aggressive and qualified officer. The only man I can think of now who might have a chance of success is Donovan.[2] I do not believe he can do any harm and being a fearless and aggressive character he might do much good. He was there before and is given some credit for the Yugoslavs entering the war against the Germans. If we decide to send him all agencies of ours now working in the Balkans should be placed under his direction and the resources we put into this effort should be at his disposal. I understand that your General Gubbins[3] is now in the Middle East. Donovan could consult with him en route.

I feel this is an urgent matter. If you are inclined to agree to my idea I will discuss the possibilities with Donovan at once.

[2] Brigadier General William J. Donovan, director of the Office of Strategic Services.

[3] General Colin Gubbins, a regular Army officer, had been the British special operations executive in London until September.

Doc. 268
CHURCHILL TO ROOSEVELT

No. 470   October 23, 1943

Your number 393.[1]

In spite of the vexatious broils between the followers of Tito[2] and Mihailović[3] in Yugoslavia and those that have broken out between the two sets of Greek guerrillas,[4] the situation in the Balkan peninsula is grievous for the enemy. It is at present being managed by General Wilson from Cairo, and the Combined Chiefs of Staff have impressed upon General Eisenhower the urgent need of passing in supplies by ship as well as by air. We British have about eighty separate missions under General Wilson's control working with partisan

[1] See above, Doc. 267.

[2] Marshal Josip Broz Tito, leader of the Communist guerrilla forces (Partisans) in Yugoslavia.

[3] General Draža Mihailović, leader of the pro-royalist Chetniks. Mihailović had been accused of collaborating with the Germans.

[4] In Greece the People's Liberation Army (ELAS) was the military arm of the National Liberation Front (EAM), both Communist-dominated organizations that were strengthening their control over the country. Other Greek factions known as the Zervas bands (EDES) were anti-Communist. None of these groups had any contact with or sympathy for the Greek government-in-exile in London.

and patriot bands scattered over these immense mountainous regions 900 miles by about 300 miles in extent. Some of our officers there of brigadier's rank are very capable and have in numerous cases been there for two years. I have great admiration for Donovan, but I do not see any centre in the Balkans from which he could grip the situation. It would take a long time to move from one of the many centres of guerrilla activity to another. If however you would like him to go to Cairo and meet General Wilson, he will be given the fullest information on the spot about the whole scene and can report to you. The fighting is of the most cruel and bloody character with merciless reprisals and execution of hostages by the Huns. But the enemy also is suffering heavily and is now consuming not less than twenty-five German and eight Bulgarian divisions in the theatre without being able to control more than key points and with increasing difficulty in maintaining railway traffic. We hope soon to compose the Greek quarrels but the differences between Tito's Partisans and Mihailović's Serbs are very deep-seated.

Eden tells me that Stalin was quite agreeable to the bombing of Sofia by us.[5] I consider this is more important and that no previous warning should be given to make the task of our airmen harder. Also that leaflets should be dropped to say that the dose they will receive is only a foretaste of what will follow if they do not withdraw their divisions from their neighbours' lands.[6]

[5] Attacks on Sofia were designed to slow the movement of German transport into the lower Balkans. On November 14 and November 24 raids were carried out against the marshaling yards over which traffic moved on the Berlin-Istanbul line.

[6] After reading Churchill's message, Roosevelt ordered General Donovan to ask General Sir Henry Wilson if he could be of assistance.

Doc. 269
CHURCHILL TO ROOSEVELT

No. 471   October 23, 1943

Your number 394.[1]

The Russians ought not to be vexed if the Americans and British closely concert the very great operations they have in hand for 1944 on

[1] Not printed. Roosevelt cabled that, as a preliminary to the full conference of the Combined Chiefs of Staff scheduled for early November, an analysis should be made of the results of the foreign ministers' conference then being held in Moscow (see below, Doc. 271, note 1). He added: "At the moment it seems to me that consideration of our relations with Russia is of paramount importance and that a meeting after our special conference with U.J. would be in order rather than one in early November." *Conferences at Cairo and Tehran*, pp. 37–38.

fronts where no Russian troops will be present. Nor do I think we ought to meet Stalin, if ever the meeting can be arranged, without being agreed about Anglo-American operations as such.

I would be content with Nov. 15th if this is the earliest date for your staffs. I thought the staffs would work together for a few days before you and I arrive, say 18th or 19th, and we could then go on together to Eureka. I do not yet know whether it is to be Nov. 20th or 25th. I had not imagined that Eureka would take more than 3 or 4 days or that large technical staffs would take part in it.

Nov. 15 would be 90 days from the beginning of Quadrant. In these 90 days events of first magnitude have occurred. Mussolini has fallen; Italy has surrendered; its fleet has come over; we have successfully invaded Italy,[2] and are marching on Rome with good prospects of success. The Germans are gathering up to 25 or more divs in Italy and the Po Valley. All these are new facts.

Our present plans for 1944 seem open to very grave defects. We are to put 15 American and 12 British divs into Overlord and will have about 6 American and 16 British or British-controlled divs on the Italian front. Unless there is a German collapse Hitler, lying in the centre of the best communications in the world, can concentrate at least 40 to 50 divs against either of these forces while holding the other. He could obtain all the necessary forces by cutting his losses in the Balkans and withdrawing to the Sava and the Danube without necessarily weakening his Russian front. The disposition of our forces between the Italian and the channel theatres has not been settled by strategic needs but by the march of events, by shipping possibilities, and by arbitrary compromises between the British and Americans. The date of Overlord itself was fixed by splitting the difference between the American and British view. It is arguable that neither the forces building up in Italy nor those available for a May Overlord are strong enough for the tasks set them.

The British staffs and my colleagues and I all think this position requires to be reviewed, and that the commanders for both fronts should be named and should be present. In pursuance of Quadrant decisions we have already prepared two of our best divs, the 50th and 51st now in Sicily, for transfer to Overlord. Thus they can play no part in the Italian battle to which they stood near, but will not come into

2 Troops of the U.S. Fifth Army had landed south of Salerno on September 9. Churchill's optimistic appraisal, designed to convince Roosevelt that great gains could be made in Italy, studiously avoided mention of the German paratroopers' rescue of Mussolini on September 12; the Italian then established a new Fascist government at Lake Como under German protection. Also Field Marshal Rommel had begun to organize northern Italian defenses, and the Germans had disarmed and shipped to internment camps some 600,000 Italian soldiers.

action again for 7 months and then only if certain hypothetical conditions are fulfilled which may very likely not be fulfilled. Early in Nov. a decision must be taken about moving landing craft from the Mediterranean to Overlord. This will cripple Mediterranean operations without the said craft influencing events elsewhere for many months. We stand by what was agreed at Quadrant but we do not feel that such agreements should be interpreted rigidly and without review in the swiftly changing situations of war.

Personally I feel that if we make serious mistakes in the campaign of 1944, we might give Hitler the chance of a startling comeback. Prisoner German General von Thoma[3] was overheard saying, "Our only hope is that they come where we can use the army upon them." All this shows the need for the greatest care and foresight in our arrangements, the most accurate timing between the two theatres, and the need to gather the greatest possible forces for both operations, particularly Overlord. I do not doubt our ability in the conditions laid down to get ashore and deploy. I am however deeply concerned with the buildup and with the situation which may arise between the 30th and the 60th days. I feel sure that the vast movement of American personnel into the United Kingdom and the fighting composition of the units requires to be searchingly examined by the commander who will execute Overlord. I wish to have both the High Commands settled in a manner agreeable to our two countries, and then the secondary commands which are of very high importance can be decided. I have the greatest confidence in General Marshall and if he is in charge of Overlord we British will aid him with every scrap of life and strength we have. My dear friend, this is much the greatest thing we have ever attempted, and I am not satisfied that we have yet taken the measures necessary to give it the best chance of success. I feel very much in the dark at present, and unable to think or act in the forward manner which is needed. For these reasons I desire an early conference.

All that you say about the plans for Eisenhower and the commanders in the Pacific which are due to be submitted on Nov. 1st would harmonise with a meeting on Nov. 15th at latest. I do not know how long you consider is required for the long-term overall plan for the defeat of Japan to be completed by the combined planners and studied by our respective Chiefs of Staff. I do not consider that the more urgent decisions to which I have referred above ought to be held up for this long-term view of the war against Japan which nevertheless should be pressed forward with all energy.

3 General Wilhelm Ritter von Thoma, who replaced Rommel as commanding general of the Afrika Korps, had been captured by the Allies in the closing days of the North African campaign.

I hope you will consider that these reasons for a meeting are solid. We cannot decide finally until an answer is received from Uncle Joe. Should Eureka not be possible it makes it all the more necessary that we should meet in the light of the information now being received from the Moscow conference. I am expecting Anthony to start home before the end of the month and am ready myself to move any day after the first week in Nov.

You will I am sure share my belief that Leros has so far managed to hold out. "The dogs under the table eat of the children's crumbs."[4]

I send you in my immediately following[5] extracts from a telegram I have sent to Eden who asked for guidance about the Russian wish to bring Turkey and Sweden immediately into the war. I wonder what you think on these subjects.

[4] Leros was recaptured by the Germans on November 16.

[5] Not printed. Churchill's message of October 23 contained three extracts from a telegram he sent to Eden on the advantages of having Sweden and Turkey enter the war. On October 26 the President telegraphed Secretary Hull àt the Moscow conference that the Joint Chiefs of Staff were opposed to Turkey and Sweden entering the war because they would require supplies intended for the cross-channel attack. See *Conferences at Cairo and Tehran*, p. 121.

Doc. 270
CHURCHILL TO ROOSEVELT

No. 474   October 25, 1943

I ought to let you know that during the last six months evidence has continued to accumulate from many sources that the Germans are preparing an attack on England particularly London by means of very-long-range rockets which may conceivably weigh 60 tons and carry an explosive charge of 10 to 20 tons. For this reason we raided Peenemünde which was their main experimental station.[1] We also demol-

[1] On November 4, 1939, the British naval attaché at Oslo, Norway, had received a report from a German scientist about secret weapons research at the German army establishment at Peenemünde on the Baltic coast. But British intelligence was unable to evaluate the technical information, and nothing more was heard of the installation until the end of 1942. Then, early in 1943, the first photographic reconnaissance of the base was made. On the night of August 17-18, 1943, 600 heavy bombers of the Royal Air Force dropped high explosives and firebombs on Peenemünde. The attack set back German rocket development by at least two months, and 120 members of the regular German staff were killed. However, during the raid RAF pilots erroneously bombed the workers' compound, killing over 600 foreign laborers, including several workers from Luxembourg who were furnishing information to British intelligence. See Walter Dornberger, *V-2* (New York, 1958), pp.

ished Watten near St. Omer which was where a construction work was proceeding the purpose of which we could not define. There are at least seven such points in the Pas de Calais and the Cherbourg peninsula and there may be a good many others we have not detected.

Scientific opinion is divided as to the practicability of making rockets of this kind but I am personally as yet unconvinced that they cannot be made. We are in close touch with your people who are ahead of us in rocket impulsion which they have studied to give aeroplanes a sendoff and all possible work is being done. The expert committee which is following this business thinks it possible that a heavy though premature and short-lived attack might be made in the middle of November and that the main attack would be attempted in the new year. It naturally pays the Germans to spread talk of new weapons to encourage their troops, their satellites, and neutrals and it may well be that their bite will be found less bad than their bark.

Hitherto we have watched the unexplained constructions proceeding in the Pas de Calais area without (except Watten) attacking them in the hopes of learning more about them. But now we have decided to demolish those we know of which should be easy as overwhelming fighter protection can be given to bombers. Your airmen are of course in every way ready to help. This may not however end the menace as the country is full of woods and quarries, and slanting tunnels can easily be constructed in hillsides.

The case of Watten is interesting.[2] We damaged it so severely that the Germans after a meeting two days later decided to abandon it altogether. There were 6,000 French workers upon it as forced labour. When they panicked at the attack a body of uniformed young Frenchmen who are used by the Germans to supervise them fired upon their countrymen with such brutality that a German officer actually shot one of these young swine. A week later the Germans seem to have reversed their previous decision and resumed the work. Three thousand more workmen have been brought back. The rest have gone to some of those other suspected places thus confirming our views. We have an excellent system of intelligence in this part of northern France and it is from these sources as well as from photographs and examination of prisoners that this story has been built up.

154–170; and David Irving, *The Mare's Nest* (Boston, 1965), pp. 15, 97–121, 149–160, 162–168.

2 The Watten rocket bunker near Calais was within easy reach of the eastern and southern coasts of England. On August 27 the U.S. Eighth Air Force had launched a 185-bomber low-altitude attack on Watten, causing extensive damage. By November 8 aerial reconnaissance had located ski-shaped launch buildings at nineteen locations in the Pas de Calais and Cherbourg area. See Irving, *Mare's Nest*, pp. 20, 123–124, 172.

I am sending you by air courier the latest report upon the subject as I thought you would like to know about it.[3]

[3] See Irving, *Mare's Nest,* pp. 33–56, 59–83.

Doc. 271
ROOSEVELT TO CHURCHILL

No. 397   October 26, 1943

The present Moscow conference[1] appears to be a genuine beginning of British-Russian-U.S. collaboration which should lead to the early defeat of Hitler. In order to further stimulate this cooperation and particularly to increase the confidence of Stalin in the sincerity of our intentions it is suggested that immediately upon our receipt of information if it turns out that he is unable to meet with us at Basra[2] or other place that is acceptable to both of us, we jointly transmit some such message as the following to him:

QUOTE. Heretofore we have informed you of the results of our combined British-American military staff conferences. You may feel that it would be better to have a Russian military representative sit in at such meetings to listen to the discussions regarding British-American operations and take note of the decisions. He would be free to make such comments and proposals as you might desire. This arrangement would afford you and your staff an intimate and prompt report of these meetings.

[1] Eden, Molotov, and Hull met in Moscow on October 18–30, 1943, to discuss measures for shortening the war and cooperation in the postwar period. At this meeting the Soviet Union's desire for information on affairs in Italy led to the establishment of the Italian Advisory Council, consisting of Great Britain, the United States, the Soviet Union, and the French Committee of National Liberation, with Greece and Yugoslavia to join later. Also, from the surrendered Italian navy the Soviet Union claimed one battleship, one cruiser, eight destroyers, four submarines, and 40,000 tons of merchant shipping. Other topics discussed at the conference included the postwar treatment of Germany, a statement on postwar measures for Austria, reparations, international economics, Polish-Soviet relations, the possible participation of Sweden and Turkey in the war, air bases in the Soviet Union for British and American planes, the exchange of weather information, the improvement of communications facilities, and a declaration on war atrocities. The conference ended with the signing of the Four Nation Declaration, which called for the establishment of a world organization after the war. The Chinese ambassador to the Soviet Union, Foo Ping-sheung, joined the three foreign ministers in signing this statement. See Hull, *Memoirs,* vol. 2, chaps. 92–93; Eden, *Memoirs,* vol. 2 book 3, chap. 10; *FR 1943,* 1: 513ff.; and William H. McNeill, *America, Britain, and Russia: Their Cooperation and Conflict 1941–1946* (New York, 1953), pp. 328ff.

[2] A city in southeastern Iraq, seventy miles from the Persian Gulf.

If you favorably consider such an arrangement we shall advise you of the date and place of the next conference as soon as they have been determined. It would be understood that the procedure outlined carried no implication of discussion of plans for purely Russian operations except as your representative might be instructed to present. UNQUOTE. If he does agree to meet us at Basra, we can discuss this matter with him at that time.[3]

[3] Churchill replied on October 27 that he disapproved of having Russian representatives in attendance at future meetings of the Anglo-American military staffs.

Doc. 272
ROOSEVELT TO CHURCHILL

No. 414   November 8, 1943

Your 474.[1]
We too have received many reports of the German rocket activity. The only information recently coming to me which might be of value to you is a statement that factories manufacturing the rocket bomb are situated in Kania Friedrichshafen, Mixtgennerth Berlin, Kugellagerwerke Schweinfurt, Wiener Neustadt,[2] and at an isolated factory on left side of the road going from Vienna to Baden just south of Vienna. Production is said to have been delayed due to death in bombing the experimental station at Peenemünde of Lieutenant General Shemiergembeinski[3] who was in charge. This came from an informer via Turkey.

[1] See above, Doc. 270.
[2] Apparently this information served only to confuse the issue. Kugellagerwerke means "ball-bearing factories" and the major ones at Schweinfurt had already suffered a massive bombing by the U.S. Eighth Air Force on October 14. Actually, the first British strike against German rocket production had come about accidentally when on June 22 the Zeppelin works at Friedrichshafen were bombed as a suspected radar factory; later British intelligence learned that this was one of the places earmarked for mass production of rockets. The other sites were Peenemünde, Wiener Neustadt, and a plant in Berlin. After the first Peenemünde raid Hitler ordered that production be concentrated in an underground plant known as the Central Works Ltd. near the town of Nordhausen in central Germany. The first rockets were shipped from this plant on January 1, 1944. The rest of the places named in Roosevelt's telegram had no connection to German rocket work. See Irving, Mare's Nest, pp. 172–173.
[3] No person of this name was involved with German rocket work. The commanding officer of the Peenemünde Rocket Research Institute was Major General Walter Dornberger.

Doc. 273
ROOSEVELT TO CHURCHILL

No. 418   November 11, 1943

Your 501.[1]

I have just heard that U.J. will come to Teheran. I received a telegram from him five days ago which made me think he would not come even to that place—this because his advisers did not wish him to leave Russian soil.

I wired him at once that I had arranged the constitutional matter here,[2] and therefore that I could go to Teheran for a short meeting with him and told him I was very happy.

Even then I was in doubt as to whether he would go through with his former offer to go to Teheran.

His latest message has clinched the matter, and I think that now there is no question that you and I can meet him there between the twenty-seventh and the thirtieth.

Thus endeth a very difficult situation, and I think we can be happy.

In regard to Cairo, I have held all along—as I know you have—that it would be a terrible mistake if U.J. thought we had ganged up on him on military action. During the preliminary meetings in Cairo the combined staffs will, as you know, be in the planning stage. That is all. It will not hurt you or me if Molotov and a Russian military representative are in Cairo too. They will not feel that they are being given the "runaround." They will have no staff and no planners. Let us take them in on the high spots.

It is only five hours ago that I received U.J.'s telegram confirming Teheran.[3] Undoubtedly, Molotov and the military representative will return there with us between the twenty-seventh and the thirtieth and, when and after we have completed our talk with U.J., they will return with us to Cairo, possibly adding other military staff to the one representative accompanying Molotov on the first trip.

I think it essential that this schedule be carried out. I can assure you there will be no difficulties.

---

[1] Not printed. On November 11 Churchill cabled about arrangements for the Cairo meeting. See *Conferences at Cairo and Tehran*, p. 79.

[2] The "constitutional matter" (see above, Doc. 262) was in fact without much substance, and had been raised by Roosevelt largely to try to get Stalin's agreement to a more convenient meeting place.

[3] On November 10 Roosevelt received a message from Stalin: "Your plan concerning the organization of our meeting in Iran, I accept. I hope [that] Mr. Churchill will agree with this proposal." *Conferences at Cairo and Tehran*, pp. 78-79.

I am sending you this at the first opportunity of letting you know about U.J.

I am just off. Happy landing to us both.

Doc. 274
CHURCHILL TO ROOSEVELT

No. 507   November 21, 1943

See St. John, chapter 14, verses 1 to 4.[1]

1 The text was typed on the message by the Map Room staff:
  "1. Let not your heart be troubled: ye believe in God, believe also in me.
  2. In my Father's house are many mansions; if it were not so, I would have told you, I go to prepare a place for you.
  3. And if I go and prepare a place for you, I will come again, and receive you unto myself; that where I am, there ye may be also.
  4. And whither I go ye know, and the way ye know."

THE CAIRO-TEHERAN CONFERENCE
NOVEMBER–DECEMBER, 1943

[The persistent efforts of Roosevelt and Churchill to arrange a conference with Stalin finally bore fruit when the Big Three met at Teheran from November 28 to December 2, 1943.

Stalin had insisted on the Iranian capital as the conference site, contending that he had to remain in close touch with developments on the Russian front. Roosevelt agreed to come to Teheran despite the problems posed by distance and poor communications facilities to the exercise of his constitutional duties at home. Churchill had wished to meet again somewhere in Africa, but he too was willing to travel the extra miles to confer with the Russian leader. The President had originally hoped to have Generalissimo Chiang Kai-shek attend the conference, but the Soviet Union was not at war with Japan, and Stalin felt it inappropriate to meet with Chiang and Roosevelt at the same time. As a result, a plan was devised for Roosevelt and Churchill to meet with Chiang at Cairo both before and after the conference with Stalin.

Churchill and Chiang were already on hand at Cairo when the President arrived there on November 22. That evening the President and the Prime Minister held a preliminary meeting with the military chiefs at which Admiral Lord Mountbatten presented his plans and requirements for a campaign in Burma. The following day Roosevelt, Churchill, and Mountbatten reviewed these plans with Chiang. The President spoke in general terms about future operations against Japan and emphasized the importance of Chinese assistance in the pending operation in Burma. The Generalissimo declared that Burma was the key to the whole Asian campaign and that, in addition to the proposed thrusts by special airborne units in northern Burma, there should be a coordinated amphibious landing in the Bay of Bengal. Churchill disagreed, and when the Cairo talks ended on November 26 no final decision had been reached on how to deliver the promised assistance to the hard-pressed Chinese.

During the Cairo meeting, Churchill again raised the subject of operations against the island of Rhodes and other points in the Aegean. This proposal had been emphatically rejected by the American military chiefs only a few weeks earlier, but the Prime Minister was unwilling to give up on his plan. More serious yet, the British military now suggested that the planned invasion of Europe—Operation Overlord—be delayed, if only briefly, to pursue the Aegean strategy and thereby persuade Turkey to enter the war on the Allied side. Because of their own strong feelings, as well as Roosevelt's instructions, the U.S. military chiefs were unwilling to accept Churchill's latest scheme, and the Cairo meeting ended without agreement on the subject.

In the political realm the gathering at Cairo gave Roosevelt an opportunity to meet with President Ismet Inönü of Turkey, King George II of Greece, and King Peter of Yugoslavia, as well as Egyptian officials. He had a brief courtesy visit with Andrei A. Vyshinsky, the Soviet representative on the Italian Advisory Council, who was en route to Algiers for a meeting of that body. The conversations disclosed the substantial political as well as military differences of opinion between Roosevelt and Churchill, such as their opposing views on whether King George II of Greece should abdicate.

Roosevelt and Churchill then proceeded to Teheran for their conference with Stalin, which opened on November 28. At their first meeting the President reviewed for Stalin the Anglo-American strategy worked out at previous conferences and the plans for the future. Roosevelt informed the Soviet leader that at their Quebec meeting four months earlier he and Churchill had tentatively agreed upon May 1944 as the date for the forthcoming invasion of Europe. Churchill remarked that while the Normandy invasion had indeed been subject to much disappointing delay, it was now definitely scheduled, although he was still uncertain about the date. He believed that there were other fronts that should be opened against the Germans and was concerned that the forces earmarked for Overlord would not be adequate to their assigned task. He repeated that Turkey should be brought into the war. Stalin, in turn, declared that Italy was not a suitable place from which to attack Germany. He felt that any forces not required for Overlord would be better employed in an attack on southern France, launched at the same time as the invasion of Normandy. Furthermore, Stalin did not believe that Turkey would break with Hitler and enter the war against him.

At their second meeting the Big Three discussed the postwar borders of Poland, the future of France, and the punishment of German war criminals. As he had done at his meeting with Foreign Secretary Eden in December 1941, Stalin insisted on his August 1939 frontier with Poland. The President acquiesced, departing from his previous stand that decisions concerning frontiers should be delayed until the end of the war. Churchill in effect agreed with Stalin, asserting that "if some reasonable formula could be devised" he was prepared to discuss the subject with the Polish government-in-exile in London and, "without telling them that the Soviet Government would accept such a solution, would offer it to them as probably the best they could obtain."

Roosevelt held two private meetings with Stalin. The first meeting was devoted primarily to discussion of France and India. The President remarked that while "Mr. Churchill was of the opinion that France would be very quickly reconstructed as a strong nation," he could not personally share that view since "many years of honest labor would be necessary before France would be reestablished." Roosevelt maintained that "the first necessity for the French, not only for the Government but the people as well, was to become honest citizens." On the subject of India's political status he told Stalin that it would be better not to raise the issue with Churchill, since the Prime Minister "had no solution of that question, and merely proposed to defer the entire question to the end of the war." The President added that he would like to talk with Stalin about India at some future date and that he felt "the best solution would be reform from the bottom, somewhat on the Soviet line."

In the second private meeting Roosevelt and Stalin talked mostly about Poland. The President mentioned the forthcoming election in 1944, noting that "there were in the United States from six to seven million Americans of Polish extraction" and that he did not wish to lose their vote. Roosevelt said he "personally agreed with the views of Marshal Stalin," indeed "would like to see the eastern border [of Poland] moved further to the west and [its] western border moved even to the River Oder." The President declared, however, that for political reasons he could not participate in any decision on the border question and "could not publicly take part in any such arrangement at the present time." Stalin replied that he understood.

At his meetings with Roosevelt and Churchill, Stalin brought up the timing and command of Overlord. Informed that no commanding officer had yet been named, the Soviet leader said he would not consider Overlord as definite until a commander had been chosen. On other matters Stalin reiterated his promise to enter the war against Japan after the defeat of Germany. In the meantime, the Americans asked for bases in Russia from which to carry out shuttlebombings against Germany, and Stalin assented to the proposal.

On the next-to-last day of the conference Churchill and his military chiefs finally agreed that the Normandy invasion should be launched in May 1944, and that a supporting invasion of southern France would be mounted at the same time. Stalin in turn promised to launch a powerful attack on the eastern front to coincide with the invasions of France. The last day of the conference was largely devoted to discussions of the new United Nations organization, the demilitarization of postwar Germany, Poland's eastern frontier, attempts to pressure Finland out of the war, and the independence and sovereignty of Iran. The Russians promised to withdraw their troops from Iran within six months after the end of the European war.

On December 2 Roosevelt, Churchill, and their staffs returned to Egypt for the second phase of the Cairo conference. The most immediate need was to reexamine the plans for the Bay of Bengal operation in the light of the Teheran decisions. Roosevelt now acceded to the British wish that the venture be canceled and informed Chiang Kai-shek accordingly. Despite his considerable disappointment, a week later Chiang gave General Joseph Stilwell command over Chinese troops in India and Burma. As the conference closed, plans for an offensive in northern Burma remained unsettled, but the Combined Chiefs of Staff set up a tentative timetable for offensive operations in the Pacific during 1944. Finally, the Combined Chiefs established a unified command for the Mediterranean theater. General Eisenhower was to have overall command and was to be responsible for all operations except strategic bombing.

Originally, the principal purpose of the second Cairo conference had been to talk to President Ismet Inönü of Turkey about taking his country into the war on the Allied side. The Americans had never shared the British military's enthusiasm for this proposal, fearing that if Turkey found itself in serious military difficulties as a result of such a decision, the United States would have to come to Turkey's aid at the expense of the main war effort. Churchill took the lead in trying to persuade the Turkish leader. But Inönü demanded so much in the way of tanks, planes, and guns as the price of abandoning Turkish neutrality that Churchill and Roosevelt were unwilling to meet his terms, with the result that Turkey declined to enter the war at that time.

Both the Cairo and the Teheran conferences were notable for the strong and undeviating positions Roosevelt and his military advisers took against Churchill and the British military leaders. By standing firm for the supremacy of Overlord over all other ventures, the Americans finally achieved what they had long sought, although Stalin's strong views on the subject were undoubtedly also important in changing Churchill's mind. Furthermore, by firmly insisting on an invasion of southern France simultaneously with Overlord, Stalin contributed significantly not only to the elimination of other proposed Mediterranean operations—which greatly pleased the Americans—but also to the abandonment of amphibious operations in the Bay of Bengal, a great relief to the British.

The Teheran conference marked the high point of Allied political unity during the war. Roosevelt, for one, was most enthusiastic. "I consider that the conference was a great success," he cabled Stalin from Cairo on December 3, "and I am sure that it was an historic event in the assurance not only of our ability to wage war together but to work in the utmost harmony for the peace to come."]

Doc. 275
CHURCHILL TO ROOSEVELT

No. 511   December 15, 1943

Am stranded amid the ruins of Carthage, where you stayed, with fever which has ripened into pneumonia. All your people are doing everything possible, but I do not pretend I am enjoying myself. I hope soon to send you some of the suggestions for the new commands. I hope you had a pleasant voyage and are fit. Love to Harry.[1]

1 Roosevelt replied to Churchill's message on December 17 while on his way up the Potomac River toward Washington. After expressing his sympathy over the Prime Minister's plight, the President added: "The Bible says you must do just what [Churchill's physician, Lord] Moran orders, but at this moment I cannot put my finger on the verse and the chapter."

Doc. 276
ROOSEVELT TO CHURCHILL

No. 427   December 27, 1943

Your number 521.[1]

It is agreed to delay the departure of fifty-six LSTs scheduled for Overlord for mounting Shingle on 20 January and on the basis that Overlord remain the paramount operation and will be carried out on the date agreed to at Cairo and Teheran. All possible expedients should be undertaken to overcome probable effect on Overlord preparation to which end the other twelve LSTs for Overlord should depart as now scheduled, and the fifteen LSTs ex-Buccaneer[2] arriving in Mediterranean on 14 January should proceed directly to U.K. I agree that Hercules[3] and Aegean must be sidetracked and that we cannot give further consideration to launching Hercules prior to Anvil.[4]

In view of the Soviet-British-American agreement reached in Teheran I cannot agree without Stalin's approval to any use of forces or equipment elsewhere that might delay or hazard the success of Overlord or Anvil.[5]

[1] Not printed. On December 26 Churchill cabled that General Sir Harold Alexander was prepared to launch operation Shingle, the amphibious landing at Anzio, Italy, about January 20, provided he got fifty-six tank landing ships (LSTs) to transport two divisions. These could be had only by delaying until February 5 the return to England of fifty-six LSTs then in the Mediterranean.

[2] Code name for the amphibious operation in the Andaman Islands, canceled at the second Cairo conference.

[3] Code name for the plan to seize the island of Rhodes.

[4] Code name for the invasion of southern France.

[5] Churchill replied on December 28: "I thank God for this fine decision which engages us once again in wholehearted unity upon a great enterprise."

1. Churchill saying good-bye at the close of the Atlantic Conference, where he and Roosevelt met for the first time, August 4–18, 1941. Roosevelt is on the arm of his son Elliott.

2. Churchill arriving for the First Washington Conference, December 22, 1941.

3. Press conference in the White House during the First Washington Conference, December 23, 1941. (UPI)

4. Leaving Christ Church, Alexandria, Virginia, January 1, 1942. Lord Halifax, British ambassador to the United States, is standing behind Churchill, who is greeting six-year-old Katrina Welles. The girl's father, Rev. E. R. Welles, is standing behind her. Roosevelt is holding the arm of Major-General Edwin M. Watson. (UPI)

5. Dinner in the President's private quarters at the White House, January 1942.

6. With the Pacific War Council at the Second Washington Conference, June 1942. *Standing left to right:* Leighton McCarthy, Canadian minister in Washington; Prime Minister William Lyon MacKenzie King of Canada; *behind King,* Lord Halifax, British ambassador to the United States; T. V. Soong, Chinese ambassador to the United States; Philippine President Manuel Quezon.

7. Preparing a joint communiqué at Casablanca during the week of January 17, 1943. *Standing left to right:* Lieutenant-General H. H. Arnold; Admiral Ernest J. King; General George C. Marshall; *seen in profile,* Lieutenant-General Hastings L. Ismay; Admiral of the Fleet Sir Dudley Pound; *without a hat,* Vice-Admiral Lord Louis Mountbatten; Air Chief Marshall Sir Charles Portal; General Sir Alan Brooke; Field Marshall Sir John Dill.

9. Churchill arriving for the fifth wartime meeting, the Third Washington Conference, May 14, 1943.

8. On the lawn of Roosevelt's villa at Casablanca with General Henri Honoré Giraud and General Charles de Gaulle.

10. Fishing at "Shangri-La," now Camp David, during the week of May 14–17, 1943.

11. At the Citadel for the First Quebec Conference, August 18, 1943, with Princess Alice, the wife of the Governor General of Canada.

12. First Quebec Conference. The Earl of Athlone, Governor General of Canada,is seated at Roosevelt's left and Canadian Prime Minister MacKenzie King is standing to Churchill's right.

13. Driving at Hyde Park following the First Quebec Conference, September 1943. In the rear seat are Brendan Bracken, the British Minister of Information, and Commander C. R. Thompson. (Wide World Photo)

14. Viewing the pyramids during the meeting at Cairo, November 1943.

15. With Generalissimo Chiang Kai-shek in Cairo prior to the Teheran Conference, November 25, 1943.

16. Roosevelt, Churchill, and Stalin at the Teheran Conference, their first joint meeting, November 29, 1943. Roosevelt is greeting WAAF officer Sarah Churchill. *Standing left to right:* Harry L. Hopkins, adviser and assistant to the President; Vyacheslav Molotov, Soviet Foreign Commissar; W. Averell Harriman, American ambassador to the Soviet Union; and Anthony Eden, British Foreign Secretary.

20. Roosevelt's longhand draft of a message to Mrs. Churchill, December 25, 1941.

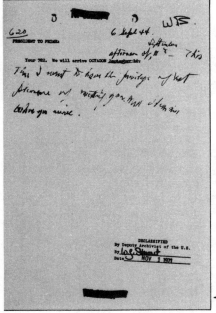

21. Roosevelt's longhand correction of a radio message to Churchill, September 6, 1944.

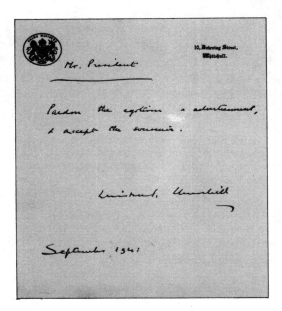

22. Churchill's longhand note accompanying his gift to Roosevelt of a specially bound collection of his writings, September 1941.

23. Aboard a warship at the Malta Conference, February 2, 1945.

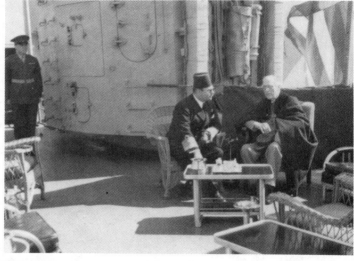

24. Conferring with King Farouk of Egypt after the Yalta Conference, February 13, 1945.

25. Conferring with King Ibn Saud of Saudi Arabia and Colonel William A. Eddy, American minister to that country, Egypt, February 1945.

26. Chatting with Emperor Haile Selassie of Ethiopia aboard the U.S.S. *Quincy,* Egypt, February 1945.

27. Arrival ceremonies at the airport before the Yalta Conference, February 3, 1945. Walking with Churchill at the far left are Secretary of State Edward R. Stettinius, Jr., and Soviet Foreign Commissar Vyacheslav Molotov.

28. Dining with Stalin at the Livadia Palace, Yalta, February 11, 1945. *Seated on the left side of the table:* Edward R. Stettinius, Jr.; Sir Alexander Cadogan, British Under-Secretary of State for Foreign Affairs; *partly obscured,* Admiral William D. Leahy; Charles E. Bohlen, assistant to the Secretary of State; and Sir Archibald Clark Kerr, British ambassador to the U.S.S.R. At the end of the table are Harry L. Hopkins and Anthony Eden, talking to Vladimir N. Pavlov, Stalin's personal secretary and interpreter. Vyacheslav Molotov is seated next to Churchill at the far right, conferring with Major Arthur Birse, Second Secretary of the British Embassy in Moscow and Churchill's interpreter.

29. Gathering at the conference table, Yalta, February 1945. *Clockwise around the table from Churchill, seated at the lower left:* Ivan Mikhailovitch Maisky, Deputy Peoples' Commissar for Foreign Affairs; Stalin; Aleksei Antonov, the Soviet Chief of Staff; *standing,* Major-General Lawrence S. Kuter, Assistant Chief of Staff for Plans, USAAF; General George C. Marshall; Admiral William D. Leahy; Roosevelt; *partly obscured,* Edward R. Stettinius, Jr.; Admiral Ernest J. King; an unidentified man; and Anthony Eden. Entering the room at the upper left are Andre Gromyko, Soviet ambassador to the United States and, behind him, Fedor T. Gusev, Soviet ambassador to the United Kingdom.

30. Seated in front of the Livadia Palace with their foreign ministers **directly** behind them (at Yalta, February 1945). *Left to right:* Churchill, with **Anthony** Eden; Roosevelt, with Edward R. Stettinius, Jr.; and Stalin, with Vyacheslav Molotov. *Standing to the left of Churchill:* Fedor T. Gusev; Charles E. Bohlen; Sir Charles McMoran Wilson, later Lord Moran, Churchill's personal **physician;** Sir Archibald Clark Kerr; *at the far right,* W. Averell Harriman.

31. A private moment at Yalta, February 1945.

PART III

January 1944
to
June 1944

Introduction to Part III

"All my hopes for the future of the world are based upon the friendship and cooperation of the western democracies and Soviet Russia."

BY THE OPENING of 1944—a year after the German disaster at Stalingrad and eighteen months after the decisive Japanese defeats at the battles of the Coral Sea and Midway—the military might of the Axis powers was slowly but steadily receding.

With their first summit conference with Stalin finally behind them, Roosevelt and Churchill began to devote their attention increasingly to the massive preparations for the forthcoming cross-channel invasion of Europe. As originally conceived, Overlord was to have been accompanied by a simultaneous landing in southern France, but the latter operation was subsequently postponed and reduced in size in order to concentrate on the Normandy landing. While Churchill had formally committed himself to both these operations, he remained somewhat uneasy about the risks of the cross-channel attack and was unconvinced of the wisdom of the planned landing in southern France, although he continued, at the same time, to point to the supposed benefits of his own peripheral strategy in the Mediterranean.

In any event, Roosevelt and Churchill now found themselves occupied with a great number of military and political problems elsewhere in Europe and the Far East. In Italy the slow advance up the peninsula against the reinforced German army was costing so much in time and men that General Sir Harold Alexander, now commander of the Fifteenth Army Group, set about establishing a second point of attack. He ordered the U.S. Fifth Army to launch an amphibious assault on the west coast of Italy, in the rear of the enemy. If the gamble succeeded, the Germans would be thrown off balance and the beach forces and the main army would soon link up, thereby quickening the drive to capture Rome. Operation Shingle, the landing at Anzio, began on January 22, 1944.

The Germans were surprised but quickly recovered, turning the American landing into a perilous defensive position on the beachhead. For two months the troops at Anzio endured heavy German attacks, and not until May 25 did the troops advancing from the south link up with those in the Anzio area. By then the Allied Fifth and Eighth Armies were in the midst of a redoubled offensive to capture Rome and to press the Germans hard before and after Overlord. Finally, Rome fell to the Allies on June 4.

In the Pacific, meanwhile, the Allies made important gains in New Guinea, the Solomons, the Marshalls, and the Admiralties. In February planes from American aircraft carriers attacked the Marianas—part of Japan's inner ring of defense—in anticipation of an American invasion of Saipan in mid-June.

Churchill was troubled that the Americans wanted to liberate Burma essentially as a prelude to increasing the flow of supplies to China. Intent on the main objective—defeating Japan—the American planners anticipated that as their island-hopping strategy brought them closer to Japan they could use the Chinese mainland as a base for launching B-29 bomber attacks on the Japanese home islands. Churchill wanted to recapture Sumatra and Malaya along with Burma, but the American strategists regarded these goals as unnecessary to defeat Japan. As things worked out, heavy troop commitments in Europe, both British and American, eventually led to a scaled-down campaign in Burma.

In March British Brigadier General Orde C. Wingate transported long-range penetration brigades by glider 100 miles inside Japanese territory in central Burma. These troops were to disrupt Japanese communications and thereby assist Chinese-American operations taking place farther north under the command of General Joseph W. Stilwell. Meanwhile an American long-range penetration group, popularly known as Merrill's Marauders, under Stilwell's command, moved from the Ledo Road into northern Burma and fought its way southward to Myitkyina. The American Joint Chiefs of Staff believed that if Myitkyina could be taken from the Japanese, this would deprive the Japanese of a fighter aircraft base, thereby making it easier for Allied planes flying supplies to China to increase their tonnage, to fly at lower altitudes, and to refuel en route. The elimination of the Japanese fighter base would also hasten the building of an all-weather road route to China. Consequently, the formal siege of Myitkyina began on June 2.

The rush of events in Europe and elsewhere also posed an increasing number of political problems. Thus the new year opened with an exchange between Roosevelt and Churchill about the conversation at Teheran on unconditional surrender. The President, however, preferred not to become involved in an extended discussion of the subject, and he and the Prime Minister likewise passed rapidly over the outrageous charge published in *Pravda*, on January 17, 1944, that there had been a secret meeting between British leaders and Nazi foreign minister Joachim von Ribbentrop "with the aim of ascertaining the terms of a separate peace with Germany."

Italy continued to claim a great deal of Roosevelt's and Churchill's time and energy. When Italy had surrendered in September 1943, the Allies worked out their armistice negotiations with Marshal Pietro Badoglio, the head of the new Italian government. The thought was that, after terms had been agreed upon, Italy could join the United Nations as a co-belligerent. In the meantime, Italy began to be plagued with growing political strife. With the Fascist dictatorship finally out of the way, new political elements began to emerge that took strongly anti-government positions. For Roosevelt and Churchill, the appearance of such groups raised the question of how far the Allies should go in encouraging—or tolerating—activity against a widely unpopular regime, which the Italian monarchy and Marshal Badoglio's government had become. The State Department appeared to favor removing King Victor Emmanuel III immediately. The British, however, strongly objected, and Roosevelt finally agreed with Churchill that changes should not be made until the military situation in Italy had substantially improved.

In the meantime, the Allies also had to face the sensitive matter of disposing of part of the Italian fleet. At the conference of foreign ministers, in Moscow, in October 1943, and again at Teheran, the Russians had expressed their desire for a share of the captured Italian vessels. Roosevelt and Churchill gave Stalin assurances that some of Italy's ships could be used by the Big Three during the war. But when the time came to turn over Italian vessels to the Russians, Churchill objected, fearing that such action would lead the crews to mutiny or to scuttle their ships. Eventually, Roosevelt, Churchill, and Stalin came to terms on the issue, but not before their relationship had been newly strained.

While preparations continued apace for the invasion of Western Europe, the Russians were beginning to score massive victories on the

Eastern front. By early 1944, the Soviets had cleared German troops from two-thirds of Russian-occupied territory, and, from the Baltic to the Balkans, they were pressing steadily ahead toward the frontiers of neighboring states. In January they ended the long siege of Leningrad, in March they opened a major offensive in the Ukraine, and in April began operations in the Crimea. There, on April 10 they retook Odessa, and on May 9 Sevastopol.

These impressive Russian military victories were bound to have important political implications, and of all the problems that confronted Roosevelt and Churchill from that time onward, none was more time-consuming, vexatious, and frustrating—or fraught with future peril—than the Polish question.

At Teheran, Roosevelt and Churchill had explored Stalin's ideas about Poland's postwar frontiers. When Stalin made his exact wishes known, the President and the Prime Minister had offered no objections, and Churchill and Foreign Secretary Eden returned to London and sought to obtain the approval of the Polish government-in-exile for Stalin's proposed boundaries. But the Polish government, which was growing increasingly fearful of what lay in store for postwar Poland, was not to be moved.

In public and private, the Poles offered a number of objections. They feared growing Soviet domination. They felt that the adjustment of boundaries ought to be the work of a formal treaty-making body—not the product of secret discussions, at however high a level, in which they had not participated. They believed, deeply, that they could make no renunciations of territory without antagonizing both people of Polish descent living abroad and the Polish underground (to say nothing of the rest of the population) at home. Both Roosevelt and Stalin were well aware of the discussions being held on these topics in London. Roosevelt and Churchill found themselves in an embarrassing situation. There was widespread support for the Polish position in the United States and Britain, which country had gone to war to protect Poland from foreign despoilation. Roosevelt's situation was further complicated by the fact that 1944 was a presidential election year, and that—as he had implied to Stalin at Teheran—Americans of Polish descent were not likely to look with favor on any candidate who yielded to Stalin's territorial demands.

The Polish problem, therefore, dragged on unresolved. Churchill continued to urge moderation and compromise on the London Poles. But, privately, he grew increasingly discouraged by Stalin's stubbornness and the occasional violence of his language, and he concluded that, for the time being at least, it was useless to continue discussions with Stalin since he was "determined to find fault and pick a quarrel on every point." Nevertheless, for all the difficulty of dealing with the Russian leader, Churchill had by no means given up hope of a fruitful postwar relationship with the Soviet Union.

Stalin's attitude toward Poland, however, was only one of the many political problems that plagued Roosevelt and Churchill with "the turn of the tide" on the battlefield. They were increasingly annoyed—and Roosevelt was especially outraged—by the attitudes, positions, and statements of General Charles de Gaulle, the head of the French Committee of National Liberation, and the President thought the time had come to break with de Gaulle. Then, too, as the invasion of Europe drew ever closer, Roosevelt and his military advisers began to have misgivings about the arrangements agreed upon for the Allied zones of occupation in Western Europe. On the surface, this seemed a largely military issue, but it had deep political overtones. American troops were slated to occupy southern Germany and Austria, and thus the supply lines of their armies would have to pass through France. After all his difficulties with de Gaulle and the French National Committee, Roosevelt seemed fearful that the United States might have to police France to safeguard those supply lines. He sought, therefore, to exchange occupation zones with the British, but Churchill refused. Neither Roosevelt nor Churchill was worried, then or later, about what might happen in divided Berlin, or on the access roads serving the city.

After Teheran, Roosevelt and Churchill also became increasingly concerned with political problems in the Balkans. In Yugoslavia, both Britain and the United States had originally supported the guerrilla forces led by General Draža Milhailović. By early 1944, however, Churchill concluded that the latter was not an effective force against the Germans, and he transferred British support to the Communist guerrillas led by the Moscow-trained Josip Broz Tito. The United States had come to similar conclusions about Mihailović, but Churchill continued to worry that London and Washington would support rival groups on Yugoslavia. Subsequently, King Peter of Yugoslavia moved to establish a new government under the Ban (or Viceroy) of Croatia. The President and the Prime Minister cooperated in setting up the new government, and they urged Tito to join with them.

To the south, meanwhile, civil war broke out in Greece between rival bands of guerrillas. One group, largely under Communist control and known by the Greek letters ELAS, opposed the anti-Communist forces (EDES). A third group, composed of royalist elements, supported King George II, although the king himself was then living in exile. Delegates from the two resistance groups traveled to Cairo to urge the king to conduct a plebescite before he returned home to

Greece. George II was receiving conflicting advice from Roosevelt and Churchill at various times, and he declined to set up the election, thus storing up future problems for the Allied leaders. Before long, a so-called National Liberation Front, known as EAM, was established in the mountains of Greece. At first it seemed to provide an alternative government for the antiroyalist factions, but it soon became more and more a Communist-front organization. In late May, after protracted negotiations in Lebanon—Greece was still occupied by German troops and British forces were not to land there until early October—a Greek Government of National Unity was finally formed. But it was not long before the Communists began once more to make unacceptable demands and the political settlement, such as it was, soon broke down.

These developments in Greece were not an isolated development. By the spring of 1944, Churchill was becoming uncomfortably aware that British and Russian policies on the future of the Balkan countries were increasingly at odds. With a sense of compromise, therefore, Churchill moved toward a more formal division of Anglo-Russian influence in the Balkans, proposing that the Russians consider Rumania within their sphere of influence and that they leave Greece as Britain's special responsibility. Stalin apparently found the idea acceptable, but Roosevelt certainly did not. The President had never favored the idea of spheres of influence, and his differences with Churchill on this subject grew wider as the war went on.

A host of other, less important political questions also demanded varying degrees of attention from Roosevelt and Churchill in the first half of 1944. Among these were efforts to secure bases in the Azores; attempts to stop the Spanish from exporting strategic materials to Germany; Churchill's concern about American interests and activities connected with oil resources in the Middle East; and efforts to deal with peace feelers from the Bulgarians. In addition, the United States was putting pressure on Argentina to break off relations with Germany and Japan and to expel resident Axis spies. Eventually, the United States decided to sever diplomatic ties with Argentina and urged the British to do the same. Churchill was willing to support his ally, but he pointed out that doing so created special risks for the United Kingdom, since the British depended on Argentina for a third of their meat supply.

In the midst of all their perplexing political problems, the two leaders discussed their concern for the well-being of women and children in German-occupied countries. Roosevelt and Churchill also looked ahead to postwar economic cooperation and the steps being taken under the United Nations organization to assure it.

In many ways, then, the first five months of 1944 were previews of many problems that lay ahead. But all the time, the Allied buildup for the greatest military invasion in history continued, and it began at last on June 6, 1944.

Messages and Notes

Doc. 277
CHURCHILL TO ROOSEVELT

No. 530

January 2, 1944

Hull tells Eden that you have no recollection of any remarks by U.J. about unconditional surrender.[1] I certainly heard, with great interest, him saying something to the effect that he thought it might be well to consider telling the Germans at some stage what unconditional surrender would involve, or perhaps what it would not involve. After that we began talking about the 50,000 and your compromise and my high falutin', and I finished up by no means certain that the Germans would be reassured if they were told what he had in mind.[2]

[1] According to Secretary of State Cordell Hull's memoirs, the British Embassy at Washington sent the State Department an *aide-mémoire* on December 22, 1943, stating that a joint announcement to the German people based on the principle of unconditional surrender had been considered at Teheran and that Stalin (U.J.) had told Roosevelt on November 29 that he thought this a bad tactic. British Foreign Secretary Anthony Eden believed that the matter should be dealt with as soon as possible. Hull asked Roosevelt for his views on December 22 and was told that the subject had not been brought up in Roosevelt's presence at Teheran. The President thought that John G. Winant, the American ambassador to Great Britain, should take the matter up with Churchill as soon as the Prime Minister got back to London. Winant was so instructed on December 24. See Cordell Hull, *The Memoirs of Cordell Hull*, 2 vols. (New York, 1948), 2: 1572. Henceforth cited as Hull, *Memoirs*.

[2] Churchill does not mention unconditional surrender in this context in his memoirs but does discuss the viewpoints of the Big Three on the matter of punish-

Find also Anthony telegraphed to the Foreign Office on November 30 as follows:

"Last night (November 29th) Marshal Stalin spoke to the President about unconditional surrender. Marshal Stalin said he considered this bad tactics vis-à-vis Germany and his suggestion was that we should together work out terms and let them be made known generally to the people of Germany."[3]

Perhaps this may give you a cue to what Anthony and I had in our memories and you may feel inclined to join with us in asking U.J. whether he would care to develop his theme to us. If, however, you prefer we can of course leave things where they are for the time being.

---

ing a large number of German leaders. See Winston S. Churchill, *Closing the Ring* (Boston, 1951) , pp. 373–374, 706.

[3] No mention of this appears in *The Memoirs of Anthony Eden, Earl of Avon*, vol. 2, *The Reckoning* (Boston, 1965) . Henceforth cited as Eden, *Memoirs*.

Doc. 278
ROOSEVELT TO CHURCHILL

No. 436.   January 6, 1944

Your 530 of 2 January.[1]

I made the following public announcement on 24 December: QUOTE. The United Nations have no intention to enslave the German people. We wish them to have a normal chance to develop in peace, as useful and respectable members of the European family. But we most certainly emphasize the word "respectable," for we intend to rid them once and for all of Nazism and Prussian militarism and the fantastic and disastrous notion that they constitute the "master race." UNQUOTE.[2]

It is my opinion that at the present time it is best to permit our understanding of unconditional surrender to rest upon that.[3]

If we should at the present time make any number of specific conditions for the surrender we might probably omit or leave open for discussion some other conditions that are now or that may in the future become of equal importance from our point of view.

In view of all the above I prefer to leave things as they are for the

---

1 See above, Doc. 277.

2 See Hull, *Memoirs*, 2: 1572–1573.

3 See Herbert Feis, *Churchill, Roosevelt, Stalin* (Princeton, N.J., 1957) , pp. 109–113, 350–358; and Anne Armstrong, *Unconditional Surrender: The Impact of the Casablanca Policy upon World War II* (New Brunswick, N.J., 1961) .

time being and we really do not know enough about opinions within Germany itself to go on any fishing expedition there at this time. I hope you and Anthony will agree.

Doc. 279
ROOSEVELT TO CHURCHILL

No. 437   January 8, 1944

As I told you in my 422,[1] Harriman[2] requested information on the action we were taking to carry out our commitments to turn over Italian ships to the Soviet by 1 February so that he could discuss the matter with Molotov[3] if he were queried. I told him it was my intention to allocate one-third of the captured Italian ships to the Soviet war effort beginning 1 February as rapidly as they could be made available.

Harriman then reminded me that Stalin's request at Teheran was a reiteration of the Soviet request originally made at Moscow in October (namely for one battleship, one cruiser, eight destroyers, and four submarines for north Russia and 40,000 tons displacement of merchant shipping for the Black Sea) and that no mention was made at Moscow or Teheran of the Russians' getting additional ships up to one-third of those captured. Accordingly Harriman regarded my cable of December 21 as being for his information and he has not discussed the question of one-third with Molotov.[4]

Harriman also emphasized the very great importance of fulfilling our pledge to yield these ships. For us to fail or to delay would in his opinion only arouse suspicion in Stalin and in his associates as to the firmness of other commitments made at Teheran.

On the other hand, the Chiefs of Staff have raised numerous objections to the transfer based on probable effects that this course would have on pending operations. They fear a loss of Italian naval and military cooperation, and the scuttling or sabotage of valuable ships which we need for Anvil[5] and Overlord.[6] They foresee no material

---

1 Not printed.

2 W. Averell Harriman, U.S. ambassador to the Soviet Union.

3 Vyacheslav M. Molotov, Soviet Foreign Minister.

4 Molotov had brought up the question on October 22, 1943, at the Moscow meeting of foreign ministers. Roosevelt cabled Hull that he was willing to turn over a third of the ships to the Soviet Union. See Hull, *Memoirs*, 2: 1284, 1301–1302.

5 Code name for the invasion of southern France.

6 Code name for the cross-channel attack.

benefit to the Russian war effort at this time since the warships are presently quite unsuited for northern waters and the Black Sea is closed to merchant vessels.

The very wise provisions of the modified Cunningham agreement[7] give the United Nations the right to make disposition of any or all Italian ships as they may think fit. It is of importance that we shall acquire and maintain the confidence of our ally and I feel that every practicable effort should be made to arrive at a solution whereby the Italian ships requested by the Soviets be turned over to them beginning about February first.

Do you believe it wise to present to U.J. the possible effect on Overlord-Anvil as expressed by our staffs, and suggest a delay in assigning Italian ships to him until after the launching of Overlord-Anvil? I am particularly desirous of having an expression of your opinion in view of the present British command of the Mediterranean theater and in order that we may reach a complete agreement as to the action to be taken. It is patently impracticable for either of us to act singly in this matter, but I think you will agree that we must not go back on what we told U.J.

7 When the Italian navy surrendered to the British at Malta on September 29, 1943, there was no recognized Italian government. Accordingly, an agreement was drawn up between Admiral Raffaele de Courten of the Italian navy and Admiral Sir Andrew Brown Cunningham of the Royal Navy. After Marshal Pietro Badoglio signed surrender terms for the Italian government, it was discovered that there was no provision for the Italian fleet. Consequently, a clause had to be added to the Cunningham–de Courten agreement. See Andrew Brown Cunningham, *A Sailor's Odyssey* (New York, 1951), pp. 572–573.

Doc. 280
CHURCHILL TO ROOSEVELT

No. 543   January 9, 1944

I entirely agree with you that we must not break faith with Stalin about the ships.[1] I have been for a week in correspondence with Anthony on subject and hope to submit a proposal to you for a joint communication from you and me in a day or two.

1 See above, Doc. 279.

Doc. 281
ROOSEVELT TO CHURCHILL

No. 441   January 14, 1944

Your 536.[1] It is my understanding that in Teheran U.J. was given a promise that Overlord be launched during May and supported by strongest practicable Anvil at about the same time and that he agreed to plan for simultaneous Russian attack on eastern front.[2]

I do not believe that we should make any decision now to defer the operations, certainly not until the responsible commanders (Eisenhower and Wilson)[3] have had full opportunity to explore all possibilities and make factual reports. In the meantime no communication should be sent to U.J. on this subject.

I think the psychology of bringing this thing up at this time would be very bad in view of the fact that it is only a little over a month since the three of us agreed on the statement in Teheran.

[1] Not printed. Churchill wrote to Roosevelt on January 6 of his meeting with Eisenhower's Chief of Staff, General Walter Bedell Smith, who reported his own and General Sir Bernard Montgomery's conviction that it would be better to strengthen the forces for Overlord than for Anvil. The men also discussed the likelihood of a few weeks' delay in mounting Overlord. Churchill considered that the change in date did not mean a breach of faith with Stalin. See Churchill, *Closing the Ring*, pp. 448–449.

[2] See Churchill, *Closing the Ring*, pp. 356–357, 369–371, 379–381, 382–384. The American record is set forth in U.S. Department of State, *The Conferences at Cairo and Tehran 1943* (Washington, 1961), pp. 563–578.

[3] General Dwight D. Eisenhower had been appointed Supreme Allied Commander for Overlord on December 24, 1943. General Sir Henry Maitland Wilson succeeded Eisenhower as commander in chief of Allied forces in the Mediterranean on January 8.

Doc. 282
CHURCHILL TO ROOSEVELT

No. 549   January 19, 1944

We are convinced that it was a misunderstanding that Salazar[1] agreed to the use of Lagens Field by an American VLR[2] squadron of Navy planes. Apparently the Germans making a virtue of necessity

[1] Antonio de Oliveira Salazar, Premier and virtual dictator of Portugal since 1932.
[2] Very long range.

have said that they respect Salazar's age-long engagements under the Anglo-Portuguese treaty but that this would not cover United States forces. At the same time Salazar is prepared to lend himself to any fiction or camouflage which would give the results we both desire.

At our talks in Washington in May 1943 we thought the prize was great and you will remember that I in particular was ready to use force if necessary to obtain it.[3] I was for a long time skeptical of the Foreign Office view that Salazar could be made to meet our needs through the invocation of the old treaty. However he has done so to a very great extent in spite of the fact that we gave no guarantee to send an army to defend Portugal at a time when things looked much more dangerous for him than they do now. All the arrangements for the ferry service are now agreed and in hand, and my impression is that the only other matter immediately outstanding is that of your Liberator squadron.[4] Although we possess overwhelming strength it would be as you yourself felt rather inconsistent with our general attitude towards small powers to override them roughly in matters of neutrality. I feel we have been spared a very difficult decision and I should not like to upset things for the sake of a single squadron.

I am told that there would be no difficulty if your squadron would operate as a British unit with British markings but with American crows wearing some badge to indicate that they are temporarily incorporated in the RAF on the analogy of the Eagle squadron.[5] Commander Huff U.S. Navy who has been advising the American legation in Lisbon on U.S. naval facilities in the Azores and is now returning to Washington favors this idea. In judging this please remember that we were quite ready to put large numbers of troops

[3] In his memoirs of the third Washington conference Churchill makes no mention of this, although he acknowledges that the Azores question was discussed. See Winston S. Churchill, *The Hinge of Fate* (Boston, 1950), p. 789. According to General Sir Alan Brooke, Chief of the Imperial General Staff, the suggestion that the British seize the Azores came from Admiral Ernest J. King, U.S. Chief of Naval Operations. See Arthur Bryant, *The Turn of the Tide* (New York, 1957) p. 545.

[4] At Cairo on December 6, 1943, the British Chiefs of Staff had prepared a memorandum on the development of facilities in the Azores in which they set forth as their requirements a total of three squadrons, two British and one American. They recommended that the American squadron be comprised of B-24 bombers (Liberators) to replace the British Hudson bombers then in use there. See *Conferences at Cairo and Tehran*, pp. 808–809.

[5] At the meeting of the Combined Chiefs of Staff at Cairo on December 7, 1943, the American Chiefs of Staff reported that they had drafted a memorandum providing for a change in the insignia of the United States aircraft to be used in the Azores. British Air Chief Marshal Sir Charles Portal replied that this was unnecessary; American planes had only to operate under the control of a British officer from a British base. General Henry H. Arnold, commander of the U.S. Army Air Force, agreed with this solution. See *Conferences at Cairo and Tehran*, p. 760.

into American uniforms at the time of Torch[6] if that would help. This is the course I would recommend. It seems to give all we want in fact.

I would at the same time send a message to Salazar pointing out to him the great importance of meeting your wishes in every way compatible with his own security. I should invoke the "friends to friends" phrase in our treaty of 1373 as a reason for his making things agreeable to you in every way and I should emphasise the extraordinary unwisdom of any abrupt step on his part which would lead to a breach with the United States which would certainly entail a change in our relations too.[7]

[6] Code name for the invasion of North Africa in November 1942.

[7] For Churchill's account of the use of this treaty to secure bases in the Azores see his *Closing the Ring*, pp. 165–166. George F. Kennan, counselor of legation at Lisbon, wrote later that he pointed out the possibilities of the Anglo-Portuguese treaty to the Department of State early in 1943 but did not receive a response. See George F. Kennan, *Memoirs 1925–1950* (Boston, 1967), pp. 144–145.

Doc. 283
CHURCHILL TO ROOSEVELT

No. 550   January 21, 1944

I deprecate the inclusion in the second of the alternatives we are putting before U.J. of an offer to obtain at once eight Italian destroyers and four Italian submarines.[1] My idea in suggesting that *Royal Sovereign*[2] and a cruiser should be offered was to avoid any immediate approach to the Italians and thus escape the dangers stressed by the Combined Chiefs of Staff. We fear that the second alternative as formulated in your draft may give us the worst of both worlds.

I, therefore, hope you will agree to the omission from the message of the following passage in your draft:

"An effort will be made at once to make available from the surrendered Italian warships eight destroyers and four submarines to be

[1] Roosevelt and Churchill had exchanged drafts of a proposed message to Stalin about the Italian ships. In his message of January 19 Roosevelt suggested that they tell Stalin that they considered such a transfer dangerous, but that if Stalin insisted on the transfer they would make a secret approach to the Italian government. As an alternative, he suggested offering the Russians a British battleship and an American light cruiser plus 20,000 tons of merchant shipping as soon as operations permitted. Furthermore, an effort would be made to deliver eight destroyers and four submarines from the Italian fleet.

[2] The British battleship *Royal Sovereign* had recently been refitted in the United States.

taken over by the Soviet as soon as they can be made available under conditions stated above for the British and U.S. ships."

Let me know if I may despatch the message as amended and the accompanying telegram on behalf of us both.[3] The British Ambassador in Moscow[4] has just been reminded by the Soviet Commissariat of Foreign Affairs that the delivery date is February 1st.

The eight destroyers could not be found from British resources since all the ships in Halifax and Bermuda are now manned and we expect to man every ship complet[ed] according to programme and will assuredly need them all to meet our huge commitments for Overlord and the battle of the Atlantic.

[3] Roosevelt agreed to Churchill's suggestion in a message of January 22.
[4] Sir Archibald Clark Kerr, British ambassador to the Soviet Union.

Doc. 284
ROOSEVELT TO CHURCHILL

No. 448   January 22, 1944

Replying to your 549,[1] it appears preferable to delay sending our VLR squadron to Lagens Field pending further efforts to obtain Salazar's agreement for the American squadron to use the field under British operational control.[2]

I hope you can succeed in influencing Salazar to permit your Air Command in the Azores to utilize in its antisubmarine campaign an American squadron under British operational control.

[1] See above, Doc. 282.
[2] Salazar refused to give his consent until July 1944. See Hull, *Memoirs,* 2: 1339–1344; Kennan, *Memoirs,* pp. 142–163; and U.S. Department of State, *Foreign Relations of the United States 1943,* 2 (Washington, 1964): 527–576, and *Foreign Relations of the United States 1943,* 4 (Washington, 1966) : 1–64. Henceforth cited as *FR.*

Doc. 285
CHURCHILL TO ROOSEVELT

No. 552   January 23, 1944

We shall help all we can about the Argentine and above all avoid any public divergence.[1] I beg you however to look into the formidable

[1] The United States had long been concerned about the relations of Argentina with the Axis and the activities of German spies there. In 1943 Secretary of State Hull asked the British for a greater coordination on Argentine policy, urging that the British delay signing an agreement on purchasing Argentine meat until Argentina agreed to prohibit the broadcasting of coded radio messages. Eventually, the

consequences which would follow from our losing their meat, hides, and other supplies. One-third of our meat supply comes from them. How are we to feed ourselves plus the American army for Overlord if this is cut? The joint examination of the supply aspects by the combined boards in Washington will show you how much these people have us in their hands. Our Chiefs of Staff consider that an immediate cessation of Argentine supplies will rupture military operations on the scale planned for this year. I cannot cut the British ration lower than it is now. We really must look before we leap. We can always save up and pay them back when our hands are clear. I must enter my solemn warning of the gravity of the situation which will follow an interruption of Argentine supplies. Even recall of Ambassadors only means that the field is left open to the Germans. These rascals have calculated very carefully and know the hold they have over us for the time being.

British cooperated and the Argentines came around. Late in 1943 Secretary Hull asked the British to exert still more economic pressure on Argentina, even to go as far as a general embargo on Argentine goods. The appeal elicited Churchill's negative reply. See *FR 1944*, 7 (Washington, 1967): 228–420; and Sir Llewellyn Woodward, *British Foreign Policy in the Second World War* (abridged ed.; London, 1962), pp. 411–413.

Doc. 286
ROOSEVELT TO CHURCHILL

No. 449   January 24, 1944

Your 552.[1] I am glad to say that the Argentine picture has changed since receipt of your telegram of January 23. This morning our Ambassador in Buenos Aires[2] telephoned urgently that the Argentine Government gave its solemn word of honor that it would break relations with Germany before Saturday noon of this week. At long last the Argentine Government apparently has suddenly discovered that the German Embassy is carrying on espionage and subversive activities in flagrant violation of assurances made to the Argentine Government.[3]

The contemplated Argentine action is convincing proof that what I have been saying all along is correct, namely that Argentina is a base of operations for activities dangerous both to our common war effort

[1] See above, Doc. 285.

[2] Norman Armour, U.S. ambassador to Argentina.

[3] When the British arrested a German agent in Trinidad, they discovered that the man was serving as a go-between for the German and Argentine governments. The United States also had evidence linking Argentina with the recent overthrow of the government of Bolivia. Argentina broke with the Axis on January 27.

and to the peace of the Americas. I think it is clear that the Argentines got word of what was up and are taking this action in an endeavor to stave off moral and possible economic sanctions against her. Although it is of real military advantage to have the German Embassy out of the way, Argentina will have to do much more in the way of housecleaning of undesirable elements and of compliance with her inter-American commitments to convince me of the sincerity of her conversion. Now is the time for us to press forward and insist that Argentina put an end to the encouragement of sinister activities that menace the conduct of the war and internal peace within several of the American republics.[4]

If you and I should refuse to deal energetically with the situation, the subversive forces in Argentina and elsewhere would construe this as a backward step and would be greatly heartened. This would prejudice our joint war effort. In addition, it would tend to destroy inter-American solidarity and place the lower part of the continent in the power of elements unfriendly to us. Our friends there would lose faith in us.

Argentina's present willingness to break with Germany shows that we here had correctly diagnosed the situation and that Argentina would not have fought back in the way you feared against the action which we earlier contemplated. We believe that that action together with any assistance which you may be willing to render should not be abandoned but merely held in abeyance pending developments.

For the present, we are merely issuing a statement to the effect that we are not recognizing the Bolivian revolutionary junta.[5] A similar statement from you would be useful.

[4] British Foreign Secretary Eden called in the Argentine ambassador to Great Britain and urged further housecleaning of Axis influences. Secretary Hull was notified of the talk on January 28.

[5] On January 25 the United States refused to recognize the Bolivian government under Major Gualberto Villarroel, which had seized power on December 21, 1943.

Doc. 287
ROOSEVELT TO CHURCHILL

No. 451   January 27, 1944

Replying to your 556,[1] I am highly pleased with Anthony's statement about Bolivia.[2] I am delighted to have your and his support.

[1] Not printed.

[2] Foreign Secretary Eden, in reply to a question in the House of Commons on Bolivia on January 25, declared that the British would not recognize the Villarroel junta.

Now that Argentina has broken relations with Germany and Japan,[3] I trust we can both press forward with the Argentine Government to bring about full cooperation by Argentina in the suppression of activities inimical to the cause of the United Nations.

[3] Actually, difficulties with Argentina continued, and the United States recalled its ambassador on June 22. Roosevelt urged Churchill to take the same step, and he and Eden reluctantly agreed to do so on July 1.

Doc. 288
CHURCHILL TO ROOSEVELT

No. 557   January 28, 1944

After much thought and talk I have sent the following signal to U.J.:

"1. On Thursday last, accompanied by the Foreign Secretary and with the authority of the War Cabinet, I saw representatives of the Polish Government in London. I informed them that the security of the Russian frontiers against Germany was a matter of high consequence to His Majesty's Government, and that we should certainly support the Soviet Union in all measures we considered necessary to that end. I remarked that Russia had sustained two frightful invasions with immense slaughter and devastation at the hands of Germany, that Poland had had national independence and existence restored after the first world war, and that it was the policy of the Great Allies to restore Poland once again after this war. I said that although we had gone to war for the sake of Poland, we had not gone to war for any particular frontier line but for the existence of a strong, free, independent Poland, which Marshal Stalin had also declared himself supporting. Moreover, although Great Britain would have fought on in any case for years until something happened to Germany, the liberation of Poland from the German grip is being achieved mainly by the enormous sacrifices and achievements of the Russian armies. Therefore Russia and her allies had a right to ask that Poland should be guided to a large extent about the frontier of the territory she should have.

"2. I then said that I believe from what had passed at Teheran that the Soviet Government would be willing to agree to the easterly frontiers of Poland conforming to the Curzon line[1] subject to discussion of

[1] At Teheran Stalin had favored establishing the western frontier of Poland on the Oder River. If part of East Prussia, including the ports of Königsberg and Tilsit, were given to the Soviet Union, he was prepared to accept the Curzon line of 1919 as

ethnographical considerations, and I advised them to accept the Curzon line as a basis for discussion. I spoke of the compensations which Poland would receive in the north and in the west. In the north there would be East Prussia; but here I did not mention the point about Königsberg. In the west they would be free and aided to occupy Germany up to the line of the Oder. I told them it was their duty to accept this task and guard the frontier against German aggression towards the east in consequence of their liberation by the Allied forces. I said that in this task they would need a friendly Russia behind them and would, I presumed, be sustained by the guarantee of the three great powers against further German attack. Great Britain would be willing to give such a guarantee if it were in harmony with her ally, Soviet Russia. I could not forecast the action of the United States, but it seemed that the three great powers would stand together against all disturbers of the peace, at any rate until a long time after the war was ended. I made it clear that the Polish Government would not be committed to the acceptance of the Curzon line as a basis of examination except as part of the arrangement which gave them the fine compensations to the north and to the west which I had mentioned.

"3. Finally I said that if the Russian policy was unfolded in the sense I had described, I would urge the Polish Government to settle now on that basis and His Majesty's Government would advocate the confirmation of such a settlement by the peace conference or by conferences for the settlement of Europe following the destruction of Hitlerism, and would support no territorial claims from Poland which went beyond it. If the Polish ministers were satisfied that agreement could be reached upon these lines, it would be their duty at the proper time not merely to acquiesce in it but to commend it to their people with courage, even though they ran the risk of being repudiated by extremists.

"4. The Polish ministers were very far from rejecting the prospects thus unfolded, but they asked for time to consider matters with the rest of their colleagues, and as a result of this they have asked a number of questions, none of which seems to me to be in conflict with

---

the eastern border of Poland—a proposal not satisfactory to the Poles. George Nathaniel Curzon (Baron Curzon of Kedleston) was British Secretary of State for Foreign Affairs, 1919 to 1924. Lord Curzon proposed the line at the time of the Paris peace conference of 1919. From 1921 to 1939 the Russo-Polish boundary lay considerably to the east; the frontier agreed upon in the Nazi-Soviet pact of August, 1939, lay somewhat further to the west of the Curzon Line. See *Conferences at Cairo and Tehran*, pp. 510, 512, 594, 598–602, 604. For Churchill's account of Teheran and of his meeting with the Poles, see his *Closing the Ring*, pp. 361–362, 394–397, 450–452.

the general outline of my suggestions to them. In particular they wish to be assured that Poland would be free and independent in the new home assigned to her; that she would receive the guarantee of the great powers against German revenge effectively; that these great powers would also assist in expelling the Germans from the new territories to be assigned to Poland; and that in regions to be incorporated in Soviet Russia such Poles as wished would be assisted to depart for their new abodes. They also enquired about what their position will be if a large part of Poland west of the Curzon line is soon occupied by the advancing Soviet armies. Will they be allowed to go back and form a more broad-based government in accordance with the popular wish and allowed to function administratively in the liberated areas in the same way as other governments who have been overrun? In particular they are of course deeply concerned about relations between the Polish underground movement and the advancing Soviet forces, it being understood that their prime desire was to assist in driving out the Germans. This underground movement raises matters important to our common war effort.[2]

"5. We also attach great importance to assimilating our action in the different regions which we hope to liberate. You know the policy we are following in Italy. There we have taken you fully into our counsels, and we want to do the same in regard to France and other countries to whose liberation we look forward. We believe such uniformity of action is of great importance, now and in the future, to the cause of the United Nations.

"6. The earliest possible agreement in principle on the frontiers of the new Polish state is highly desirable to allow of a satisfactory arrangement regarding these two very important points.

"7. While however everyone will agree that Soviet Russia has the right to recognise or refuse recognition to any foreign government, do you not agree that to advocate changes within a foreign government comes near to that interference with internal sovereignty to which you and I have expressed ourselves as opposed? I may mention that this view is strongly held by His Majesty's Government.

"8. I now report this conversation which expresses the policy of His Majesty's Government at the present time upon this difficult question

---

[2] Hull had sent Roosevelt a summary report on Polish-Soviet relations on November 23, 1943. The Secretary of State recommended urging a resumption of Polish-Soviet relations but added: "If this is not possible at the moment, I believe we should exert all our influence to persuade the Polish Government to give instructions to its underground army to launch at the opportune moment a full-fledged attack on the Germans behind their lines and to assist the Red Army in its battle." *Conferences at Cairo and Tehran*, pp. 381–385. In this way the Polish government could show its desire to make a material contribution to shortening the war.

to my friend and comrade, Marshal Stalin. I earnestly hope these plans may be helpful. I had always hoped to postpone discussions of frontier questions till the end of the war when the victors would be round the table together. The dangers which have forced His Majesty's Government to depart from this principle are formidable and imminent. If, as we may justly hope, the successful advance of the Soviet armies continues and a large part of Poland is cleared of the German oppressors, a good relationship will be absolutely necessary between whatever forces can speak for Poland and the Soviet Union. The creation in Warsaw of another Polish government different from the one we have recognised up to the present, together with disturbances in Poland, would raise issues in Great Britain and the United States detrimental to that close accord between the three great powers upon which the future of the world depends.

"9. I wish to make it clear that this message is not intended to be any intervention or interference between the Governments of the Soviet Union and Poland. It is a statement in broad outline of the position of His Majesty's Government in Great Britain in regard to matters in which they feel themselves deeply concerned.

"10. I should like myself to know from you what steps you would be prepared to take to help us all to resolve this serious problem. You could certainly count on our good offices, for what they would be worth.

"11. I am sending a copy of this message to the President of the United States with a request for complete secrecy."[3]

[3] Stalin replied on February 16 that since the Poles had rejected the Curzon line there was no possibility of agreement on the Polish-Soviet frontier. Also, since the Polish government-in-exile was hostile to the Soviet Union, future friendly relations were doubtful.

Doc. 289
CHURCHILL TO ROOSEVELT

No. 562   February 1, 1944

The following has just arrived from U.J. and as I do not know whether you have a separate copy I repeat it to you with the following comment: "What can you expect from a bear but a growl?"

"From Premier Stalin to Prime Minister [Churchill] and President Roosevelt. Personal and secret.

"I received on the January 23rd both your joint messages, signed by you, Mr. Prime Minister, and you, Mr. President, regarding the question of the handing over of Italian shipping for the use of the Soviet Union.[1]

"I must say that, after your joint affirmative reply at Teheran to the question which I raised of the handing over to the Soviet Union of Italian shipping by the end of January 1944,[2] I considered this question settled and the thought never entered my mind of the possibility of any kind of reconsideration of this decision which was taken and agreed between the three of us. All the more so since, as we agreed at the time, this question was to be completely settled with the Italians. Now I see that this is not so and that nothing has ever been mentioned to the Italians on the subject.

"In order however not to complicate this question, which is of such great importance for our common struggle against Germany, the Soviet Government is prepared to accept your proposal regarding the despatch from British ports to the U.S.S.R. of the battleship *Royal Sovereign* and one cruiser, and regarding the temporary use of these vessels by the Naval High Command of the U.S.S.R. until such time as the appropriate Italian shipping is made available to the Soviet Union. Similarly we shall be prepared to accept from the U.S.A. and Great Britain 20,000 tons of merchant shipping which will also be used by us until such time as a similar tonnage of Italian shipping is handed over to us. It is important that there should be no delays now regarding the matter and that all the shipping indicated should be handed over to us during the month of February.

"In your reply however there is no mention of the handing over to the Soviet Union of 8 Italian destroyers and 4 submarines, to the handing over of which to the Soviet Union at the end of January you, Mr. Prime Minister, and you, Mr. President, agreed in Teheran. Meanwhile, for the Soviet Union this very question, the question of destroyers and submarines, without which the handing over of one battleship and one cruiser has no significance, is of capital importance. You understand yourselves that a cruiser and a battleship are powerless without escorting destroyers. Since the whole of Italy's fleet is under your control, to carry out the decision which was taken at Teheran to hand over for the use of the Soviet Union 8 destroyers and

---

[1] The Combined Chiefs of Staff had recommended not transferring the Italian ships because doing so would interfere with Italian cooperation and might lead to the scuttling of the ships, thereby jeopardizing the invasions of Normandy and southern France. See Ministry of Foreign Affairs of the U.S.S.R., *Correspondence Between the Chairman of the Council of Ministers of the U.S.S.R. and the Presidents of the U.S.A. and the Prime Ministers of Great Britain During the Great Patriotic War of 1941–1945* (New York, 1958), vol. 2, no. 116. Henceforth cited as *Stalin's Correspondence*.

[2] See *Conferences at Cairo and Tehran*, p. 597.

4 submarines out of that fleet should present no difficulties. I am agreeable (literally 'I agree') that, instead of Italian destroyers and submarines, a similar number of American or British destroyers and submarines should be handed over to the Soviet Union for our use. Moreover, the question of the handing over of destroyers and submarines cannot be postponed, but must be settled at one and the same time with the handing over of the battleship and cruiser, as was definitely agreed between us at Teheran."[3]

[3] For Roosevelt's reply to Churchill see below, Doc. 292. For the President's reply to Stalin, see below, Doc. 306.

Doc. 290
CHURCHILL TO ROOSEVELT

No. 564   February 3, 1944

I earnestly hope that the existing regime in Italy will be allowed to function at least until the great battles now being fought by the soldiers of our two countries have resulted in our capture of Rome. I am sure that a disturbance now of such authority as remains in the Italian state and the attempt to create a new authority out of political groups with no real backing will add greatly to our difficulties. Moreover these groups when formed into a government, in order to win credit from the Italian people, would feel it essential to assert Italian interests in a much stronger form than the King and Badoglio dare to do. I feel it would be a great pity if Badoglio threw in his hand, and our reports show that the Italian navy might be powerfully affected by action against the King. Much British and American blood is flowing, and I plead that military considerations should carry weight.[1]

[1] Roosevelt was criticized for dealing with the Italian government under Marshal Pietro Badoglio on the grounds that doing so violated the unconditional surrender formula established at the Casablanca conference. Also, both Churchill and Roosevelt were aware that Italian leftist parties were trying to depose both King Victor Emmanuel and Badoglio. At the time of the Anzio landings, Hull urged a thorough reorganization of the Italian government, but Roosevelt reassured Churchill that no changes in the current arrangements were imminent. For Roosevelt's reply, see below, Doc. 300. See also Hull, *Memoirs*, 2: 1548–1553.

Doc. 291
CHURCHILL TO ROOSEVELT

No. 565   February 3, 1944

Further to my 562.[1] We could revert to the idea of asking the King and Badoglio to hand us over 8 destroyers and 4 submarines for transfer to the Russians. This might easily cause a mutiny in the Italian fleet at the present very dangerous time. I am told that the Italian navy is already worried by the attacks that are made on the government they have hitherto obeyed. I should think it quite likely that Badoglio would throw in his hand rather than agree to this demand. As he is so often being told that he is to be kicked out as soon as we get to Rome, he does not seem to have much to lose. There are only 7 Italian destroyers in the whole Italian navy and these are all being used in the heavy operations now in progress in the Mediterranean.

In these circumstances His Majesty's Government is prepared to find 8 destroyers for loan to the Russians pending delivery of the Italian vessels. These will of course be old destroyers, most of them, those that we got from you in 1941. They are however serviceable and will steam and fight. The Russians will not use them in the same continuous sea service as we are accustomed to maintain. They will probably lie in harbour in northern Russian ports. Here they will be available for training crews which can man the Italian destroyers when these are handed over and have been fitted for Arctic work. In view of the ungracious tone of Stalin's reply and evident Soviet refusal to try to understand our position which was so patiently and considerately explained, I have little doubt that they will reproach us upon the quality of these vessels. It is however the best we can do.

It will be more difficult for us to find 4 old submarines, and we cannot spare any of the new ones which are in constant action. We should be glad therefore if you could supply these on loan until we can get the Italian craft.

Let me know how you feel about all this, and I will then submit to you a draft from us both to Uncle Joe.

1 See above, Doc. 289.

Doc. 292
ROOSEVELT TO CHURCHILL

No. 456   February 4, 1944

Referring to your 562[1] and 565[2] it is suggested that our reply to U.J. should be in effect as follows:

QUOTE. The receipt is acknowledged of your message in regard to handing over Italian shipping to the Soviet.

It is our intention to carry out the transfer agreed to at Teheran at the earliest date practicable without hazarding the success of Anvil and Overload which operations we all agree should be given first priority in our common effort to defeat Germany at the earliest possible date.

There is no thought of not carrying through the transfers discussed at Teheran. The British battleship and the American cruiser can be made available without any delay, and an effort will be made at once to make available from the British Navy the eight destroyers. Four submarines will be taken from Italy.

I am convinced that disaffecting the Italian navy at this time would be what you have so aptly termed an unnecessary diversion and that it would adversely affect the prospects of our success in France. UNQUOTE.[3]

If we send to U.J. a message similar to the above, it will involve making available the battleship and cruiser at once, sending the merchant shipping to him without avoidable delay, and taking from Italy four submarines from those now in our possession which I believe number about thirty.

Under the conditions existing at present and prior to a success in landing Overlord and Anvil I would prefer that the U.K. find the destroyers for this contribution as so kindly offered in your 565. I need all of ours that can be made available for current and pending operations in the Pacific.

It seems to me that, if this matter of joining with Britain and the United States in providing Russia with needed ships should be diplomatically presented, the Italian Government could offer no valid objection to taking part in the common effort by the provision of four submarines at this time, or it might be best to simply direct the Allied

1 See above, Doc. 289.
2 See above, Doc. 291.
3 The text suggested by Roosevelt was sent to Stalin as a joint message on February 7 and was received on February 24. See *Stalin's Correspondence*, vol. 2, no. 158.

commander in the Mediterranean, Wilson, to send four Italian submarines in tow to a port in U.K. without making any explanation to the Italians of their future use.

Please let me have your reaction to these suggestions and your draft of a proposed reply to U.J.'s growl.

Doc. 293
CHURCHILL TO ROOSEVELT

No. 566   February 5, 1944

I have not yet received any answer from Uncle J to my telegram about Poland which was repeated to you in my number 557.[1] Ambassador Kerr has however had an encouraging interview with him about the questions posed on behalf of the Poles in my telegram.[2] Uncle J replied that of course Poland would be free and independent and he would not attempt to influence the kind of government they cared to set up after the war. If Poland wished to ask for a guarantee she would get it. She could count upon all the help she needed in expelling the Germans. All Poles would be free to move out of the regions to be assigned to Russia and he would ask for the same freedom on behalf of the Ukrainians now west of the Curzon line. The Poles need have no anxiety about their position when Poland west of the Curzon line was occupied by the Red armies. Of course the Polish Government would be allowed to go back and to establish the broad-based kind of government they had in mind. Poland was their country and they were free to return to it.

On the other hand Uncle J continues to press for the expulsion from the Polish Government of Sosnkowski,[3] Kot,[4] and Kukiel,[5] and I doubt very much whether he will deal with the Poles while they remain in. I am seeing Premier Mikolajczyk[6] tomorrow and shall point out to him the very great advantages of regaining Russian recognition and obtaining a definite settlement now with Russia which can be approved by the Allies. The greatest inducement will be

1 See above, Doc. 288.

2 Sir Archibald Clark Kerr, the British ambassador in Moscow, had met with Stalin on February 2.

3 General Kazimierz Sosnkowski, commander in chief of the Polish armed forces.

4 Stanislaw Kot, former Polish ambassador to the Soviet Union and at the time Minister of Information of the Polish government-in-exile.

5 General Marian Kukiel, Minister of Defense of the Polish government-in-exile.

6 Stanislaw Mikolajczyk, Prime Minister of the Polish government-in-exile.

the possibility of his going back to Warsaw after the advance of the Russian armies to the westward has passed it, and being able to constitute there a Polish government and state.

I will report to you again after I have heard from Uncle J and have seen Premier Mikolajczyk.[7] Meanwhile I am more hopeful than I have yet been. I can understand that you are unable to join in any guarantee other than those general arrangements for maintaining world peace which we have to make at the end of the war.

[7] See *FR 1944*, 3 (Washington, 1965) : 1249–1257.

Doc. 294
CHURCHILL TO ROOSEVELT

No. 570

February 6, 1944

In the swiftly changing course of events a number of questions have arisen since the Chiefs of Staff parted at Cairo. The Turkish problem,[1] the great battle on the Italian front including Shingle,[2] Anvil—its place and scale, the preparations for Overlord which are on a gigantic scale, all require direct consultation. Could you send your Chiefs of Staff over here, or at any rate General Marshall,[3] in the next few days? This will give a far better opportunity of coming to agreement than if they continue to correspond by telegraph. I am sure the time has come for a further talk on the highest staff level. The Overlord Commanders in Chief must know where they stand and every day counts.

[1] Turkey hesitated to enter the war until it was satisfied that the Germans would not retaliate. Churchill wanted to issue an ultimatum, but the Foreign Office pointed out that support from Turkey against Russia might be needed after the war. Finally, Turkey put an embargo on chrome exports to Germany in May and broke diplomatic relations in August. See Woodward, *British Foreign Policy* (abridged ed.), pp. 328–329, and the forthcoming fourth volume of the unabridged series.

[2] Code name for the amphibious landing at Anzio, Italy, on January 22, 1944.

[3] George C. Marshall, U.S. Army Chief of Staff.

Doc. 295
ROOSEVELT TO CHURCHILL

February 7, 1944

I share your concern over the potential dangers of the present Polish-Soviet situation, and I understand the spirit in which you sent your number 33 to U.J.[1] Isn't there a possibility that the wording of paragraphs 7 and 8 will give him the impression that you are wedded to the present personalities of the Polish Government-in-exile and are determined to see them reinstated as the future government of Poland? He may interpret this as evidence of a design on your part to see established along the borders of the Soviet Union a government which rightly or wrongly they regard as containing elements irrevocably hostile to the Soviet Union. I know that this is not your intention and that you are only interested in preserving the principle of the right of all countries to choose their government without interference, and specifically to avoid the creation by the Soviet Government of a rival Polish government. Might it not be well to make this clear to U.J. by some reference to the possibility that the Polish Government would of its own accord, if a real solution on the frontier and other questions with Russia was in the offing, accept the resignation of these persons known to be particularly objectionable to the Soviet Government?

I recognize that because of treaty obligations with both sides you are more directly concerned with the immediate issues between the U.S.S.R. and Poland. Our primary concern is the potential dangers of this situation to the essential unity which was so successfully established at Moscow and Teheran. It is for this reason that I have confined the official action of this Government to a tender of good offices looking towards the resumption of relations between Poland and the Soviet Union. Feeling, however, that this unity and the larger issues connected therewith are now definitely at stake, I have just sent the following message to U.J.:

"I have followed with the closest attention the recent developments in your relations with Poland. I feel that I am fully aware of your views on the subject and am therefore taking this opportunity of communicating with you on the basis of our conversations at Teheran. First of all, let me make it plain that I neither desire nor intend to attempt to suggest much less to advise you in any way as to where the interests of Russia lie in this matter since I realize to the full that the future security of your country is rightly one of your primary concerns. The observations which I am about to make are prompted solely by the larger issues which affect the common goal towards which we are both working.

"The overwhelming majority of our people and Congress, as you know, welcomed with enthusiasm the broad principles subscribed to at the Moscow and Teheran conferences, and I know that you agree with me that it is of the utmost importance that faith in these understand-

[1] See above, Doc. 288.

ings should not be left in any doubt. I am sure that a solution can be found which would fully protect the interests of Russia and satisfy your desire to see a friendly, independent Poland, and at the same time not adversely affect the cooperation so splendidly established at Moscow and Teheran. I feel that it is of the utmost importance that we should bear in mind that the various differences which inevitably arise in the conduct of international relations should not be permitted to jeopardize the major all-important question of cooperation and collaboration among nations which is the only sound basis for a just and lasting peace.

"I have given careful consideration to the views of your Government as outlined by Mr. Molotov to Mr. Harriman on January 18[2] regarding the impossibility from the Soviet point of view of having any dealings with the Polish Government-in-exile in its present form and Mr. Molotov's suggestion that the Polish Government should be reconstituted by the inclusion of Polish elements at present in the United States, Great Britain, and the Soviet Union. I fully appreciate your desire to deal only with a Polish government in which you can repose confidence and which can be counted upon to establish permanent friendly relations with the Soviet Union, but it is my earnest hope that while this problem remains unsolved neither party shall by hasty word or unilateral act transform this special question into one adversely affecting the larger issues of international collaboration. While public opinion is forming in support of the principle of international collaboration, it is especially incumbent upon us to avoid any action which might appear to counteract the achievement of our long-range objective. I feel I should ill serve our common interest if I failed to bring these facts to your attention.

"Prime Minister Churchill tells me that he is endeavoring to persuade the Polish Prime Minister to make a clean-cut acceptance as a basis for negotiation of the territorial changes which have been proposed by your Government. Is it not possible on that basis to arrive at some answer to the question of the composition of the Polish Government which would leave it to the Polish Prime Minister himself to make such changes in his government as may be necessary without any evidence of pressure or dictation from a foreign country?

"As a matter of timing it seems to me that the first consideration at this time should be that Polish guerrillas should work with and not against your advancing troops. That is of current importance and some assurance on the part of all Poles would be of great advantage as a first step."[3]

2 Harriman's telegram is printed in *FR 1944*, 3: 1230–1232.
3 Stalin received this message on February 11. See *Stalin's Correspondence*, 2: 149.

Doc. 296
ROOSEVELT TO CHURCHILL

No. 457   February 7, 1944

Combined Chiefs of Staff have reached an impasse on the subject of countries and areas to be occupied by British and United States forces in Rankin or following Overlord.[1] U.S. Chiefs of Staff have pointed out that a changeover from spheres of responsibility connect[ing] Overlord to spheres of later occupational responsibility desired by U.S. is militarily feasible and no vital objection can be made on that score. Matter now appears necessary for study by you and me in order to have decision before Overlord and to proceed with plans. United States proposals are set out in CCS four two six slant one paragraph eighteen. (Report to President and Prime Minister, Sextant Conference.) [2]

I am absolutely unwilling to police France and possibly Italy and the Balkans as well. After all, France is your baby and will take a lot of nursing in order to bring it to the point of walking alone. It would be very difficult for me to keep in France my military force or management for any length of time.

[1] Early in 1943 the planning group of the Chief of Staff to the Supreme Allied Commander (COSSAC) had taken up the question of occupying Germany in connection with preparations for the invasion of Europe. Churchill asked the group to prepare plans for three possible circumstances: (1) the collapse of Germany, (2) the decline of German efforts, and (3) the surrender of German satellites. The plan to be followed in the first contingency was called Rankin: the quick dispatch of troops to key political, economic, and communications centers in lieu of an invasion. Then, in the summer of 1943, a British committee sent COSSAC a memorandum describing the British and American occupation zones. In November Roosevelt expressed concern about an American zone in Germany south of the Moselle River, as well as in France; he preferred to have the United States in northwestern Germany. Following the President's line of reasoning, at the second Cairo conference the American Chiefs of Staff asked for a change in the occupation zones. But COSSAC subsequently reported that the target date for Overlord would be affected by any such replanning and that the only practical solution would be for the British and Americans to change zones later. The British Chiefs of Staff objected to the idea of trading zones, and the matter was referred back to the President who eventually accepted the British position.

[2] The report of the Combined Chiefs of Staff (CCS) to the President and Prime Minister on the second Cairo conference is printed in *Conferences at Cairo and Tehran*, pp. 810–815.

Doc. 297
ROOSEVELT TO CHURCHILL

No. 461   February 9, 1944

Replying to your 570,[1] my Chiefs of Staff are now involved in an important and difficult study of the provision of troops for both the Pacific and Atlantic and of the strategy to be followed in the Pacific in the immediate future which makes it difficult for them to be absent from Washington at this time.

We are informed that the combined planning staff in Washington reports that by the end of May facilities will be available in the U.K. and in the Mediterranean to launch a five- to seven-division assault in Overlord and a two-division assault in Anvil.

If this report of the planning staff is accepted by your staff in London there does not appear to be any essential necessity for a meeting of our Chiefs of Staff in the immediate future.

Messages exchanged between Marshall and Eisenhower and between Bedell Smith[2] and General Handy[3] indicate that an agreement on the Overlord-Anvil problem will be reached within the next twenty-four hours.[4]

I hope an early meeting of our Chiefs of Staff with yours can be delayed unless the general situation gets more complicated.

[1] See above, Doc. 294.

[2] Lieutenant General Walter Bedell Smith, Eisenhower's Chief of Staff.

[3] General Thomas T. Handy, head of the Operations Division of the War Department.

[4] For the Marshall-Eisenhower and other exchanges relating to the Overlord-Anvil planning, see Alfred D. Chandler, Jr., et al., eds., *The Papers of Dwight David Eisenhower: The War Years* (Baltimore and London, 1970), 3: 1707–1804. Henceforth cited as *PDDE*. The Overlord-Anvil debate is set forth in John Ehrman, *Grand Strategy*, vol. 5, *August 1943–September 1944* (London, 1956), pp. 225–263; and Gordon A. Harrison, *Cross-Channel Attack* (Washington, 1951), pp. 164–173. General Marshall's role in the controversy is described in Forrest C. Pogue, *George C. Marshall: Organizer of Victory* (New York, 1973), pp. 326–343.

Doc. 298
ROOSEVELT TO CHURCHILL

No. 463   February 9, 1944

I have received an unconfirmed report that the Bulgarian Government desires to send a mission to Istanbul to discuss conditions under which Bulgarian army would join the Allies.[1]

If this report should prove to be true it appears to me that it would be worthwhile for us to make some concessions such as suspending the bombing attacks on Bulgaria for a limited period and with your sending representatives to meet the Bulgarian mission at Istanbul. Probably the Russians should be in on this too.

It is assumed that your sources of information in Turkey have heard the same story if it has any validity.

I am repeating this to you only for what it is worth in anticipation of possible future developments.[2]

[1] Bulgaria was an ally of Germany, although it had not declared war on the Soviet Union. In view of this ambiguity, the United States did not declare war on Bulgaria until June 5, 1942. Then, in October 1943, the Combined Chiefs of Staff asked General Eisenhower to give Bulgaria "a sharp lesson." He complied by ordering the Italian-based bombers to carry out two raids against Bulgaria, on November 14 and November 24. These and later raids evidently persuaded Bulgarian officials to reach an understanding with the Allies.

[2] As things turned out, Bulgaria began surrender negotiations with the Allies on August 26, 1944, and signed an armistice on October 28.

Doc. 299
CHURCHILL TO ROOSEVELT

No. 575   February 10, 1944

Eden and I are agreed here that the bombing of Bulgarian targets as weather permits should not be stopped because of the peace overtures. If the medicine has done good, let them have more of it.

Doc. 300
ROOSEVELT TO CHURCHILL

No. 464 February 11, 1944

Your 573.[1] I have directed the Department of State to take no action toward effecting any change in the existing government of Italy at the present time and until our military situation in the Italian campaign is sufficiently improved to warrant risking the disaffection of those Italians who are now assisting the Allied forces.[2]

I think though that you and I should regard this only as a temporary reprieve for the two old gentlemen.[3]

1 Not printed. According to Churchill's memoirs, the President's message was a reply to Churchill's cable of February 3. See above, Doc. 290.

2 Roosevelt sent Hull this directive on February 10.

3 King Victor Emmanuel III and Marshal Pietro Badoglio.

Doc. 301
CHURCHILL TO ROOSEVELT

No. 576 February 12, 1944

Many thanks for your telegram number 463 of February 9th.[1]

It seems to me most undesirable that a Bulgarian mission should open conversations in Constantinople. If the Bulgarian Government really mean business, they should be told to send a fully qualified mission to meet representatives of the three powers at a place which will be indicated and might be Cyprus or Cairo. Cyprus is absolutely secret and nearer.

Our bombing of Sofia appears in fact to have had exactly the effect we hoped for, in that the Bulgarians are falling over each other in their haste to make contact with us. That being so, would it not be a mistake to suspend it at the request of the first-comer who no doubt hopes for a respite during protracted conversations?

If you agree, therefore, I hope we may send identical instructions to our representatives in Moscow on the above lines and get Molotov's agreement to our proposed line of action.[2]

1 See above, Doc. 298.

2 For documents on the armistice negotiations, see FR 1944, 3: 300–514.

Doc. 302
ROOSEVELT TO CHURCHILL

No. 465   February 12, 1944

I wholly agree with your 576.[1] Let the work go on.

Please send me a draft of the message which you consider sending to our representatives in Moscow for delivery to Molotov with the purpose of getting his approval.[2]

[1] See above, Doc. 301.
[2] For Churchill's reply, see below, Doc. 304.

Doc. 303
ROOSEVELT TO CHURCHILL

No. 467   February 15, 1944

I believe that as a result of our suspension of tanker loadings the Spanish situation is developing satisfactorily and that if both our Governments hold firm we can obtain a complete and permanent Spanish embargo on the export of wolfram to any country.[1] Our information indicates that the Germans are very short of wolfram and that supplies obtained at this time can be directly translated into terms of British and American casualties. We have had indications of a disposition on the part of your Ambassador and ours at Madrid to accept some compromise short of a complete embargo. I do not consider this satisfactory and I see no danger that our joint insistence upon a complete embargo before resuming loading of Spanish tankers will produce any serious reaction in Spain which would adversely affect the Allied position. The establishment of a complete embargo

[1] At the first Quebec conference the U.S. Chiefs of Staff had argued for "a stern and frankly demanding policy toward Spain." But the British, dependent on Spanish food supplies, urged that economic and political pressures be used to get the Spanish to discontinue shipping raw materials to Germany. A particularly important commodity here was wolfram, an element vital to the production of high-grade steel. Still taking the hard line, in November 1943 Secretary Hull demanded an immediate embargo on wolfram, with the threat of stopping shipments of petroleum to Spain. The shipments were stopped at the end of January 1944. See U.S. Department of State, *The Conferences at Washington and Quebec 1943* (Washington, 1970), pp. 480, 1099–1101, 1130–1131; Woodward, *British Foreign Policy* (abridged ed.), pp. 366–368; Hull, *Memoirs*, 2: 1326–1329; and *FR 1944*, 4: 297–337.

would be entirely within Franco's[2] announced policy of neutrality and I hope you will send instructions to Hoare[3] to stand firm as we are doing to Hayes.[4] We know that the Portuguese are watching the Spanish situation carefully and our insistence upon the embargo should have a helpful effect in obtaining satisfaction with regard to wolfram from Salazar.[5]

[2] General Francisco Franco led the victorious anti-Republican rebel army in the Spanish Civil War, 1936–1939. Subsequently he became president and chief of state of Spain.

[3] Sir Samuel Hoare, British ambassador to Spain.

[4] Carlton J. H. Hayes, U.S. ambassador to Spain.

[5] On February 8 Ambassador Hayes telegraphed to Hull: "It appears though that the Doctor [Salazar], like Br'er Rabbit, is lying low pending developments in Spain." *FR 1944*, 4: 92. For a recent account, see J. K. Sweeney, "The Portuguese Wolfram Embargo: A Case Study in Economic Warfare," *Military Affairs*, 38 (1974) : 23–26.

Doc. 304
CHURCHILL TO ROOSEVELT

No. 580   February 15, 1944

I would propose to telegraph as follows to Ambassador Clark Kerr: "Your United States colleague,[1] who will be receiving from Washington identical instructions to those contained in this telegram, will be able to furnish you with full details of proposals made on February 6th by Bulgarian Minister to Turkey on behalf of the regent,[2] the Bulgarian Prime Minister,[3] and the principal opposition leaders for the initiation of discussions with the U.S.A. with a view to Bulgaria joining the United Nations.

"These proposals have been considered by the President and the Prime Minister whose views are as follows: It is undesirable that a Bulgarian mission should open conversations in Constantinople. If the Bulgarian Government really mean business it would be a mistake to rebuff them because they do not at the outset offer unconditional surrender. They should be told to send a fully qualified mission to meet United States, Soviet, and British representatives at a place which will be indicated and which might be Cyprus or Cairo. Advantage of Cyprus is that it is nearer to Bulgaria and absolutely secret.

[1] W. Averell Harriman.

[2] Prince Cyril, brother of King Boris who died in August 1943.

[3] Petko Stainov.

"This Bulgarian peace feeler shows that the air bombing of Sofia appears to have had exactly the effect which was hoped for. In these circumstances it would be a mistake to suspend it at the request of the Bulgarian Minister to Turkey before it is known whether the Bulgarian proposals really are serious ones and when it is probable that the Bulgarian Government hope for a respite from bombing during protracted conversations. It is therefore proposed to continue with the bombing of Bulgarian targets.

"In concert with your United States colleague, please convey views of President and Prime Minister to Molotov and seek his agreement to proposed line of action."

On hearing from you that you consider this message suitable, I would at once despatch it.

Meanwhile you will no doubt have informed the Jadwin[4] mission of our decision.

[4] Colonel C. L. Jadwin, U.S. Army, the former military attaché in Bulgaria, was in Turkey to negotiate with representatives of Bulgaria.

Doc. 305
ROOSEVELT TO CHURCHILL

No. 469   February 16, 1944

Replying to your 580,[1] I am in agreement with your proposed telegram to Clark Kerr and I am today sending identical instructions to Harriman together with such details of the Bulgarian proposal as are available here.

I have also informed Jadwin of our decision.

[1] See above, Doc. 304.

Doc. 306
ROOSEVELT TO CHURCHILL

No. 470   February 17, 1944

I have today sent the following quoted message to Uncle Joe:

QUOTE. Replying to your message of January 29,[1] I am pleased to inform you that the following United States ships are available for temporary use by the Naval Command of the U.S.S.R. until adequate

[1] See above, Doc. 289.

Italian tonnage to replace them can be placed at the disposal of the Soviet Union.

The merchant ship (10,000 tons) *Harry Percy,* now at Glasgow.

The merchant ship *John Gorrie* (10,000 tons) , now at Liverpool.

The cruiser *Milwaukee* will arrive in some port in the United Kingdom March 8. UNQUOTE.

Doc. 307
ROOSEVELT TO CHURCHILL

No. 471   February 18, 1944

Replying to your number 581,[1] as you know the project for very-long-range bomber operations (B-29s) from China against Japan was approved at Sextant.[2] A necessary part of this project is the fighter protection required. In relating available resources to agreed operations at Sextant provision was made for the movement of these two groups from the Mediterranean to China. These new, powerful, and very-long-range bombers demand adequate protection. In making preparation for the use of the B-29s we have run into considerable difficulty particularly as to construction of airfields in China. I have urged the Generalissimo[3] to aid in every way possible. The Generalissimo in a message to me said this: "While favoring your view that very-long-range air operations against Japan proper from China should do much to heighten the morale of both our nations I am strongly of the opinion that in order to assure the success of these operations the present American air force stationed in China should

1 Not printed. On February 16 Churchill expressed distress that two groups of fighter planes were slated to leave the Mediterranean for China. He had given up operations in the Aegean Sea in favor of the cross-channel attack. Yet this sacrifice would not help the situation in Italy or the Anvil operation in southern France if the aircraft were sent to China.

2 A memorandum by the U.S. Chiefs of Staff of December 3, 1943, at the second Cairo conference (Sextant) stated that among the specific operations for the defeat of Japan to be carried out in 1944 were those in China: "Our efforts in the China area should have as their objective the intensification of land and air operations in and from China and the buildup of the USAAF [U.S. Army Air Force] and the Chinese army and air forces. It shall include also the establishing, without materially affecting other approved operations, of a very-long-range strategic bombing force at Calcutta, with advanced bases at Chengtu [in China's Szechwan province] to attack vital targets in the Japanese 'inner zone' "—including Japan, Manchuria, Korea, northern China, Formosa, and the Japanese-held part of Sakhalin Island. See *Conferences at Cairo and Tehran,* pp. 780, 814.

3 Chiang Kai-shek.

be immediately increased to such an extent as to be able to protect our air bases from attack or destruction by the enemy." In reply I told the Generalissimo that we had been planning to provide this protection by dispatching the two fighter groups in question. The movement is now actually in progress. The bulk of the crews and maintenance personnel have been in process of movement for a month with the special equipment required. The final increment is scheduled for transportation before the end of the month.[4] I am informed that Slessor[5] in his study of air requirements in the Mediterranean stated that if Hardihood[6] were abandoned there would be enough planes to take care of China as well as sparing some units for Overlord if this were considered essential.

I am confident that Overlord's fighter strength can be adequately taken care of by fully utilizing the fighter planes available in the U.K.

[4] See *Conferences at Cairo and Tehran*, pp. 172–173; and *FR 1944*, 6 (Washington, 1967) : 4, 21–22, 28–29.

[5] Air Marshal Sir John Slessor, commander of British air forces in the Mediterranean.

[6] Code name for the British plan to send military aid to Turkey in the event of that country's entering the war against Germany.

Doc. 308
CHURCHILL TO ROOSEVELT

No. 583   February 20, 1944

I have been watching lately with increasing misgiving the official telegrams about the oil business.[1] I am very glad you have consented

[1] In July 1943 the United States had established the Petroleum Reserves Corporation to safeguard American supplies of oil by the acquisition and development of oil fields outside the country. This agency soon ran into difficulties with the American oil companies and with the Department of State. Secretary of the Interior Harold L. Ickes, who headed the corporation, wanted to carry out negotiations himself on a Cabinet level, while the State Department wanted to arrange for a general discussion with the United Kingdom on oil reserves. Accordingly, on December 2, 1943, the State Department invited the British to exchange views on the Middle East oil reserves. Originally both sides were in agreement that the discussions would be held between experts in the field, but by mid-February the Americans had decided that their delegation would be at the Cabinet level. The British Embassy in Washington protested this change, and the Foreign Office told Churchill that a Cabinet-level discussion would draw public attention to the issue and might result in demands that the British give up their rights to participate in the conference. Especially since the United Kingdom was dependent on the production, refining, and shipment

to delay for a few days the publication of a purely American statement. You may be sure I should only wish to arrive at what is fair and
just between our two countries. Surely this can be patiently considered
between us before it is flung into public discussion on both sides of the
Atlantic. A wrangle about oil would be a poor prelude for the tremendous joint enterprise and sacrifice to which we have bound ourselves.

Lord Halifax[2] has explained to me the difficulties of the situation
on your side. We too have our difficulties which may become very
formidable in Parliament. There is apprehension in some quarters
here that the United States has a desire to deprive us of our oil assets
in the Middle East on which, among other things, the whole supply of
our Navy depends. This sensitiveness has of course been greatly
aggravated by the Five Senators.[3] I am sure these suspicions are
entirely unfounded so far as the Government of the United States is
concerned. When however it is announced that you are to open a
conference upon oil in Persia and the Middle East and that the Secretary of State is to be the leader of the American delegation the whole
question will become one of first magnitude in Parliament. It will be
felt that they are being hustled and may be subjected to pressure. I am
sure to be asked for an assurance that the question of no transfer of
property will arise and I shall be unable to give such an assurance.
Moreover great expectations will certainly be aroused in the United
States by a conference on oil opened under your auspices. Will there
not be unceasing pressure upon you from those elements in the United
States which are least friendly to us to gratify those expectations at our
expense?

International conferences at the highest level should surely be carefully prepared beforehand and I would beg you to consider whether it
would not be more advisable to proceed as a first step for official and
technical talks on the lines which had, I understand, already been
agreed between the State Department and ourselves.

---

capacities of the United States, a refusal to discuss the oil question would be
embarrassing and might cause great harm to the United Kingdom. See Woodward,
British Foreign Policy (abridged ed.), pp. 396–397; and *FR 1944*, 5 (Washington,
1965): 8–23.

2 British ambassador to the United States.

3 Churchill was apparently referring to the Special Senate Committee to Investigate Petroleum Resources, chaired by Francis T. Maloney of Connecticut.

Doc. 309
CHURCHILL TO ROOSEVELT

No. 585   February 20, 1944

My immediately preceding telegram.[1] Following is text of telegram which I have sent to Marshal Stalin:

"1. The Foreign Secretary and I have had numerous long discussions with the Polish Prime Minister and Foreign Minister.[2] I shall not attempt to repeat all the arguments which were used but only to give what I conceive to be the position of the Polish Government in the upshot.

"2. The Polish Government are ready to declare that the Riga line[3] no longer corresponds to realities and with our participation to discuss with the Soviet Government as part of the general settlement a new frontier between Poland and the Soviet Union together with the future frontiers of Poland in the north and west. Since however the compensations which Poland is to receive in the north and west cannot be stated publicly or precisely at present time the Polish Government clearly cannot make an immediate public declaration of their willingness to cede territory as indicated above because the publication of such an arrangement would have an entirely one-sided appearance with the consequence that they would immediately be repudiated not only by a large part of their people abroad but by the underground movement in Poland with which they are in constant contact. It is evident therefore that the Polish-Soviet territorial settlement which must be an integral part of the general territorial settlement of Europe could only formally be agreed and ratified when the victorious powers are gathered round the table at the time of an armistice or peace.

"3. For the above reasons the Polish Government until it has returned to Polish territory and been allowed to consult the Polish people can obviously not formally abdicate its rights in any part of Poland as hitherto constituted, but the vigorous prosecution of the war against Germany in collaboration with the Soviet armies would be greatly assisted if the Russian Government will facilitate the return of the Polish Government to the territory of liberated Poland at the

---

[1] Not printed.

[2] Churchill's report to Roosevelt on one of these meetings is printed in *FR 1944*, 3: 1249–1257. See also Woodward, *British Foreign Policy*, 3 (London, 1971): 154–174.

[3] The Treaty of Riga, signed on March 18, 1921, defined the border between Poland and Russia at the end of their six months' war in the aftermath of the Russian Revolution.

earliest possible moment; and in consultation with their British and American allies as the Russian armies advance arrange from time to time with the Polish Government for the establishment of the civil administration of the Polish Government in given districts. This procedure would be in general accordance with those to be followed in the case of other countries as they are liberated. The Polish Government are naturally very anxious that the districts to be placed under Polish civil administration should include such places as Vilna and Lwow, where there are large concentrations of Poles, and that the territories to the east of the demarcation line should be administered by the Soviet military authorities with the assistance of representatives of the United Nations. They point out that thus they would be in the best position to enlist all such able-bodied Poles in the war effort. I have informed them and they clearly understand that you will not assent to leaving Vilna and Lwow under Polish administration. I wish on the other hand to be able to assure them that the area to be placed under Polish civil administration will include at least all Poland west of the Curzon line.

"4. At the frontier negotiations contemplated in paragraph 2 above, the Polish Government, taking into consideration the mixed character of the population of eastern Poland, would favour a frontier drawn with a view to assuring the highest degree of homogeneity on both sides while reducing as much as possible the extent and hardships of an exchange of populations. I have no doubt myself, especially in view of the immediate practical arrangements contemplated by the Polish Government as set out in paragraph 3 above, that these negotiations will inevitably lead to the conclusion you desire in regard to the future Polish-Soviet frontier, but it seems to me unnecessary and undesirable publicly to emphasise this at this stage.

"5. As regards the war with Germany which they wish to prosecute with the utmost vigour, the Polish Government realise that it is imperative to have a working agreement with the Soviet Government in view of the advance of the liberating Russian armies onto Polish soil from which these armies are driving the German invader. They assure me emphatically that they have at no time given instructions to the underground movement to attack 'partisans.' On the contrary, after consultation with the leaders of their underground movement and with their accord they have issued orders to all Poles now in arms or about to revolt against the Hitlerite tyranny as follows: When the Russian army enters any particular district in Poland the underground movement is to disclose its identity and meet the requirements of the Soviet commanders, even in the absence of a resumption of Polish-Soviet relations. The local Polish military commander, accompanied by the local civilian underground authority, will meet and declare to the commander of the incoming Soviet troops that, following the instructions of the Polish Government, to which they remain faithful, they are ready to coordinate their actions with him in the fight against the common foe. These orders which are already in operation seem to me, as I am sure they will to you, of the highest significance and importance.

"6. For the first time on February 6th I told the Polish Government that the Soviet Government wished to have the frontier in east Prussia drawn to include, on the Russian side, Königsberg.[4] The information came as a shock to the Polish Government who see in such a decision a substantial reduction in the size and in economic importance of the German territory to be incorporated in Poland by way of compensation. But I stated that in the opinion of His Majesty's Government this was a rightful claim on the part of Russia. Regarding as I do this war against German aggression as all one and as a thirty years' war from 1914 onwards I reminded Monsieur Mikolajczyk of the fact that the soil of this part of East Prussia was dyed with Russian blood expended freely in the common cause. Here the Russian armies advancing in August 1914 and winning the battle of Gumbinnen[5] and other actions had, with their forward thrusts and with much injury to their mobilisation, forced the Germans to recall two army corps from the advance on Paris, which withdrawal was an essential part in the victory of the Marne. The disaster at Tannenberg[6] did not in any way undo this great result. Therefore it seemed to me that the Russians had an historic and well-founded claim to this German territory.

"7. As regards the composition of the Polish Government, the Polish Government cannot admit any right of a foreign intervention. They can however assure the Russian Government that by the time they have entered into diplomatic relations with the Soviet Government, they will include among themselves none but persons fully determined to cooperate with the Soviet Union. I am of the opinion that it is much better that such changes should come about naturally and as a result of further Polish consideration of their interests as a whole. It might well be, in my opinion, that the moment for a resumption of these relations in a formal manner would await the reconstitution of a Polish government at the time of the liberation of Warsaw, when it would arise naturally from the circumstances attending that glorious event.

"8. It would be in accordance with assurances I have received from

---

[4] Königsberg subsequently became known as Kaliningrad.

[5] The battle of Gumbinnen, August 19–20, 1914.

[6] During World War I the Germans stopped the Russian invasion of East Prussia at the battle of Tannenberg, August 26–30, 1914.

you that, in an agreement covering the points made above, the Soviet Government should join with His Majesty's Government in undertaking vis-à-vis each other and Poland first to recognise and respect the sovereign independence and territorial integrity of the reconstituted Poland and the right of each to conduct its domestic affairs without interference: secondly, to do their best to secure in due course the incorporation in Poland of the free city of Danzig, Oppeln Silesia,[7] East Prussia west and south of a line running from Königsberg, and of as much territory up to the Oder as the Polish Government see fit to accept: thirdly, to effect the removal from Poland, including the German territories to be incorporated in Poland, of the German population: and, fourthly, to negotiate the procedure for an exchange of population between Poland and the Soviet Union, and for the return to their mother country of nationals of the powers in question. All the above undertakings to each kingdom[8] should, in my view, be drawn up in such a form that they could be embodied in a single instrument or exchange of letters.

"9. I informed the Polish ministers that should the settlement which has now been outlined in the various telegrams that have passed between us become a fact and be observed in the spirit by all parties to it, His Majesty's Government would support that settlement at the conference after the defeat of Hitler, and also that we would guarantee that settlement in after-years to the best of our ability."

[7] Upper Silesia, a province of East Prussia.
[8] Churchill meant the governments of the Soviet Union and Poland.

Doc. 310
CHURCHILL TO ROOSEVELT

No. 586   February 21, 1944

Sir Samuel Hoare had [sic] already been instructed to give his fullest support to your Ambassador[1] and I have now seen reports of the further representations made by our Ambassadors at Madrid.

These show that a settlement which I should myself regard as eminently satisfactory can now be reached on all points, if we act quickly. This settlement would include the complete cessation of Spanish wolfram exports to Germany for six months. If all goes as we hope, I do not think we need anticipate much difficulty in maintaining this position when the six months have elapsed.

[1] Carlton J. H. Hayes.

The Foreign Secretary is telegraphing in greater detail to the State Department. I hope you will agree that we should immediately clinch matters on the above basis, which I am sure would represent a major political victory over the enemy.

We have just had a stick of bombs around 10 Downing Street and there are no more windows. Clemmie[2] and I were at Chequers[3] and luckily all the servants were in the shelter. Four persons killed outside.[4]

2 Mrs. Winston S. Churchill.

3 The Prime Minister's official country residence.

4 Roosevelt replied on February 23: "It is very pleasing to know that a settlement of our current controversy with Spain promises to be accomplished quickly.

"I am happy to know that you and Clemmie were absent at the time of the bombing and that none of your people were injured."

Doc. 311
CHURCHILL TO ROOSEVELT

No. 587   February 21, 1944

My telegram number 585.[1] While the Polish ministers cannot formally authorise us to proceed on this basis, they are ready that we should do so on their behalf and assure us that they will not subsequently disavow our actions. For the reasons explained in my message they cannot however themselves come out formally and publicly at this stage in the sense of this message. There is the further difficulty that three of the four parties represented in the Polish Government, i.e., all except the Peasant party, refuse to authorise Monsieur Mikolajczyk to go as far as we would have wished. The present proposals therefore represent agreement with Monsieur Mikolajczyk, Monsieur Romer,[2] and Count Raczynski[3] for which they would hope subsequently to secure the support of the Polish Government and the Polish underground movement in Poland if it proves acceptable to U.J.

You will see that my message goes very far to meet Soviet requirement insofar as:

(1) Orders have already been issued to the Polish underground movement to cooperate with the Soviet forces (see paragraph 5 of my telegram).

(2) The Polish Government will accept a position under which the Soviet Government hand over to them for administration only those

1 See above, Doc. 309.

2 Tadeusz Romer, Polish Minister of Foreign Affairs.

3 Count Eduard Raczyński, Polish ambassador to Great Britain.

areas of Poland west of the Curzon line (this abandonment of large Polish agglomerations in Vilna and Lwow areas means a great sacrifice to them).

(3) The Polish Government agree and are ready to declare that the Riga line no longer corresponds to realities. They realise that while reserving their formal rights their acceptance of a demarcation line based on the Curzon line in fact prejudges the future frontier about which they are ready and indeed anxious to open negotiations soon. It has been made very clear to the Polish ministers in this connexion that His Majesty's Government regard the Curzon line as the appropriate future frontier and will support this at the postwar settlement.

Clark Kerr has been instructed to emphasise the above points when communicating my message to U.J., and also to stress the necessity for reserving the formal settlement of future Polish frontiers until we are in a position to deal with the western and northern as well as the eastern frontiers.

Instructions to Clark Kerr conclude:

"The Polish ministers have recently shown great restraint by refusing to enter into polemics as a result of the bitter and unjustified attacks upon them in the recent *Pravda* article.[4] They are showing realism and courage in enabling us to proceed on the present basis despite the contrary view held by large sections of the Polish Government and population in Poland and abroad and despite their own misgivings regarding the overwhelming Soviet power. We doubt very much whether we can push them any further and we should feel alarmed about the effect upon opinion here and in the U.S.A., and therefore upon the United Nations war effort, of a Soviet refusal to give sympathetic consideration to the present proposals. You should make use of the above arguments in your representations to Marshal Stalin."

[4] The attack on the Polish government appeared in the February 12, 1944, issue of *Pravda*.

Doc. 312
ROOSEVELT TO CHURCHILL

No. 473   February 21, 1944

Your 585[1] and 587.[2] I have sent the following message to U.J.:

QUOTE. I am informed as to the text of the message sent to you on February 20th by Mr. Churchill on the subject of a tentative settle-

[1] See above, Doc. 309.
[2] See above, Doc. 311.

ment of the Polish postwar boundary by agreement between the Soviet and the Polish Governments.

This suggestion by the Prime Minister, if accepted, goes far toward advancing our prospects of an early defeat of Germany and I am pleased to recommend that you give to it favorable and sympathetic consideration.

As I intimated before, I think the most realistic problem of the moment is to be assured that your armies will be assisted by the Poles when you get into Poland. UNQUOTE.

You are to be congratulated on getting the Polish Government-in-exile to agree to your proposed compromise and I hope Stalin will also agree and take his share in the settlement of this very serious difficulty.

Doc. 313
ROOSEVELT TO CHURCHILL

No. 475   February 23, 1944

Reference your 565[1] and 567.[2]

The following message from Stalin and my reply thereto are quoted for your information:

QUOTE. Stalin to Roosevelt. I have received your message of February 18.[3] Thank you for the information.

It, however, does not exhaust the question since there is nothing mentioned in it about the Anglo-American destroyers and submarines instead of Italian ones (8 destroyers, 4 submarines), as it was agreed upon at Teheran. I hope to receive a speedy reply regarding these questions, touched in my communication of January 29th. UNQUOTE.

QUOTE. Roosevelt to Stalin. I have received your message of February 21 regarding the loan of Anglo-American ships to the Soviet navy.

It was my understanding that Great Britain would provide the one battleship, the eight destroyers, and the four submarines. I have telegraphed to Prime Minister Churchill in regard to this and will let you know when I hear from him. UNQUOTE.[4]

---

1 See above, Doc. 291.
2 Not printed.
3 See above, Doc. 306.

4 On February 25 Stalin received a message from Roosevelt stating that he had heard from Churchill and that "our understanding as expressed to you is now confirmed." *Stalin's Correspondence*, 2: 167.

Doc. 314
CHURCHILL TO ROOSEVELT

No. 589   February 23, 1944

Reference your telegram number 457[1] on the question of countries and areas to be occupied by British and U.S. forces in Rankin, or after Overlord, the position seems to me to be as follows.

COSSAC'S[2] original plan suggested three zones to be occupied by our forces, your forces, and the Russians, respectively. Our sphere included NW Germany, Norway, Belgium, Luxembourg, Holland, and Denmark: your sphere southern Germany, France, and possibly Austria. The Russian sphere lay to the east of the British area.

On the basis of this allocation which was approved in principle at Quadrant,[3] planning proceeded both for Overlord and Rankin. At Sextant, when plans were already far advanced, your Chiefs of Staff proposed that the allocation should be virtually reversed, but gave no reason.

I agree that your proposals might be militarily feasible for the true Rankin case "O" (i.e., the collapse of Germany before the launching of Overlord). But even then there would, from our point of view, be the following serious objections:

(1) The whole of the German coastline in the North Sea and a large part of their coastline in the Baltic, and therefore all the German naval establishments of any importance and the majority of the naval and shipbuilding yards, would be included in the United States area. The naval disarmament of Germany is a matter of peculiar interest to us and we are better equipped and situated than any other power to ensure that this process is carried out with the maximum thoroughness.

(2) There is close liaison between the Royal Air Force and the Norwegian and Netherlands air force which we have trained and organised, and it is desirable that this should be continued after the war. It will be extremely difficult to maintain this association of these countries which are outside our zone of responsibility. On the other hand, you have had the major responsibility for reequipping the French land and air forces.

If, however, the collapse of Germany occurs after Allied forces have

1 See above, Doc. 296.
2 Chief of Staff to the Supreme Allied Commander. See above, Doc. 296, note 1.
3 Code name for the Quebec conference in August 1943.

been committed to the Continent in Overlord, which seems almost certain, most serious practical objections must be added to those in paragraph 1 and paragraph 2 above. Our forces would be operating on the left flank of Overlord with their overseas bases in the Havre-Cherbourg area, whilst the United States forces, on the right flank, would have their overseas bases in the Brittany ports.

Your proposals therefore would involve either the crossing of the land lines of communication of the two parts of the Allied forces advancing on Germany, or the withdrawal and reembarkation of the U.S. forces. Both these would cause severe administrative difficulties and delays. It is obviously too late to replan Overlord with British forces on the right and U.S. forces on the left.

In view of the serious objections which I have described and the fact that at this late stage all our thoughts and energies must be given to making a success of Overlord, I consider that only reasons of overriding importance could justify such a fundamental change of plan as that proposed.

As I understand it your proposal arises from an aversion to undertaking police work in France and a fear that this might involve the stationing of U.S. forces in France over a long period. I rather think, however, that I can put a different complexion on this matter.

I agree that our connexion with France will be closer than yours and that it will be primarily our concern to see that she is if possible restored as a strong power, without whose cooperation the controlling of Germany is going to be much more difficult. But surely the question of policing does not arise. Under the new directive (which I hope is now agreed) we are, I think, going to recognise some provisional government as soon as we can, and we must hope that such a government will be able to establish its authority over the whole country.

I recognise that you must protect your communications, but I hardly think that the mere fact that your communications pass through France would involve you generally in the policing of France against your will.

I believe indeed that if you have the southern zone, the French, so far from holding more of your men in Europe for longer than you wish, may prove the means for releasing some of your men more quickly than you had hoped. If a satisfactory regime were set up in France and you were anxious to withdraw some of your troops from Germany there would probably be little difficulty in French troops being moved into the southern German zone to take over from your men; the French would in those circumstances be only too anxious to assume this responsibility.

All these reasons make it most undesirable to make a change which would alter the whole basis of our work and planning over the last 6 to 9 months and which must lead to serious complications in the future.

Doc. 315
ROOSEVELT TO CHURCHILL

No. 476   February 23, 1944

In recent months a number of important steps have been taken by the governments of the United Nations toward laying the foundations for postwar cooperative action in the various fields of international economic relations. You will recall that the United Nations Conference on Food and Agriculture, held in May 1943, gave rise to an interim commission which is now drafting recommendations to lay before the various governments for a permanent organization in this field. More recently, there has been established—and is now in operation—the United Nations Relief and Rehabilitation Administration.[1] For nearly a year, there have been informal technical discussions at the expert level among many of the United Nations on mechanisms for international monetary stabilization; these discussions are preparatory to a possible convocation of a United Nations monetary conference.[2] Similar discussions have been taking place, though on a more restricted scale, with regard to the possibility of establishing mechanisms for facilitating international developmental investment. To some extent, informal discussions have taken place among some of the United Nations with regard to such questions as commercial policy, commodity policy, and cartels. Discussions are in contemplation on such questions as commercial aviation, oil, and others. In April a conference of the International Labor Organization will take place, in part for the purpose of considering the future activities of that organization.

In a document presented by the Secretary of State at the Moscow meeting of foreign ministers, entitled "Bases of Our Program for International Economic Cooperation,"[3] the need was emphasized for

[1] Roosevelt had signed the agreement establishing the United Nations Relief and Rehabilitation Administration on November 9, 1943. The State Department intended that it be published as an executive agreement, but the Senate objected. It was submitted to Congress and approved on March 28, 1944, as House Joint Resolution 192, 78th Cong., 2d sess., 58 Stat. 122.

[2] The Monetary and Financial Conference met at Bretton Woods, New Hampshire, on July 1–22, 1944.

[3] The text of this document, dated October 20, 1943, is printed in U.S. Department of State, *Postwar Foreign Policy Preparation 1939–1945* (Washington, 1949), app. 30, pp. 560–562.

both informal discussions and formal conferences on various economic problems. It was suggested that "the time has come for the establishment of a commission comprising representatives of the principal United Nations and possibly certain others of the United Nations for the joint planning of the procedures to be followed in these matters."

It is clear to me that there is a manifest need for United Nations machinery for joint planning of the procedures by which consideration should be given to the various fields of international economic cooperation, the subjects which should be discussed, the order of discussion, and the means of coordinating existing and prospective arrangements and activities. I do not mean to raise at this time and in this connection the broader issues of international organization for the maintenance of peace and security. Preliminary discussions on this subject are currently in contemplation between our three Governments under the terms of the Moscow protocol.[4] What I am raising here is the question of further steps toward the establishment of United Nations machinery for postwar economic collaboration, which was raised by the Secretary of State at the Moscow meeting and was discussed by you, Marshal Stalin, and myself at Teheran.

I should appreciate it very much if you would give me your views on the suggestion made by the Secretary of State at Moscow, together with any other thoughts as to the best procedures to be followed in this extremely important matter.[5]

[4] The Moscow Protocol of November 1, 1943, dealt with proposals for shortening the war against Germany, including the Normandy invasion in the spring of 1944, the attempt to get Turkey to enter the war, and to get air bases in Sweden.

[5] Churchill replied on April 15 that the coming visit to London of Undersecretary of State Edward R. Stettinius, Jr., would provide an opportunity for a preliminary discussion of the best procedure for dealing with these economic questions. Roosevelt also sent a copy of his message to Stalin, who replied on March 10 that it was time to determine the ways and means of promoting economic cooperation in accordance with the decisions reached at the Moscow and Teheran conferences. See *Stalin's Correspondence*, vol. 2, no. 176.

Doc. 316
CHURCHILL TO ROOSEVELT

No. 591   February 24, 1944

Your telegram of February 22nd[1] was brought to me by Winant[2] and I told him that I was much concerned at the way things were developing. Our Cabinet are quite willing to have a technical enquiry into the oil position throughout the world. We should then know how we both stood.

The Cabinet however have definitely expressed the following view, namely:

First, that the enquiry should be on the official level in the first instance in order to ascertain the facts.

Secondly, they would prefer that it should take place here in London, and

Thirdly, that we should be authorised to state to Parliament that no proposal will be made to change the existing ownership of oil interests in the Middle East on which, as you know, our Navy depends, or elsewhere.

Your telegram dismisses all these points and if you will allow me to say so seemed to convey your decision on these matters.

When I read the telegram to the Cabinet this evening I found them also very much disturbed at the apparent possibility of a wide difference opening between the British and United States Governments on such a subject and at such a time. I have called for reports from the ministers particularly concerned and will bring the matter before the Cabinet again in a few days. Meanwhile I trust you will not commit yourself to any public announcement because I am by no means sure that we could endorse it. Should the matter become public, otherwise than by agreement, debates will take place in Parliament at which all

[1] Not printed. In his telegram Roosevelt noted that while Churchill was worried about American interest in the Middle Eastern oil, he had heard that the British were "eyeing" U.S. reserves in Saudi Arabia. Rumors like this underscored the need for a basic understanding between the two governments, and the importance of oil to postwar economic and security arrangements convinced the President that the technical discussions by experts should take place under the guidance of a Cabinet-level group. Roosevelt wanted to preside over the first meeting and to hold it at the White House. Actually, he preferred discussions should be held in Washington, where there would be no limitations on the problems discussed, so that the broadest possible agreement might be reached.

[2] John G. Winant, U.S. ambassador to Great Britain.

kinds of things would be said which would darken counsel and be resented on your side of the ocean.

I am deeply grieved that all these troubles should arise at a time when you have so many worries to contend with, and you may be sure that I will on every occasion do my best to be helpful. But I feel sure that to open up these matters with the maximum publicity without knowing where they will lead us might do real harm to Anglo-American relations.[3]

3 Exploratory discussions between American and British experts took place in Washington from April 18 to May 3, 1944. A draft memorandum of understanding was prepared and presented to both governments for study. Cabinet-level conversations on petroleum were held in Washington from July 25 to August 3. *FR 1944*, 3: 111–121.

Doc. 317
ROOSEVELT TO CHURCHILL

No. 480   February 24, 1944

My Chiefs of Staff are agreed that the primary intermediate objective of our advance across the Pacific lies in the Formosa-China coast-Luzon area. The success of recent operations in the Gilberts and Marshalls indicates that we can accelerate our movement westward.[1] There appears to be a possibility that we can reach the Formosa-China-Luzon area before the summer of 1945. From the time we enter this vital zone until we gain a firm lodgment in this area, it is essential that our operations be supported by the maximum air power that can be brought to bear. This necessitates the greatest expansion possible of the air strength based in China.

I have always advocated the development of China as a base for the support of our Pacific advances and now that the war has taken a greater turn in our favor, time is all too short to provide the support we should have from that direction.

It is mandatory therefore that we make every effort to increase the flow of supplies into China. This can only be done by increasing the air tonnage or by opening a road through Burma.

1 U.S. forces had landed on Tarawa and Makin atolls in the Gilbert Islands on November 20, 1943, and had succeeded in ending organized resistance there in three days. Other atolls were occupied without opposition. U.S. forces landed on Kwajalein atoll, the core of the Marshall Islands, on January 31, 1944, and Eniwetok atoll on February 17. Again, the conquest of both was completed within a few days, and other points in the Marshall Islands were seized without fighting.

Our occupation of Myitkyina[2] will enable us immediately to increase the air lift to China by providing an intermediate air transport base as well as by increasing the protection of the air route.

General Stilwell[3] is confident that his Chinese-American force can seize Myitkyina by the end of this dry season and, once there, can hold it, provided Mountbatten's[4] IV Corps from Imphal secures the Shwebo-Monywa area.[5] I realize this imposes a most difficult task, but I feel that with your energetic encouragement Mountbatten's commanders are capable of overcoming the many difficulties involved.

The continued buildup of Japanese strength in Burma requires us to undertake the most aggressive action within our power to retain the initiative and prevent them from launching an offensive that may carry them over the borders into India.

I am gravely concerned over the recent trends in strategy that favor an operation toward Sumatra and Malaya in the future rather than to face the immediate obstacles that confront us in Burma.[6] I fail to see how an operation against Sumatra and Malaya, requiring tremendous resources and forces, can possibly be mounted until after the conclusion of the war in Europe. Lucrative as a successful Culverin[7] might be, there appears much more to be gained by employing all the resources we now have available in an all-out drive into Upper Burma so that we can build up our air strength in China and ensure the essential support for our westward advance to the Formosa-China-Luzon area.

I most urgently hope, therefore, that you back to the maximum a vigorous and immediate campaign in Upper Burma.[8]

[2] The capture of Myitkyina, the northern terminus of the Burmese road and railroad networks, was deemed essential to the eventual reopening of surface communications with China, as well as to air transport over the Himalayas.

[3] General Joseph W. Stilwell, deputy supreme commander of Allied forces in Southeast Asia.

[4] Admiral Lord Louis Mountbatten, supreme Allied commander in Southeast Asia.

[5] Imphal is in northwestern Burma near the Indian province of Assam. Southeast of it on the Chindwin River are the settlements of Monywa and Shwebo, which lie on the railway line running from Rangoon through Mandalay and on to Myitkyina.

[6] Churchill's plan to capture the northern tip of Sumatra and from there possibly move on to Malaya had been introduced to the Americans at the Washington conference in May 1943. The plan was rejected then, as it was again at the Quebec meeting in August 1943 and at the Cairo conference at the end of the year. On January 10 Churchill took up with Admiral Mountbatten a Sumatra operation, and he kept pushing variations of the plan into the fall of 1944.

[7] Code name for the proposed assault on Sumatra.

[8] Churchill remained unenthusiastic about the campaign in Upper Burma. In a telegram to the President on February 25 he continued to support Culverin as being a cheaper alternative and marshaled other arguments for his favorite plan. But the

War Department planners had decided against the operation independent of Stilwell, even though both Churchill and Mountbatten suspected Stilwell's influence on the case.

Doc. 318
ROOSEVELT TO CHURCHILL

February 29, 1944

Dear Winston:

I have been worrying a good deal of late on account of the tendency of all of us to prepare for future events in such detail that we may be letting ourselves in for trouble when the time arrives.

As you doubtless remember, at Quebec last summer the staff people took a shot at drawing up terms of surrender for Italy. The American draft was short and to the point and was finally adopted and presented.

But later on the long and comprehensive terms, which were drawn up by your people, were presented to Badoglio.

I did not like them because they attempted to foresee every possibility in one document. But, as so often happens, when such an attempt is made, certain points were omitted and additional protocols with respect to naval and other questions had to be later presented.

That is a good deal the way I feel about all this detailed planning that we are jointly and severally making in regard to what we do when we get into France. I have been handed pages and pages with detailed instructions and appendices. I regard them as prophecies by prophets who cannot be infallible.

Therefore, I redrew them with the thought of making the Commander in Chief[1] solely responsible for Overlord and for the maintenance of law, order, and reasonable justice for the first few months after we get into France. I have suggested that he get in touch with local persons and representatives of the French National Committee in such places as they have military status, but that he and his staff bear the sole responsibility.

Now comes this business of what to do when we get into Germany. I understand that your staff presented a long and comprehensive document—with every known kind of terms—to the European Advisory Commission,[2] and that the Russians have done somewhat the same.

[1] General Eisenhower.

[2] The European Advisory Commission had been established at the Moscow conference of foreign ministers in October 1943 to consider all questions that might arise

My people over here believe that a short document of surrender terms should be adopted. This, of course, has nothing to do with the locality of the occupying forces after they get into Germany, but it is an instrument of surrender which is in conformity with the general principles.

I am enclosing (a) an argument—facts bearing on the problem,[3] and (b) a proposed acknowledgment of unconditional surrender by Germany.[4]

I hope much that you will read the argument. I think it is very cogent.

I am trying as hard as I can to simplify things—and sometimes I shudder at the thought of appointing as many new committees and commissions in the future as we have in the past!

I note that in the British proposal the territory of Germany is divided up in accordance with the British plan. "Do please don't" ask me to keep any American forces in France. I just cannot do it! I would have to bring them all back home. As I suggested before, I denounce and protest the paternity of Belgium, France, and Italy. You really ought to bring up and discipline your own children. In view of the fact that they may be your bulwark in future days, you should at least pay for their schooling now!

With my warm regards,

As ever yours,

---

between Great Britain, the United States, and the Soviet Union regarding the surrender of Germany and the terms of surrender. See Bruce Kuklick, "The Genesis of the European Advisory Commission," *Journal of Contemporary History,* 4 (October 1969) : 189–210; and Philip Mosely, *The Kremlin and World Politics* (New York, 1960) , chs. 5–6.

3 Not printed.

4 Not printed.

Doc. 319
ROOSEVELT TO CHURCHILL

No. 484

March 2, 1944

Your number 597.[1] In view [of] agreement for alternate origination and your origination last month,[2] I propose the following statement for release March 10th:

1 Not printed. Churchill sent statistics on the amount of Allied shipping lost as a result of enemy actions in February 1942, 1943, and 1944. The last was the lowest monthly record since the United States entered the war.

2 Roosevelt and Churchill agreed to alternate the work of drafting the joint monthly statement on the war against the German U-boats in the Atlantic Ocean.

QUOTE. Despite the increasing traffic of United Nations shipping in the Atlantic, February 1944 was the lowest month as to tonnage of Allied merchant ship losses to enemy U-boat action since the United States entered the war; and February was the second lowest month of the entire war.

Again there were more U-boats destroyed than merchant vessels sunk, so the exchange rate remains favorable to the United Nations. In actual numbers a few more U-boats were sunk in February than in January.

The lack of aggressiveness on the part of the U-boat continues. UNQUOTE.[3]

3 Churchill replied on March 6 that the British would omit the last sentence in their release.

Doc. 320
ROOSEVELT TO CHURCHILL

No. 486   March 3, 1944

In reply to insistent questioning at a press conference today I stated that Italian merchant ships and warships are now being used in our war effort by the Allied Mediterranean command and that some of the Italian ships or substitutes therefor from the British and American tonnage will be allocated to the Soviet navy to assist in their requirements for their war effort.[1]

1 Roosevelt attached a copy of a Reuters news release on the press conference, which began: "President Roosevelt today announced that Italian warships are ready to be sent to the Russian navy. Discussions for transferring roughly ⅓ of the Italian fleet to Russia, the President said, were about half completed."

Doc. 321
ROOSEVELT TO CHURCHILL

No. 487   March 3, 1944

Referring your 596.[1] In agreement with your suggestion we have instructed Jadwin mission to inform Minister of Bulgaria that representatives of the three Allies are prepared to confer in Cairo with a

1 Not printed.

fully qualified Bulgarian mission. Jadwin also directed to telegraph immediately to Washington any reply that he may receive.

In view of the inclusion of the Balkans in General Wilson's area it seems to me that he is the correct official to control any mission to discuss surrender terms of Bulgaria.

Doc. 322
CHURCHILL TO ROOSEVELT

No. 601   March 4, 1944

Your number 485.[1] Thank you very much for your assurances about no sheep's eyes at our oil fields at Iran and Iraq. Let me reciprocate by giving you the fullest assurance that we have no thought of trying to horn in upon your interests or property in Saudi Arabia. My position on this, as in all matters, is that Great Britain seeks no advantage, territorial or otherwise, as the result of the war. On the other hand she will not be deprived of anything which rightly belongs to her after having given her best services to the good cause—at least not so long as your humble servant is entrusted with the conduct of her affairs. I will bring the matter before the Cabinet on Monday and hope to telegraph you immediately thereafter. . . .

About the Italian ships et cetera. I was much startled by the press accounts of your talk with them.[2] The Russians have never asked for one-third of the Italian ships. But only for the specific vessels mentioned at Moscow and agreed to by us at Teheran. See list which follows.[3] We have never agreed, as you know, to anything beyond this. We shall now see what the Italian reaction will be and whether the Combined Chiefs of Staff were right in their apprehensions set forth in JSM[4] 1372 dated 28th-12-43. From your 483[5] I infer that we are to

1 Not printed. In it Roosevelt said in part: "I am having the oil question studied by the Department of State and my oil experts, but please do accept my assurances that we are not making sheep's eyes at your oil fields in Iraq or Iran." He added: "I cannot hold off conversations much longer." On February 22 the Interdivisional Petroleum Committee produced the first draft of a policy document entitled "Foreign Petroleum Policy of the United States," which stated that the first objective of the United States was to implement the "equal access" provision of the Atlantic Charter in regard to petroleum. See *FR 1944*, 5: 27–33.

2 *Complete Presidential Press Conferences of Franklin Delano Roosevelt*, 25 vols. in 12 (New York, 1972), 23: 76–77.

3 See below, Doc. 324.

4 Joint Staff Memorandum.

5 Not printed. But see above, Doc. 313.

go on with the policy of loaning U.J. some British and American ships till we can get the Italians'. I therefore suggest the following joint message to U.J. from you and me. Begins:

"Although the Prime Minister instructed Ambassador Clark Kerr to tell you that the destroyers we are lending you were old, this was only for the sake of absolute frankness. In fact they are good, serviceable ships, quite efficient for escort duty. There are only 7 fleet destroyers in the whole Italian navy, the rest being older destroyers and torpedo boats. Moreover these Italian destroyers, when we do get them, are absolutely unfitted for work in the north without very lengthy refit. Therefore we thought the 8 which the British Government have found would be an earlier and more convenient form of help to you. The Prime Minister regrets that he cannot spare any new destroyers at the present time. He lost 2 last week, one in the Russian convoy; and for the landing at Overlord alone he has to deploy, for close inshore work against the batteries, no fewer than 42 destroyers, a large proportion of which may be sunk. Every single vessel that he has of this class is being used to the utmost pressure in the common cause. The movement of the Japanese fleet to Singapore creates a new situation for us both in the Indian Ocean.[6] The fighting in the Anzio bridgehead and generally throughout the Mediterranean is at its height. The vast troop convoys are crossing the Atlantic with the United States Army of Liberation. The Russian convoys are being run up to the last minute before Overlord with very heavy destroyer escorts. Finally there is Overlord itself. The President's position is similarly strained, but in this case mainly because of the great scale and activity of the operations in the Pacific. Our joint intentions to deliver to you the Italian ships agreed upon at Moscow and Teheran remain unaltered, and we shall put the position formally to the Italian Government at the time when it is broadened and the new ministers take over their responsibilities. There is no question of our right to dispose of the Italian navy, but only of exercising that right with the least harm to our common interests. Meanwhile, all our specified ships are being prepared for delivery to you on loan as already agreed. Signed: Roosevelt. Churchill." Message to Stalin ends.

I must send you my warmest congratulations on the grand fighting of your troops, particularly the United States Third Division in the

---

6 The Central Pacific offensive began in late January 1944 when naval, ground and air units under Admiral Chester Nimitz struck at the Marshall Islands. Amphibious landings were made on Kwajalein atoll on January 31, on Eniwetok on February 17. As the result of the seizure of these and other points, the Japanese pulled their fleet back to the Philippines, Netherlands East Indies, and New Guinea barrier.

Anzio bridgehead.[7] I am always deeply moved to think of our men fighting side by side in so many fierce battles and of the inspiring additions to our history which these famous episodes will make. Of course I have been very anxious about the bridgehead where we have so little ground to give. The stakes are very high on both sides now and the suspense is long-drawn. I feel sure we shall win both here and at Cassino.[8]

We certainly do have plenty to worry us now that our respective democracies feel so sure the whole war is as good as won.

[7] Since the landings at Anzio, on January 22, Allied forces on the beachhead had been under heavy counterattack. Meanwhile, the U.S. Fifth Army's drive to capture Cisterna in central Italy had encountered stiff enemy opposition. Between February 28 and March 3 the Germans launched their final major assault on the Anzio beachhead and this attack was largely contained by the U.S. Third Infantry Division.

[8] Before the Anzio landings, according to Allied plans, the Fifth Army was to attack Cassino, a strongpoint in the Rapido River valley and a part of the Germans' Gustav line. The attack came on January 17, and the intense struggle ended only on May 18. The fall of Cassino enabled the Fifth Army to break through to the beachhead at Anzio, and the combined Allied forces went on to capture Rome on June 4.

Doc. 323
CHURCHILL TO ROOSEVELT

No. 605   March 4, 1944

Following is Stalin's reply referred to in my number 604.[1]

"I received both your messages of the 20th February[2] on the Polish question from Sir A. Clark Kerr on the 27th February.

"I have studied the detailed account of your conversations with the members of the Émigré Polish Government and have come more and more to the conclusion that such people are not capable of establishing normal relations with the U.S.S.R. Suffice it to point to the fact that not only do they not wish to recognise the Curzon line but they still lay claim to Lwow as well as Vilna. As regards designs to place under foreign control the administration of certain Soviet territories, we cannot accept for discussion such aspirations since we consider even the very raising of a question of such a kind insulting for the Soviet Union.

"I have already written to the President that the solution of the question of Soviet-Polish relations has not yet matured.[3]

[1] Not printed.
[2] See above, Doc. 309.
[3] See *FR 1944*, 3: 1266.

"It is necessary once more to affirm the justness of this conclusion. 3rd March 1944."

Doc. 324
CHURCHILL TO ROOSEVELT

No. 608   March 7, 1944

I have never agreed nor have you ever asked me to agree to a division of the Italian fleet into 3 shares.[1] If this claim were to be based on the fact that we 3 powers signed the Italian armistice together, what about all the other powers that fought Italy? Greece for instance would have an irrefutable claim. It was not until after the Cairo conference that I heard you had mentioned about the 1/3 for Russia. Averell[2] was however able to assure you that nothing of the sort had been said to the Russians. See your number 437.[3] You are therefore quite uncommitted so far as they are concerned.

His Majesty's Government would not be able to agree to a division of the Italian fleet by 1/3 or a pro rata division among signatories to the armistice. We hold very strongly that losses entailed in the Italian war must be considered. We bore the whole weight of that war from 1940 onwards until British and American troops entered Tunisia as the result of Torch. Our naval losses alone have been very heavy indeed.[4]

At the Moscow conference the Russians asked for certain specified types of Italian ships, namely

1 battleship
1 cruiser
8 destroyers
4 submarines

and 40,000 tons of merchant shipping. At Teheran we assented to this. The Combined Chiefs of Staff subsequently became alarmed lest the announcement that we meant to turn over Italian ships to the Soviets should impair cooperation by the Italian naval forces and possibly lead to scuttling. You and I then agreed to propose to Russia that we lend her the same quantity of ships until the matter could be adjusted

1 See above, Doc. 279 and Doc. 322.

2 W. Averell Harriman.

3 See above, Doc. 279.

4 From 1939 until Italy's surrender, the Royal Navy's losses in the Mediterranean consisted of 1 battleship, 2 aircraft carriers, 14 cruisers, 48 destroyers, 13 destroyer escorts, 3 fast minelayers, 2 depot ships, 1 monitor, and 40 submarines, as well as 129 merchant ships totaling 780,000 tons.

with the Italians after the present critical stage of the war in Italy and in the Mediterranean was over. This was accepted by the Russians. I am sure you will recognise that the British Admiralty made a generous contribution to the plan by providing in fact 13 warships out of 14 and half the merchant tonnage. This plan is in actual process of being carried out.

Our relations with the Italian Government in this matter must also be considered. They surrendered their fleet and there is no doubt of the ultimate right of the Allies to dispose of it as they may decide. However Admiral Andrew Cunningham, with General Eisenhower's full assent,[5] made an agreement at Taranto in consequence of which the Italian fleet, which had bravely escaped from the clutches of the Germans not without heavy loss, thenceforward became actively employed in the Allied interest. A relationship has been established between the Italian fleet and the British and American fleets alongside of whom they are operating which certainly implies that we should treat them properly and with due consideration. A prisoner of war is one thing but once you accept a man's services and he fights at your side against the common enemy, a different status and relationship are established. I hope this may be patiently looked into because at present the British Admiralty feel uncomfortable about the position into which we have got.

I shall no doubt have to make a statement to Parliament in the near future and would propose, subject to your agreement, something as follows:

"As President Roosevelt has said the question of the future employment and disposal of the Italian fleet has been the subject of some discussion. In particular consideration has been given to the immediate reinforcement of the Soviet navy either from Anglo-American or Italian resources. On these discussions I have no statement to make other than to say that at present no change is contemplated in the arrangements with the Italian naval authorities under which Italian ships and their crews take part in the common struggle against the enemy in the theatres where they now operate. It may well be found that the general question of enemy or ex-enemy fleet disposal should best be left over till the end of the war against both Germany and Japan, when the entire position can be surveyed by the victorious Allies and what is right and just can be done."[6]

5 General Eisenhower had conveyed the point most emphatically to General Marshall on September 6, 1943: "The armistice terms I insisted upon leave no doubt that the United Nations can do with these ships exactly as we please." *PDDE*, 2: 1389.

6 In May 1944 British warships were given to the Soviet Union in lieu of the Italian ships. See Churchill, *Closing the Ring*, pp. 714–715.

Doc. 325
CHURCHILL TO ROOSEVELT

No. 609   March 7, 1944

Following is the text of reply which I have sent, at the desire of the War Cabinet, to U.J. in reply to his message of March 3rd repeated to you in my No. 605.[1]

"1. I thank you for your message of March 3rd about the Polish question.

"2. I made it clear to the Poles that they would not get either Lwow or Vilna, and the references to these places, as my message shows, merely suggested a way in those areas in which the Poles thought they could help the common cause. They were certainly not intended to be insulting either by the Poles or by me. However since you find them an obstacle pray consider them withdrawn and expunged from the message.

"3. The proposals I submitted to you make the occupation by Russia of the Curzon line a de facto reality in agreement with the Poles from the moment your armies reach it, and I have told you that, provided the settlement you and we have outlined in our talks and correspondence was brought into being, His Britannic Majesty's Government would support it at the armistice or peace conferences. I have no doubt it would be equally supported by the United States. Therefore you would have the Curzon line de facto with the assent of the Poles as soon as you get there, and with the blessing of your Western allies at the general settlement.

"4. Force can achieve much but force supported by the good will of the world can achieve more. I earnestly hope that you will not close the door finally to a working arrangement with the Poles which will help the common cause during the war and give you all you require at the peace. If nothing can be arranged and you are unable to have any relations with the Polish Government, which we shall continue to recognise as the government of the ally for whom we declared war upon Hitler, I should be very sorry indeed. The War Cabinet ask me to say that they would share this regret. Our only comfort will be that we have tried our very best.

"5. You spoke to Ambassador Clark Kerr of the danger of the Polish question making a rift between you and me. I shall try earnestly to prevent this. All my hopes for the future of the world are based upon

1 See above, Doc. 323.

the friendship and cooperation of the Western democracies and Soviet Russia."

Doc. 326
ROOSEVELT TO CHURCHILL

No. 490   March 7, 1944

Our advices from Italy indicate that the political situation there is rapidly deteriorating to our disadvantage and that an immediate decision in breaking the impasse between the present government and the six opposition parties is essential.[1]

General Wilson has had to forbid a strike called by three of the anti-Fascist parties in the Naples area. I fear we are moving into a situation in which the Allied authorities will have to use force against the anti-Fascist leaders and groups.

One of General Wilson's telegrams of February 29[2] reports that the government and the opposition are waiting for an indication of Allied policy with regard to their respective plans. I would like to give General Wilson an immediate reply. As you know, we prefer the program put forward by the six opposition parties which involves the abdication of Victor Emmanuel and the delegation of the powers of his successor to a QUOTE lieutenant UNQUOTE of the realm, acceptable to the six political parties. Croce[3] has been mentioned as their probable choice. General Wilson and his advisers have recommended the acceptance of this proposal and are awaiting our approval. My feeling is that we should assure at the earliest opportunity the active coopera-

[1] Late in January the six opposition parties had agreed on a program whereby Crown Prince Umberto would ascend the throne in return for a promise not to use his powers until a constituent assembly decided the constitutional question. When he was asked for assistance in putting this program into effect, General Sir Henry Maitland Wilson recommended that the six parties agree to support all the Allies' arrangements with Marshal Badoglio. Then the Allies would insist that King Victor Emmanuel abdicate and would direct the Crown Prince to ask a member of one of the opposition parties to form a new government. See Harry L. Coles and Albert K. Weinberg, *Civil Affairs: Soldiers Become Governors* (Washington, 1964), pp. 442–444; and C. R. S. Harris, *Allied Military Administration of Italy 1943–1945* (London, 1957), pp. 129–141.

[2] Wilson reported that Victor Emmanuel had agreed to retire in favor of the Crown Prince, whom he would appoint as lieutenant of the realm. See Coles and Weinberg, *Civil Affairs*, p. 444.

[3] Benedetto Croce, the distinguished anti-Fascist philosopher and historian, was a leader of the movement to persuade or force Victor Emmanuel to step down in favor of his son.

tion of the liberal political groups by bringing them into the Italian Government.

If you will send instructions to your Chiefs of Staff here, we can send an agreed directive to General Wilson in the early part of the week.

Doc. 327
ROOSEVELT TO CHURCHILL

No. 493   March 8, 1944

Your 609.[1] The reply to U.J. contained therein seems to be a very clear and concise statement of the British attitude in the Polish controversy.

It will be of assistance to me in handling our Polish complications here.[2]

[1] See above, Doc. 325.
[2] Polish-American politicians, editors, and other spokesmen were threatening to cut off their support for Roosevelt if he did not stand behind the anti-Communist Polish government. See Jan Ciechanowski, *Defeat in Victory* (Garden City, N.Y., 1947) , pp. 264–282.

Doc. 328
CHURCHILL TO ROOSEVELT

No. 610   Mar_n 8, 1944

Your number 490[1] causes me concern. It is a departure from your agreement with me of February 11 (your 464) [2] which you kindly reaffirmed in your number 483[3] describing the matter as "finished business." On the strength of the first assurances I made my statement to Parliament.

My advices do not lead me to believe that any new facts of importance have arisen or that the Allied forces are not capable of maintaining order in the regions they have occupied as the result of the "unconditional surrender" of Italy. It would in my opinion be a very serious mistake to give way to agitation especially when accompanied by threats on the part of groups of office-seeking politicians. We should

[1] See above, Doc. 326.
[2] See above, Doc. 300.
[3] Not printed.

then be liable to set up in Italy an administration which might not command the allegiance of the armed forces, but which would endeavour to make its position with the Italian people by standing up to the Allies. In fact we should have another but more intractable version of the de Gaullist Committee. Meanwhile in the midst of a heart-shaking battle we are to get rid of the tame and helpful government of the King and Badoglio which is doing its utmost to work its passage and aid us in every way.

I readily admit that the course you recommend would be the most popular and would have at least a transitory success. But I am sure that for the victorious conquerors to have their hands forced in this way by sections of the defeated population would be unfortunate. So also would be the obvious open division between you and me and between our two Governments. I gave you and the State Department loyal and vigorous support over the Darlan affair.[4] Unity of action between our two Governments was never more necessary than at the present time considering the great battles in which we are engaged and which lie ahead.

I am quite ready to take up with you now the proposals put forward by General Wilson, set out in his number 634, whereby the Crown Prince becomes lieutenant of realm. I have no confidence in either Croce or Sforza[5] for this job. Macmillan[6] tells me Croce is a dwarf professor about 75 years old who wrote good books about aesthetics and philosophy. Vyshinsky[7] who has tried to read the books says they are even duller than Karl Marx. Sforza has definitely broken his undertaking given in his letter to Mr. Berle of September 23.[8] I hope

4 See above, the Introduction to Part II.

5 Count Carlo Sforza was a prominent Italian liberal who had been in exile in America. Before Mussolini came to power he had served as Foreign Minister, and during his exile he gained an international reputation as a statesman, scholar, and anti-Fascist.

6 Harold Macmillan, formerly Minister at Allied Force Headquarters and political advisor to the Allied Commander in the Mediterranean area, as well as ambassador to France, had been appointed United Kingdom High Commissioner to the Italian Advisory Council. For his experiences on that troubled body, see his *The Blast of War, 1939–1945* (New York, 1967), pp. 467ff.

7 Andrei A. Vyshinsky, Soviet representative on the Italian Advisory Council.

8 In a letter dated September 23, 1943, Sforza had told Assistant Secretary of State Adolf A. Berle, Jr., that regardless of party all Italians had a duty to work together to drive the Germans out of Italy. He was therefore willing to support Badoglio. Churchill had interviewed Sforza in London while the latter was en route to Italy in October 1943, and the Prime Minister felt he had secured a pledge from Sforza to work with the King and Badoglio until Rome was captured. Sforza evidently had a different understanding of his obligations. On Oct. 1, Sforza had issued a statement declaring "I would consider it almost an act of treason against Italy to oppose the

therefore we may open discussions with you on the basis of the Foreign Secretary's telegram number 1783 to Halifax.[9] I repeat I am most anxious to see a broadly based government assume power in Italy, but this ought not to be done under duress by the Allies and can certainly be done with far better advantage when the battle has been gained or, best of all, when Rome is taken. Macmillan is returning at once.

Badoglio government so long as it organizes and leads war against Germany in full accord with the Allied armies." *FR 1943, 2* (Washington, 1964) p. 406, note 62.

[9] An *aide-mémoire* of March 6, 1944, was based on Foreign Secretary Eden's telegram. See *FR 1944, 3:* 1037–1038.

Doc. 329
CHURCHILL TO ROOSEVELT

No. 615   March 9, 1944

You will be glad to hear that the latest Russian convoy has now got safe home, and that four U-boats out of the pack that attacked it were certainly sunk on the voyage by the escort.

Doc. 330
ROOSEVELT TO CHURCHILL

No. 498   March 13, 1944

With further reference to your No. 610,[1] I am sorry if my earlier messages were not clear. I did not at any time intend to convey to you my agreement that we postpone all political decisions until after Rome had been taken. The political situation in Italy has developed rapidly since our earlier messages; the military situation has not kept pace. The capture of Rome is still remote and major political decisions must be taken.

I do not like having to use stern measures against our friends in Italy, except for good reason. In the present situation the Commander

[1] See above, Doc. 328. In an earlier message, sent on March 8, Roosevelt asked Churchill for suggestions on how to deal with the threat of strikes reported by General Wilson. He concluded: "It is my strongest wish that you and I should continue to work in complete harmony in this matter as in all others. We may differ on timing but things like that can be worked out, and on the big objectives like self-determination we are as one."

in Chief[2] and his political advisers, both British and American, have recommended that we give immediate support to the program of the six opposition parties. Thus we have, happily for once, our political and military considerations entirely in harmony.

We do not need to intervene beyond informing the executive junta of our support of their program, as described in NAF 622, 624, and 628,[3] and confirm this to the King if necessary. The Italians can present the solution to the King and work out the program among themselves.

I cannot for the life of me understand why we should hesitate any longer in supporting a policy so admirably suited to our common military and political aims. American public opinion would never understand our continued tolerance and apparent support of Victor Emmanuel.

2 General Sir Henry Maitland Wilson.
3 See Coles and Weinberg, *Civil Affairs,* pp. 442–444.

Doc. 331
CHURCHILL TO ROOSEVELT

No. 620   March 14, 1944

I feel you will be interested to hear about the operation just completed to fly two of Wingate's[1] long-range penetration brigades into enemy territory in north Burma. Landing strips in two areas were selected, one 60 miles north of Katha and one 20 miles south of it, from which the brigades could advance westwards primarily to interrupt the Japanese lines of communication and so assist the American-Chinese operations taking place further north. The strips were 100 miles inside enemy territory and 260 miles from the transport base.

1 Brigadier General Orde C. Wingate had made a reputation as a leader of irregular forces in Abyssinia and as a jungle fighter in Burma. Churchill was fascinated by him and brought him to the Quebec conference in August 1943, where he impressed Roosevelt and the Combined Chiefs of Staff. Wingate was the originator of the long-range penetration brigade, an infantry group dropped behind enemy lines and moved in conjunction with advances by the main body of the army. The British Chiefs of Staff formed six long-range groups at Wingate's behest, hoping to seize enough of northern Burma to open a road to China. An American group was subsequently organized; it was popularly known as "Merrill's Marauders." Three of Wingate's brigades were intended to divert the Japanese from the Myitkyina area while Chinese forces under General Stilwell crossed the Salween River from China's Yünnan province and fought the Japanese in northern Burma. Wingate was killed in an air crash in March 1944.

First landings were made by gliders whose occupants then prepared the strips to receive transport aircraft. Between March 6th and March 11th, 7,500 men with all their gear and with mules were successfully landed. The only losses were a number of gliders, and some of these should be repairable. The brigades have now started their advance but a small holding party has been left at one of the strips to receive a flight of Spitfires and a squadron of Hurricane fighter-bombers which were to fly in to protect the base and provide air support.

Only serious mishap occurred on the first night. One of the strips in the northern area was found to have been obstructed by the Japanese, and surface of remaining strip was much worse than expected, causing crashes which blocked the strip and prevented further landings that night. A few of the gliders had to be turned back in the air and failed to reach our territory. Another strip was immediately prepared in this area and was ready for landings two days later. The total of killed, wounded, and missing is at most 145.

The operation appears to have been a complete surprise for Japanese. There has been no enemy air action against the strips in the northern area, and the one in the south was only bombed on 10th March after our men had left it. As it happened, the enemy were concentrating aircraft at airfields in the Mandalay area as part of their own plans. In consequence, the strong air forces we had collected to protect the landings had a very good bag, and in 2 days destroyed 61 enemy aircraft for the loss of only 3 of our own.

We are all very pleased that Wingate's venture has started so well, and the success of this flying-in operation augurs well for the future. Your men have played an important part both in the transport squadrons and in the supporting air operations.[2]

[2] The American Air Transport Wing, which flew supplies from India to China, provided the planes and the support for Wingate's operation.

Doc. 332
CHURCHILL TO ROOSEVELT

No. 621　　　　　　　　　　　　　　　　　　　　March 15, 1944

I consulted the War Cabinet this morning on the proposal that the British and American Governments should accept the six-party programme without further delay.[1] The War Cabinet asked me to assure you that they agree fully with your wish to establish a more broadly based government in Italy and that the future form of government of the Italian people can only be settled by self-determination. They also

[1] See above, Doc. 330.

agree with you that the point to consider is the timing. On this they have no doubt that it would be far better to wait till we are masters of Rome before parting company with the King and Badoglio, because from Rome a more representative and solidly based administration can be constructed than is possible now. They feel that nothing could be worse for our joint interests and for the future of Italy than to set up a weak democratic government which flopped. Even a settlement reached at Rome could not be final because it would be necessary to review it when the northern provinces and great industrial centres favourable to us and essential to a democratic solution, like Milan and Turin, have been liberated. They do not consider that the six parties are representative in any true sense of the Italian democracy or Italian nation or that they could at the present time replace the existing Italian government which has loyally and effectively worked in our interests.

In reaching these conclusions the War Cabinet have of course had before them the telegrams sent by the Allied Commander in Chief whose views on this subject they do not share. Meanwhile we should be quite ready to discuss the suggestions put to the State Department in paragraph 3 of the Foreign Secretary's number 1783.[2] It is also of course recognised that should the capture of Rome be unduly protracted, say for 2 or 3 months, the question of timing would have to be reviewed.

Finally they ask me to emphasise the great importance of not exposing to the world any divergencies of view which may exist between our two Governments, especially in face of the independent action taken by Russia in entering into direct relations with the Badoglio government without consultation with other Allies.[3] It would be a great pity if our respective viewpoints had to be argued out in Parliament and the press when waiting a few months may make it possible for all three Governments to take united action.

2 See above, Doc. 328, note 9.

3 General Eisenhower had established the Allied Control Commission on November 10, 1943, to carry out the terms of the armistice and to align the Italian economy to support the war against Germany. The commission acted through the Italian government. Its president was the supreme Allied commander in the Mediterranean theater, Sir Henry Maitland Wilson. On March 14 the governments of Italy and the Soviet Union announced their agreement to establish direct relations. The Allied commission pointed out to the Italian foreign minister, Renato Prunas, that Italy was not in a position to enter into an agreement with any foreign power without the consent of the supreme commander through the Allied commission. The Russians subsequently explained that their representative would have only the rank of counselor or minister and that he would be under the jurisdiction of the Soviet Union's representative on the Italian Advisory Council. See Coles and Weinberg, *Civil Affairs*, pp. 446–447; and Harris, *Allied Administration of Italy*, pp. 116–117, 141–142.

Doc. 333
ROOSEVELT TO CHURCHILL

No. 499   March 15, 1944

Your 620.[1] I am thrilled by the news of our success under Wingate. If you wire him please give him my hearty good wishes. May the good work go on. This marks an epic achievement for airborne troops, not forgetting the mules.

[1] See above, Doc. 331.

Doc. 334
ROOSEVELT TO CHURCHILL

No. 501   March 15, 1944

We have lately been giving further thought to the matter of limited feeding programs for children and nursing and expectant mothers in the German-occupied countries of Europe.[1] Ambassador Winant will shortly take up with your Government a proposal under which such programs might be put into effect initially in Belgium, France, the Netherlands, and Norway.

I bespeak your most earnest consideration of this proposal. I am convinced that the time has arrived when the continued withholding of food from these categories of the population of the occupied countries is likely to hurt our friends more than our enemies and consequently to be injurious to the United Nations cause.[2]

[1] This message was composed in the State Department.
[2] For Churchill's reply, see below, Doc. 349.

Doc. 335
ROOSEVELT TO CHURCHILL

No. 502   March 17, 1944

Thank you for your number 621, March 15,[1] reporting the decisions of the War Cabinet with respect to the Italian political situation. I am

[1] See above, Doc. 332.

in full agreement with you and them that we should not permit our divergent views to become known publicly particularly at this time.

However, I still feel that if the pressure of the six opposition parties comes to a point where it will have an adverse effect on the situation, we should support their program. I think that we should watch political developments carefully in Italy for the present with that in mind and keep the matter continually before the Advisory Council.[2]

2 On March 26 Palmiro Togliatti, one of the leaders of the Italian Communist party, arrived in Italy after an exile of eighteen years in the Soviet Union. He announced that in the interest of getting a maximum national effort against the Germans he would be willing to serve under the King and Badoglio, and the five other parties agreed to do the same. On April 12 Victor Emmanuel announced that he would retire as soon as Allied troops entered Rome, delegating his powers to Crown Prince Umberto as lieutenant-general of the realm. Badoglio subsequently broadened his government to include the six parties. Croce, Sforza, Togliatti, and two other prominent political leaders all became ministers without portfolio in the new government. The King formally withdrew from public affairs on June 5, the day after Rome was occupied.

Doc. 336
CHURCHILL TO ROOSEVELT

No. 622   March 17, 1944

We have had a most immediate telegram from Mountbatten operative part of which I am sending you in my immediately following.[1]

Upshot is that Japanese are staging an offensive with the apparent object of capturing [I]mphal plain. Mountbatten thinks he has a good chance of inflicting a sharp defeat on the enemy greater than that achieved in recent Arakan operations.[2]

Everything depends on flying up from Arakan the operational portion of 5 Division, ordering the troops to stand fast in places where they cannot be supplied by ordinary means, and supplying them by Ving[3] any opportunity offered to use Wingate's two remaining bri-

1 Not printed.

2 On February 4 Japanese forces had attacked the British Fifteenth Army Corps in the Arakan coastal sector of Burma. While the Seventh Indian Division held its position, the Twenty-sixth and Fifth Indian Divisions moved against the Japanese from the north and south. By February 14 the British offensive was successfully concluded.

3 Error in transmission. Mountbatten's telegram, on which Churchill's message is based, says in part: "It may also be necessary to order troops to stand fast in places where they cannot be supplied by ordinary means and to supply them by U.S. air. At the same time, an opportunity may offer of using Wingate's two remaining brigades of his second wave behind Japanese formations."

gades to harass the enemy in the rear. These brigades also would have to be supplied by air.

To do this, Mountbatten needs 30 C-47s or the equivalent in load-carrying capacity of C-46s to be diverted from the Hump[4] for about a month starting 18 March. He is going ahead unless contrary instructions are issued. The stakes are pretty high in this battle and victory would have far-reaching consequences.

British Chiefs of Staff have telegraphed their entire agreement with Mountbatten's proposals to Washington. We trust that U.S. Chiefs of Staff will agree.[5]

[4] World War II slang for the Himalayas.
[5] For Roosevelt's reply, see below, Doc. 338.

Doc. 337
CHURCHILL TO ROOSEVELT

No. 625   March 18, 1944

Following is latest from U.J. about Poland. No leakage has occurred for which we are responsible.[1] We did not tell the Poles anything. On the other hand the *Observer* newspaper was unduly well informed about Stalin's attitude. This we think could only have come from the Russian Embassy. The matter is of relative unimportance. What matters is that our talks with him on this subject are at an end. He has definitely avoided seeing Ambassador Clark Kerr. Presently I shall have to make some statement in Parliament which I do not expect he will like very much.[2] Meanwhile I do not propose to send any answers. Telegram from U.J. begins:

"I received from Sir A. Clark Kerr on March 12th your message of March 7th on the Polish question.[3]

"Thank you for the explanations which you made in this message.

"In spite of the fact that our correspondence is considered secret and personal the contents of my letter to you have for some time begun to appear in the English press, and, moreover, with many distortions which I have no possibility of refuting.

"I consider this to be a breach of secrecy. This fact makes it difficult

[1] Stalin's complaint in the message printed here was that his last message (see above, Doc. 323) had been leaked to the press.
[2] Churchill's statement in the House of Commons on May 24 was an effort to dispel the suspicions of the Soviet Union about Britain's motivations on the Polish question.
[3] See above, Doc. 325.

for me to express my opinion freely. I hope that you have understood me."[4]

Telegram from U.J. ends.

[4] The British Foreign Office traced the leak to the Soviet Embassy in London, but Soviet officials denied this. See Woodward, *British Foreign Policy*, 3: 181.

Doc. 338
ROOSEVELT TO CHURCHILL

No. 503   March 19, 1944

Receipt is acknowledged of your 622[1] and 623.[2] The American Chiefs of Staff have issued instructions authorizing the diversion of 30 C-47s or the equivalent C-46 aircraft from the Hump program to meet Mountbatten's immediate necessity with instructions to the American Commander of the Air Forces, India-Burma Sector,[3] that these planes should be returned to the Air Transport Command at the earliest possible time.

The American Chiefs of Staff have advised the Commanding General, American Army Air Forces, and the Commanding General, American Army Forces,[4] in that area that Mountbatten should request the British Chiefs of Staff to provide the additional transport aircraft which he needs to support his operations during the remainder of this dry season.

[1] See above, Doc. 336.
[2] Not printed.
[3] Major General George E. Stratemeyer.
[4] Lieutenant General Joseph W. Stilwell.

Doc. 339
CHURCHILL TO ROOSEVELT

No. 630   March 21, 1944

Reference my telegram number 625.[1]
I have today sent following reply to Uncle J. So what!
"Prime Minister to Marshal Stalin. Personal and [most secret].
"Your telegram of March 16th.

[1] See above, Doc. 337.

"1. First of all I must congratulate you again on all the wonderful victories your armies are winning and also on the extremely temperate way in which you have dealt with the Finns.² I suppose they are worried about interning the nine German divisions in Finland for fear that the nine German divisions should intern them. We are much obliged to you for keeping us in touch with all your action in this theatre.

"2. With regard to the Poles, I am not to blame in any way about revealing your secret correspondence. The information was given both to the American *Herald Tribune* correspondent and to the London *Times* correspondent by the Soviet Embassy in London. In the latter case it was given personally by Ambassador Gusev.³

"3. I shall have very soon to make a statement to the House of Commons about the Polish position.⁴ This will involve my saying that the attempts to make an arrangement between the Soviet and Polish Governments have broken down; that we continue to recognise the Polish Government with whom we have been in continuous relations since the invasion of Poland in 1939; that we now consider all questions of territorial change must await the armistice or peace conferences of the victorious powers; and that in the meantime we can recognise no forcible transferences of territory.

"4. I am repeating this telegram to the President of the United States. I only wish I had better news to give him for the sake of all.

"5. Finally, let me express the earnest hope that the breakdown which has occurred between us about Poland will not have any adverse effect upon our cooperation in other spheres where the maintenance of our common action is of the greatest consequence."

2 Soviet forces reached Tarnopol in southern Russia on March 9; overran Berislav on the Dnieper River on March 11; crossed the Dnieper and captured Kherson on March 13; broke through German defenses on the Bug River on March 15; took Yampol on the eastern bank of the Dniester River on March 18; and crossed the river on a broad front the next day. By March 20 the highway and rail junction at Vinnitsa were in Russian hands. Meanwhile, on March 17, Finland rejected the peace terms offered by the Soviet Union, and hostilities on that front did not cease until the truce agreement of September 4, 1944. Roosevelt and Churchill attempted to mediate between Stalin and the Finns at the Teheran conference and indicated that they would oppose Finland's being absorbed into the Soviet Union. The unconditional surrender formula was not applied. Finland became the only Axis nation to the east of Germany that was not occupied by Soviet troops. See G. A. Gripenberg, *Finland and the Great Powers: Memoirs of a Diplomat* (Lincoln, Neb., 1965), pp. 298ff.

3 Feodor T. Gusev, Soviet ambassador to Great Britain.

4 Churchill's statement is published in *Parliamentary Debates*, Commons, 5th ser. (1909–), vol. 400, cols. 778–779.

Doc. 340
ROOSEVELT TO CHURCHILL

March 21, 1944

Dear Winston,

As I told you in my letter of February 29th,[1] I have been putting the finishing touches on a directive to Eisenhower which would make him solely responsible for Overlord and for the administration of good order and reasonable justice when we get ashore.[2]

The paper is now being cleared through the usual channels of the Combined Chiefs of Staff for presentation to Eisenhower, and I am sending you a copy herewith.

I hope you will agree that my efforts to keep it simple and to provide primarily for the first few months of occupation are on a sound basis and have not been in vain.

With warm regards,

As ever,

[1] See above, Doc. 318.
[2] Roosevelt set out priorities for Eisenhower: (1) the defeat of Germany; (2) the liberation of France as soon as possible; and (3) the fostering of democratic methods and conditions so that the French people might choose their own government. See Coles and Weinberg, *Civil Affairs*, pp. 667–668.

Doc. 341
ROOSEVELT TO CHURCHILL

No. 508   March 22, 1944

Your 630.[1] Thank you for the information as to the present status of the Anglo-Soviet disagreement about Poland. I hope your strategy will accomplish the best possible advantage to both of us.

[1] See above, Doc. 339.

Doc. 342
CHURCHILL TO ROOSEVELT

No. 632   April 1, 1944

1. I send you in my immediately following[1] the recent telegrams I have received from U.J. The War Cabinet did not think there was

[1] See below, Doc. 343.

much use in going on with the personal correspondence on this subject at this time as evidently he is determined to find fault and pick a quarrel on every point. We are therefore instructing Ambassador Clark Kerr as in my next following telegram.[2]

2. I have a feeling that the bark may be worse than its bite and that they have a great desire not to separate themselves from their British and American allies. Their conduct about Finland has been temperate and their attitude towards Rumania and Bulgaria seems to be helpful.[3] It may be that, while unwilling to say anything of a reassuring nature to us about Poland, they will in fact watch their step very carefully. This may be of great benefit to the Poles in Poland. It would, I believe, help the situation if you invited Monsieur Mikolajczyk to pay his visit to the United States on your return from your holiday[4] and thus show the Russians the interest which the United States takes in the fate and future of Poland.[5]

[2] Not printed.

[3] Peace feelers from Rumania had first come during the Moscow conference of foreign ministers in October 1943, at which time Molotov thought that the terms should be unconditional surrender. As the Russian army advanced toward the frontier of Rumania in March 1944, the Rumanians attempted to find out what Great Britain and the United States would do to protect them from the Soviet troops. They were advised to surrender to the three powers, not to oppose the Russians, and to contribute to the defeat of Germany. These terms were not accepted. On April 1, as the Soviet army was about to invade Rumania, the Soviet government informed the United States and Great Britain that it intended to take back the formerly-Russian provinces of Bessarabia and Bucovina but would take no other Rumanian territory and would use no force to change the Rumanian social system. The subsequent armistice terms offered by the Allies were lenient: Rumanian troops had the option of surrendering to the Russians or joining them in fighting against the Germans; Rumania was compensated for the territory ceded to the Soviet Union with a larger part of Transylvania taken from Hungary; and a military occupation of Rumania and a war indemnity were imposed. The Rumanian government tried in vain to separate the Allies and to get better terms. Finally, on August 23, 1944, it surrendered unconditionally to the Soviet Union and two days later declared war on Germany. Armistice terms were signed on September 12.

In the case of Bulgaria the British and American governments inquired of the Soviet Union whether the Axis government might not surrender if it knew the terms in advance. The Russians replied in March that (from their point of view) the question was not urgent. The Soviet Union was not at war with Bulgaria at this time and Soviet troops were far from the borders of that country. In August, Bulgaria attempted to assert its neutrality, which the Allies refused to accept. On September 5 the U.S.S.R. declared war on Bulgaria, invaded the country and overthrew the government by coup d'état, replacing it with a predominantly Communist administration, which declared war on Germany.

[4] Roosevelt had suffered a slight attack of pneumonia and was looking worn and debilitated. On the night of April 8, he went to Hyde Park for two weeks of rest.

[5] Mikolajczyk arrived in Washington on June 5 for a nine-day visit, during which he talked with the President, Secretary Hull, and other officials. Roosevelt had

originally invited Mikolajczyk to come on January 15, but had postponed the visit at Churchill's request.

Doc. 343
CHURCHILL TO ROOSEVELT

No. 633   April 1, 1944

My immediately preceding telegram.[1] Following are recent telegrams I have received from U.J. Begins:

"1. Premier J. V. Stalin to Mr. Prime Minister W. Churchill 23.3.44 rec'd 25.3.44.

"I have recently received from you two messages on the Polish question and have studied the statement which Sir A. Clark Kerr made to V. M. Molotov on your instructions on the same question. I was unable to reply at the time as matters at the front often take me away from nonmilitary questions.

"I now reply on these questions.

"It is patent that your messages, and especially the statement of Sir A. Clark Kerr, are full of threats concerning the Soviet Union. I should like to draw your attention to this fact, as the method of threats is not only incorrect in the mutual relations of allies but is also harmful and can lead to contrary results.

"In one of your messages, you qualified the efforts of the Soviet Union in the matter of the maintenance and realisation of the Curzon line as a policy of force. This means that you now seek to qualify the Curzon line as inequitable and the struggle for it as unjust. I can, on no account, agree with such an attitude. I cannot but remind you that at Teheran you, the President, and I agreed as to the justice of the Curzon line. You considered then the attitude of the Soviet Union regarding this question as perfectly just, and you said that the representatives of the Émigré Polish Government would be mad to refuse the Curzon line. Now you maintain something which is directly the contrary. Does this not mean that you no longer acknowledge what we agreed upon at Teheran, and that by this very fact you are breaking the Teheran agreement? I have no doubt that if you had continued to stand firmly, as before, by the attitude you adopted at Teheran, the dispute with the Polish Émigré Government would already have been settled. As for myself and the Soviet Government, we continue to stand by the attitude we adopted at Teheran and have no intention of departing from it, since we consider that the realisation of the Curzon

1 See above, Doc. 342.

line is not a manifestation of a policy of force but a manifestation of the policy of the restoration of the legal rights of the Soviet Union to those territories which even Curzon and the Supreme Council of the Allied Powers recognised in 1919 as being non-Polish.

"You state in your message of the March 7th[2] that the question of the Soviet-Polish frontier will have to be deferred until the summoning of the armistice conference. I think we have here some misunderstanding. The Soviet Union is not waging war and has no intention of waging war against Poland. The Soviet Union has no dispute with the Polish people and considers itself the ally of Poland and the Polish people. For this very reason, the Soviet Union is shedding blood for the sake of the liberation of Poland from German oppression. For this reason, it would be strange to speak of an armistice between the U.S.S.R. and Poland. But the Soviet Government has a dispute with the Émigré Polish Government, which does not reflect the interests of the Polish people and does not express its hopes. It would be even more strange to identify with Poland the Émigré Polish Government in London separated (literally 'torn away') from Poland. I find it difficult even to point to the difference between the Émigré Government of Poland and the similar Émigré Government of Yugoslavia or between certain generals of the Polish Émigré Government and the Serbian General Mihailović.[3]

"In your message of the March 21st[4] you state that you intend to make a statement in the House of Commons to the effect that all questions of territorial changes must be deferred until the armistice or the peace conference of the victorious powers, and that, until then, you cannot recognise any transferences of territories carried out by force. I understand this to mean that you represent the Soviet Union as a power hostile to Poland, and that the essence of the matter is that you deny the emancipatory character of the war of the Soviet Union against German aggression. This is equivalent to attempting to ascribe to the Soviet Union what is not in fact the case and to discrediting it thereby. I have no doubt that such a statement of yours will be taken by the peoples of the Soviet Union and the world public opinion as an undeserved insult directed at the Soviet Union.

"Of course, you are free to make whatever statement you please in the House of Commons—that is your affair. But if you do make such a statement, I shall consider that you have committed an unjust and unfriendly act towards the Soviet Union.

2 See above, Doc. 325.

3 Draža Mihailović, Yugoslav resistance leader. For developments in the Yugoslav resistance movement, see below, Doc. 345, notes 2–3.

4 See above, Doc. 339.

"In your message you express the hope that failure over the Polish question will not influence our collaboration in other spheres. As for myself, I stood for, and continue to stand for, collaboration. But I fear that the method of threats and discrediting, if it continues in the future, will not conduce to our collaboration. Stalin."

"2. Premier Stalin to Prime Minister 25.3.44.

"I have carried out a thorough enquiry into your statement that the disclosure of the correspondence between us occurred between the fault of the Soviet Embassy in London and of Ambassador F. T. Gusev personally.

"This enquiry has shown that neither the Embassy nor F. T. Gusev personally were at all guilty in this matter and that they did not even have in their possession certain of the documents the contents of which were published in the English newspapers. Thus the leakage occurred not on the Soviet but on the English side.

"Gusev is willing to undertake any investigation of this matter in order to prove that he and the members of his staff are in no way implicated in the matter of the disclosure of the contents of our correspondence. It seems to me that you have been led astray with regard to Gusev and the Soviet Embassy. Stalin."

Doc. 344
ROOSEVELT TO CHURCHILL

No. 512 April 4, 1944

I have studied with considerable care your message number 631 of March 30[1] with regard to our negotiations with Spain concerning wolfram. I am most reluctant to accept any compromise on this matter with the Spanish Government. It can hardly be helpful in the present wolfram negotiations with the Portuguese.[2] At the same time I appreciate that in the absence of full agreement between us on the measures to be adopted we cannot anticipate an early successful conclusion of these negotiations. I am therefore asking the Department of State to

1 Not printed. Churchill urged a compromise on the wolfram embargo, since the Spanish might cut off the iron ore and potash shipments to Great Britain and since the limited quantity of wolfram reaching Germany was of little help to its war effort. Churchill reminded Roosevelt that he had supported the United States in regard to Argentina and now asked help for Britain's interests in Spain.

2 Churchill had written to Dr. Salazar on March 15 asking why Portugal was helping to prolong the war by shipping wolfram to Germany. In his reply on March 28, Salazar justified his course of action. See Woodward, *British Foreign Policy* (abridged ed.), pp. 383-384; and *FR 1944*, 4: 99-101.

work out with your Embassy a mutually agreeable line to take with the Spanish.[3]

[3] The State Department drew back from its demand for a complete embargo, and the British and American ambassadors were given identical instructions in regard to this issue. Churchill cabled his thanks to the President on April 6. See *FR 1944*, 4: 377–378.

Doc. 345
CHURCHILL TO ROOSEVELT

No. 638   April 6, 1944

It is said that OSS[1] have received instructions, which have been approved by you, to arrange for a small intelligence mission to be infiltrated to General Mihailović's headquarters, and we have been asked to organise the necessary arrangements.[2]

We are now in process of withdrawing all our missions from Mihailović and are pressing King Peter to clear himself of this millstone, which is dragging him down in his own country and works only to the assistance of the enemy. If, at this very time, an American mission arrives at Mihailović's headquarters, it will show throughout the Balkans a complete contrariety of action between Britain and the United States. The Russians will certainly throw all their weight on Tito's side, which we are backing to the full.[3] Thus we shall get altogether out of step. I hope and trust this may be avoided.

[1] Office of Strategic Services, a United States intelligence organization organized in 1941.

[2] After the defeat of the Yugoslav army in 1941, Colonel (later General) Draža Mihailović established a resistance force known as the Chetniks in the mountains of Serbia. Mihailović's political views were pan-Serbian, which made him unappealing to many Yugoslavs of other ethnic backgrounds. After Germany attacked the Soviet Union, the Yugoslav Communists organized partisan bands to harass Axis forces occupying Yugoslavia; the most important of these bands was a group led by Marshal Josip Broz, self-styled Tito. In November 1941 Mihailović made an agreement, observed only briefly, with the Communists to act in a common cause against the Germans. Later, the British Foreign Office tried to get the Soviet Union to bring the two groups together, but the Russians accused Mihailović of collaborating with the enemy and refused to deal with him.

[3] The British hoped that Tito would agree to support King Peter of Yugoslavia if the latter dismissed Mihailović from his office in the resistance. Tito replied that both the King and Mihailović must go and insisted that the Allies recognize the National Council of Liberation as the government of Yugoslavia. Wanting to aid Tito's struggle against the Germans, the British tried again to unify the two groups. In a letter to Churchill in January 1944 Tito said that he understood the Allies' position on the King and would avoid further attacks on him, and in February the British withdrew their liaison officers from Mihailović's forces. See *FR 1944*, 4: 1330–1357. See Woodward, *British Foreign Policy*, 3: 278ff.

Doc. 346
ROOSEVELT TO CHURCHILL

No. 515   April 8, 1944

Your 638.[1] My thought in authorizing an OSS mission to the Mihailović area was to obtain intelligence and the mission was to have no political functions whatever.

In view however of your expressed opinion that there might be misunderstanding by our allies and others, I have directed that the contemplated mission be not *repeat* not sent.

[1] See above, Doc. 345.

Doc. 347
ROOSEVELT TO CHURCHILL

No. 516   April 8, 1944

In view of prospective change in plans for Anvil I believe that U.J. should be fully informed at once when we reach decision in regard to Anvil on recommendation of the Combined Chiefs of Staff.[1]

[1] The invasion of southern France was being held up because of slow progress on the Italian front, which made it impossible to build up the necessary forces in time. After some disagreement with the British, Eisenhower agreed to a postponement of the operation.

Doc. 348
ROOSEVELT TO CHURCHILL

No. 518   April 8, 1944

I am a good deal concerned by the French National Committee's demands in regard to military matters.[1] The tone of these communica-

[1] The French National Committee was demanding to treat directly with the Allied governments and not the Combined Chiefs of Staff. Further, the committee wanted to be fully informed of plans before consenting to the use of French forces and insisted on communicating directly and secretly between French commands without going through Allied channels. See *FR 1944*, 3: 668–669.

tions verges on the dictatorial, especially when we consider the simple facts.[2]

Personally I do not think that we can give military information to a source which has a bad record in secrecy. The implied threat to stay out of operations in France would, if carried out, do the Committee and its leader irreparable harm.[3]

If de Gaulle wants to come over here to visit me[4] I shall be very glad to see him and will adopt a paternal tone, but I think it would be a mistake for me to invite him without an intimation from him that he wants to come.

[2] Roosevelt was still angry over an earlier confrontation with de Gaulle. On December 21, 1943, the French leader had ordered the arrest of Marcel Peyrouton, Pierre Boisson, and Pierre-Étienne Flandin, all major Vichy figures who had been helpful to the Allied cause. Both Churchill and Eisenhower expressed their concern to Roosevelt who responded on December 22 with a directive to Eisenhower to take no action against these men and the observation to Churchill "that this is the proper time to eliminate the Jeanne d'Arc complex and return to realism." Roosevelt ultimately took a more moderate line, and Churchill tried to smooth things over at a luncheon with de Gaulle on January 12. See Milton Viorst, *Hostile Allies* (New York, 1965), pp. 186ff., and Charles de Gaulle, *The Complete War Memoirs* (New York, 1964), 1: 546–547.

[3] In his reply of April 12 Churchill agreed that military information should be withheld from the French National Committee in the case of Overlord but not in the case of Anvil, since French divisions might be employed in that operation and necessarily would have to be informed.

[4] De Gaulle had been about to depart for the United States in December 1942 when the assassination of Admiral Jean François Darlan made him change his plans. Subsequently he met the President at the Casablanca conference. In 1944 Roosevelt and Hull were still unwilling to recognize de Gaulle as head of the French state. As the date of the invasion of France drew nearer, Churchill and the British attempted to mediate, particularly to get the Americans to recognize the French Committee of National Liberation and to work out arrangements for the administration of civil affairs in areas taken from the Germans. The British finally succeeded in setting up a Washington visit for de Gaulle on July 6, without either a formal invitation or an acceptance. De Gaulle's side of the story is set forth in *De Gaulle Memoirs*, 1: 569–577.

Doc. 349
CHURCHILL TO ROOSEVELT

No. 641   April 8, 1944

The proposals of your Government for a limited relief scheme[1] were put forward by Mr. Riefler[2] on March 29th and have been most

[1] See above, Doc. 334.

[2] Winfield Riefler, an official of the Foreign Economic Administration and special assistant to the U.S. ambassador in London, John G. Winant.

earnestly considered by my colleagues and by myself. I share your desire to do everything possible to ameliorate the lot of the peoples of the occupied countries insofar as this is possible without detriment to the war effort. I find it however difficult to accept the view that the maintenance of our blockade policy is likely to hurt our friends more than our enemies.

The whole question seems to me to be governed by the impending military operations for the invasion of Europe. Our experience of the working of the Greek relief scheme has conclusively shown that it causes considerable difficulties for, and imposes restriction on, our naval and air forces, and these difficulties will increase as new operations are begun. The opening of further channels of importation into Europe at the present moment would, in our view, be wholly incompatible with the naval and military situation which is developing. It would involve not only the granting of safe-conducts for ships to sail to designated ports within the operational zones, but also the preservation of routes of inland transport from those ports to the countries in which the food is to be distributed. It would clearly be impossible to undertake to keep any ports or routes to them open, or to keep intact any railways between now and the end of this year: and if it were possible to give such an undertaking we should thereby give the Germans valuable information as to our military intentions. Any relief action now undertaken would therefore inevitably hamper impending military operations.

Even if military considerations were not decisive there are also grave objections from the blockade point of view. These are being explained in detail to Mr. Winant and I do not think I need trouble you with them, if we are agreed that nothing can be allowed to hamper or interfere with forthcoming operations.[3]

[3] The President forwarded this message to Admiral William D. Leahy, his Chief of Staff, with the comment: "I don't know but what the Prime is right on this." See *FR 1944, 2* (Washington, 1967): 252–300.

Doc. 350
ROOSEVELT TO CHURCHILL

No. 519 April 8, 1944

Your 641.[1] While I remain of the opinion that it would be humane and wise to provide such relief as is practicable to the undernourished women and children of friendly people in Nazi-occupied Europe, I am

[1] See above, Doc. 349.

in complete agreement with you that nothing should be done that will interfere with or hamper forthcoming operations.

Doc. 351
CHURCHILL TO ROOSEVELT

No. 644   April 14, 1944

Would it not be well for you and me to send a notice to Uncle J about the date of Overlord? I do not see why this particular communication should not go from us both unitedly. I suggest for your consideration the following message. Message begins:

"1. Pursuant to our talks at Teheran, the general crossing of the sea will take place around the date mentioned in my immediately following, with 3 days' margin on either side for weather. We shall be acting at our fullest strength.

"2. Our action in the Mediterranean theatre will be designed to hold the maximum number of German divisions away from the Russian front and from Overlord. The exact method by which this will be achieved will depend on the outcome of the heavy offensive which we shall launch in Italy with all our strength about mid-May.

"3. Since Teheran your armies have gained and are gaining a magnificent series of unforeseen victories for the common cause. Even in months when you thought they would not be active they have gained these great victories. We ask you to let us know, in order to make our own calculations, what scale your effort will take in the 3 months following the date mentioned, when we shall certainly strike. We send you our very best wishes and hope we may all fall on the common foe together. Signed Roosevelt-Churchill." Message ends.

Please let me have your amendments to this and I will send it off.[1]

1 For Roosevelt's reply, see below, Doc. 353.

Doc. 352
CHURCHILL TO ROOSEVELT

No. 646   April 15, 1944

To safeguard the security of Overlord, we have decided to prohibit foreign representatives in this country from sending or receiving uncensored communications, whether cypher telegrams or diplomatic bags. We shall also forbid couriers or other members of diplomatic staffs from leaving the country. The ban will come into force from midnight Monday, April 17, and continue until after the launching of the operation. It will not, of course, apply to your representatives or to the Soviet representatives; but it will cover both neutral representatives and representatives of other Allied governments, including representatives of the French Committee of Liberation and exiled governments in this country.

We are imposing this ban because of our desire to leave nothing undone which might promote the success of Overlord, and we have been much influenced by the view of General Eisenhower, who pressed strongly for it.[1]

We shall explain to the foreign governments that the ban is being imposed for compelling military reasons and that many other restrictions are being imposed on our own people in the interests of security.

We hope that no foreign government will be tempted to retaliate by forbidding our diplomatic representatives to send uncensored communications. If, however, any were to do so, may we count on the help of your representative in the country concerned to enable us to continue to send and receive uncensored communications?

So much information about military plans is constantly passing between here and Washington that valuable information might well reach the enemy through cypher telegrams sent by representatives of foreign governments in the United States.

I have no doubt that you will be ready to consider whether some corresponding action should be taken to prevent leakages through diplomatic representatives in the United States.[2]

[1] Eisenhower had written to General Sir Alan Brooke on April 9 about secrecy concerning Overlord: "I feel bound to say frankly that I regard this source of leakage [diplomatic communications] as the gravest risk to the security of our operations and to the lives of our sailors, soldiers, and airmen. Appreciating as I do the difficulties involved in the suspension of diplomatic privileges, I cannot conceal my opinion that these difficulties are far outweighed by the greater issues that are at stake." *PPDE*, 3: 1636.

[2] Roosevelt's reply, dated midnight April 18, said: "The situation here is so different from that in the United Kingdom that restrictions here would have to be handled differently. We are nevertheless considering what can be done to tighten up, and are consulting our military people on the point."

In the end Eisenhower got what he wanted, even though nearly all the Allied governments protested, and the French Committee of National Liberation broke off negotiations with headquarters Allied Expeditionary Force, the Normandy invasion force.

Doc. 353
ROOSEVELT TO CHURCHILL

No. 522   April 16, 1944

Replying to your 644[1] as the Combined Chiefs of Staff dispatched a message on April 6th to General Burrows,[2] head of your mission in Moscow, and General Deane,[3] who heads our mission, with instructions to inform the Soviet General Staff that in accordance with the agreement reached at Teheran it is our firm intention to launch Overlord on the agreed date (which date was furnished in a succeeding message), I do not believe we should repeat to U.J. information which has already been given to the Russian military authorities. In this same message, Deane and Burrows were instructed to pay a handsome tribute to the magnificent progress of the Soviet armies and to ask the Soviet General Staff to confirm that they, for their part, would fulfill the undertaking given at Teheran by Marshal Stalin to organize a large-scale offensive at the appropriate time to assist Overlord by containing the maximum number of German divisions in the east.

With reference to paragraph two of your proposed message, it would be better to wait until our Chiefs of Staff have come to a firm agreement on the scope and timing of operations in the Mediterranean.

As to the question regarding the scale of the Soviet effort raised in paragraph three of your proposed message, U.J. made a definite commitment at Teheran, and I believe he meant it. The CCS message to Deane and Burrows directed them to ask for confirmation of the Soviet Teheran undertaking.

The British Chiefs of Staff did not consider it advisable to ask directly for Soviet plans or scale of effort because the Soviet decisions must depend on the development of their operation between now and the middle of May. The U.S. Chiefs of Staff took the same view. I am inclined to agree that U.J. should not be asked this specific question unless you have strong reasons to the contrary.

1 See above, Doc. 351.
2 Major General M. B. Burrows, the British military attaché in Moscow. The British military mission was established after the signing of the Anglo-Russian treaty of May 26, 1942.
3 Major General John R. Deane, the U.S. military attaché. The American mission was established following the Moscow foreign ministers' conference in October 1943. See Deane's *The Strange Alliance* (New York, 1947).

If you feel it timely to dispatch a message, I suggest the following redraft to which you may attach my signature if you concur:

"1. Pursuant to our talks at Teheran, the general crossing of the sea will take place around a date which Generals Deane and Burrows have recently been directed to give the Soviet General Staff.[4] We shall be acting at our fullest strength.

"2. We are launching an offensive on the Italian mainland at maximum strength about mid-May.

"3. Since Teheran your armies have been gaining a magnificent series of victories for the common cause. Even in the months when you thought they would not be active, they have gained these great victories. We send you our very best wishes and trust that your armies and ours, operating in unison in accordance with our Teheran agreement, will (soon) crush the Hitlerites."[5]

[4] Deane and Burrows had told the Chief of Staff of the Red Army on April 10 that the cross-channel attack would take place on May 31 but that the date might be shifted two or three days before or after that depending on tides and weather. See *Stalin's Correspondence*, 2: 293, note 57.

[5] For Churchill's reply, see below, Doc. 355.

Doc. 354
ROOSEVELT TO CHURCHILL

No. 523   April 17, 1944

Your 648.[1] Thank you for the information regarding recent difficulties encountered in Greek participation in our Allied effort.

I join with you in a hope that your line of action toward the problem may succeed in bringing the Greeks back into the Allied camp and to a participation against the barbarians that will be worthy of traditions established by the heroes of Greek history. Frankly, as one whose family and who personally have contributed by personal help to Greek independence for over a century, I am unhappy over the present situation and hope that Greeks everywhere will set aside petti-

[1] Not printed. Churchill reported that following the establishment of a political committee by the National Liberation Front in the mountains of Greece, elements in the Greek armed forces in the Middle East mutinied and demanded the resignation of the existing government and the establishment of a republic. King George II of Greece was unwilling to accept such a government and insisted that order be restored before any changes were made. Churchill agreed. The King flew to Cairo, formed a new government, and awaited suppression of the mutiny. See Churchill, *Closing the Ring*, pp. 532–552; and Woodward, *British Foreign Policy*, 3: 383–437. For American documents, see *FR 1944*, 5: 84–104.

ness and regain their sense of proportion. Let every Greek think of
their glorious past and show a personal unselfishness which is so necessary now. You can quote me if you want to in the above sense.

Doc. 355
CHURCHILL TO ROOSEVELT

No. 650   April 18, 1944

Your number 522.[1]
I certainly think that it would be a good thing to send the message
as redrafted by you beginning at "1. Pursuant to our talks" and
ending "will crush the Hitlerites." This engages Stalin's direct personal attention and is more worthy of the tremendous event to which
we are committed heart and soul than a staff notification. It may even
be followed by a friendly response.[2] I have ventured to omit the word
"soon" as it seems safer, and have sent it off over our joint signatures.

1 See above, Doc. 353.
2 Stalin's reply of April 22 was most cordial. It expressed gratification at the
news and promised "maximum support" through a new Red Army offensive. See
Stalin's Correspondence, 2: 188.

Doc. 356
CHURCHILL TO ROOSEVELT

No. 651   April 18, 1944

Your number 523.[1]
Thank you so much. I have told our people to make use of your
message to the King and his new ministers, and to read it to the
mutinous brigade and recalcitrant ships. It may have a most salutary
effect.[2] I am not publishing anything here.

1 See above, Doc. 354.
2 Emmanuel J. Tsouderos, the Greek Minister of Foreign Affairs and Minister of
Finance, had resigned on April 3, and on April 9 the Greek National Liberation
Front accepted his invitation for a conference. The mutiny was put down by April
25, and King George II returned to England.

Doc. 357
ROOSEVELT TO CHURCHILL

No. 529   April 21, 1944

Your 649.[1] As you say, the only point which divides us on Spanish policy is whether to resume oil shipments concurrently with the resumption of wolfram shipments from Spain to Germany to the extent of 60 tons over the three months of April, May, and June, or whether to do all in our power by a united effort to continue the suspension of wolfram shipments until July 1 in the hope and belief that thereafter shipments in the second half of the year in the amounts agreed to will not be practicable. It seems to us that to agree to the resumption of wolfram shipments prior to July 1st would frustrate the efforts which we are jointly making in Sweden and Turkey and would impair our position in dealing with Switzerland and Portugal. To these negotiations we attach great importance, as I know you do also.[2]

Furthermore, our public attaches the greatest importance to Spanish shipments of wolfram and is most critical of oil supplies going to that country while these shipments continue. They are most insistent upon a policy of firmness in this matter and a contrary course on the eve of military operations would, I believe, have the most serious consequences.

The Duke of Alba's[3] repudiated proposal to which you refer required shipments of only half the wolfram now proposed for the rest of 1944 and even in that case we said that only as a last resort would we consent to shipments before July 1st.

We have gone a very long way to meet your difficulties as you describe them in your long cable to me. Will you not, therefore, reconsider an instruction to our two Ambassadors to join in a determined effort to settle the matter upon the basis of a suspension of

[1] Not printed. Churchill cabled that the only difference between the American and British policies was nine tons over a three-month period, and this was not worth the risk of having 1,000 tons of wolfram near the border turned over to the Germans.

[2] In Sweden efforts were being made to restrict the shipments of ball bearings to Germany, and Turkey was being urged to discontinue shipping chrome ore. In December 1943 the Swiss had agreed to reduce by 45 percent their exports of arms, ammunition, and machinery and by 40 percent the sale of precision tools, fuses, ball bearings, and arms.

[3] Spanish ambassador to Great Britain.

shipments during the first half-year? I do not believe that we have yet done all that is possible along this line.[4]

[4] See James W. Cortada, *United States–Spanish Relations, Wolfram and World War II* (Barcelona, 1971).

Doc. 358
ROOSEVELT TO CHURCHILL

No. 531   April 25, 1944

Referring to your 655,[1] I have today authorized Hull to accept Halifax's proposal to restrict shipments of wolfram from Spain.

[1] Not printed. Churchill made a final plea on this hard-argued point, with the success disclosed above.

Doc. 359
CHURCHILL TO ROOSEVELT

No. 663   April 26, 1944

King Peter is very anxious to have the Ban of Croatia over here as soon as possible.[1] I am most anxious he should form a government which will not tie him to Mihailović, a weight which cannot well be borne. The Ban is essential to his plans for forming a broad-based administration not obnoxious to the Partisans.[2] Could you find the gentleman and put him on an aeroplane as early as possible? He may need a little encouragement. Halifax will do this if the Ban is directed to the British Embassy.[3]

[1] In August 1939 King Peter of Yugoslavia had appointed Ivan Subasić Ban (or Viceroy) of Croatia under a decree which gave a measure of autonomy to that area. In 1941 Subasić left Yugoslavia and for a time was in the United States working to unify Yugoslav groups.
[2] Tito's guerrilla followers.
[3] Roosevelt replied on May 13: "I am informed that the Ban of Croatia is now in England. I am generally opposed to any kind of ban but have no objection to this variety." Churchill answered on May 14: "Ban duly lifted and safely received."

Doc. 360
CHURCHILL TO ROOSEVELT

No. 669   May 7, 1944

The War Cabinet have been much concerned during the last three weeks about the number of Frenchmen killed in the raids on the railway centres in France. We have had numerous staff meetings with our own officers and I have discussed the matter with Generals Eisenhower and Bedell Smith.[1] There were and are great differences of opinion in the two air forces not between them but crisscross about the efficacy of the "Railway Plan" as a short-term project. In the end Eisenhower, Tedder,[2] Bedell Smith, and Portal[3] all declare themselves converted. I am personally by no means convinced that this is the best way to use our air forces in the preliminary period, and still think that the GAF should be the main target.[4] The matter has been discussed in very great detail on the technical side, and it would not be wise to dismiss lightly the arguments for or against.

When this project was first put forward a loss of 80,000 French civilian casualties including injured, say 20,000 killed, was mentioned. The War Cabinet could not view this figure without grave dismay on account of the apparently ruthless use of the air forces, particu-

1 Eisenhower wrote Churchill on April 5 that one of the fundamental factors behind Overlord was the superiority of Allied air power. The bombing of French transportation centers would increase the chance of success of the invasion. Eisenhower thought that warnings would accomplish little in the way of keeping people away from target areas. He also felt that the estimated civilian casualties were exaggerated.

Eisenhower reported to General Marshall on April 12 that the wisdom of bombing population centers was being discussed "constantly with political authorities." He wrote to Churchill again on May 2 declaring that some targets where the estimated civilian casualties would be most severe would not be hit until the later stages of the operation. See *PDDE*, 3: 1809–1810, 1817, 1842–1844; Churchill, *Closing the Ring*, pp. 527–530; and Ehrman, *Grand Strategy*, 5: 297–304.

2 Air Chief Marshal Sir Arthur W. Tedder, deputy commander in chief for Overlord.

3 Air Chief Marshal Sir Charles Portal, head of the Royal Air Force.

4 The Transportation Plan evinced much discussion, including the argument that the German air force (GAF) should be knocked out first. Air Chief Marshal Portal had met with representatives of the two factions on the question and had decided that for the time being the primary effort would be against the German fighter plane industry, and then in support of the Transportation Plan. Portal reported the results of this meeting to Churchill on March 29, and this in turn led to the War Cabinet discussions.

larly of the Royal Air Force on whom the brunt of this kind of work necessarily falls, and the reproaches that would be made upon the inaccuracy of night bombing. The results of the first, say, three-sevenths of the bombing have however shown that the casualties to French civil life are very much less than was expected by the commanders; in fact Air Chief Marshal Tedder has now expressed the opinion that about 10,000 killed, apart from injured, will probably cover the job.

I am satisfied that all possible care will be taken to minimise this slaughter of friendly civilian life. Nevertheless the War Cabinet share my apprehensions of the bad effect which will be produced upon the French civilian population by these slaughters, all taking place so long before Overlord D Day. They may easily bring about a great revulsion in French feeling towards their approaching United States and British liberators. They may leave a legacy of hate behind them.[5] I have just now received the telegram contained in my immediately following[6] from our Ambassador at Algiers,[7] which I am pretty sure represents a serious wave of opinion in France. It may well be that the French losses will grow heavier on and after D Day, but in the heat of battle, when British and United States troops will probably be losing at a much higher rate, a new proportion establishes itself in men's minds. It is the intervening period that causes me most anxiety. We are of course doing everything in our power by leaflets, etc., to warn the French people to keep clear of dangerous spots, and this may prove beneficial in the remaining interval. However both on technical and political grounds, which latter are very gravely involved, the War Cabinet feel very great distress and anxiety.

Accordingly they ask me to invite you to consider the matter from the highest political standpoint and to give us your opinion as a matter between governments. It must be remembered on the one hand that this slaughter is among a friendly people who have committed no crimes against us, and not among the German foe with all their record of cruelty and ruthlessness. On the other hand we naturally feel the hazardous nature of Operation Overlord and are in deadly earnest

---

[5] When Major General Pierre J. Koenig, head of the First Free French Division in the United Kingdom, was informed of the plan on June 4, his reaction was: "This is war, and it must be expected that people will be killed. We would take twice the anticipated loss to be rid of the Germans." *PDDE*, 3: 1810, note 3.

[6] See below, Doc. 362, note 2.

[7] The Right Honourable Alfred Duff Cooper was named Representative of His Majesty's Government in the United Kingdom with the French Committee of National Liberation on January 1, 1944. He had the personal rank of ambassador. After he arrived in Algiers on January 4, Macmillan no longer dealt with French affairs.

about making it a success. I have been careful in stating this case to you to use only the most moderate terms, but I ought to let you know that the War Cabinet is unanimous in its anxiety about these French slaughters, even reduced as they have been, and also in its doubts as to whether almost as good military results could not be produced by other methods. Whatever is settled between us, we are quite willing to share responsibilities with you.[8]

8 For Roosevelt's reply, see below, Doc. 362.

Doc. 361
ROOSEVELT TO CHURCHILL

No. 536   May 10, 1944

I believe we should inform Marshal Stalin that Anvil will not be launched in conjunction with the Overlord assault. If you agree to the following message, will you send it as being from both of us?

"In order to give maximum strength to the attack across the sea against northern France, we have transferred part of our landing craft from the Mediterranean to England. This, together with the need for using our Mediterranean land forces in the present Italian battle, makes it impracticable to attack the Mediterranean coast of France in conjunction with the Overlord assault. We are expecting to make such an attack later.[1] In order to keep the greatest number of German forces away from northern France and the eastern front, we are attacking the Germans in Italy at once on a maximum scale and, at the same time, are maintaining a threat against the Mediterranean coast of France."

1 In the final version of this message the third sentence was amended to read: "We are planning to make such an attack later, for which purpose additional landing craft are being sent to the Mediterranean from the United States." Stalin received the message on May 14. See *Stalin's Correspondence*, 2:140.

Doc. 362
ROOSEVELT TO CHURCHILL

No. 537   May 11, 1944

Replying to your 669[1] and 670,[2] I share fully with you your distress at the loss of life among the French population incident to our air preparations for Overlord.

I share also with you a satisfaction that every possible care is being and will be taken to minimize civilian casualties. No possibility of alleviating adverse French opinion should be overlooked, always provided that there is no reduction of our effectiveness against the enemy at this crucial time. The message from your Ambassador at Algiers referred to the good psychological effect to be obtained if a French transport expert were consulted by the target committee.[3] This matter should be referred to the responsible military commanders for their decision.

However regrettable the attendant loss of civilian lives is, I am not prepared to impose from this distance any restriction on military action by the responsible commanders that in their opinion might militate against the success of Overlord or cause additional loss of life to our Allied forces of invasion.[4]

[1] See above, Doc. 360.

[2] Not printed. Churchill sent Roosevelt a report from the British ambassador at Algiers of a meeting with René Massigli, the Free French Minister of Foreign Affairs. Massigli presented a memorandum on the Allied bombing of targets in France and the serious psychological effect it was having on the population. The suggestion was made that sabotage might bring better results with less cost in lives.

[3] The military group responsible for selecting bomber targets.

[4] Roosevelt's reply settled the issue, but Churchill continued to watch the operations closely. An intelligence estimate a week before D Day said that nothing of importance had been accomplished by the attacks on railroads, but later reports indicated that by June 6 the French transportation system was on the point of total collapse. Civilian casualties were much lower than anticipated but there is no reliable estimate of the number. See Harrison, *Cross-Channel Attack*, pp. 217–230; and Forrest C. Pogue, *The Supreme Command* (Washington, 1954), pp. 127–134.

Doc. 363
CHURCHILL TO ROOSEVELT

No. 677 May 18, 1944

I send you herewith a message which I have sent to Marshal Tito, which I hope you will like. The King[1] hopes to announce his new government on Monday. He has just left me, and seems in very good form. Telegram runs as follows:

"This morning, as the result of British advice, King Peter II dismissed Monsieur Purić's[2] administration, which included General Mihailović as Minister of War. He is now about to form a small government under the Ban of Croatia. This course has the strong approval of His Britannic Majesty's Government.

"We do not know what will happen in the Serbian part of Yugoslavia. Mihailović certainly holds a powerful position locally as Commander in Chief, and it does not follow that his ceasing to be Minister of War will rob him of his influence. We cannot predict what he will do. There is also a very large body, amounting perhaps to 200,000, of Serbian peasant proprietary who are anti-German but strongly Serbian and who naturally hold the views of a peasants' ownership community. My object is that these forces may be made to work with you for a united, independent Yugoslavia which will expel from the soil of Yugoslavia the filthy Hitlerite murderers and invaders till not one remains.

"It is of importance to the common cause and to our relations with you that these changes should be given a fair chance to develop in a favourable way to the main object. I should greatly regret it if you were at all in a hurry to denounce them in public. Crucial events impend in Europe. The battle in Italy goes in our favour. General Wilson assures me of his resolve to aid you to the very utmost. I feel therefore that I have a right to ask you to forbear any utterance adverse to this new event, at least for a few weeks till we have exchanged telegrams upon it.

"Brigadier Maclean,[3] who is with me now, will be with you in less

---

1 Peter II of Yugoslavia.

2 Bozhidar Purić, Prime Minister of Yugoslavia.

3 Brigadier General Fitzroy H. R. Maclean, commander of the Allied military mission to the Partisans in Yugoslavia. Maclean had been a member of the Foreign Office from 1933 to 1941, when he resigned to join the Army and entered Parliament.

than 3 weeks with all the views he has gathered here, and I hope that at the very least you will await his return.

"Meanwhile, I congratulate you once more upon the number of enemy divisions which you are holding gripped on your various fronts. You will realise, Marshal Tito, that the war will soon come to a very high pitch of intensity and that British, American, and Russian forces will all hurl themselves on the common foe. You must be at your strongest during this climax. While I cannot guarantee a speedy breakdown of the enemy's power, there is certainly a chance of it."[4]

[4] See Churchill, *Closing the Ring*, pp. 461–478; Eden, *Memoirs*, 2: 510–512; and Woodward, *British Foreign Policy*, 3: 278–335.

Doc. 364
ROOSEVELT TO CHURCHILL

No. 540   May 18, 1944

I am delighted with your telegram to Marshal Tito and I wish you would tell King Peter that I am heartily in accord.[1] I sent him yesterday a letter in reply to a very nice letter I had from him.[2]

Incidentally, do you remember my telling you over a year ago of my talk with Peter in which I discussed the possibility of three nations in place of the one, he to be the head of a reconstituted Serbia? This created no excitement on his part or that of Purić.

The King, with real fire in his eyes, remarked that he was a Serb. I think that you and I should bear some such possibility in mind in case the new government does not work out. Personally I would rather have a Yugoslavia, but three separate states with separate governments in a Balkan confederation might solve many problems.

[1] See above, Doc. 363.

[2] In a letter to Roosevelt on April 17 King Peter had expressed concern over the agreement to drop Mihailović. He said that Tito had no more than 30,000 men, and that the Yugoslav nation repudiated communism. He asked the President to intervene so that the question of Yugoslavia, if not all of the Balkans, would not be decided without common discussion and under a common guarantee among the United States, Great Britain, the Soviet Union, and Yugoslavia. See *FR 1944*, 4: 1359–1361.

Roosevelt argued, in reply, that the Partisan movement was stronger and had more popular support than the King realized. He pledged the United States to work with the governments of Great Britain and the Soviet Union concerning Yugoslavia, adding that, while the United States "may be considered to have a less direct interest in southeastern Europe, we treasure the friendship of your people." *FR 1944*, 4: 1366–1368.

Doc. 365
CHURCHILL TO ROOSEVELT

May 21, 1944

My dear Mr. President,

Many thanks for letting me see General Hurley's[1] memorandum on Persia, which I am returning to you herewith as requested. I am sorry to have delayed answering it, but several Departments of State had to be consulted on the points which it raised. The General seems to have some ideas about British imperialism which I confess make me rub my eyes. He makes out, for example, that there is an irrepressible conflict between imperialism and democracy. I make bold, however, to suggest that British imperialism has spread and is spreading democracy more widely than any other system of government since the beginning of time.

As regards Persia, however, I do not think that "British imperialism" enters into the picture. It is true that we, like the United States, are inevitably concerned about our strategic supplies of oil, the more so because, unlike the United States, we have no metropolitan sources. From the same security point of view, we have responsibilities which we cannot at present abandon for the western frontier of India and the eastern frontier of Iraq. Apart from this, we have the same wartime interest as the United States in the safety of the trans-Persian supply route to Russia. For all these reasons we want a strong and friendly government in Persia, and have no wish to see the establishment of foreign "zones of influence." In short, we are certainly no less interested than the United States in encouraging Persian independence, political efficiency, and national reform.

I agree with what you say about Persia's need for outside assistance. Whether she would welcome the principle of international trusteeship seems open to doubt. It sounds rather like the mandatory system. I

1 Brigadier General Patrick J. Hurley, the President's personal representative in the Near East in 1943. Hurley's report, dated May 13, 1943, is printed in *FR 1943*, 4 (Washington, 1964): 363-370. Roosevelt sent this to Churchill on February 29, "for your eyes only": "I rather like his general approach to the care and education of what used to be called backward countries. From your and my personal observation I think we could add something about personal cleanliness as well. The point of all this is that I do not want the United States to acquire a zone of influence—or any other nation for that matter. Iran certainly needs Trustees. It will take thirty to forty years to eliminate the graft and the feudal system. Until that time comes, Iran may be a headache to you, to Russia and to ourselves."

think that our best way of helping the Persians is through the American advisers. Dr. Millspaugh[2] and his colleagues have undertaken a very necessary but a long, arduous, and thankless task. We are giving them, and intend to continue giving them, all the help in our power, as we have since made clear in our discussions with the Stettinius mission.[3]

I assume that you have had no reply from Stalin to your suggestion for a free port at the head of the Persian Gulf, and for international management of the Persian railway.[4] On this point we might await Russian reactions. I am by no means certain that after the war, when the Black Sea ports are again open, the trans-Persian route will continue to be necessary for Russian trade, or indeed could be operated under such conditions as would enable it to compete commercially with the Black Sea route.

I quite recognise that the position of the UKCC[5] and the use of lend-lease supplies in Persia, to which Hurley drew your attention, required some looking into. I am glad to be able to say that since the date of your letter to me, the matter has been discussed with your people and a mutually satisfactory arrangement reached. I think they also appreciate that we have no intention whatever of trying to establish a British monopoly through the UKCC which is under instructions not to interfere with private trade unless absolutely necessary for the purposes of the war.[6]

[2] Arthur C. Millspaugh, head of the sixty-man American financial mission to Iran. See *FR 1944*, 5: 390–442.

[3] Five State Department officials, including Undersecretary of State Edward R. Stettinius, Jr., and Wallace Murray, Director of the Office of Near Eastern and African Affairs, had been sent to London on March 30 as a special mission to explore all outstanding Allied problems. See *FR 1944*, 3: 3ff.

[4] This issue had been raised at the Teheran conference. A year later, on December 8, 1944, Roosevelt recalled the circumstances in a memorandum to Secretary Hull: "The Teheran agreement [Declaration of the Three Powers Regarding Iran, December 1, 1943, signed by Churchill, Roosevelt, and Stalin] was pretty definite and my contribution was to suggest to Stalin and Churchill that three or four Trustees build a new port in Iran at the head of the Persian Gulf (free port), take over the whole [Iranian state] railroad from there into Russia, and run the thing for the good of all. Stalin's comment was merely that it was an interesting idea and he offered no objection." *FR 1944*, 5: 483. For the text of the declaration, see *Conferences at Cairo and Tehran*, pp. 646–647.

[5] The United Kingdom Commercial Corporation, an organization charged with the procurement of commodities for the Soviet Union for delivery through the Persian corridor. According to General Hurley, the Iranians claimed that the corporation had bought up war materials and now enjoyed a complete monopoly of their foreign trade.

[6] The British side of the story is in Woodward, *British Foreign Policy* (abridged ed.), pp. 314–316. American documents are in *FR 1944*, 5: 306–335.

I return General Hurley's memorandum, of which I have kept a copy.

Yours sincerely,

Doc. 366
ROOSEVELT TO CHURCHILL

No. 544   May 27, 1944

Your 682[1] received. I am in complete agreement with you that the French National Spirit should be working with us in Overlord to prevent unnecessary loss of American and British lives.

You are fully informed in regard to my belief that Allied military power should not be used to impose any particular group as the Government of the French people.

At the present time I am unable to see how an Allied establishment of the Committee as a government of France would save the lives of any of our men.

Any assistance that the Committee or any other Frenchmen can give to our Army of Liberation is of course highly desirable from our point of view as well as to the interest of France.

I am hopeful that your conversations with General de Gaulle will result in inducing him to actually assist in the liberation of France without being imposed by us on the French people as their Government.[2] Self-determination really means absence of coercion.

1 Not printed.
2 On May 26 the French Committee of National Liberation passed a measure by which it took the title of provisional government of the French republic. Meanwhile, on May 23, Churchill invited de Gaulle to come to London but suggested no specific date. De Gaulle arrived on June 3.

Doc. 367
ROOSEVELT TO CHURCHILL

No. 545   May 27, 1944

I propose that the Combined Chiefs of Staff be directed by both of us to send the following message to Eisenhower:

QUOTE. You are hereby directed to make such plans as are practicable to send American troops to the Netherlands and northwest

Germany as forces of occupation when hostilities with Germany cease. For planning purposes, the area in Germany to be occupied by U.S. forces will comprise the states of Schleswig, Hanover, Brunswick, Westphalia, Hesse-Nassau, and the Rhine province.

It will be assumed in this plan that France, Austria, and the Balkans will not be included in an American zone of responsibility and that Berlin will be occupied jointly by the U.S., British, and Soviet forces. UNQUOTE.[1]

[1] At Roosevelt's request, this message was drafted by General Marshall. After the President saw it, he returned it to Marshall with a recommendation that it first be sent to Churchill for his approval. It was never sent to Eisenhower.

Doc. 368
CHURCHILL TO ROOSEVELT

No. 686   May 31, 1944

Reference your number 545.[1] As you had not reverted to the question of the zones of occupation by our respective forces since I sent you my number 589 of 23rd February,[2] I had the impression that all this was settled.

It has however occurred to me that in sending your number 545 you might possibly have overlooked the arguments in my number 589 which, in our view, are just as cogent now as they were in February last.

I hope that if there has been a misunderstanding we can clear it up, as a change of policy such as you now propose would have grave consequences.[3]

[1] See above, Doc. 367.
[2] See above, Doc. 314.
[3] For Roosevelt's reply, see below, Doc. 370.

Doc. 369
CHURCHILL TO ROOSEVELT

No. 687   May 31, 1944

There have recently been disquieting signs of a possible divergence of policy between ourselves and the Russians in regard to the Balkan countries and in particular towards Greece. We therefore suggested to the Soviet Ambassador here that we should agree between ourselves as a practical matter that the Soviet Government would take the lead in Rumanian affairs, while we would take the lead in Greek affairs, each Government giving the other help in the respective countries. Such an arrangement would be a natural development of the existing military situation since Rumania falls within the sphere of the Russian armies and Greece within the Allied command under General Wilson in the Mediterranean.

The Soviet Ambassador here told Eden on May 18th that the Soviet Government agreed with this suggestion but before giving any final assurance in the matter they would like to know whether we had consulted the United States Government and whether the latter had also agreed to this arrangement.

I hope you may feel able to give this proposal your blessing. We do not of course wish to carve up the Balkans into spheres of influence and in agreeing to the arrangement we should make it clear that it applied only to war conditions and did not affect the rights and responsibilities which each of the three great powers will have to exercise at the peace settlement and afterwards in regard to the whole of Europe. The arrangement would of course involve no change in the present collaboration between you and us in the formulation and execution of Allied policy towards these countries. We feel, however, that the arrangement now proposed would be a useful device for preventing any divergence of policy between ourselves and them in the Balkans.

Meanwhile Halifax has been asked to raise this matter with the State Department on the above lines.[1]

1 Lord Halifax raised the issue with Hull on May 30; the Secretary of State advised that it would be unwise to abandon the broad declarations of policy, principles, and practice set forth by the Allied governments. In sum, he was opposed to spheres of influence. See Hull, *Memoirs*, 2: 1451–1453. Hull drafted the President's reply to Churchill of June 10. See below, Doc. 378.

Doc. 370
ROOSEVELT TO CHURCHILL

No. 549   June 2, 1944

Referring back to your message of February twenty-third, No. 589,[1] and in reply to your 686,[2] my telegram No. 457 of February seventh[3]

1 See above, Doc. 314.
2 See above, Doc. 368.
3 See above, Doc. 296.

on this subject contained the following statement: QUOTE I am absolutely unwilling to police France and possibly Italy and the Balkans as well UNQUOTE.

I am worried lest you also did not receive my letter to you of February twenty-ninth[4] and I was really waiting to hear from you in response to that letter of mine.

I am worried because I fear you did not get it and that that was the reason for your silence until the other day.

A good part of the letter does not refer to the subject but I am now quoting it to you in full lest it did not reach you. . . .

As a result of this exchange back in February and March, I believed until recently that at least tentative plans would be made for occupation of northwestern Germany by American forces.

I am just as strongly for this point of view as I was before, and your special problems can be perfectly easily handled on the naval side even if American forces are in northwest Germany.

In view of my clearly stated inability to police the south and southwestern areas now occupied by the Germans, I really think it is necessary that General Eisenhower shall even now make such plans as are practical to use American forces of occupation in northwestern Europe during the occupation period. Such plans as it is practicable for Eisenhower to prepare in advance would help to meet the contingency of your not being able to provide forces of occupation in all of the surrendered and liberated areas not occupied by the Soviets and of my inability to police the southern areas—France, Italy, etc.

There is ample time for this unless Germany suddenly collapses because, as you and I know, the present timetable proves the point.

Under my plan all of your needs can and will be taken care of in the northwest area, but I hope you will realize that I am in such a position that I cannot go along with the British General Staff plan. The reasons are political, as you well know, though, as a result, they enter necessarily into the military.

Over here new political situations crop up every day but so far, by constant attention, I am keeping my head above water.[5]

---

[4] See above, Doc. 318.

[5] This telegram was not answered by Churchill but was taken up at the second Quebec conference in September 1944.

June 1944
to
April 1945

Introduction to Part IV

". . . [W]hen the war of the giants is over, the wars of the pygmies will begin."

O N THE MORNING of June 6, 1944, Allied forces began their long and carefully planned invasion of Hitler's Europe.

Assisted by tactical surprise and vastly superior firepower in overcoming fierce German resistance, the Allied forces managed within a few days to establish a firm beachhead in Normandy. During the first forty-eight hours alone some 250,000 troops poured ashore, and despite the most strenuous efforts of Hitler's legions the Germans could not dislodge the Allied troops and drive them back into the sea. By breaching the elaborately constructed defenses of *Festung Europa*, the Allies thus scored a decisive initial victory in their struggle to destroy Nazi Germany. Stalin was undoubtedly correct when, in a generous message to Churchill on June 11, he hailed the successful invasion of Europe: "History will record this deed as an achievement of the highest order."

Yet the initial Allied victory did not lead immediately to further successes. Hitler had ordered his commanders in France to hold every foot of territory, and for nearly six weeks German forces managed to contain the Allied troops in their initial landing area. Nonetheless, for the Allies the delay was time well spent. By July 25 Allied troops in France numbered 1.45 million, of which 810,000 were Americans and 640,000 British and Canadians. On that date the Allies, aided once again by their overwhelming supremacy in men and firepower, could at last overturn enemy resistance and begin the strategic breakout that led them, by the last week of August, to the liberation of Paris and most of northern France. Between June and September the Germans suffered tremendous losses, including 400,000 killed, wounded, or taken prisoner, 1,300 tanks, 1,500 field guns, and 20,000 vehicles.

Although most of their time and energy was centered on destroying their Nazi foe, Churchill, Roosevelt, and de Gaulle did not allow D Day to witness any significant diminution of their behind-the-scenes hostility. Both during the initial stages of the Normandy invasion and for some weeks thereafter, the Prime Minister, the President, and the head of the Free French Committee were locked in one unpleasant dispute after another. On the eve of the initial landings de Gaulle refused General Eisenhower's request that he broadcast a message to the French people asking their support of the Allied invasion. Once the Allied forces were securely established in France, de Gaulle refused another request—to endorse the currency the Allied forces planned to circulate—thus imperiling the Allies' attempts to restore normal economic activity. Underlying his sometimes petty and annoying maneuvers was de Gaulle's determination to force Britain and the United States to recognize him as the head of liberated France. This role neither Roosevelt nor Churchill was prepared to accord him; and for several months the British and American leaders exchanged a long series of messages on how to deal with the obstructionist French general.

Italy posed problems of a very different sort for the President and the Prime Minister. Rome had been liberated on June 4, but after that date, while the Allies were scoring impressive gains in France, their forces in Italy found themselves stymied by fierce and effective German resistance. They were further handicapped when seven divisions were withdrawn to support Operation Anvil, the Allied landing in southern France, scheduled for August 15. Although such a diversionary landing had long been planned—indeed at the Teheran conference Roosevelt and Churchill had assured Stalin that a movement into southern France would be an integral part of the planned second front—Churchill now strongly opposed the withdrawal of troops from Italy for this purpose. He contended that the Allied forces in Italy could most effectively assist General Eisenhower by continuing to tie down and attack the substantial numbers of German troops still remaining in Italy. At first the British military chiefs strongly supported the Prime Minister, but after a visit from General Marshall on June 19, Field Marshal Sir Henry Maitland Wilson, the Mediterranean commander, came out in favor of proceeding with Anvil as scheduled.

When the Combined Chiefs of Staff became deadlocked on the question, Churchill appealed directly—and with characteristic eloquence—to Roosevelt. A dramatic exchange of messages ensued. At one point Roosevelt suggested that they lay their disagreement before

Stalin, but nothing came of this idea. At another, Churchill told Roosevelt that he regarded the decision to proceed with the invasion "as the first major strategical and political error for which we two have to be responsible." The President, however, refused to yield, and the Allied landing in southern France, renamed Operation Dragoon, took place as scheduled. Once ashore, the Allied forces moved ahead fairly rapidly. On August 25 French troops liberated Marseilles and Toulon, and on September 11 Allied forces coming up from the south to Dijon met Eisenhower's main army pressing down from the north.

For the Russians, the summer of 1944 was a time of almost unchecked advances, with significant military victories in Poland and in the Balkans following one another in rapid order. On July 3 the Russians took Minsk and on July 16 Vilna; on July 31 they occupied Kovno, the Lithuanian capital, and a month later took both Brest-Litovsk and Bucharest, as well as Ploesti, the heart of the Rumanian oil country.

The growing stalemate in Italy and the rapid westward advance of the Russian armies created a new series of problems for Roosevelt and Churchill. In the first place, Churchill, who had long wanted to mount a more substantial attack on Hitler's Europe from the Mediterranean, was much chagrined by the evident failure of the Allied armies, commanded by General Sir Harold Alexander, to make more rapid progress north of Rome. Indeed, the result of the Italian stalemate in the latter half of 1944 was to delay, if not to obliterate, Churchill's fond hopes for a significant push into the Po Valley, past Trieste and the Ljubljana gap in Yugoslavia—Churchill's objective always being to meet the Russian forces as far east as possible and to see Vienna liberated by British rather than Russian troops.

If Churchill was discomfited by his inability to change Roosevelt's mind on Dragoon, he was no less troubled by what he regarded as the increasingly dangerous political consequences of the rapid Russian advance to the west. As noted in the official American history of joint strategic planning, "by the summer of 1944 the war was entering a new era, and Churchill was already looking at the European continent with one eye on the retreating Germans and the other on the advancing Russians." Churchill's principal concern, of course, was that the advance of the Red Army would enable the Russians to impose Communist governments on large parts of Eastern Europe, a development that Churchill would oppose bitterly. The Prime Minister was especially concerned about events in Poland, where the Russians were apparently planning to install the Moscow-directed, Communist-dominated Committee of National Liberation, better known as the Lublin Committee, as the new Polish government.

Even in the busy months after D Day, Churchill's concern over the future of Poland was not an isolated aspect of his continuing interest in political matters. Indeed, hardly had the Allied forces landed in Normandy than Churchill began to concern himself, far more than Roosevelt, with the political and other internal affairs of friendly and formerly enemy countries. As early as June 10 he denounced the replacement of Marshal Pietro Badoglio as head of the Italian government by Ivanoe Bonomi, an old anti-Fascist leader. In the following months Britain began to play a far more interventionist role in Italian politics than Roosevelt was prepared to undertake. By November 1944 substantial differences developed between Washington and London over Italian political affairs, with Churchill in effect vetoing the appointment of Count Carlo Sforza as the new Italian Foreign Minister. Secretary of State Edward R. Stettinius, Jr., who succeeded Cordell Hull on December 1, refused to follow Churchill's lead, and the State Department issued a communiqué—to which Churchill took strong exception—describing Sforza's appointment as "purely an internal affair."

Palmiro Togliatti, the veteran Communist leader, returned to Italy after years of exile in Moscow in April 1944 and became Deputy Prime Minister in November 1944. But Churchill evidently was not disturbed by the prospect of Communist gains in Italy. There were no Communist troops in Italy, which was in any case still under the nominal control of an Allied military government.

In Poland and elsewhere in Eastern Europe the situation was very different, and it was the political future of those areas, newly taken over by the Red Army, that most immediately troubled Churchill. Yet the Prime Minister was agreeable to Russian control of some parts of Eastern Europe. Shortly after the Allied landings in France Roosevelt and Churchill disagreed over a British proposal, only recently revealed to Roosevelt, for an Anglo-Soviet agreement on spheres of influence in the Balkans. As Churchill explained the matter, in the spring of 1944 Anthony Eden, the British Foreign Secretary, made "a general suggestion . . . that the U.S.S.R. should temporarily regard Rumanian affairs as mainly their concern under war conditions, while leaving Greece" to Great Britain's direction. On May 30 the State Department told Lord Halifax, the British ambassador in Washington, that the United States was unwilling to approve the proposed arrangement, and on June 10 Roosevelt formally informed Churchill of the U.S. position. The Prime Minister declared himself "most concerned" by Roosevelt's response. For the moment, however, he stood his ground, arguing that "events will always outstrip the changing situation in these Balkan regions. Somebody must have the power to plan and act."

In the end Churchill let the matter drop, but this did not solve the question of the political status of liberated areas. Churchill continued to be concerned about the future of Eastern Europe, but his interest was initially as pragmatic as it was ideological. Churchill became deeply involved in Greek affairs in order to prevent a Communist takeover in that country, while in neighboring Yugoslavia he was willing to support Marshal Tito, the Communist guerrilla leader, and to urge Tito to collaborate with Dr. Ivan Subasić, Prime Minister of the Yugoslav government-in-exile in London. On August 12–13, Churchill conferred at Naples with both Tito and Subasić. The results of the meeting, as he indicated to Roosevelt, seemed satisfactory. If he had any premonition of future difficulty with the Yugoslav Communist leader, no suggestion of it appeared at this time. Roosevelt, in turn, congratulated Churchill on his "prospect of success in bringing together the opposing factions in Yugoslavia." As Churchill recalled later: "Tito assured me that, as he had stated publicly, he had no desire to introduce the Communist system into Yugoslavia, if only because most European countries after the war would probably be living under a democratic regime. . . . I asked Tito if he would reaffirm his statement about communism in public, but he did not wish to do this as it might seem to have been forced upon him." Tito's reply evidently satisfied Churchill.

Poland remained a far more intractable issue. Both Britain and the United States continued to recognize the Polish government-in-exile as the legitimate government of that country. But it was not long before Roosevelt and Churchill had to wrestle with the problem of how to bring about an agreement between the London Poles, headed by Stanislaw Mikolajczyk, and the Lublin Committee. It seems clear that both Roosevelt and Churchill hoped that some sort of compromise could be arranged between Mikolajczyk and Stalin. They viewed with a mixture of anticipation and concern Mikolajczyk's repeated trips to Moscow to confer with the Russian leader, hoping that the two could find some *modus vivendi*. But as 1944 drew to a close, with Russian troops taking control of additional Polish territory, it became evident that Stalin would not agree to anything beyond superficial changes in the Communist-sponsored Polish regime.

Another aspect of the Polish situation that troubled Churchill and Roosevelt was the Russian attitude toward the heroic Warsaw uprising of August 1, 1944. The attack on German forces by the Warsaw underground seems to have been inspired not only by the proximity of the Russian army but also by calls to arms broadcast over Russian-controlled radio stations. Yet once the partisan uprising began, the Russians refused to accelerate their efforts to liberate Warsaw. Also, following an acrimonious exchange between Churchill and Stalin, they refused to allow American or British aircraft to land on Russian airfields after raiding German positions in the Warsaw area or dropping supplies to the embattled partisans. As a result, the Warsaw uprising was doomed almost from the start, and after a magnificent struggle the underground was brutally crushed by the Germans early in October; thousands of surviving resistance fighters were shipped off to extermination camps.

Whatever its actual or symbolic importance, the Warsaw struggle was soon overshadowed by the great international conferences. From August 21 to October 9 representatives of the United States, Britain, the Soviet Union, and China gathered at Dumbarton Oaks, formerly the estate of Mr. and Mrs. Robert Woods Bliss, in Washington to draw up plans for a postwar international organization to keep the peace. Although Roosevelt and Churchill were not closely involved in the detailed work of the conference—indeed between September 11 and September 19 they were meeting at Quebec and Hyde Park—they were greatly concerned over two issues that divided the Dumbarton Oaks conferees. In the first place, the Russians proposed that each of the sixteen Soviet republics be given a seat in the General Assembly of the new organization. Second, the British proposed that in the Security Council the great powers not be able to veto decisions in cases in which they were involved; eventually the United States came to support this proposal. As regards the seating problem, Roosevelt persuaded Stalin to postpone the issue until the next summit conference; on the question of voting procedures, no final agreement was reached. Churchill began to change his mind, however, under the influence of Jan Christiaan Smuts, the distinguished Prime Minister of South Africa. In a letter to Churchill in September Smuts declared that "the principle of unanimity among the great powers has much to recommend it at least for the years immediately following on this war. If this principle proves unworkable in practice the situation could subsequently be reviewed when mutual confidence had been established and a more workable basis laid down."

While the Dumbarton Oaks conference was in session, Roosevelt and Churchill and their advisers met for the second time at Quebec, from September 11 to 16, and then on September 18–19 at Hyde Park. The two men were understandably buoyed by the triumphant advance of the Allied forces in Western and Eastern Europe. The late summer of 1944 had witnessed the liberation of Paris (August 25), Marseilles and Toulon (August 28), Bucharest (August 31), and Antwerp (September 4). Also, armistices were signed with Finland (September 4) and Bulgaria (September 8), followed by the landing of British troops in Greece on October 4. Roosevelt and Churchill reached speedy agreement on British participation in the war against Japan, on modification of the Italian armistice, and on the final zones of occupation in western Germany. In addition, the British heard with satisfaction Secretary of the Treasury Henry Morgenthau's proposal that Britain should receive $3.5 billion in lend-lease assistance between the end of the war in Europe and the defeat of Japan, along with a loan of $3 billion for nonmilitary purposes. On the other hand, to the regret of Churchill and his colleagues, it was agreed that no additional forces were to be assigned to the Mediterranean area and that the United States would not participate in the liberation of Greece.

The most spectacular event of the second Quebec conference was the proposal, likewise advanced by Secretary Morgenthau, for the dismantling of German industry after the war and the "pastoralization" of its economy. Churchill, who had had no advance notice of Morgenthau's plan, "at first . . . violently opposed this idea" but subsequently joined Roosevelt in initialing a memorandum for its approval. A few days later, however, word of the scheme leaked out, and public opposition was so immediate and widespread that Roosevelt and Churchill quickly dropped the plan.

The future of Poland—and for that matter the postwar governance of the Balkans—was not discussed at length at Quebec or Hyde Park. But by the time Churchill returned to London he realized that the continued advance of the Red Army made Eastern Europe a subject that could not be postponed much longer. Since Roosevelt—then in the midst of an increasingly active campaign for a fourth term in the White House—found it impossible, as well as politically undesirable, to hold another summit conference with Stalin before January, Churchill, accompanied by Eden, set off for Moscow once more.

Roosevelt evidently viewed Churchill's trip with some misgivings. He may have been worried that Churchill and Stalin would agree to a division of the Balkans into spheres of influence, the sort of postwar agreement that Roosevelt generally opposed as unwise and premature. And indeed no sooner had Churchill and Stalin commenced their discussions in the Kremlin on October 9 than the Prime Minister proposed, and Stalin at once accepted, just this sort of political formula for the Balkans. The details of the arrangement appear not to have been communicated to Roosevelt.

Churchill was greatly satisfied to learn, as he wrote later, "that the Soviets intended to enter the war against Japan as soon after the defeat of Germany as they could collect the necessary forces and supplies in the Far East." He cabled Roosevelt, while flying home on October 22, that there had been fruitful and productive discussions on a wide range of other issues, from the treatment of war criminals to the revision of the Montreux Convention of 1936, governing the passage of warships through the Dardanelles.

On one subject only—Poland—had progress been limited or uncertain. "Under dire threats," as Churchill put it in a message to Harry Hopkins on October 12, he had "persuaded" Mikolajczyk to come immediately from London to Moscow. At the meeting, Churchill tried to browbeat the Polish Prime Minister into accepting the Curzon line as the new Russo-Polish frontier and to move the London Poles toward an agreement with the Lublin Committee. On the other hand, he sought to persuade Stalin that unless Mikolajczyk "had 50/50 plus himself the Western world would not be convinced that the transaction was bona fide and would not believe that an independent Polish government had been set up." Churchill may have come away from Moscow believing that his political negotiations with Stalin were destined to bear lasting fruit, but the events of the next few months certainly disabused him of that comforting notion.

The closing months of 1944 marked a period of notable Allied successes, as well as a number of setbacks. In mid-September the Allies failed in a dramatic attempt to secure the key Rhine bridgehead at Arnhem. Even more serious was Hitler's last desperate attempt, in the middle of December, to attack the weak American position in the Ardennes and to drive to the river Meuse and ultimately to Antwerp, thus cutting the Allied line in two and in effect threatening the entire Allied left flank. Aided by tactical surprise and calling upon massed remnants of Hitler's air and ground forces as well as numerous agents disguised in Allied uniforms, the Germans at first scored some impressive and ominous gains. But before Christmas the worst was past, and by the end of December the American forces, which had been bearing the brunt of Hitler's attack, were able to take up the counteroffensive. By the end of January 1945 the Germans were driven back almost to their starting positions, with heavy losses.

But the setbacks at Arnhem and the battle of the Bulge, disappointing and even threatening as they appeared to be, were nothing compared with the steady inroads the Allies continued to make on German-held territory, even though opposition stiffened as they neared the frontiers of the Reich. In the weeks and months after Quebec the Allies took Sofia (September 18), Reval and Tallinn (September 21–22), Calais (September 30), Riga (October 13), Athens and Corfu (October 15), Petsamo (October 17), Belgrade (October 19), Aachen (October 20), Salonika (November 2), Mulhouse (November 21), Metz and Belfort (November 22), Strasbourg (November 23), and Ravenna (December 5). Allied forces landed on Leyte (October 22), triumphed in the battle of Leyte Gulf (October 23–26), sank the German battleship *Tirpitz* (November 12), reopened Antwerp harbor (December 3), began a new offensive in the Baltic

(December 22), encircled Budapest (December 24), and broke the German siege of Bastogne (December 27).

Despite all these achievements, Churchill became increasingly concerned about the pace of Allied progress. On December 6—about ten days before the beginning of the German offensive in the Ardennes— he sent Roosevelt a long and gloomy assessment of the Allied military situation in Europe and the Far East, remarking on "the serious and disappointing war situation which faces us at the close of the year. . . . [W]e have definitely failed to achieve the strategic object which we gave to our armies five weeks ago." Roosevelt responded: "Perhaps I am not close enough to the picture to feel as disappointed about the war situation as you are, and also because six months ago I was not as optimistic as you were on the time element."

It is idle to speculate on what had led Churchill to this assessment of the military situation, although he could have had in mind a variety of political and military conditions. His and Roosevelt's endlessly trying relationship with General de Gaulle was scarcely improved by the American and British recognition of his provisional French government as the de facto government of that country. Also, Churchill was distressed by mounting disorder in Italy, the deteriorating political situation in Poland, the alarming military condition of the Burma-China theater, and, above all, the growing crisis in Greece, which early in December erupted into Communist revolt and open civil war. Throughout these developments, Churchill was obliged to watch Britain's limited resources being steadily drained away, while Roosevelt declined to give any assurances of postwar American support and while British policy—in Italy and Greece particularly—was being subjected to increasing American criticism and left-wing opposition at home.

Churchill and Roosevelt had already exchanged some rather strongly worded messages on the Italian political situation, and the Prime Minister was no less passionate in replying to his critics in the House of Commons on the Greek question on December 8: "We are told that because we do not allow gangs of heavily armed guerrillas to descend from the mountains and install themselves, with all the bloody terror and vigour of which they are capable, in power in great capitals, we are traitors to democracy. I repulse that claim. . . ." For all his concern, Churchill avoided the larger international implications of the Greek Communist revolt, in particular the question of whether it marked the onset of a new relationship of hostile confrontation between the Western democracies and their Communist ally.

In any event, when Churchill asked his government for a vote of confidence, the House of Commons supported him 279–30, and his political victory gained him a congratulatory message from Roosevelt as well. But Churchill did not take time to wait for assurances. When the Greek Communist rebels disobeyed the order of General Ronald Scobie to evacuate Athens and Piraeus and replied by attempting to seize control of the capital, Churchill informed the British commander that "we have to hold and dominate Athens. It would be a great thing for you to succeed in this without bloodshed if possible, but also with bloodshed if necessary." A few days later, an American journalist published virtually an exact copy of the Churchill message, an action that stoked still further the disagreement on both sides of the Atlantic. Churchill must have been particularly dismayed when, shortly after, he received a message from Roosevelt saying, "No one will understand better than yourself that I, both personally and as head of state, am necessarily responsive to the state of public feeling. It is for these reasons that it has not been possible for this Government to take a stand along with you in the present course of events in Greece."

By the end of December Churchill was able to establish a semblance of political order in Greece. Flying to Athens with Eden on December 28, he persuaded King George II to appoint Archbishop Damaskinos as regent. The Archbishop was expected to form a new government without Communists and to continue the struggle against them until Athens was free of guerrillas or until the Communists had agreed to a ceasefire.

On December 30 King George finally stepped aside, and by early January the Communist forces realized the futility of further military action against superior British military power. Early in January the Communists retreated from the Athens-Piraeus area, but not before they "had carried out mass executions in areas under [their] control and taken perhaps as many as 30,000 hostages from Attica alone. . . . [A]lmost 4,000 of these victims of [Communist] brutality were destined to die in the hands of their captors."

There were renewed Allied military victories in the first months of 1945: American forces landed on Luzon (January 9), the Russians broke through German lines on the Vistula (January 12), the Germans had to evacuate Warsaw (January 17), the Russians crossed the Oder River in Lower Silesia (January 23), American forces reached the German border (January 27), and another American detachment liberated Manila (February 4). These victories, along with their mounting political problems and disagreements, prompted Roosevelt and Churchill to arrange to meet Stalin for a second time at Yalta in the Crimea early in February 1945.

Arrangements for the Yalta meeting proved to be as involved and time-consuming as preparations for the Teheran conference fourteen months earlier. Roosevelt and Churchill planned to meet at Malta on the way to the Crimea, but Roosevelt arrived only at the last moment and no significant discussions were held on the island. Once convened at Yalta, the Big Three plunged into a week of strenuous meetings, making substantial progress on most of the issues before them. Even so, the other conferees showed concern about Roosevelt's physical appearance and condition and wondered whether he was prepared for the urgent matters before the conference.

In the end Roosevelt, Churchill, and Stalin accepted the American formula for voting procedures in the Security Council of the United Nations organization and agreed on separate seats in the General Assembly for the Ukraine and White Russia. They set April 25 as the opening date for a conference in San Francisco to prepare a charter for the new international body. The Big Three provided for a French zone of occupation in Germany, issued a Declaration on Liberated Europe, and agreed on the conditions under which a new Polish government was to be formed. Finally, they agreed that the Russians should join the war against Japan within two or three months of the German surrender and that in return they would receive substantial territorial compensation, including Port Arthur and southern Sakhalin—territories that Russia had lost at the end of the Russo-Japanese war of 1904–1905. This last agreement was worked out in the strictest secrecy between Roosevelt and Stalin, and not even Secretary of State Stettinius was informed about it. Churchill signed the accords with considerable reluctance.

When Roosevelt and Churchill returned home, the Yalta agreements—or the part of them made known at the time—were almost unanimously hailed. Churchill told the House of Commons: "The impression I brought back from the Crimea, and from all my other contacts, is that Marshal Stalin and the Soviet leaders wish to live in honourable friendship and equality with the Western democracies. I feel also that their word is their bond." Roosevelt addressed a joint session of Congress in equally optimistic terms on March 1.

For the time being, public response to the Yalta agreements on both sides of the Atlantic was one of satisfaction and hope. Allied military victories in Europe now came with mounting rapidity. Russian forces captured Budapest (February 13), and American troops breached the main Siegfried line (February 14). In March Eisenhower's forces crossed the Rhine and occupied Cologne (March 7) and Frankfurt (March 29), while the Russians captured Brandenburg (March 20), occupied Danzig and entered Austria (March 30). In the Pacific, too, the weeks following Yalta witnessed a succession of major Allied victories. American forces landed on Iwo Jima (February 19), on Panay (March 19), and on Okinawa (April 1). By April 7 Russian forces had entered Vienna, and on April 9 the Allies began their last offensive in Italy.

In his memoirs of World War II Anthony Eden recorded that "at Yalta the Russians had seemed relaxed and, so far as we could judge, friendly. . . . Within a few weeks all that had changed." Even at Yalta Roosevelt was concerned that the concession of three votes to the Soviet Union in the General Assembly would be badly received at home, and as if to prepare for such an eventuality, he wrote to Churchill (and in similar vein to Stalin) that he might find it "necessary to work out some way of giving the United States additional votes in order to ensure parity." Both Churchill and Stalin—the latter even more explicitly—agreed at once to Roosevelt's request.

But the public outcry that greeted the disclosure of Roosevelt's concession on the voting-rights issue (the United States having refrained from pressing a claim to additional votes in the General Assembly) was only one of the problems that developed between the Western Allies and the Soviet Union. The Prime Minister was perturbed to learn of the Americans' intention to sign a bilateral air agreement with the Republic of Ireland. And there remained problems of strategy and tactics in the embattled Burma-China theater, where Allied forces were doing considerably less well than in Europe or in other parts of the Pacific.

There also remained questions of military and psychological tactics in Europe, including the possibility of issuing a proclamation to the German army and people to rise against their leaders and the matter of how to protect the populace in German-occupied areas against last-minute brutalities and terror. On March 29 Roosevelt suggested that heavily armed, unmanned bombers be launched against Germany, but Churchill and his advisers successfully resisted the plan. Roosevelt had not forgotten about Greece, and late in March he proposed that a tripartite economic mission assist that broken country to return to some degree of normalcy. Churchill, for his part, was outraged by the Communist coup in Rumania, directed by Soviet Deputy Foreign Minister Andrei Vyshinsky, at the end of February. In truth, there was little that he and Roosevelt could hope to accomplish on this front, especially since Churchill had made an agreement with Stalin in Moscow in October 1944 giving 90 percent predominance in Rumania to the Russians.

The Communist coup in Rumania was only one source of friction among the Big Three. In the weeks after Yalta W. Averell Harriman, Roosevelt's trusted ambassador in Moscow, began to bombard the President with a series of messages indicating that the Russians' formal courtesy was rapidly turning into a total lack of cooperation. For example, the Russians were reluctant to assist with the repatriation of liberated American prisoners of war in Poland, leading Roosevelt, on

March 17, to send a stiff message to Stalin: "This Government had done everything possible to meet each of your requests. I now request you to meet mine in this particular matter." Stalin was unmoved by Roosevelt's message and sent the President an evasive reply. Early in April Stalin accused Roosevelt and Churchill of conducting secret peace negotiations with the Germans in Switzerland, to which Roosevelt replied, with considerable heat, that he resented these "vile misrepresentations."

It was Poland, however, long the focal point of East-West differences, that became and remained the center of bitter disagreement between Roosevelt, Churchill, and Stalin. The President and the Prime Minister regarded the Polish question, not incorrectly, as symbolic of the future relations of the Big Three powers. Although the Russians sought to exclude British and American observers from Poland, it was clear that the Communist authorities in charge there were rapidly silencing or liquidating their opponents, and there remained no hope of the "free and unfettered elections" agreed on at Yalta.

In the voluminous messages that crossed the Atlantic in March and early April, Churchill pressed for the strongest possible protests against Russian violations of the Yalta agreements. Roosevelt, on the other hand, seemed for a time to hang back, reluctant to address himself to Stalin when he sensed that his appeals would meet with no positive response. Roosevelt's reluctance led Churchill at one point, almost in despair, to warn the President: "We realise how hopeless the position would become for Poland if it were ever known that we were not in full accord."

Recent evidence suggests that Roosevelt was by no means indifferent to the information reaching him from Ambassador Harriman, who cautioned the President on April 3 that "failure to stand our ground is interpreted as a sign of weakness." On April 6 Roosevelt came to the conclusion—as he put it to Churchill—that "our armies will in a very few days be in a position that will permit us to become 'tougher' than has heretofore appeared advantageous to the war effort." Even so, to Churchill's dismay, Roosevelt—and his military chiefs, who accepted as binding the political agreements Roosevelt had previously entered into—continued to resist Churchill's desire to march on to Berlin or to seize Vienna and Prague. In short, Roosevelt did not agree with Churchill's insistence that the Western allies meet the Russians as far east as possible, in order to reap whatever political advantages such gains might give the United States and Britain in the postwar world.

In virtually his last message to Churchill, drafted by himself and sent on April 11, Roosevelt expressed his desire to "minimize the

general Soviet problem as much as possible because these problems
. . . seem to straighten out. . . . We must be firm, however, and our
course thus far is correct."

The following afternoon, April 12, 1945, at Warm Springs, Georgia,
where he had gone for an extended rest, President Roosevelt died
suddenly of a cerebral hemorrhage.

Messages and Notes

Doc. 371
ROOSEVELT TO CHURCHILL

No. 550

June 6, 1944

Your 691.[1] I am in full agreement with you as to the high desirability of reopening the northern convoys to Russia at the earliest practicable date after the results of Overlord[2] are known to us.

We should give to the Soviet attack on Germany all the support and assistance that we can provide.[3]

[1] Not printed.

[2] Operation Overlord, the Allied invasion of Europe, began early on the morning of June 6.

[3] A massive new Russian offensive was launched on June 22. See Earl F. Ziemke, *Stalingrad to Berlin: The German Defeat in the East* (Washington, 1968), pp. 319ff.

Doc. 372
CHURCHILL TO ROOSEVELT

No. 694   June 7, 1944

You will have seen from Eisenhower's No. SH 2511[1] part of General de Gaulle's activities over here. He has arrived without the three commissioners, Massigli,[2] Le Troquer,[3] and d'Astier,[4] whom we understood he was going to bring. This is to make clear his position that he will not discuss the civil administration of France only with us, and that an American representative fully charged must be present.

You have probably been informed of his attitude in refusing to allow the French liaison officers to go with our forces into France until the civil administration question has been settled. Under severe pressure from the Foreign Secretary[5] he consented at last to broadcast, though not in Eisenhower's series.[6] You will no doubt read the broadcast for yourself. It is remarkable, as he has not a single soldier in the great battle now developing. Further, he has also modified his attitude about the liaison officers and will allow some of them to go. It is probable that all would go in any case, whatever he said, if called upon by General Eisenhower and their British and American comrades.

I can assure you that every courtesy and personal attention was lavished upon General de Gaulle. After a full discussion with his two generals and Monsieur Viénot,[7] his representative here, we have had

1 On June 4 General Dwight D. Eisenhower, supreme commander of the Allied Expeditionary Force for Overlord, informed the Combined Chiefs of Staff that de Gaulle had arrived in London "anxious to assist in every possible way. . . . As a result of conferences on military subjects attended by the Prime Minister, General de Gaulle, my Chief of Staff, and others, General de Gaulle has agreed to prepare a broadcast on the lines suggested by us." Alfred D. Chandler, Jr., *et al.* eds., *The Papers of Dwight David Eisenhower: The War Years* (Baltimore and London, 1970), vol. 3, no. 1733. Hereafter cited as *PDDE*.

2 René Massigli, Free French Minister of Foreign Affairs.

3 André Le Troquer, Free French Minister of War and Air and civil delegate to Supreme Headquarters, Allied Expeditionary Force.

4 Emmanuel R. d'Astier de la Vigerie, Free French Minister of the Interior.

5 Anthony Eden.

6 For the background of de Gaulle's address, see *The Complete War Memoirs of Charles de Gaulle*, 2 (New York, 1964): 254ff. Henceforth cited as de Gaulle, *War Memoirs*. See also *PDDE*, vol. 3, no. 1907, note 3; Arthur Layton Funk, *De Gaulle: The Crucial Years 1943–1944* (Norman, Okla., 1959), pp. 256ff.; and Forrest C. Pogue, *George C. Marshall: Organizer of Victory* (New York, 1973), p. 399.

7 Pierre Viénot, Free French ambassador to Great Britain.

luncheon in my train, and the Foreign Secretary and I then took him personally to see General Eisenhower at his headquarters in a woodland camp. Generals Eisenhower and Bedell Smith[8] went to the utmost limit in their endeavour to conciliate him, making it clear that in practice events would probably mean that the Committee would be the natural authority with whom the Supreme Commander would deal. It was after this that he proceeded to London and acted in the sense of my paras 1 and 2.

We are still persevering. We have told de Gaulle that if he sends for three or four of his commissioners, we will then begin conversations designed to clarify and smooth the difficulties about the civil administration in France. Meanwhile, I have assured General Eisenhower that we will certainly support him in making the necessary proclamation about currency.

It is not impossible that the commissioners will differ from de Gaulle and may show themselves disposed to make friendly arrangements with the American and British Governments. There might even be a sort of isolation of de Gaulle.

If he refuses to send for the commissioners, we shall suggest he had better go back to Algiers. If he accepts, I hope you will consider whether Winant[9] might not sit in in order to give you an American slant on the talks. After this we will let you know what our view is. I have repeatedly told de Gaulle and he acknowledged it without irritation that failing an agreement, I stand with you.

Supposing all this fails, we shall express the hope that he will return to Algiers and then later proceed to Washington as the result of your message sent through Admiral Fénard[10] or if he cares he can stay here and proceed by the dates named. I think it would be a great pity if you and he did not meet. I do not see why I should have all the luck.

[8] Lieutenant General Walter Bedell Smith, Eisenhower's Chief of Staff.

[9] John G. Winant, U.S. ambassador to Great Britain.

[10] Vice Admiral Raymond Fénard, chief of the French naval mission to the United States.

Doc. 373
CHURCHILL TO ROOSEVELT

No. 696

June 9, 1944

I want to know your wishes about the notes[1] issued for the troops in France. Eisenhower has urgent need to make a proclamation announc-

[1] The currency to be issued by Allied forces liberating France.

ing it. De Gaulle is quite ready to make a supporting proclamation but there is reason to expect he will press for his proclamation to contain the words "provisional government of France" or "of the French Republic" and publish it in the *Official Journal of the French Republic* which he produces at Algiers. We shall naturally endeavour to persuade him to stick to the French Committee of National Liberation but he fights at every point. The Treasury fear that if he does not endorse the issue, the notes will have no backing behind them and alternatively I feel that Eisenhower's proclamation will commit our two Governments jointly or separately to redeem them. How does this stand in your mind?

Others even say that he might denounce the notes as false money. I do not myself think that he will dare. I should myself think, if I were a French shopkeeper, that a note printed in the United States tendered to me by a British or American soldier and declared legal by General Eisenhower was well worth having whether de Gaulle endorsed it or not.

Would you please let me know what is your view? Shall we get de Gaulle to take responsibility for these notes as President of the provisional government of France in which case the French nation will ultimately face the problem of redeeming them? Or shall we say the United States and Great Britain assume responsibility for these notes and will fix the ultimate responsibility at the peace settlement? I should be grateful for an early answer.

Doc. 374
CHURCHILL TO ROOSEVELT

No. 697   June 9, 1944

Further to my No. 696.[1] I have now seen the specimens of the notes in question. They do not strike us as very reassuring. They look very easy to forge. Nothing is said on whose responsibility they are issued and who is responsible for redeeming them. Surely there must be some authority behind them.

These views expressed after seeing the notes affect paragraph 2 of my No. 696 and make it all the more necessary that someone should take responsibility for meeting them when they are presented. Please, my dear friend, look at them for yourself and say what we ought to do. Should we let de Gaulle obtain new status as his price for backing

1 See above, Doc. 373.

these notes or should we take the burden on ourselves for the time being and improve the issue later on and settle up at the peace table where there will be many accounts to be presented?[2]

2 For Roosevelt's reply, see below, Doc. 382.

Doc. 375
ROOSEVELT TO CHURCHILL

No. 556   June 9, 1944

Your 694[1] received. It appears that de Gaulle is performing in accordance with his previous record of lack of cooperation in our effort to liberate France.

He may visit Washington at the end of this month or about mid-July but there is no indication yet that he will be helpful in our efforts in the interest of his country. I will do my best to attract his interest to the Allied war effort.

1 See above, Doc. 372.

Doc. 376
CHURCHILL TO ROOSEVELT

No. 698   June 10, 1944

I have received the following from U.J.:[1]

"I have received your message of the 7th June with the information of the successful development of the operation Overlord. We all greet you and the valiant British and American armies and warmly wish you further successes.

"The preparation of the summer offensive of the Soviet armies is concluding. Tomorrow, the 10th June, the first stage will open in our summer offensive on the Leningrad front."

1 Uncle Joe—Joseph V. Stalin.

Doc. 377
CHURCHILL TO ROOSEVELT

No. 699   June 10, 1944

I think it is a great disaster that Badoglio should be replaced by this group of aged and hungry politicians.[1] He has been a useful instrument to us from the time when he delivered the fleet, in spite of the enemy, safely into our hands. I thought it was understood that he was to go on, at any rate till we could bring the democratic north in and have a thoroughly sound Italian government. Instead we are confronted with this absolutely unrepresentative collection. As far as I can make out, the Italian Advisory Committee[2] have not been consulted. I have had no opportunity of bringing the matter before the Cabinet, nor I suppose have you had much time to consider it. I was not aware, at this present time, that we had conceded to the Italians who have cost us so dear in life and material the power to form any government they chose without reference to the victorious powers, and without the slightest pretence of a popular mandate. I take a most serious view of the situation, and I hope before you take a final decision you will let me know your views and give me an opportunity of replying.

[1] The government of Marshal Pietro Badoglio in Italy had been succeeded by a coalition Cabinet on June 8. See Harold Macmillan, *The Blast of War 1939–1945* (London, 1967), pp. 499–501.

[2] The Italian Advisory Council had been established at the foreign ministers' conference in Moscow in October 1943. According to Annex 3 of the secret protocol of the conference, signed on November 1, the council was to "have the duty in particular of watching the machinery of control in Italy which will be enforcing the terms of surrender" and was to advise the Allied commander in chief, General Eisenhower, "on general policy connected with the work of control." U.S. Department of State, *Foreign Relations of the United States 1943*, 1 (Washington, 1963): 758. Henceforth cited as *FR*. The initial members of the council included Robert D. Murphy (U.S.A.), Harold Macmillan (U.K.), Andrei Vyshinsky, succeeded by Alexander Bogolomov (U.S.S.R.), and René Massigli (French Committee of National Liberation). For an informative account of the council's troubled history, see Macmillan, *Blast of War*, pp. 467ff.

Doc. 378
ROOSEVELT TO CHURCHILL

No. 557   June 10, 1944

The proposed agreement between your Government and Russia concerning Rumania and Greece, outlined in your telegram No. 687

of May 31,[1] was discussed by Lord Halifax[2] with Mr. Hull[3] on May 30. The State Department has communicated to Lord Halifax the reasons why this Government is unwilling to approve the proposed arrangement. Briefly, we acknowledge that the militarily responsible government in any given territory will inevitably make decisions required by military developments but are convinced that the natural tendency for such decisions to extend to other than military fields would be strengthened by an agreement of the type suggested. In our opinion, this would certainly result in the persistence of differences between you and the Soviets and in the division of the Balkan region into spheres of influence despite the declared intention to limit the arrangement to military matters.

We believe efforts should preferably be made to establish consultative machinery to dispel misunderstandings and restrain the tendency toward the development of exclusive spheres.

[1] See above, Doc. 369.
[2] British ambassador to the United States.
[3] Cordell Hull, U.S. Secretary of State.

Doc. 379
CHURCHILL TO ROOSEVELT

No. 700   June 11, 1944

I am much concerned to receive your number 557.[1] Action is paralysed if everybody is to consult everybody else about everything before it is taken. The events will always outstrip the changing situations in these Balkan regions. Somebody must have the power to plan and act. A consultative committee would be a mere obstruction, always overridden in any case of emergency by direct interchanges between you and me, or either of us and Stalin.

See, now, what happened at Easter when I had charge not only of the Foreign Office but of the British armed forces. We were able to cope with this mutiny of the Greek forces entirely in accordance with your own views.[2] This was because I was able to give constant orders to the military commanders, who at the beginning advocated conciliation and, above all, no use or even threat of force. Very little life was lost. The Greek situation has been immensely improved and, if firmness is maintained, will be rescued from confusion and disaster. The Russians are ready to let us take the lead in the Greek business,

[1] See above, Doc. 378.
[2] See above, Doc. 354, note 1.

which means that EAM[3] and all its malice can be controlled by the national forces of Greece. Otherwise, civil war and ruin to the land you care about so much. I always reported to you and I always will report to you. You shall see every telegram I send. I think you might trust me in this.

Similarly, troubles arose in Egypt, where King Farouk wished to sack Nahas[4] and put in his court minister to rig the elections. This might easily have led to widespread riots and disorder throughout Egypt. Here again the military advised that no action should be taken which involved the use of force. I was in a position to give the necessary orders to the military without having to consult anybody, and none is more pleased than they are at the result. Here again I kept you informed, and Lord Killearn[5] kept your Ambassador at Cairo[6] informed. All passed off happily without the slightest struggle.[7]

If, in either of these two difficulties, we had had to consult other powers and a set of triangular or quadrangular telegrams got started, the only result would have been chaos or impotence.

It seems to me, considering the Russians are about to invade Rumania in great force and are going to help Rumania recapture part of Transylvania from Hungary, provided the Rumanians play which they may, considering all that, it would be a good thing to follow the same leadership considering that neither you nor we have any troops there at all and that they will probably do what they like anyhow. Moreover I thought their terms, apart from indemnity, very sensible and even generous. The Rumanian army has inflicted many injuries upon the Soviet troops and went into the war against Russia with glee. I see no difficulty whatever in our addressing the Russians at any time on any subject, but please let them go ahead upon the lines agreed as they are doing all the work.

Similarly with us in Greece. We are an old ally of Greece. We had 40,000 casualties in trying to defend Greece against Hitler, not counting Crete. The Greek King[8] and the Greek Government have placed themselves under our protection. They are at present domiciled in Egypt. They may very likely move to the Lebanon which would be a better atmosphere than Cairo. Not only did we lose the 40,000 men

---

[3] The Greek National Liberation Front.

[4] Mustafa an-Nahas, Pasha, the Egyptian prime minister.

[5] British ambassador to Egypt.

[6] Alexander C. Kirk, U.S. ambassador to the government of Greece in Egypt and U.S. minister in Egypt.

[7] For an account of the political difficulties in Egypt in 1942, see Trefor E. Evans, ed., *The Killearn Diaries 1934–1946: The Diplomatic and Personal Record of Lord Killearn* (London, 1972), pp. 194ff.

[8] George II.

above mentioned in helping Greece, but a vast mass of shipping and warships, and by denuding Cyrenaica to help Greece, we also lost the whole of Wavell's[9] conquests in Cyrenaica. These were heavy blows to us in those days. Your telegrams to me in the recent crisis worked wonders. We were entirely agreed, and the result is entirely satisfactory. Why is all this effective direction to be broken up into a committee of mediocre officials such as we are littering about the world? Why can you and I not keep this in our own hands considering how we see eye to eye about so much of it?

To sum up, I propose that we agree that the arrangements I set forth in my number 687[10] may have a trial of three months, after which it must be reviewed by the three powers.

9 General Sir Archibald Wavell, commander in chief of British forces in the Middle East until June 1943.
10 See above, Doc. 369.

Doc. 380
ROOSEVELT TO CHURCHILL

No. 558   June 11, 1944

Your 699.[1] Before forming an opinion on this question I should like to have a recommendation[2] from the Italian Advisory Committee and General Wilson.[3]

1 See above, Doc. 377.
2 Churchill replied in full on June 11: "I entirely agree."
3 General Sir Henry Maitland Wilson, commander in chief of Allied Forces in the Mediterranean.

Doc. 381
CHURCHILL TO ROOSEVELT

No. 702   June 12, 1944

I have just received the following from Premier Stalin:

"1. I have received your message about the departure of Badoglio. To me, too, the departure of Badoglio was unexpected. It seemed to me that without the consent of the Allies, the British and the Americans, the removal of Badoglio and the appointment of Bonomi[1] could

1 Ivanoe Bonomi, head of the new Italian government.

not take place. From your message, however, it is evident that this took place regardless of the will of the Allies. One must assume that certain Italian circles purpose to make an attempt to change to their advantage the armistice conditions. In any case, if for you and the Americans circumstances suggest that it is necessary to have another government in Italy and not the Bonomi government, then you can count on there being no objections to this from the Soviet side.

"2. I have also received your message of the 10th June.[2] I thank you for the information. As is evident, the landing, conceived on a grandiose scale, has succeeded completely. My colleagues and I cannot but admit that the history of warfare knows no other like undertaking from the point of view of its scale, its vast conception, and its masterly execution. As is well known, Napoleon in his time failed ignominiously in his plan to force the channel. The hysterical Hitler, who boasted for two years that he would effect a forcing of the channel, was unable to make up his mind even to hint at attempting to carry out his threat. Only our allies have succeeded in realising with honour the grandiose plan of the forcing of the channel. History will record this deed as an achievement of the highest order."

2 In that message Churchill told Stalin: "The whole world can see the Tehran design appearing in our concerted attacks upon the common foe." Ministry of Foreign Affairs of the U.S.S.R., *Correspondence Between the Chairman of the Council of Ministers of the U.S.S.R. and the Presidents of the U.S.A. and the Prime Ministers of Great Britain During the Great Patriotic War of 1941–1945* (New York, 1958), vol. 1, no. 277. Henceforth cited as *Stalin's Correspondence*.

Doc. 382
ROOSEVELT TO CHURCHILL

No. 559   June 12, 1944

I share your view that this currency issue is being exploited to stampede us into according full recognition to the Comité.[1] Personally I do not think the currency situation referred to in your cable[2] is as critical as it might first appear, nor do I feel that it is essential from the point of view of the acceptability of the supplemental currency that de Gaulle make any statement of support with respect to such currency. I propose that de Gaulle should be informed as follows:

We intend to continue to use the supplementary franc currency in exactly the same manner as we have planned and as we have agreed

1 The French Committee of National Liberation, headed by General de Gaulle.
2 See above, Docs. 373 and 374.

with the British Treasury and as has been fully understood by Messrs. Monnet[3] and Mendès-France[4] of the French Comité.

If for any reason the supplementary currency is not acceptable to the French public, General Eisenhower has full authority to use yellow seal dollars and British military authority notes. Accordingly, if de Gaulle incites the French people into refusing to accept supplementary francs then the Comité will have to bear the full responsibility for any bad effects resulting from the use of yellow seal notes and BMA[5] notes in France. One of the certain consequences will be the depreciation of the French franc in terms of dollars and sterling in a black market which will accentuate and reveal the weaknesses of the French monetary system. This is one of the important reasons why we accepted the request of the French Comité that we not use yellow seal dollars and BMA notes as a spearhead currency. There would be other adverse effects which would be apparent to de Gaulle and his advisers.

I would certainly not importune de Gaulle to make any supporting statement whatever regarding the currency. Provided it is clear that he acts entirely on his own responsibility and without our concurrence he can sign any statement on currency in whatever capacity he likes, even that of the King of Siam.

As far as the appearance of the notes is concerned, I have seen them before but I have looked at them again and think them adequate. I am informed by the Bureau of Engraving and Printing counterfeiting experts that they will be extremely difficult to counterfeit by virtue of the intricate color combination. I am also informed that the British Treasury officials approved the note and that the French representatives here not only approved the note but were satisfied with the designs and the color.

It seems clear that prima donnas do not change their spots.

[3] Jean Monnet, member of the French Committee of National Liberation and French representative in Washington.
[4] Pierre Mendès-France, member of the French Committee of National Liberation.
[5] British military authority.

Doc. 383
ROOSEVELT TO CHURCHILL

No. 560   June 12, 1944

Your 700.[1] I am in agreement with your proposal in paragraph seven of subject message.

[1] See above, Doc. 379.

We must be careful to make it clear that we are not establishing any postwar spheres of influence.

Doc. 384
CHURCHILL TO ROOSEVELT

No. 703   June 14, 1944

Your number 560.[1] I am deeply grateful to you for your reply to my number 700.[2] I have asked the Foreign Secretary to convey the information to Monsieur Molotov[3] and to make it clear that the reason for the three months' limit is in order that we should not prejudge the question of establishing postwar spheres of influence.

Your number 558.[4] Please note the remarks I had had on this question from Marshal Stalin. I share your opinion that the matter should be examined by the Joint Advisory Committee[5] and that they should report to the three Governments, who will consult together and give a united answer. Meanwhile Badoglio remains nominally in charge, and the delay in bringing the new government into office is to be explained by the needs of consulting the victorious powers. This is what Badoglio and Bonomi have, I believed, settled amicably at Salerno, whither they have both repaired. It appears that they are quite friendly and I see great difficulties in persuading Badoglio to resume the thankless task he has quitted, at his great age. I consider that if we cannot do this it will be detrimental to the interests of the Allies.

When de Gaulle arrived here at my invitation, in my first efforts to make him friendly I held out the hopes that he would plant his foot upon the soil of France. After making as much trouble for us as was in his power, he has now expressed a great desire that these should be made good. I have therefore consented that he should visit the British sector in France today, 14th, where he will be received by General Montgomery[6] at his headquarters and may possibly be allowed to go to Bayeux. No demonstrations will be permitted on military grounds, as crowds might attract bombardment. He will give no addresses there,

1 See above, Doc. 383.
2 See above, Doc. 379.
3 Vyacheslav M. Molotov, Soviet Foreign Minister.
4 See above, Doc. 380.
5 The Italian Advisory Council. See above, Doc. 377, note 2.
6 General Sir Bernard L. Montgomery, Commanding General of the Twenty-first Army Group, and of all the Allied ground forces in Normandy.

but a statement, which we shall have the power to censor, may be made on his return. I did not want to give him the grievance that we had refused him his desire to set foot on his native soil, and also I was a bit compromised myself by our first conversation. I imparted the above decision of mine, that he should go to our sector, to Eisenhower, and Bedell Smith, and the responsibility for it is mine. I hope you will not think I was wrong.

I understand that you issued a statement last night about the currency.[7] You may be sure I shall try to support you in every way. I am quite sure that if an old woman in Bayeux sells a cow to an American quartermaster and is paid in these notes, when she presents them at Morgenthau's[8] office in Washington he will have to see that she is no loser on the transaction. My information from France last night was that the French people are taking the notes.

I had a jolly day on Monday on the beaches and inland. There is a great mass of shipping extending more than fifty miles along the coast. It is being increasingly protected against weather by the artificial harbours, nearly every element of which has been a success, and will soon have effective shelter against bad weather. The power of our air and of our anti-U-boat forces seems to ensure it a very great measure of protection. After doing much laborious duty, we went and had a plug at the Hun from our destroyer, but although the range was 6,000 yards he did not honour us with a reply.

Marshall[9] and King[10] came back in my train. They were greatly reassured by all they saw on the American side, and Marshall wrote out a charming telegram to Dickie,[11] saying how many of these new craft had been produced under his organisation and what a help they had been. You used the word "stupendous" in one of your early telegrams to me. I must admit that what I saw could only be described by that word, and I think your officers would agree as well. The marvelous efficiency of the transportation exceeds anything that has ever been known in war. A great deal more has to be done, and I think more troops are needed. We are working up to a battle which may well

7 At his press conference on June 13 Roosevelt explained at length the issuance of special currency for American and British forces in France, adding: "As soon as there is an appropriate French authority recognized by the Allied governments, we will of course fully accept any currency which it issues." *Complete Presidential Press Conferences of Franklin Delano Roosevelt*, 25 vols. in 12 (New York, 1972), 23: 263. Hereafter cited as *PPC*.

8 Secretary of the Treasury Henry Morgenthau, Jr.

9 General George C. Marshall, U.S. Army Chief of Staff.

10 Admiral Ernest J. King, U.S. Chief of Naval Operations.

11 Admiral Lord Louis Mountbatten, supreme commander of Allied forces in Southeast Asia.

be a million a side. The Chiefs of Staff are searching about for the best solution of these problems as between the Mediterranean and Overlord.

How I wish you were here.

Doc. 385
ROOSEVELT TO CHURCHILL

No. 561   June 14, 1944

Your 703.[1] I can see no objection to your action in permitting de Gaulle to visit France and feel that his visit may have the good effect of stimulating that part of the French underground over which he has authority or which he can influence to work against the common enemy.

In my opinion we should make full use of any organization or influence he may have insofar as is practicable without imposing him by force of our arms upon the French people as their Government or giving recognition to his outfit as the provisional government of France. After all, the Germans control over 99% of the area of France.

His unreasonable attitude toward our supplementary French currency does not disturb me. My reaction to his action in the matter of currency is fully covered in my number 559 of 12 June.[2]

I join with you in a hope that the Italian situation will clear up to the advantage of our military effort in Italy and elsewhere, and I regret exceedingly that it was not possible for me to be with you on your visit with our splendid soldiers who have made the first breach in Hitler's "citadel of Europe."[3] But don't do it again without my going with you.

[1] See above, Doc. 384.
[2] See above, Doc. 382.
[3] Churchill had visited the British and American sectors in Normandy on June 10–12.

Doc. 386
CHURCHILL TO ROOSEVELT

No. 705

June 17, 1944

Your No. 562.[1]

I have reluctantly come to the conclusion that it will not be possible to press the return of Badoglio, and I am so informing U.J. We ought I think to wait for his answer before taking final action. Also matters should be regularised through the Advisory Council.

The important thing now is to make sure that all these ministers who have elected themselves to office shall be cognisant of all the engagements into which Badoglio entered. We also think the time has come to publish the long terms of surrender.[2]

[1] Not printed. Roosevelt wrote that "it would be a grave mistake for us not to permit the Bonomi Cabinet to be promptly installed. Though regretting Badoglio's withdrawal, I nevertheless feel that this may be of distinct advantage to us. . . . I understand that the new Cabinet have pledged themselves to assume all the commitments the Badoglio government contracted with the Allies, including both the long terms of surrender and the postponement of the institutional question until the hostilities are ended. . . . Interference on our part at this late moment in the establishment of what appears to be a representative government would have, I fear, serious repercussions both at home and in Italy, to the detriment of the military situation and the profit of mischievous elements there, and would not this be in direct violation of our announced policy to let the people choose their own government?"

[2] For the full text of the Italian terms of surrender, see Albert N. Garland and Howard McGaw Smyth, assisted by Martin Blumenson, *Sicily and the Surrender of Italy* (Washington, 1965), app. D.

Doc. 387
CHURCHILL TO ROOSEVELT

No. 706

June 18, 1944

The following looks good.

Doctor Subasić and Tito agreed today [on] the following joint communiqué which will be issued by Tanjug[1] afternoon of June 18th. I should be grateful if wide publicity and warm welcome could be given to it in local press.

[1] Yugoslav news agency.

"The 'New Yugoslav' News Agency has been authorised to issue the statement: 'From June 14th to June 17th discussions have been going on in liberated territory of Yugoslavia between the President of the National Liberation Committee of Yugoslavia, Marshal Josip Broz Tito, and Prime Minister of the Royal Yugoslav Government, Dr. [Ivan] Subasić. Several members of the National Liberation Committee of Yugoslavia and of the Presidium of Anti-Fascist Council of National Liberation Yugoslavia took part in these discussions. These negotiations have been led from both sides in a spirit of mutual effort towards strengthening the liberation fight of the nations of Yugoslavia and with the aim of achieving broadest unity of the national forces. Agreement and mutual accord was reached regarding many questions. This will undoubtedly help to strengthen still further our relations with the Allies and help the peoples of Yugoslavia to liberate their country as speedily as possible.' "

Doc. 388
CHURCHILL TO ROOSEVELT

No. 707   June 20, 1944

I hope de Gaulle will come to you because it would be a good thing all round if some sort of arrangement could be fixed. This need not involve recognising the French National Committee as the provisional government of France. In practice, however, I think it would be found that de Gaulle and the French National Committee represent most of the elements who want to help us. Vichy is a foe and there is a large middle body who only wish to be left alone and eat good meals from day to day.[1] The energising factor of de Gaulle must not be forgotten in our treatment of the French problem.

Your operations in the Pacific assume every day a more vehement and compulsive course.[2] Admiral King gave me a full account in the several good talks I had with him. Everything went well at the meeting of the Chiefs of Staff.

[1] For the last phase of the Vichy regime, see Arnold Toynbee and Veronica M. Toynbee, eds., *Hitler's Europe* (London, 1954), pp. 426ff.; and Robert O. Paxton, *Vichy France: Old Guard and New Order 1940–1944* (New York, 1972), pp. 326ff.

[2] American forces had landed on Saipan in the Marianas on June 15, and on June 19–20 a great naval battle was fought in the Philippine Sea between American and Japanese forces. See Samuel Eliot Morison, *History of United States Naval Operations in World War II*, vol. 8, *New Guinea and the Marianas, March 1944–August 1944* (Boston, 1953), chaps. 13–17.

However, it is most desirable we have a meeting before October. How about August 20 at the Citadel Quebec? A week in those surroundings and cool air would do you no end of good.

Your troops are fighting magnificently and I should not think that Cherbourg would hold out long.[3] Anyhow, the synthetic harbours,[4] which are a miracle of rapid construction, would each of them handle more traffic than Cherbourg, and I hope you will honour one of them with your arrival.

[3] Cherbourg was liberated on June 27.

[4] Prefabricated breakwaters, code-named Mulberries, were towed across the channel and sunk off the Normandy beaches.

Doc. 389
CHURCHILL TO ROOSEVELT

No. 708   June 20, 1944

The man I think best capable of stating the British case in the oil conference[1] is without question Beaverbrook.[2] While naturally we must choose our own representative to put our own point of view, I should be grateful if you would let me know in personal privacy whether you would foresee any American political or party difficulties in this choice by me. I should greatly regret if he were not acceptable as I believe he is far and away the best man to work towards a solution by cordial agreement.

At this moment a flying bomb[3] is approaching this dwelling. We think we are getting the best of them. We have received the greatest consideration from Eisenhower and Spaatz,[4] and I have given it out

[1] After initial meetings by technical experts, formal Anglo-American conversations on petroleum began in Washington on July 25. See FR 1944, 3 (Washington, 1965): 119ff. The two nations reached an accord on August 8, but when the agreement was submitted to the Senate for its advice and consent, the chairman of the Foreign Relations Committee, Senator Tom Connally of Texas, declined to hold hearings until after the November elections. Certain sections of the American oil industry opposed the agreement, indicating, as the State Department informed the President on December 27, 1944, "concern lest implementation of the Agreement might lead to the mandatory regulation of its operations." FR 1944, 3: 127. On January 10, 1945, the President withdrew the agreement.

[2] Lord Beaverbrook, Lord Privy Seal, had been named head of the British delegation to the petroleum talks. See A. J. P. Taylor, Beaverbrook (London, 1972), p. 557.

[3] German V-1 rockets, the so-called flying bombs, had been falling on London since June 13. See Basil Collier, The Battle of the V-Weapons 1944–1945 (London, 1964), chap. 6.

[4] Lieutenant General Carl Spaatz, commander of the U.S. strategic air forces in Europe.

that nothing is to impede the battle. This perpetual bombardment is a new feature, but I do not think it will seriously affect production in London. Up to date there are 7,000 casualties of which half are light. The Guards' Chapel where 300 [casualties] occurred was a sad episode.[5] General Bedell Smith was invited by Colonel Ivan Cobbold who was killed to attend the service but did not go.

I consider the battle on land is progressing favourably but the weather has not been kind for June. Bomb has fallen some way off, but others are reported. We have exploded more than half our visitors today by fighter aircraft harmlessly. As you know, tomorrow is a great effort on Berlin.[6] This will give them something else to rejoice about. Every good wish.

[5] On June 18 a German rocket had struck the Guards' Chapel at Wellington Barra.ks in London.

[6] On June 21 nearly 2,500 RAF planes attacked the German capital. See Hilary St. George Saunders, *Royal Air Force, 1939–1945*, vol. 3, *The Fight Is Won* (London, 1954), p. 159; Wesley Frank Craven and James Lee Cate, eds., *The Army Air Forces in World War II*, 3 (Chicago, 1950): 284–285.

Doc. 390
CHURCHILL TO ROOSEVELT

No. 710   June 21, 1944

We are much concerned at the consequences of the directions which have been given by Admiral King to Admiral Stark[1] about transferring the great mass of American ships from the Overlord battle to the Mediterranean. This is surely not the time to withdraw such a great American naval component without consultation with the Admiralty and the Supreme Commanders concerned, or the specific approval of the Combined Chiefs of Staff.[2]

Very important strategic decisions have to be taken by the Combined Chiefs of Staff and by you and me about the form of diversion from the forces against Overlord to be effected from the Mediterranean. These grave matters are now under close and urgent consideration by General Wilson and General Eisenhower, following the

[1] Admiral Harold R. Stark, commander of U.S. naval forces in European waters.
[2] For the background of Churchill's opposition to such withdrawal, see Winston S. Churchill, *Triumph and Tragedy* (Boston, 1953), pp. 57ff.; John Ehrman, *Grand Strategy*, vol. 5, *August 1943–September 1944* (London, 1956), pp. 345ff.; Robert W. Coakley and Richard M. Leighton, *Global Logistics and Strategy 1943–1945* (Washington, 1968), pp. 374ff.; and Pogue, *Marshall: Organizer of Victory*, pp. 405ff.

lead given to them by the Combined Chiefs of Staff, and arising from the discussions which they had so recently here in London together.[3] No decisions can be taken until we have had the considered view of the two Supreme Commanders concerned.

I understand that Eisenhower has telegraphed to you also on this subject.[4]

[3] See Maurice Matloff and Edwin M. Snell, *Strategic Planning for Coalition Warfare 1943–1944* (Washington, 1959), pp. 467ff.

[4] On June 20 Eisenhower cabled General Marshall: "[T]he Combined Chiefs of Staff have long ago decided to make Western Europe the base from which to conduct decisive operations against Germany. To authorize any departure from this decision seems to me to be ill advised and potentially dangerous. . . . I think that [General] Wilson should be directed to undertake Operation Anvil at the earliest date." *PDDE*, vol. 3, no. 1765.

Doc. 391
ROOSEVELT TO CHURCHILL

No. 565   June 22, 1944

With reference to your 687[1] and my 560[2] regarding matters in the Balkans, I am a bit worried and so is the State Department. I think I should tell you frankly that we were disturbed that your people took this matter up with us only after it had been put up to the Russians and they had inquired whether we were agreeable.[3] Your Foreign Office apparently sensed this and has now explained that the proposal "arose out of a chance remark" which was converted by the Soviet Government into a formal proposal. However, I hope matters of this importance can be prevented from developing in such a manner in the future.

[1] See above, Doc. 369.

[2] See above, Doc. 383.

[3] For the background of what Churchill described as Roosevelt's "pained message," see Churchill, *Triumph and Tragedy*, pp. 71ff.; and Sir Llewellyn Woodward, *British Foreign Policy in the Second World War*, 3 (London, 1971): 115–116.

Doc. 392
CHURCHILL TO ROOSEVELT

No. 712   June 23, 1944

The Russians are the only power that can do anything in Rumania and I thought it was agreed between you and me that on the basis of their reasonable armistice terms, excepting indemnities, they should try to give coherent direction to what happened there. In point of fact, we have all three cooperated closely in handling in Cairo the recent Rumanian peace feelers.[1] On the other hand, the Greek burden rests almost entirely upon us and has done so since we lost 40,000 men in a vain endeavour to help them in 1941. Similarly, you have let us play the hand in Turkey, but we have always consulted you on policy and I think we have been agreed on the line to be followed. It would be quite easy for me, on the general principle of slithering to the left, which is so popular in foreign policy, to let things rip when the King of Greece would probably be forced to abdicate and EAM would work a reign of terror in Greece, forcing the villagers and many other classes to form security battalions under German auspices to prevent utter anarchy. The only way I can prevent this is by persuading the Russians to quit boosting EAM and ramming it forward with all their force. Therefore, I proposed to the Russians a temporary working arrangement for the better conduct of the war. This was only a proposal and had to be referred to you for your agreement.

I cannot admit that I have done anything wrong in this matter. It would not be possible for three people in different parts of the world to work together effectively if no one of them may make any suggestion to either of the others without simultaneously keeping the third informed. A recent example of this is the message you have sent quite properly to U.J. about your conversations with the Poles of which, as yet, I have heard nothing from you.[2] I am not complaining at all of this because I know we are working for the general theme and purposes and I hope you will feel that has been so in my conduct of the Greek affair.

I have, also, taken action to try to bring together a union of the Tito forces with those in Serbia and with all adhering to the Royal Yugoslav Government, which we have both recognised. You have been informed at every stage of how we are bearing this heavy burden which at present rests mainly on us. Here again, nothing would be easier than to throw the King and the Royal Yugoslav Government to the wolves and let a civil war break out in Yugoslavia to the joy of the Germans. I am struggling to bring order out of chaos in both cases and concentrate all efforts against the common foe. I am keeping you constantly informed: and I hope to have your confidence and help within the spheres of action in which initiative is assigned to us.

On the other hand, I send you my sincere apologies for Oliver

1 See *FR 1944,* 4 (Washington, 1966) : 151 ff.
2 See below, Doc. 396.

Lyttelton's foolish remark[3] which I fear may cause you trouble. If there is anything I can say usefully, pray let me know.

Let me congratulate you most wholeheartedly upon the brilliant fighting of the American troops in the Cherbourg peninsula as well as in Italy. We have immense tasks before us. Indeed, I cannot think of any moment when the burden of the war has laid more heavily upon me or when I have felt so unequal to its ever more entangled problems. I greatly admire the strength and courage with which you face your difficulties, especially in a year when you have, what I may venture to call, other preoccupations.[4]

[3] In an address to the American Chamber of Commerce in London on June 20, Oliver Lyttelton, the British Minister of Production, had made some remarks that were embarrassing to the British. To the House of Commons, Lyttelton later explained: "I was trying, in a parenthesis, to make clear the gratitude which this country feels for the help given us in the war against Germany, before Japan attacked the United States. The words I used, however, when read textually, and apart from the whole tenor of my speech, seem to mean that the help given us against Germany provoked Japan to attack. This is manifestly untrue." *Parliamentary Debates*, Commons, 5th ser. (1909–), vol. 401, cols. 200–201.

[4] The reference is clearly to the forthcoming American presidential election.

Doc. 393
ROOSEVELT TO CHURCHILL

No. 567 June 23, 1944

Your 707.[1] I join with you in a hope that a visit by de Gaulle in Washington will have a corrective effect on what is now a very unsatisfactory situation.

We are informed by your Embassy that your Government plans discussions with the Committee prior to de Gaulle's visit with the thought of "being helpful to the Washington conversations."

I hope you will not make any agreements with the Committee prior to giving me an opportunity to comment thereon.

I should not like to be faced with a fait accompli when de Gaulle arrives in Washington.

[1] See above, Doc. 388.

Doc. 394
CHURCHILL TO ROOSEVELT

No. 714   June 25, 1944

I have just read memorandum CCS 603 from the United States Chiefs of Staff[1] and also the immediately following containing the proposed draft orders. These very grave questions will immediately be examined by the British Chiefs of Staff and by the War Cabinet. I earnestly hope you will consent to hear both sides. Our answer will be given within 48 hours.

[1] The message of the Combined Chiefs of Staff raised a heated debate over whether to proceed as planned with the invasion of southern France. Roosevelt, the U.S. Joint Chiefs, and the Combined Chiefs strongly backed Eisenhower, who favored launching the invasion as scheduled in mid-August and withdrawing troops from Italy for that purpose. Churchill and the British Chiefs vigorously opposed this plan, contending that it would seriously weaken Italian operations. See Forrest C. Pogue, *The Supreme Command* (Washington, 1954) , pp. 220ff.; Ehrman, *Grand Strategy*, 5: 349ff.; Pogue, *Marshall: Organizer of Victory*, pp. 410ff.; and *PDDE*, vol. 3, no. 1785.

Doc. 395
ROOSEVELT TO CHURCHILL

No. 570   June 26, 1944

Your number 712.[1]

It appears that both of us have inadvertently taken unilateral action in a direction that we both now agree to have been expedient for the time being.

It is essential that we should always be in agreement in matters bearing on our Allied war effort. . . .

Oliver Lyttelton's remark reminds me of the well-known old prayer that we be spared from our friends—I think that is now a dead issue that should not be resurrected.

Local problems are no doubt occupying much of the time of both of us,[2] but I am sure we do not admit preoccupation with anything but the war.

[1] See above, Doc. 392.
[2] A rash of flying bombs was then falling on Britain. Also, the Republican National Convention, then meeting in Chicago, was bitterly critical of Roosevelt's foreign and domestic policies. The Republicans nominated Governor Thomas E. Dewey of New York for President and Governor John W. Bricker of Ohio for Vice President.

Doc. 396
ROOSEVELT TO CHURCHILL

No. 571   June 26, 1944

The following is an accurate paraphrase of the message sent to Stalin on 17 June 1944:

QUOTE. The Polish Prime Minister, Mr. Mikolajczyk,[1] as you know, has just completed a short visit here. I deemed his visit at this time as desirable and necessary for reasons which Ambassador Harriman[2] has already explained to you.

Therefore, you know that his visit was not connected with any attempt on my part to insert myself into the merits of the differences which exist between the Soviet Government and the Polish Government-in-exile. I can assure you that no specific plan or proposal in any way affecting Polish-Soviet relations was drawn up, although we had a frank and beneficial exchange of views on a wide variety of subjects affecting Poland. However, I think you would be interested in his attitude towards the problems confronting his country and in my personal impression of him.

He impressed me as a very reasonable and sincere person whose only aim is to do what is best for his country. Being fully aware that the entire future of Poland depends upon the establishment of really good relations with the Soviet Union, he will, in my opinion, exert every effort to achieve that goal.

His first immediate concern is the vital necessity for setting up the fullest kind of collaboration between the forces of the Polish underground and the Red Army in the common struggle against our enemy. It is his belief that cooperation between the organized Polish underground and your armies is a military factor of the greatest importance not only to your armies in the east but also to the main task of finishing off by our combined efforts the Nazi beast in his lair.

The Prime Minister gave me the impression that he will not let any minor considerations stand in the way of his attempts to reach a solution with you and that he is thinking only of Poland and the Polish people. If he felt that you would welcome such a step on his part, it is my firm belief that he would not hesitate to go to Moscow in order to discuss with you frankly and personally the problems involving your two countries, in particular the urgency of immediate military col-

1 Stanislaw Mikolajczyk, Prime Minister of the Polish government-in-exile.
2 W. Averell Harriman, U.S. ambassador to the Soviet Union.

laboration. You will understand, I know, that I am in no way trying to press my personal views upon you in a matter which is of special concern to you and your country, when I make this observation. However, I felt that a frank account of the impressions I received in talking with the Polish Prime Minister were due you. UNQUOTE.

Doc. 397
CHURCHILL TO ROOSEVELT

No. 716   June 27, 1944

Your No. 570.[1] Let me withdraw at once the word "preoccupation" in para 5 of my 712[2] and substitute the word "trials." Thank you very much for what you say. You may be very sure I shall always be looking to our agreement in all matters before, during, and after.

I have read your message to Stalin about Mikolajczyk.[3] I think it will be most helpful. Every good wish.

[1] See above, Doc. 395.
[2] See above, Doc. 392.
[3] See above, Doc. 396.

Doc. 398
CHURCHILL TO ROOSEVELT

No. 717   June 28, 1944

The deadlock between our Chiefs of Staff raises most serious issues.[1] Our first wish is to help General Eisenhower in the most speedy and effective manner. But we do not think this necessarily involves the complete ruin of all our great affairs in the Mediterranean, and we take it hard that this should be demanded of us.

I am sending you, in a few hours, a very full argument on the whole matter which I have prepared with my own hands, and which is endorsed by the Chiefs of Staff.[2] I shall consult the War Cabinet on the subject tomorrow, 29th, and I have already circulated the paper to them. Those who have seen it completely endorse it, including those members who belong to the Defence Committee. I have very little doubt of unanimous support upon this issue.

[1] See above, Doc. 394, note 1.
[2] Not printed. See Ehrman, *Grand Strategy*, 5: 345ff.

I most earnestly beg you to examine this matter in detail for yourself. I think the tone of the United States Chiefs of Staff is arbitrary and, certainly, I see no prospect of agreement on the present lines. What is to happen then? It was such a pity that they all separated before this issue arose, just like we separated before the Italian climax after Quadrant.[3]

Please remember how you spoke to me at Teheran about Istria, and how I introduced it at the full conference.[4] This has sunk very deeply into my mind, although it is not, by any means, the immediate issue we have to decide.

I am shocked to think of the length of the message that I shall be sending you tonight.[5] It is a purely personal communication between you and me in our capacity as heads of the two Western democracies.

[3] Code name for the conference at Quebec in August 1943.

[4] No specific reference to this matter has been found in U.S. Department of State, *The Conferences at Cairo and Tehran 1943* (Washington, 1961).

[5] Not printed. Churchill again vigorously opposed the invasion of southern France, declaring that "supreme priority must naturally be accorded to the support of 'Overlord.' . . . Let us reinforce 'Overlord' directly, to the utmost limit of landings from the west. . . . [But] let us resolve not to wreck one great campaign [Italy] for the sake of winning the other. Both can be won." Churchill, *Triumph and Tragedy*, pp. 716ff.

Doc. 399
ROOSEVELT TO CHURCHILL

No. 573   June 28, 1944

Your 714.[1]

I have examined the problem of assistance for Overlord by operations in the Mediterranean which our Chiefs of Staff have been discussing. On balance I find I must completely concur in the stand of the U.S. Chiefs of Staff.[2] General Wilson's proposal for continued use of practically all the Mediterranean resources to advance into northern Italy and from there to the northeast is not acceptable to me, and I really believe we should consolidate our operations and not scatter them.[3]

It seems to me that nothing can be worse at this time than a deadlock in the combined staffs as to future course of action. You and I must prevent this and I think we should support the views of the

[1] See above, Doc. 394.

[2] See Pogue, *Marshall: Organizer of Victory*, pp. 411–412.

[3] See *PDDE*, vol. 3, no. 1765, note 1.

Supreme Allied Commander.[4] He is definitely for Anvil[5] and wants action in the field by August 30th, preferably earlier.

It is vital that we decide at once to go ahead with our long-agreed policy to make Overlord the decisive action. Anvil, mounted at the earliest possible date, is the only operation which will give Overlord the material and immediate support from Wilson's forces.

[4] General Eisenhower.
[5] Code name for the invasion of southern France.

Doc. 400
CHURCHILL TO ROOSEVELT

No. 721   July 1, 1944

We are deeply grieved by your telegram.[1] There are no differences whatever between my War Cabinet colleagues and the British Chiefs of Staff. The splitting up of the campaign in the Mediterranean into two operations neither of which can do anything decisive, is, in my humble and respectful opinion, the first major strategic and political error for which we two have to be responsible.

At Teheran you emphasised to me the possibilities of a move eastward when Italy was conquered and mentioned particularly Istria. No one involved in these discussions has ever thought of moving armies into the Balkans: but Istria and Trieste in Italy are strategic and political positions, which as you saw yourself very clearly might exercise profound and widespread reactions, especially now after the Russian advances.

After Teheran I was made doubtful about Anvil by General Eisenhower's dislike for it. You will remember his words at Cairo when "General Eisenhower stressed the vital importance of continuing the maximum possible operations in an established theatre since much time was invariably lost when the scene of action was changed, necessitating, as it did, the arduous task of building up a fresh base."[2]

Furthermore, I was impressed by General Montgomery's arguments when at Marrakesh,[3] after he had been nominated to the Overlord command, he explained that it would take 90 days for a force landed at Anvil to influence the Overlord operation.

[1] See above, Doc. 399.
[2] No direct reference to this matter can be found in *Conferences at Cairo and Tehran.*
[3] General Montgomery visited Churchill in Marrakesh December 31–January 1, while the Prime Minister was resting there.

Both these opinions are in contrast to SCAF 54.[4] It is no reflexion on these officers that they should now express a different view. But their opinions, expressed so decidedly, make me less confident about an Anvil operation. Moreover in those days the date was to be early in June. There is no doubt that an advance up the Rhone Valley begun at the end of August could easily be blocked and stemmed by a smaller number of German troops, who could come either through the tunnels from Italy or from southern Germany. I doubt whether you will find that three American divisions, supported by seven French 80 percent native divisions from Morocco, Algeria, and Tunis, will have any important strategic effect on the tremendous battle which Eisenhower and Montgomery are fighting 500 miles away to the north. It seems more likely to prove a cul-de-sac into which increasing numbers of United States troops will be drawn, and I fear that further demands will be made even upon what is left to us in Italy. It would no doubt make sure of de Gaulle having his talons pretty deeply dug into France.

I should not be frank if I did not assure you that I fear a costly stalemate for you unless far more American divisions, at the expense of Eisenhower, are thrust into Anvil to make it good at all costs by the great power of the United States. Little account is to be taken of Alexander's[5] operations. The last decision given by the British and American Chiefs of Staff here a fortnight ago was: "The destruction of the German armed forces in Italy south of the Pisa-Rimini line must be completed. There should be no withdrawal from the battle of any Allied forces that are necessary for this purpose" (telegram number 3116 dated June 14th from CCS to Generals Wilson and Eisenhower). . . .

I have considered your suggestion that we should lay our respective cases before Stalin. The passage in the very nice telegram I have received from him yesterday (which follows this immediately) [6] seems to suggest that he does not underrate the Italian front. I do not know what he would say if the issue was put to him to decide. On military

4 General Eisenhower's message to the Combined Chiefs of Staff, dated June 26, 1944, outlined some of the substantial land, sea, and air forces Eisenhower was prepared to make available to a landing in southern France. The message concluded: "All of the above, I repeat, will entail certain sacrifices for Overlord, but these will be made gladly because we are convinced of the transcendent importance of Anvil." *PDDE*, vol. 3, no. 1780. See also Pogue, *Supreme Command*, pp. 222–223. "SCAF" is Supreme Commander Allied Forces.

5 General Sir Harold Alexander, commanding general of the Fifteenth Army Group.

6 Not printed. Stalin told Churchill: "While the scale of the operations in Northern France is becoming more and more powerful and menacing for Hitler, the successful development of the Allied offensive in Italy, too, is worthy of the greatest attention and praise." *Stalin's Correspondence*, 1: 232–233.

grounds he might be greatly interested in the eastward movement of Alexander's army which, without entering the Balkans, would profoundly affect all the forces there and which, in conjunction with any attacks he may make upon Rumania or with Rumania against Hungarian Transylvania, might produce the most far-reaching results. On a long-term political view, he might prefer that the British and Americans should do their share in France in the very hard fighting that is to come, and that east, middle, and southern Europe should fall naturally into his control. However it is better to settle the matter for ourselves and between ourselves.

What can I do, Mr. President, when your Chiefs of Staff insist on casting aside our Italian offensive campaign, with all its dazzling possibilities, relieving Hitler of all his anxieties in the Po basin (vide Boniface) ,[7] and when we are to see the integral life of this campaign drained off into the Rhone Valley in the belief that it will in several months carry effective help to Eisenhower so far away in the north?

If you still press upon us the directive of your Chiefs of Staff to withdraw so many of your forces from the Italian campaign and leave all our hopes there dashed to the ground, His Majesty's Government, on the advice of their Chiefs of Staff, must enter a solemn protest. I need scarcely say that we shall do our best to make a success of anything that is undertaken. We shall therefore forward your directive to General Wilson as soon as you let us know that there is no hope of reconsideration by your Chiefs of Staff or by yourself. Our Chiefs of Staff are letting yours know the corrections on points of detail which they think necessary in the previous draft.

It is with the greatest sorrow that I write to you in this sense. But I am sure that if we could have met, as I so frequently proposed, we should have reached a happy agreement. I send you every personal good wish. However we may differ on the conduct of the war, my personal gratitude to you for your kindness to me and for all you have done for the cause of freedom will never be diminished.

[7] British term given to certain information supplied by Churchill to Roosevelt. See, for instance, Churchill's letter of September 12, 1944. U.S. Dept. of State, *The Conference at Quebec 1944* (Washington, 1972) , p. 42.

Doc. 401
ROOSEVELT TO CHURCHILL

No. 577   July 1, 1944

Your 721.[1]

I appreciate deeply your clear exposition of your feelings and views

[1] See above, Doc. 400.

on this decision we are making. My Chiefs of Staff and I have given the deepest consideration to this problem and to the points you have raised. We are still convinced that the right course of action is to launch Anvil at the earliest possible date.[2]

Perhaps I am more optimistic than you are, but I feel that our commanders in Italy will, with the forces left to them, continue to do great things and attain all the essential objectives there.

I do not believe we should delay further in giving General Wilson a directive. We have had indicated to us the changes which the British Chiefs of Staff think necessary in the directive and they are acceptable to us. Will you ask your Chiefs to dispatch it to General Wilson at once?

As a matter of fact I personally cannot see [how] in the short distance to go in Italy to the Pisa-Rimini line we can destroy even a major part of the German army. North of that line if we clear the Po Valley we gain very little in the destruction of Germans as they can retreat even further north.

At Teheran what I was thinking of was a series of raids in force in Istria if the Germans started a general retirement from the Dodecanese and Greece. But it has not happened yet and Tito appears to be in a less strong position than he was then.

On the same line the country in Istria has bad combat terrain in the wintertime—worse than southern France.

Therefore I am compelled by the logic of not dispersing our main efforts to a new theater to agree with my Chiefs of Staff and I think we can jointly cut any idea of 90 days to 60 if you and I insist on it.

I honestly believe that God will be with us as He has in Overlord and in Italy and in North Africa. I always think of my early geometry: "A straight line is the shortest distance between two points."

2 See Pogue, *Marshall: Organizer of Victory*, p. 409.

Doc. 402
ROOSEVELT TO CHURCHILL

No. 580   July 6, 1944

Referring to my 571[1] transmitting a message sent by me to U.J. the following quoted reply is received this date:

QUOTE. Thank you for the information regarding your meeting with Mr. Mikolajczyk.

If to bear in mind the establishment of military cooperation be-

1 See above, Doc. 396.

tween the Red Army and forces of the Polish underground movement [in] the fighting against Hitlerite invaders,[2] then this, undoubtedly, is now an essential matter for the final rout of our common foe.

Great significance, of course, has in this respect the correct solution of the question of Soviet-Polish relations. You are familiar with the point of view of the Soviet Government and its endeavor to see Poland strong, independent, and democratic, and the Soviet-Polish relations good-neighborly and based upon durable friendship. The Soviet Government sees the most important premises of this in the reorganization of the Émigré Polish Government, which would provide the participation in it of Polish statesmen in England, as well as Polish statesmen in the United States and the U.S.S.R., and especially Polish democratic statesmen in Poland itself, and also in the recognition by the Polish Government of the Curzon line as the new border between the U.S.S.R. and Poland.

It is necessary to say, however, that from the statement of Mr. Mikolajczyk in Washington it is not seen that he makes in this matter any steps forward. That is why it is difficult for me at the present moment to express any opinion in respect to Mr. Mikolajczyk's trip to Moscow.

Your opinion on the question of Soviet-Polish relations and your efforts in this matter are highly valued by all of us. UNQUOTE.

2 Garbled in the original.

Doc. 403
ROOSEVELT TO CHURCHILL

No. 582   July 10, 1944

Re your 713,[1] I am prepared to accept Committee as temporary de facto authority for civil administration in France provided two things are made clear—first, complete authority to be reserved to Eisenhower to do what he feels necessary to conduct effective military operations, and, second, that French people be given opportunity to make free

1 Not printed. In that message, dated June 24, Churchill informed Roosevelt that "the conversations now proceeding with . . . the de Gaullist Ambassador in London . . . [have as their object] to discover a basis that we might accept for the operation of civil affairs in liberated areas of France in regard to which both the United States Government and we ourselves have agreed that the French Committee on National Liberation should take the leadership. . . . Our people have no power to conclude any agreement. . . . You will certainly not be faced by His Majesty's Government with any fait accompli."

choice of their own Government. I have asked officials here to take British drafts as a base and modify them to ensure these points, and they will shortly be in touch with your people here. Suggest you authorize your political and military officials here to work out details immediately with our officials for final clearance through the Combined Chiefs of Staff. General de Gaulle is leaving behind officials qualified to deal with this matter. I urge that no publicity be given these arrangements until they are finally cleared.

The visit has gone off very well.[2]

[2] General de Gaulle visited Washington from July 6 to July 8. At a luncheon at the White House on July 7, President Roosevelt spoke of their relationship in cordial terms: "I think we will all agree that this is an historic occasion we will remember all the rest of our lives. There are no great problems between the French and the Americans, or between General de Gaulle and myself. They are all working out awfully well, without exception. They are going to work out all right, if they will just leave a few of us alone to sit around the table. . . . And, therefore, it has been a great privilege to have General de Gaulle come over here to talk about these things. . . ." Samuel I. Rosenman, ed., *The Public Papers and Addresses of Franklin Delano Roosevelt*, 13 vols. (New York, 1938–1951), 13: 194–195. Hereafter cited as *PPR*. For de Gaulle's rather less flattering account of his conversations with Roosevelt, see his *War Memoirs*, 2: 268ff.

Doc. 404
CHURCHILL TO ROOSEVELT

No. 726   July 13, 1944

Your number 582.[1]

I am glad to hear that the de Gaulle visit went off well and that you agree that the British drafts will do as a basis for agreement with the French Committee.

We agree with the procedure you suggest, and we are instructing our people in Washington accordingly.

In regard to your two points. I entirely agree that Eisenhower must have all the authority which he wants for his military operations. This was the paramount aim of our officials in the discussions and the necessity was fully recognised by the French. It was not easy to find a form of words which reconciled Eisenhower's supremacy with French susceptibilities but we were satisfied that we had fully safeguarded the position by the agreed wording of articles one to five of the draft main agreement (see my immediately following message).[2] If your people

[1] See above, Doc. 403.

[2] Not printed. In that long telegram Churchill set forth in detail his views concerning administrative policies to be pursued by General Eisenhower and the

can improve the wording and persuade the French to accept it, we shall, of course, be content. I am sure though that it would be a mistake to delay unduly. Now, after your successful meeting, is the moment to clear the whole business up.

Your second point is very important but we did not feel that it was an appropriate provision to insert in an agreement confined to practical administrative and other questions arising out of Allied operations for the liberation of France. Moreover, the French Committee, as you know, have provided in their decree of April 21st for the holding of elections and the appointment of a provisional government by the resultant representative assembly as soon as two-thirds of France, including Paris, have been liberated. I think we can be sure that the very democratically minded civilian members of the Committee and of the assembly and the French people inside France will see that these elections are held. We ourselves are satisfied on this point and I hope that you will not press for it to be covered in the actual agreement. Indeed, I do not see how it could be.

When the texts have been finally cleared through the Combined Chiefs of Staff, I take it that you will wish to proceed as in the case of the agreements about other Allied liberated territory, and that you will wish Eisenhower to sign for you on the military level. On our side the Foreign Secretary will sign with a representative of the French Committee. As we, for our part, are already prepared to accept the London texts and it appears from your telegram that there is not much difference between us, I hope that the talks which your people are having with the French in Washington will shortly be concluded and that we can get the various memoranda finally settled within a very few days.

I entirely agree that no publicity be given these arrangements until they are finally cleared.

French Committee of National Liberation following the liberation of French territory. See Woodward, *British Foreign Policy*, 3: 69–70.

Doc. 405
ROOSEVELT TO CHURCHILL

No. 583   July 13, 1944

The receipt is acknowledged of your 726[1] and 727.[2] I feel that the small differences between the British and American drafts of the

[1] See above, Doc. 404.
[2] Not printed.

agreement can be adjusted by your and my representatives here working with representatives of the French Committee.

It is essential that Eisenhower have all the authority that is necessary for the conduct of his military operations at the smallest cost in life to the American and British soldiers.

I am off on my trip and will be gone several weeks but can always be reached.[3]

[3] On July 13 President Roosevelt left Washington by train for the West Coast. There he embarked on the heavy cruiser *Baltimore* for a trip to Pearl Harbor and Honolulu, where he conferred with his top military and naval commanders in the Pacific.

Doc. 406
CHURCHILL TO ROOSEVELT

No. 732   July 16, 1944

When are we going to meet and where? That we must meet soon is certain. It would be better that U.J. came too. I am entirely in your hands. I would brave the reporters at Washington or the mosquitoes of Alaska! Surely we ought now to fix a date and then begin negotiating with U.J. His Majesty's Government would wish to propose Eureka II[1] for the last ten days of August. For details see my immediately following telegram.[2] Failing this, Casablanca, Rome, or even Teheran present themselves and many other places too. But we two must meet and if possible three. Please let me have your ideas on all this.[3]

[1] A reference to the code name for the Big Three conference at Teheran in November 1943.

[2] Not printed.

[3] On the following day, Churchill proposed that the meeting be held at Invergordon, Scotland, with the three participants using their own battleships as headquarters. Roosevelt was intrigued by this idea, suggesting only that the date be postponed until September 10–15. When Roosevelt broached the proposal to Stalin, the Soviet leader rejected the idea of any meeting "in the immediate future." Roosevelt ultimately changed his mind about going to Scotland and instead met with Churchill in September at Quebec. See below, Doc. 412.

Doc. 407
CHURCHILL TO ROOSEVELT

No. 735   July 25, 1944

Please see U.J.'s telegram to me of July 23rd and the answer I have
sent off after discussion with Anthony,[1] the text of which immediately
follows this.[2]

We have pressed Mikolajczyk strongly to go with his ministers and
to make contact with Stalin. It may well be they will receive a friendly
welcome, but of course their outburst last night about "usurpers" et
cetera may have worsened the situation.[3] However we still have hope,
and aim at fusion of some kind.

Meanwhile it is of the utmost importance that we do not desert the
orthodox Polish Government,[4] and Anthony will give answers in the
House tomorrow making it clear that our relations remain unchanged.[5]

[1] Foreign Secretary Eden.

[2] See below, Doc. 408.

[3] In a statement issued on July 25 concerning the establishment of the Soviet-
created Committee of National Liberation in Poland, the Polish Telegraph Agency
in London declared: "It was an attempt by a handful of usurpers to impose on the
Polish nation a political leadership, which is at variance with the overwhelming
majority." General Sikorski Historical Institute, *Documents on Polish-Soviet Relations 1939–1945* (London, 1961), vol. 2, no. 165. The preceding day Mikolajczyk had
handed Churchill a strongly worded memorandum on the same subject and had sent
an analogous memorandum to R. E. Schoenfeld, the U.S. chargé d'affaires to the
Polish government-in-exile. Mikolajczyk maintained that the Soviet Union clearly
intended "to impose on the Polish people an illegal administration which has
nothing in common with the will of the nation. All this is happening contrary to
the repeated assurances of Marshal Stalin that he desires the restoration of an
independent Poland. . . . An immediate démarche in Moscow of the British Government seems, therefore, to be indispensable. Moreover, in order to avoid further
confusion, it would be highly desirable if the British Government would seize an
early public occasion in order to reiterate the Prime Minister's declaration of May 24
[concerning] 'the Polish Government which we recognize and which we have always
recognized.' " *Polish-Soviet Relations,* vol. 2, no. 164.

[4] The Polish government-in-exile in London.

[5] On July 26 Eden reiterated the British position in the House of Commons:
"There has been no change in the attitude of His Majesty's Government, who
continue to recognise the Polish government, [led] by M. Mikolajczyk, as the
Government of Poland." He immediately added: "Since, however, we are here
concerned with relations between two of our Allies, I would ask the House not to
press me further at this stage." *Parliamentary Debates,* Commons, 5th ser., vol. 402,
col. 761.

In private, Eden was considerably less optimistic. He put no stock in Roosevelt's
promises to Mikolajczyk: "The President will do nothing for the Poles, any more

Anything you say to U.J. that will induce him to give Mikolajczyk a good welcome and realise the importance of founding a united Polish government will be invaluable. The great hope is fusion of some kind between the Poles relying on Russia and Poles relying on U.S.A. and G.B. We are sure that U.J. will be much influenced by your view of these things.

---

than Mr. Hull did at Moscow or the President did himself at Tehran. The poor Poles are sadly deluding themselves if they place any faith in these vague and generous promises. The President will not be embarrassed by them thereafter, any more than by the specific undertaking he has given to restore the French Empire." *The Memoirs of Anthony Eden, Earl of Avon,* vol. 2, *The Reckoning* (Boston, 1965), pp. 539–540. Henceforth cited as Eden, *Memoirs.*

Doc. 408
CHURCHILL TO ROOSEVELT

No. 736   July 25, 1944

Following are telegrams referred to in paragraph 1 of my immediately preceding telegram.[1]

"Premier Stalin to Prime Minister. Dated July 23rd.

"I have received your message of July 20th. I am writing to you now only on the Polish question.

"Events in our front are proceeding at an extremely rapid tempo. Lublin, one of the large towns of Poland, was occupied today by our troops, who are continuing to advance.

"In these circumstances the question of administration on Polish territory has arisen for us in a practical form. We do not wish to have and shall not set up our administration on the territory of Poland, for we do not wish to interfere in the internal affairs of Poland. The Poles themselves must do this. We therefore considered it necessary to establish contact with the Polish Committee of National Liberation, which was recently set up by the National Council of Poland, which was itself constituted in Warsaw at the end of last year out of representatives of the democratic parties and groups, as you must already have been informed by your Ambassador in Moscow.[2] The Polish Committee of National Liberation intends to undertake the setting up of administration on Polish territory, and this, I hope, will be accomplished. In Poland we have not found any other forces which could have set up a Polish administration. The so-called underground

1 See above, Doc. 407.
2 Sir Archibald Clark Kerr.

organisations, directed by the Polish government in London, proved ephemeral and devoid of influence. I cannot consider the Polish Committee as the Government of Poland, but it is possible that, in due course, it will serve as a nucleus for the formation of a provisional Polish government out of democratic forces.

"As regards Mikolajczyk, I shall of course not refuse to receive him. It would however be better if he were to address himself to the Polish National Committee, whose attitude would be friendly towards Mikolajczyk."

Doc. 409
CHURCHILL TO ROOSEVELT

No. 740   July 29, 1944

This seems to me the best ever received from U.J.:[1]

"I have received your messages of the 25th and 27th July on the subject of the departure of Mikolajczyk. M. Mikolajczyk and his party will be given the necessary assistance on arrival in Moscow.

"You know our point of view on the question of Poland who is our neighbour and relations with whom have an especial importance for the Soviet Union. We welcome the National Committee which has been created on the territory of Poland from democratic forces and I think that by the creation of this Committee a good start has been made for the unification of Poles friendly disposed towards Great Britain, the U.S.S.R., and the United States and for the surmounting of opposition on the part of those Polish elements who are not capable of unification with democratic forces.

"I understand the importance of the Polish question for the common cause of the Allies and for this very reason I am prepared to give assistance to all Poles and to mediate in the attainment of an agreement between them. The Soviet forces have done and are doing everything possible to hasten the liberation of Poland from the German usurpers and to help the Polish people in the restoration of their freedom and in the matter of the welfare of their country."

Message of 25th July is contained in my 736 to you.[2] Following is text of my message to U.J. of 27th July:

"1. Mikolajczyk and his colleagues have started.[3] I am sure Miko-

---

[1] Stalin's message was dated July 28.

[2] See above, Doc. 408.

[3] On July 27 Mikolajczyk and two other Polish officials left London for Moscow, where they met with Stalin from August 1 to August 10.

lajczyk is most anxious to help a general fusion of all Poles on the lines on which you and I and the President are, I believe, agreed. I believe that Poles who are friendly to Russia should join with Poles who are friendly to Great Britain and the United States in order to establish the strong, free, independent Poland, the good neighbour of Russia and an important barrier between you and another German outrage. We will all three take good care there are other barriers also.

"2. It would be a great pity and even disaster if the Western democracies found themselves recognising one body of Poles and you recognising another. It could lead to constant friction and might even hamper the great business which we have to do the wide world over. Please therefore receive these few sentences in the spirit in which they are sent which is one of sincere friendship and our 20 years' alliance."

Doc. 410
ROOSEVELT TO CHURCHILL

No. 593   August 3, 1944

Your 740,[1] received at sea,[2] indicated that we have reason to hope that the Stalin-Mikolajczyk conversation may bring about a settlement of the Polish controversy that can be accepted by all of us.

My inspection journey to the Pacific has already been fully justified by my conferences with the High Commands.[3]

[1] See above, Doc. 409.

[2] For a good account of President Roosevelt's trip to the Pacific, see James MacGregor Burns, *Roosevelt: Soldier of Freedom* (New York, 1970) , pp. 488ff.; and Morison, *History of U.S. Naval Operations*, vol. 12, *Leyte, June 1944–January 1945* (Boston, 1958) , pp. 8ff.

[3] For an account of the President's meeting at Honolulu with General Douglas MacArthur and Admiral Chester Nimitz, see William D. Leahy, *I Was There* (New York, 1950) , pp. 250ff.; and Samuel I. Rosenman, *Working with Roosevelt* (New York, 1952) , pp. 455ff. The principal question, as Roosevelt put it to MacArthur, was: "Douglas, where do we go from here?" MacArthur, contending that "both national honor and sound strategy required the liberation of the Philippines before we went further," replied: "Leyte, Mr. President, and then Luzon!" It should be noted, however, that the Joint Chiefs of Staff "do not seem to have been particularly impressed by this top-level accord, since they continued to argue the question, 'Luzon, Formosa, or what?' for months thereafter." Morison, *History of U.S. Naval Operations*, 12: 9–11.

Doc. 411
CHURCHILL TO ROOSEVELT

No. 745   August 10, 1944

I send you the following telegram from Premier Stalin. The mood is more agreeable than we have sometimes met, and I think that we should persevere.

"Aug. 8. Premier Stalin to Prime Minister.

"I wish to inform you about my meeting with Mikolajczyk, Grabski,[1] and Romer.[2] My talk with Mikolajczyk convinced me that he has unsatisfactory information about affairs in Poland. At the same time, I was left with the impression that Mikolajczyk is not opposed to the finding of ways to unite the Poles.

"Para two. As I did not consider it possible to press any decision on the Poles, I suggested to Mikolajczyk that he and colleagues should meet and themselves discuss their questions with representatives of the Polish Committee of National Liberation and, above all, the question of the speediest possible union of all the democratic forces of Poland on liberated Polish territory. These meetings have taken place. I have been informed about them by both sides. The delegation of the National Committee proposed that the 1921 constitution should be taken as the basis of the activity of the Polish Government, and, in the event of agreement, offered Mikolajczyk's group four portfolios, among them the post of Prime Minister for Mikolajczyk. Mikolajczyk, however, could not bring himself (literally 'did not decide') to give his agreement to this. Unfortunately, these meetings have not yet led to the desired results, but they have all the same had a positive significance, inasmuch as they have permitted both Mikolajczyk and also Morawski[3] and Berut,[4] who had only just arrived from Warsaw, to inform each other in a broad way about their points of view and especially of the fact that both the Polish National Committee and Mikolajczyk expressed the wish to work together and to seek the practical possibilities to that end. One may consider this as the first

1 Stanislaw Grabski, chairman of the Polish National Council, a Soviet-sponsored body.
2 Tadeusz Romer, Minister of Foreign Affairs of the Polish government-in-exile in London.
3 Edward Boleslaw Osòbka-Morawski, chairman of the Soviet-sponsored Polish Committee of National Liberation.
4 Boleslaw Berut, chairman of the National People's Council of Poland. The latter group, established in Warsaw on January 1, 1944, unified the Polish partisan groups into a People's Army which in turn formed the nucleus of the Lublin Committee.

stage in relations between the Polish Committee and Mikolajczyk and his colleagues. We shall hope that the business will go better in future."

Doc. 412
CHURCHILL TO ROOSEVELT

No. 750   August 10, 1944

I have a very bad report on the climatic conditions in Bermuda in the first or second week of September.[1] It is said to be extremely hot and steamy whether ashore or afloat. There is also a persistent southerly wind reported very sticky and unpleasant. I most deeply regret your inability to visit Scotland. The King[2] seemed very much disappointed when I told him. However, I quite see that, with Stalin not coming, you may wish to defer this promised visit. I, therefore, recommend the Quadrant area.[3] Mackenzie King[4] assured me he would be enchanted. I have no doubt all could be arranged to your comfort and convenience.

I agree about reduced staff on the Teheran scale, but I hope that the meeting will not be delayed beyond the early part of September. There are several serious matters in the military sphere which must be adjusted between our staffs. I, too, would greatly welcome a few frank talks with you on matters it is difficult to put on paper. We have to settle the part the British Empire should take in the war against Japan after German's unconditional surrender. The situation in Burma causes me much anxiety. We have suffered very heavy losses through disease and the prospect of the whole forces of the British Indian Army being tied down indefinitely in the worst part of the country is unattractive.[5] Other tangled questions arise about the position of Alexander's army in Italy including whether it is to be bled white for Dragoon[6] and thus stripped of all initiative. It is impossible to resolve

---

[1] Roosevelt had proposed Bermuda as a possible site for the September summit meeting.

[2] George VI of England.

[3] Quebec.

[4] William Lyon Mackenzie King, Prime Minister of Canada.

[5] For an account of British plans and operations in Burma at this time, see S. Woodburn Kirby, *The War Against Japan*, vol. 4, *The Reconquest of Burma* (London, 1956), pp. 101ff.

[6] Code name for the forthcoming invasion of southern France (formerly Anvil).

these thorny matters by correspondence and I am sure that, if we and the staffs were together, good working agreements could be reached.

It will be a very great pleasure for me to see you again. I do hope your tour[7] has done you good. Let me know your wishes as soon as possible.

7 During the election campaign, Roosevelt made a secret trip between July 13 and August 17, visiting the West Coast, Hawaii, and Alaska.

Doc. 413
CHURCHILL TO ROOSEVELT

No. 751   August 11, 1944

The following telegram received from Ambassador Clark Kerr[1] dated 10 Aug. '44 contains our latest news of Polish affairs.

"M. Mikolajczyk left this morning. I did not see him again after his visit to Stalin last night, but he sent me a message to say that the atmosphere at the Kremlin had been much more cordial than last time. Both Stalin and Molotov had shown marked friendliness. Stalin had answered the question I had suggested with a categorical assurance that he had no intention of communising Poland. He had emphasised the need for an alliance between Poland and the U.S.S.R. but had said that the Poles must have ties with the West also, 'alliances with Great Britain, the United States, and France.'

"Stalin had agreed to send help to the Poles in Warsaw, and had said that arrangements must at once be made for Marshal Rokossovski[2] to send a Soviet officer to Polish headquarters here with cyphers and wireless.

"The talk had then turned on Germany. Stalin had said he would do 'everything possible and impossible' to ensure that Germany could never again reap revenge. Mikolajczyk had told Stalin that a German officer captured in Normandy had said that Germany would go Communist after the war, and would find in the Communist part of the world an outlet for the German capacity for organisation. To this, Stalin had replied that communism was 'no more fit for Germany than a saddle for a cow.' This had surprised and pleased the Poles, who had recalled the German origins of the Communist theory.

"Mikolajczyk now felt that speed was the first essential.

1 British ambassador to the Soviet Union.
2 General Konstantin Rokossovski, commander of the first Byelorussian Front. Earlier in August, he had tried unsuccessfully to cross the Vistula River south of Warsaw.

"It is clear that this talk has put cheerfulness where there has been gloom in the hearts of the Poles."

Doc. 414
CHURCHILL TO ROOSEVELT

No. 753   August 14, 1944

I have had meetings during the last 2 days with Marshal Tito and the Yugoslav Prime Minister.[1] I told both the Yugoslav leaders that we had no thought but that they should combine their resources so as to weld the Yugoslav people into one instrument in the struggle against the Germans. Our aim was to promote the establishment of a stable and independent Yugoslavia, and the creation of a united Yugoslav government was a step towards this end.

The two leaders reached a satisfactory agreement on a number of practical questions. They agreed that all the Yugoslav naval forces will now be united in the struggle under a common flag. This agreement between the Yugoslav Prime Minister and Marshal Tito will enable us with more confidence to increase our supplies of war material to the Yugoslav forces.[2]

They agreed between themselves to issue [an announcement] simultaneously in a few days time, which I hope will strengthen and intensify the Yugoslav war effort. They are going off together today to Vis to continue their discussions.

I am informing Marshal Stalin of the result of these meetings.

1 Churchill met with Marshal Tito and Prime Minister Ivan Subasić at Caserta, Italy, on August 12–13. See Churchill, *Triumph and Tragedy*, pp. 88ff.

2 Eden was skeptical of Tito's forthrightness, and Churchill soon developed doubts of his own. On August 31 he sent Eden a memorandum, remarking, as Eden recalled later, "upon our responsibility for supplying Tito with arms with which he could subjugate Yugoslavia." Eden replied in effect that the Foreign Office had been warning of such a danger for many months. "I have," he told Churchill, "certainly never lost sight of this danger, which has arisen largely because our policy towards Yugoslavia has had to be dictated on grounds of short-term military expediency rather than those of long-term political interest." Eden, *Memoirs*, 2: 546.

Doc. 415
ROOSEVELT TO CHURCHILL

No. 599   August 14, 1944

Your 753.[1] Congratulations on your prospects of success in bringing together the opposing factions in Yugoslavia which should bring to an end the civil war in that country and be of assistance to us in the rapidly approaching defeat of the Nazis.

1 See above, Doc. 414.

Doc. 416
CHURCHILL TO ROOSEVELT

No. 755   August 17, 1944

We have always marched together in complete agreement about Greek policy, and I refer to you on every important point. The War Cabinet and Foreign Secretary are much concerned about what will happen in Athens, and indeed in Greece, when the Germans crack or when their divisions try to evacuate the country. If there is a long hiatus after German authorities have gone from [the] city before organised government can be set up, it seems very likely that EAM and the Communist extremists will attempt to seize the city and crush all other form of Greek expression but their own.

You and I have always agreed that the destinies of Greece are in the hands of the Greek people, and they will have the fullest opportunity of deciding between a monarchy or republic as soon as tranquility has been restored, but I do not expect you will relish more than I do the prospect of chaos and street fighting or of a tyrannical Communist government being set up. This could only serve to delay and hamper all the plans which are being made by UNRRA[1] for the distribution of relief to the sorely tried Greek people. I therefore think that we should make preparations through the Allied staff in the Mediterranean to have in readiness a British force, not exceeding 10,000 men, which could be sent by the most expeditious means into the capital when the time is ripe. The force would include parachute troops, for which the help of your air forces would be needed. I do not myself

1 United Nations Relief and Rehabilitation Administration.

expect that anything will happen for a month, and it may be longer but it is always well to be prepared. As far as I can see there will be no insuperable difficulty. I hope, therefore, you will agree that we may make these preparations by the staffs out here in the usual way. If so, the British Chiefs of Staff will submit to the Combined Chiefs of Staff draft.

Doc. 417
CHURCHILL TO ROOSEVELT

August 18, 1944[1]

"Para 1. After the conversation with M. Mikolajczyk I gave orders that the command of the Red Army should drop arms intensively in the Warsaw sector. A parachutist liaison officer was also dropped who, according to the report of the command, did not reach his objective as he was killed by the Germans.

"Further, having familiarised myself more closely with the Warsaw affair, I am convinced that the Warsaw action represents a reckless and terrible adventure which is costing the population large sacrifices. This would not have been if the Soviet command had been informed before the beginning of the Warsaw action and if the Poles had maintained contact with it.[2]

"In the situation which has arisen the Soviet command has come to the conclusion that it must dissociate itself from the Warsaw adventure as it cannot take either direct or indirect responsibility for the Warsaw action.[3]

1 This message from Stalin was sent by the American military attaché in London with a prefatory sentence stating that the Prime Minister wanted the President to see it.

2 On August 17 Ambassador Harriman cabled Roosevelt that "for some time the Soviet radio has been urging the Poles to throw caution aside and rise against the Germans." *FR 1944*, 3: 1378. For background on the Warsaw uprising see Stanislaw Mikolajczyk, *The Rape of Poland: Pattern of Soviet Aggression* (New York, 1948), chap. 6; *Polish-Soviet Relations*, 2: 324ff.; George L. Bruce, *The Warsaw Uprising, 1 August–2 October 1944* (London, 1972); and for a differing Polish view, see Jan M. Ciechanowski, *The Warsaw Rising of 1944* (Cambridge, 1974).

3 In a message to President Roosevelt on August 18 Mikolajczyk asked for immediate American assistance to the embattled Warsaw resistance, noting that "Moscow Radio on July 29 at 8:15 P.M. in a broadcast in Polish appealed to Warsaw to strike at the Germans. On the other hand M. Molotov told me in Moscow on the 31 of July that Soviet troops were only 10 km from Warsaw and Marshal Stalin informed me that the Soviet Army expected to enter the city on the 6 of August.

"Para 2. I have received your communication regarding the meeting with Marshal Tito and Prime Minister Subasić. I thank you for the communication.

"Para 3. I am very pleased at the successful landing of Allied forces in the south of France.[4] I wish success from my heart."

Hearing the sound of battle on the outskirts of Warsaw the Commander of the Home Army General Broz had all the reasons to give the order for rising." *Polish-Soviet Relations*, vol. 2, no. 202.

[4] American, British, and French forces had landed in southern France on August 15.

Doc. 418
CHURCHILL TO ROOSEVELT

No. 760   August 18, 1944

The refusal of the Soviet to allow the U.S. aircraft to bring succour to the heroic insurgents in Warsaw[1] added to their own complete neglect to fly in supplies when only a few score of miles away constitutes an episode of profound and far-reaching gravity. If, as is almost certain, the German triumph in Warsaw is followed by a wholesale massacre no measure can be put upon the full consequences that will arise. I am willing to send a personal message to Stalin if you think this wise and if you will yourself send a separate similar message.

Better far than two separate messages would be a joint message signed by us both. I have no doubt we could agree on the wording.

The situation in Europe is being vastly changed by the glorious and gigantic victories being achieved in France by the U.S. and British forces and it may well be that our armies will gain a victory in Normandy[2] which far exceeds in scale anything that the Russians have done on any particular occasion. I am inclined to think, therefore, that they will have some respect for what we say so long as it is plain and simple. It is quite possible Stalin would not resent it but even if he did we are nations serving high causes and must give true counsels towards world peace.

[1] As the Soviet forces approached Warsaw, the Polish underground in the city launched a major uprising on August 1.

[2] The breakout from Normandy had begun on July 28. See Martin Blumenson, *Breakout and Pursuit* (Washington, 1961), chaps. 13–24. Several weeks later, in the wake of numerous Allied advances in Normandy, Hitler reportedly said: "The 15th of August was the worst day of my life." Felix Gilbert, ed., *Hitler Directs His War: The Secret Records of His Daily Military Conferences* (New York, 1950), p. 102.

Doc. 419
ROOSEVELT TO CHURCHILL

No. 601   August 19, 1944

Your 760.[1] The following is suggested as a joint message to U.J. which if you approve you may send over both our signatures:
QUOTE. We are thinking of world opinion if the anti-Nazis in Warsaw are in effect abandoned. We believe that all three of us should do the utmost to save as many of the patriots there as possible. We hope that you will drop immediate supplies and munitions to the patriot Poles in Warsaw, or will agree that our planes should do it very quickly. We hope you will approve. The time element is of extreme importance. UNQUOTE.[2]

1 See above, Doc. 418.
2 For Churchill's reply, see below, Doc. 421.

Doc. 420
CHURCHILL TO ROOSEVELT

No. 761   August 20, 1944

Further to my 760.[1]
You should see the following telegram which I have just received from Foreign Secretary:
"The Polish Government have reminded me that Soviet broadcasting stations have for a considerable time past repeated appeals to the Polish population to drop all caution and start a general rising against the Germans. As late as July 29th, i.e., three days before the Warsaw rising began, the Moscow radio station broadcast an appeal from the Union of Polish Patriots[2] to the population of Warsaw which, after referring to the fact that the guns of liberation were now within hearing, called upon them as in 1939 to join battle with the Germans, this time for decisive action: 'For Warsaw, which did not yield but fought on, the hour of action has already arrived.' " . . .

1 See above, Doc. 418.
2 The nucleus of the first pro-Soviet government in Poland, established in March 1943. The group's president was Wanda Wassilewska, a member of the Supreme Soviet of the U.S.S.R. and wife of the Vice Commissar for Foreign Affairs.

Doc. 421
CHURCHILL TO ROOSEVELT

No. 762   August 20, 1944

The message in your number 601[1] has been sent on to U.J. over our two signatures. Our thoughts are one.

Following telegram received from our Ambassador in Moscow, dated 17 August:

"United States Ambassador[2] and I are asking urgently for interview with M. Stalin. If his instructions do not arrive in time he will support me on his own responsibility.

"You should, however, know that last night Vyshinsky[3] asked the United States Ambassador to call, and explaining that he wished to avoid the possibility of misunderstanding about what he had said to us the previous afternoon, read out the following statement. Begins:

" 'The Soviet Government cannot, of course, object to English or American aircraft dropping arms in the region of Warsaw since this is American and British affair. But they decidedly object to American or British aircraft, after dropping arms in the region of Warsaw, landing on Soviet territory, since the Soviet Government do not wish to associate themselves either directly or indirectly with the adventure in Warsaw.' "

[1] See above, Doc. 419.
[2] W. Averell Harriman.
[3] Andrei A. Vyshinsky, Deputy Minister of Foreign Affairs, was also a Soviet representative on the Italian Advisory Council.

Doc. 422
CHURCHILL TO ROOSEVELT

No. 765   August 23, 1944

After much pressure from Weizmann[1] I have arranged that the War Office shall raise a Jewish brigade group in what you would call a regimental combat team. This will give great satisfaction to the Jews when it is published and surely they of all other races have the right to strike at the Germans as a recognisable body. They wish to have their own flag, which is the Star of David on a white background with two

[1] Chaim Weizmann, head of the World Zionist Organization.

light blue bars. I cannot see why this should not be done. Indeed I think that the flying of this flag at the head of a combat unit would be a message to go all over the world. If the usual silly objections are raised I can overcome them, but before going ahead I should like to know whether you have any views upon it.[2]

2 For Roosevelt's reply, see below, Doc. 427.

Doc. 423
ROOSEVELT TO CHURCHILL

No. 603   August 23, 1944

Your 759,[1] 761,[2] and 762.[3] We must continue to hope for agreement by the Soviet to our desire to assist the Poles in Warsaw.

1 See above, Doc. 417.
2 See above, Doc. 420.
3 See above, Doc. 421.

Doc. 424
CHURCHILL TO ROOSEVELT

No. 769   August 25, 1944

Uncle Joe's reply adds nothing to our knowledge and he avoids the definite questions asked.[1] I suggest following reply:

"We are most anxious to send American planes from England. Why should they not land on the refuelling ground which has been assigned to us behind the Russian lines without enquiry as to what they have done on the way? This should preserve the principle of your Government's dissociation from this particular episode. We feel sure that if wounded British or American planes arrive behind the lines of your armies, they will be succoured with your usual consideration. We do not try to form an opinion about the persons who instigated this rising which was certainly called for repeatedly by Radio Moscow. Our sympathies are, however, for the 'almost unarmed people' whose

1 On August 22 Stalin replied to Roosevelt and Churchill's joint message of August 20 (see above, Doc. 419). Rejecting their appeal to aid the Warsaw patriots, he declared: "Sooner or later the truth about the handful of power-seeking criminals who launched the Warsaw adventure will out." *Stalin's Correspondence*, vol. 2, no. 223.

special faith has led them to attack German guns, tanks, and aircraft. We cannot think that Hitler's cruelties will end with their resistance. On the contrary, it seems probable that that is the time when they will begin with full ferocity. The massacre in Warsaw will undoubtedly be a very great annoyance to us when we all meet at the end of the war. Unless you directly forbid it, therefore, we propose to send the planes."

If he will not give any reply to this I feel we ought to go and see what happens. I cannot conceive that he would maltreat or detain them. Since signing this, I have seen that they are even trying to take away your airfields at Poltava and elsewhere.

Doc. 425
CHURCHILL TO ROOSEVELT

No. 770   August 25, 1944

Could you very kindly give me an answer to my telegram of August 16th (number 755) ?[1] We are getting on with the preparations and the crisis may come soon. Should you feel you do not wish to express an opinion on the subject I am quite willing to go ahead on my own.[2]

[1] See above, Doc. 416, dated August 17.
[2] For Roosevelt's reply, see below, Doc. 428, note 5.

Doc. 426
ROOSEVELT TO CHURCHILL

No. 606   August 26, 1944

Your 769.[1] In consideration of Stalin's present attitude in regard to relief of the Polish underground in Warsaw as expressed in his messages to you and to me, and his definite refusal to permit the use by us of Soviet airfields for that purpose, and in view of current American conversations in regard to the subsequent use of other Soviet bases, I do not consider it advantageous to the long-range general war prospect for me to join with you in the proposed message to U.J.

I have no objection to your sending such a message if you consider it advisable to do so.[2]

[1] See above, Doc. 424.
[2] Churchill did not send the proposed message.

Doc. 427
ROOSEVELT TO CHURCHILL

No. 609

August 28, 1944

Your 765.[1] I perceive no objection to your organizing a Jewish brigade as suggested.

1 See above, Doc. 422.

Doc. 428
CHURCHILL TO ROOSEVELT

No. 771

August 29, 1944

To take part in the conference[1] I shall only bring 14 or 15 persons but I must explain to you that as I and the Chiefs of Staff have to conduct a very great number of important affairs from day to day it will be necessary to have considerable numbers of persons for that purpose. For instance. My own party and private secretaries 7. Secretariat and administration 6. Clerical 42. Cypher staff 30. Royal Marine Guard 36. There will also be a small contingent from our element in Washington. These however are only the machinery with which I carry on my work and without which I could not leave the country. You have all your great departments immediately under your hand a few hours away by air.

The glorious events in France[2] and in the Balkans[3] have completely altered the whole outlook of the war and with people like the Germans anything might happen. Last time Bulgaria proved the lynchpin which when pulled brought everything crashing down.[4]

I must express my admiration to you not only for the valour but for the astonishing mobility and manoeuvering power of the great armies

1 Roosevelt and Churchill had agreed to meet in Quebec on September 11.

2 Allied forces had liberated Paris on August 25. Three days later French forces took Marseilles and Toulon.

3 Rumania had surrendered unconditionally on August 23, and Bulgaria followed suit on August 25. Russian forces occupied Brest-Litovsk on August 28.

4 Bulgaria had accepted the Allied armistice terms on September 30, 1918, which set in motion the collapse of the central powers, culminating in the German armistice of November 11.

trained in the United States. I am looking forward immensely to seeing you again and trying to clear up with you in the light of our friendship some of the difficulties which beset even the path of dazzling victory. Thank you very much for your telegram about Greece.[5]

[5] Not printed. In that message, dated August 26, Roosevelt told the Prime Minister: "I have no objection to your making preparations to have in readiness a sufficient British force to preserve order in Greece when the German forces evacuate that country. There is also no objection to the use by General Wilson of American transport airplanes that are available to him at that time and that can be spared from his other operations." *FR 1944,* 4: 133–134.

Doc. 429
CHURCHILL TO ROOSEVELT

No. 776   September 1, 1944

I see that General Donovan[1] has sent an American mission to General Milhailović.[2] I thought from your telegram No. 515,[3] in response to my No. 638,[4] that such a step would not be taken. We are endeavouring to give Tito the support and, of course, if the United States back Mihailović, complete chaos will ensue. I was rather hoping things were going to get a bit smoother in these parts, but if we each back different sides, we lay the scene for a fine civil war. General Donovan is running a strong Mihailović lobby, just when we have persuaded King Peter[5] to break decisively with him and when many of the Chetniks[6] are being rallied under Tito's National Army of Liberation. The only chance of saving the King is the unity between his Prime Minister, the Ban of Croatia,[7] and Tito. I have been able to arrange for the fusion of the Yugoslav air and naval forces under the title and with the emblem of the Royal Yugoslav Air Force and the Royal Yugoslav Navy.

[1] Brigadier General William J. Donovan, director of the U.S. Office of Strategic Services.

[2] General Draža Mihailović, Yugoslav resistance leader and a political opponent of Marshal Tito.

[3] See above, Doc. 346.

[4] See above, Doc. 345.

[5] Peter II of Yugoslavia.

[6] Followers of General Mihailović.

[7] Dr. Ivan Subasić.

Doc. 430
ROOSEVELT TO CHURCHILL

No. 617   September 3, 1944

Your No. 776.[1]
The mission of OSS[2] is my mistake. I did not check with my previous action of last April 8th.[3] I am directing Donovan to withdraw his mission.

1 See above, Doc. 429.
2 Office of Strategic Services.
3 Roosevelt had agreed in April that no OSS mission should be sent to Mihailović's headquarters. See above, Doc. 346. See also Walter R. Roberts, *Tito, Mihailović, and the Allies, 1941–1945* (New Brunswick, 1973), pp. 254ff.

Doc. 431
CHURCHILL TO ROOSEVELT

No. 779   September 4, 1944

1. The War Cabinet are deeply disturbed at the position in Warsaw and at the far-reaching effect on future relations with Russia of Stalin's refusal of airfield facilities.[1]

2. Moreover as you know Mikolajczyk has sent his proposals to the Polish Committee of Liberation for a political settlement.[2] I am afraid that the fall of Warsaw will not only destroy any hope of progress but will fatally undermine the position of Mikolajczyk himself.

3. My immediately following telegram[3] contains the text of a telegram which the War Cabinet in their collective capacity have sent to our Ambassador in Moscow and also of a message which the women of Warsaw have communicated to the Pope and which has been handed by the Vatican to our Minister.[4]

1 See above, Doc. 418.
2 See *Polish-Soviet Relations*, vol. 2, no. 214.
3 See below, Doc. 432.
4 The message from the women of Warsaw to Pope Pius XII concluded: "Holy Father, no one is helping us. The Russian armies which have been for three weeks at the gates of Warsaw have not advanced a step. The aid coming to us from Great Britain is insufficient. The world is ignorant of our fight. God alone is with us. Holy Father, Vicar of Christ, if you can hear us, bless us Polish women who are fighting for the Church and for freedom." Churchill, *Triumph and Tragedy*, p. 143.

4. The only way of bringing material help quickly to the Poles fighting in Warsaw would be for United States aircraft to drop supplies using Russian airfields for the purpose. Seeing how much is in jeopardy we beg that you will again consider the big stakes involved. Could you not authorise your air forces to carry out this operation, landing if necessary on Russian airfields without their formal consent? In view of our great successes in the west, I cannot think that the Russians could reject this fait accompli. They might even welcome it as getting them out of an awkward situation. We would of course share full responsibility with you for any action taken by your air forces.

Doc. 432
CHURCHILL TO ROOSEVELT

No. 780   September 4, 1944

Following is text of telegram sent to Moscow this evening mentioned in my immediately preceding telegram:[1]

"1. The War Cabinet at their meeting today considered the latest reports of the situation in Warsaw which show that the Poles fighting against the Germans there are in desperate straits.

"2. The War Cabinet wish the Soviet Government to know that public opinion in this country is deeply moved by the events in Warsaw and by the terrible sufferings of the Poles there. Whatever the rights and wrongs about the beginnings of the Warsaw rising, the people of Warsaw themselves cannot be held responsible for the decision taken. Our people cannot understand why no material help has been sent from outside to the Poles in Warsaw. The fact that such help could not be sent on account of your Government's refusal to allow United States aircraft to land on aerodromes in Russian hands is now becoming publicly known. If on top of all this the Poles in Warsaw should now be overwhelmed by the Germans, as we are told they must be within two or three days, the shock to public opinion here will be incalculable. The War Cabinet themselves find it hard to understand your Government's refusal to take account of the obligations of the British and American Governments to help the Poles in Warsaw. Your Government's action in preventing this help being sent seems to us at variance with the spirit of Allied cooperation to which

1 See above, Doc. 431.

you and we attach so much importance both for the present and the future."

Doc. 433
ROOSEVELT TO CHURCHILL

No. 619   September 5, 1944

Replying to your 779,[1] 780,[2] and 781,[3] I am informed by my Office of Military Intelligence that the fighting Poles have departed from Warsaw and that the Germans are now in full control.[4]

The problem of relief for the Poles in Warsaw has therefore unfortunately been solved by delay and by German action and there now appears to be nothing we can do to assist them.

I have long been deeply distressed by our inability to give adequate assistance to the heroic defenders of Warsaw and I hope that we may together still be able to help Poland and be among the victors in this war with the Nazis.

[1] See above, Doc. 431.
[2] See above, Doc. 432.
[3] Not printed.
[4] The Warsaw resistance was not actually defeated until October 3.

THE SECOND QUEBEC CONFERENCE
SEPTEMBER 1944

[Roosevelt and Churchill held their second meeting in Quebec between September 11 and September 16, 1944, at the conference known by the code name Octagon. They were accompanied by their top military chiefs—Roosevelt brought along Admiral Leahy, General Marshall and Admiral King, General Henry H. Arnold, and Treasury Secretary Morgenthau, while Churchill had with him Generals Sir John Dill and Sir Alan Brooke, his Chief of Staff Sir Hastings Ismay, Admiral Sir Andrew Browne Cunningham, Air Marshal Sir Charles Portal, and Major General Leslie C. Hollis, a member of the secretariat of the Combined Chiefs of Staff, as well as Anthony Eden, Lord Cherwell, and Sir Alexander Cadogan, whom he ordered to come from Washington where the conference on postwar international organization was then in session. Canadian Prime Minister Mackenzie King participated in several sessions, and Roosevelt had a notable teatime conversation with Archduke Otto of Austria.

Before the opening of the meeting, Roosevelt had informed Undersecretary of State Edward R. Stettinius, Jr., that "Quebec is to be entirely military," and military, or quasi-military, issues were indeed the first order of business between the President and the Prime Minister. The main lines of Allied grand strategy had, of course, been agreed upon at the summit conferences of 1943 and were now in process of being carried out. The time had come, therefore, to look ahead and plan for the time after the defeat of Nazi Germany. Roosevelt and Churchill rapidly agreed on British participation in the war against Japan, on modification of the Italian armistice, and on the zones of occupation in Germany. To Churchill's regret, it was also agreed that no additional forces were to be assigned to the Mediterranean theater and that the United States was not to participate in the liberation of Greece. The British revived their earlier proposal for a concerted drive on Vienna, but American resistance to the plan produced less bad feeling at Quebec than it had at earlier meetings. Even so, Churchill, shocked at Stalin's unwillingness to rescue the Warsaw patriots or even to permit British and American planes to use Russian-controlled airfields to supply the Polish fighters, was quoted as saying that "he preferred to get into Vienna before the Russians did, as one did not know what Russia's policy would be after she took it."

Despite Roosevelt's plans for the meeting, and specific assurances to Stettinius, the President and the Prime Minister took up a number of important political and diplomatic issues. Roosevelt discussed atomic energy problems with Churchill's scientific adviser, Lord Cherwell, and reviewed with Churchill and Eden the problem of voting rights in the Security Council of the proposed new international organization (a subject on which the ongoing Dumbarton Oaks conference in Washington was making no progress). Indeed, on this particular subject Churchill admitted that he had not studied the papers, and Cadogan feared that "neither Churchill nor the President had a complete understanding of what was involved." On another matter, Churchill was delighted with Secretary Morgenthau's proposal that Great Britain receive $3.5 billion in lend-lease assistance between the end of the war in Europe and the defeat of Japan, along with an American loan of $3 billion for nonmilitary purposes.

The most striking development at the second Quebec conference was Morgenthau's proposal for reducing postwar Germany to an agrarian economy. When Morgenthau first explained the plan at a dinner with Roosevelt and Churchill on September 13, Churchill—

according to Morgenthau's account—turned loose "the full flood of his rhetoric, sarcasm, and violence." According to Lord Moran, Churchill's personal physician, the Prime Minister said: "I am all for disarming Germany but we ought not to prevent her living decently. . . . You cannot indict a whole nation. . . . [W]hat is to be done should be done quickly. Kill the criminals, but don't carry on the business for years."

But by the time Churchill met two days later with Roosevelt, Morgenthau, and Eden, he had changed his mind and now favored the scheme, pointing out to his Foreign Secretary "what this meant in the way of trade; [England] would get the export trade of Germany." Eden remained unconvinced and suggested that Secretary Hull be consulted. The disagreement grew into a heated public exchange. Eden wrote later: "This was the only occasion I can remember when the Prime Minister showed impatience with my views before foreign representatives. He resented my criticism of something which he and the President had approved, not I am sure on his account, but on the President's." Yet in the end it was Eden's—not Churchill's or Roosevelt's—judgment that carried the day. A few days later, word of the Morgenthau Plan leaked out, and there was such widespread opposition to it that Roosevelt and Churchill dropped the proposal, and nothing further was heard of it. At the end of the conference Roosevelt and Churchill cabled Stalin a summary of their principal military decisions.

By September 18, Roosevelt and Churchill had returned to Hyde Park where, in a top-secret aide mémoire, they agreed that work on the atomic bomb should be continued in "utmost secrecy," that when one had been completed, "it might, perhaps, after mature consideration, be used against the Japanese, who should be warned that this bombardment will be repeated until they surrender," and they further agreed that full Anglo-American collaboration on atomic energy for peaceful and military purposes should be continued after Japan's defeat until and unless terminated by mutual agreement. They also drafted, but did not send, a cable to Stalin expressing "certain anxieties which are much in our minds about political developments in Europe," and referred specifically to Yugoslavia, Greece, and Poland.

On the evening of September 19 the Churchill party, including the Prime Minister's wife and daughter Mary, left Hyde Park for New York, where they embarked on the *Queen Mary* for the voyage home. The President was well satisfied with their work. As he told the press at the close of the Quebec conference: "We have reached not only a complete unanimity, but we have made plans as far as any person can make plans today."]

Doc. 434
CHURCHILL TO ROOSEVELT

No. 784   September 22, 1944

About our Italian manifesto.[1] Anthony has made some valid comments which you no doubt have now seen.[2] The argument against publication of long armistice terms[3] at this stage is I feel conclusive. I do not think the omission of words "on basis of exchange of goods" would detract from the value of concessions.

I hear that a very bad impression has been produced in England by the Rome lynching.[4] It might therefore be wise to delay a week or so before making the announcement. This will also give time for a review of French situation which I am anxious to go into on my return and about which I will presently cable you.[5] Thank you so much for our delightful visit to your home. Every good wish. May we soon meet again.

[1] At the close of their conversations at Hyde Park, following the meeting at Quebec, Roosevelt and Churchill had agreed on a statement granting increased self-government to Italy, announcing "first steps" toward the reconstruction of the Italian economy and permitting Italy to send direct representatives to London and Washington. In their statement the President and the Prime Minister declared that the Italian people had "in these last twelve months demonstrated their will to be free, to fight on the side of the democracies, and to take a place among the United Nations devoted to the principles of peace and justice." *FR 1944*, 3: 1153–1154.

[2] Eden hoped that the President would "agree to leave out paragraph referring to a revision of long armistice terms. . . . We could not do this without prior consultation with Russia who is also a party to armistice terms. To omit such consultation would cause great offence." *FR 1944*, 3: 496–497.

[3] For the text of the Italian armistice terms, signed at Malta on September 29, 1943, by Marshal Badoglio and General Eisenhower, see Garland and Smyth, *Sicily and the Surrender of Italy*, app. D.

[4] A reference to the lynching of Rome police chief Pietro Caruso on September 18, 1944, during the "Social Republic" and the subsequent lynching of a former governor of the Regina Coeli prison, Donato Carretta. See C. R. S. Harris, *Allied Military Administration of Italy 1943–1945* (London, 1957), p. 213.

[5] See below, Doc. 443.

Doc. 435
CHURCHILL TO ROOSEVELT

No. 785   September 25, 1944

You will wish to read the following telegram I have received from Smuts.[1] Begins:

"I feel deeply perturbed over deadlock with Russia in world organisation talks.[2] This crisis, in any case, comes at most unfortunate moment before final end of war. I fear we are being rushed at breakneck pace into momentous decisions, and not in this case only. International aviation,[3] telecommunications, etc., all tell the same tale. Here, however, the consequences may be particularly disastrous. I may therefore be pardoned for sending a warning note about this impasse.

"At first, I thought the Russian attitude absurd[4] and their contention one not to be conceded by other great powers, and not unlikely to be turned down by smaller powers also. But second thoughts have tended the other way. I assume that Russian attitude is sincerely stated by Molotov and correctly interpreted by Clark Kerr and Cadogan[5] as one involving honour and standing of Russia among her allies. She asks whether she is trusted and treated as an equal or is still the outlaw and pariah. A misunderstanding here is more than a mere difference. It touches Russian *amour propre* and produces an inferiority complex and may poison European relations with far-reaching results. Russia, conscious of her power, may become more grasping than ever. Her

1 Jan Christiaan Smuts, Prime Minister of the Union of South Africa.

2 A reference to the conference on postwar international organization then being held at Dumbarton Oaks in Washington. The meeting had two phases: the first, between representatives of the United States, Great Britain, and the Soviet Union, lasted from August 21 to September 28; the second, between representatives of the United States, Great Britain, and China, lasted from September 29 to October 7. *FR 1944*, 1 (Washington, 1966): 713ff. In his subsequent account of the conference Secretary Hull noted that "there were now five questions concerning the United Nations organization left unsettled, for future decision. They were: voting in the [Security] Council (the deadlock Smuts mentions); statute of the International Court of Justice . . . ; initial membership; trusteeships; and liquidation of the League of Nations." Cordell Hull, *The Memoirs of Cordell Hull*, 2 vols. (New York, 1948), 2: 1706. Henceforth cited as Hull, *Memoirs*.

3 See below, Docs. 462, 468, and 470.

4 The Soviet Union insisted on an unconditional veto in the Security Council of the new world organization and on membership for each of the sixteen Soviet republics. See Hull, *Memoirs*, 2: 1678–1680.

5 Sir Alexander Cadogan, Permanent Undersecretary of State for Foreign Affairs.

making no attempt to find a solution shows her reaction and sense of power. What will be her future relations with Germany and Japan, even France, not to mention lesser countries? If a world organisation is formed with Russia out of it, she will become the power centre of another group and we shall be heading for World War III. If no such organisation is formed by the United Nations, they will stand stulti- fied before history. The dilemma is a very grave one, and the position into which we may be drifting should be avoided at all costs.

"In view of these dangers, the smaller powers should be prepared to make a concession to Russia's *amour propre* and should not on this matter insist on theoretical equality of status. Such insistence may have most devastating results for smaller powers themselves. Where questions of power and security are concerned, it would be most unwise to raise theoretical issues of sovereign equality, and United Kingdom and United States of America should use their influence in favour of common sense and safety first rather than status for the smaller countries.

"On the merits there is much to be said for unanimity among the great powers, at least for the years immediately following on this war. If in practice the principle proves unworkable, the situation could be reviewed later when mutual confidence has been established and a more workable basis laid down. At the present stage, a clash should be avoided at all costs. If unanimity for the powers is adopted, even including their voting on questions directly concerning their interests, the result would be that the United Kingdom and the United States of America will have to exert all their influence on Russia to be moderate and sensible and not to flout world opinion. And in this they are likely to be largely successful. If Russia proves impossible, the world organi- sation may have to act; but the blame will be here. At worst the principle of unanimity will only have the effect of a veto, of prevent- ing action where it may be wise or even necessary. It will be negative and slow down action. But it will also make it impossible for Russia to embark on crises disapproved of by United Kingdom and United States of America.

"Where people are drunk with new-won power, it may not be so bad a thing to have a brake-like unanimity. I do not defend it, I dislike it, but I do not think it at present so bad that the future of world peace and security should be sacrificed on this issue.

"The talks have so far been on an official advisory level although, no doubt, there may have been intervention on a higher level. I think, before definite decisions are reached on the highest level, the whole situation should be most carefully reconsidered in all its far-reaching implications, and some *modus vivendi*, even if only of a temporary character, should be explored among the great powers, which would prevent a catastrophe of the first magnitude. We simply must agree and cannot afford to differ where so much is at stake for the future."

Doc. 436
ROOSEVELT TO CHURCHILL

No. 623   September 28, 1944

Your 788.[1] I am pleased to know that our Italian announcement[2] went well in the U.K. It seems also to have been well received here.

In regard to the "French provisional government" I believe it would be wise to delay any action on our part until the German troops are expelled from all of France including Alsace and Lorraine.

I have no information as yet that General de Gaulle has expressed any desire for the setting up of any "zones of the interior" which would be the first change from a military to a civilian administration of the government.

1 Not printed.

2 The joint Anglo-American declaration stated, among other things, that Italy should henceforth be regarded as a friendly co-belligerent and no longer as an enemy state. See Woodward, *British Foreign Policy*, 3: 444ff.

Doc. 437
ROOSEVELT TO CHURCHILL

No. 624   September 28, 1944

Your 785.[1] I have read with great interest your telegram from Field Marshal Smuts, and I think we are all in agreement with him as to the necessity of having the U.S.S.R. as a fully accepted and equal member of any association of the great powers formed for the purpose of preventing international war.

It should be possible to accomplish this by adjusting our differences through compromise by all the parties concerned and this ought to tide things over for a few years until the child learns how to toddle.

1 See above, Doc. 435.

Doc. 438
CHURCHILL TO ROOSEVELT

No. 789   September 29, 1944

Your number 624.[1] I am repeating this to Field Marshal Smuts who will be much gratified.

U.J. was most expansive and friendly in a conversation with Averell[2] and Clark Kerr the other night. He however "grumbled about his own health." He said he was never well except at Moscow and his doctors did not like him flying. Even his visits to the front did him harm and it took him a fortnight to get over Teheran, etc.

In these circumstances Anthony and I are seriously considering flying there very soon. The route is shorter now. We have not yet heard from U.J. in reply to our suggestion. Our two great objects would be, first, to clinch his coming in against Japan and, secondly, to try to effect a friendly settlement with Poland. There are other points too about Greece and Yugoslavia which we would also discuss. We should keep you informed of every point. We would of course welcome Averell's assistance, or perhaps you could send Stettinius[3] or Marshall. I feel sure that personal contact is most necessary.

Your number 623.[4] You may be sure that we shall not take any action with the French except after full consultation with you. I hope nothing I said yesterday embarrassed you.[5] I see you use the expression "French provisional government" in your 623. It seems to me there would not be much harm in this phrase coming into use without any formal instrument being agreed between the Governments. After all they are the French provisional government and it is fully admitted even in the Boniface series[6] that they represent all France.

It seems to me pretty clear that Germany is not going to be conquered this year. Omar Bradley[7] in a telegram I have seen is already

1 See above, Doc. 437.

2 W. Averell Harriman.

3 Edward R. Stettinius, Jr., U.S. Undersecretary of State.

4 See above, Doc. 436.

5 On September 28, Churchill told the House of Commons that the French Consultative Assembly should be made more representative before Britain could recognize the provisional government. *Parliamentary Debates*, Commons, 5th ser., vol. 403, cols. 495–496.

6 See above, Doc. 400, note 6.

7 Lieutenant General Omar N. Bradley, commander of the U.S. Twelfth Army Group.

talking about an operation across the Rhine in the middle of November and I see many other signs of the German resistance stiffening.

Off the record—I have read your speech with much gusto and was delighted to see you in such a vigorous form.[8]

Every good wish.

[8] Roosevelt had addressed the International Brotherhood of Teamsters at a dinner in Washington on September 23. He said in part: "I am accustomed to hearing malicious falsehoods about myself. . . . But I think I have a right to resent, to object to libelous statements about my dog [Fala]." *PPR*, 13: 284–292.

Doc. 439
CHURCHILL TO ROOSEVELT

No. 790   October 3, 1944

Anthony and I start Saturday and hope in two or three days to reach U.J.[1] We should like you to send a message to him saying that you approve of our mission and that Averell will be available to take part in discussions.[2]

Will you tell Averell or General Deane[3] what can be said about your Far Eastern plans and let us know what you have told them, so that we all keep within the limits prescribed? We want to elicit the time it will take after the German downfall for a superior Russian army to be gathered opposite the Japanese on the frontiers of Manchukuo and to hear from them the problems of this campaign, which are peculiar owing to the lines of communication being vulnerable in the later stages.

Of course the bulk of our business will be about the Poles, but you and I think so much alike about this that I do not need any special guidance as to your views.

The point of Dumbarton Oaks[4] will certainly come up and I must tell you that we are pretty clear that the only hope is that the three great powers are agreed. It is with great regret that I have come to this

[1] For the diplomatic background of Churchill's and Eden's trip to Moscow, see Eden, *Memoirs*, 2: 555ff.; Woodward, *British Foreign Policy*, 3: 146ff.; and Lynn Ethridge Davis, *The Cold War Begins: Soviet-American Conflict over Eastern Europe* (Princeton, 1974), chap. 5.

[2] Roosevelt sent such a telegram to Stalin on October 5, but Stalin replied on October 8 that he was "somewhat puzzled" by the message, since he did not know "what points Mr. Churchill and Mr. Eden want to discuss in Moscow."

[3] Major General John R. Deane, U.S. military attaché in Moscow.

[4] The conference on postwar international organization, held near Washington. See *FR 1944*, 1: 713ff.

conclusion contrary to my first thought.[5] Please let me know if you have any wishes about this matter, and also instruct Averell accordingly.

[5] On October 4 Roosevelt replied that he would prefer to postpone a decision on the question of arrangements for voting in the new international organization. See below, Doc. 440, note 2.

Doc. 440
CHURCHILL TO ROOSEVELT

No. 791   October 5, 1944

Your number 626.[1]

Thank you very much for what you say and for your good wishes. I am very glad that Averell should sit in at all principal conferences; but you would not, I am sure, wish this to preclude private tête-à-têtes between me and U.J. or Anthony and Molotov, as it is often under such conditions that the best progress is made. You can rely on me to keep you constantly informed of everything that affects our joint interests apart from the reports which Averell will send.

I gather from your last sentence but one that you have sent some general account of your Pacific plans to your people in Moscow which will be imparted to U.J. and which I shall see on arrival. This will be most convenient.

Should U.J. raise the question of voting[2] as he very likely will do, I will tell him that there is no hurry about this and that I am sure we can get it settled when we are all three together.

[1] Not printed. See above, Doc. 439, note 5.
[2] The Russians originally wanted all the sixteen Soviet republics to be charter members of the United Nations. The western Allies objected strongly at first, but Churchill and some other leaders came to see the Soviet demand in a more favorable light, although their final positions on the question were not yet settled.

Doc. 441
CHURCHILL TO ROOSEVELT[1]

No. 794   October 11, 1944

In an informal discussion we have taken a preliminary view of the situation as it affects us and have planned out the course of our

[1] This telegram was sent as a joint message by Churchill and Stalin.

agreement, social and otherwise.[2] We have invited Messrs. Mikolajczyk, Romer, and Grabski to come at once for further conversations
with us and with the Polish National Committee.[3] We have agreed
not to refer in our discussions to Dumbarton Oaks issues and that
these shall be taken up when we three can meet together. We have to
consider the best way of reaching an agreed policy about the Balkan
countries including Hungary[4] and Turkey.[5] We have arranged for
Mr. Harriman to sit in as an observer at all meetings where business of
importance is to be transacted and for General Deane to be present
whenever military topics are raised. We have arranged for technical
contacts between our high officers and General Deane on military
aspects, and for any meetings which may be necessary later in our
presence and that of the two Foreign Secretaries together with Mr.
Harriman. We shall keep you fully informed ourselves about the
progress we make.

We take this occasion to send you our heartiest good wishes and to
offer our congratulations on prowess of United States forces and upon
the conduct of the war in the west by General Eisenhower.

[2] Churchill and Eden arrived in Moscow on October 9 for nine days of talks with
Stalin.

[3] For minutes of the meetings of the Polish delegation with Churchill, Stalin, and
their advisers, held at the Russian Foreign Office on October 13, see *Polish-Soviet
Relations,* vol. 2, nos. 237, 239, 241. At one point during the talks Churchill burst
out at the London Poles: "You are callous people who want to wreck Europe. . . .
You have only your own miserable interests in mind. . . . I will have to call on the
other Poles, and this Lublin government may function very well. . . . If you want
to conquer Russia we shall leave you to do it. . . . I don't know whether the British
Government will continue to recognise you."

[4] On September 23 the Hungarian government had sent Colonel General Istvan
Naday, former commander of the Hungarian First Army, to Caserta, Italy, to seek an
armistice with the Allies. See *FR 1944,* 3: 887ff.

[5] Turkey had severed diplomatic and economic relations with Germany on August
1. See *FR 1944,* 5 (Washington, 1965) : 891ff.

Doc. 442
CHURCHILL TO ROOSEVELT

No. 795   October 11, 1944

We have found an extraordinary atmosphere of good will here, and
we have sent you a joint message.[1] You may be sure we shall handle
everything so as not to commit you. The arrangements we have made
for Averell are I think satisfactory to him and do not preclude neces-

[1] See above, Doc. 441.

sary intimate contacts which we must have to do any good. Of all these I shall give you a faithful report.

It is absolutely necessary we should try to get a common mind about the Balkans, so that we may prevent civil war breaking out in several countries when probably you and I would be in sympathy with one side and U.J. with the other. I shall keep you informed of all this, and nothing will be settled except preliminary agreements between Britain and Russia, subject to further discussion and melting down with you. On this basis I am sure you will not mind our trying to have a full meeting of minds with the Russians.[2]

I have not yet received your account of what part of the Pacific operations we may mention to Stalin and his officers.[3] I should like to have this because otherwise in conversation with him I might go beyond what you wish to be said. Meanwhile I will be very careful. We have not touched upon Dumbarton Oaks except to say it is barred, at your desire. However Stalin at lunch today spoke in praise of the meeting and of the very great measure of agreement that has been arrived at there. Stalin also in his speech at this same luncheon animadverted harshly upon Japan as being an aggressor nation. I have

[2] For details of Churchill's and Eden's discussions with the Russians, see Churchill, *Triumph and Tragedy*, chap. 15; Eden, *Memoirs*, 2: 558; and Woodward, *British Foreign Policy*, 3: 150ff. Churchill and Eden reached Moscow on October 9, and despite Roosevelt's strong opposition to "spheres of influence," he lost no time in trying to strike a bargain of sorts with Stalin for the Balkans. At his first meeting with Stalin, Churchill took a small sheet of paper and wrote on it a series of figures that he may or may not have calculated in advance. According to Churchill's proposal, the Russians might have a 90% predominance in Rumania, the British the same in Greece. Yugoslavia was to be shared on a 50–50 basis, as was Hungary. In Bulgaria, the Soviet Union was to have 75% predominance. Stalin may have been taken aback by Churchill's proposal, but he made an approving mark on the paper. Actually, this was not the end of the bargaining. On October 11 Churchill drafted a letter to Stalin saying that the percentages were "no more than a method by which in our thoughts we can see how near we are together. . . . [The percentages] would be considered crude, and even callous, if they were exposed to the scrutiny of the Foreign Offices and diplomats all over the world. Therefore they could not be the basis of any public document, certainly not at the present time." (Woodward, *British Foreign Policy*, 3: 150–152.) Roosevelt was not entirely unaware what Churchill was doing in Moscow. On October 11 Ambassador Harriman cabled the President that Churchill "has been using the unpopular term 'sphere of influence' but as Eden describes his objectives it is to work out a practical agreement on how the problems of each country are going to be dealt with and the relative responsibility of the Russians [and] the British. [Churchill and Eden] stated that they have explained to Stalin and Molotov that they have no authority to commit us and whatever is worked out will be submitted to us." (*FR 1944*, 4: 109–110)

[3] On October 22, Roosevelt deferred discussion of the Pacific war effort to the forthcoming Big Three meeting.

little doubt from our talks that he will declare war upon them as soon as Germany is beaten. But surely Averell and Deane should be in a position not merely to ask him to do certain things, but also tell him, in outline at any rate, the kind of things you are going to do yourself, and we are going to help you to do.

Doc. 443
CHURCHILL TO ROOSEVELT

No. 798   October 14, 1944

I have been reflecting about the question of recognition of the French provisional government. I think events have now moved to a point where we could take a decision on the matter consistently with your own policy and my latest statement in the House of Commons.

In your telegram number 623[1] you said that you thought that we should wait until France was cleared of the enemy and you implied that in any case de Gaulle must first show himself ready to take over from Eisenhower full responsibility for the administration of part of France as an interior zone. I for my part took the line in Parliament that the reorganisation of the consultative assembly on a more representative basis ought to precede recognition. . . .

There is no doubt that the French have been cooperating with Supreme Headquarters and that their provisional government has the support of the majority of French people. I suggest therefore that we can now safely recognise General de Gaulle's administration as the provisional government of France.

One procedure might be to tell the French now that we will recognise as soon as the enlarged assembly has met and has given de Gaulle's administration a vote of confidence.

An alternative procedure would be to recognise as soon as the interior zone has been formally established. I am inclined to think that this alternative is preferable as it would connect recognition with what will be a mark of satisfactory cooperation between the French authorities and AEF[2] in the common cause against Germany.

Please tell me what you think. If you agree that we should settle the matter by one or other of the procedures suggested above, the Foreign Office and State Dept might at once compare their ideas upon the

1 See above, Doc. 436.
2 Allied Expeditionary Force.

actual terms in which we should give recognition. It is important that we should take the same line although we need not necessarily adopt exactly the same wording. We should have of course also to inform the Soviet Government of what we intend.

Recognition would not of course commit us on the separate question of French membership of the European Advisory Commission[3] or similar bodies.[4]

[3] The European Advisory Commission, comprised of representatives from the United States, Britain, and the Soviet Union, had been established at the Moscow foreign ministers' conference in October 1943. Its purpose was to consider all questions of Allied policy concerning the defeat of Germany and the terms of surrender. For the work of the commission in 1944, see *FR 1944*, 1: 1–483, esp. 100ff. See also above, Doc. 318.

[4] For Roosevelt's reply, see below, Doc. 446.

Doc. 444
CHURCHILL TO ROOSEVELT

No. 799   October 18, 1944

I send you in my immediately following[1] text of document to which Mikolajczyk's delegation agreed together with two amendments on which Stalin insisted. Mikolajczyk said that if he accepted the first of these amendments he would be repudiated by his own people. Stalin's position is that in this case it is not worthwhile proceeding to the difficult discussions arising out of the second amendment. These could probably have been surmounted had the first been accepted.

Both the London and the Lublin Poles[2] will now return home to consult their colleagues on outstanding points and our communiqué from here will explain that progress has been made and differences narrowed. Meanwhile, only the London Poles and Russians know of this document and every endeavour will be made to prevent it leaking out, though London Poles will have to consult some of their people.

You will see I have not gone at all beyond the position adopted by His Majesty's Government in your presence at Teheran,[3] though possibly the regions to be ceded by Germany have been more precisely

[1] See below, Doc. 445.
[2] The Soviet-sponsored Polish Committee of National Liberation, based in Lublin.
[3] See *Conferences at Cairo and Tehran*, pp. 596ff.; Winston S. Churchill, *Closing the Ring* (Boston, 1951), pp. 361–362, 394ff.; and Woodward, *British Foreign Policy*, 3: 224–231. For Mikolajczyk's account, see *The Rape of Poland*, pp. 93–97.

stated. I have made it clear throughout that you are not committed in any way by what I have said and done. It only amounts to a promise on the part of His Majesty's Government to support the Curzon line and its compensations at the armistice or peace conference, which alone can give a final and legal validity to all territorial changes. I have already informed Parliament in open session of our support of Curzon line as a basis for frontier settlement in the east, and our twenty-year treaty with Russia makes it desirable for us to define our position to a degree not called for from the United States at the present time.

I should however mention, though no doubt Averell will have reported, that Molotov stated at our opening meeting with the London Poles that you had expressed agreement with Curzon line at Teheran. I informed Stalin afterwards that neither I nor Eden could confirm this statement. Stalin thereupon said that he had had a private conversation with you, not at the table, when you had concurred in the policy of the Curzon line, though you had expressed a hope about Lwow being retained by the Poles.[4] I could not, of course, deal with this assertion. Several times in the course of my long talks with him, he emphasised his earnest desire for your return at the election and of the advantage to Russia and to the world which that would be. Therefore, you may be sure that no indiscretion will occur from the Russian side.

Meanwhile, in other directions, considerable advantages have been gained. You have already been informed about the obvious resolve of the Soviet Government to attack Japan on the overthrow of Hitler, of their detailed study of the problem, and of their readiness to begin inter-Allied preparations on a large scale. When we are vexed with other matters, we must remember the supreme value of this in shortening the whole struggle.

Arrangements made about the Balkans are, I am sure, the best that are possible. Coupled with our successful military action recently[5] we should now be able to save Greece, and I have no doubt that agreement to pursue a fifty-fifty joint policy in Yugoslavia[6] will be the best solution for our difficulties in view of Tito's behaviour and changes in the local situation, resulting from the arrival of Russian and Bulgarian forces under Russian command to help Tito's eastern flank.

---

[4] See *Conferences at Cairo and Tehran*, p. 884.

[5] Allied forces had liberated Athens on October 13, and the German garrison on Corfu had surrendered on October 15.

[6] A reference to Churchill's and Stalin's recognition of equality of interest in Yugoslavia. See Woodward, *British Foreign Policy*, 3: 151.

The Russians are insistent on their ascendancy in Rumania[7] and Bulgaria[8] as the Black Sea countries.

Although I hear most encouraging accounts from various quarters about United States politics, I feel the suspense probably far more than you do or more than I should if my own affairs were concerned in this zone. My kindest regards and warmest good wishes.

[7] On September 15 Harriman had cabled Secretary Hull from Moscow that "it was evident that the Russians entered upon [the Rumanian armistice] negotiations with the determination that . . . we should give them pretty much of a free hand in arranging the armistice terms and the subsequent treatment of the Rumanians. . . . The United States attitude throughout the negotiations tended to bear them out in the feeling described above and was appreciated by them accordingly. They believe, I think, that we lived up to a tacit understanding that Rumania was an area of predominant Soviet interest in which we should not interfere." *FR 1944*, 4: 234–235.

[8] On October 17 Harriman cabled Hull that "the [State] Department is . . . presumably aware that in the case of Bulgaria, the Russians steadfastly refused to consider the inclusion in the armistice terms of any specific reference to an equal voice in the [Allied] Control Commission [for Bulgaria] for the three powers after the termination of hostilities with Germany." *FR 1944*, 3: 459.

Doc. 445
CHURCHILL TO ROOSEVELT

No. 800   October 18, 1944

This is text referred to in paragraph one of my immediately preceding telegram.[1] Text begins:

"British and Soviet Governments, upon conclusions of discussions at Moscow in October 1944 between themselves and with Polish Government, have reached the following agreement.

"2. 'Upon unconditional surrender of Germany, territory of Poland in west will include the free city of Danzig, the regions of East Prussia, west and south Königsberg, the administrative district of Oppeln in Silesia and lands desired by Poland to east of line of the Oder. It is further agreed that possession of these territories shall be guaranteed to Poland by Soviet and British Governments. It is understood that Germans in said regions shall be repatriated to Germany and that all Poles in Germany shall at their wish be repatriated to Poland.'

"3. In consideration of foregoing agreement, the Polish Government accept Curzon line as basis for frontier between Poland and U.S.S.R.

"4. Separate Soviet-Polish agreements will regulate reciprocal transfer and repatriation of population of both countries and release of

[1] See above, Doc. 444.

persons detained. It is agreed that necessary measures will be taken for the transfer of all persons of both countries desiring to change their allegiance in accordance with their freely expressed wishes.

"5. It is agreed that a Polish government of national unity under Prime Minister Mikolajczyk will be set up at once in territory already liberated by Russian arms.

"6. The Soviet Government take this occasion of reaffirming their unchanging policy of supporting establishment within the territorial limits set forth of a sovereign, independent Poland, free in every way to manage its own affairs, and their intention to make a treaty of durable friendship and mutual aid with Polish Government, which it is understood will be established on an anti-Fascist and democratic basis.

"7. The treaties and relationships existing between Poland and other countries will be unaffected by this settlement, the parties to which declare again their implacable resolve to wage war against Nazi tyranny until it has surrendered unconditionally." End of text.

Herewith amendments to text:

Paragraph five should read as follows:

"It is agreed that Polish government of national unity in accordance with agreement (or understanding) reached between the Polish government in London and Polish Committee of National Liberation in Lublin will be set up at once in territory already liberated by Russian armies." (Amendment to para five ends.)

(Further amendment.) Note reference to second amendment. Stalin said he agreed that M. Mikolajczyk should be Prime Minister. End of amendment.

Doc. 446
ROOSEVELT TO CHURCHILL

No. 631   October 19, 1944

Replying to your 798.[1] I think until the French set up a real zone of interior that we should make no move towards recognizing them as a provisional government. The enlargement of the consultative assembly which has already been extended and made more representative is almost as important and I should be inclined to hang recognition on the effective completion of both these acts. I would not be satisfied with de Gaulle merely saying that he was going to do it.

1 See above, Doc. 443.

I agree with you that there must be no implication, if and when we do recognize a provisional government, that this means a seat on the European Advisory Council, etc. These matters can be taken up later on their merits.

I am anxious to handle this matter, for the present, directly between you and me and would prefer, for the moment, that the *modus operandi* not become a matter of discussion between the State Department and your Foreign Office.

Let me know your views upon this message.

Harriman's messages indicate that you have had a good and useful conference and I shall be anxiously waiting to get a final summation from you.

I do hope you are free of the temperature and really feeling all right again.

Doc. 447
CHURCHILL TO ROOSEVELT

No. 801   October 22, 1944

Many thanks for your number 631.[1]

On our last day at Moscow Mik[2] saw Berut who admitted his difficulties. Fifty of his men had been shot in the last month. Many Poles took to the woods rather than join his forces. Approaching winter conditions behind the front could be very hard as the Russian army moved forward using all transport. He insisted however that if Mik were Premier he must have 75% of the Cabinet. Mik proposed that each of the five Polish parties should be represented, he naming four out of the five of their best men whom he would pick from personalities not obnoxious to Stalin.

Later at my request Stalin saw Mik and had one and one-quarter hours' very friendly talk.[3] Stalin promised to help him, and Mik promised to form and conduct a government thoroughly friendly to the Russians. He explained his plan but Stalin made it clear that the Lublin Poles must have the majority.

After the Kremlin dinner we put it bluntly to Stalin that unless Mik had 50/50 plus himself the Western world would not be convinced

---

1 See above, Doc. 446.

2 Mikolajczyk. Boleslaw Berut was chairman of the Communist-sponsored Polish National Council.

3 See *Polish-Soviet Relations*, vol. 2, no. 246.

that the transaction was bona fide and would not believe that an independent Polish government had been set up. Stalin at first replied he would be content with 50/50 but rapidly corrected himself to a worse figure. Meanwhile Eden took the same line with Molotov who seemed more comprehending. I do not think the composition of the government will prove an insuperable obstacle if all else is settled. Mik had previously explained to me that there might be one announcement to save the prestige of the Lublin government and a different arrangement among the Poles behind the scenes.

Apart from the above Mik is going to urge upon his London colleagues the Curzon line including Lwow for the Russians. I am hopeful that even in the next fortnight we may get a settlement. If so I will cable you the exact form so that you can say whether you want it published or delayed.

Major war criminals. U.J. took an unexpectedly ultrarespectable line. There must be no executions without trial; otherwise the world would say we were afraid to try them. I pointed out the difficulties in international law but he replied if there were no trials there must be no death sentences, but only lifelong confinements. In face of this view from this quarter I do not wish to press the memo I gave you which you said you would have examined by the State Department.[4] Kindly therefore treat it as withdrawn.

We also discussed informally the future partition of Germany. U.J. wants Poland, Czecho, and Hungary to form a realm of independent anti-Nazi pro-Russian states, the first two of which might join together. Contrary to his previously expressed view, he would be glad to see Vienna the capital of a federation of south German states, including Austria, Bavaria, Wurtemburg [sic], and Baden. As you know, the idea of Vienna becoming the capital of a large Danubian federation has always been attractive to me, though I should prefer to add Hungary, to which U.J. is strongly opposed.

As to Prussia, U.J. wished the Ruhr and the Saar detached and put out of action and probably under international control and a separate state formed in the Rhineland. He would also like the internationalisation of the Kiel Canal. I am not opposed to this line of thought. However, you may be sure that we came to no fixed conclusions pending the triple meeting.

I was delighted to hear from U.J. that you had suggested a triple meeting towards the end of November at a Black Sea port. I think this a very fine idea, and hope you will let me know about it in due course. I will come anywhere you two desire.

4 See *Conference at Quebec 1944*, pp. 489–490.

U.J. also raised formally the Montreux Convention,[5] wishing for modification for the free passage of Russian warships. We did not contest this in principle. Revision is clearly necessary as Japan is a signatory and Inönü[6] missed his market last December. We left it that detailed proposals should be made from the Russian side. He said they would be moderate.

About recognising the present French administration as the provisional government of France, I will consult the Cabinet on my return. Opinion of U.K. is very strongly for immediate recognition. De Gaulle is no longer sole master, but is better harnessed than ever before. I am sure he will make all the mischief he can, but I still think that when Eisenhower proclaims a large zone of the interior for France it would not be possible to delay this limited form of recognition. Undoubtedly de Gaulle has the majority of the French nation behind him and the French Government hold support against potential anarchy in large areas. I will however cable you again from London. I am now in the air above Alamein of blessed memory.[7] Kindest regards.

[5] Stalin was concerned about Turkish control of the Dardanelles, specifically Turkey's right to prevent the passage of Soviet warships between the Black Sea and the Mediterranean. For the text of the Convention of Montreux Regarding the Régime of the Straits, July 20, 1936, see *League of Nations Treaty Series*, vol. 173, p. 213.

[6] Ismet Inönü, President of Turkey.

[7] Churchill returned to London after spending a day in Cairo.

Doc. 448
ROOSEVELT TO CHURCHILL

No. 632   October 22, 1944

Your 795,[1] 796,[2] 797,[3] 799,[4] 800,[5] and 801[6] received.

I am delighted to learn of your success at Moscow in making progress toward a compromise solution of the Polish problem.

When and if a solution is arrived at, I should like to be consulted as to the advisability from this point of view of delaying its publication for about two weeks. You will understand.[7]

Everything is going well here at the present time.

[1] See above, Doc. 442.
[2] Not printed.
[3] Not printed.
[4] See above, Doc. 444.
[5] See above, Doc. 445.
[6] See above, Doc. 447.
[7] The presidential election took place on November 7.

Your statement of the present attitude of U.J. towards war criminals, the future of Germany, and Montreux Convention is most interesting. We should discuss these matters together with our Pacific war effort at the forthcoming three-party meeting.

In regard to recognizing a provisional government of France, I will communicate with you on this matter as soon as Eisenhower reports having established a zone of the interior which is expected within the next few days.

The selection of a Black Sea port for our next meeting seems to be dependent upon our ability to get through the Dardanelles safely as I wish to proceed by ship. Do you think it is possible to get U.J. to come to Athens or Cyprus?[8]

8 For Churchill's reply, see below, Doc. 450.

Doc. 449
CHURCHILL TO ROOSEVELT

No. 803   October 23, 1944

In view of your number 631[1] in reply to my number 798[2] I was naturally surprised at the very sharp turn taken by the State Department and on arrival here I find the announcement[3] is to be made tomorrow. We shall, of course, take similar and simultaneous action. I think it likely that the Russians will be offended.[4] Molotov in conversation said that he expected they would be made to appear the ones who were obstructing, whereas they would have recognised long ago but had deferred to American and British wishes. I hope therefore it has been possible to bring them in.

1 See above, Doc. 446.
2 See above, Doc. 443.
3 American recognition of the French provisional government. See Woodward, *British Foreign Policy*, 3: 82ff.
4 In an earlier version of this message Churchill "opined" that the Russians would be offended. See Woodward, *British Foreign Policy*, 3: 84.

Doc. 450
CHURCHILL TO ROOSEVELT

No. 804   October 23, 1944

Para 1. I am bewildered by the reference in your No. 632[1] to recognising the provisional government in France. Matters have already

1 See above, Doc. 448.

moved far beyond the stage mentioned in your third sentence from the end. However I am in full agreement with the result which is to be announced tonight at five-thirty GMT.[2]

Para 2. U.J.'s doctors do not like him flying and I suppose there would be the same difficulties in Russian warships coming out of the Black Sea as of American and British warships coming in. One way would be for Turkey to declare war, which I expect she would be very willing to do. . . . From what I saw of the Crimea it seems much shattered and I expect all other Black Sea ports are in a similar state. We should therefore in all probability have to live on board our ships. I am enquiring about Athens from Eden who will be there in a day or two. Personally I should think it a splendid setting and here again we should have our ships handy. Cyprus is of course available where absolute secrecy, silence, and security can be guaranteed together with plain comfortable accommodation for all principals. Will you telegraph to U.J. on the subject, or shall I? Or, better still, shall we send a joint message?[3]

Para 3. I was delighted to see the proofs of your robust vigour in New York. Nevertheless I cannot believe that four hours in an open car and pouring rain with a temperature of 40 and clothes wet through conform to those limits of prudence which you would be so ready to prescribe if it were my case.[4] I earnestly hope you are none the worse and should be grateful for reassurance. I cannot think about anything except this (group undecypherable) election.

2 Greenwich Mean Time.

3 For Roosevelt's reply, see below, Doc. 452.

4 For an account of Roosevelt's open-car campaign tour of New York City on the eve of the election, see Burns, *Roosevelt: Soldier of Freedom*, p. 526, and Jim Bishop, *FDR's Last Year: April 1944–April 1945* (New York, 1974) , pp. 168ff.

Doc. 451
ROOSEVELT TO CHURCHILL

No. 633   October 23, 1944

Replying to your 803,[1] I am informed that Moscow as well as London had timely information as to time of release of announcement regarding provisional government of France.

I regret that my absence from Washington resulted in more precipitate action by State Department than was contemplated in my 631 to you.[2]

I hope that the final result will be beneficial.

1 See above, Doc. 449.

2 See above, Doc. 446.

Doc. 452
ROOSEVELT TO CHURCHILL

No. 635   October 24, 1944

Your 804.[1] Regarding the provisional government mixup, I hope it has now cleared to a satisfactory conclusion.

I have today sent the following to U.J.:

"I am delighted to learn from reports made by Ambassador Harriman and from your message of October 19 of the success attained by you and the Prime Minister in approaching agreement on a number of questions of high interest to all of us in our common desire to secure and maintain a durable and satisfactory peace. I am sure that the progress made during your conversations in Moscow will facilitate and expedite our work in the next meeting when we three should come to a full agreement on our future activities, policies, and mutual interests.

"All of us must investigate the practicability of various places where our November meeting can be held, i.e., from the standpoint of living accommodations, security, accessibility, and so forth. I would appreciate receiving your suggestions.

"I have been considering the practicability of Cyprus, Athens, or Malta in the event that my entering the Black Sea on a ship should be too difficult or impracticable. I prefer traveling and living on a ship. We know that security and living conditions in Cyprus and Malta are satisfactory.

"I am looking forward to seeing you again with much pleasure.

"I would be pleased to have your advice and suggestions."

I would, of course, prefer to have him come to the Mediterranean which would be more convenient for all of us.

My journey to New York was useful and rain does not hurt an old sailor. Thank you for your advice nevertheless. I am in top form for the [indecipherable] election.

1 See above, Doc. 450.

Doc. 453
CHURCHILL TO ROOSEVELT

No. 807   October 24, 1944

Please see my number 802.[1]

I am anxious to get this settled. When I passed through Naples three days ago, I had long talks with General Wilson, Macmillan,[2] and other authorities there.[3] The situation in Italy is not good and might sharply deteriorate. There was a serious riot in Sicily and there has been trouble at Pisa. General Wilson spoke to me with anxiety about the whole position, particularly that the Allied Control Commission[4] had been without a head now for nearly ten weeks. I certainly take my full share of the blame for this, but I should like to get it settled now; otherwise, there may be trouble for all of us.

[1] Not printed. Churchill wanted a joint announcement of Harold Macmillan's appointment as head of the Allied Control Commission for Italy.

[2] Harold Macmillan, British representative on the Italian Advisory Council.

[3] See Macmillan, *Blast of War*, pp. 554–555, 591.

[4] See above, Doc. 332, note 3. Similar control commissions were planned for the other Axis countries.

Doc. 454
ROOSEVELT TO CHURCHILL

No. 641   November 2, 1944

Referring to my 635,[1] I have received a reply from U.J. which is not very helpful in the selection of a place for our next meeting. He states that if our meeting on the Soviet Black Sea coast is acceptable he considers it an extremely desirable plan.

His doctors to whose opinion he must give consideration do not wish him to make any "big trips."

He gave me no information as to location of the meeting, accessibility, living conditions, etc., except to express a hope that it will be possible to provide a safe entrance for my ship into the Black Sea.

He will be glad to see me as soon as I find it possible to make the trip.

[1] See above, Doc. 452.

I do not wish to go to the Black Sea if it can be avoided, first because the Congress will be in session at that time which makes it imperative that I be at all times within rapid mail communication with Washington by air mail, and, second, because of sanitary conditions.

Dr. McIntire[2] tells me that health conditions in Black Sea ports such as Odessa are very bad, and we must think of the health of our staff and our ships' crews as well as ourselves.

What do you think of the possibility of our inducing U.J. to meet with us in Piraeus, Salonika, or Constantinople? Any of these would not be a "big trip" for him. . . .

I fear that Uncle Joe will insist on the Black Sea. I do think it important that we three should meet in the near future.

All advice and assistance that you can contribute to the solution of this problem will be appreciated.

2 Vice Admiral Ross T. McIntire, the President's personal physician. For his account of the President's health during the latter stages of the war, see his *White House Physician* (in collaboration with George Creel) (New York, 1946), which should be compared, however, with the revelations in Bishop, *FDR's Last Year*.

Doc. 455
CHURCHILL TO ROOSEVELT

No. 816   November 8, 1944

I always said that a great people could be trusted to stand by the pilot who weathered the storm.[1] It is an indescribable relief to me that our comradeship will continue and will help to bring the world out of misery.

I send you, as you have forgotten it, a copy of the telegram I sent you in 1940,[2] much of which is true today.

1 President Roosevelt was reelected to a fourth term on November 7, defeating Republican Governor Thomas E. Dewey of New York. Senator Harry S Truman of Missouri was elected Vice President, succeeding Henry A. Wallace.

2 See above, Doc. 31.

Doc. 456
ROOSEVELT TO CHURCHILL

No. 646   November 10, 1944

Your 816[1] and 817.[2] Thank you for your friendly message and for your repetition of the 1940 message which I certainly had not for-

1 See above, Doc. 455.
2 Not printed.

gotten. We should now be permitted to continue our work together until this worldwide agony is ended and a better future ensured.

Doc. 457
ROOSEVELT TO CHURCHILL

No. 647   November 13, 1944

The death of the *Tirpitz* is great news.[1] We must help the Germans by never letting them build anything like it again, thus putting the German Treasury on its feet.

[1] The German battleship *Tirpitz*, anchored near the Norwegian part of Tromsö, was sunk by British aircraft on November 12. See S. W. Roskill, *The War at Sea 1939–1945*, 3 vols. (London, 1961), vol. 3, part 2, pp. 168–169.

Doc. 458
ROOSEVELT TO CHURCHILL

No. 648   November 14, 1944

The more I think it over the more I get convinced that a meeting of the three of us just now may be a little less valuable than it would be after I am inaugurated on the twentieth of January. The location of a meeting now is very difficult. All my people advise strongly against the Black Sea. I do not think there is a chance that U.J. would agree to Jerusalem, Egypt, or Malta.

But there is a real chance that by the end of January or early February he could get rail transportation to [the] head of the Adriatic. He might be willing to come to Rome or the Riviera. I would of course stop in England going or returning. I do not think he wants to fly or take a very difficult and long rail journey to Haifa.

Incidentally it would be far easier for me as I am undergoing the throes of the old session and preparing for the new session on January third.[1]

Ever so many thanks for your wire.[2] I finally got angry toward the end of the campaign and replied to the worst type of opposition I have ever met.[3] However it worked and people are now sitting back trying to catch their breath.

[1] The Seventy-ninth Congress was scheduled to open on January 3, 1945.
[2] See above, Doc. 455.
[3] For an excellent account of the 1944 presidential campaign, see Burns, *Roosevelt: Soldier of Freedom*, pp. 507ff.

What do you think of the postponement? It appeals to me greatly. My best to you on your Parisian trip.[4] Don't turn up in French clothes.

4 Churchill and Eden had arrived in Paris on November 10 for talks with de Gaulle.

Doc. 459
CHURCHILL TO ROOSEVELT

No. 822   November 16, 1944

Your number 647.[1]
Thank you so much. It is a great relief to us to get this brute[2] where we have long wanted her.
Your number 648.[3]
I am very sorry that you are inclined to make no further effort to procure a triple meeting in December, and I will send you a separate telegram making some further suggestions about this.[4]
Thank you for your kind wishes about the Paris-de Gaulle trip. I certainly had a wonderful reception from about half a million French in the Champs Élysées and also from the party opposition centre at the Hotel de Ville. I reestablished friendly private relations with de Gaulle, who is better since he has lost a large part of his inferiority complex.[5]
I see statements being put out in the French press and other quarters that all sorts of things were decided by us in Paris. You may be sure that our discussions on important things took place solely on an ad referendum basis to the three great powers, and of course especially to you who have by far the largest forces in France. Eden and I had a two hours' talk with de Gaulle and two or three of his people after luncheon on the 11th. De Gaulle asked a number of questions which made me feel how very little they were informed about anything that had been decided or was taking place. He is of course anxious to obtain full modern equipment for eight more divisions

1 See above, Doc. 457.
2 The German battleship *Tirpitz*.
3 See above, Doc. 458.
4 Not printed. Churchill acquiesced reluctantly in delaying the meeting until the end of January because of Roosevelt's fourth inaugural and the opening of Congress. Churchill was particularly sorry that Roosevelt could not leave sooner and visit Great Britain.
5 For de Gaulle's recollections of Churchill's and Eden's visit, see his *War Memoirs*, 3: 55ff.

which can only be supplied by you. SHAEF[6] reasonably contends that these will not be ready for the defeat of Germany in the field and that shipping must be devoted to the upkeep of the actual forces that will win the battles of the winter and spring. I reinforced this argument.

At the same time I sympathise with the French wish to take over more line, to have the best share they can in the fighting or what is left of it, and there may be plenty, and not to have to go into Germany as a so-called conqueror who has not fought. I remarked that this was a sentimental point which ought nevertheless to receive consideration. The important thing for France was to have an army prepared for the task which it would actually have to discharge, namely their obligation first to maintain a peaceful and orderly France behind the front of our armies, and secondly to assist in the holding down of parts of Germany later on.

On this second point the French pressed very strongly to have a share in the occupation of Germany not merely as subparticipation under British or American command but as a French command. I expressed my sympathy with this, knowing well that there will be a time not many years distant when the American armies will go home and when the British will have great difficulty in maintaining large forces overseas, so contrary to our mode of life and disproportionate to our resources, and I urged them to study the type of army fitted for that purpose, which is totally different in form from the organisation by divisions required to break the resistance of a modern war-hardened enemy army. They were impressed by this argument but nevertheless pressed their view.

I see a Reuters message, emanating no doubt unofficially from Paris, that it was agreed France should be assigned certain areas, the Ruhr, the Rhineland, etc., for their troops to garrison. There is no truth in this and it is obvious that nothing of this kind can be settled on such a subject except in agreement with you. All I said to de Gaulle on this was that we had made a division of Germany into Russian, British, and United States spheres: roughly, the Russians had the east, the British the north, and the Americans the south. . . .

. . . Here is another reason why we should have a triple meeting if U.J. will not come, or a quadruple meeting if he will. In the latter case the French would be in on some subjects and out on others. One must always realise that before five years are out there must be made a French army to take on the main task of holding down Germany. The main question of discussion between Eden and Bidault[7] was Syria, which was troublesome, lengthy, and inconclusive but primarily our worry.

[6] Supreme Headquarters, Allied Expeditionary Force.
[7] Georges Bidault, Foreign Minister of the French provisional government.

I thought I would give you this account at once in case of further tendentious statements being put out in the press.

I thought very well of Bidault. He looks like a younger and better-looking Reynaud,[8] especially in speech and smiling. He made a very favourable impression on all of us and there is no doubt that he has a strong share in the power. Giraud[9] was at the banquet apparently quite content. What a change in fortunes since Casablanca.[10] Generally I felt in the presence of an organised government, broadly based and of rapidly growing strength, and I am certain that we should be most unwise to do anything to weaken it in the eyes of France at this difficult, critical time. I had a considerable feeling of stability in spite of Communist threats, and that we could safely take them more into our confidence. I hope you will not consider that I am putting on French clothes when I say this. Let me know your thoughts. I will cable you later about the meeting and the meat.

8 Paul Reynaud, Premier of France in 1940.

9 General Henri Giraud was then inspector general of the French army, an honorific post.

10 In January 1943 General Giraud had been French high commissioner in Africa and commander of French military forces there. On January 24 he had held a press conference together with Roosevelt and Churchill.

Doc. 460
ROOSEVELT TO CHURCHILL

No. 649   November 18, 1944

Your 822.[1] I am sending you in a message to follow[2] a copy of a message I have just sent to Uncle Joe on the subject of our next meeting. It does not seem to me that the French provisional government should take part in our next conference, as such a debating society would confuse our essential issues. The three of us can discuss the questions you raise in regard to turning over parts of Germany to France after the collapse of Nazism and the further problems of helping to build up a strong France.

Regardless of available shipping and availability of material in the United States, I have no authority at present to equip an eight-division postwar French army. I, of course, sympathize with the French point of view and hope that we may all be able to help her meet

1 See above, Doc. 459.

2 Not printed. Roosevelt suggested a late January meeting at several possible sites around the Mediterranean. See U.S. Department of State, *The Conferences at Malta and Yalta 1945* (Washington, 1955), pp. 15–16.

postwar responsibilities. You know, of course, that after Germany's collapse I must bring American troops home as rapidly as transportation problems will permit. I shall be glad to have your views about the time and place of our next meeting.

Doc. 461
CHURCHILL TO ROOSEVELT

No. 825   November 19, 1944

Naturally I am very sorry to receive your numbers 649[1] and 650.[2]

Your message to U.J. will, of course, make it certain that he will not come anywhere before the end of January. Also you yourself give independently the important reasons which make it difficult for you to come earlier.

These reasons, I fear, destroy the hope which we had cherished that you would now pay your long-promised visit to Great Britain, and that we two could meet here in December and ask U.J. to send Molotov, who would be an adequate deputy. It is a great disappointment to me that this prospect should be indefinitely postponed.

There is, in my opinion, much doubt whether U.J. would be willing or able to come to an Adriatic port by January 30th, or that he would be willing to come on a non-Russian vessel through this extremely heavily mined area. However, if he accepts we shall, of course, be there. I note you do not wish the French to be present. I had thought they might come in towards the end in view of their vital interests in the arrangements made for policing Germany, as well as in all questions affecting the Rhine frontiers.

Even if a meeting can be arranged by the end of January, the two and a half intervening months will be a serious hiatus. There are many important matters awaiting settlement. For example, the treatment of Germany and the future world organisation, relations with France, the position in the Balkans, as well as the Polish question, which ought not to be left to moulder.

Para two of your 649 causes me alarm. If after Germany's collapse you "must bring the American troops home as rapidly as transportation problems will permit" and if the French are to have no equipped postwar amy or time to make one, or to give it battle experience, how will it be possible to hold down western Germany beyond the present Russian occupation line? We certainly could not undertake the task without your aid and that of the French. All would therefore rapidly

[1] See above, Doc. 460.
[2] Not printed.

disintegrate as it did last time. I hope, however, that my fears are groundless. I put my faith in you.[3]

3 For Roosevelt's reply, see below, Doc. 466.

Doc. 462
ROOSEVELT TO CHURCHILL

No. 654   November 21, 1944

The aviation conference[1] is at an impasse because of a square issue between our people and yours. We have met you on a number of points, notably an arrangement for regulation of rates and an arrangement by which the number of planes in the air shall be adjusted to the amount of traffic. This is as far as I can go. In addition, your people are now asking limitations on the number of planes between points regardless of the traffic offering. This seems to me a form of strangulation. It has been a cardinal point in American policy throughout that the ultimate judge should be the passenger and the shipper. The limitations now proposed would, I fear, place a dead hand on the use of the great air trade routes. You don't want that any more than I do.

The issue will be debated tomorrow. I hope you can get into this yourself and give instructions, preferably by telephone, to your people in Chicago so that we can arrange, if possible, to agree. It would be unfortunate indeed if the conference broke down on this issue.[2]

1 The conference on international civil aviation met in Chicago from November 1 to December 7, 1944. See *FR 1944*, vol. 2 (Washington, 1967): 355ff. The Soviet Union had declined in advance to participate. See Woodward, *British Foreign Policy*, 3: 567. For Berle's diaries and memoranda relating to the Chicago conference, see Beatrice Bishop Berle and Travis Beal Jacobs, eds., *Navigating the Rapids, 1918–1971: From the Papers of Adolf A. Berle* (New York, 1973), pp. 498ff.

2 For Churchill's reply, see below, Doc. 468, note 2.

Doc. 463
ROOSEVELT TO CHURCHILL

No. 655   November 22, 1944

Apparently the Chiefs of SHAEF would like something done by top level to help break down German morale.[1]

1 In a message to the Combined Chiefs of Staff on November 20, Eisenhower declared it "of vital importance that we should redouble our efforts to find a solution to the problem of reducing the German will to resist. . . . I have in mind particularly the employment of deception methods in addition to propaganda and other possible means." *PDDE*, vol. 4, no. 2131.

I can think of nothing except a joint statement from you and me and therefore suggest something along the line of the following:

QUOTE. We have viewed the overall iron discipline of the Wehrmacht[2] and stranglehold of the Nazi party over the individuals of the German nation and we have considered the problem of getting the truth to the people of Germany, for they have been flooded with Nazi propaganda that the Allies seek the destruction of the German people and the devastation of Germany.

Once more we wish to make it clear to the German people that this war does not seek to devastate Germany or eliminate the German people.

Once more we want to make it clear to the people of Germany that we seek the elimination of Nazi control and the return of the German people to the civilization of the rest of the world.

We are winning. There is no question of that.

But we want to save lives and to save humanity.

We hope that this slaughter of Germans can be brought to an end but we are going to bring this war to a conclusion which will satisfy civilization and seek to prevent future wars. The answer lies in the hands of the German people. They are being pressed the whole length of their boundaries on the Rhine. They are being pressed by overwhelming numbers and inexhaustible resources in Poland and Czechoslovakia and Hungary. German towns are daily being destroyed and your enemies draw closer in the closing of an inexorable ring. The simple fact remains that the Allies are united in demanding a complete military victory.

The choice lies with the German people and the German army. Do not prolong the days of death and suffering and destruction. Join all the other people in Europe and Africa and America and Asia in this great effort for decency and peace among human beings. UNQUOTE.

2 German armed forces.

Doc. 464
CHURCHILL TO ROOSEVELT

No. 828   November 24, 1944

Your number 655.[1] I have consulted the Cabinet and separately the Chiefs of Staff and we all gravely doubt whether any such statement should be made. I do not think that the Germans are very much afraid of the treatment they will get from the British and American armies or

1 See above, Doc. 463.

Governments. What they are afraid of is a Russian occupation, and a large proportion of their people being taken off to toil to death in Russia, or as they say, Siberia. Nothing that we can say will eradicate this deep-seated fear.

Moreover, U.J. certainly contemplates demanding two or three million Nazi youth, Gestapo men, etc., doing prolonged reparation work, and it is hard to say that he is wrong. We could not therefore give the Germans any assurances on this subject without consultations with U.J.

It seems to me that if I were a German soldier or general, I should regard any such statement at this juncture, when the battle for Cologne is at its height, as a confession of weakness on our part and as proof positive of the advantages of further desperate resistance. The Chiefs of the Staff and Ministry of Information both independently agree with me that this might well be the consequence of any such announcement now. I do not see any alternative to the General Grant attitude "to fight it out on this line, if it takes all summer." We, therefore, are opposed to any reassurance being volunteered by us at this juncture.

The brilliant French success in the south, your capture of Metz, and the breakthrough of the Seventh American Army upon Strasbourg now taken are substantial facts which must be added to the intense pressure of the American First and Ninth Armies and our own British efforts towards Venlo.[2] Even if we do not conquer at the strongest point towards Cologne, enough has been already gained to make the battle a notable step towards our goal. Words, I am sure, would play no part now and we can, it seems to me, speak no words of which the Russians, who are still holding on their front double the number of divisions opposite us, are not parties.

I, therefore, earnestly hope that we shall fight the battle out till winter comes about the middle of December and throw extra weight into the points of penetration. I am sure it would be hurtful to our prestige and even to our initiative if we seemed to try high-level appeals to the Germans now. All kinds of propaganda can be thrown across the battlefronts locally as they do to us, and the staffs are working at a plan, on which a separate telegram will be sent, which is designed to meet Eisenhower's desire to get at German morale by underground methods.[3] But to make the great Governments respon-

2 French forces liberated Mulhouse and Belfort on November 21 and November 22. The U.S. Third Army liberated Metz on November 22, and French forces liberated Strasbourg on November 23. See L. F. Ellis, *Victory in the West*, vol. 2, *The Defeat of Germany* (London, 1968), p. 160.

3 Ultimately Churchill declined to join Roosevelt in a joint statement, and Eisenhower supported the Prime Minister's decision.

sible for anything which would look like appeasement now would worsen our chances, confess our errors, and stiffen the enemy resistance. Please, however, do not hesitate to correct me if you think I am wrong. Meanwhile, I remain set where you put me on unconditional surrender.[4]

[4] By November 27 Eisenhower had abandoned his interest in a propaganda proposal. See *PDDE*, vol. 4, nos. 2140, 2142.

Doc. 465
CHURCHILL TO ROOSEVELT

No. 831   November 26, 1944

Cherwell[1] has told me how very kind the U.S. Army and Navy were in showing him their latest developments in many fields and in entertaining him at their various establishments. Perhaps if you thought it well, you would transmit my thanks to them and especially to General Groves[2] who went to so much trouble to show Cherwell the latest developments in his particular field.

Perhaps you might also think fit to express my gratitude to the Tuve establishment[3] at Silver Springs whose work on the proximity fuses has proved so valuable in defending London against the robot bombs.

[1] Lord Cherwell, Paymaster General and private scientific adviser to Churchill.

[2] Major General Leslie R. Groves, head of the Manhattan Project, which was developing atomic energy for military purposes.

[3] A reference, apparently, to Dr. Merle A. Tuve, head of the U.S. Army's research section on shell proximity fuses since early 1941. British physicists had for some time been working on fuses for bombs and antiaircraft rockets, but they had regarded the difficulties of developing shell fuses as "virtually insuperable." See Constance McLaughlin Green, Harry C. Thomson, and Peter C. Roots, *The Ordnance Department: Planning Munitions for War* (Washington, 1955) , p. 363.

Doc. 466
ROOSEVELT TO CHURCHILL

No. 658   November 26, 1944

Your 825.[1] Uncle Joe has now replied[2] to my message in regard to the tripartite meeting forwarded to you in my 650.[3]

[1] See above, Doc. 461.

[2] For the text of Stalin's message of November 23, 1944, see *Conferences at Malta and Yalta,* p. 18.

[3] See above, Doc. 460, note 2.

He expresses regret that my naval advisers doubt the expediency of meeting on the shore of the Black Sea. He does not object to a meeting at the end of January or the beginning of February, but he has in mind that we shall choose as a meeting place one of the Soviet port cities. He must consider the opinion of his doctors that a long trip would be a danger to him.

He hopes that we will now or soon finally agree upon a meeting place that will be acceptable to all of us.

I have a feeling that we will not succeed in getting U.J. to travel beyond the Black Sea unless the Germans should have surrendered by that time.

In regard to paragraph six of your 825, there should be no difficulty for us in equipping so much of a French occupation force as they may need in a disarmed Germany from the military equipment that we will take from the German army when it surrenders or is destroyed.

In any event, I have at the present time no authority under which it would be possible for me to equip any postwar foreign army, and the prospect of getting such authority from the Congress is more than doubtful.

Doc. 467
CHURCHILL TO ROOSEVELT

No. 834

November 27, 1944

Your 657.[1] Thank you very much. Please tell us if there is anything you think we ought to do.

Your 658.[2] I agree with your conclusion that U.J. will not travel beyond the Black Sea but I am sure the ports there will be unfit for us until the winter has passed.

Your last paragraph. We have not got to this point yet and I agree with you we should collect a good many arms from the Germans. Still, I think when American divisions begin to return home there would be a strong case for their leaving some of their heavy weapons and equipment behind for the French to take over the job.

[1] Not printed. In that message, dated November 27, Roosevelt said he accepted Churchill's "attitude toward the proposed joint statement" to the German people and had accordingly informed General Eisenhower. The President added: "I share . . . your earnest hope that both the British and American armies can throw extra weight into the effort and succeed in destroying the German Westwall armies by the end of this year."

[2] See above, Doc. 466.

Doc. 468
CHURCHILL TO ROOSEVELT

No. 836   November 28, 1944

Winant has brought me your message about the air[1] in reply to my number 827,[2] and naturally it has caused me much anxiety. I agree with you that this is a grave matter in which not only governments but parliaments and peoples may become deeply agitated, with consequences which cannot fail to be disastrous both to the prosecution of the war and to the prevention of future wars. I feel it my duty, therefore, to place before you in simple terms the issue as it presents itself to me after hearing all the advice of the special committee under Beaverbrook, of which Stafford Cripps[3] is an important member, as well as the unanimous views of the War Cabinet.

The foundations of our position at this conference, which is being held at the time and place which you proposed, are:

(A) The British Empire is asked to put invaluable and irreplaceable bases for air transport all over the world at the disposal of such

[1] Not printed. In a message sent on November 23, Roosevelt denied that the American delegation to the civil aviation conference had brought forth new proposals even after agreement had been reached and emphasized that "the important thing is that the [joint] draft of November 17, as interpreted by your people, does not set up the conditions for operable routes which pass through any considerable number of countries, and particularly which go to distant countries, for instance, a route from the United States to South Africa. It would make a round-the-world route almost impossible. . . . We know perfectly well that we ought not to set up a situation in which our operators could wreck the local establishments between nearby countries, or so fill the air on long routes that nobody else could get in and survive." *FR 1944*, 2: 587–588.

[2] Not printed. In that message, dated November 22, Churchill noted that to "reach a common agreement, we have agreed to throwing open our airfields all over the world to aircraft of other nationalities and to such planes being able to carry not only through traffic but local traffic between two neighbouring countries on the route." The present difficulties had arisen, Churchill added, "because of the new proposals brought forward by your delegation on the evening of November 18 after the agreement had been reached. Since these proposals demand a share of the local traffic between two neighbouring countries by aircraft of a third country far beyond that which the granting of the right to take up traffic on through service would warrant, we could not accept them." Churchill therefore proposed that, unless Roosevelt could confirm the agreement reached on November 17, the conference should "finalise the valuable technical agreements which have been arrived at," and that other matters should be adjourned "for a period during which we can . . . see whether we can arrive at some solution of the problem." *FR 1944*, 2: 585–586.

[3] Minister of Aircraft Production.

nations as are capable of using them. This means of course primarily and in bulk placing them at the disposal of the United States.

(B) It was agreed between us as a war measure that you should make the transport aircraft and specialise upon them on account of the character of the war, the need to supply China over the Hump, the vast distances of the Pacific Ocean, etc., and that we should concentrate our efforts upon fighting types. In consequence the United States are in an incomparably better position than we are to fill any needs of air transport that may arise after the war is over, and to build up their civil aircraft industry. We would venture most earnestly to suggest that these two points are not receiving adequate consideration.

However, in partial recognition of the above two points, Lord Swinton[4] believed that he had reached an agreement with Mr. Berle[5] at Chicago on November 17th about the amount of aircraft capacity that should be put into service by our respective countries (frequencies) on a basis of "embarked traffic." Agreement was also reached about fares to prevent undercutting, unfair subventions, etc.

All the above was satisfactory to us and, I think, to the world. On November 18, however, your side of the table put forward an entirely new set of ideas and arguments which, in our judgement, took away with one hand what had been given with the other in consideration of our fundamental position set forth above in paragraphs (A) and (B).

For instance, the escalator clause was sought, not only for traffic to and from your country but also for traffic between any two foreign countries. This meant that the number of services on any route could be increased when an airline achieved a load equal to 65% of its full capacity. We had already agreed, reluctantly, that this escalator clause should apply to traffic to and from an aircraft's own country. We had also agreed to a so-called fifth freedom which would grant to an aircraft on through services the right to pick up and set down traffic between foreign countries at intermediate stops. It is true that provision was made for a differentiation of fares to safeguard the local traffic. That seemed to me a valuable line to explore.

Mr. Berle then asked for a combination of the escalator clause and the fifth freedom which would enable American aircraft to carry most of the traffic between the United Kingdom and the Dominions and India and all foreign countries, as well as between all nations of the Commonwealth. It would, in fact, give to United States airlines the right to everything save sabotage. . . .

I have the opinion that both this point of linking the escalator clause and the fifth freedom together, and the claim for duplication on foreign air routes, require further patient study with a view to reach-

4 Minister of Aviation.

5 Adolf A. Berle, Jr., Assistant Secretary of State.

ing agreement between our two countries. Thus, we could make sure that Great Britain and the Dominions and many other countries as well are not in fact run out of the air altogether as a result of your flying start with no regard to the fact that we are willing to throw all our bases all over the world into the common pool. I am sure I could not obtain the agreement of the Cabinet or of either house of Parliament to anything which wore that aspect. Nor would I try.

It may be that you will say I have not rightly posed the issues. If this be so, I should be most grateful if you would state them in your own words. . . .

Should it not be possible for us to reach an agreement at this stage on Freedoms III, IV,[6] and V, when great battles in which our troops are fighting side by side are at their height and when we are preparing for immense new further efforts against Japan? I cannot see that a temporary adjournment to allow of the aforesaid patient discussions would do any serious harm. On the contrary, I believe that it would be as readily understood as was the postponement of final decision at Dumbarton Oaks.[7] There is always the great body of technical matter upon which agreement has been secured. Therefore, unless complete agreement is reached, I plead that there shall be an adjournment. Such adjournment for a short time, if asked for by an intimately allied power like us, ought not to be denied, nor ought we to be confronted with such very serious contingencies as are set out in your message received on Saturday.[8] An open dispute carried out by Parliament and Congress, both of which would have to be informed, and in our voluble free press on both sides, would do far more harm to the war effort and to our hopes of the future than an adjournment of a few weeks or even months, while both parties persevered behind the scenes for a settlement.

It is my earnest hope that you will not bring on this air discussion the prospect of our suffering less generous treatment on lend-lease than we had expected from the Quebec discussions.[9] But even if I thought

[6] The third of Roosevelt's Four Freedoms is freedom from want, and the fourth is freedom from fear. See Doc. 35, note 4.

[7] The delegates at Dumbarton Oaks had postponed a final decision regarding voting procedures in the Security Council of the future United Nations organization.

[8] Roosevelt warned Churchill that without unanimity on the aviation agreement, Congress might not be "in a generous mood" about Britain's lend-lease needs.

[9] For the lend-lease agreement signed at Quebec, see *Conference at Quebec 1944*, p. 344. According to Treasury Secretary Henry Morgenthau, Jr., "Churchill was quite emotional about this agreement, and at one time he had tears in his eyes. When the thing was finally signed, he told the President how grateful he was, thanked him most effusively, and said that this was something they were doing for both countries." *Conference at Quebec 1944*, p. 361. See also John Morton Blum, *Roosevelt and Morgenthau* (Boston, 1970), pp. 550ff.

that we were to be so penalised, I would not feel myself able to agree to a decision contrary to the merits, as we see them, on this matter.

I should be ready, of course, to accept impartial arbitration on the points outstanding at the Chicago conference, provided that they were discussed in relation to the general framework. We have not yet got our World Court again, but there are friendly states and neutral states from whom competent judges might be found.

Let me say also, that I have never advocated competitive "bigness" in any sphere between our two countries in their present state of development. You will have the greatest navy in the world. You will have, I hope, the greatest air force. You will have the greatest trade. You have all the gold. But these things do not oppress my mind with fear because I am sure the American people under your reacclaimed leadership will not give themselves over to vainglorious ambitions, and that justice and fair play will be the lights that guide them.[10]

10 For Roosevelt's reply, see below, Doc. 470.

Doc. 469
CHURCHILL TO ROOSEVELT

No. 839   November 29, 1944

In a telegram received today (SEACOS 265) Admiral Mountbatten reports that he has received a warning from General Carton de Wiart[1] that Generalissimo Chiang Kai-shek contemplates withdrawing the divisions which he requires in China from the Chinese army in India, which is now engaged in carrying out its share of Operation Capital.[2]

The Chiefs of Staff endorse what Admiral Mountbatten says about the deplorable effect of these withdrawals on our operations in Burma. I suggest that you and I send the Generalissimo the following message of protest. If you agree with this suggestion, and with the terms of the message to the Generalissimo, pray send it off as a joint message from us both, with such minor alterations or additions as you think fit.

"Message from President and Prime Minister to Generalissimo.

"Admiral Mountbatten reports that he has received a message from General Carton de Wiart saying that you contemplate the withdrawal of two of your best divisions from the north Burma front as soon as Bhamo has fallen.

1 General Sir Adrian Carton de Wiart, personal representative of Prime Minister Churchill and Admiral Mountbatten in Chungking.
2 Code name for the operation to reopen the Burma Road. See Kirby, *War Against Japan*, 4: 4ff.

"The withdrawal of these forces from north Burma will inevitably bring the southward thrust through Bhamo to a standstill, thus jeopardising the success of the whole campaign and the security of the Mogaung-Myitkyina air base.

"Your two divisions are now in contact with the enemy. If they are withdrawn from the battle in Burma by land route they will spend these critical months in weary marches over the rough track northwards. If they are withdrawn by air, they will use up aircraft which might otherwise be carrying to China the supplies you badly need. In neither case could their heavy transport and equipment be moved with them.

"We earnestly request you therefore to reconsider any idea of weakening your gallant forces which are cooperating so successfully with ours with the intention of reestablishing firm communications between China and her allies."[3]

[3] For Roosevelt's reply, see below, Doc. 471.

Doc. 470
ROOSEVELT TO CHURCHILL

No. 661   November 30, 1944

I have given careful thought to your 836[1] and to the problems which you cite. You know that I have no desire for any arrangement by which our people would profit from the sacrifices which yours have made in this war. Your confidence in the justice and fair play of the American people is, I am sure, justified. I have equal confidence that your people have the same qualities in the same measure. I know that they want equal opportunity in the air and unquestionably they should have it. I cannot believe that they would want aviation, in which you as well as we have a great future, stifled and suffocated because they were for a moment in a less favorable competitive position.

You say that the British Empire is being asked to put bases all over the world at the disposal of other nations. Of course it is. Would you like to see a world in which all ports were closed to all ships but their own or open to one foreign ship, perhaps two, if they carried only passengers and cargo bound all the way from Liverpool to Shanghai? Where would England be if shipping were subjected to such limitations? Where will it be if aviation is? I am unable to believe that you do not want an agreement at this time.

I cannot agree that the answer is to hold everyone back. It must be

[1] See above, Doc. 468.

rather to go forward together. I know the handicaps under which your aviation industry has labored during the war. We have found ways to help you before and I am confident that we can find ways to help you in overcoming this. We are prepared to make transport aircraft freely available to you on the same terms as our own people can get them. Our only stipulation is that aviation must be permitted to develop, subject only to reasonable safeguards, as far and as fast as human ingenuity and enterprise can take it.

We have no desire to monopolize air traffic anywhere. I do not see how increased frequencies on long routes would dominate traffic on short ones, when all lines would have the same right to increase their frequencies on the same basis. Nor do I see how in the long term such an arrangement would favor us over others, despite our head start.

You asked that I give further consideration to the fundamentals of your position and that I state the issues as I see them. I have done both and I am more convinced than ever that the answer is not to hold back but to go forward together.

I feel the conference can still reach an agreement vastly helpful both in the air and in wider fields. Swinton and Berle on November 27 publicly stated our respective positions. The smaller states have spoken and, if I may say so, our position seemed to have by far the greater support. If it is not possible to reach complete agreement when our delegations have so closely approached it, the reasons, despite our best will, would be all too clear.

You speak of impartial arbitration within the general framework. The Canadians undoubtedly see both points of view, have labored tirelessly to bring us together, and on November 27 brought out a new formula which might provide a reasonable line of compromise if the small nations would indeed accept so limited a formula. I will give Berle latitude for one more try on the lines of that formula if you will give Swinton the same.

Given, on both sides, that spirit of justice and fair play of which you speak, I know that an agreement can be reached which will be equally beneficial to both our interests and to the world.

Doc. 471
ROOSEVELT TO CHURCHILL

No. 663   December 1, 1944

Since the receipt of your message number 839[1] of November 29th reference Mountbatten's SEACOS 265 a message has been received

1 See above, Doc. 469.

from General Wedemeyer[2] outlining the gravity of the situation in China and stating that he concurs in the decision of the Generalissimo to transfer the two best-trained divisions of Chinese troops from Burma to the Kunming area.[3] You have undoubtedly seen this message which went to Mountbatten and has been furnished to your mission here in Washington so I shall not repeat it.

We have General Wedemeyer's views on the ground as to the gravity of the situation along with his knowledge of the situation and the plans for operations in Burma. I feel that he is better informed as to the general situation and requirements than any other individual at this moment. Furthermore we are faced by the fact that the Generalissimo, in a grave crisis which threatens the existence of China, has decided that he must recall these two divisions in order to check the Japanese drive on Kunming. It would avail us nothing to open a land line to China if the Japanese seized the Kunming terminal for air and ground. Under the circumstances I therefore am of the opinion that we are not in a position to bring pressure on the Generalissimo to alter his decision.

The U.S. Chiefs of Staff propose to send to General Wedemeyer a message which approves his recommendation in support of the Generalissimo's decision but requests him to endeavor to develop a scheme for using other units which might make possible the retention in India of one or even both of the two crack Chinese divisions. The U.S. Chiefs have explained their intention to the British Chiefs of Staff and have requested that they concur with this action and inform Mountbatten accordingly.

2 Lieutenant General Albert C. Wedemeyer, commander in chief of of U.S. Army forces in the China theater and Chief of Staff to Generalissimo Chiang Kai-shek.

3 For the background of Wedemeyer's immediate problems, see his *Wedemeyer Reports!* (New York, 1958) , pp. 290ff.

Doc. 472
CHURCHILL TO ROOSEVELT

No. 842   December 3, 1944

I am deeply grateful to you for your most kind message on my birthday,[1] which gave me the greatest pleasure, and also for the framed quotation from Abraham Lincoln with your own charming note upon it.[2] This reached me, by sure hands, when I awoke.

1 Churchill had celebrated his seventieth birthday on November 30.

2 The quotation was inscribed "For Winston on his birthday—I would even go to Teheran to be with him again." Elliott Roosevelt, ed. (assisted by Joseph P. Lash) , *F.D.R.: His Personal Letters 1928–1945* (New York, 1950) , 2: 1558.

I cannot tell you how much I value your friendship or how much I hope upon it for the future of the world, should we both be spared.

Doc. 473
ROOSEVELT TO CHURCHILL

No. 666   December 5, 1944

In view of the fact that prospects for an early meeting between you, Marshal Stalin, and myself are unsettled and because of my conviction, with which I am sure you agree, that we must move forward as quickly as possible in the convening of a general conference of the United Nations on the subject of international organization, I am taking this means of placing before you my present views on the important subject of voting procedure in the Security Council. This and other questions will, of course, have to be agreed between us before the general conference will be possible.[1] I am also taking up this matter with Marshal Stalin.[2]

I am certain that the following draft provision should be eminently satisfactory to everybody concerned:

PROPOSAL FOR SECTION C OF THE CHAPTER
ON THE SECURITY COUNCIL

"C. *VOTING*
1. Each member of the Security Council should have one vote.
2. Decisions of the Security Council on procedural matters should be made by an affirmative vote of seven members.
3. Decisions of the Security Council on all other matters should be made by an affirmative vote of seven members including the concurring votes of the permanent members, provided that, in decisions under Chapter VIII, Section A, and under paragraph 1 of Chapter VIII, Section C, a party to a dispute should abstain from voting."

You will note that the proposal provides for the unanimity of the permanent members in all decisions of the Council which relate to a determination of a threat to the peace or to action for the removal of

[1] At the end of the Dumbarton Oaks conference two major issues remained unresolved between the United States, Great Britain, and the Soviet Union: voting procedures in the Security Council and invitations to the conference to draft a charter for the new world organization. See *Conferences at Malta and Yalta*, p. 55.

[2] For the text of Roosevelt's almost identical message to Stalin, received December 14, 1944, see *Stalin's Correspondence*, 2: 247.

such a threat or for the suppression of aggression or other breaches of the peace. I am prepared to accept in this respect the view expressed by the Soviet Government in its memorandum on an international security organization presented at the Dumbarton Oaks meeting.[3] This means, of course, that in decisions of this character the permanent members would always have a vote.[4]

At the same time I am sure that the maintenance of the moral prestige of the great powers is an essential element in any successful system of international cooperation. I am certain therefore that those powers should not insist on exercising a veto in such judicial or quasi-judicial procedures as the international organization may employ in promoting voluntary peaceful settlement of disputes. I am certain that willingness of the permanent members to abstain from the exercise of their voting rights on questions of this sort would immensely strengthen their own position as the principal guardians of the future peace and would make the whole plan far more acceptable to all nations.[5]

If you should be inclined to give favorable consideration to some such approach to the problem of voting in the Council, would you be willing that there be held as soon as possible a meeting of representatives designated by you, by me, and by Marshal Stalin to work out a complete provision on this question and to discuss the arrangements necessary for a prompt convening of a general United Nations conference?

[3] See *FR 1944*, 1: 706–711, 834–836.

[4] Roosevelt's proposal followed closely the compromise formula suggested at Dumbarton Oaks by Sir Alexander Cadogan. See David Dilks, ed., *The Diaries of Sir Alexander Cadogan, O.M.*, 1938–1945 (London, 1971), pp. 665, 669, 685; *The Memoirs of Lord Gladwyn* (London, 1972), pp. 147ff.; and Woodward, *British Foreign Policy* (abridged ed., London, 1962), pp. 460ff. Cadogan's proposal called for abandoning the veto on procedural questions and on decisions dealing with the peaceful settlement of disputes but provided for retaining it in cases where there was a threat to the peace or where action was proposed against breaches of the peace.

[5] Churchill said he could not understand what Roosevelt had in mind and asked Eden to explain it to him. See Woodward, *British Foreign Policy* (abridged ed.), p. 467.

Doc. 474
CHURCHILL TO ROOSEVELT

No. 844   December 6, 1944

As we are unable to meet, I feel that the time has come for me to place before you the serious and disappointing war situation which faces us at the close of this year. Although many fine tactical victories have been gained on the western front and Metz and Strasbourg are trophies,[1] the fact remains that we have definitely failed to achieve the strategic object which we gave to our armies five weeks ago. We have not yet reached the Rhine in the northern part and most important sector of the front and we shall have to continue the great battle for many weeks before we can hope to reach the Rhine and establish our bridgeheads. After that again, we have to advance through to Germany.

In Italy the Germans are still keeping 26 divisions, equivalent to perhaps 16 full strength or more, on our front. They could however at any time retreat through the Brenner and Ljubljana and greatly shorten their line by holding from Lake Garda to (say) mouth of the Adige. By this they might save half their Italian forces for home defence. Even after that there are the Alps to which they could fall back, thus saving more men. It seems to me that their reason for standing so long in Italy may have been to extricate the twelve divisions in the Balkans, etc., which are now fighting their way back to Hungary and Austria. Apart from the air and partisans and small commando forces, there are no means of preventing this, and my opinion is that the greater part will escape. About half of these might be available for adding to what may be saved from Italy. This would be a powerful reinforcement to the German homeland available, according to events, either in the east or in the west.

We have secured weighty advantages from Dragoon for the battle on the main front, but the reason why the Fifteenth Group of Armies has not been able to inflict a decisive defeat on Kesselring[2] is that, owing to the delay caused by the weakening of our forces for the sake of Dragoon, we did not get through the Apennines till the Valley of the Po had become waterlogged. Thus neither in the mountains nor on the plains have we been able to use our superiority in armour.

On account of the obstinacy of the German resistance on all fronts we did not withdraw the five British and British-Indian divisions from Europe in order to enable Mountbatten to attack Rangoon in March, and for other reasons also this operation became impracticable. Mountbatten therefore began, as we agreed at Quebec, the general advance to Burma downstream from the north and the west,[3] and this has made satisfactory progress. Now, owing to the advance of the Japanese in China, with its deadly threat to Kunming and perhaps Chungking to the Generalissimo and his regime, two and possibly more Chinese

---

1 See above, Doc. 464, note 2.
2 Field Marshal Albert Kesselring, German field commander in Italy.
3 See Churchill, *Triumph and Tragedy*, p. 160.

divisions have to be withdrawn for the defence of China.[4] I have little doubt that this was inevitable and right. The consequences however are serious so far as Mountbatten's affairs are concerned, and no decision has yet been taken on how to meet this new misfortune, which at one stroke endangers China and your air terminal as well as the campaign in northern Burma. All my ideas about a really weighty blow across the Adriatic or across the Bay of Bengal have equally been set back.

The vast-scale operations which you have conducted in the Pacific are at present the only part of the war where we are not in a temporary state of frustration.

We have however happily to consider what the Russians will do. We have Stalin's promise for a winter campaign starting I presume in January. On most of his immense front he seems to have been resting and preparing, though only about three or four German divisions have come over to face Eisenhower. I am not in a position to measure the latest attacks he has launched to the southwest of Budapest. We may however I think look forward to more assistance from this and other Russian actions than we have had lately, and the German position is so strained that any heavy penetration might bring about a partial if not a total collapse.

I have tried to survey the whole scene in its scope and proportion and it is clear that we have to face in varying degrees of probability—

(a) a considerable delay in reaching and still more in forcing the Rhine on the shortest road to Berlin,
(b) a marked degree of frustration in Italy,
(c) the escape home of a large part of the German forces from the Balkan peninsula,
(d) frustration in Burma,
(e) elimination of China as a combatant.

When we contrast these realities with the rosy expectations of our peoples in spite of our joint efforts to damp them down, the question very definitely arises:

"What are we going to do about it?"

My anxiety is increased by the destruction of all hopes of an early meeting between the three of us and the indefinite postponement of another meeting of you and me with our staffs. Our British plans are dependent on yours, our Anglo-American problems at least must be surveyed as a whole, and the telegraph and the telephone more often than not only darken counsel. Therefore I feel that if you are unable to come yourself before February, I am bound to ask you whether you could not send your Chiefs of Staff over here as soon as possible, where

4 See above, Doc. 471. See also Kirby, *War Against Japan*, vol. 4, chap. 11.

they would be close to your main armies and to General Eisenhower and where the whole stormy scene can be calmly and patiently studied with a view to action as closely concerted as that which signalised our campaigns of 1944.[5]

[5] The German offensive in mid-December prevented the Chiefs of Staff from leaving Washington.

Doc. 475
CHURCHILL TO ROOSEVELT

No. 845   December 6, 1944

In view of the State Department's communiqué on Italy issued yesterday,[1] there will no doubt be a debate in Parliament. I shall be called upon to reply to its strictures by implication upon His Majesty's Government's policy and action not only in Italy but in Greece and possibly in Belgium.[2] This I am quite prepared to do and I hope you will realise that I must have all liberty in this matter.

I should be very much obliged to you if you would authorise me to read the terms of Count Sforza's[3] letter to Mr. Berle of September [23, 1943.[4] It was on the faith of this letter that the British Government withdrew their opposition which they had a right to have considered to the sending of Count Sforza into Italy. When Count Sforza passed through London I went through this letter with him almost line by line, before witnesses who are available, and he made the strongest declaration amounting to a gentleman's word of honour that this represented his position. However no sooner had he got to Italy than he worked busily at the intrigues which destroyed the Badoglio gov-

[1] In a communiqué issued on December 5 the State Department declared that the composition of the Italian government was a purely Italian affair, except where important military factors were concerned. The statement went on: "This policy would apply to an even more pronounced degree with regard to the Governments of the United Nations in their liberated territories." *Department of State Bulletin*, December 10, 1944, p. 722.

[2] For the background of British concern about the State Department communiqué, see Woodward, *British Foreign Policy*, 3: 458ff. According to the official historian of British foreign policy during this period, Eden felt that Churchill had been deeply hurt by the statement and considered the last sentence in the communiqué "especially serious, since it implied a severe censure of our handling of Greek affairs." Woodward, *British Foreign Policy*, 3: 461.

[3] Count Carlo Sforza, a prominent Italian liberal and minister without portfolio in the new Italian government.

[4] See above, Doc. 328, note 8.

ernment. On account of this behaviour I have regarded him as a man in whom no trust could be placed. It has never been our policy, and we have no power, to veto the appointment of particular Italian ministers to particular positions. But it is certain that were Count Sforza to obtain the premiership or the foreign secretaryship, the relations between the British Government and the Italian Government would suffer very much from our complete want of confidence in him. If you do not feel able to allow me to quote the letter, I shall nonetheless feel entitled to mention the substances of the undertakings given by Count Sforza to me.

I was much astonished at the acerbity of the State Department's communiqué to the public, and I shall do my best in my reply to avoid imitating it. I feel however entitled to remind you that on every single occasion in the course of this war I have loyally tried to support any statements to which you were personally committed; for instance, in the Darlan affair[5] I made the greatest possible exertions as you may remember to sustain the action of the United States Government and commander, which was and still is much criticised in quarters ever ready to be critical. Also, in the matter of the division of the Italian fleet I not only did all in my power to avoid the slightest appearance of difference between us, though the difference was considerable, but His Majesty's Government have actually supplied fourteen out of the fifteen warships lent to the Russians to make up for their one-third share of the Italian fleet to which you had referred.[6] Finally, it was I who proposed to you the bulk of the mitigations which were introduced into our relationship with Italy as the result of our talks at Quebec and Hyde Park.[7]

In all these circumstances I was much hurt that a difference about Count Sforza should have been made the occasion for an attempt on the part of the State Department to administer a public rebuke to His Majesty's Government. In the very dangerous situation in which the war is now it will be most unfortunate if we have to reveal in public controversy the natural differences which arise inevitably in the move-

[5] See above, Introduction to Part II.

[6] See above, Docs. 320, 322, and 324.

[7] See above, Doc. 434, note 1. For Churchill's personal interest in changing Italy's status from that of an enemy power to that of "a friendly co-belligerent," and the proposals he had in mind to this end, see Woodward, British Foreign Policy, 3: 446–447. Churchill believed that Italy ought to receive $50 million from the United Nations Relief and Rehabilitation Administration in the way of supplies, that the United States and Britain should declare that the 600,000 Italians interned in Germany should be accorded the status of prisoners of war, and that "appropriate measures" should be taken against those maltreating them. It is unclear, however, from the American documents to what extent Roosevelt and Churchill discussed the latter's specific ideas either at Quebec or at Hyde Park.

ment of so great an alliance. I do not remember anything that the State Department has ever said about Russia or about any other Allied state comparable to this document with which Mr. Stettinius has inaugurated his assumption of office.[8] I am sure such things have never been said by the State Department about Russia even when very harsh communications have been received and harsher deeds done.

[8] Stettinius had succeeded Cordell Hull as Secretary of State on December 1.

Doc. 476
CHURCHILL TO ROOSEVELT

No. 846   December 6, 1944

I have replied as follows to Stalin's enquiry[1] for my advice on the two questions raised with him by de Gaulle:[2]

"1. Your telegram about de Gaulle's visit and the two questions he will raise. We have no objection whatever to a France-Soviet pact of mutual assistance similar to the Anglo-Soviet pact.[3] On the contrary, His Majesty's Government consider it desirable and an additional link between us all. Indeed, it also occurs to us that it might be best of all if we were to conclude a tripartite treaty between the three of us which would embody our existing Anglo-Soviet treaty with any improvements. In this way the obligations of each one of us would be identical and linked together. Please let me know if this idea appeals to you as I hope it may. We should both of course tell the United States.

"2. The question of changing the eastern frontier of France to the left bank of the Rhine or alternatively of forming a Rhenish-Westphalian province under international control, together with other alternatives, ought to await settlement at the peace table. There is, however, no reason why, when the three heads of governments meet, we should not come much closer to conclusions about all this than we have done so far. As you have seen, the President does not expect de

[1] For the text of Stalin's message to Churchill, dated December 2, see *Stalin's Correspondence*, 1: 277-278.

[2] General de Gaulle visited Moscow from December 2 to December 10. Of that visit de Gaulle later wrote: "During the fifteen or so hours which comprised the total of my interviews with Stalin, I discovered the outlines of his ambitious and cryptic policy. As a Communist disguised as a Marshal, a dictator preferring the tactics of guile, a conqueror with an affable smile, he was a past master of deception." De Gaulle, *War Memoirs*, 3: 69.

[3] The Anglo-Soviet treaty of May 26, 1942. See above, Doc. 134. See also Winston S. Churchill, *The Hinge of Fate* (Boston, 1950), pp. 326ff.; and Woodward, *British Foreign Policy*, 2 (London, 1971): 244-256.

Gaulle to come to the meeting of the three. I would hope that this could be modified to his coming in later on when decisions, especially affecting France, were under discussion.

"3. Meanwhile, would it not be a good thing to let the European Advisory Commission sitting in London, of which France is a member, explore the topic for us all without committing in any way the heads of governments?

"4. I am keeping the President informed."

There seems much to be said for a tripartite Anglo-France-Soviet pact. In that way we can be sure that our mutual obligations to each other are harmonised from the beginning. Public opinion too would think such a joint agreement more satisfactory than an arrangement whereby relations between the French and ourselves were governed by agreements which each of us had entered into separately with Russia.

I should welcome your views.

Doc. 477
ROOSEVELT TO CHURCHILL

No. 668   December 6, 1944

I have this date sent the following message to U.J.:

QUOTE. Thank you for your two informative messages of December two[1] and December three.[2]

In regard to a proposed Franco-Soviet pact along the lines of the Anglo-Soviet pact of mutual assistance, this Government would have no objection in principle if you and General de Gaulle considered such a pact in the interests of both your countries and European security in general.

I am in complete agreement with your replies to General de Gaulle with regard to the postwar frontier of France. It appears to me at the present time that no advantage to our common war effort would result from an attempt to settle this question now and that its settlement subsequent to the collapse of Germany is preferable. UNQUOTE.

I will reply to your 846[3] in a subsequent message.[4]

1 See *Stalin's Correspondence,* vol. 2, no. 243.

2 In his message of December 3 Stalin informed Roosevelt that "General de Gaulle, as I had anticipated, brought up . . . the French frontier on the Rhine [i.e., shifting the frontier to the left bank of the Rhine]. . . . I said, in effect, that the matter could not be settled without the knowledge and consent of our chief Allies." *Stalin's Correspondence,* vol. 2, no. 244.

3 See above, Doc. 476.

4 See below, Doc. 480.

Doc. 478
CHURCHILL TO ROOSEVELT

No. 848   December 6, 1944

Thank you for your telegram number 664.[1]

Although I have always felt that these discussions were premature and throw too heavy a burden on our minds at a time when so many anxieties of war weigh down upon us, yet I can assure you that I sympathise completely with your desire to take advantage of these pregnant negotiations at Chicago. It is our considered view, however, that further and, in the end, swifter progress will be made if we have an opportunity here to review the position in every one of its aspects and in its general setting in the world economy.

It is our desire, as it is yours, to reconcile the greatest possible freedom of air commerce with a broad justice to all nations, large and small.

It is your desire, as it is ours, that the free play of enterprise should not degenerate into an exploitation of national advantages which would in the end be found generally intolerable.

We are not satisfied, however, that the projects which have succeeded one another in such profusion during the intricate discussions at Chicago represent the final contribution of human ingenuity towards a solution.

Apart from our own views, we have to take account of Parliament and public opinion.

Criticisms of the Chicago proposals are already appearing in quarters of the press which are in no sense reactionary or narrowly nationalistic. These are symptoms which in the interest of ultimate agreement we cannot ignore. They serve to fortify us in our conviction that we should at this stage consult with our people. From such a consultation we shall expect to reach a clearer comprehension of issues which now seem to us extremely confused and to propound fresh constructive approaches.

1 Not printed. On December 2 the President wrote that the civil aviation conference in Chicago "apparently still feels, as do I, that agreement should be reached if possible. I would accordingly appreciate your further urgent consideration of the matter."

Doc. 479
ROOSEVELT TO CHURCHILL

No. 669   December 6, 1944

Your 845.[1]

As you know, the letter to Berle merely transmitted Sforza's message to Badoglio and in no way involved this Government. I see no reason why you should not use the message itself in any way you see fit. I believe the message has already been made public, having been given to the press by Badoglio at the time of its receipt.

I deplore any offense which the press release on Italy may have given you personally or any implication of my lack of understanding of your responsibility before your country. You must recognize, however, the untenable position in which we were put by Mr. Eden's prior statement in the House regarding the British Government's representations to the Italian Government on the position of Sforza in any new government.[2] While military operations continue, Italy is an area of combined Anglo-American responsibility and our silence on this step made it appear that we agreed with the action taken. Actually this move was made without prior consultation with us in any quarter and it is quite contrary to the policy which we have tried to follow in Italy, since the Moscow conference last year,[3] in accepting democratic solutions in government worked out by the Italian people themselves.[4] In the circumstances we had no other choice than to make our own position clear.

You will remember my feeling on this score expressed to you at the time Bonomi succeeded Badoglio in forming a government last June.[5]

1 See above, Doc. 475.

2 Eden had told the House of Commons on December 1 that, inasmuch as Count Sforza had not kept the promises he had made when he returned to Italy, Britain did not wish to see him appointed Foreign Minister. See *Parliamentary Debates*, Commons, 5th ser., vol. 406, cols. 305–306.

3 See above, Doc. 271, note 1.

4 See Woodward, *British Foreign Policy*, 2: 588.

5 See above, Doc. 386, note 1.

Doc. 480
ROOSEVELT TO CHURCHILL

No. 670   December 6, 1944

Your 846.[1]
You will have seen from my reply to Stalin on his talks with de
Gaulle[2] that our views are identical on the two questions which he
raised.

I still adhere to my position that any attempt to include de Gaulle
in the meeting of the three of us would merely introduce a complicat-
ing and undesirable factor.

In regard to your suggestion to Uncle Joe that the question of
France's postwar frontiers be referred to the European Advisory Commission I feel that since the Commission is fully occupied with
questions relating to the surrender of Germany, it would be a mistake
to attempt to bring up at this stage before it any questions of postwar
frontiers. It seems to me preferable to leave this specific topic for
further exploration between us.

I fully appreciate the advantages which you see in a possible tripartite Anglo-Franco-Soviet pact. I am somewhat dubious, however, as
to the effect of such an arrangement on the question of an international security organization to which, as you know, I attach the very
highest importance. I fear that a tripartite pact might be interpreted
by public opinion here as a competitor to a future world organization,
whereas a bilateral arrangement between France and the Soviet Union
similar to the Soviet-British pact would be more understandable. I
realize, however, that this is a subject which is of primary concern to
the three countries involved.

1 See above, Doc. 476.
2 See above, Doc. 477.

Doc. 481
ROOSEVELT TO CHURCHILL

No. 672   December 9, 1944

Your 844.[1] I am at Warm Springs in Georgia taking ten days off
after the campaign and everything in the personal line is going well.

1 See above, Doc. 474.

Perhaps I am not close enough to the picture to feel as disappointed about the war situation as you are and perhaps also because six months ago I was not as optimistic as you were on the time element. On the European front I always felt that the occupation of Germany up to the left bank of the Rhine would be a very stiff job. Because in the old days I bicycled over most of the Rhine terrain, I have never been as optimistic as to the ease of getting across the Rhine with our joint armies as many of the commanding officers have been.

However, our agreed broad strategy is developing according to plan. You and I are now in the position of Commanders in Chief who have prepared their plans, issued their orders, and committed our resources to battle according to those plans and orders. For the time being, even if a little behind schedule, it seems to me the prosecution and outcome of the battles lie with our field commanders in whom I have every confidence. We must remember that the winter season is bringing great difficulties but our ground and air forces are day by day chewing up the enemy's dwindling manpower and resources, and our supply flow is much improved with the opening of Antwerp.[2]

General Eisenhower estimates that on the western front line he is inflicting losses in excess of the enemy's capability to form new units.[3] I still cannot see clearly just when, but soon a decisive break in our favor is bound to come.

As to the Italian front, Alexander's forces are doing their bit in keeping those German divisions in Italy, and we must remember that the Germans are really free to withdraw to the line of the Alps if they so decide.

The same thing applies to their troops in the Balkans. I have never believed that we had the power to capture any large German forces in the Balkans without assistance by the Russians.

On the Russian front we must also give full allowance to the vile weather and the Russians seem to be doing their bit at the present time.[4] This, of course, you know more about than I do.

The Far Eastern situation is, of course, on a somewhat different footing and I am not at all happy about it.[5]

2 Antwerp harbor had been cleared of mines and reopened on November 28, eighty-five days after the liberation of the city. See John Ehrman, *Grand Strategy*, vol. 6, *October 1944–August 1945* (London, 1956), p. 32.

3 For Eisenhower's assessment of the military situation on December 3 and his subsequent top-secret message to General Marshall on December 5, see *PDDE*, vol. 4, nos. 2148 and 2154. In the latter message Eisenhower observed that Hitler "is throwing in the line some divisions with only six weeks' training, a fact that contributes materially to his high casualty rate."

4 The Soviet armies were moving steadily toward Budapest. See Ziemke, *Stalingrad to Berlin*, pp. 382ff.

5 The Japanese had resumed the offensive in Burma in September.

From the long-range point of view other than the measures Wede-meyer is now taking,[6] we can do very little to prepare China to conduct a worthwhile defense, but Japan is suffering losses in men and ships and materials in the Pacific area that are many times greater than ours and they, too, cannot keep this up.[7] Even the Almighty is helping. This magnificent earthquake and tidal wave is a proof.[8]

The time between now and spring when the freeze is over will develop many things. We will know a lot more than we know now.

My Chiefs of Staff are now devoting all of their abilities and energies in directing their organizations toward carrying out the plans we have made and in supporting our forces throughout the world. Practically all of these forces are, for the time being, committed. That is why I do not feel that my Chiefs should leave their posts at this time since no requirement exists for broad strategic decisions to guide our field commanders.

I think I can leave after Inauguration Day.[9] I hoped that Uncle Joe could come to Rome or Malta or Taormina or Egypt, but if he will not—and insists on the Black Sea—I could do it even at great difficulty on account of Congress. Harriman suggested Batum which has an excellent climate. You and I could fly there from Malta or Athens, sending ahead one of my transport flagships on which to live. Yalta is also intact, though the roadstead is open and we should probably have to live ashore.

Congratulations on the vote.[10]

6 On December 3 General Wedemeyer had informed the Chiefs of Staff in Wash-ington that he was moving 60,000 Chinese troops from Sian and two days later asked Lieutenant General Daniel I. Sutton, commander of the India-Burma theater, for two combat cargo squadrons to speed up troop movement. See Kirby, *War Against Japan*, 4: 128.

7 In the battle of Leyte Gulf (October 22–27) the Japanese had suffered heavy losses, including three battleships, four aircraft carriers, and twenty other vessels. By the end of November nearly 250,000 Americans had landed on Leyte, and on December 7 American forces landed at Ormoc, where they fought off Japanese efforts to interdict the invasion and inflicted serious losses. See Morison, *History of U.S. Naval Operations*, 12: 375ff.

8 On December 7 a violent earthquake, registered throughout the world, struck central Japan, causing tidal waves and landslides. The Japanese sought to minimize the damage, but seismologists in the United States, Britain, and India described the shock as "one of the greatest ever recorded." See *The New York Times*, December 8 and December 9, 1944.

9 January 20, 1945.

10 On December 8 Churchill received a 279–30 vote of confidence from the House of Commons. During the debate leading up to the vote, Churchill and his govern-ment were also attacked for their policy in Greece.

Doc. 482
ROOSEVELT TO CHURCHILL

No. 673   December 13, 1944

I have been as deeply concerned as you have yourself in regard to the tragic difficulties you have encountered in Greece.[1] I appreciate to the full the anxious and difficult alternatives with which you have been faced. I regard my role in this matter as that of a loyal friend and ally whose one desire is to be of any help possible in the circumstances. You may be sure that in putting my thoughts before you I am constantly guided by the fact that nothing can in any way shake the unity and association between our two countries in the great tasks to which we have set our hands.

As anxious as I am to be of the greatest help to you in this trying situation, there are limitations imposed in part by the traditional policies of the United States and in part by the mounting adverse reaction of public opinion in this country.[2] No one will understand

[1] On December 5 Churchill had authorized the British commander in Greece, General Ronald M. Scobie, "to destroy or neutralise" all Communist forces approaching Athens, promising him additional British reinforcements for that purpose. On the night of December 12–13 a group of Communist guerillas, disguised as British soldiers, entered the British barracks in Athens, taking over 100 prisoners, and were not driven off until after more than twelve hours of fighting. See Churchill, *Triumph and Tragedy*, pp. 289ff.

[2] In a memorandum to the President on December 13 Secretary of State Stettinius wrote: "Public opinion has been stirred to an unprecedented degree by the Greek crisis. . . . In this country the public has strongly supported the Department's declared position, but many demands are accumulating for: (1) strong representations to the British; (2) United States mediation; and (3) establishment in Greece of a United States-Soviet-British Commission to ensure a fair deal." *FR 1944*, 5: 149. Amidst mounting opposition in the United States (and Britain) to the latter's policy in Greece, Churchill sought repeatedly to enlist Harry Hopkins' support. On December 11, for instance, he wrote him: ". . . the President might be reminded of our very close agreement on so many occasions about the Greek situation. I must frankly confess I never knew E.A.M. would be so powerful. I only wish they had fought one-tenth as well against the Germans. We have got many troops coming in now but I certainly do not want to fight another war against E.L.A.S. If, using this telegram or the facts in it as you think best, you can get any word of approval spoken by the United States in favour of the Allied intervention in Athens by British troops, you may save many British and Greek lives and set free soldiers who are needed elsewhere." Hopkins was evidently not much moved. On December 16 he cabled Churchill: "Public opinion is deteriorating rapidly because of Greek situation and your statement in Parliament about the United States and Poland." Churchill, *Triumph and Tragedy*, p. 302. For Churchill's remarks on Poland, see below, Doc. 484, note 1.

better than yourself that I, both personally and as head of state, am necessarily responsive to the state of public feeling. It is for these reasons that it has not been possible for this Government to take a stand along with you in the present course of events in Greece. Even to attempt to do so would bring only temporary value to you and would in the long run do injury to our basic relationships. I don't need to tell you how much I dislike this state of affairs as between you and me. My one hope is to see it rectified so we can go along in this, as in everything, shoulder to shoulder. I know that you, as the one on whom the responsibility rests, desire with all your heart a satisfactory solution of the Greek problem and particularly one that will bring peace to that ravished country. I will be with you wholeheartedly in any solution which takes into consideration the factors I have mentioned above. With this in mind I am giving you at random some thoughts that have come to me in my anxious desire to be of help.

I know that you have sent Macmillan there with broad powers to find such a solution and it may be that he will have been successful before you get this.[3] I of course lack full details and am at a great distance from the scene, but it has seemed to me that a basic reason— or excuse, perhaps—for the EAM attitude has been distrust regarding the intentions of King George. I wonder if Macmillan's efforts might not be greatly facilitated if the King himself would approve the establishment of a regency in Greece and would make a public declaration of his intention not to return unless called for by popular plebiscite. This might be particularly effective if accompanied by an assurance that elections will be held at some fixed date, no matter how far in the future, when the people would have full opportunity to express themselves.

Meanwhile, might it not be possible to secure general agreement on the disarmament and dissolution of all the armed groups now in the country, including the Mountain Brigade and the Sacred Battalion,[4] leaving your troops to preserve law and order alone until the Greek national forces can be reconstituted on a nonpartisan basis and adequately equipped?

I shall be turning over in my mind this whole question and hope you will share your thoughts and worries with me.

3 See Macmillan, *Blast of War*, pp. 592ff.
4 Two Greek units that fought with the British Eighth Army in Italy. Churchill was honorary commander of the Third Mountain Brigade.

Doc. 483
CHURCHILL TO ROOSEVELT

No. 851   December 15, 1944

Your number 673.[1]

I will send you a considered answer to your telegram, for the kindly
tone of which I thank you, over the weekend. I hope that the British
reinforcements now coming steadily into Attica may make a more
healthy situation in Athens. You will realise how very serious it would
be if we withdrew, as we easily could, and the result was a frightful
massacre, and an extreme left-wing regime under Communist inspira-
tion installed itself, as it would, in Athens. My Cabinet colleagues here
of all parties are not prepared to act in a manner so dishonourable to
our record and name. Ernest Bevin's speech to the Labour conference
won universal respect.[2] Stern fighting lies ahead, and even danger to
our troops in the centre of Athens. The fact that you are supposed to
be against us, in accordance with the last sentence of Stettinius' press
release,[3] as I feared has added to our difficulties and burdens. I think
it probable that I shall broadcast to the world on Sunday night and
make manifest the purity and disinterestedness of our motives
throughout and also of our resolves.

Meanwhile I send you a letter I have received from the King of
Greece,[4] to whom we have suggested the policy of making the Archbishop of Athens[5] regent. The King refuses to allow this. Therefore an
act of constitutional violence will be entailed if we finally decide upon
this course. I know nothing to the credit of the Archbishop, except
that our people on the spot think he might stop a gap or bridge a
gully.

[1] See above, Doc. 482.

[2] In an address to an overwhelmingly hostile audience at the Labor party conference in London on November 13 Ernest Bevin, a leading member of that party and
Minister of Labor in the Churchill Cabinet, declared: "These steps which have been
taken in Greece are not the decision of Winston Churchill. They are the decision of
the Cabinet. . . . I am a party to the decisions that have been taken, and . . . I
cannot bring it to my conscience that any one of the decisions was wrong." Alan
Bullock, *The Life and Times of Ernest Bevin*, vol. 2, *Minister of Labour 1940–1945*
(London, 1967), p. 344.

[3] The statement caused much resentment in London. See above, Doc. 475, note 1.

[4] Not printed.

[5] Archbishop Damaskinos.

Doc. 484
ROOSEVELT TO CHURCHILL

No. 674   December 15, 1944

I have seen the newspaper reports of your statement in the House on the Polish question.[1] In order that we may cooperate fully in this matter I would appreciate receiving the benefit of your ideas as to what steps we can now take in regard to this question. Particularly I would like to have your evaluation of the possibility of Mikolajczyk's coming back into power[2] with sufficient authority to carry out his plans and what action you feel we should take in the event the Lublin Committee should declare itself to be the provisional government of Poland and Stalin should recognize it as such. In view of this possibility I wonder if it would be helpful if I should send a message to Stalin suggesting that he postpone any positive action on the Polish question until the three of us can get together.

You will recall the contents of the letter I sent to Mikolajczyk by Mr. Harriman which he showed to you and which outlines our policy in regard to Poland.[3] I anticipate strong pressure here for the position

[1] In the course of a lengthy statement in the House of Commons on the Polish question on December 15, Churchill reaffirmed British recognition of the Polish government-in-exile but expressed his faith in "the friendship and help of Marshal Stalin" in unifying the Polish government. Churchill also supported Soviet claims to the Curzon line as the eastern frontier of Poland, which he described as "the great gift [the Poles] have to make to Russia." Finally, Churchill addressed himself to the role of the United States in the Polish question: "The friendship of the United States Government for Poland, no less than our own, the large mass of Poles who have made their homes in the United States, and are, or are becoming, American citizens, the constitutional difficulties of the United States in making treaties and foreign agreements of every kind—all these have not enabled the Government of that great nation to speak in the terms which I have thought it my duty, with the assent of my colleagues, to use in this House." *Parliamentary Debates*, Commons, 5th ser., vol. 406, cols. 1480-1481, 1483, 1486, 1487.

[2] Mikolajczyk had resigned as Prime Minister of the Polish government-in-exile in November and a new Cabinet had been formed by Tomasz Arciszewski.

[3] In his letter to Mikolajczyk of November 17 the President had stressed four major points of U.S. policy toward Poland: (1) that the United States stood "unequivocally for a strong, free, and independent Polish state"; (2) that the United States would offer no objection if an agreement on future Polish boundaries, including compensation from Germany, were reached by direct negotiations between Poland, Britain, and the Soviet Union; (3) that the United States would not oppose, and would assist in, the transfer of minority groups in Poland; and (4) that the United States was prepared, "subject to legislative authority," to assist in "the postwar economic reconstruction of the Polish state." *Polish-Soviet Relations*, vol. 2, no. 268.

of this Government to be made clear, and I may therefore have to make public in some form the four points outlining our position contained in my letter to Mikolajczyk referred to above.

Knowing that we have in mind the same basic objectives in regard to Poland I want to be sure to coordinate with you any steps which I may contemplate in this matter.

Doc. 485
CHURCHILL TO ROOSEVELT

No. 853   December 16, 1944

I thank you cordially for your telegram number 674[1] about Poland. I trust you will carry out your proposal to send a message to Stalin suggesting that he postpone any positive action on the Polish question until the three of us can get together. This suggestion is most valuable and also I feel extremely urgent. Would it be possible for you to do this today, as I apprehend Stalin may make some move recognising the Lublin Committee as the Government of Poland?[2]

We will send you a fuller account of our views on the other questions you raise as soon as possible, probably tomorrow. I can however tell you at once that the War Cabinet feel that the four points mentioned in your letter to Mikolajczyk are very much in line with our ideas, and that the publication of them could do nothing but good. I also hope to send you a statement about Greece in answer to your number 673.[3]

I do hope you have benefited by your brief rest at Hot Springs after so strenuous and successful a campaign.

[1] See above, Doc. 484.
[2] For Roosevelt's reply, see below, Doc. 487.
[3] See above, Doc. 482.

Doc. 486
CHURCHILL TO ROOSEVELT

No. 854   December 16, 1944

In your telegram number 674[1] you asked for my estimate of the possibility of Mikolajczyk returning to power with enough authority to carry out his plans.

When he resigned it looked to us for the time as though efforts by

[1] See above, Doc. 484.

other Poles to form a government might fail and Mikolajczyk be called back soon. Now that Arciszewski's[2] government has established itself, we no longer see any immediate prospect of this. The majority of the Poles here appear to have accepted Arciszewski *faute de mieux* and to be in a fatalistic mood of waiting for something to turn up. But with the Poles these moods do not last. In London Mikolajczyk has the support of all his own Peasant party and of important elements of the Socialist and Christian Labour parties. We have indications that the people in Poland are unhappy about Mikolajczyk's absence from the government. I am hopeful therefore that Mikolajczyk's return to power will still be possible in the new year.

You also asked about the Lublin Committee. We do not regard it as in any way representative of Polish opinion and whatever developments there may be in the Soviet Government's attitude we do not, at present, intend to recognise it. We shall maintain our recognition of the London government, which is the legal Government of Poland and the authority to which the large Polish forces fighting under British command owe allegiance. We hope that we can keep in step and consult beforehand on all this.

2 Tomasz Arciszewski had succeeded Mikolajczyk as Prime Minister of the Polish government-in-exile on November 29.

Doc. 487
ROOSEVELT TO CHURCHILL

No. 675   December 16, 1944

Your number 853.[1] I have today sent the following message to U.J.:

"In view of the interest raised in this country by Prime Minister Churchill's statement in the House of Commons yesterday[2] and the strong pressure we are under to make known our position in regard to Poland, I believe it may be necessary in the next few days for this Government to issue some statement on the subject. This statement, if issued, will outline our attitude somewhat along the following lines:

"QUOTE. 1. The United States Government stands unequivocally for a strong, free, independent, and democratic Poland.

"2. In regard to the question of future frontiers of Poland, the United States, although considering it desirable that territorial questions await the general postwar settlement, recognizes that a settlement before that time is in the interest of the common war effort and

1 See above, Doc. 485.
2 See above, Doc. 484, note 1.

therefore would have no objection if the territorial questions involved in the Polish situation, including the proposed compensation from Germany, were settled by mutual agreement between the parties directly concerned.

"3. Recognizing that the transfer of minorities in some cases is feasible and would contribute to the general security and tranquility in the areas concerned, the United States Government would have no objection if the Government and the people of Poland desire to transfer nationals and would join in assisting such transfers.

"4. In conformity with its announced aim, this Government is prepared to assist, subject to legislative authority, and insofar as may be practicable, in the economic reconstruction of countries devastated by Nazi aggression. This policy applies equally to Poland as to other such devastated countries of the United Nations. UNQUOTE.

"The proposed statement, as you will note, will contain nothing, I am sure, that is not known to you as the general attitude of this Government and is I believe insofar as it goes in general accord with the results of your discussion with Prime Minister Churchill in Moscow in the autumn, and for this reason, I am sure, you will welcome it.

"I feel it is of the highest importance that until the three of us can get together and thoroughly discuss this troublesome question there be no action on any side which would render our discussions more difficult. I have seen indications that the Lublin Committee may be intending to give itself the status of a provisional government of Poland. I fully appreciate the desirability from your point of view of having a clarification of Polish authority before your armies move further into Poland. I very much hope, however, that because of the great political implications which such a step would entail you would find it possible to refrain from recognizing the Lublin Committee as a government of Poland before we meet, which I hope will be immediately after my inauguration on January 20. Could you not until that date continue to deal with the Committee in its present form? I know that Prime Minister Churchill shares my views on this point."

Doc. 488
CHURCHILL TO ROOSEVELT

No. 855   December 17, 1944

About Greece. The present position is that our representatives on the spot, Macmillan and Leeper,[1] have strongly recommended the

---

[1] Reginald Leeper, British ambassador to Greece. For Leeper's account of the Greek rebellion, see his *When Greek Meets Greek* (London, 1950), chap. 7.

appointment of the Archbishop as regent. This is obnoxious to the Papandreou[2] government though they might be persuaded to advocate a regency of three, namely the Archbishop, General Plastiras,[3] and Dragoumis.[4] There is suspicion that the Archbishop is ambitious of obtaining chief political power and that, supported by EAM, he will use it ruthlessly against existing ministers. Whether this be true or not I cannot say. The facts are changing from hour to hour. I do not feel at all sure that in setting up a one-man regency we might not be imposing a dictatorship in Greece.

There is also to be considered the fact that the King refuses, I think inflexibly, to appoint a regency, certainly not a one-man regency of the Archbishop, whom he distrusts and fears. According to the Greek constitution the Crown Prince is regent in the absence of the King. The King also states that all his ministers under Papandreou advise him against such a step and that, as a constitutional monarch, he cannot be responsible for it.

The War Cabinet decided to await for three or four days the course of military operations. Our reinforcements are arriving rapidly and the British General Staff Intelligence says that there are not more than 12,000 ELAS[5] in Athens and the Piraeus. The Greek King's estimate is 15[,000] to 22,000. Anyhow we shall, by the middle of next week, be far superior in numbers. I am not prepared, as at present informed, to give way to unconstitutional violence in such circumstances.

Our immediate task is to secure control of Athens and the Piraeus. According to the latest reports ELAS may agree to depart. This will give us a firm basis from which to negotiate the best settlement possible between the warring Greek factions. It will certainly have to provide for the disarming of the guerrilla forces. The disarmament of the Greek Mountain Brigade, who took Rimini, and the Sacred Squadron, who fought so well at the side of British and American troops, would seriously weaken our forces, and in any case we could not abandon them to massacre. They may however be removed elsewhere as part of a general settlement.

I am sure you would not wish us to cast down our painful and thankless task at this time. We embarked upon it with your full consent (see my number 755[6] and your reply[7]). We desire nothing from Greece but to do our duty by the common cause. In the midst of

---

2 George Papandreou, Prime Minister of Greece.

3 General Nikolas Plastiras, a republican with appeal to liberal supporters of the Communist National Liberation Front (EAM).

4 Philip Dragoumis, a close friend of King George II.

5 The Communist National Popular Liberation Army.

6 See above, Doc. 416.

7 See above, Doc. 428, note 5.

our task of bringing food and relief and maintaining the rudiments of order for a government which has no armed forces, we have become involved in a furious, though not as yet very bloody, struggle. I have felt it much that you were unable to give a word of explanation for our action but I understand your difficulties.

Meanwhile the Cabinet is united and the Socialist ministers approve Mr. Bevin's declarations at the Labour conference[8] which, on this matter, endorse the official platform by a majority of 2,455,000 to 137,000 votes.[9] I could at any time obtain, I believe, a ten-to-one majority in the House of Commons. I am sure you will do whatever you can. I will keep you constantly informed.

[8] See above, Doc. 483, note 3.
[9] See Bullock, *Life of Ernest Bevin,* 2: 346.

Doc. 489
CHURCHILL TO ROOSEVELT

No. 856   December 17, 1944

Your number 675.[1] I am most grateful to you for sending this telegram to U.J. It can do nothing but good.

[1] See above, Doc. 487.

Doc. 490
CHURCHILL TO ROOSEVELT

No. 857   December 23, 1944

I and my military advisers entirely agree with Eisenhower (see his SCAF 155)[1] that it is essential for us to obtain from the Russians, at the earliest possible moment, some indication of their strategical and tactical intentions. We think it hopeless to try to get this information

[1] In that message, dated December 21, Eisenhower told the Combined Chiefs of Staff: "There has been a tendency recently for German divisions formed or reforming in the east of Germany to move to the western front. The arrival of these divisions obviously influences the events in my area, and if this trend continues it will affect the decisions which I have to make regarding future strategy in the West. I therefore consider it essential that we should obtain from the Russians at the earliest possible moment some indication of their strategical and tactical intentions." *PDDE,* vol. 4, no. 2190.

through our military mission, or indeed to ask the Russians to commit it to writing. The best if not the only hope of getting what we want is for you and me to send a joint telegram to U.J. suggesting that he should allow us to send a high-ranking officer, nominated by General Eisenhower, to Moscow at once, in order that he may explain our present dispositions and future intentions on the western front to the Soviet Government and obtain reciprocal information from them.[2]

2 For Roosevelt's and Churchill's request on this subject to Stalin, dated December 24, and Stalin's agreement, see *Stalin's Correspondence*, vol. 2, nos. 250, 251.

Doc. 491
CHURCHILL TO ROOSEVELT

No. 859   December 28, 1944

Many thanks for your number 680[1] which encouraged me amidst many difficulties. Ambassador MacVeagh[2] called yesterday and we had a talk. Like everyone else here he is convinced that a regency under the Archbishop is the only course open at the moment. I have seen the Archbishop several times and he made a very good impression on me by the sense of power and decision which he conveyed as well as by his shrewd political judgements. You will not expect me to speak here on his spiritual qualities for I really have not had sufficient opportunity to measure these.

Greek conference, of which you will have had from other sources full account, was unanimous in recommending a regency. This was strongly supported by EAM; however I do not consider Archbishop is at all left-wing in Communist sense. On the contrary he seems to be an extremely determined man bent on establishing a small, strong executive in Greece to prevent the continuance of civil war.

I am therefore returning with Anthony to England to press upon the King of Greece to appoint the Archbishop regent. Effect of this, if King agrees, will of course mean that Archbishop will form a government of ten or less of the best will. I gathered that he would make Plastiras Prime Minister and that Papandreou would not be included. Naturally I could not probe too far while all these matters are hypothetical.

1 Not printed. In that message, dated December 26, Roosevelt acknowledged Churchill's aid in meeting with Greek leaders, adding: "I am ready to be of all assistance I can in this difficult situation. I hope that your presence there on the spot will result in achieving an entirely satisfactory solution." Churchill and Eden flew to Greece on Christmas Eve, arriving there the next day.

2 Lincoln MacVeagh, U.S. ambassador to Greece.

On our return we shall advise our colleagues, who are already inclined to this course, that we should put the strongest pressure on Greek King to accept advice of his Prime Minister, Monsieur Papandreou, who changes his mind about three times a day but has now promised to send a telegram in his own words but in sense of my immediately following.[3]

If Ambassador MacVeagh's report should on these matters correspond with mine I should greatly hope that you would feel yourself able to send a personal telegram to the King of Greece during the next few days supporting the representation we shall make to him, of which we shall keep you informed.[4] My idea is that the regency should be only for one year or till a plebiscite can be held under conditions of what is called "normal tranquility."

The Archbishop has left this matter entirely in my hands so that I can put the case in most favourable manner to the King. Of course if after these difficulties have been surmounted and Archbishop is regent you felt able [to] send him a telegram of support, that would make our task easier. Mr. President, we have lost over 1,000 men and though the greater part of Athens is now clear, it is a painful sight to see this city with street fighting raging now here now there and the poor people all pinched and only kept alive in many cases by rations we are carrying, often at loss of life, to them at the various depots. Anything that you can say to strengthen this new layout as the time comes will be most valuable and may bring about acceptance by ELAS of the terms of truce set forth by General Scobie.[5] For the rest we are reinforcing as is necessary and military conflict will go on. The vast majority of the people long for a settlement that will free them from the Communist terror.

We have to think of an interim arrangement which can be reviewed when our long hope for meeting takes place. This date should not now be far distant. It will then be possible to correlate our opinions and actions. In the meanwhile we have no choice but to recommend creation of a new and more competent executive government under regency of Archbishop, and to press on with our heavy and unsought task of clearing Athens from very dangerous, powerful, well-organised, and well-directed elements which are now pressing the area advance. I should value a telegram when I return on Friday morning.

3 Not printed.
4 Roosevelt sent a telegram to the King of Greece on December 28, 1944. *FR 1944*, 5: 177.
5 General Ronald M. Scobie, British commander in Greece.

Doc. 492
CHURCHILL TO ROOSEVELT

No. 861   December 29, 1944

Your 676.[1] I send you in my immediately following[2] the Admiralty report on Yalta. If this place is chosen, it would be well to have a few destroyers on which we can live if necessary. There would be no difficulty in flying from the great air base and weather centre at Caserta. I, myself, landed in a York at Simferopol. I daresay, however, Stalin will make good arrangements ashore. Our party will be kept to the smallest dimensions. I think we should aim at the end of January. I shall have to bring Anthony and Leathers.[3]

1 Not printed. On December 23 Roosevelt sent Churchill the text of a message to Ambassador Harriman: "If Stalin cannot manage to meet us in the Mediterranean I am prepared to go to the Crimea and have a meeting at Yalta. . . . I would plan to leave America very soon after the inauguration on a naval vessel. . . . I still hope the military situation will permit Marshal Stalin to meet us halfway." *Conferences at Malta and Yalta,* p. 21.

2 Not printed.

3 Lord Leathers, Minister of War Transport.

Doc. 493
CHURCHILL TO ROOSEVELT

No. 864   December 30, 1944

Anthony and I sat up with the King of Greece till 4:30 this morning at the end of which time His Majesty agreed to the announcement in my immediately following telegram.[1] I have sent this to Ambassador Leeper in Athens in order that the Archbishop may go to work at once.[2] The Greek translation is now being made and I will furnish you with a copy of it at the earliest moment.

This has been a very painful task to me. I had to tell the King that if he did not agree the matter would be settled without him and that

1 Not printed. On December 30 King George of Greece agreed to an announcement appointing Archbishop Damaskinos as regent and proposing a plebiscite on the future form of the Greek Government. See Churchill, *Triumph and Tragedy,* p. 322.

2 See Leeper, *When Greek Meets Greek,* chap. 8.

we should recognise the new government instead of him. I hope you will be able to give every support and encouragement to the Archbishop and his government.

Your number 681[3] enclosing Stalin's reply about Poland shows how serious will be the difficulties we shall have to face. I have consulted the Foreign Secretary and the Cabinet about it and their clear view is that we shall continue to press Stalin not to recognise the Lublin Committee as the Government of Poland and tell him plainly that we shall not do so. The matter should be reserved for the coming conference.

[3] Not printed. In that message, dated December 29, Roosevelt included Stalin's message of December 27, which expressed renewed Russian support for the Lublin Committee and proposed the exchange of diplomatic representatives, with a view to the committee's eventual recognition "as the lawful Government of Poland." *Stalin's Correspondence*, vol. 2, no. 254.

Doc. 494
ROOSEVELT TO CHURCHILL

No. 684   December 30, 1944

Your 864.[1] I have today sent the following to Stalin. You will see that we are in step.

QUOTE. I am disturbed and deeply disappointed over your message of December 27 in regard to Poland in which you tell me that you cannot see your way clear to hold in abeyance the question of recognizing the Lublin Committee as the provisional government of Poland until we have had an opportunity at our meeting to discuss the whole question thoroughly. I would have thought no serious inconvenience would have been caused your Government or your armies if you could have delayed the purely juridical act of recognition for the short period of a month remaining before we meet.

There was no suggestion in my request that you curtail your practical relations with the Lublin Committee nor any thought that you should deal with or accept the London government in its present composition. I had urged this delay upon you because I felt you would realize how extremely unfortunate and even serious it would be at this period in the war in its effect on world opinion and enemy morale if your Government should formally recognize one government of Poland while the majority of the other United Nations including the United States and Great Britain continue to recognize and to maintain diplomatic relations with the Polish government in London.

[1] See above, Doc. 493.

I must tell you with a frankness equal to your own that I see no prospect of this Government's following suit and transferring its recognition from the government in London to the Lublin Committee in its present form. This is in no sense due to any special ties or feelings for the London government. The fact is that neither the Government nor the people of the United States have as yet seen any evidence either arising from the manner of its creation or from subsequent developments to justify the conclusion that the Lublin Committee as at present constituted represents the people of Poland. I cannot ignore the fact that up to the present only a small fraction of Poland proper west of the Curzon line has been liberated from German tyranny, and it is therefore an unquestioned truth that the people of Poland have had no opportunity to express themselves in regard to the Lublin Committee.

If at some future date following the liberation of Poland a provisional government of Poland with popular support is established, the attitude of this Government would of course be governed by the decision of the Polish people.

I fully share your view that the departure of Mr. Mikolajczyk from the government in London has worsened the situation. I have always felt that Mr. Mikolajczyk, who I am convinced is sincerely desirous of settling all points at issue between the Soviet Union and Poland, is the only Polish leader in sight who seems to offer the possibility of a genuine solution of the difficult and dangerous Polish question. I find it most difficult to believe from my personal knowledge of Mr. Mikolajczyk and my conversations with him when he was here in Washington and his subsequent efforts and policies during his visit at Moscow[2] that he had knowledge of any terrorist instructions.[3]

I am sending you this message so that you will know the position of this Government in regard to the recognition at the present time of the Lublin Committee as the provisional government. I am more than ever convinced that when the three of us get together we can reach a solution of the Polish problem, and I therefore still hope that you can hold in abeyance until then the formal recognition of the Lublin Committee as a government of Poland. I cannot, from a military angle, see any great objection to a delay of a month. UNQUOTE.

2 See above, Doc. 402.
3 Stalin accused Mikolajczyk of tacitly supporting terrorist activities directed against Soviet troops in Poland.

Doc. 495
CHURCHILL TO ROOSEVELT

No. 870   December 31, 1944

Many thanks for your 683.[1] The Greek King behaved like a gentleman and with the utmost dignity,[2] and I am sure a private message from you would give him comfort.[3] I shall send only a civil acknowledgement to ELAS for the published message they have sent me, and hand the matter over to the Archbishop. It is clearly his job now.

I have read your 684[4] to Anthony, and he and I are in entire agreement with it. It will be most valuable to see what Stalin's reaction to it is. We shall of course send a supporting message at any moment you tell us it would be useful. The reason for delay is that you do not state in your 684 whether you have told Stalin that you have shown your message to me.

It is very satisfactory that we seem to be getting into step on both these tangled questions.

The great battle in the west[5] seems to be turning steadily in our favour and I remain of the opinion that Rundstedt's[6] sortie is more likely to shorten than to lengthen the war.[7]

---

[1] Not printed. On December 30 Roosevelt cabled Churchill: "I am happy to know of your safe arrival [in Greece] and wish you every success in the solution of the Greek problem which seems very promising as a result of your journey."

[2] See above, Doc. 493, note 1.

[3] For Roosevelt's message to George II, see *FR 1944,* 5: 177.

[4] See above, Doc. 494.

[5] The German offensive in the Ardennes, which had begun on December 16.

[6] Field Marshal Gerd von Rundstedt, German supreme commander on the western front.

[7] For accounts of the German offensive, see Hugh M. Cole, *The Ardennes: The Battle of the Bulge* (Washington, 1965); John S. D. Eisenhower, *The Bitter Woods* (New York, 1969); and John Toland, *The Battle of the Bulge* (New York, 1960). For a German point of view, see Percy Ernst Schramm, ed., *Kriegstagebuch des Oberkommandos der Wehrmacht (Wehrmachtführungsstab)*, vol. 4, pt. 1 (Frankfurt, 1961), pp. 430ff. For General Eisenhower's account of operations until December 23, see his top-secret memorandum of that date, *PDDE*, vol. 4, no. 2198.

Doc. 496
ROOSEVELT TO CHURCHILL

No. 689   January 2, 1945

Replying to your 867,[1] you are aware of the difficulty of my getting involved in any operations in the Balkans that are not essential to the early defeat of Nazi Germany.

Assuming that you will make the necessary arrangements with Stalin, I offer no objections to your sending to Moscow a representative of the Mediterranean theater.

In regard to sending Alexander, is it not possible that having British officers as the two senior members of the conference might be a less advantageous arrangement?

With this thought in mind, would it not be wise for you to give favorable consideration to sending the American deputy from the Mediterranean?[2]

It is very important to our operations in France and Belgium that Eisenhower's representatives should not be delayed to await the representative from the Mediterranean.

[1] Not printed. Churchill sent Roosevelt a copy of the Combined Chiefs of Staff's instructions to Eisenhower asking him not to let his representative at the forthcoming Moscow meeting, Air Marshal Tedder, discuss coordination of Russian and British forces. General Alexander was prepared to go to Moscow for that purpose. Tedder asked Stalin for an offensive to relieve hard-pressed Allied troops in the Battle of the Bulge.

[2] Lieutenant General Joseph T. McNarney.

Doc. 497
CHURCHILL TO ROOSEVELT

No. 874   January 4, 1945

Your 690.[1]

In none of your telegrams about Argonaut[2] have you mentioned whether U.J. likes this place and agrees to it and what kind of

[1] Not printed. On January 3 Roosevelt told Churchill that he planned to arrive at Yalta by February 2, adding: "In considering itinerary of visit to Black Sea, it has developed much to my regret that because of my extended absence from Washington it is necessary for me to postpone my projected visit to the United Kingdom until a later date. I will make every effort to arrange to visit the U.K. in May or June."

[2] Code name for the forthcoming Big Three summit conference at Yalta.

accommodation he can provide. I am looking forward to receiving this. It has occurred to some of us that he might come back and say, "Why don't you come on the other four hours and let me entertain you in Moscow?" However, I am preparing for Y[3] and am sending a larger liner which will cover all our troubles.

Would it not be possible for you to spend 2 or 3 nights at Malta and let the staffs have a talk together unostentatiously? Also, Eisenhower and Alexander could both be available there. We think it very important that there should be some conversation on matters which do not affect the Russians, e.g., Japan, and also about future use of the Italian armies. You have but to say the word and we can arrange everything.

We are very sorry indeed you will not come to our shores on this journey. We should feel it very much and a very dismal impression would be made if you were to visit France before you come to Britain. In fact, it would be regarded as a slight on your closest ally. I gather however that you will only go to the Mediterranean and Black Sea, in which case it is merely a repetition of Teheran.

The CIGS[4] and I have passed two very interesting days at Eisenhower's headquarters at Versailles. Quite by chance de Gaulle arrived at the same time on the business about which he has sent you and me, as heads of governments, a telegram concerning the southern sector.[5] We had an informal conference and the matter has been satisfactorily adjusted so far as he is concerned. Eisenhower has been very generous to him.

I am now in Eisenhower's train going to visit Montgomery, the weather having made flying impossible. The whole country is covered with snow. I hope to be back in England Saturday. Every good wish.

[3] Yalta.

[4] Chief of the Imperial General Staff, General Sir Alan Brooke.

[5] De Gaulle had appealed to both Roosevelt and Churchill to prevent the evacuation of Allied troops from Strasbourg, but Roosevelt rejected the appeal on the grounds that "the decision was a purely military one." Eisenhower, *The Bitter Woods*, p. 400.

Doc. 498
CHURCHILL TO ROOSEVELT

No. 876   January 6, 1945

Your number 691.[1]
Thank you for the information and it is interesting to see that the "Presidium of the Supreme Soviet of the U.S.S.R." has now been brought up into the line.
You may rest assured of our entire support.

[1] Not printed. On January 4 Roosevelt sent Churchill Stalin's telegram of January 1. Stalin understood Roosevelt's request that he postpone recognition of the Lublin Committee but added that "one circumstance makes me powerless to fulfill your wish"—namely, that the Presidium of the Supreme Soviet of the U.S.S.R. had informed the Lublin Committee that "it intends to recognize the provisional government of Poland as soon as it is formed." *Conferences at Malta and Yalta*, pp. 225–226.

Doc. 499
CHURCHILL TO ROOSEVELT

No. 877   January 7, 1945

CIGS and I have passed the last two days with Eisenhower and Montgomery and they both feel the battle very heavy but are confident of success.[1] I hope you understand that, in case any troubles should arise in the press, His Majesty's Government have complete confidence in General Eisenhower and feel acutely any attacks made on him.[2]

[1] In a cable of this date to the Combined Chiefs of Staff General Eisenhower declared: "I have no doubt but that the Germans are making a supreme and all-out effort to achieve victory in the west in the shortest possible time." *PDDE*, vol 4, no. 2226.

[2] These attacks included demands, successfully resisted by Eisenhower and Marshall, for the appointment of a single ground commander. See Pogue, *Supreme Command*, pp. 389ff., and *Marshall: Organizer of Victory*, pp. 509ff. "No sooner had the time of danger ended," General Bradley was later to write, "than the period of recrimination began. During the bitter, strained weeks that followed, the Allied amity that Eisenhower had sought to preserve suffered a severe setback." Omar N. Bradley, *A Soldier's Story* (New York, 1951), p. 483. In the midst of this criticism Eisenhower received a supportive phone call from Churchill, who told him: "I assure you that British troops will always deem it an honor to enter the same battle as their American friends." Dwight D. Eisenhower, *Crusade in Europe* (Garden City, N.Y., 1948), p. 356.

He and Montgomery are very closely knit and also Bradley and Patton,[3] and it would be disaster which broke up this combination which has, in nineteen forty-four, yielded us results beyond the dreams of military avarice. Montgomery said to me today that the breakthrough would have been most serious to the whole front but for the solidarity of the Anglo-American army.

Although I regret our divisions only amount to seventeen and two-thirds, all units are absolutely up to strength and we have seven or eight thousand reinforcements all ready in addition in France awaiting transfer to their units. The measures we have taken to bring another 250,000 into or nearer the front line enable me to say with confidence that at least our present strength will be maintained throughout the impending severe campaign.

I am deeply impressed with the need of sustaining the foot who bear two-thirds of the losses but are very often the last to receive reinforcements. More important even than the sending over of large new units is the keeping up of the infantry strength of divisions already engaged. We are therefore preparing a number of infantry brigades, including several from the Marines, of which the Navy has 80,000. These brigades will liberate mobile divisions from quasi-static sectors and, at the same time, do the particular work which is needed in them. Montgomery welcomed this idea most cordially as regards the Twenty-first Army Group. I gathered from General Eisenhower that he takes the same view and that he is longing for more infantry drafts, i.e., rifle and bayonet, to maintain the U.S. divisions at their proper establishment.

I most cordially congratulate you on the extraordinary gallantry which your troops have shown in all this battle, particularly at Bastogne and two other places which Montgomery mentioned to me on his own front, the exact location of which I do not carry in my mind, one at the peak of the salient where the First and Ninth American Divisions fought on and won after extremely heavy losses, and the other in connection with the Seventh U.S. Armoured Division, which seems to have performed the highest acts of soldierly devotion.[4] Also many troops of the First Army have fought to the end holding crossroads in the area of incursion which averted serious perils to the whole armies of the north at heavy personal sacrifice.

As I see there have been criticisms in the American papers of our troops having been kept out of the battle, I take this occasion to assure you that they stand absolutely ready at all times to obey General

3 Lieutenant General George S. Patton, Jr., commander of the U.S. Third Army.
4 The Seventh U.S. Armored Division defended St. Vith; the Ninth U.S. Army was attached to Montgomery, and the First was briefly attached to his command during the Battle of the Bulge.

Eisenhower's commands. I believe that the dispositions which he and Marshal Montgomery under him have made are entirely in accordance with strict military requirements, both as regards the employment of troops in counterattack and their lateral movement, having regard to crisscross communications. I have not found a trace of discord at the British and American headquarters but, Mr. President, there is this brute fact: we need more fighting troops to make things move.

I have a feeling this is a time for an intense new impulse, both of friendship and exertion, to be drawn from our bosoms and to the last scrap of our resources. Do not hesitate to tell me of anything you think we can do.

Doc. 500
CHURCHILL TO ROOSEVELT

No. 880   January 8, 1945

I am still thinking it of high importance that our military men should get together for a few days before we arrive at Argonaut. There will no doubt be opportunities for them to confer together at Sevastopol on days when we are engaged in politics and do not require technical advice. All the same, there are a tremendous lot of questions which should be looked at beforehand, and our agenda ought really to be considered.

Even further to this I would add that there would be great advantages in a preliminary conference of about a week's duration between the Foreign Ministers. If these could be gathered at the Pyramids or Alexandria, about which arrangements are very easy, and could join us at Argonaut, an immense amount of preliminary work would be done. I do not know whether you are bringing Stettinius with you, or whether you would bring him for such a conference. If so, I should greatly welcome it, and the moment that such a decision has been taken, we would invite Molotov to come to the rendezvous. You will remember that advantages were gained last time by the discussions which took place in Moscow before we met at Teheran. Pray let me know whether this appeals to you at all.

What are your ideas of the length of our stay at Argonaut? This may well be a fateful conference, coming at a moment when the Great Allies are so divided and the shadow of the war lengthens out before us. At the present time I think the end of this war may well prove to be more disappointing than was the last.

Doc. 501
CHURCHILL TO ROOSEVELT

No. 884   January 10, 1945

Your number 696.[1]
Thank you very much about the Combined Chiefs of Staff's preliminary meeting.

Eden has particularly asked me to suggest that Stettinius might come on 48 hours earlier to Malta with the United States Chiefs of Staff so that he (Eden) can run over the agenda with him beforehand, even though Molotov were not invited. I am sure this would be found very useful. I do not see any other way of realising our hopes about world organisation in five or six days. Even the Almighty took seven. Pray forgive my pertinacity.

I have now read very carefully your message to Congress and I hope you will let me say that it is a most masterly document.[2] Every good wish.

[1] Not printed. On January 10 Roosevelt informed Churchill that "in regard to an advance conference between the Foreign Ministers and the Secretary of State, in view of my absence from Washington during the time required to proceed by sea to Malta, it is impracticable for Stettinius to be out of the country for the same extended period."

[2] For the text of Roosevelt's State of the Union message to Congress, see *PPR* 13: 483–507.

Doc. 502
CHURCHILL TO ROOSEVELT

No. 887   January 14, 1945

Tube alloys.[1]
I should like Field Marshal Wilson to succeed Field Marshal Dill[2] on the Combined Policy Committee[3] and hope that this will be agreeable to you.

[1] Code name for atomic energy.

[2] General Sir John Dill, head of the British military mission in Washington since 1941, had died on November 9, 1944.

[3] The Combined Policy Committee on Atomic Energy was created under the terms of an agreement signed by Roosevelt and Churchill at Quebec on August 19, 1943. U.S. Department of State, *United States Treaties and Other International Agreements* (Washington, 1955), 5: 1114.

Doc. 503
CHURCHILL TO ROOSEVELT

No. 888　　　　　　　　　　　　　　　　　　　January 14, 1945

Halifax is giving the State Department a full account of the recent talks which Eden and I have had with King Peter of Yugoslavia.[1] We have, with the approval of the War Cabinet, been urging him in his own interests to accept the Tito-Subasić agreements[2] which preserve the principle of the monarchy and which are the best we think he can hope for in the circumstances. We told him that he could preserve his own position by making it clear in a suitable declaration that he could not, while outside Yugoslavia, assume actual responsibility for the way in which the agreements were fulfilled and that he accepted them on the clear understanding that they would be loyally carried out in the spirit and the letter.[3]

On Thursday, however, King Peter, without consultation with us or with his own Prime Minister, issued a declaration stating his own views on the Tito-Subasić agreements.[4] You know my views on these matters so well that I do not need to repeat that we should insist, so far as is possible, on full and fair elections deciding the future regime of the Yugoslav people or peoples.

We are now examining the situation to see how we can save the agreements and preserve the title of the Royal Yugoslav Government until the people or peoples of those mountainous regions have a chance of going to the poll. We have telegraphed to Stalin[5] on the

[1] Churchill and Eden had met with King Peter on January 9. See Woodward, *British Foreign Policy*, 3: 358.

[2] The primary agreement, dated November 1, 1944, provided that King Peter should appoint a council of three regents to represent him in Yugoslavia, pending a final decision on the future form of Yugoslav government. See *FR 1944*, 4: 1418–1419; and *Conferences at Malta and Yalta*, pp. 250–254.

[3] Churchill considered the agreements "entirely one-sided," meaning "nothing but the dictatorship of Tito, that well-drilled Communist." Woodward, *British Foreign Policy*, 3: 357.

[4] On January 11 King Peter set forth his objections to the agreements and his refusal to adhere to them. See Woodward, *British Foreign Policy*, 3: 359; and *Conferences at Malta and Yalta*, p. 258.

[5] On the night of January 11–12 Churchill suggested to Stalin that "we make the Tito-Subasić agreement valid and simply bypass King Peter II. . . . However, before we can express ourselves finally on this subject we must put the matter to the United States, who would be most offended if they were not informed." *Stalin's Correspondence*, vol. 2, no. 387.

lines which are explained in our telegram to Halifax, which shows our views at length. I should be glad to talk this over with you when we meet.

Doc. 504
CHURCHILL TO ROOSEVELT

No. 890   January 15, 1945

One of the questions which I think should be discussed at our meeting with Stalin, or between the Foreign Secretaries, is that of Persia.

In the declaration about Persia which we and Stalin signed at Teheran in December 1943,[1] it is stated that "the Governments of the United States of America, the U.S.S.R., and the United Kingdom are at one with the Government of Iran in their desire for the maintenance of the independence, sovereignty, and territorial integrity of Iran."

You will have seen reports of the recent attitude of the Russians in Persia.[2] We here feel that the various forms of pressure which they have been exerting constitute a departure from the statement quoted above. They have refused to accept the Persian decision to grant no concessions until after the war:[3] and they have brought about the fall of a Persian Prime Minister[4] who, believing that there could be no free or fair negotiations so long as Russian (or other foreign) troops were in Persia, refused the immediate grant of their oil demands. The

[1] *Conferences at Cairo and Tehran 1943*, pp. 646–647.

[2] See, for instance, *Conferences at Malta and Yalta*, pp. 330ff. On November 1, 1944, the U.S. ambassador to Iran, Leland B. Morris, had cabled the State Department from Teheran that "measures which smack of Hitlerian methods continue to be used in increasing crescendo by the Soviet authorities here." On January 18, according to a State Department memorandum, the Iranian ambassador in Washington visited the director of the Office of Near Eastern and African Affairs "to impress upon [him] the desperate situation in which he said his Government finds itself by reason of the attitude of the Russian military authorities in occupation of northern Iran. According to the Minister, the Russians . . . are in fact acting in such a way that all Iranian administration in the north may soon become impossible." At his government's request, the Iranian ambassador asked that "particular attention be given to the desperate situation in Iran at the forthcoming high-level conference." *FR 1945*, 8 (Washington, 1969) : 361.

[3] On October 9, 1944, the Iranian cabinet had stopped granting further oil concessions. See *FR 1944*, 5: 456ff.

[4] Mirza Mohammed Khan Saed had resigned on November 9, 1944.

new Persian Prime Minister,[5] supported by the Parliament, has maintained his predecessor's attitude on this question. But the Russians have indicated that they do not intend to drop their demands.

This may be something of a test case. Persia is a country where we, yourselves, and the Russians are all involved: and we have given a joint undertaking to treat the Persians decently. If the Russians are now able not only to save their face by securing the fall of the Persian Prime Minister who opposed them, but also to secure what they want by their use of the big stick, Persia is not the only place where the bad effect will be felt.

Please let me know whether you agree that this should be taken up with the Russians: and if so, whether you feel that it should be handled by ourselves with Stalin (as signatories of the Teheran declaration) or by the Foreign Secretaries. I think it should be our object to induce the Russians to admit that the Persians are within their rights in withholding a concession if they wish to do so. We could agree, if necessary, that the oil question should be further reviewed after the withdrawal of foreign troops from Persia.

We do not wish the Russians to be able to represent that they were not warned in time of the strength of our feelings on this matter. If, therefore, you agree generally with my suggestion, I propose that we should separately or jointly let Stalin know now that we think Persia should be discussed at our next meeting (or by the Foreign Secretaries) . . . .

5 Mustafa Qoli Khan Bayat.

Doc. 505
CHURCHILL TO ROOSEVELT

No. 891   January 21, 1945

I suggest that the press should be entirely excluded from Argonaut, but that each of us should be free to bring not more than three or four uniformed service photographers to take "still" and cinematograph pictures to be released when we think fit. Please let me know if you agree.[1]

There will of course be the usual agreement communiqué, or communiqués.

I am sending a similar telegram to U.J.[2]

1 Roosevelt replied on January 22: "I am in full agreement with the suggestion regarding press representatives and photographers." *Conferences at Malta and Yalta*, p. 38.

2 For the text of Churchill's message to Stalin, dated January 24, see *Conferences at Malta and Yalta*, p. 39.

Doc. 506
CHURCHILL TO ROOSEVELT

No. 894   January 24, 1945

It would be a great pity if Eisenhower and Alexander only come to Cricket[1] and if we do not have them with us at Magneto.[2] This will really make it impossible for the heads of government to enter fully into the military problems. I hope therefore they may be instructed as originally proposed to come to Magneto as well as Cricket and if they have to be absent from either, it should be Cricket.

The above of course is subject to battle exigencies.[3]

1 Code name for the Malta meeting.

2 Code name for the Yalta meeting (formerly Argonaut).

3 The generals did not attend either conference, although Eisenhower's chief of staff was present at Malta.

Doc. 507
CHURCHILL TO ROOSEVELT

No. 897   January 27, 1945

I have just heard from Dublin that your people are asking the Government of Southern Ireland[1] to sign a bilateral civil aviation agreement.[2] Naturally everyone here is astonished that this should have been started without our being told beforehand. We already complained when they were invited to the Chicago conference without a mention to us.[3] We were together at Hyde Park and I thought you felt that my attitude deserved consideration. It was because of their behaviour in the war[4] that the Southern Irish were not asked to talk civil aviation with the rest of the British Commonwealth and Empire at Montreal.[5] I cannot feel sure this affair has been brought to your

1 The Irish Republic (Eire).

2 This agreement was signed in Washington on February 3. See *FR 1945*, 6 (Washington, 1969) : 289; and *Conferences at Malta and Yalta*, p. 959.

3 See *FR 1944*, 2: 554–555.

4 Eire maintained German and Italian missions as late as February 1945. See *Conferences at Malta and Yalta*, p. 774.

5 The Commonwealth countries, minus Eire, had met in Montreal on October 23–28, 1944, in preparation for the international aviation conference in Chicago in November and December of that year. See above, Docs. 462 and 468.

notice and I am certain that you would have wished at least to acquaint us with your intentions beforehand.

The War Cabinet have very strong feelings on this episode and we all earnestly hope as good friends that you will consider the matter personally yourself. We went far to meet your requests about the Argentine meat[6] in spite of the grave and growing injury to ourselves and the risk to the general war effort, which is now becoming evident. I am sure we may ask you to postpone these negotiations with the Southern Irish until at least you and I have a chance of talking it over together.[7]

[6] See above, Docs. 285 and 286.

[7] The printed U.S. documents contain no evidence that Churchill and Roosevelt discussed this subject at Yalta. On February 7, however, Secretary Stettinius, then at Yalta, cabled Washington that "the British are disturbed over our having entered into an aviation agreement with Ireland without consulting or informing them." He asked Acting Secretary of State Joseph Grew for an "appropriate explanation for us to present to the British." The next day Grew replied that, when it became increasingly doubtful that a general agreement could be reached at Chicago, the United States had moved toward bilateral agreements. After signing an air agreement with Spain on December 2, the United States had intended to draw up similar agreements with a number of other countries. Grew concluded: "Ireland was naturally one of these in view of its obvious geographic importance to American air routes. We saw no reason to consult the United Kingdom particularly since the agreement followed the standard form drawn up with British participation at Chicago." See *Conferences at Malta and Yalta*, pp. 959–960.

THE MALTA-YALTA CONFERENCE
JANUARY-FEBRUARY 1945

[On January 22, 1945, two days after his fourth inauguration, President Roosevelt left Norfolk, Virginia, on board the cruiser USS *Quincy* for his last meeting with Churchill and Stalin.

Since Churchill had insisted on seeing the President before their meeting with Stalin, Roosevelt agreed to stop off at Malta on February 2, where he was joined by General Marshall, Admiral King, and Secretary of State Stettinius. The President dined with Churchill on board the *Quincy* and, together with the Prime Minister, attended a meeting of the Combined Chiefs of Staff, who had been in session at Malta for several days discussing operations in Europe, the Mediterranean, and the Far East. To them, Roosevelt "expressed his appreciation of the amount of progress which had been made in so short a time in the military discussions."

However, Roosevelt avoided political discussions with Churchill, and Anglo-American preparations for the Yalta conference were as inadequate as they had been for Teheran. This greatly disturbed Foreign Secretary Eden, who told Harry Hopkins that "we are going into a decisive conference and had so far neither agreed what we would discuss nor how to handle matters with a bear who would certainly know his mind."

On February 3 Roosevelt and Churchill flew in separate planes to Saki in the Crimea—a distance of 1,375 miles—and then they motored the remaining eighty miles to Livadia Palace, on the outskirts of Yalta. Stalin arrived from Moscow by train and car the following morning. The first session of the Yalta conference was held that afternoon, and the last—a meeting of foreign ministers—on the afternoon of February 11.

The Yalta conference took place against a background of renewed Allied victories on all fronts. The German offensive in the Ardennes in December 1944 had thrown a brief scare into Allied ranks, but by late January both German and Japanese forces were once more on the retreat. By the eve of Yalta General George S. Patton's First Army had crossed the German frontier at several points from Belgium and Luxembourg, while in East Prussia Soviet forces, having taken most of Poland, neared Königsberg and were preparing to invade Pomerania, less than seventy miles from Berlin. In the Pacific the U.S. First Cavalry was moving steadily ahead on Luzon toward Manila, which was liberated on the first day of the Yalta conference.

Assisted closely by their foreign ministers and military chiefs, Roosevelt, Churchill, and Stalin covered a broad range of issues but centered their attention on three areas—postwar Europe, the war in the Pacific, and a new international organization to keep the peace. They agreed swiftly on many of the important issues before them. Accepting in principle the future dismemberment of Germany, the Big Three gave formal approval to the zones of occupation previously drawn up by the European Advisory Commission; but largely at Churchill's insistence, they added a French zone of occupation in southwestern Germany. They also approved the Curzon line as Poland's new eastern frontier (with some minor digressions in Poland's favor) and compensated Poland with "substantial accessions of territory in the north and west." They further agreed that Poland's western boundary should be drawn permanently at a later peace conference, but both Roosevelt and Churchill in effect accepted the Oder River—though not the Neisse, farther west, as the Russians wished—as Poland's new western frontier. The Big Three likewise agreed on the establishment of an Allied council for occupied Germany but made no final decision on a Soviet request for $20 billion in reparations.

On the future of the liberated areas and especially the government of Poland, the Big Three soon encountered serious differences of opinion. By February 1945 the communization of Soviet-occupied Eastern and Balkan Europe was well advanced. After lengthy discussion Roosevelt, Churchill, and Stalin agreed to the President's proposal for a Declaration on Liberated Europe, which—reaffirming the Atlantic Charter principle of "the right of all peoples to choose the form of government under which they will live"—called for the formation of "interim governmental authorities broadly representative of all domestic elements in the population and pledged to the earliest possible establishment through free elections of governments responsive to the will of the people." Roosevelt, however, already disillusioned with the European Advisory Commission, failed to press the State Department's recommendation for a European high commission to supervise the implementation of the new declaration. As things turned out, this omission deprived the United States and Great Britain of any effective presence in the newly liberated areas in Eastern and Balkan Europe.

The issue that more than any other divided the Big Three and their foreign ministers was the future government of Poland. Since Great Britain had gone to war against Germany in September 1939 in order to maintain Poland's freedom and independence, Churchill and Roosevelt were hardly in a position to overlook the disturbing reports about Poland over the last months. In the end, after protracted debate and numerous drafts and redrafts, the Big Three agreed upon the establishment of a new Polish coalition government comprised of democratic leaders from home and abroad; the new interim government was formally "pledged to the holding of free and unfettered elections as soon as possible."

In accepting this particular formulation, Roosevelt made it clear that "it was very important for him in the United States that there be some gesture made for the six million Poles there indicating that the United States was in some way involved with the question of freedom of elections." He added, however, that in his judgment "it was only a matter of words and details." The President's optimism was not generally shared. Eden later wrote that Roosevelt "was deluding himself. . . . [W]e finally reached agreement on words, but it was not long before we learned that the difference remained untouched. Only if a genuinely representative government had been formed in Poland quickly would the pledge of free and unfettered elections have had any meaning. . . . This was true of all we did at Yalta; it was the execution which mattered."

Yet the Big Three did reach a number of other important agreements. In regard to the new world organization, the Russians retreated from their insistence on unanimity among the great powers on all issues before the Security Council, reserving unanimity for substantive issues only. On the other hand, Stalin persuaded Roosevelt and Churchill to agree that White Russia and the Ukraine should have separate seats in the General Assembly, although Churchill and Stalin were quick to approve Roosevelt's written notice that in order to "ensure wholehearted acceptance by the Congress and people of the United States," he might have to ask for additional votes for the United States to achieve voting parity. Both Stalin and Roosevelt (as the latter had indicated at Teheran) would have preferred to have the future peace of the world maintained by "the Four Policemen," but they agreed to convene a conference in San Francisco in April to draft the charter of the new world organization.

Finally, there was the increasingly urgent question of Russia's entry into the war against Japan, and the price to be paid for such assistance. This subject had already been discussed at Teheran, and the agreement reached at Yalta followed the lines of the earlier discussions. At a secret Roosevelt-Stalin meeting on February 8—which Churchill learned about only the following day—the Russian leader finally agreed to enter the war against Japan within two or three months after the defeat of Hitler, but his price was high. Roosevelt agreed that the Russians were to receive back all the rights and territories the Japanese had wrested from them in the war of 1904–1905; the status quo in Outer Mongolia would be preserved; and that the Soviet Union would receive the Kurile Islands, some of which they had voluntarily exchanged for Sakhalin under a treaty with Japan in 1875. Following Chiang Kai-shek's acceptance of these conditions—which Roosevelt undertook to obtain—Stalin also promised that China would retain full sovereignty over Manchuria and that the Soviet Union would conclude a treaty of friendship and alliance with the Chinese government.

Churchill knew nothing of all this—nor for that matter did Secretary Stettinius. Not until the last day of the conference did Roosevelt take Churchill into his confidence. Churchill in turn informed Secretary Eden, who regarded the Roosevelt-Stalin negotiations as "discreditable" and counseled Churchill not to sign the agreement. Churchill seemed less troubled and concurred with Roosevelt's bargain on the ground that, if the British declined to sign the Roosevelt-Stalin agreement, their authority in the Far East would suffer.

Although relations between Roosevelt and Churchill were on the whole close and cordial at Yalta, the President could not completely escape the temptation of baiting Churchill about the Empire, as he had at Teheran, and of trying to gain favor with Stalin at Churchill's expense. Thus at the secret meeting with Stalin on February 8 Roosevelt told the Soviet leader that he "hoped that the British would give back the sovereignty of Hong Kong to China and that it would then become an international free port." He added, however, that he "knew that Mr. Churchill would have strong objections to this suggestion."

Yalta closed in a sea of amity. Even the usually waspish Sir Alexander Cadogan—who at one time observed that "the Great Men don't know what they're talking about and have to be educated"—was carried away: "The P.M. and Anthony [Eden] are well satisfied—if not more—and I think they are right."

Following the close of the Yalta conference, Roosevelt flew to Suez, where he reboarded the *Quincy;* and after meeting briefly with King Farouk of Egypt, King Ibn Saud of Saudi Arabia, and Emperor Haile Selassie of Ethiopia, he and his party began the long voyage home. The President was by then in failing health, and the return journey was overshadowed by other illnesses and by death. Hopkins, his closest adviser, was rapidly wasting away, and General Edwin M. Watson, his devoted military aide, who had been in apparently excellent health, suffered a cerebral hemorrhage and died on board ship on February 20, two days out of Algiers.

Roosevelt returned to Washington and promptly reported to Congress: "I come home from the Crimea conference with a firm belief that we have made a good start on the road to a world of peace. . . . [The peace] cannot be a structure of complete perfection at first. But it can be a peace—and it will be a peace—based on the sound and just principles of the Atlantic Charter, on the concept of the dignity of the human being, and on the guarantees of tolerance and freedom of religious worship."]

Doc. 508
CHURCHILL TO ROOSEVELT

No. 901   February 28, 1945

Accept my deep sympathy in your personal loss through the death of General Watson.[1] I know how much this will grieve you.

You will probably see the accounts of our three days' debate which began yesterday.[2] Today 21 Conservatives are moving a hostile

1 Major General Edwin M. Watson, President Roosevelt's military aide, had died on February 20.

2 In the debate that began in the House of Commons on February 27, Churchill said: "Most solemn declarations have been made by Marshal Stalin and the Soviet Union that the sovereign independence of Poland is to be maintained. . . . The Poles will have their future in their own hands, with the single limitation that they must honestly follow, in harmony with their Allies, a policy friendly to Russia. . . .

amendment in favour of Poland,[3] and Greenwood, who speaks for the Labour party, made a foolish and hostile speech.[4] We shall no doubt defeat the amendment by an overwhelming majority.[5] Nevertheless there is a good deal of uneasiness in both parties that we are letting the Poles down, etc.[6]

In these circumstances it is of the utmost importance that as many representative Poles as possible should be invited as soon as possible to

---

It will be for the Poles themselves, with such assistance as the Allies are able to give them, to agree upon the composition and constitution of the new Polish government of National Unity." Churchill went on to say that there would be no Lublin Committee or Provisional Government in Poland today if the Polish government-in-exile "had accepted our faithful counsel given them a year ago. . . . Even in October [1944] M. Mikolajczyk could have gone from Moscow to Lublin, with every assurance of Marshal Stalin's friendship, and become the Prime Minister of a more broadly constructed government." *Parliamentary Debates,* Commons, 5th ser., vol. 408, cols. 1278–1279, 1282.

3 On February 28 Mr. Petherick moved an amendment stating that Great Britain remember that it "took up arms in a war of which the immediate cause was the defense of Poland against German aggression and in which the overriding motive was the prevention of the domination by a strong nation of its weaker neighbours, regrets the decision to transfer to another power the territory of an ally contrary to treaty and to Article 2 of the Atlantic Charter and furthermore regrets the failure to ensure to those nations which have been liberated from German oppression the full right to choose their own government free from the influence of any other power." *Parliamentary Debates,* Commons, 5th ser., vol. 408, cols. 1421–1422.

4 In his reply to Churchill's address, Arthur Greenwood, the Deputy Leader of the Labor party, declared that "it is foreign to the principles of British justice that the fate of a nation should be decided in its absence and behind its back. . . . I do not hold any brief for the Polish Government. I do not think it has been too well treated by His Majesty's Government. I think it has made mistakes. I have told my Polish friends that it has made mistakes. I admit all that, but I say it really is a cardinal sin for these Great Powers—one of whom has an interest which we have not got—in the absence of the people whose lives are being bartered away, to determine the future of any country." *Parliamentary Debates,* Commons, 5th ser., vol. 408, cols. 1298–1299.

5 The government majority vote, on February 28, was 396 to 25.

6 Toward the end of the debate, on February 28, Mr. Petherick quoted from a hitherto secret protocol of December 15, 1939, attached to the Anglo-Polish mutual assistance agreement of August 25, 1939, that "the undertakings mentioned in Article 6 of the Agreement, should they be entered into by one of the Contracting Parties with a Third State, would of necessity be so framed that their execution should at no time prejudice either the sovereignty or territorial inviolability of the other Contracting Party." To the revelation of this secret protocol, Foreign Secretary Eden replied that "these measures only applied to aggression by Germany, and it does not in the least surprise me, if I may say so. . . . I do not ask my honourable Friend how he obtained this secret Protocol." *Parliamentary Debates,* Commons, 5th ser., vol. 408, cols. 1425, 1510. For the text of the Anglo-Polish agreement and the secret protocol, see *Polish-Soviet Relations,* vol. 1, app. 5.

the consultations in Moscow[7] and, above all, that Mikolajczyk who is the leading test case should be invited. The London Polish government is of course trying to prevent any Poles leaving here for Moscow or Poland, and is playing for a breakdown.

Clark Kerr telegraphs that Molotov spontaneously offers to allow British and American observers to go into Poland and see what is going on for themselves.[8] I think this is of the highest importance. Nor can I feel that the acceptance of the offer would imply any recognition of the Lublin government. There are many stories put about of wholesale deportations by the Russians and of liquidations by the Lublin Poles of elements they do not like, and I have no means of verifying or contradicting these assertions.

I do hope you have benefited by the voyage and will return refreshed. The battle seems to be going well and I propose to visit the front at the weekend, seeing both Eisenhower and Montgomery. I cannot help feeling there might easily be a good breakthrough in the west. Every good wish to you and all. I hope Harry[9] is recovering.

[7] The Moscow Commission on Poland, established at the Yalta conference and composed of Ambassadors Harriman and Clark Kerr and Soviet Foreign Minister Molotov, met for the first time on February 23, 1945.

[8] Churchill wrote later that Molotov "had offered to allow us to send observers to Poland, and had been disconcerted by the readiness and speed with which we had accepted." Churchill, *Triumph and Tragedy*, p. 418. See below, Doc. 510.

[9] Harry L. Hopkins, special assistant to the President, had become seriously ill at the close of the Yalta conference and had flown home ahead of Roosevelt and his party.

Doc. 509
CHURCHILL TO ROOSEVELT

No. 904   March 6, 1945

On January 27 I sent you my telegram 897[1] about the aviation agreement with the Government of Southern Ireland. You could not at the time reply because of wireless silence. At Yalta, and also later at Alexandria,[2] I understood from you that you did not approve this step and that it had been taken without your agreement. Mr. Stettinius

[1] See above, Doc. 507.

[2] Roosevelt and Churchill had met on board the USS *Quincy* in Alexandria harbor on February 15. No written record of that meeting has been found, but apparently "the conversation dealt with the prosecution of the war against Japan and the coordination of Anglo-American policy in Italy." *Conferences at Malta and Yalta*, p. xi.

also made this clear so far as he was concerned. At the same time as we sent out 897 to you, Lord Halifax was instructed to let the State Department have a copy of the telegram at once so that they should hold their hand until you had had an opportunity to comment on it.

On January 31 the State Department confirmed that negotiations had been in progress but said that they had not reached readiness for signature. On February 3, however, without further warning, Lord Halifax was informed that the agreement had been signed and shortly afterwards it was published.

Our special concern with Eire is obvious on political and geographical grounds, and it is indeed much closer than that of the United States with the Argentine. We and the United States have, moreover, throughout kept in close touch in our general policy towards Eire, e.g., over the recent United States approach to de Valera[3] for the removal of the Axis representatives.[4] For this reason the political effect of the United States action in concluding an agreement with Southern Ireland on an important issue without consulting us seemed to us bound to injure our relations with de Valera politically, and may be embarrassing to the United States also, as it can only encourage him to try to play off one against the other. It has, in fact, been hailed in Southern Ireland as a diplomatic success for them.

I trust therefore that you will be able to take the necessary steps to have the agreement annulled. So far no response has been made to our telegrams or representations whether addressed personally to you or handed formally to the State Department.[5]

[3] Eamon de Valera, Prime Minister of Eire.

[4] For the background of these efforts, which began in 1944, see Nicholas Man-sergh, *Survey of British Commonwealth Affairs*, vol. 2, *Problems of Wartime Cooperation and Postwar Change 1939–1952* (London, 1958), pp. 161ff. In February 1944 the United States had requested the recall of Axis diplomats in Dublin, but the government of Eire had flatly rejected the request.

[5] See below, Doc. 516.

Doc. 510
CHURCHILL TO ROOSEVELT

No. 905   March 8, 1945

I feel sure that you will be as distressed as I am by recent events in Rumania.[1] The Russians have succeeded in establishing the rule of a

[1] In December 1944 a new Rumanian Cabinet had been formed under General Nicolai Radescu. This government included a minority of Communists, who controlled the Ministry of Interior and the Ministry of Justice. Following a visit to

Communist minority by force and misrepresentation. We have been hampered in our protests against these developments by the fact that, in order to have the freedom to save Greece, Eden and I at Moscow in October recognised that Russia should have a largely preponderant voice in Rumania and Bulgaria while we took the lead in Greece.[2] Stalin adhered very strictly to this understanding during the thirty days' fighting against the Communists and ELAS in the city of Athens, in spite of the fact that all this was most disagreeable to him and those around him.[3]

Peace has now been restored in Greece and, though many difficulties lie before us, I hope that we shall be able to bring about in the next few months free, unfettered elections, preferably under British, American, and Russian supervision, and that thereafter a constitution and Government will be erected on the indisputable will of the Greek people, which remains our supreme ultimate objective in all cases, and with which I know you are in sympathy.[4]

Stalin is now pursuing the opposite course in the two Black Sea Balkan countries, and one which is absolutely contrary to all democratic ideas. Since the October Anglo-Russian conversations in Moscow Stalin has subscribed on paper to the principles of Yalta which are certainly being trampled down in Rumania. Nevertheless I am most anxious not to press this view to such an extent that Stalin will say, "I did not interfere with your action in Greece, why do you not give me the same latitude in Rumania?"

This again would lead to comparisons between the aims of his action and those of ours. On this neither side would convince the other. Having regard to my personal relations with Stalin, I am sure it would be a mistake for me at this stage to embark on the argument.

Again I am very conscious of the fact that we have on our hands the much more important issue of Poland, and I do not therefore want to do anything as regards Rumania which might prejudice our prospects of reaching a Polish settlement. Nevertheless, I feel that he should be informed of our distress at the developments which led to the setting up by force of a government in Rumania of a Communist minority,

---

Moscow by leading Rumanian Communists, agitation began against the Radescu government. On February 26 Soviet Deputy Foreign Minister Vyshinsky appeared in Bucharest and demanded that King Michael appoint a new, Communist-controlled government.

2 See above, Doc. 3, 442, 444.

3 At the sixth plenary meeting at Yalta on February 9 Stalin had expressed "complete confidence in British policy in Greece." *Conferences at Malta and Yalta,* p. 849.

4 For the Greek situation after the appointment of Archbishop Damaskinos as regent, see Macmillan, *Blast of War,* pp. 527ff.

since this conflicts with the conclusions of the Declaration on Liberated Europe upon which we were agreed at the Crimea conference.[5]

More especially I am afraid that the advent of this Communist government may lead to an indiscriminate purge of anti-Communist Rumanians, who will be accused of fascism much on the lines of what has been happening in Bulgaria. This is as good as foretold in the Moscow broadcast of yesterday, the text of which I have telegraphed to our Embassy.

I would suggest, therefore, that Stalin should be asked to see to it that the new government does not immediately start a purge of all political elements which are in opposition to their views on the ground that they have been encouraged to do so by the Yalta declaration.

We will, of course, give you every support, and if you will show me the text of any message you feel inclined to send Stalin, I will also send one to him supporting it. There is, of course, complete agreement between our representatives on the spot and yours.

The news from Moscow about Poland is also most disappointing. I must let you know that the government majorities here[6] bear no relation to the strong undercurrent of opinion among all parties and classes and in our own hearts against a Soviet domination of Poland.

Labour men are as keen as Conservatives, and Socialists as keen as Catholics. I have based myself in Parliament on the assumption that the words of the Yalta declaration will be carried out in the letter and the spirit. Once it is seen that we have been deceived and that the well-known Communist technique is being applied behind closed doors in Poland, either directly by the Russians or through their Lublin puppets, a very grave situation in British public opinion will be reached.

How would the matter go in the United States? I cannot think that you personally or they would be indifferent. Thus just at the time when everything military is going so well in Europe and when the Japanese policy is also satisfactorily arranged, there would come an open rift between us and Russia not at all confined, in this country at any rate, to government opinion, but running deep down through the masses of the people.

After a fairly promising start Molotov is now refusing to accept any interpretation of the Crimea proposals except his own extremely rigid

---

[5] In their Declaration on Liberated Europe Roosevelt, Churchill, and Stalin agreed that "the establishment of order in Europe and the rebuilding of national economic life must be achieved by processes which will enable liberated people to destroy the last vestiges of Nazism and Fascism and to create democratic institutions of their own choice. This is a principle of the Atlantic Charter." *Conferences at Malta and Yalta,* p. 972.

[6] See above, Doc. 508, note 5.

and narrow one.[7] He is attempting to bar practically all our candidates from the consultations, is taking the line that he must base himself on the views of Berut and his gang, and has withdrawn his offer that we should send observers to Poland.[8]

In other words, he clearly wants to make a farce of consultations with the "non-Lublin" Poles—which means that the new government in Poland would be merely the present one dressed up to look more respectable to the ignorant—and also wants to prevent us from seeing the liquidations and deportations that are going on and all the rest of the game of setting up a totalitarian regime before elections are held and even before a new government is set up. As to the upshot of all this, if we do not get things right now, it will soon be seen by the world that you and I by putting our signatures to the Crimea settlement have underwritten a fraudulent prospectus.

I am in any case pledged to Parliament to tell them if the business of setting up a new Polish government etc. cannot be carried out in the spirit of the Yalta declaration. I am sure the only way to stop Molotov's tactics is to send a personal message to Stalin and in that message I must make clear what are the essential things we must have in this business if I am to avoid telling Parliament that we have failed.

I think you will agree with me that far more than the case of Poland is involved. I feel that this is the test case between us and the Russians of the meaning which is to be attached to such terms as democracy, sovereignty, independence, representative government, and free and unfettered elections.

I therefore propose to send to Stalin a message on the lines set out below. It is as you will see based on the ideas in Eden's telegram to Halifax number 2078 which has been communicated to State Department.[9] I hope you will be ready to send Stalin a similar message containing the same minimum requirements. I shall not send my message till I hear from you. Message begins.

"I am sorry to say that the discussions in the Moscow Commission on Poland show that M. Molotov has quite a different view from us as to how the Crimea decision on Poland should be put into effect. As you know, nobody here believes that the present Warsaw administration is

---

7 See *FR 1945*, 5 (Washington, 1967) : 142–144.

8 At a meeting with Molotov and Harriman on March 6 Ambassador Clark Kerr raised the question of a British mission going to Poland "as a means of getting more information." According to Harriman, Molotov "interrupted by stating he did not feel he could now even take this question up with the Warsaw government because of Mr. Eden's recent 'offensive remarks' about the Warsaw government in the House." *FR 1945*, 5: 144.

9 See Woodward, *British Foreign Policy*, 3: 494ff.

really representative, and [there has been] criticism of the decision in Parliament to the line that the discussion in Moscow would not result in a really representative government being set up and that, if this was so, all hope of free elections disappeared. All parties were also exercised about the reports that deportations, liquidations, and other oppressive measures were being put into practice on a wide scale by the Warsaw administration against those likely to disagree with them.

"Feeling confident of your cooperation in this matter, Eden and I pledged ourselves to Parliament that we would inform them if the fears of our critics were fulfilled. I am bound to tell you that I should have to make a statement of our failure to Parliament if the Commission in Moscow were not in the end able to agree on the following basis:

" (A) M. Molotov appears to be contending that the terms of the Crimea communiqué established for the present Warsaw administration an absolute right of prior consultation on all points. In the English text the passage of the communiqué in question, which was in American draft, cannot bear this interpretation. M. Molotov's contention therefore cannot be accepted.

" (B) All Poles nominated by any of the three governments shall be accepted for the consultations unless ruled out by unanimous decision of the Commission and every effort made to produce them before the Commission at the earliest possible moment: The Commission should ensure to the Poles invited facilities for communicating with other Poles whom they wish to consult whether in Poland or outside and the right to suggest to the Commission the names of other Poles who should be invited to its proceedings. All Poles appearing before the Commission would naturally enjoy complete freedom of movement and of communication among themselves while in Moscow and would be at liberty to depart whither they chose upon the conclusion of the consultations. M. Molotov has raised objections to inviting M. Mikolajczyk but his presence would certainly be vital.

" (C) The Poles invited for consultations should discuss among themselves with a view to reaching agreement upon the composition of a government truly representative of the various sections of Polish opinion present before the Commission. The discussions should also cover the question of the exercise of the presidential functions. The Commission should preside over these discussions in an impartial arbitral capacity.

" (D) Pending the conclusion of the Commission's discussions the Soviet Government should use its utmost influence to prevent the "Warsaw" administration from taking any further legal or administrative action of a fundamental character affecting social, constitutional, economic, or political conditions in Poland.

"(E) The Soviet Government should make arrangements to enable British and American observers to visit Poland and report upon conditions there in accordance with the offer spontaneously made by M. Molotov at an earlier stage in the Commission's discussions.

"We must not let Poland become a source of disagreement and misunderstanding between our two peoples. For this reason I am sure you will understand how important it is for us to reach an early settlement on the basis of the Yalta decision, and it is because I am confident that you will do your utmost to bring this about that I am now telegraphing you." Ends.

I should be grateful to know your views. Pray let this telegram be between you and me.[10]

Many congratulations on your statement to Congress.[11] Every good wish.

10 For Roosevelt's reply, see below, Doc. 513.

11 A reference to the President's generally optimistic report on the Yalta conference delivered to a joint session of Congress on March 1, 1945: "I am confident that the Congress and the American people will accept the results of this conference as the beginnings of a permanent structure of peace. . . ." *PPR* 13: 586.

Doc. 511
CHURCHILL TO ROOSEVELT

No. 907   March 10, 1945

I have now read the instructions[1] to Mr. Harriman which were shown to our Ambassador[2] today. I need not say how cordially I agree with all the first part of these instructions,[3] but I am distressed at the conclusion[4] which I fear may lead us into great difficulties.

1 See *FR 1945*, 5: 150–152.

2 Sir Archibald Clark Kerr.

3 "The United States Government is concerned at the difficulties which the Moscow Commission has encountered in its first efforts to carry out the terms of the Crimean decision on Poland. It is felt that a clear statement of the understanding of this Government not only as to the intent and purpose of the decision but also the role of the Commission itself would be of value in overcoming these difficulties which appear to be in large measure a question of interpretation." *FR 1945*, 5: 150.

4 "In the opinion of the United States Government, as an essential condition for the successful negotiations in Moscow for the formation of the new provisional government as well as for the eventual carrying out by that new government of its pledge of the 'holding of free and unfettered elections' as provided in the [Yalta] communiqué, there should be the maximum amount of political tranquility inside Poland during the period of negotiations." *FR 1945*, 5: 151.

I do not know what the answer of the London Polish government would be to a request for a political truce. They continue to assert, with a wealth of detail, that their friends in Poland are being arrested, deported, and liquidated on a large scale. At the best they would make conditions of an impossible character.

As to the Lublin Poles, they may well answer that their government can alone ensure "the maximum amount of political tranquility inside," that they already represent the great mass of the "democratic forces in Poland," and that they cannot join hands with émigré traitors to Poland or Fascist collaborationists and landlords, and so on according to the usual technique.

Meanwhile we shall not be allowed inside the country or have any means of informing ourselves upon the position. It suits the Soviet very well to have a long period of delay so that the process of liquidation of elements unfavourable to them or their puppets may run its full course.

This would be furthered by our opening out now into proposals of a very undefined character for a political truce between these Polish parties (whose hatreds would eat into live steel) in the spirit and intent of the Crimea decision and might well imply the abandonment of all clear-cut requests such as those suggested in my last telegram to you.[5] Therefore I should find it very difficult to join in this project of a political truce.

I have already mentioned to you that the feeling here is very strong. Four ministers have abstained from the divisions and two have already resigned.

I beg therefore that you will give full consideration to my previous telegram number 905[6] and will suspend the delivery of the latest Harriman instructions till I have received your reply and can reply to it.

[5] See above, Doc. 510.
[6] See above, Doc. 510.

Doc. 512
ROOSEVELT TO CHURCHILL

No. 713   March 11, 1945

Your 907.[1]

I had drafted and released for transmission my reply to your 905, March 8,[2] before I had received your 907 of March 10. I did not hold

[1] See above, Doc. 511.
[2] See above, Doc. 510.

up on my first message as I don't believe that the main issues in that reply are basically affected by the points you raise in your 907.

With reference to your observations on the last part of the instructions to Ambassador Harriman in regard to a political truce in Poland, I can assure you that our objectives are identical, namely, to bring about a cessation on the part of the Lublin Poles of the measures directed against their political opponents in Poland to which you refer and vice versa. The only difference as I see it is one of tactics. You would prefer that the demand in regard to the Lublin Poles be put squarely to the Soviet Government as such whereas we feel that the chances of achieving our common objective would be immeasurably increased if it were done under the guise of a general political truce. You will recall at Yalta that Stalin made quite a point of the QUOTE terrorist END QUOTE activities of the underground forces of the London government against the Red Army and the Lublin Poles.[3] Whether or not these allegations have any foundation in fact is beside the question since it is definitely the position of the Soviet Government. In view of Stalin's attitude we feel we would be inviting certain refusal if we merely demanded that the Lublin Poles alone be forced to cease their persecutions of political opponents. Furthermore, we must be careful not to give the impression that we are proposing a halt in the land reforms. This would furnish the Lublin Poles with an opportunity to charge that they and they alone defend the interests of the peasants against the landlords. However, in view of your feeling on this point we have made sure that Harriman will not deliver those instructions until Clark Kerr has received his. I would also be very glad to consider any suggestions which you may have in order to strengthen this point bearing in mind the considerations which I have set forth above.

The question of sending in observers is being pressed by Harriman under other instructions. We feel, however, that more would be accomplished by pressing for low-level observers at this point who would certainly see as much if not more than some more spectacular body.[4] If you feel strongly that some reference to observers should go into the present instructions to Harriman, I will have no objection. Since we wish to get on as speedily as possible with the business of the Commission in Moscow, I would appreciate your letting me have

3 See *Conferences at Malta and Yalta*, pp. 670, 681. However, Stalin had made this charge even before the Yalta conference. In a telegram to Roosevelt dated December 27, 1944, he declared that "terrorists instigated by Polish emigrants kill in Poland soldiers and officers of the Red Army, lead a criminal fight against Soviet troops which are liberating Poland, and directly aid our enemies, whose allies they in fact are." *Conferences at Malta and Yalta*, p. 221.

4 See below, Doc. 515.

urgently your views on my two messages so that instructions can be issued to Harriman and Clark Kerr for transmission to Molotov.

Doc. 513
ROOSEVELT TO CHURCHILL

No. 714   March 11, 1945

Your 905.[1]

I have of course had very much in mind the considerations in regard to Rumania and to the Polish question raised in your 905, March 8, and share your concern over these developments. I am fully determined, as I know you are, not to let the good decisions we reached at the Crimea slip through our hands and will certainly do everything I can to hold Stalin to their honest fulfillment. In regard to the Rumanian situation Averell has taken up and is taking up again the whole question with Molotov invoking the Declaration on Liberated Europe and has proposed tripartite discussions to carry out these responsibilities. It is obvious that the Russians have installed a minority government of their own choosing, but apart from the reasons you mentioned in your message, Rumania is not a good place for a test case. The Russians have been in undisputed control from the beginning, and with Rumania lying athwart the Russian lines of communications it is moreover difficult to contest the plea of military necessity and security which they are using to justify their action. We shall certainly do everything we can, however, and of course will count on your support.

As to the Polish negotiations in Moscow I most certainly agree that we must stand firm on the right interpretation of the Crimean decision. You are quite correct in assuming that neither the Government nor the people of this country will support participation in a fraud or a mere whitewash of the Lublin government, and the solution must be as we envisaged it at Yalta. We have recently sent instructions to Harriman,[2] a copy of which has been given to your Embassy here, to address a communication to Molotov making this clear[3] and in

---

1 See above, Doc. 510.

2 See FR *1945*, 5: 510–511.

3 In his formal note to Molotov, Harriman pointed out that "American opinion is watchful of the responsibilities of the United States Government with respect to the former Axis satellite states, as set forth in the Crimea Declaration [on Liberated Europe]." He added: "My Government considers this matter an urgent one." *FR 1945*, 5: 512–513. Harriman was not optimistic, however, that Anglo-American pro-

general very much along the lines of the Foreign Office's suggestions contained in the telegram to Halifax to which you refer. I understand that Clark Kerr will be instructed along similar lines. In the circumstances I feel that it would be much better to await the result of these steps by our Ambassadors before either you or I intervene personally with Stalin, particularly since there is no question of either of our Governments yielding to Molotov's interpretation. I feel that our personal intervention would best be withheld until every other possibility of bringing the Soviet Government into line has been exhausted. I very much hope, therefore, that you will not send any message to Uncle Joe at this juncture—especially as I feel that certain parts of your proposed text might produce a reaction quite contrary to your intent. We must, of course, keep in close touch on this question.

---

tests would produce any results. On March 14 he cabled Secretary Stettinius that "Russian policy in Rumania is probably in line with their long-range plans established some time ago for the Balkan and Eastern European states." *FR 1945*, 5: 511.

Doc. 514
ROOSEVELT TO CHURCHILL

No. 715   March 12, 1945

Your No. 909[1] points directly to an urgent necessity of our taking every practicable means of accomplishing the corrective measures in Poland that are envisaged in the agreements reached at Yalta.

The Yalta agreements, if they are followed, should correct most of the abuses alleged in your 909.

In my opinion as expressed in my 714,[2] we should leave the first

1 Not printed. On March 10 Churchill sent Roosevelt a lengthy summary of information from the Polish underground, transmitted by Prime Minister Arciszewski in London. Covering the period from January 17 to March 1, the summary stated: "The Sovietisation of Poland is proceeding apace. . . . From 5th February Poles in important positions (professors, doctors and so on) have been forced to sign a memorandum condemning the Polish Government in London . . . and praising the Lublin Committee. . . . The NKVD [Russian secret police] are keeping those arrested in cellars, air raid shelters, and in every possible place. . . . In the course of interrogations, the NKVD beat prisoners, torture them morally, keep them in the cold without clothes. They accuse those arrested of espionage on behalf of the British and of the Polish Government in London, and of collaboration with the Germans. There is a high rate of mortality among the prisoners. . . . Please inform the British. Allied intervention necessary." The report concluded: "Most people in Poland consider the present state of affairs as Soviet occupation."

2 See above, Doc. 513.

steps to our Ambassadors from which we may hope to obtain good results.

When and if it should become necessary because of failure of the Ambassadors we may have to appeal to Marshal Stalin for relief for the oppressed inhabitants of Poland.

Doc. 515
CHURCHILL TO ROOSEVELT

No. 910   March 13, 1945

1. Your numbers 713,[1] 714,[2] and 715.[3]

I thank you for your full and considerate replies to my various messages on Poland. We can, of course, make no progress at Moscow without your aid, and if we get out of step the doom of Poland is sealed.

A month has passed since Yalta and no progress of any kind has been made. Soon I shall be questioned in Parliament on this point and I shall be forced to tell them the truth. Time is, of course, all on the side of Lublin, who are no doubt at work to establish their authority in such a way as to make it impregnable.

2. I am willing to defer addressing Stalin directly for the time being on this subject. But, in that case, I must beg you to agree that the instructions to our Ambassadors should deal with the points which I have proposed to put to Stalin in (A) to (E) of . . . my number 905.[4]

You say that some of these might have the opposite effect to what we intend. I wonder which you have in mind. We might be able to improve the wording. But I am convinced that unless we can induce the Russians to agree to these fundamental points of procedure, all our work at Yalta will be in vain.

3. When the discussions following Yalta began at Moscow, we had a perfectly simple objective, namely, to bring together for consultation representative Poles from inside Poland and elsewhere and to promote the formation of a new reorganised Polish government sufficiently representative of all Poland for us to recognise it.

A test case of progress in this direction would be the inviting of Mikolajczyk and two or three of his friends who have resigned from

1 See above, Doc. 512.
2 See above, Doc. 513.
3 See above, Doc. 514.
4 See above, Doc. 510.

the London Polish government because they realise that a good understanding must be reached with Russia.

4. I fear that your present instructions to Averell will lead to little if any progress on all this, as the only definite suggestion is that there should be a truce between Polish parties. Here we should enter ground of great disadvantage to us both. The Russians would almost at once claim that the truce was being broken by the anti-Lublin Poles and that Lublin therefore could not be held to it.

I have little doubt that some of the supporters of the Polish government in London and more particularly the extreme right-wing underground force, the so-called NSZ, are giving and would give the Russians and Lublin ground for this contention.

As we are not allowed to enter the country to see what the truth is, we shall be at the mercy of assertions. After a fortnight or so of negotiations about the truce, we shall be farther back than in the days before Yalta when you and I were agreed together that anyhow Mikolajczyk should be invited.

5. At Yalta also we agreed to take the Russian view of the frontier line. Poland has lost her frontier. Is she now to lose her freedom? That is the question which will undoubtedly have to be fought out in Parliament and in public here.

I do not wish to reveal a divergence between the British and the United States Governments, but it would certainly be necessary for me to make it clear that we are in presence of a great failure and an utter breakdown of what was settled at Yalta, but that we British have not the necessary strength to carry the matter further and that the limits of our capacity to act have been reached.

The moment that Molotov sees that he has beaten us away from the whole process of consultations among Poles to form a new government, he will know that we will put up with anything. On the other hand, I believe that combined dogged pressure and persistence, along the lines on which we have been working and of my proposed draft message to Stalin, would very likely succeed.

6. We are also in presence of the Soviet memorandum of March 9 about inviting representatives of the Lublin Poles to San Francisco.[5] This would amount to a de facto recognition of Lublin. Are we not

5 In an *aide-mémoire* to the State Department on March 9, 1945—and in a similarly worded note delivered to the British Foreign Office on that date—the Soviet Union proposed that if a Polish government of national unity had been agreed upon by late April, it should be invited to send its representatives to the forthcoming San Francisco conference, which was scheduled to convene on April 25 to draft a charter for the new United Nations organization. The Russians added, however, that if, "due to the complication of this question, the reorganization of the Polish provisional government is not achieved or completed," then representatives of the Lublin government should be invited. *FR 1945*, 1 (Washington, 1967) : 113.

both pledged not to recognise the Lublin government until it has been reorganised in accordance with the declaration and spirit of Yalta, and consequently to continue to recognise the London Polish government as the only one in existence?[6]

The only possible course if no agreement is reached is to invite neither of the present governments. This is in fact the line agreed upon between us. On the other hand, this very invitation question is well suited to bring matters to a head at the Moscow conference and make the Soviets see that they must reach a fair and honourable conclusion in accordance with the decisions of Yalta. . . .

[6] On March 11 the Polish government-in-exile delivered identical notes to the United States, Britain, and China strongly protesting its exclusion from the San Francisco conference: "The fact that Poland, whose Constitutional President and Government are recognized by all the United Nations as well as all neutral nations with the exception of one Power only, is not invited . . . is the first disturbing example of the application of the right of veto of the Big Powers exercised by them even before the United Nations have agreed to and carried out the suggestions to be submitted to them relating to the future establishment of a world security organization." *FR 1945*, 1: 114–115. A slightly different wording is found in *Polish-Soviet Relations*, vol. 2, no. 324. On March 22 Secretary of State Stettinius responded that "the invitations to the conference have been extended by agreement of the sponsoring Governments. . . . Fully appreciating the importance of Polish representation at the San Francisco conference, the United States Government earnestly hopes that it will be possible to establish the new Polish provisional government before the conference is convened, and that the Governments sponsoring the conference will agree to extend an invitation to it." *FR 1945*, 1: 145.

Doc. 516
ROOSEVELT TO CHURCHILL

No. 717   March 15, 1945

I am surprised at your 904.[1] There must have been some misunderstanding of my position. Furthermore, the circumstances of the agreement with Ireland were fully explained to your people, Cadogan in particular, at Yalta.[2]

During the latter days of the Chicago conference when it became increasingly doubtful that full agreement on aviation would be reached on a multilateral basis we held preliminary discussions looking toward bilateral agreements, as Berle publicly stated, with a number of countries represented there. Ireland was naturally one of

[1] See above, Doc. 509.

[2] There is no reference to such a discussion in *Conferences at Malta and Yalta*. But see above, Doc. 507, note 7.

these in view of its obvious geographic importance to American air routes. The agreement followed the standard form drawn up with the assistance of your people at Chicago and in no way prejudices your right to make similar arrangements. In the circumstances we saw no need to do more than advise your people, which we authorized Gray[3] to do, before signature. One hour before the scheduled time of signature a copy of your 897[4] was brought to the attention of Acting Secretary Grew.[5] He advised me that in view of your message he was postponing signature until February 3 to give me time to comment but that, the negotiations having been satisfactorily concluded, we could not in good faith refuse to sign nor could we risk the damage to Anglo-American relations which would result should it become known that your Government had objected to our concluding this agreement with Ireland. I saw no reason to instruct the State Department not to sign on February 3 and I fully approve of its action. There can of course be no question of annulling the agreement. I am sorry but there it is.

I fully realize your concern on political grounds and your opinion, which I share, of Ireland's role during the war. We instructed Gray to make clear to the Irish that signature of the agreement indicated no change whatsoever in our attitude toward Ireland any more than our signature of a similar agreement with Spain indicated any change in our attitude toward Franco.

This agreement is however a postwar matter. You will recall how earnestly I endeavored to secure your cooperation on the future of aviation during the Chicago conference. These bilateral aviation agreements were made necessary by the failure of that conference to reach a multilateral agreement permitting the natural development of aviation. While I fully understand your own position, I think it only fair to tell you that aviation circles in this country are becoming increasingly suspicious that certain elements in England intend to try to block the development of international flying in general until the British aviation industry is further developed. Of course any feeling of complacence, even though wholly unwarranted at any time, on the part of the Irish has now been somewhat deflated by their being left out of the San Francisco conference.

3 David Gray, U.S. ambassador to Eire.
4 See above, Doc. 507.
5 Joseph C. Grew, Acting Secretary of State.

Doc. 517
ROOSEVELT TO CHURCHILL

No. 718   March 15, 1945

· I cannot but be concerned at the views expressed in the second paragraph of point 5 of your 910.[1] I do not understand what you mean by a divergence between our Governments on the Polish negotiations. From our side there is certainly no evidence of any divergence of policy. We have been merely discussing the most effective tactics and I cannot agree that we are confronted with a breakdown of the Yalta agreement until we have made the effort to overcome the obstacles incurred in the negotiations at Moscow. I also find puzzling your statement in paragraph 4 that the only definite suggestion in our instructions to Averell is for a political truce in Poland. Those instructions, of which you have a copy, not only set forth our understanding of the Yalta agreement but they make the definite point that the Commission itself should agree on the list of Poles to be invited for consultation and that no one of the three groups from which the reorganized government is to emerge can dictate which individuals from the other two groups ought to be invited to Moscow.[2] I must in all fairness point out that while fully aware that time is working against us Averell has had his instructions since March 9 but has not acted on them at your request in order that other points could be included. Our chief purpose at that time was and remains without giving ground to get the negotiations moving again and tackle first of all the point on which they had come to a standstill. I cannot urge upon you too strongly the vital importance of agreeing without further delay on instructions to our Ambassadors so that the negotiations may resume. The need for new instructions to our Ambassadors arose out of the unwillingness of Molotov to accept our proposal concerning the list of Poles to be invited in the first instance. Since our Ambassadors informed him that the matter was being referred to their Governments, the negotiations are held up pending those instructions. With this in mind I have examined the points which you propose to submit to Stalin in your 905[3] and have the following comments to make:

[1] See above, Doc. 515.
[2] For the text of Harriman's instructions, see *FR 1945*, 3 (Washington, 1968) : 150–152.
[3] See above, Doc. 510.

We are in agreement on point (A) and this is covered in our instructions to Averell.

I cannot believe that Molotov will accept the proposal contained in point (B) that any Pole can be invited unless all three members of the Commission object and I am opposed to putting forward such a suggestion at this time as it would, in my view, almost certainly leave us in a stalemate which would only redound to the benefit of the Lublin Poles. I also think the demand for freedom of movement and communication would arouse needless discussion at this stage in the negotiations.

On point (C) we are agreed that the Poles invited for consultation should discuss the composition of the government among themselves with the Commission presiding in an impartial arbitral capacity so far as possible. Harriman has already been instructed to this effect but feels, and I agree, that this might be pressed later.

I have covered your point (D) in my previous message[4] and continue to feel that our approach would be better calculated to achieve the desired result. With reference to point (E) you will recall that this had been agreed to by Molotov who took fright when Clark Kerr revealed that you were thinking of a large special mission. I am willing to include in Averell's instructions the wording you propose in point (E).

Please let me know urgently whether you agree that in the light of the foregoing considerations, our Ambassadors may proceed with their instructions.

I heartily agree that we cannot invite the Lublin Poles to San Francisco, and the State Department is coordinating a reply to the Soviet note with your Foreign Office.[5] . . .

[4] Not printed.

[5] In an *aide-mémoire* of March 29 the State Department informed the Russian Embassy that it "found itself unable to agree" to the Soviet request of inviting the Lublin Poles to the San Francisco conference. *FR 1945*, 1: 147–148, 164.

Doc. 518
CHURCHILL TO ROOSEVELT

No. 912   March 16, 1945

Thank you for your No. 718 of 16 March.[1] I am most relieved that you do not feel that there is any fundamental divergence between us and I agree that our differences are only about tactics.

[1] See above, Doc. 517. No. 718 is dated March 15.

You know, I am sure, that our great desire is to keep in step with you and we realise how hopeless the position would become for Poland if it were ever seen that we were not in full accord.[2] . . .

With regard to point (B),[3] what happens if Molotov vetoes every one of our suggestions? And, secondly, what is the use of anyone being invited who has no freedom of movement and communications? We had in fact not understood that Molotov had disputed this latter point when it was raised with him earlier, but Mikolajczyk has made it a condition of going to Moscow and I gravely doubt whether we could persuade him to leave unless we had some definite assurance to convey to him. . . .

In regards point (D) I fear I cannot agree that your truce plan would achieve the desired result. How can we guarantee that nothing will be said or done in Poland or by the Polish Government's supporters here, which the Russians could not parade as a breach of the truce?

I fear that the truce plan will lead us into interminable delays and a dead end in which some at least of the blame may well be earned by the London Polish government. I fear therefore that it is impossible for us to endorse your truce proposal, for we think it actively dangerous. . . .

At present all entry into Poland is barred to our representatives.[4] An impenetrable veil has been drawn across the scene. This extends even to the liaison officers, British and American, who were to help in bringing out our rescued prisoners of war. According to our information the American officers as well as the British who had already reached Lublin have been requested to clear out.

There is no doubt in my mind that the Soviets fear very much our seeing what is going on in Poland. It may be that apart from the Poles they are being very rough with the Germans. Whatever the reason, we are not to be allowed to see. This is not a position that could be defended by us.

---

[2] Churchill then urged Roosevelt to accept the text of a proposed message to Stalin drafted by Ambassador Clark Kerr and went on to express his serious reservations concerning portions of a proposed American message, which Roosevelt had communicated to him. See Woodward, *British Foreign Policy*, 3: 500ff.

[3] Point (B) voiced the British and American requirement that Mikolajczyk be invited to the consultation; (D) concerned land reform.

[4] The British had unsuccessfully attempted to send observers to Poland as early as March 1. See Woodward, *British Foreign Policy*, 3: 494–495.

Doc. 519
CHURCHILL TO ROOSEVELT

No. 913   March 17, 1945

I hear that there are certain difficulties between Mountbatten and Wedemeyer about activities in Indochina. As Wedemeyer is now in Washington it seems a good moment to try to clear them up.

Under existing decisions of the Combined Chiefs of Staff Indochina is still within the China theatre. But Mountbatten has a vital interest in Indochina as well as in Siam, since it is through them that runs the Japanese land and air reinforcement route to Burma and Malaya: and as you know he has an oral understanding with Chiang Kai-shek that both he and the Generalissimo shall be free to attack Siam and Indochina and that the boundaries between the two theatres shall be decided when the time comes in accordance with the progress made by their respective forces. The Generalissimo agreed after Sextant[1] that this understanding extended to pre-occupational activities.

I am told that Wedemeyer feels difficulty in recognising this oral understanding in the absence of instructions to that effect from his superior authorities.

This is a situation from which much harmful friction may spring. Could not you and I clear it up by jointly endorsing the oral understanding which seems a sensible and workable arrangement?

I well understand Wedemeyer's interest in Indochina and it is clear that there ought to be the closest liaison about it between him and Mountbatten. If you agree, we might, when endorsing the understanding, direct that appropriate arrangements be made by the Combined Chiefs of Staff for full and frank exchange of intentions, plans, and intelligence between Wedemeyer and Mountbatten as regards Indochina and indeed as regards all matters of mutual concern.[2]

[1] Code name for the conference at Cairo in November 1943.
[2] For Roosevelt's reply, see below, Doc. 527.

Doc. 520
CHURCHILL TO ROOSEVELT

No. 914   March 17, 1945

I hope that the rather numerous telegrams I have to send you on so many of our difficult and intertwined affairs are not becoming a bore to you.[1] Our friendship is the rock on which I build for the future of the world so long as I am one of the builders. I always think of those tremendous days when you devised lend-lease, when we met at Argentia,[2] when you decided with my heartfelt agreement to launch the invasion of Africa, and when you comforted me for the loss of Tobruk by giving me the 300 Shermans of subsequent Alamein fame.[3] I remember the part our personal relations have played in the advance of the world cause now nearing its first military goal.

I am sending to Washington and San Francisco most of my ministerial colleagues on one mission or another, and I shall on this occasion stay at home to mind the shop. All the time I shall be looking forward to your long-promised visit. Clemmie[4] is off to Russia next week for a Red Cross tour as far as the Urals to which she has been invited by Uncle Joe (if we may venture to describe him thus), but she will be back in time to welcome you and Eleanor.[5] My thoughts are always with you all.

Peace with Germany and Japan on our terms will not bring much rest to you and me (if I am still responsible). As I observed last time, when the war of the giants is over, the wars of the pygmies will begin. There will be a torn, ragged, and hungry world to help to its feet: and what will Uncle Joe or his successor say to the way we should both like to do it? It was quite a relief to talk party politics the other day.[6] It

[1] "Although I had no exact information about the President's state of health," Churchill wrote later, "I had the feeling that, except for occasional flashes of courage and insight, the telegrams he was sending us were not his own. I therefore sent him a message in a personal vein to ease the uphill march of official business." Churchill, *Triumph and Tragedy*, p. 429. The records of the Roosevelt Library, in particular the pertinent action sheets, do not indicate that there was a significant change in the preparation of the Roosevelt-to-Churchill messages, the supervision, if not the actual drafting, of which continued to be the responsibility of Admiral Leahy, the President's Chief of Staff. More recently, Charles Bohlen, then a liaison officer between the State Department and the White House, has written that he was responsible for drafting many of the important post-Yalta messages to Churchill and Stalin. Charles E. Bohlen, *Witness to History 1929–1969* (New York, 1973), p. 207. All of this is not to say that Roosevelt did not have final word on the content of the messages or that he did not sometimes apply a personal touch to them.

[2] Site of the first meeting between Roosevelt and Churchill, August 9–12, 1941.

[3] In June 1942, meeting with Roosevelt at the White House, Churchill received word that British forces at Tobruk had surrendered to Rommel, with 25,000 men taken prisoner. Churchill felt disgraced. The President asked him: "What can we do to help?" The Prime Minister replied: "Give us as many Sherman tanks as you can spare, and ship them to the Middle East as quickly as possible." See Burns, *Roosevelt: Soldier of Freedom*, p. 235.

[4] Mrs. Churchill.

[5] Mrs. Roosevelt.

[6] On March 15 Churchill had delivered a rousing address to the Conservative party conference at Central Hall, Westminster. See *The Times* (London), March 16, 1945.

was like working in wood after working in steel. The advantage of this telegram is that it has nothing to do with shop except that I had a good talk with Rosenman[7] about our daily bread. All good wishes.

[7] Since March 2 Samuel I. Rosenman, counsel to the President, had been on an extended trip to England and the Continent. For an account of his meetings with Churchill, see Rosenman, *Working with Roosevelt*, p. 542.

Doc. 521
ROOSEVELT TO CHURCHILL

No. 719   March 18, 1945

Your No. 912.[1]
The State Department and your Embassy have prepared instructions to our Ambassadors in Moscow closely following the draft suggested by Clark Kerr and have agreed upon a text which I have approved and which I believe meets both our views.[2] I hope that you will concur.[3]

[1] See above, Doc. 518.
[2] See Woodward, *British Foreign Policy*, 3: 505–506.
[3] Churchill concurred, and on March 19 the American and British ambassadors in Moscow sent separate, but identical, notes to Molotov.

Doc. 522
ROOSEVELT TO CHURCHILL

No. 720   March 19, 1945

I would very much appreciate it if you would see Bernie Baruch[1] as soon as convenient to you, and also appreciate it if you could wire him as he counts you one of his oldest friends and would much prefer having your approval before he goes.[2]

[1] Bernard M. Baruch, an American industrialist who headed the War Industries Board during World War I, was regarded as an elder statesman during World War II, whose advice on various problems was sought by many leaders, including Roosevelt.
[2] According to Samuel Rosenman, Baruch went to London to discuss "with Churchill and the British War Cabinet various matters of industrial, financial, and economic importance." Rosenman, *Working with Roosevelt*, p. 547. The visit was not, however, a spur-of-the-moment idea on Roosevelt's part. As Baruch remembered it, the President asked him to come to the White House on January 22, 1945, and in the presence of Stettinius and Hopkins told him: "I want you to go to see Winston. I'll have a memo for you." To this Hopkins is said to have added: "The only man who can talk to him is you." Margaret L. Coit, *Mr. Baruch* (Boston, 1957), p. 545.

Doc. 523
CHURCHILL TO ROOSEVELT

No. 917   March 21, 1945

I am greatly looking forward to seeing Bernie, who is one of my older friends.[1] I am telegraphing him to say how glad I am that he is coming. I should like to know when he will see me.[2]

[1] In his Christmas message of December 5, 1944, transmitted by Ambassador Halifax, Churchill had told Baruch: "It is always a pleasure to hear from you and usually wise to follow your advice." Coit, *Mr. Baruch*, p. 545.
[2] Baruch flew to London in late March in the President's personal plane, the *Sacred Cow*. See Rosenman, *Working with Roosevelt*, p. 547.

Doc. 524
ROOSEVELT TO CHURCHILL

No. 721   March 21, 1945

I have given careful consideration to your No. 915,[1] and it is my considered opinion that at the present time it is not appropriate for us to issue a proclamation to the German army[2] such as that suggested by you.

It seems to me that a correct means of getting this information to the German army and to the German people is through our established propaganda agencies.

[1] Not printed. For Anglo-American concern about the safety of their prisoners in German hands see *FR 1945*, 3: 697ff.
[2] Reports of the surrender of large numbers of German troops to the advancing Allied forces apparently made it unnecessary to issue any such proclamation.

Doc. 525
ROOSEVELT TO CHURCHILL

No. 723   March 21, 1945

What would you think of sending a special mission for developing the productive power of Greece rapidly by concerted, nonpolitical action? Such a mission could consist of people like Lyttelton, Mikoyan —the People's Commissar for Foreign Trade of U.S.S.R.,[1] and Donald Nelson,[2] who is back after a very successful similar mission in China. It would not take them long and might have a highly constructive effect on world opinion at this time.

I take it that they could meet in Greece in about a month's time.

I am not taking it up with the Soviet Government until I get your slant.[3]

[1] Anastas I. Mikoyan.
[2] Donald M. Nelson, chairman of the War Production Board, 1942–1944, and in 1945 a member of the War Mobilization Committee.
[3] For Churchill's reply, see below, Doc. 538.

Doc. 526
CHURCHILL TO ROOSEVELT

No. 920   March 22, 1945

I have seen your recent exchange of messages with Marshal Stalin on prisoners-of-war matters.[1] As regards the general question of Allied prisoners in German hands, I entirely agree with you that we ought to arrange matters now, so that we are in a position to do something quickly at the right time.

We have long foreseen danger to these prisoners, arising either in consequence of chaotic conditions resulting from a German collapse or, alternatively, out of a deliberate threat by Hitler and his associates to murder some, or all, of the prisoners. The object of this manoeuvre might be either to avoid unconditional surrender, or to save the lives of the more important Nazi gangsters and war criminals, using this threat as a bargaining counter, or to cause dissension among the Allies in the final stages of the war. With this in mind we put to the United States and Soviet Governments last October, through our diplomatic representatives in Washington and Moscow, a proposal for an Anglo-American-Russian warning to the Germans (for text please see my immediately following telegram[2]) but have so far received no reply.

On March 2nd last the British Minister in Bern was informed by the head of the Swiss Political Department that he had received reports

[1] See FR 1945, 5: 1067ff.
[2] No. 921, not printed. In that message Churchill repeated, with minor variations, a warning to the Germans proposed in a British note to the State Department of October 19, 1944. See also FR 1944, 1: 1258.

from Berlin which he could not confirm, that the Germans intended to liquidate, i.e., massacre, such prisoners of war as were held in camps in danger of being overrun by the advancing Allies forces, rather than try to remove the prisoners or allow them to fall into Allied hands. In addition, we have in recent months received various indications that the Nazis might, in the last resort, either murder Allied prisoners in their hands or hold them as hostages.

Various proposals of a practical nature for bringing immediate military aid and protection to prisoners-of-war camps in Germany have been under consideration by British and United States military authorities. I believe the issue, at the appropriate moment, of a joint warning on the lines we have proposed would be a powerful aid to such practical measures as it may be possible to take. An SS general is now in charge of prisoners-of-war matters in the German Ministry of Defence and SS and Gestapo are believed to be taking over the control of camps. On such people a warning will have only limited effect, though at the worst it can do no harm. On the other hand, it is by no means certain that SS have completely taken over from regular army officers and on the latter the warning might have real effect. We should be sure to miss no opportunity of exploiting any duality of control.

I would therefore earnestly invite you and Marshal Stalin, to whom I am repeating this message, to give this proposal your personal attention and I very much hope you will agree to go forward with us in issuing it at the appropriate moment.[3]

3 On March 22 the President replied: "If Marshal Stalin agrees, I will go forward with you in issuing the joint warning. . . ."

Doc. 527
ROOSEVELT TO CHURCHILL

No. 724   March 22, 1945

As you say in your No. 913,[1] Indochina is still within the China theater, even though Admiral Mountbatten and the Generalissimo have agreed that at the appropriate time Chinese forces will attack Indochina and Thailand from the north and Mountbatten is expected to attack from the south, and that the boundaries between the two theaters shall be adjusted at that time.[2] This appears perfectly sound

1 See above, Doc. 519.
2 For details of General Wedemeyer's plan, see his *Wedemeyer Reports!*, pp. 270–271.

to me. However, there appears to be considerable obscurity as to the intent of the parties concerned as to any agreement dealing with pre-occupational activities in Indochina by Mountbatten. I understand that the Generalissimo has insisted that he should control, through his Chief of Staff General Wedemeyer, all clandestine activities by other than Chinese forces which may be conducted within the China theater including Indochina.

I am told that both Mountbatten and Wedemeyer are now each independently conducting in Indochina air operations and intelligence activities as well as supporting guerrilla forces. This appears to be a likely source of confusion and wasted effort and might result in placing the two theaters unintentionally in direct conflict. I believe it essential that some definite coordination of the activities in Indochina of these two commanders be quickly provided. Also the Generalissimo is involved.

It seems to me the best solution at present is for you and me to agree that all Anglo-American-Chinese military operations in Indochina, regardless of their nature, be coordinated by General Wedemeyer as Chief of Staff to the Generalissimo, who is Supreme Commander of the China theater, at least until any adjustment of theater boundaries is made in connection with an advance by Mountbatten's forces into Indochina from the south. This would place on Wedemeyer the normal responsibilities of a theater commander and appears to be readily workable and also consistent since I understand Mountbatten now controls similarly operations from China into Burma. At the same time it would provide coordination between future Chinese and American operations in Indochina and any operations by Mountbatten which may be necessary.

If you agree to this proposal, I suggest that you direct Mountbatten to coordinate his activities in Indochina with Wedemeyer; and I will direct Wedemeyer to take any steps necessary to ensure coordination of all Allied operations in the China theater including Indochina.

Your suggestion for the full, free, and frank exchange of plans, intentions, and intelligence between Wedemeyer and Mountbatten as regards Indochina and in all matters of mutual concern is excellent. I think we both should issue instructions to this end.[3]

[3] It was decided that Mountbatten would operate in Chiang's theater only by prearrangement. Charles F. Romanus and Riley Sunderland, *Time Runs Out in CBI* (Washington, 1959), p. 260.

Doc. 528
CHURCHILL TO ROOSEVELT

No. 925   March 27, 1945

1. I am extremely concerned at the deterioration of the Russian attitude since Yalta.[1]

2. About Poland, you will have seen that Molotov in his reply to the agreed communication made to him by our Ambassadors on the 19th March,[2] and in their discussion on the 23rd March, returned a series of flat negatives on every point he dealt with and ignored others.[3]

He persists in his view that the Yalta communiqué merely meant the addition of a few other Poles to the existing administration of Russian puppets and that these puppets should be consulted first. He maintains his right to veto Mikolajczyk and other Poles we may suggest and pretends that he has insufficient information about the names we have put forward long ago.

Nothing is said about our proposal that the Commission[4] should preside in an arbitral capacity over discussions among the Poles. Nothing on our point that measures in Poland affecting the future of the Polish state and action against individuals and groups likely to disturb the atmosphere should be avoided.

He ignores his offer about observers and tells us to talk to the

[1] For the background of this and Churchill's succeeding messages, see Roger Parkinson, *A Day's March Nearer Home: The War History from Alamein to V-E Day Based on the War Cabinet Papers of 1942 to 1945* (New York, 1974) , pp. 468ff. Of "the final shattering of the Yalta spirit," Parkinson writes: "Churchill's disillusionment six weeks after the high hopes of the Crimea paralleled Neville Chamberlain's transition after Hitler's breach of the Munich agreement" (p. 470) .

[2] For the agreed communications to Molotov, see *FR 1945*, 5: 172ff. These included a proposal that "British and American observers should visit Poland to report upon conditions there. . . . The United States Government must therefore urgently press Soviet Government to make the necessary arrangements to this end." See above, Doc. 521, note 3.

[3] For a summary of the discussions with Molotov, see Woodward, *British Foreign Policy*, 3: 509–510; and *FR 1945*, 5: 180ff. As regards American and British observers, Molotov replied that the Soviet Government "learned with amazement" of this "intention . . . inasmuch as this proposal can sting the national pride of the Poles to the quick, the more so since in the decisions of the Crimea conference this subject is not even touched upon." *FR 1945*, 5: 176ff. In fact, however, at the fifth plenary session of that conference, Stalin had remarked that "he had heard complaints from the Prime Minister that he had no information in regard to the situation in Poland" and did not see "why Great Britain and the United States could not send their own people to Poland." *Conferences at Malta and Yalta*, p. 779.

[4] The Moscow Commission on Poland set up at the Yalta Conference.

Warsaw puppets about this.[5] It is as plain as a pike staff that his tactics are to drag the business out while the Lublin Committee consolidate their power.

3. Clark Kerr's proposal for dealing with this was to try by redrafting to build something on the four-point formula included in Molotov's reply. We cannot see that any real progress towards getting an honest Polish settlement can possibly be made in this way.[6]

It would merely mean that we allowed our communication to be sidetracked, negotiated on the basis of Molotov's wholly unsatisfactory reply, and wasted time finding formulae which do not decide vital points. We therefore instructed Clark Kerr that he should not proceed on this basis, and that we are discussing matters with you.

4. As you know, if we fail altogether to get a satisfactory solution on Poland and are in fact defrauded by Russia, both Eden and I are pledged to report the fact openly to the House of Commons. There I advised critics of the Yalta settlement to trust Stalin.[7] If I have to make a statement of facts to the House, the whole world will draw the deduction that such advice was wrong. All the more so that our failure in Poland will result in a setup there on the new Rumanian model.[8]

In other words, Eastern Europe will be shown to be excluded from the terms of the Declaration on Liberated Europe[9] and you and we shall be excluded from any jot of influence in that area.

5. Surely we must not be manoeuvred into becoming parties to imposing on Poland, and on how much more of Eastern Europe, the Russian version of democracy. (You no doubt saw Vyshinsky's public explanations in Rumania of this doctrine.)[10] There seems to be only one possible alternative to confessing our total failure. That alternative is to stand by our interpretation of the Yalta declaration.

But I am convinced it is no use trying to argue this any further with Molotov. In view of this, is it not now the moment for a message from us both on Poland to Stalin? I will send you our rough idea on this in my immediately following.[11] I hope you can agree.

6. I see nothing else likely to produce good results. If we are rebuffed, it will be a very sinister sign, taken with the other Russian

---

5 "The American Government," Molotov said in this regard, "could best explore this question if it were to address itself directly to the [Polish provisional government]." *FR 1945*, 5: 178.

6 See Woodward, *British Foreign Policy*, 3: 510.

7 See above, Doc. 508, note 2.

8 For Anglo-American policy as regards Rumania, see *FR 1945*, 5: 461ff.; and Woodward, *British Foreign Policy*, 3: 561ff.

9 See above, Doc. 510, note 5.

10 For Vyshinsky's role in Rumanian politics, see *FR 1945*, 5: 487ff.

11 See below, Doc. 529.

actions at variance with the spirit of Yalta; such as Molotov's rude questioning of our word in the case of Crossword,[12] the unsatisfactory proceedings over our liberated German prisoners,[13] the coup d'état in Rumania, the Russian refusal to allow the Declaration on Liberated Europe to operate, and the blocking of all progress in the EAC[14] by the Russians.

7. What also do you make of Molotov's withdrawal from San Francisco?[15] It leaves a bad impression on me. Does it mean that the Russians are going to run out or are they trying to blackmail us? As we have both understood them, the Dumbarton Oaks proposals, which will form the basis of discussion at San Francisco, are based on the conception of great-power unity.

If no such unity exists on Poland, which is after all a major problem of the postwar settlement—to say nothing of the other matters just mentioned—what, it will legitimately be asked, are the prospects of success of the new world organisation? And is it not indeed evident that, in the circumstances, we shall be building the whole structure of future world peace on foundations of sand?

8. I believe, therefore, that if the success of San Francisco is not to be gravely imperilled, we must both of us now make the strongest possible appeal to Stalin about Poland and if necessary about any other derogations from the harmony of the Crimea. Only so shall we have any real chance of getting the world organisation established on lines which will commend themselves to our respective public opinions.

---

12 In February the German commander of the SS troops in Italy, General Karl Wolff, had contacted representatives of the U.S. Office of Strategic Services in Switzerland concerning the possible surrender of German forces. On March 8 he met in Zurich with Allen W. Dulles, then head of the OSS mission in Switzerland. On March 19 a second exploratory meeting was held with Wolff, who was told that German forces would have to surrender unconditionally. Churchill gave the undertaking the code name Crossword. Dulles and his associates named it Sunrise. See Allen W. Dulles, *The Secret Surrender* (New York, 1966), chaps. 7–8. On March 21 Sir Archibald Clark Kerr informed the Soviet government of the meetings that had taken place. The following day Molotov handed the British ambassador an insulting reply, accusing the British and American commands of negotiating "behind the backs of the Soviet Union." When Clark Kerr protested this unfounded charge, Molotov replied: "In this instance the Soviet Government sees not a misunderstanding but something worse."

13 See, for instance, *FR 1945*, 5: 1072ff.

14 European Advisory Commission.

15 On March 23, the Soviet Embassy in Washington had informed the State Department that the Russian delegation to the San Francisco conference would be headed by Andrei A. Gromyko, Soviet ambassador to the United States. Acting Secretary of State Grew pointed out that "with the exception of Ambassador [Gromyko] this is not a high-ranking delegation." *FR 1945*, 1: 151–152.

Indeed, I am not sure that we should not mention to Stalin now the deplorable impression Molotov's absence from San Francisco will cause.

Doc. 529
CHURCHILL TO ROOSEVELT

No. 926   March 27, 1945

1. My immediately preceding telegram.[1] Could we not both tell him that we are distressed that the work of the Polish Commission is held up because misunderstandings have arisen about the interpretation of the Yalta decisions? The agreed purpose of those decisions was that a new government of national unity was to be established after consultations with representatives of Lublin and other democratic Poles which both our Governments could recognise.

We have not got any reply on the various Polish names we have suggested, pleading lack of information. We have given him plenty of information. There ought not to be a veto by one power on all nominations. We consider that our nominations for the discussions have been made in the spirit of confidence which befits allies, and of course there could be no question of allowing Lublin to bar them. We will accept any nominations he puts forward, being equally confident that the Soviet Government will not suggest pro-Nazi or anti-democratic Poles.

The assembled Poles should then discuss the formation of a new government among themselves. The Commission should preside as arbitrators to see fair play. Monsieur Molotov wants the Lublinites to be consulted first. The communiqué does not provide for this. But we have no objection to his seeing them first.

We cannot authorise our representatives to do so since we think it contrary to the spirit of the communiqué. Also, to our surprise and regret, Molotov, who suggested at an earlier stage that we might like to send observers, has now withdrawn the offer.

Indeed, he appears to suggest that it had never been made, and has suggested that we should apply to the present Warsaw administration. Stalin will understand that the whole point of the Yalta decision was to produce a Polish government we could recognise and that we obviously cannot therefore deal with the present administration.

1 See above, Doc. 528. For the background of this and Churchill's preceding telegram, see Woodward, *British Foreign Policy*, 3: 510–512.

We feel sure he will honour the offer to send observers, and his influence with his Warsaw friends is so great that he will overcome with ease any reluctance they may show in agreeing.

2. Also, Stalin will surely see that while the three Great Allies are arranging for the establishment of the new government of national unity, those in power in Poland should not prejudice the future. We have asked that the Soviet Government should use their influence with their friends in temporary power there. Stalin will, we feel confident, take steps to this end.

3. Stalin will find all this set out in most reasonable terms in our communication of the 19th March. Will he cast his eye over it and judge whether our suggestions are not all in line with the spirit of the Yalta decision, and should they not all be met by our ally in order that the aim of the Yalta settlement of Poland, viz., the setting up of a representative government which Britain and the U.S.A. can recognise, may be carried out without further delay?[2]

[2] For Roosevelt's reply, see below, Doc. 531.

Doc. 530
ROOSEVELT TO CHURCHILL

No. 728   March 29, 1945

My Chiefs of Staff have undertaken during the past few months a project for the employment of war-weary U.S. bombers to be launched against large industrial targets in Germany, each bomber to be loaded with some 20,000 pounds of high explosives and set on course to its target with an appropriate timing device to determine its flight duration.[1]

Your Chiefs of Staff originally concurred in the development and employment of this project but have recently withdrawn their concurrence because, it is understood, of the British Government's apprehension that retaliatory action against London by the Germans might result if pilotless bombers were employed.[2]

My Chiefs of Staff inform me that they consider this weapon to be

[1] For the background of this project, see Craven and Cate, eds., *Army Air Forces in World War II*, 3: 727.

[2] The subject had been raised again at Malta on January 30. Air Chief Marshal Sir Charles Portal offered the opinion that "the possibility of [German] retaliation against the unique target of London had been felt to outweigh the advantages of the employment of this weapon." *Conferences at Malta and Yalta*, p. 468. The proposal was thereupon dropped.

most valuable in our all-out offensive against Germany. Since the original proposal was made last December, developmental work has progressed to a point where we are now able to direct its flight to the target by remote technical control. In view of the large explosive charge carried by each airplane and the present advanced stage of development in remote control, many lucrative targets in the industrial areas in Germany can be leveled and the German war effort correspondingly weakened.

I am assured that pilotless bombers will be launched only from bases on the Continent, which would appear to minimize the chances of retaliatory action against England. I believe that if the enemy were able to take effective measures against the cities of England with this type of weapon he would have done so regardless of any use by us of pilotless aircraft. In addition, combat experience with this weapon on the Continent will make possible the most effective use of this type of weapon in the battle against the highly concentrated areas of the Japanese homeland.

In order that the enemy may feel the full weight of our resources at this propitious hour, it is requested that you ask your Chiefs of Staff to reconsider their withdrawal of concurrence in this project.[3]

[3] Churchill's response in mid-April, though "nominally favorable," was "couched in such unmistakable terms of opposition that President Truman, who had just taken office, did not press the question further." Craven and Cate, eds., *Army Air Forces in World War II, 3: 728.*

Doc. 531
ROOSEVELT TO CHURCHILL

No. 729 March 29, 1945

Your 925[1] and 926.[2]

I have likewise been watching with anxiety and concern the development of Soviet attitude since the Crimea conference. I am acutely aware of the dangers inherent in the present course of events not only for the immediate issues involved and our decisions at the Crimea but also for the San Francisco conference and future world cooperation. Our peoples and indeed those of the whole world are watching with anxious hope the extent to which the decisions we reached at the Crimea are being honestly carried forward. For our part (and I know for yours) we intend to shirk no responsibility which we have assumed

1 See above, Doc. 528.
2 See above, Doc. 529.

under those decisions. I agree with you that we should not neglect any step calculated to demonstrate to the Soviet Government the vital importance of their doing likewise. It is for this reason and because of the magnitude of the issues involved that I consider it essential to base ourselves squarely on the Crimea decisions themselves and not allow any other considerations, no matter how important, to cloud the issue at this time. I have this particularly in mind with respect to the Polish negotiations.

You will recall that the agreement on Poland at Yalta was a compromise between the Soviet position that the Lublin government should merely be QUOTE enlarged UNQUOTE and our contention that we should start with a clean slate and assist in the formation of an entirely new Polish government. The wording of the resulting agreement reflects this compromise, but if we attempt to evade the fact that we placed, as clearly shown in the agreement, somewhat more emphasis on the Lublin Poles than on the other two groups from which the new government is to be drawn I feel we will expose ourselves to the charge that we are attempting to go back on the Crimean decision. It by no means follows, however, and on this we must be adamant, that because of this advantage the Lublin group can in any way arrogate to itself the right to determine what Poles from the other two groups are to be brought in for consultation. For the foregoing reasons I feel strongly that we should first of all bring the matter to a head on the question that falls clearly within the Yalta agreement, namely, our right to call for consultation a group of Polish leaders that are truly representative, and that it is for the Commission and the Commission alone to decide which Poles are representative. Our Ambassadors in Moscow appear to be in agreement that we should proceed on the basis of their redraft, designed to reconcile our basic instructions with the points put forward by Molotov. They will at the same time make it absolutely clear that we have not receded in the slightest from the other points in our instructions of March 19 and shall revert to them at a later stage. . . .

I agree with you, however, that the time has come to take up directly with Stalin the broader aspects of the Soviet attitude (with particular reference to Poland) and my immediately following telegram[3] will contain the text of the message I propose to send.

I hope you will let me have your reaction as soon as possible.[4]

3 Not printed.
4 For Churchill's reply, see below, Doc. 533.

Doc. 532
CHURCHILL TO ROOSEVELT

No. 927

March 30, 1945

I am delighted to see from the abundance of messages I have received from you this morning that you are back in Washington[1] and in such vigour. I saw Bernie yesterday and he is coming tonight for the weekend.[2] He seems in great form. As you know, I think he is a very wise man. Winant is coming tomorrow. Clemmie is in flight for Moscow and will be flying about there for at least a month, all of which hangs on my mind. By the way, did you ever receive a telegram from me of a purely private character, No. 914?[3] It required no answer. But I should like to know that you received it.[4]. . .

1 Roosevelt had been at his country home at Warm Springs, Georgia.
2 See above, Docs. 522 and 523.
3 See above, Doc. 520.
4 Roosevelt's reply, see below, Doc. 535.

Doc. 533
CHURCHILL TO ROOSEVELT

No. 928

March 30, 1945

1. Thank you for your 729[1] and 730.[2] I am glad you agree that the time has come for us both to address Stalin directly. We consider the draft in your 730 is a grave and weighty document and, although there are a few points in which it does not give full expression to our own views, we will wholeheartedly accept it and I will also endorse it in my parallel message to Stalin, the text of which I will send you before it goes.[3]

2. Perhaps however before deciding on your final text you would consider the importance of making it clear that we shall not enter into any arrangements with the Lublinites before the arrival of our own Poles. There is no harm in discussing with the Lublinites, but I am

1 See above, Doc. 531.
2 Not printed. Roosevelt sent a copy of his proposed telegram to Stalin. See *FR 1945*, 5: 194–196.
3 See below, Doc. 534.

sure that Mikolajczyk for instance will stipulate that the field shall be open when he arrives. We should be glad if you would provide for this in your draft.

3. More important still is to get rid of Molotov's veto on our candidates. You indicate this in a most polite manner, but would it not be well to emphasise the point by adding a sentence at the appropriate place to the effect that none of the three of us should veto each other's candidates? Otherwise he will simply veto every one that the Lublin Poles wish him to.

4. Finally, could you not mention in the last paragraph of your draft that it was Molotov himself who originally made the suggestion of observers?[4]

5. I do not ask you to delay the dispatch of your draft on account of these desired additions by us. We leave it in your hands. Meanwhile I agree that our two Ambassadors should give Molotov the redraft of the latter's basic principles, making it clear in doing so that we have not receded in the slightest from the other points in our instructions of March 19th and will revert to them at a later stage.

[4] In response to this suggestion, Roosevelt added the following sentence in his message to Stalin: "As you will recall Mr. Molotov himself suggested this [that American and British representatives of the Moscow Commission should be permitted to visit Poland] at an early meeting of the Commission and only subsequently withdrew it." *FR 1945, 5:* 196.

Doc. 534
CHURCHILL TO ROOSEVELT

No. 929   March 31, 1945

Following is text of message I propose to send to Stalin. Please let me know what you think. I will not send it off till I hear from you. Text begins:

"Prime Minister to Marshal Stalin. Personal and top secret.

"1. You will by now I hope have received the message from the President of the United States which he was good enough to show to me before he sent it.

"It is now my duty on behalf of His Majesty's Government to assure you that the War Cabinet desire me to express to you our wholehearted endorsement of this message of the President's, and that we associate ourselves with it in its entirety.

"2. There are two or three points which I desire specially to emphasise. First, that we do not consider we have retained in the

Moscow discussions the spirit of Yalta nor indeed, at points, the letter. It was never imagined by us that the Commission we all three appointed with so much good will would not have been able to carry out their part swiftly and easily in a mood of give and take.

"We certainly thought that a Polish government 'new' and 'reorganised' would by now have been in existence, recognised by all the United Nations. This would have afforded a proof to the world of our capacity and resolve to work together for its future. It is still not too late to achieve this.

"3. However, even before forming such a new and reorganised Polish government, it was agreed by the Commission that representative Poles should be summoned from inside Poland and from Poles abroad, not necessarily to take part in the government but merely for free and frank consultation.

"Even this preliminary step cannot be taken because of the claim put forward to veto any invitation, even to the consultation, of which the Soviets or the Lublin government do not approve. We can never agree to such a veto by any one of us three. This veto reaches its supreme example in the case of Monsieur Mikolajczyk who is regarded throughout the British and American world as the outstanding Polish figure outside Poland.

"4. We also have learned with surprise and regret that Monsieur Molotov's spontaneous offer to allow observers or missions to enter Poland has now been withdrawn. We are therefore deprived of all means of checking for ourselves the information, often of a most painful character, which is sent us almost daily by the Polish government in London.

"We do not understand why a veil of secrecy should thus be drawn over the Polish scene. We offer the fullest facilities to the Soviet Government to send missions or individuals to visit any of the territories in our military occupation.

"In several cases this offer has been accepted by the Soviets and visits have taken place to mutual satisfaction. We ask that the principle of reciprocity shall be observed in these matters, which would help to make so good a foundation for our enduring partnership.

"5. The President has also shown me messages which have passed between him and you about Monsieur Molotov's inability to be present at the conference at San Francisco.[1] We had hoped the

---

[1] In a telegram to Stalin on March 24 Roosevelt had expressed his disappointment at Molotov's withdrawal from the San Francisco conference, adding: "If his pressing and heavy responsibilities in the Soviet Union make it impossible for him to stay for the entire conference, I very much hope that you will find it possible to let him come at least for the opening vital sessions." *FR 1945*, 1: 156. On March 27 Stalin replied: "I and Mr. Molotov regret it extremely but the convening, on request of the

presence there of the three Foreign Ministers might have led to a
clearance of many of the difficulties which have descended upon us in
a storm since our happy and hopeful union at Yalta. We do not
however question in any way the weight of the public reasons which
make it necessary for him to remain in Russia.

"6. Like the President, I too was struck with the concluding sentence of your message to him. What he says about the American people
also applies to the British people and to the nations of the British
Commonwealth, with the addition that His Majesty's present advisers
only hold office at the will of the Universal Suffrage Parliament.

"If our efforts to reach an agreement about Poland are to be
doomed to failure, I shall be bound to confess the fact to Parliament
when they return from the Easter recess. No one has pleaded the cause
of Russia with more fervour and conviction than I have tried to do. I
was the first to raise my voice on June 22, 1941.[2]

"It is more than a year since I proclaimed to a startled world the
justice of the Curzon line for Russia's western frontier,[3] and this

---

deputies of the Supreme Soviet, in April, of a session of the Supreme Soviet of the
U.S.S.R. where the presence of Mr. Molotov is absolutely necessary, is excluding the
possibility of his participation even in the first meetings of the conference." *FR 1945*,
1: 165.

[2] In a BBC broadcast on the evening of June 22, 1941, Churchill had declared:
"The Nazi regime is indistinguishable from the worst features of Communism. . . .
No one has been a more consistent opponent of Communism than I have for the last
twenty-five years. I will unsay no word that I have spoken about it. But all this fades
away before the spectacle which is now unfolding. . . . Any man or state who fights
on against Nazidom will have our aid. . . . It follows, therefore, that we shall give
whatever help we can to Russia and the Russian people. We shall appeal to all our
friends and allies in every part of the world to take the same course and pursue it,
as we shall faithfully and steadfastly to the end. . . . The Russian danger is,
therefore, our danger, and the danger of the United States, just as the cause of any
Russian fighting for his hearth and home is the cause of free men and free peoples
in every quarter of the globe. Let us learn the lessons already taught by such cruel
experience. Let us redouble our exertions, and strike with united strength while life
and power remain." Winston S. Churchill, *The Grand Alliance* (Boston, 1950), pp.
371–373.

[3] In the course of a lengthy review of the war and the international situation,
Churchill had told the House of Commons on February 22, 1944: "Here I may
remind the House that we ourselves have never in the past guaranteed, on behalf of
His Majesty's Government, any particular frontier line to Poland. . . . I have an
intense sympathy with the Poles, that heroic race whose national spirit centuries of
misfortune cannot quench, but I also have sympathy with the Russian standpoint.
. . . Russia has the right of reassurance against future attacks from the West, and
we are going all the way with her to see she gets it, not only by the might of her
arms but by the approval and assent of the United Nations. I cannot feel that the
Russian demand for a reassurance about her Western frontiers goes beyond the limit
of what is reasonable or just." *Parliamentary Debates*, Commons, 5th ser., vol. 397,
cols. 697–698.

frontier has now been accepted by both the British Parliament and the President of the United States.

"It is as a sincere friend of Russia that I make my personal appeal to you and to your colleagues to come to a good understanding about Poland with the Western democracies and not to smite down the hands of comradeship in the future guidance of the world which we now extend."

Doc. 535
ROOSEVELT TO CHURCHILL

No. 731   March 31, 1945

Your 927.[1] I did receive your very pleasing message No. 914.[2]

The efforts of Bernie, who is a wise man of wide experience, should be of much assistance to both of us.

We hope that Clemmie's long flying tour in Russia will first be safe and next be productive of good which I am sure it will be.

The war business today seems to be going very well from our point of view[3] and we may now hope for the collapse of Hitlerism at an earlier date than had heretofore been anticipated.[4]

1 See above, Doc. 532.
2 See above, Doc. 520.
3 General Montgomery's forces and the U.S. Ninth Army had crossed the Rhine on March 23–24.
4 Sir Alexander Cadogan entered in his diary on March 27: "[Churchill] had a telegram this morning from Monty [General Montgomery] saying German army was beat." Dilks, ed., *Cadogan Diaries*, p. 725.

Doc. 536
ROOSEVELT TO CHURCHILL

No. 732   March 31, 1945

Thank you for your 928 of March 30[1] in regard to my proposed message to Stalin. I am very pleased to find that we are in such substantial agreement. I have carefully considered the helpful suggestions that you have made, and I am making the following three additions to

1 See above, Doc. 533.

cover the points you raise. In regard to the point raised in your paragraph 2 I am adding immediately after the words QUOTE Yalta decisions on this point UNQUOTE the following sentence: QUOTE it is of course understood that if the Lublin group comes first no arrangements would be made independently with them before the arrival of the other Polish leaders called for consultation. UNQUOTE.

In your paragraph 3 after the words QUOTE accorded the same confidence UNQUOTE, I am adding the phrase QUOTE and that any candidate for consultation presented by any one of the Commission be accepted by the others in good faith UNQUOTE.

In regard to your point 4 after the words QUOTE permitted to visit Poland UNQUOTE, I would add the following sentence: QUOTE As you will recall Mr. Molotov himself suggested this at an early meeting of the Commission and only subsequently withdrew it UNQUOTE.

I have just received your 929,[2] and as I concur in your proposed message, I have sent mine to Stalin with the foregoing additions.[3]

2 See above, Doc. 534.

3 On April 2 Ambassador Winant cabled the President that Churchill was "delighted" to get his message no. 732, adding that "Churchill feels that if the Russians get tough and ask that the acceptance of the Lublin Committee be a condition of their attending at San Francisco, he would be set on going through with the conference. Although Eden does not think that such action on the part of the Russians is likely, he is of the same mind."

Doc. 537
CHURCHILL TO ROOSEVELT

No. 931   April 1, 1945

You will have read the telegrams between the British Chiefs of Staff and their United States colleagues. I think there is some misunderstanding on both sides, which I am anxious to disperse without more ado.[1]

1 On March 28, without informing or consulting the Combined Chiefs of Staff, General Eisenhower had sent Stalin a personal message informing him that his immediate plans now called for the encirclement and destruction of German forces in the Ruhr, followed by a drive toward Erfurt, Leipzig, and Dresden, to link up with Russian forces and cut Germany in two. "Before deciding firmly on my future plans," Eisenhower told Stalin, "I think it most important that they should be coordinated as closely as possible with yours both as to direction and timing. Could you, therefore, tell me your intentions, and let me know how far the proposed operations outlined in this message conform to your probable action?" On April 5 Stalin replied that Eisenhower's plan "entirely coincides with the Plan of the Soviet High Command. . . . Berlin has lost its former strategic importance. The Soviet

We are very much obliged to the United States Chiefs of Staff for their paragraph which gives time for a reasonable interchange of views between our two Chiefs of Staff Committees.

I am however distressed to read that it should be thought that we wish in the slightest degree to discredit or lower the prestige of General Eisenhower in his increasingly important relations with the Russian commanders in the field. All we sought was a little time to consider the far-reaching changes desired by General Eisenhower in the plans that had been concerted by the Combined Chiefs of Staff at Malta and had received your and my joint approval. The British Chiefs of Staff were naturally concerned by a procedure which apparently left the fortunes of the British Army, which though only a third of yours still amounts to over a million men, to be settled without the slightest reference to any British authority.[2] They also did not fully understand from General Eisenhower's message what actually was intended. In this we may be excused, because General Deane was similarly puzzled and delayed delivery of General Eisenhower's mes-

High Command therefore plans to allot secondary forces in the direction of Berlin. . . ." PDDE, vol. 4, nos. 2363, 2394, note 1. In the meantime, Churchill, General Montgomery, and the British Chiefs of Staff were greatly agitated by what they regarded as Eisenhower's sudden change of strategy and his communicating with Stalin without first consulting his own advisers, the Combined Chiefs of Staff, or the British. The British Chiefs of Staff immediately protested to their American counterparts, who supported Eisenhower. See Eisenhower, Crusade in Europe, pp. 398ff.; Churchill, Triumph and Tragedy, pp. 460ff.; Pogue, Supreme Command, pp. 441ff.; Ehrman, Grand Strategy, 6: 131ff; Arthur Bryant, Triumph in the West 1943-1946 (London, 1959), pp. 336ff.; Stephen E. Ambrose, Eisenhower and Berlin 1945: The Decision to Halt at the Elbe (New York, 1967), pp. 54ff.; and his Supreme Commander—The War Years of General Dwight D. Eisenhower (New York, 1970), pp. 625ff. and chap. 20; Peter Lyon, Eisenhower: Portrait of the Hero (Boston, 1974), pp. 332ff.; Ellis, Victory in the West, 2: 297; and Pogue, Marshall: Organizer of Victory, pp. 555ff. The best brief treatment, from the American point of view, is Forrest C. Pogue, "The Decision to Halt at the Elbe (1945)," in Kent Roberts Greenfield, ed., Command Decisions (New York, 1959).

By this time Churchill was beginning to have serious doubts about neglecting Berlin. He put his position to Eisenhower directly: "If we deliberately leave Berlin to [the Russians] even if it should be in our grasp, [it] may strengthen their conviction, already apparent, that they have done everything. Further, I do not consider myself that Berlin has yet lost its military and certainly not its political significance. . . . [W]hile Berlin remains under the German flag, it cannot, in my opinion, fail to be the most decisive point in Germany." Churchill, Triumph and Tragedy, p. 463.

2 On March 31 Eisenhower cabled General Marshall: "You may be sure that in future policy cables passing between myself and Military Mission to Moscow will be repeated to the Combined Chiefs and the British Chiefs." PDDE, vol. 4, no. 2379, note 2. "It is noteworthy . . . that in future when such an occasion arose [Eisenhower] consulted the Combined Chiefs of Staff before approaching Russia." Ellis, Victory in the West, 2: 304.

sage to Stalin for twenty hours in order to ask for background.[3] I am in full agreement in this instance with the procedure proposed by your Chiefs of Staff, and I am sorry we did not think of it ourselves.

At this point I wish to place on record the complete confidence felt by His Majesty's Government in General Eisenhower, our pleasure that our armies are serving under his command, and our admiration of the great and shining qualities of character and personality which he has proved himself to possess in all the difficulties of handling an Allied command.[4] Moreover, I should like to express to you, Mr. President, as I have already done orally in the field to General Eisenhower, my heartfelt congratulations on the glorious victories and advances by all the armies of the United States centre in the recent battles on the Rhine and over it. . . .

Having dealt with and I trust disposed of these misunderstandings between the truest friends and comrades that ever fought side by side as allies, I venture to put to you a few considerations upon the merits of the changes in our original plans now desired by General Eisenhower. It seems to me the differences are small and, as usual, not of principle but of emphasis. Obviously, laying aside every impediment and shunning every diversion, the Allied armies of the north and centre should now march at the highest speed towards the Elbe. Hitherto the axis has been upon Berlin. General Eisenhower, on his estimate of the enemy's resistance, to which I attach the greatest importance, now wishes to shift the axis somewhat to the southward and strike through Leipzig, even perhaps as far south as Dresden. He withdraws the Ninth United States Army from the northern group of armies, and in consequence stretches its front southward. I should be sorry if the resistance of the enemy was such as to destroy the weight and momentum of the advance of the British Twenty-first Army Group and to leave them in an almost static condition along the Elbe when and if they reach it. I say quite frankly that Berlin remains of

[3] When Eisenhower complied with General Deane's request for additional information concerning the composition of his Army groups and his estimate of enemy dispositions, the Combined Chiefs of Staff ordered that the information not be given to Stalin, and Eisenhower so cabled Deane. See *PDDE*, vol. 4, nos. 2371, 2376, 2379.

[4] On April 3 Eisenhower thanked Churchill for his warm tribute: "The generosity of your language is equalled only by my continued determination that every action of mine shall be governed by the single purpose of winning this campaign at the earliest possible moment. In doing so I shall likewise devote myself toward sustaining among the forces of the United States and Great Britain those feelings of mutual respect and unification that have been the mainspring of effectiveness in this command. Specifically I have always planned that U.S. and British forces should advance shoulder to shoulder and there will never be a change in this policy. If Berlin can be brought into the orbit of our success the honors will be equitably shared." *PDDE*, vol. 4, no. 2387.

high strategic importance. Nothing will exert a psychological effect of despair upon all German forces of resistance equal to that of the fall of Berlin. It will be the supreme signal of defeat to the German people. On the other hand, if left to itself to maintain a siege by the Russians among its ruins, and as long as the German flag flies there, it will animate the resistance of all Germans under arms.

There is moreover another aspect which it is proper for you and me to consider. The Russian armies will no doubt overrun all Austria and enter Vienna. If they also take Berlin will not their impression that they have been the overwhelming contributor to our common victory be unduly imprinted in their minds, and may this not lead them into a mood which will raise grave and formidable difficulties in the future? I therefore consider that from a political standpoint we should march as far east into Germany as possible, and that should Berlin be in our grasp we should certainly take it. This also appears sound on military grounds.

To sum up, the difference that might exist between General Eisenhower's new plans and those we advocated, and which were agreed upon beforehand, would seem to be the following, viz., whether the emphasis should be put on an axis directed on Berlin or on one directed on Leipzig and Dresden. This is surely a matter upon which a reasonable latitude of discussion should be allowed to our two Chiefs of Staff Committees before any final commitment involving the Russians is entered into.

I need hardly say that I am quite willing that this message, which is my own personal message to you and not a staff communication, should be shown to General Marshall.

Doc. 538
CHURCHILL TO ROOSEVELT

No. 932 April 3, 1945

I am attracted [by] the suggestion in your No. 723[1] that a high-powered economic mission should visit Greece, but I am rather doubtful whether this is an appropriate moment to bring the Russians in. We cannot expect any help from the Russians in the economic sphere, and to include them in the mission would be a purely political gesture. As such, it might be valuable if we could be sure that the Russian representative would behave correctly and make a public

1 See above, Doc. 525.

demonstration of his solidarity with our policy, but this assumption seems very doubtful. There is the further disadvantage that at a time when the Russians are firmly excluding both you and us from any say in the affairs of Rumania, it would be rather odd to invite them unsolicited to assume some degree of responsibility in Greek affairs.

We have ourselves been giving some thought to the future Allied organisation in Greece. I am, of course, most anxious to reduce the number of British troops in the country at the earliest possible moment, but it is clear that this will not be the end of our responsibility there. In fact the Greek Government must for some time be given advice and guidance in many spheres of the administration if they are to govern the country effectively. Without this help, they will be unable to resume control throughout the country, and the withdrawal of our forces may be seriously delayed.

Advice for the Greek Government has hitherto been provided mainly under the authority of General Scobie as General Officer Commanding British troops in Greece. We hope, however, that the "operational phase" is now over and it therefore seems appropriate that Scobie should be relieved of many of the responsibilities which he has so far borne, and that these should be transferred to our two Embassies where they more properly belong. As you will know, it is proposed that UNRRA should take over relief work from the military on April 1, and this seemed to be a convenient date on which the other changes could be made. The War Cabinet have therefore agreed that on the British side the Embassy will be responsible as from April 1 for tendering advice to the Greek Government. This advice will be particularly important on economic and financial questions, and I much hope that we can count on the continued collaboration of the United States Embassy in Athens. If you agree, I suggest that a joint Anglo-American committee should be established, comprising the appropriate British and American experts and responsible to our two Embassies. Although members of this committee have not been invited by the Greek Government to advise, I have no doubt that they will in fact exercise great influence over the economic and financial policies of the Greek Government.

I feel that this committee should be set in motion before we consider sending a mission on the lines you suggest. A further reason for postponement would be in order to see how the transference of relief from the military authorities to UNRRA works out. Once all this new machinery has begun to work, a high-powered mission on the lines you suggest might do great good by smoothing out difficulties and getting things moving. By that time we might also have resolved the troubles in Rumania and be in a position to invite the Russians to join the mission.

We should, of course, welcome the assistance of Donald Nelson at any time, and if it [is] convenient for him to visit Greece now, I would certainly not suggest that he should delay his journey until a full Allied mission can be sent. The problems to be overcome in Greece are so formidable and urgent that his presence there even for a short visit would be of the greatest value.[2]

2 For Roosevelt's reply, see below, Doc. 543.

Doc. 539
ROOSEVELT TO CHURCHILL

No. 733   April 4, 1945

I have given your personal message No. 931[1] a very careful reading and have gone over the various papers involved, some of which I had not previously read. Further I have just received a copy of Eisenhower's directive to his Army group commanders, dated April 2.[2]

I personally, as you do, deplore any misunderstanding between us in general, particularly at a time of great victories by our armies. I think you have misunderstood the presentation of the American Chiefs of Staff regarding the matter of Eisenhower's prestige and especially regarding the achievements of the 21st Army Group.[3] In the first instance they were endeavoring to make a point in their argument by enunciating a military principle well known to us all, and not making any accusation.

Regarding the implications that you find in the references to the 21st Army Group, I know that in general the same explanation can be given: the U.S. Chiefs of Staff were discussing a problem in possibly too technical a manner, without going into details with which we are all familiar as to the character of the military obstacles, the strength and quality of the German opposing forces, etc.[4]

1 See above, Doc. 537.

2 Eisenhower implemented the strategy outlined to Stalin on March 28: "Operations to isolate the Ruhr . . . having been completed, it is my intention to divide and destroy the enemy forces by launching a powerful thrust on the axis Kassel-Leipzig. It is hoped that this advance will make a junction with the Soviet forces in that area." *PDDE*, vol. 4, no. 2385.

3 Eisenhower transferred the U.S. Ninth Army from Montgomery to General Bradley in preparation for his main drive into Germany. Churchill thought this deprived Montgomery of his offensive power, thereby negating the chance to take Berlin.

4 See Pogue, *Supreme Command*, pp. 441–443. For the Joint Chiefs' support of Eisenhower, see Ehrman, *Grand Strategy*, 6: 139–140.

As to the "far-reaching changes desired by General Eisenhower in the plans that had been concerted by the Combined Chiefs of Staff at Malta and had received your and my joint approval,"[5] I do not get the point. For example, the strength and all the resources agreed upon for the northern group of armies were made available to Montgomery. Following the unexpected Remagen bridgehead [capture][6] and the destruction of the German armies in the Saar basin there developed so great a weakness on those fronts that the secondary efforts realized an outstanding success. This fact must have a very important relation to the further conduct of the battle. However, General Eisenhower's directive of April 2, it seems to me, does all and possibly a little more to the north than was anticipated at Malta. Leipzig is not far removed from Berlin, which is well within the center of the combined effort. At the same time the British Army is given what seems to me very logical objectives on the northern flank.

As to the Ninth Army, it is a matter of record that Eisenhower previously placed the Ninth Army and a large portion of the First Army under Field Marshal Montgomery during the Ardennes affair; he again placed or continued the Ninth Army under the command of Montgomery for the crossing of the Rhine. In all probability he intends to again place the Ninth Army under Montgomery for the operation to the north once the general advance has broken through the German resistance.[7]

I appreciate your generous expressions of confidence in Eisenhower and I have always been deeply appreciative of the backing you have given him and the fact that you yourself proposed him for this command. I regret that the phrasing of a formal discussion should have so disturbed you but I regret even more that at the moment of a great victory by our combined forces we should become involved in such unfortunate reactions.

It appears reasonable to expect that under Eisenhower's present

[5] See *Conferences at Malta and Yalta*, p. 829; Pogue, *Supreme Command*, pp. 413ff.; Ehrman, *Grand Strategy*, 6: 87ff.; Bryant, *Triumph in the West*, pp. 392ff.; Ellis, *Victory in the West*, 2: 209ff., 301; and Pogue, *Marshall: Organizer of Victory*, pp. 513ff. At Malta the Combined Chiefs of Staff had "engaged in the most violent disagreements and disputes of the war. (One can read the official minutes of these meetings without suspecting that a single harsh word had been exchanged, but some of those who were present tell a much more colorful story of what went on)." Robert E. Sherwood, *Roosevelt and Hopkins* (New York, 1948), p. 848.

[6] On March 7 a detachment of the U.S. First Army had crossed the Rhine on the Ludendorff Bridge, which the Germans, waiting for the crossing of their own units on the right bank, had not yet blown up. Of the sensational Remagen crossing General Eisenhower wrote: "That was one of my happy moments of the war. . . . [T]his was completely unforeseen." Eisenhower, *Crusade in Europe*, p. 380.

[7] The German counteroffensive had begun on December 16, 1944.

plans the great German army will in the very near future be completely broken up into separate resistance groups, while our forces will remain tactically intact and in a position to destroy in detail the separated parts of the Nazi army.

You have my assurance of every cooperation.

Doc. 540
CHURCHILL TO ROOSEVELT

No. 933   April 5, 1945

I still think it was a pity that Eisenhower's telegram[1] was sent to Stalin without anything being said to our Chiefs of Staff, or to our deputy, Air Chief Marshal Tedder,[2] or to our Commander-in-Chief, Field Marshal Montgomery. The changes in the main plan have now turned out to be very much less than we at first supposed.[3] My personal relations with General Eisenhower are of the most friendly character. I regard the matter as closed, and to prove my sincerity I will use one of my very few Latin quotations: *Amantium irae amoris integratio est.*[4]

1 See above, Doc. 537, note 1.

2 Sir Arthur W. Tedder.

3 In his memoirs, General Bradley recalled that "when Eisenhower asked me what I thought it might cost us to break through from the Elbe to Berlin, I estimated 100,000 casualties. 'A pretty stiff price to pay for a prestige objective,' I said, 'especially when we've got to fall back and let the other fellow take over.' . . . Had the occupation zones not yet been established, I might have agreed that the attack would be politically worthwhile. But I could see no justification for taking casualties in the capture of a city we would probably hand over to the Russians." Bradley, *A Soldier's Story*, pp. 535–537. It remained for General Eisenhower to raise the issue with General Marshall one last time on April 7: "I am the first to admit that a war is waged in pursuance of political aims, and if the Combined Chiefs of Staff should decide that the Allied effort to take Berlin outweighs purely military considerations in the theater, I would cheerfully adjust my plans and my thinking so as to carry out such an operation." *PDDE*, vol. 4, no. 2401. But according to Admiral Leahy, the Combined Chiefs of Staff never took up the issue, and there is no evidence that they responded to General Eisenhower's question. Leahy, *I Was There*, p. 351. See also Pogue, *Supreme Command*, p. 446.

4 According to Ronald Lewin, the classicists in the War Department rendered the Latin as "Lovers' quarrels are a part of love." Actually, "the phrase . . . means a renewing or restoring of love. This was more apt." Ronald Lewin, *Churchill as Warlord* (New York, 1973), p. 261. The source of the quotation is Terence, *Andria (The Woman of Andros)*, III.3.23. For identifying this quotation we are indebted to Professor Kristine Gilmartin of the Rice University Department of Classics.

Doc. 541
CHURCHILL TO ROOSEVELT

No. 934   April 5, 1945

Your No. 734.[1]

1. I am astounded that Stalin should have addressed to you a message so insulting to the honour of the United States and also of Great Britain. His Majesty's Government cordially associate themselves with your reply and the War Cabinet have instructed me to send to Stalin the message in my immediately following.[2]

2. There is very little doubt in my mind that the Soviet leaders, whoever they may be, are surprised and disconcerted at the rapid advance of the Allied armies in the west and the almost total defeat of the enemy on our front, especially as they say they are themselves in no position to deliver a decisive attack before the middle of May. All this

---

[1] Not printed. In that message, dated April 4, Roosevelt sent Churchill a copy of Stalin's telegram of April 3 and his reply thereto. Referring to the conversations between American and German officials at Bern (see above, Doc. 528, note 11), Stalin told the President that he was "apparently not fully informed. . . . [M]y military colleagues are sure that negotiations did take place and that they ended in an agreement with the Germans, whereby the German Commander on the Western Front, Marshal Kesselring, is to open the front to Anglo-American troops and let them move east, while the British and Americans have promised, in exchange, to ease the armistice terms for the Germans." *Stalin's Correspondence*, vol. 2, no. 206. The President replied that he received Stalin's message "with astonishment" and repeated what he had told Stalin about the Bern meetings. Roosevelt added: "I have complete confidence in General Eisenhower and know that he would certainly inform me before entering into any agreement with the Germans. . . . I am certain that there were no negotiations at Bern at any time. . . . Finally I would say this, it would be one of the great tragedies of history if at the very moment of the victory, now within our grasp, such distrust, such lack of faith should prejudice the entire undertaking after the colossal losses of life, matériel, and treasure involved. Frankly I cannot avoid a feeling of bitter resentment toward your informers, whoever they are, for such vile misrepresentations of my actions or those of my trusted subordinates." *FR 1945*, 3: 745–746.

[2] Not printed. Churchill sent the President a copy of a message to Stalin refuting Soviet charges of Anglo-American infidelity: "There were no negotiations in Switzerland even for a military surrender of Kesselring's army. Still less did any political-military plot, as alleged in your telegram to the President, enter our thoughts, which are not as suggested of so dishonourable character. . . . With regard to the charges which you have made in your message to the President of April 3, which also asperse His Majesty's Government, I associate myself and my colleagues with the last sentence of the President's reply." Churchill, *Triumph and Tragedy*, pp. 449–451.

makes it the more important that we should join hands with the Russian armies as far to the east as possible and, if circumstances allow, enter Berlin.

3. I may remind you that we proposed and thought we had arranged six weeks ago provisional zones of occupation in Austria,[3] but since Yalta the Russians have sent no confirmation of these zones. Now that they are on the eve of taking Vienna[4] and very likely will occupy the whole of Austria, it may well be prudent for us to hold as much as possible in the north.

4. We must always be anxious lest the brutality of the Russian messages does not foreshadow some deep change of policy for which they are preparing. On the whole I incline to think it is no more than their natural expression when vexed or jealous. For that very reason I deem it of the highest importance that a firm and blunt stand should be made at this juncture by our two countries in order that the air may be cleared and they realise that there is a point beyond which we will not tolerate insult. I belive this is the best chance of saving the future. If they are ever convinced that we are afraid of them and can be bullied into submission, then indeed I should despair of our future relations with them and much else.

[3] See *FR 1945*, 3: 1ff.
[4] Russian forces entered Vienna on April 7.

Doc. 542
ROOSEVELT TO CHURCHILL

No. 736   April 6, 1945

I am in general agreement with your opinion expressed in 934,[1] and I am pleased with your very clear strong message to Stalin No. 935.[2]

We must not permit anybody to entertain a false impression that we are afraid.

Our armies will in a very few days be in a position that will permit us to become "tougher" than has heretofore appeared advantageous to the war effort.

[1] See above, Doc. 541.
[2] See above, Doc. 541, note 2.

Doc. 543
ROOSEVELT TO CHURCHILL

No. 737   April 8, 1945

I recognize the force of the observations on the Russian angle in your 932[1] and agree that it might be better not to go forward with a tripartite economic mission at the present time. On the other hand I think it would be a mistake to set up a bilateral mission. This would look as though we, for our part, were disregarding the Yalta decision for tripartite action in liberated areas and might easily be interpreted as indicating that we consider the Yalta decisions as no longer valid. Such is certainly not the case, as you know, and I therefore feel that we must be careful not to do anything that would weaken the effectiveness of our efforts to get the Russians to honor those decisions on their side.

Our Ambassador at Athens[2] recently put up to us, at the instance of Mr. Leeper, the suggestion of a joint Anglo-American committee of experts, responsible to our two Embassies, to advise the Greek Government on financial and economic policies. Having the above considerations in mind, we told him we could not approve a formal setup of this kind, but that the Embassy experts should of course continue to keep in close touch with their British colleagues and the Greek authorities and offer the latter such informal advice and assistance as might be called for. We have agreed with your people to accept the Greek Government's invitations to you and to us to send transportation experts to Greece. This is a very specific situation where a coordinated recommendation is essential, since there will be a joint interest in the supply of any equipment necessary to get transportation going again in Greece. Our people are also doing all they can to help UNRRA to do a good job in Greece.

The Greeks have approached us informally for help[3] and we are anxious to give them what economic support we can. We have suggested that they send a competent supply mission to Washington to present their claims to our supply agencies.[4] While it seems impracticable at the moment to set up an economic mission in Greece on a tripartite or bilateral basis, I think it might be helpful if I send

1 See above, Doc. 538.
2 Lincoln MacVeagh.
3 See FR 1945, 8: 208, note 9. The initial Greek request for technical assistance had been made on February 17.
4 See FR 1945, 8: 204–205.

Donald Nelson out anyway, with a few assistants, to make a survey of the needs and possibilities for me. I shall discuss this with him and keep you informed of any developments.

Doc. 544
ROOSEVELT TO CHURCHILL

No. 739   April 10, 1945

I assume Stalin repeated to you his reply to my message on Poland,[1] since he sent me his reply to yours.[2] We shall have to consider most carefully the implications of Stalin's attitude and what is to be our next step. I shall, of course, take no action of any kind, nor make any statement, without consulting you, and I know you will do the same.

[1] See above, Doc. 533, notes 2 and 4. On April 7 Stalin replied to Roosevelt: "Matters on the Polish question have really reached a dead end. What are the reasons for it? The reasons for it are that the Ambassadors of the United States and England in Moscow—members of the Moscow Commission—have departed from the principles of the Crimea conference and have introduced into the matter new elements not provided at the Crimea conference." *FR 1945,* 5: 201–204.

[2] See above, Doc. 534. In his reply to Churchill on April 9 Stalin declared: "You wonder why the Polish theatre of military events should be secret. In reality there is no secret. You overlook the circumstances that sending to Poland of British observers or other foreign observers is considered by the Poles as insult to their national dignity. . . . [T]he Soviet Government . . . cannot but take into consideration the negative attitude of the provisional Polish government." *FR 1945,* 5: 204–205.

Doc. 545
ROOSEVELT TO CHURCHILL

No. 740   April 10, 1945

Your No. 938.[1]

I agree in principle with your proposal to give notice to the German Government that it is responsible for the sustenance of the civil population in those parts of Holland that remain in German occupation.

In view of Stalin's recent allegations in regard to Crossword,[2] I believe that before making any arrangement through the Red Cross with any German authority we should inform Stalin.

[1] Not printed.
[2] See above, Doc. 541, note 1.

Doc. 546
CHURCHILL TO ROOSEVELT

No. 940   April 11, 1945

Your No. 734[1] about Crossword. I send you a private message I have received from Stalin[2] covering the official telegram which he has sent to you with copy to me. I have a feeling that this is about the best we are going to get out of them, and certainly it is as near as they can get to an apology.

However, before considering any answer at all from His Majesty's Government, please tell me how you think the matter should be handled so that we may keep in line together.

[1] Not printed. See above, Doc. 541, note 1.

[2] In that telegram Stalin reiterated that "the Russian point of view is the correct one," adding: "If, however, you are going to regard every frank statement of mine as offensive, it will make this kind of communication very difficult. I can assure you that I had and have no intention of offending anyone." *FR 1945*, 3: 753.

Doc. 547
CHURCHILL TO ROOSEVELT

No. 944   April 11, 1945

Your 739.[1]

1. Stalin sent me a copy of his reply to your message on Poland. He also sent me an additional private message, of which the last sentence in para 1, if seriously intended, would be important. I send this message in my immediately following.[2] Please let these personal introductions to his official messages be guarded absolutely as between you and me.

2. I have to make a statement in the House of Commons next Thursday and of course I shall like to know your views about how we

[1] See above, Doc. 544.

[2] Not printed. Churchill forwarded a copy of a private message from Stalin. See *Stalin's Correspondence*, vol. 1, no. 418. The sentence referred to by the Prime Minister read: "However, if you deem it necessary, I shall try to induce the provisional Polish government to withdraw its objections to inviting Mikolajczyk providing he publicly endorses the decisions of the Crimea conference on the Polish question and declares in favour of establishing friendly relations between Poland and the Soviet Union."

should answer Stalin as soon as possible. I have a feeling that they do not want to quarrel with us, and your telegram about Crossword may have seriously and deservedly perturbed them. Our angle of approach and momentum remain exactly what they have been in both the matters under dispute as set forth in our telegrams.

Doc. 548
ROOSEVELT TO CHURCHILL

No. 742   April 11, 1945

Your 944.[1] I would minimize the general Soviet problem as much as possible because these problems, in one form or another, seem to arise every day and most of them straighten out as in the case of the Bern meeting.

We must be firm, however, and our course thus far is correct.[2]

[1] See above, Doc. 547.

[2] "There is no question from the correspondence," Samuel Rosenman wrote later, "that the 'course' the President was referring to was not the general wartime policy toward the Soviet Union but the firm, even tough, position that he and Churchill had taken with Stalin on Poland." Rosenman, *Working with Roosevelt*, p. 538. It is believed that Roosevelt wrote this message himself, but the original draft has not been located.

Chronology

Chronology

October 1939

Doc. 2   3   Pan-American Conference decrees 300-mile safety zone.

6   Hitler demands peace on his terms and threatens a war of destruction.

9   German raider captures USS *City of Flint*.

11   Roosevelt writes to Soviet President Mikhail Kalinin concerning Finland.

Doc. 3   14   German submarine sinks British battleship *Royal Oak* at anchor at Scapa Flow.

November 1939

4   U.S. Congress passes Neutrality Act of 1939, eliminating arms embargo and placing sales on cash-and-carry basis.

28   British order-in-council extends contraband control to German exports.

29   Soviet Union breaks diplomatic relations with Finland. United States offers mediation.

30   Russians invade Finland.

December 1939

3   Finland appeals to League of Nations.

8   United States protests British order-in-council of November 28.

10   United States grants $10 million credit to Finland.

Doc. 4   13   British cruisers attack German raider *Admiral Graf Spee* off Montevideo.

14   Soviet Union expelled from League of Nations over Finnish issue.

20   United States bans sale of plans, plants, rights, and technical information on production of aviation gasoline "to certain countries."

Doc. 7   23   Twenty-one American republics protest to Britain, France, and Germany over *Graf Spee* incident.

January 1940

2   United States protests British interference with mails.

20   Churchill warns European neutrals and asks them to join Allies.

26   U.S.-Japanese commercial treaty expires.

February 1940

9 Undersecretary of State Sumner Welles leaves on "peace mission" to London, Paris, Berlin, and Rome.

19 United States extends "moral embargo" on aviation fuel to Soviet Union.

March 1940

6 France and Italy sign trade agreement.

12 Russo-Finnish war ends.

21 Paul Reynaud becomes Premier of France, replacing Édouard Daladier.

28 Supreme War Council of Allies resolves on "no separate peace."

30 Japan sets up puppet government for China at Nanking.

April 1940

8 Britain and France mine Norwegian waters.

9 Germans invade Norway and Denmark. Norway appeals for British help. Denmark submits.

10 United States freezes Norwegian and Danish funds. Iceland suspends relations with Denmark.

14 Allied forces land in Norway.

16 Iceland asks to enter direct relations with United States.

24 Germany takes control of Norway.

29 Roosevelt appeals to Mussolini to use his influence for a just and stable peace.

May 1940

1 United States establishes provisional consulate in Greenland.

9 British troops occupy Iceland.
Germans attack Belgium, the Netherlands, and Luxembourg.

Docs. 8, 10, 11 10 Churchill succeeds Neville Chamberlain as Prime Minister.
Germans invade France.

11 Allied troops occupy Aruba and Curaçao.

Doc. 10 15 Dutch army capitulates.
             Committee to Defend America by Aiding the Allies
             founded in United States.
             Churchill first asks for U.S. destroyers.

         16 Roosevelt requests new defense appropriations.

         20 Germans capture Amiens and Abbeville.

         28 Belgian army capitulates.
             Roosevelt again appeals to Mussolini to avoid war.
             British begin evacuation of forces at Dunkirk.

June 1940

              4 Churchill tells House of Commons that Britain would
                 fight on even if England were invaded and subjugated.

Docs. 13, 14 5 Final battle of France begins.

              9 Norway orders its troops to cease hostilities.

Doc. 12   10 Italy declares war on Great Britain and France.

             12 Britain orders blockade of Italy.

             13 United States adopts hemisphere defense plan (Rain-
                 bow IV).
                 Roosevelt promises redoubled efforts to aid France and
                 the Allies.

Doc. 17   14 Germans enter Paris.

             15 Russians take over Lithuania.

Docs. 17, 18 16 Henri Philippe Pétain replaces Reynaud as Premier of
                 France and asks Germans for armistice terms.

             17 Russians take over Latvia and Estonia.
                 United States freezes French assets.
                 United States notifies Germany and Italy that it will
                 not recognize any transfer of territory in Western Hemis-
                 phere.

             18 General Charles de Gaulle makes first broadcast appeal
                 in name of "Free French."

             19 Roosevelt forms coalition Cabinet by appointing Henry
                 Stimson Secretary of War and Frank Knox Secretary of
                 the Navy.
                 Polish and Belgian governments-in-exile move to London.

             22 French accept German armistice terms.

             28 Congress passes National Defense Act.
                 British recognize de Gaulle as leader of Free French.
                 Russia seizes Bessarabia and northern Bukovina from
                 Rumania.

July 1940

3   British sink three French battleships and a destroyer near Oran.

5   France breaks diplomatic relations with Britain.

9   French warships demilitarized at Alexandria.

10   Roosevelt asks Congress for new defense appropriations.

17   Japanese force British to close Burma Road.

19   Hitler makes new peace offer to British.

20   Roosevelt signs bill providing for "two-ocean Navy."

21   Hitler first mentions attacking Russia.
Prince Fumumaro Konoye becomes Prime Minister of Japan.

26   United States places an embargo on export of gas, oil, and metal to Japan.

30   Pan-American Conference at Havana puts European colonies in Western Hemisphere under joint trusteeship.

August 1940

1   Hitler issues directive for air and naval war against Britain.

8   Britain offers new constitution and postwar partnership to India.

9   British withdraw forces from Shanghai.

17   Hitler declares total blockade of British Isles.

18   Roosevelt meets Canadian Prime Minister Mackenzie King to plan joint defense measures. Joint Defense Board established.

Doc. 21   20   Churchill announces willingness to lease Western Hemisphere bases to United States.

September 1940

Docs. 9, 11, 17,   2   Destroyer-bases "deal" consummated.
19, 20, 21,
23, 24, 41, 44

4   America-First Committee founded.

7   Germans begin day and night air attacks on London.

13   Italian offensive in Libya begins.

15   Battle of Britain reaches its height.

| | 16 | Roosevelt signs Burke-Wadsworth Act—first peacetime draft in American history. |

           16 Roosevelt signs Burke-Wadsworth Act—first peacetime draft in American history.

           22 Japanese begin occupation of French Indochina.

Doc. 26   23 British attempt to seize Dakar fails.

           25 United States makes $25 million loan to China.

           26 Roosevelt places embargo on scrap iron and steel to Japan.

Doc. 27   27 Germany, Italy, and Japan sign Tripartite Pact in Berlin.

October 1940

           4 Hitler and Mussolini meet at Brenner Pass.

           5 Prince Konoye predicts war between Japan and United States.

           8 Germans begin occupation of Rumania.

           12 Hitler calls off invasion of Britain for 1940.

Doc. 27   17 Burma Road reopened.

Doc. 30   22–24 French and Spanish leaders meet with Hitler.

Doc. 45   28 Italians invade Greece. Greeks appeal for British help.

           31 Battle of Britain ends with defeat of Luftwaffe.

November 1940

           1 British troops land in Crete.

Doc. 31   5 Roosevelt reelected.

           14–19 German planes raid Coventry and Birmingham.

           20 Hungary joins Tripartite Pact.

           23 Rumania joins Tripartite Pact.

           30 United States lends another $100 million to China.

December 1940

Doc. 36   6 British offensive in western Sahara begins.

           17 Roosevelt, at press conference, suggests "lending" arms to Britain.

           18 Hitler issues "Barbarossa" directive for Russian invasion.

           20 Alien registration goes into effect in United States.

           22 Anthony Eden becomes British Foreign Secretary.

Doc. 35   29 Roosevelt pledges that the United States will become "the great arsenal of democracy."

January 1941

6 Roosevelt recommends lend-lease aid to Britain and enunciates Four Freedoms.

10 Lend-lease bill introduced in Congress.

11 Hitler orders force to be prepared for North Africa.

22 Tobruk captured by British.

Docs. 38, 39   24 U.S.-British staff talks begin.

February 1941

6 Hitler issues directive for economic war on Britain.

14 Hitler demands Yugoslavia join Axis.

Doc. 40   16 Britain mines Singapore waters.

March 1941

1 Bulgaria joins Axis.

Doc. 46   10 Murphy-Weygand agreement approved.

Docs. 42, 43,   11 Lend-lease bill becomes law.
49, 92, 94

Doc. 50   25 Roosevelt authorizes repair of British vessels in U.S. navy yards.

Yugoslavia joins Axis.

Docs. 45, 48   27 Hitler postpones "Barbarossa."

Yugoslav coup brings in government friendly to the Allies.

United States appropriates $7 billion for lend-lease aid.

30 Field Marshal Erwin Rommel launches German counter-offensive in Africa.

Doc. 51   31 Roosevelt orders Coast Guard to seize thirty Axis and thirty-five Danish merchant ships in American ports.

April 1941

3 Pro-Nazi military government established in Iraq.

Doc. 52   6 Germans invade Yugoslavia and Greece.

8 Germans occupy Salonika.

May 1941

June 1941

12 Russo-Japanese trade agreement signed.
14 United States freezes Axis assets.
16 United States closes German and Italian consulates.
17 United States and Canada set up Joint Economic Committee.
18 German-Turkish friendship pact signed.
21 Allies occupy Damascus.
22 Germans invade Russia.
    Churchill declares support for Russia.
24 Roosevelt releases Russian credits and promises U.S. aid.
25 Sweden allows transit of one German division from Norway to Finland.

July 1941

1   Germans enter Riga.
5   Germans reach Dnieper.
6   Russian counterattack launched on Latvian frontier.

Doc. 58   7   United States occupies Iceland.

12 Anglo-Soviet mutual assistance agreement signed.
21 France accepts Japanese demand for military control of Indochina.
    Germans launch first air raid on Moscow.
24 United States denounces Japanese actions in Indochina.
25 United States freezes Japanese and Chinese assets.
30 United States recognizes Czech government-in-exile.

August 1941

1   United States issues embargo on all exports of aviation fuel.
2   United States and Russia exchange notes on economic assistance.
8   Japan suggests Konoye-Roosevelt meeting in Honolulu.

Docs. 68, 69,   9   Roosevelt and Churchill open Atlantic conference
70   aboard USS Augusta.

10 Britain and Russia send notes to Turkey promising aid if attacked.
12 Atlantic conference ends.
    Pétain announces full collaboration with Germany.

24 U.S. forces occupy Surinam.
United States grants lend-lease aid to Free French.

Docs. 82, 83,   26 United States makes counterproposal to Japan.
84   Lebanon becomes independent.

December 1941

6 Roosevelt asks Japanese to remove troops from Indochina.
Red Army launches major counteroffensive on central front.

Docs. 85, 86   7 Japan attacks Pearl Harbor.
Doc. 87   8 United States and Britain declare war on Japan.
Japanese invade Thailand, Malaya, and Philippines.

9 China declares war on Japan, Germany, and Italy.

10 British battleships *Repulse* and *Prince of Wales* sunk off Malaya.
Japanese seize Guam.

11 Germany and Italy declare war on United States.
Japanese invade Burma.

13 British forces launch attack in Libya.

16 Japanese invade British Borneo.

18 Japanese invade Hong Kong.

19 Hitler takes personal command of German army.

Docs. 88, 89   22 Churchill arrives in United States for first Washington conference.

23 General Douglas MacArthur decides to evacuate Manila.

Doc. 93   24 St. Pierre and Miquelon seized by Free French.

25 British garrison of Hong Kong surrenders to Japanese.

27 British commandos raid enemy base on islands off Norway.

January 1942

1 Declaration by the United Nations signed by twenty-six nations.

7 U.S. troops in Philippines retreat to Bataan.

11 Japanese invade Dutch East Indies and Dutch Borneo.

14 First Washington conference ends.

18 German-Japanese-Italian military convention signed in Berlin.

20 Russians recapture Mozhaisk.

21   Rommel counterattacks in Libya.
General Joseph Stilwell named as Allied Chief of Staff attached to Chiang Kai-shek.

25   Rommel's forces push eastward across Libya.

Doc. 93   26   First convoy of U.S. troops arrives in Northern Ireland.

29   ANZAC command established.

February 1942

1   Germans proclaim Vidkun Quisling Premier of Norway.

6   Great Britain and United States establish Combined Chiefs of Staff.

9   Pacific War Council established in London.

Doc. 95   12   German warships *Scharnhorst, Gneisenau,* and *Prinz Eugen* escape from Brest and reach North Sea.

14   Japanese invade Sumatra.

Doc. 96   15   Japanese capture Singapore.

16   German submarines attack Aruba.

19   Naval base at Darwin, Australia, attacked by Japanese aircraft.

22   Roosevelt orders MacArthur to leave Philippines.

23   Japanese submarine shells oil refinery near Santa Barbara, California.

27   Naval battle of Java Sea begins.

March 1942

Doc. 102   7   Japanese complete conquest of Java.
British evacuate Rangoon.

Docs. 105, 109   16   MacArthur appointed commander of Pacific theater.

17   MacArthur arrives in Australia.

Docs. 101, 106, 117, 119,132   22   Cripps mission arrives in India.

26   Roosevelt orders acceleration of shipments to Russia.

27   U.S. Chiefs of Staff issue proposals for cross-channel invasions in 1942 and 1943.

30   New, enlarged Pacific War Council set up in Washington.

April 1942

1   United States begins mass evacuation of Japanese citizens and aliens from Pacific coast states.

	3	Japanese open all-out offensive against Bataan line.
	6	U.S. troops arrive in Australia.
Doc. 115	7	Russians open rail link to besieged Leningrad.
Docs. 114, 119	8	General George C. Marshall and Harry Hopkins arrive in London for talks with British military leaders.
	9	U.S. forces on Bataan surrender.
Docs. 103, 114, 121, 124	14	British approve Operation Bolero—cross-channel invasion buildup.
	18	United States launches first air attack on Tokyo.
	29	Japanese capture terminus of Burma Road.

May 1942

	2	United States grants lend-lease aid to Iran and Iraq.
	3	Japanese capture Tulagi.
Docs. 107, 108, 128, 129	5	British invade Madagascar.
	6	General Jonathan M. Wainwright surrenders Corregidor and remaining Philippine forces to Japan. U.S. forces arrive in Liberia.
Doc. 113	7	U.S. aircraft carriers *Wasp* and *Eagle* ferry Spitfires to Malta.
	8	Battle of Coral Sea ends in U.S. victory.
Doc. 132	12	First large detachment of U.S. Eighth Air Force arrives in Britain.
	14	President Manuel Quezon establishes Philippine government-in-exile in Washington.
Docs. 124, 125	20	Vyacheslav Molotov, Soviet Foreign Minister, arrives in London.
	21	Hitler postpones conquest of Malta.
Doc. 134	26	Anglo-Russian twenty-year mutual assistance treaty signed.
	27	Nazi police chief Reinhard Heydrich assassinated by Czech patriots.
	28	Russians defeated at battle of Kharkov.
Docs. 135, 136, 137	29	Molotov arrives in Washington.
	30	1,000-plane RAF raid devastates Cologne.

June 1942

	1	Japanese midget submarines sink Australian boat in Sydney harbor.

	3	Japanese bomb Dutch Harbor and Fort Mears, Alaska.
	4	British Eighth Army counterattacks in Libya.
		Japanese decisively defeated in main battle of Midway.
	5	United States declares war on Bulgaria, Hungary, and Rumania.
	7	Japanese invade Aleutians.
	10	Czech village of Lidice destroyed by Germans to avenge assassination of Heydrich.
Doc. 136	11	U.S.-USSR mutual aid agreement signed.
	12	U.S. planes based in Africa bomb Rumanian oil fields at Ploesti.
Docs. 138, 139	18	Churchill arrives in United States for second Washington conference.
	20	Roosevelt and Churchill decide on North African invasion.
	21	Tobruk falls to Germans.
	24	Rommel begins drive into Egypt.
	27	Second Washington conference ends.
	28	Germans launch main summer offensive in Russia.
	30	British Eighth Army makes stand at El Alamein.

July 1942

	1	Sevastopol falls to Germans.
	2	Churchill wins vote of confidence 475–25.
Doc. 171	4	United States launches first air operations against Western Europe.
	6	Voronezh falls to the Germans.
Doc. 144	17	Marshall, Hopkins, and Admiral Ernest J. King fly to London to urge invasion of Continent.
	21	Admiral William D. Leahy becomes Roosevelt's Chief of Staff.
Docs. 140, 142	22	British refuse to launch cross-channel attack in 1942.
	24	Rostov falls to Germans.
Docs. 145, 146, 153, 154	25	Combined Chiefs of Staff agree on command setup for Operation Torch—the invasion of North Africa.

August 1942

	5	Great Britain repudiates Munich Pact.
Doc. 154	7	Churchill visits British Eighth Army in Egypt.
Doc. 171	7–8	U.S. forces land on Tulagi and Guadalcanal in Solomons.

8 All-India Congress party demands immediate British withdrawal from India.

Docs. 147, 148, 151, 152, 156, 157, 158, 159, 160

12 Churchill arrives in Moscow for four-day talks with Stalin.

14 General Dwight D. Eisenhower named commander for Torch.

19 British commandos raid Dieppe.

23 Germans launch attack on Stalingrad.

September 1942

3 Germans reach suburbs of Stalingrad.

Docs. 161, 162, 163, 164, 165, 166, 167, 169, 172

5 Operation Torch set for November 8. Landings projected for Algiers, Oran, and Casablanca.

6 Germans capture Novorossiysk.

9 Lone Japanese plane drops incendiary bombs in Oregon.

16 Street fighting begins in Stalingrad.

October 1942

1 German attack halted at Stalingrad.

6 General Sir Bernard Montgomery issues instructions for El Alamein offensive in western Sahara.

9 Allies launch daylight air attacks on Lille.

11 U.S. forces win naval battle at Cape Esperance in Solomons.

17 Torch convoys begin assembling at Firth of Clyde.

Doc. 177 23 Eleanor Roosevelt arrives in London.
U.S. naval forces leave Hampton Roads, Virginia, for Africa.

23–29 Axis and British forces meet at battle of El Alamein.

29 Alcan Highway opened.

November 1942

5 Eisenhower flies to Gibraltar to establish Allied command post for Operation Torch.

8   Allied troops invade French North Africa on Algerian and Moroccan coasts to begin Operation Torch.
    Vichy France severs diplomatic relations with United States.

9   Germans invade Tunisia.
    General Henri Giraud arrives on Algerian front.

Doc. 183   10   Admiral Jean Darlan broadcasts ceasefire announcement.
    Oran surrenders to Allies.

Doc. 181   11   French resistance in North Africa ends.
    British Eighth Army drives Axis forces out of Egypt and enters Libya.
    Axis troops march into unoccupied France.

Doc. 185   13   British Eighth Army recaptures Tobruk.
    Eisenhower flies to Algiers to conclude agreement with Admiral Darlan.

19   Russian army opens winter offensive.

22   Soviet forces complete encirclement of German Sixth Army at Stalingrad.

27   Allies scuttle French fleet in harbor of Toulon to prevent its capture by Germans.

December 1942

4   North African-based U.S. bombers (B-24s) launch first attack on Italy.

8   Joint Chiefs of Staff give Roosevelt a proposal for Operation Anakim—the recapture of Burma.

12   Landing of first U.S. troops in Iran completed.

Docs. 202, 203, 204   24   Admiral Darlan assassinated in Algiers.

January 1943

2   Allies capture Buna mission in New Guinea.

12   Soviet forces raise the siege of Leningrad.

Docs. 190, 192, 194, 197, 198, 200, 206   14   Casablanca conference begins.

15   British Eighth Army opens drive on Tripoli.

22   Papuan campaign ends in New Guinea with fall of Sanananda—first Allied land victory against Japanese.

23 Casablanca conference ends.

27 British-based U.S. Eighth Air Force makes first air attack on Germany.

30 Germans break through French and U.S. positions in North Africa.

February 1943

2 German resistance at Stalingrad ends.

Doc. 211   4 British Eighth Army crosses into Tunisia.

8 Seventy-seventh Indian Brigade (Chindits) under Brigadier General Orde Wingate begins guerrilla warfare behind Japanese lines in Burma.

9 Organized Japanese resistance on Guadalcanal ends.

14 Soviet army retakes Rostov.

25 RAF begins round-the-clock air offensive against Germany.
Allies recover Kasserine Pass in North Africa.

March 1943

4 Battle of the Bismarck Sea ends in Allied victory.

9 Rommel leaves Africa.

14 General Giraud restores representative government in French North Africa and suppresses Vichy French organizations.

26 Allies turn back Japanese attempt to reinforce their position in Aleutian Islands.

April 1943

Doc. 218   23 Combined Chiefs of Staff issue directive for establishment of an Anglo-American staff to plan invasion of Western Europe.

May 1943

3 General Stilwell receives Roosevelt's directive for a major U.S. air effort in China and continued preparations for a modified Operation Anakim.

10 U.S. forces invade Attu Island in Aleutians—beginning of rollback of Japanese.

September 1943

3   British troops land on Calabrian coast of Italian boot.
9   Troops of U.S. Fifth Army land at Salerno, Italy.
25   Russian troops take Smolensk.
29   Marshal Badoglio and General Eisenhower sign terms for the surrender of Italy on board a British ship off Malta.

October 1943

1   British troops enter Naples.
13   Italy declares war on Germany.

Doc. 271   19–30   Conference of foreign ministers held in Moscow.

November 1943

5   U.S. Fifth Army begins attack on German winter line in Italy.
6   Germans withdraw from Kiev.

Doc. 266   7   British troops in India launch limited offensive on coast of Burma.

8   General Sir Harold Alexander orders U.S. Fifth Army to prepare for amphibious landing on west coast of Italy.

Docs. 254, 256, 258, 259   12   German troops invade Leros in the Aegean Sea.

16   Admiral Lord Louis Mountbatten activates Southeast Asia command.

20   Central Pacific offensive begins with landings by U.S. forces on Tarawa and Makin atolls in Gilbert Islands.

Docs. 269, 271   22   First phase of Cairo conference opens.

23   Organized Japanese resistance on Tarawa and Makin atolls ends.

25   China-based U.S. Fourteenth Air Force makes first bombing attack on Formosa.

26   First phase of Cairo conference ends.

Docs. 250, 255, 262, 273   28   Roosevelt and Churchill meet with Stalin at Teheran conference—continues through December 2.

December 1943

Doc. 275   2–7   Roosevelt, Churchill, and Chiang Kai-shek meet for second phase of Cairo conference.

14   Soviet troops begin winter offensive.

18   Chiang Kai-shek gives General Stilwell command of Chinese troops in India and Burma.

21   General Stilwell arrives at Ledo, India, to take charge of campaign in northern Burma.

24   Roosevelt and Churchill announce appointment of General Eisenhower as supreme commander of the Allied Expeditionary Force for Operation Overlord— the invasion of France.

January 1944

3   Soviet troops make first crossing of prewar Polish frontier northwest of Kiev.

4   U.S. planes begin flying supplies from Britain to underground forces in Western Europe.

11   Allies launch Operation Pointblank—strategic air offensive against German air force and industry—in preparation for Overlord.

Doc. 290   22   Troops of U.S. Fifth Army land at Anzio, Italy, behind German lines.

Docs. 285, 286, 287   26   Argentina breaks off diplomatic relations with Germany and Japan.

29   800 U.S. bombers raid Frankfurt—largest American air strike to date against Germany.

31   U.S. forces invade Kwajalein atoll in Marshall Islands.

February 1944

Doc. 297   17   U.S. troops invade Eniwetok atoll.

23   U.S. carrier-based planes begin aerial attacks on Mariana Islands in western Pacific.

Docs. 317, 331, 333   24   U.S. force (Merrill's Marauders) begins ground campaign in northern Burma.

29   U.S. forces land on Los Negros Island in Admiralties.

March 1944

	4	United States launches first air attack on Berlin.
Docs. 331, 333, 336, 338	5	General Wingate's long-range penetration brigades begin landing behind Japanese lines in central Burma.
	12	Joint Chiefs of Staff issue orders to General MacArthur and Admiral Chester Nimitz for a dual advance to the Luzon-Formosa area by February 1945.
Docs. 297, 347, 351	22	British Chiefs of Staff recommend that plans for Operation Anvil—the invasion of southern France—be dropped in favor of a greater effort in Italy.

April 1944

Doc. 353	8	Soviet troops open offensive in the Crimea.
	10	Russians take Odessa.
	16	Russians capture Yalta.
	17	Japanese open last major offensive in China.
	22	U.S. forces land in Hollandia region of Dutch New Guinea.

May 1944

	9	Soviet troops take Sevastopol.
Doc. 361	11	U.S. Fifth Army and British Eighth Army in Italy begin an offensive with Rome as the goal.
	18	U.S. campaign in Admiralties ends.
	25	U.S. Fifth Army breaks through to link up with Anzio beachhead forces.

June 1944

	2	U.S. Fifteenth Air Force begins shuttlebombing runs between Italy and Russia.
	4	U.S. Fifth Army takes Rome.
Docs. 351, 352, 353, 360, 362	6	Allied forces invade France.
Doc. 384	10	Churchill, Admiral King, General Marshall, and General Henry H. Arnold visit Normandy beachhead.

Doc. 419 20 Roosevelt and Churchill appeal to Stalin to aid Warsaw insurgents.

21 Big Four representatives meet at Dumbarton Oaks for conference on future world organization.

Doc. 428 23 King Michael of Rumania organizes coup d'état against his pro-German government and surrenders to Soviet forces.

Doc. 428 25 American and French forces liberate Paris.
Rumania declares war on Germany.

28 French troops liberate Marseilles and Toulon.

September 1944

1 American forces enter Belgium.

4 British troops liberate Antwerp.
Russia and Finland agree to armistice.

5 Russia declares war on Bulgaria.

8 First German V-2 rockets launched against Britain.

9 Russia and Bulgaria agree to armistice.

11 Second Quebec conference begins.
Allied troops liberate Luxembourg.
American forces reach German border north of Trier.
British forces occupy Le Havre.

Docs. 435, 437, 439 15 Soviet and Tito forces join.
Dumbarton Oaks conference adjourns.

16 Second Quebec conference ends.

18 Russian forces enter Sofia.

19 American troops occupy Brest.

22 Russians occupy Talinin, capital of Estonia.

28 Canadian forces capture Calais.

29 Roosevelt rejects Morgenthau Plan.

October 1944

3 Germans evacuate Athens.
Warsaw uprising crushed.

Docs. 439, 440, 441, 442, 446, 447, 448 9 Churchill and Eden arrive in Moscow for nine-day meetings with Stalin.

13 Russians occupy Riga.

November 1944

December 1944

January 1945

February 1945

2 Malta conference ends.
3 1,000 U.S. planes bomb Berlin.
4 Conference at Yalta begins.
   American forces enter Manila.
   Russian forces enter Posen.
11 Conference at Yalta ends.
13 Russians occupy Budapest.
14 American forces breach main Siegfried line.
16 American forces recapture Bataan.
19 Americans land on Iwo Jima.
23 Americans begin offensive toward Cologne.
   Turkey declares war on Germany and Japan.
24 Egyptian Prime Minister Nahas Pasha assassinated after
   reading declaration of war on Germany and Japan.
26 1,200 U.S. planes bomb Berlin.

March 1945

1 Americans occupy Trier.
2 Americans liberate Corregidor.
7 Americans occupy Cologne.
Doc. 514   9 Roosevelt agrees with Churchill to "stand firm" on
              Polish question.
19 American forces land on Panay.
20 Russians capture Brandenburg.
   British liberate Mandalay.
Doc. 525   21 Roosevelt suggests U.S.-British-Russian mission to re-
              vive Greek economy.
30 Russians occupy Danzig.
   Russian forces enter Austria.
   American military government established in Frankfurt.

April 1945

1 Americans land on Okinawa.
Doc. 541   5 Russians enter Vienna suburbs.
9 Last Allied offensive in Italy begins.
   Russians enter center of Vienna.
Doc. 548   11 Roosevelt, minimizing current problems with Russians,
              declares present Anglo-American course is correct.
12 American forces cross Elbe River and capture Weimar.
   Russians capture Königsberg.
   Roosevelt dies at Warm Springs, Georgia, and is suc-
   ceeded by Vice President Harry S Truman.

Maps

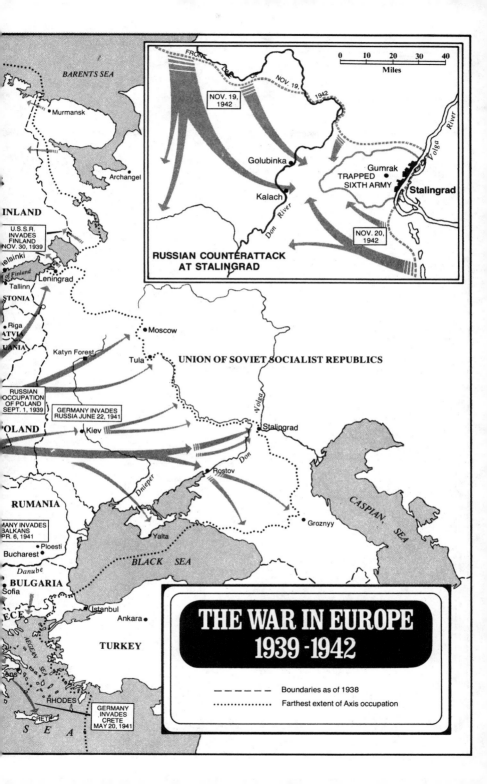

RUSSIAN COUNTERATTACK AT STALINGRAD

NOV. 19, 1942

NOV. 20, 1942

Golubinka

Kalach

Gumrak

TRAPPED SIXTH ARMY

Stalingrad

Don River

Volga River

0 10 20 30 40 Miles

BARENTS SEA

Murmansk

Archangel

FINLAND

U.S.S.R. INVADES FINLAND NOV. 30, 1939

Helsinki

of Finland

Leningrad

Tallinn

ESTONIA

Riga

LATVIA

LITHUANIA

Katyn Forest

Moscow

Tula

UNION OF SOVIET SOCIALIST REPUBLICS

RUSSIAN OCCUPATION OF POLAND SEPT. 1, 1939

GERMANY INVADES RUSSIA JUNE 22, 1941

POLAND

Kiev

Volga

Stalingrad

Don

Rostov

Dnieper

CASPIAN SEA

RUMANIA

GERMANY INVADES BALKANS APR. 6, 1941

Ploesti

Bucharest

Danube

BULGARIA

Sofia

Yalta

BLACK SEA

Groznyy

GREECE

Istanbul

Ankara

TURKEY

AEGEAN SEA

RHODES

GERMANY INVADES CRETE MAY 20, 1941

CRETE

SEA

THE WAR IN EUROPE 1939-1942

– – – – Boundaries as of 1938

.... Farthest extent of Axis occupation

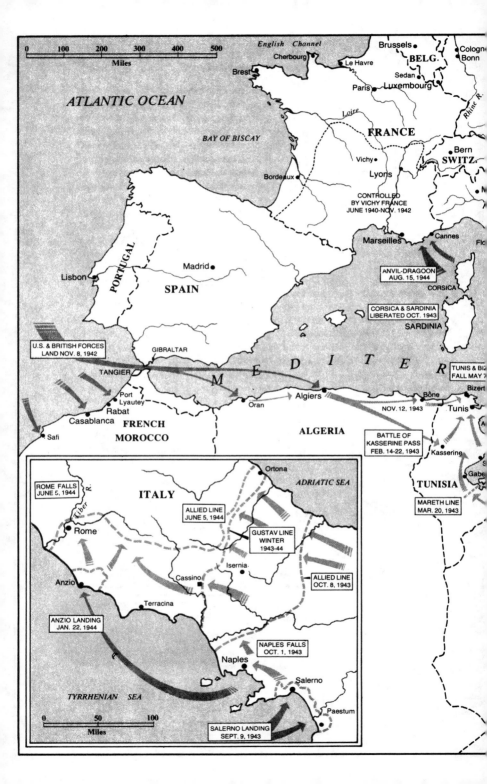

THE MEDITERRANEAN THEATER
1942-1944

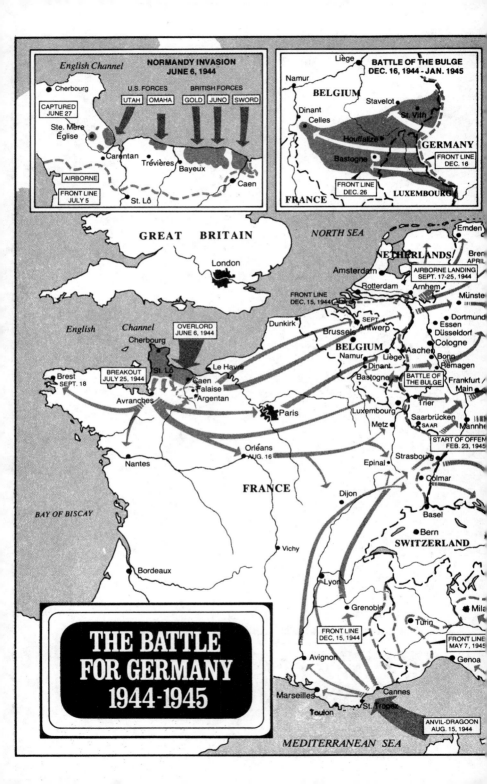

NORMANDY INVASION JUNE 6, 1944

English Channel

- Cherbourg
- CAPTURED JUNE 27
- Ste. Mere Église
- AIRBORNE
- FRONT LINE JULY 5
- Carentan
- Trévières
- Bayeux
- Caen
- St. Lô

U.S. FORCES UTAH OMAHA
BRITISH FORCES GOLD JUNO SWORD

BATTLE OF THE BULGE DEC. 16, 1944 - JAN. 1945

- Liège
- Namur
- BELGIUM
- Dinant
- Celles
- Stavelot
- St. Vith
- Houffalize
- Bastogne
- GERMANY
- FRONT LINE DEC. 16
- FRONT LINE DEC. 26
- FRANCE
- LUXEMBOURG

GREAT BRITAIN

NORTH SEA

- London
- Emden
- NETHERLANDS
- Bren APRIL
- Amsterdam
- AIRBORNE LANDING SEPT. 17-25, 1944
- Rotterdam
- Arnhem
- Münste
- FRONT LINE DEC, 15, 1944
- Dortmund
- Essen
- Düsseldorf
- Cologne
- SEPT. 4
- Brussels
- Antwerp
- BELGIUM
- Aachen
- Bonn
- Remagen
- Namur
- Liège
- Dinant
- Bastogne
- BATTLE OF THE BULGE
- Frankfurt Main
- *English Channel*
- OVERLORD JUNE 6, 1944
- Cherbourg
- Dunkirk
- Le Havre
- Brest SEPT. 18
- BREAKOUT JULY 25, 1944
- St. Lô
- Caen
- Falaise
- Argentan
- Avranches
- Paris
- Luxembourg
- Trier
- Saarbrücken
- SAAR
- Mannhe
- Metz
- START OF OFFEN FEB. 23, 1945
- Nantes
- Orléans AUG. 16
- Strasbourg
- Epinal
- Colmar
- **FRANCE**
- Dijon
- Basel
- **BAY OF BISCAY**
- Bern
- **SWITZERLAND**
- Bordeaux
- Vichy
- Lyon
- Grenoble
- FRONT LINE DEC, 15, 1944
- Turin
- Mila
- FRONT LINE MAY 7, 1945
- Avignon
- Genoa

THE BATTLE FOR GERMANY 1944-1945

- Marseilles
- Toulon
- Cannes
- St. Tropez
- ANVIL-DRAGOON AUG. 15, 1944

MEDITERRANEAN SEA

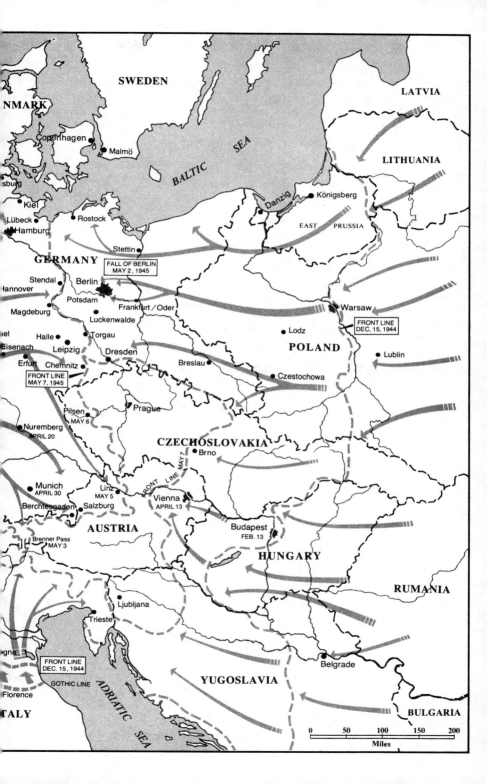

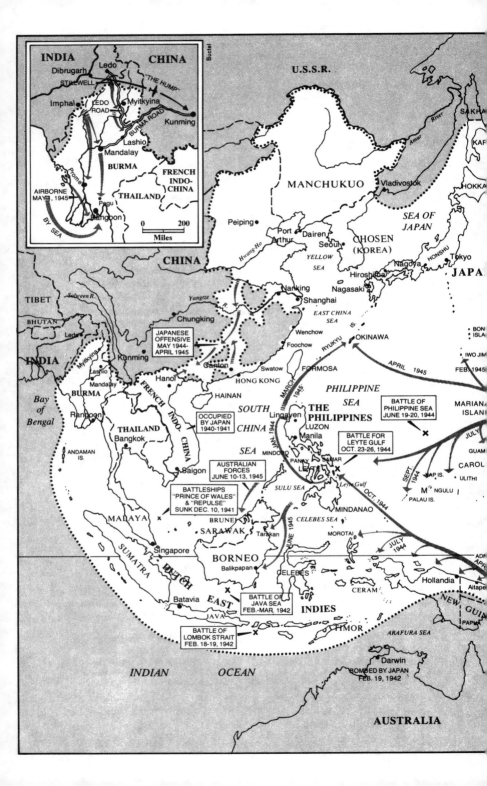

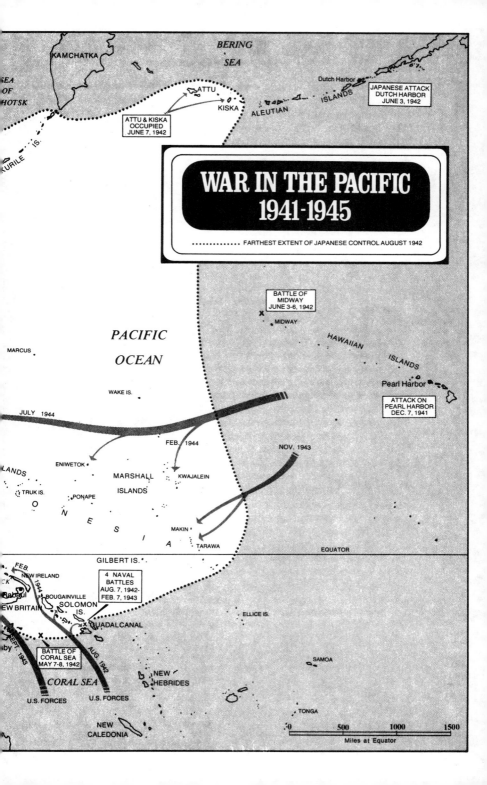

Bibliography
(of Works Cited)

Bibliography

(of Works Cited)

Ambrose, Stephen E. *Eisenhower and Berlin 1945: The Decision to Halt at the Elbe*. New York: 1967.

———. *The Supreme Commander—The War Years of General Dwight D. Eisenhower*. New York: 1970.

Anglin, Douglas G. *The St. Pierre and Miquelon Affair of 1941*. Toronto: 1966.

Armstrong, Anne. *Unconditional Surrender: The Impact of the Casablanca Policy upon World War II*. New Brunswick, N.J.: 1961.

Arnold, Henry H. *Global Mission*. New York: 1949.

Bailey, Thomas A. *Woodrow Wilson and the Great Betrayal*. New York: 1945.

Baldwin, Hanson W. *Great Mistakes of the War*. New York: 1950.

———. *Battles Won and Lost—Great Campaigns of World War II*. New York: 1966.

Barnes, Harry Elmer, ed. *Perpetual War for Perpetual Peace*. Caldwell, Idaho: 1953.

The Battle of Greece (Government White Paper). Athens: 1949.

Berle, Beatrice Bishop and Jacobs, Travis Beal, eds. *Navigating the Rapids 1918–1971: From the Papers of Adolf A. Berle*. New York: 1973.

Bernstein, Barton J., ed. *Toward a New Past—Dissenting Essays in American History*. New York: 1968.

———, ed. *Politics and Policies of the Truman Administration*. Chicago: 1970.

Bernstein, Marvin D., and Loewenheim, Francis L. "Aid to Russia—the First Year," in Harold Stein, ed., *American Civil-Military Decisions*. Montgomery, Ala.: 1963.

Birkenhead, The Earl of. *Halifax*. London: 1965.

Bishop, Donald G. *The Roosevelt–Litvinov Agreements—The American View*. Syracuse, N.Y.: 1965.

Bishop, Jim. *FDR's Last Year: April 1944–1945*. New York: 1974.

Blum, John Morton. *Roosevelt and Morgenthau*. Boston: 1970.

Blumenson, Martin. *Breakout and Pursuit*. Washington: 1961.

———. *The Kasserine Pass*. New York: 1966.

———. *The Patton Papers, 2, 1940–1945*. New York: 1974.

Bohlen, Charles E. *The Transformation of American Foreign Policy*. New York: 1969.

———. *Witness to History, 1929–1969*. New York: 1973.

Bradley, Omar N. *A Soldier's Story*. New York: 1951.

Bruce, George L. *The Warsaw Uprising, 1 August–2 October 1944*. London: 1972.

Bryant, Arthur. *The Turn of the Tide: A History of the War Years Based on the Diaries of Field Marshall Lord Alanbrooke, Chief of the Imperial General Staff*. Garden City, N.Y.: 1957.

———. *Triumph in the West 1943–1946*. London: 1959.

Bullitt, Orville H., ed. *For the President Personal and Secret: Correspondence between Franklin D. Roosevelt and William C. Bullitt*. Boston: 1972.

Bullock, Alan. *The Life and Times of Ernest Bevin*. Vol. 2. *Minister of Labour, 1940–1945*. London: 1967.

Burns, James MacGregor. *Roosevelt: Soldier of Freedom*. New York: 1970.

Butler, J. R. M. *Grand Strategy*. Vol. 2. *September 1939–June 1941*. London: 1957.

———. *Lord Lothian (Philip Kerr) 1882–1940*. London and New York: 1960.

Butow, R. J. C. *Tojo and the Coming of the War*. Princeton, N.J.: 1961.

Chadwin, Mark Lincoln. *The Hawks of World War II*. Chapel Hill, N.C.: 1968.

Chandler, Alfred D., Jr. et al., eds. *The Papers of Dwight David Eisenhower: The War Years*. 5 vols. Baltimore and London: 1970.

Charlottesville, Virginia. Box 231, University of Virginia Library. Edward R. Stettinius, Jr., papers.

Churchill, Winston S. "The Bond Between Us," *Collier's* (November 4, 1933).

———. "While the World Watches," *Collier's* (December 29, 1934).

———. *The Gathering Storm*. Boston: 1948.

———. *Their Finest Hour*. Boston: 1949.

———. *The Grand Alliance*. Boston: 1950.

———. *The Hinge of Fate*. Boston: 1950.

———. *Closing the Ring*. Boston: 1951.

———. *Triumph and Tragedy*. Boston: 1953.

Ciechanowski, Jan. *Defeat in Victory*. Garden City, N.Y.: 1947.

Ciechanowski, Jan M. *The Warsaw Rising of 1944*. Cambridge: 1974.

Clark, Mark W. *Calculated Risk*. New York: 1950.

Cline, Ray S. *Washington Command Post—The Operations Division*. Washington: 1951.

Coakley, Robert W., and Leighton, Richard M. *Global Logistics and Strategy, 1943–1945*. Washington: 1968.

Coit, Margaret L. *Mr. Baruch*. Boston: 1957.

Cole, Hugh M. *The Ardennes: The Battle of the Bulge*. Washington: 1965.

Cole, Wayne S. *America First—The Battle against Intervention 1940–1941*. Madison, Wis.: 1953.

Coles, Harry L., and Weinberg, Albert K. *Civil Affairs: Soldiers Become Governors*. Washington: 1964.

Collier, Basil. *The Battle of the V-Weapons 1944–1945*. London: 1964.

Complete Presidential Press Conferences of Franklin Delano Roosevelt. 25 vols. in 12. New York: 1972.

Compton, James V. *The Swastika and the Eagle—Hitler, the United States, and the Origins of World War II*. Boston: 1967.

Conn, Stetson *et al. Command Decisions*. Washington: 1959.

Conn, Stetson, and Fairchild, Byron. *The Framework of Hemisphere Defense*. Washington: 1960.

Cortada, James W. *United States–Spanish Relations, Wolfram and World War II*. Barcelona: 1971.

Craven, Wesley Frank, and Cate, James Lee, eds. *The Army Air Forces in World War II*. 7 vols. Chicago: 1948–1958.

Crozier, Brian. *De Gaulle: The Warrior*. London: 1973 and New York: 1973.

Cunningham, Andrew Brown. *A Sailor's Odyssey*. New York: 1951.

Davis, Kenneth S. *FDR—The Beckoning of Destiny 1882–1928*. New York: 1972.

Davis, Lynn Ethridge. *The Cold War Begins: Soviet-American Conflict over Eastern Europe*. Princeton: 1974.

Dawson, Raymond H. *The Decision to Aid Russia 1941—Foreign Policy and Domestic Politics*. Chapel Hill, N.C.: 1959.

Deakin, F. W. *The Brutal Friendship—Mussolini, Hitler and the Fall of Italian Fascism*. London: 1963.

Deane, John R. *The Strange Alliance*. New York: 1947.

De Gaulle, Charles. *The Complete War Memoirs*. 3 vols. in 1. New York: 1964.

Dilks, David, ed. *The Diaries of Sir Alexander Cadogan, O.M., 1938–1945*. London: 1971.

Divine, Robert A. *Roosevelt and World War II*. Baltimore: 1969.

———. *Second Chance—The Triumph of Internationalism in America during World War II*. New York: 1971.

Dornberger, Walter. *V-2*. New York: 1958.

Dulles, Allen W. *The Secret Surrender*. New York: 1966.

Eade, Charles, ed. *The War Speeches of the Rt. Hon. Winston Churchill*. 3 vols. 2d ed. London: 1965.

Eden, Anthony. *The Memoirs of Anthony Eden, Earl of Avon*. 2 vols. Vol. 2, *The Reckoning*. Boston: 1965.

Ehrman, John. *Grand Strategy*. Vol. 5. *August 1943–September 1944*. London: 1956.

———. *Grand Strategy*. Vol. 6. *October 1944–August 1945*. London: 1956.

Eisenhower, Dwight D. *Crusade in Europe*. Garden City, N.Y.: 1948.

Eisenhower, John S. D. *The Bitter Woods*. New York: 1969.

Ellis, L. F. *The War in France and Flanders 1939–1940*. London: 1953.

———. *Victory in the West*. 2 vols. London: 1962–1968.

Esthus, Raymond A. "President Roosevelt's Commitment to Britain to Intervene in a Pacific War," *Mississippi Valley Historical Review*, 50 (June 1963).

Evans, Trefor E., ed. *The Killearn Diaries 1934–1946: The Diplomatic and Personal Record of Lord Killearn*. London: 1972.

Feingold, Henry L. *The Politics of Rescue: The Roosevelt Administration and the Holocaust*. New Brunswick, N.J.: 1970.

Feis, Herbert. *Churchill, Roosevelt, Stalin*. Princeton: 1957.

FitzGibbon, Louis. *Katyn—A Crime Without Parallel*. London: 1971.

Ford, Corey. *Donovan of OSS*. Boston: 1970.

Freidel, Frank. *Franklin Roosevelt: The Apprenticeship*. Boston: 1952.

Friedlander, Saul. *Prelude to Downfall—Hitler and the United States 1939–1941*. New York: 1967.

Frye, Alton. *Nazi Germany and the American Hemisphere 1933–1941*. New Haven: 1967.

Funk, Arthur Layton. *De Gaulle: The Crucial Years 1943–1944*. Norman, Okla.: 1959.

Gaddis, John L. *The United States and the Origins of the Cold War 1941–1947*. New York: 1972.

Gardner, Lloyd C., "From Liberation to Containment," in William Appleman Williams, ed., *From Colony to Empire: Essays in the History of American Foreign Relations*. New York: 1972.

Gardner, Lloyd C., LaFeber, Walter F., and McCormick, Thomas J. *Creation of the American Empire* in *U.S. Diplomatic History*. Chicago: 1973.

Garland, Albert N., and Smyth, Howard McGaw (assisted by Martin Blumenson). *Sicily and the Surrender of Italy*. Washington: 1965.

General Sikorski Historical Institute. *Documents on Polish-Soviet Relations 1939–1945*. Vols. 1–2, London: 1961–1967.

Gilbert, Felix, ed. *Hitler Directs His War: The Secret Records of His Daily Military Conferences*. New York: 1950.

Gladwyn, Hubert Miles Gladwyn Jebb, Baron. *The Memoirs of Lord Gladwyn*. New York: 1972.

Gowing, Margaret. *Britain and Atomic Energy 1939–1945*. London: 1964.

Green, Constance McLaughlin, Thompson, Harry C., and Roots, Peter C. *The Ordinance Department*. Vol. I. *Planning Munitions for War*. Washington: 1955.

Greenfield, Kent Roberts, ed. *American Strategy in World War II: A Reconsideration*. Baltimore: 1963.

———. *Command Decisions*. New York: 1959.

Gripenberg, G. A. *Finland and the Great Powers: Memoirs of a Diplomat*. Lincoln, Nebr.: 1965.

Gwyer, J. M. A., and Butler, J. R. M. *Grand Strategy*. Vol. 3. *June 1941–August 1942*. London: 1964.

Haight, John McVickar. *American Aid to France 1938–1940*. New York: 1970.

Halifax, Lord. *Fullness of Days.* New York: 1957.

Hall, H. Duncan. *North American Supply.* London: 1955.

Hall, H. Duncan, and Wrigley, C. C. *Studies of Overseas Supply.* London: 1956.

Hamilton, James Douglas. *Motive for a Mission—The Story Behind Hess's Flight to Britain.* London: 1971.

Hancock, Sir Keith, and Gowing, Margaret M. *British War Economy.* London: 1949.

Harris, C. R. S. *Allied Military Administration of Italy 1943–1945.* London: 1957.

Harrison, Gordon A. *Cross-Channel Attack.* Washington: 1951.

Hart, B. H. Liddell, ed. *The Rommel Papers.* New York: 1953.

Hayes, Carlton J. H. *Wartime Mission in Spain, 1942–1945.* New York: 1945.

Herring, George C., Jr. "The United States and British Bankruptcy 1944–1945: Responsibilities Deferred," *Political Science Quarterly,* 86 (June 1971).

————. *Aid to Russia—1941–1946: Strategy, Diplomacy, the Origins of the Cold War.* New York and London: 1973.

Hess, Gary R. *American Encounters India 1941–1947.* Baltimore: 1971.

Hillgruber, Andreas. *Hitlers Strategie—Politik und Kriegführung 1940–1941.* Frankfurt, 1965.

Hoptner, J. B. *Yugoslavia in Crisis 1931–1941.* New York: 1962.

Howard, Michael. *The Mediterranean Strategy in the Second World War.* London: 1968.

————. *Grand Strategy.* Vol. 4. *August 1942–September 1943.* London: 1972.

Howe, George F. *Northwest Africa—Seizing the Initiative in the West.* Washington: 1957.

Hull, Cordell. *The Memoirs of Cordell Hull.* 2 vols. New York: 1948.

Hyde Park, New York. FDR Library. Map Room File; President's Personal File; and President's Secretary's File.

Ike, Nobotaka. *Japan's Decision for War—Records of the 1941 Policy Conferences.* Stanford, Calif.: 1967.

Independence, Missouri. Harry S Truman Library. George M. Elsey papers.

Irving, David. *The Mare's Nest.* Boston: 1965.

Ismay, Hastings. *The Memoirs of General Lord Ismay.* New York: 1960.

Jonas, Manfred. *Isolationism in America 1935–1941.* Ithaca, N.Y.: 1966.

Jones, Robert Huhn. *The Roads to Russia: United States Lend-Lease to the Soviet Union.* Norman, Okla.: 1969.

Kennan, George F. *Russia and the West under Lenin and Stalin.* Boston: 1961.

————. *Memoirs 1925–1950.* Boston: 1967.

Kennedy, Sir John. *The Business of War.* New York: 1958.

Kimball, Warren F. *The Most Unsordid Act: Lend-Lease, 1939–1941.* Baltimore: 1969.

————. "Lend Lease and the Open Door: The Temptation of British Opulence 1937–1942," *Political Science Quarterly,* 86 (June 1971).

King, Ernest J., and Whitehill, Walter Muir. *Fleet Admiral King*. New York: 1952.

Kirby, S. Woodburn. *The War against Japan*. 4 vols. London: 1957–1965.

———. *Singapore—The Chain of Disaster*. New York: 1971.

Kirkpatrick, Sir Ivone. *Mussolini—A Study of a Demagogue*. London: 1964.

Kolko, Gabriel. *The Politics of War—The World and United States Foreign Policy 1943–1945*. New York: 1968.

Kolko, Joyce, and Kolko, Gabriel. *The Limits of Power—The World and United States Foreign Policy 1945–1954*. New York: 1972.

Koskoff, David E. *Joseph P. Kennedy: A Life and Times*. Englewood Cliffs, N.J.: 1974.

Kuklick, Bruce. "The Genesis of the European Advisory Commission," *Journal of Contemporary History*, 4 (October 1969).

Langer, William L., *Our Vichy Gamble*. New York: 1947.

Langer, William L. and Gleason, S. Everett. *The Challenge to Isolation, 1937–1940*. New York: 1952.

———. *The Undeclared War, 1940–1941*. New York: 1953.

League of Nations. *League of Nations Treaty Series and International Engagements*. 205 vols. Geneva: 1920–1946.

Leahy, William D. *I Was There*. New York: 1950.

Leeper, Reginald. *When Greek Meets Greek*. London: 1950.

Leighton, Richard M., and Coakley, Robert W. *Global Logistics and Strategy, 1940–1943*. Washington: 1955.

Leutze, James, ed. *The London Journal of General Raymond E. Lee, 1940–1941*. Boston: 1971.

Lewin, Ronald. *Churchill as Warlord*. New York: 1973.

Loewenheim, Francis L. "The Diffidence of Power—Some Notes and Reflections on the American Road to Munich," *Rice University Studies*, 58 (Fall 1972).

———, ed. *The Historian and the Diplomat—The Role of History and Historians in American Foreign Policy*. New York: 1967.

Lukas, Richard C. *Eagles East: The Army Air Forces and the Soviet Union*. Tallahassee, Fla.: 1970.

Lyon, Peter. *Eisenhower: Portrait of the Hero*. Boston: 1974.

Macmillan, Harold. *The Blast of War, 1939–1945*. London: 1967.

Maisky, Ivan. *Memoirs of a Soviet Ambassador—The War 1939–1945*. New York: 1968.

Majdalany, Fred. *The Battle of El Alamein—Fortress in the Sand*. Philadelphia: 1965.

Mansergh, Nicholas. *Survey of British Commonwealth Affairs*. Vol. 2. *Problems of Wartime Cooperation and Postwar Change, 1939–1952*. London: 1958.

Marder, Arthur. "Winston Is Back: Churchill at the Admiralty 1939–1940," *The English Historical Review*, Supp. 5 (1972).

Martin, James J. *American Liberalism and World Politics 1931–1941*. 2 vols. New York: 1964.

Matloff, Maurice, and Snell, Edwin M. *Strategic Planning for Coalition Warfare, 1943–1944.* Washington: 1953.

May, Ernest R. *The World War and American Isolation 1914–1917.* Cambridge, Mass.: 1959.

————. *"Lessons" of the Past—The Use and Misuse of History in American Foreign Policy.* New York: 1973.

McCarthy, Dudley. *South-West Pacific Area—First Year: Kokoda to Wau.* Canberra: 1959.

McIntire, Ross T. (in collaboration with George Creel). *White House Physician.* New York: 1946.

McNeill, William H. *America, Britain, and Russia: Their Cooperation and Conflict 1941–1946.* New York: 1953.

Middleton, Drew. *Retreat from Victory—A Critical Appraisal of American Foreign and Military Policy from 1920 to the 1970s.* New York: 1973.

Mikolajczyk, Stanislaw. *The Rape of Poland: Pattern of Soviet Aggression.* New York: 1948.

Miller, John, Jr. *Guadalcanal: The First Offensive.* Washington: 1949.

Ministry of Foreign Affairs of the U.S.S.R. *Correspondence Between the Chairman of the Council of Ministers of the U.S.S.R. and the Presidents of the U.S.A. and the Prime Ministers of Great Britain during the Great Patriotic War of 1941–1945.* 2 vols. New York: 1958.

Montgomery of Alamein, Viscount. *The Memoirs of Field Marshal the Viscount Montgomery.* Cleveland, Ohio: 1958.

Moran, Lord. *Churchill.* Boston: 1966.

Morison, Samuel Eliot. *History of the United States Naval Operations in World War II.* 15 vols. Boston: 1947–1962.

————. *Strategy and Compromise.* Boston: 1958.

Morton, Louis. *The Fall of the Philippines.* Washington: 1953.

————. *The War in the Pacific—Strategy and Command: The First Two Years.* Washington: 1962.

Mosely, Philip. *The Kremlin and World Politics.* New York: 1960.

Motter, T. H. Vail. *The Persian Corridor and Aid to Russia.* Washington: 1952.

Murphy, Robert. *Diplomat among Warriors.* Garden City, New York: 1964.

Namier, Sir Lewis. *Diplomatic Prelude 1936–1940.* London: 1948.

————. *Europe in Decay 1936–1940.* London: 1950.

————. *In the Nazi Era.* New York: 1952.

Nevins, Allan. *Herbert H. Lehman and His Era.* New York: 1963.

New Haven, Connecticut. Stirling Library, Yale University. Henry L. Stimson diary.

Norman, Dorothy, ed. *Nehru—The First Sixty Years.* 2 vols. New York: 1965.

Parkinson, Roger. *Blood, Toil, Tears, and Sweat—The War History from Dunkirk to Alamein.* New York: 1973.

————. *A Day's March Nearer Home: The War History from Alamein to V-E Day Based on the War Cabinet Papers of 1942 to 1945.* New York: 1974.

Parliamentary Debates (Great Britain), Commons, 5th series, vols. 361–408.

Paxton, Robert O. *Vichy France: Old Guard and New Order 1940–1944.* New York: 1972.

Playfair, I. S. O., and Molony, C. J. C. *The Mediterranean and the Middle East.* Vol. 4, *The Destruction of the Axis Forces in Africa.* London: 1966.

Pogue, Forrest C. *The Supreme Command.* Washington: 1954.

———. *George C. Marshall: Ordeal and Hope, 1939–1943.* New York: 1966.

———. *George C. Marshall: Organizer of Victory, 1943–1945.* New York: 1973.

———. "The Wartime Chiefs of Staff and the President," *Soldiers and Statesmen: Proceedings of the Fourth Military Symposium.* Washington: 1973.

Postan, M. M. *British War Production.* London: 1952.

Richards, Denis. *Royal Air Force 1939–1945.* 3 vols. London: 1953–1954.

Rigdon, William M. *White House Sailor.* New York: 1962.

Roberts, Walter R. *Tito, Mihailović, and the Allies 1941–1945.* New Brunswick, N.J.: 1973.

Romanus, Charles F., and Sunderland, Riley. *Time Runs Out in CBI.* Washington: 1959.

Roosevelt, Elliott (with Joseph P. Lash), eds. *F.D.R.: His Personal Letters 1928–1945.* 2 vols. New York: 1950.

Rose, Lisle A. *Dubious Victory, the United States and the End of World War II (The Coming of the American Age, 1945–1946).* Kent, Ohio: 1973.

Rosenman, Samuel I., ed. *The Public Papers and Addresses of Franklin Delano Roosevelt.* 13 vols. New York: 1938–1951.

———. *Working with Roosevelt.* New York: 1952.

Roskill, S. W. *The War at Sea 1939–1945.* 3 vols. London: 1954–1961.

Rozek, Edward J. *Allied Wartime Diplomacy—A Pattern in Poland.* New York: 1958.

Russett, Bruce M. *No Clear and Present Danger—A Skeptical View of the United States Entry Into World War II.* New York: 1972.

Saunders, Hilary St. George. *Royal Air Force 1939–1945.* 3 vols. London: 1953–1954.

Schlesinger, Arthur M., Jr. *The Imperial Presidency.* Boston: 1973.

Schramm, Percy Ernst, ed. *Kriegstagebuch des Oberkommandos der Wehrmacht (Wehrmachtführungsstab).* Frankfurt: 1961.

Sherwin, Martin. "The Atomic Bomb and the Origins of the Cold War: U.S. Atomic Energy Policy and Diplomacy 1941–1945," *American Historical Review* (October 1973).

Sherwood, Robert E. *Roosevelt and Hopkins.* New York: 1948.

Slessor, Sir John. *The Central Blue.* London: 1956 and New York: 1957.

Smith, Gaddis. *American Diplomacy during the Second World War, 1941–1945.* New York: 1965.

Smith, Robert Freeman. "American Foreign Relations 1920–1942," in Barton J. Bernstein, ed. *Toward a New Past—Dissenting Essays in American History.* New York: 1968.

Smith, R. Harris. *OSS: The Secret History of America's First Central Intelligence Agency.* Berkeley, Calif.: 1972.

Smyth, Henry D. *Atomic Energy for Military Purposes*. Princeton: 1945.

Spaak, Paul-Henri. *The Continuing Battle—Memoirs of a European 1936–1966*. Boston: 1972.

Stacey, C. P. *Official History of the Canadian Army in the Second World War*. Vol. I. *Six Years of War—The Army in Canada, Britain, and the Pacific*. Ottawa: 1957.

Stimson, Henry L., and Bundy, McGeorge. *On Active Service in Peace and War*. New York: 1948.

Sweeney, J. K. "The Portuguese Wolfram Embargo: A Case Study in Economic Warfare," *Military Affairs*, 38 (1974): 23–26.

Swetterham, John Alexander. *The Tragedy of the Baltic States*. New York: 1954.

Sykes, Christopher. *Orde Wingate*. Cleveland, Ohio, and New York: 1959.

Taylor, A. J. P. *Beaverbrook*. London and New York: 1972.

Taylor, A. J. P. et al. *Churchill Revised: A Critical Assessment*. New York: 1969.

Theoharis, Athan. "Roosevelt and Truman on Yalta: The Origins of the Cold War," *Political Science Quarterly*, 87 (June 1972).

Thomson, Harry C., and Mayo, Linda. *The Ordinance Department—Procurement and Supply*. Washington: 1960.

Thompson, Reginald W. *Generalissimo Churchill*. New York: 1973.

Toland, John. *The Battle of the Bulge*. New York: 1960.

Tolley, Kemp. *The Cruise of the "Lanikai."* Annapolis, Md.: 1973.

————. "The Strange Mission of the Lanikai," *American Heritage* (October 1973).

Tompkins, Peter. *The Murder of Admiral Darlan—A Study in Conspiracy*. New York: 1965.

Toynbee, Arnold, and Toynbee, Veronica M., eds. *Hitler's Europe*. London: 1954.

Tulloch, Derek. *Wingate in Peace and War*. London: 1972.

U.S. Congress. *Congressional Record*, 78th Cong., 1st sess., 39 parts.

U.S. Congress. *Hearings Before the Joint Committee on the Investigation of the Pearl Harbor Attack*. 79th Cong. 1st sess. Washington: 1946, 39 vols.

U.S. Department of State. *Department of State Bulletin* (December 10, 1944).

————. *Postwar Foreign Policy Preparation 1939–1945*. Washington: 1949.

————. *United States Treaties and Other International Agreements*. Washington: 1955.

————. *The Conferences at Malta and Yalta 1945*. Washington: 1955.

————. *Foreign Relations of the United States, 1939–1945*. Washington: 1956–1969.

————. *Documents on German Foreign Policy 1918–1945*. Washington: 1960, series D, Vol. 9.

————. *The Conferences at Cairo and Tehran 1943*. Washington: 1961.

————. *The Conferences at Washington 1941–1942 and Casablanca 1943*. Washington: 1968.

————. *The Conferences at Washington and Quebec 1943*. Washington: 1970.

————. *The Conference at Quebec 1944*. Washington: 1972.

Vandenberg, Arthur H., Jr. *The Private Papers of Senator Vandenberg.* Boston: 1952.

Verrier, Anthony. *The Bomber Offensive.* New York: 1969.

Viorst, Milton. *Hostile Allies: FDR and De Gaulle.* New York: 1965.

Walker, Richard L. *E. R. Stettinius, Jr.* New York: 1965.

Webster, Sir Charles, and Frankland, Noble. *The Strategic Air Offensive against Germany 1939–1945.* London: 1961.

Wedemeyer, Albert C. *Wedemeyer Reports!* New York: 1958.

Westerfield, H. Bradford. *Foreign Policy and Party Politics: Pearl Harbor to Korea.* New Haven: 1955.

Whalen, Richard J. *The Founding Father—The Story of Joseph P. Kennedy.* New York: 1964.

Wigmore, Lionel. *The Japanese Thrust: Australia in the War of 1939–1945.* Vol. 5. Canberra: 1957.

Willoughby, Malcolm F. *The U.S. Coast Guard in World War II.* Annapolis, Md.: 1957.

Wilmot, Chester. *The Struggle for Europe.* New York: 1952.

Wilson, Theodore A. *The First Summit—Roosevelt and Churchill at Placentia Bay 1941.* Boston: 1969.

Woodward, Sir Llewellyn. *British Foreign Policy in the Second World War.* Abridged ed. London: 1962.

———. *British Foreign Policy in the Second World War.* 3 vols. London: 1970–1971.

Young, G. M. *Stanley Baldwin.* London: 1952.

Ziemke, Earl F. *Stalingrad to Berlin: The German Defeat in the East.* Washington: 1968.

Zowandny, J. K. *Death in the Forest—The Story of the Katyn Forest Massacre.* South Bend, Ind.: 1962.

Index

Index

*(Page numbers in the Index
refer to both text and notes)*

as provisional government, recognition of, asked by, 64, 72, 501, 508, 515, 523-524, 534, 536, 550
Roosevelt's views on, 335, 344-345, 361, 456, 483-484, 501, 530-531, 534, 541, 550-551, 552-553
see also Free French
French Empire, 305
revolt in, as possibility, 118
French Equatorial Africa, 306
French Indochina, *see* Indochina
French North Africa, 19
invasion of, *see* North African invasion
political authority in, 59-60, 267-268, 274, 278-281, 282, 293-294, 302, 303, 305, 314, 344-345
refugee facilities planned in, 351-353
U.S. economic aid to, 134, 197-198
French West Africa, 81, 115, 245
invasion of, *see* North African invasion
Fulbright Resolution (1943), 368
Fulton, Dr. James R., 202

Gallipoli, Battle of, 15
Gamelin, Gen. Maurice, 99
George, David Lloyd, 3, 5
George II, King of Greece, 61, 395, 407-408, 489, 490, 516, 528, 540, 629, 630, 635
regency recommended to, 634-635, 637, 638, 639-640, 642
George VI, King of England, 36, 341, 559
Georges, Gen. Alphonse, 335, 338, 347
Georges, Gen. Joseph, 99
German air force (GAF; Luftwaffe):
in Balkans, 371
British lifeline threatened by, 118, 126
in convoy attacks, 254, 323
effect of second front on, 218
North African invasion and, 254
pre-Overlord decimation of, 28, 33, 337, 493, 496
Rotterdam raid of, 94
takeover of French bases by, as threat, 115, 122
German-occupied Europe, *see* Europe, German-occupied
Germany:
air offensive against, 189, 273, 276, 308, 333; Churchill's views on, 28, 151-152, 154, 201, 264, 284, 538; after Italian surrender, 358; Roosevelt

on, 289, 325, 358, 518, 688-689; Stalin informed of, 235, 337, 343, 364
Allied advance into, disputed plans for, 36-37, 574, 696-699, 701-703, 704-705
Allied forces in, 516, 517, 654, 695
anti-Jewish program of, 351, 352
in Atlantic conference plans, 154
Balkan weak points of, 371, 385, 386
blitzkrieg of, 50, 80
blockade of, 134, 151, 154, 179
in "Bulge" counteroffensive (1944), 42, 514, 642, 643, 645-646, 654, 702
collapse of, contingency plans for, 432, 449-450, 504, 562
forced labor of, 389, 390
France and, *see* France; France, Vichy
French zone of occupation in, 517, 600, 602-603, 607
Greece invaded by, 132
Iranian colony of, 155
Italian campaign and, 33, 273, 387, 403-404, 461, 508, 617, 626
Italian defeat and, consequences of, 342-343, 356, 357, 358, 367
Morgenthau plan for, 513, 574-575
naval operations of, 135, 179, 180, 224, 323-324; off South America, 90-93
in North African campaign, *see* North Africa
North African invasion and, 236, 240, 241, 243, 244, 245, 246-247, 254, 255, 319-320
occupation of, plans for, 12, 36, 37, 432, 449-450, 457, 501-502, 504, 512-513, 517, 600, 602-603, 607, 654, 703
occupied, Allied council for, 654
oil supplies of, 91, 130, 312
partition of, 591, 600
postwar demilitarization of, plans for, 397
psychological warfare on, 603-606
rocket warfare of, 36, 274, 389-391, 392, 537-538, 606
Soviet advance into, 654; Churchill's concerns about, 39, 43, 519, 696-699, 703; cold-war perspective on, 42-43
Soviet campaign of, *see* Soviet Union, German war with
Soviet pact (1939) with, 57, 65, 271, 421
Soviet and Polish claims to territory in, 444, 445, 591
Spain and, *see* Spain
Stalin's assurances to Poles on future of, 560

THE EDITORS

FRANCIS L. LOEWENHEIM, Professor of History at Rice University, received his Ph.D. at Columbia University in 1952. Formerly a member of the faculty at Princeton University, he also held visiting appointments at the College of William and Mary, the University of Illinois, Michigan State University, the University of Michigan, and the University of St. Thomas. He served as Assistant to Edward Meade Earle, Director of the School of Historical Studies at the Institute for Advanced Study, as Research Associate on the Twentieth-Century Fund Study of U.S. Civil-Military Relations, and as a member of the Historical Division of the U.S. Department of State. He has edited or contributed to numerous works, including *Political Community and the North Atlantic Area* (1957), *American Civil-Military Decisions* (1963), *Theory and Practice in American Politics* (1964), *Peace or Appeasement? Hitler, Chamberlain, and the Munich Crisis* (1965), *The Historian and the Diplomat: The Role of History and Historians in American Foreign Policy* (1967), *Some Pathways in Twentieth Century History* (1969), *The Czech Renascence of the Nineteenth Century* (1970), *Genesis and Destiny: Western Civilization — The Modern Heritage, 1500 to the Present* (1971), *The 'Foreign Affairs' 50-Year Bibliography, 1920-1970* (1972), *Studies in History* (1973), *Franklin D. Roosevelt — His Life and Times* (1985), *Foreign Visitors to the Capitol* (1989), *The Harry S. Truman Encyclopedia* (1989), and *Julian Huxley — Biologist and Statesman of Science* (1990).

HAROLD D. LANGLEY is Curator of Naval History at the Smithsonian Institution and Adjunct Professor at the Catholic University of America. He received his Ph.D. from the University of Pennsylvania in 1960. Formerly a manuscript specialist at the University of Pennsylvania and the Library of Congress and a diplomatic historian at the U.S. State Department, he has also taught at Marywood College, Montgomery Junior College, and George Washington University. He is the author of *Social Reform in the U.S. Navy, 1798-1862* (1967) and *St. Stephen Martyr, Church and Community, 1867-1967,* as well as the editor of *Documents on the International Aspects of the Exploration and Use of Outer Space, 1952-1962* (1963), *To Utah with the Dragoons* (1974), and *So Proudly We Hail: The History of the United States Flag* (1981).

MANFRED JONAS is John Bigelow Professor of History at Union College, where he served as Chair of the Department from 1970 to 1981. A Harvard University Ph.D., he has also taught at the City College of New York, Northeastern University, and what is now Widener University. From 1959 to 1962 he served as Visiting Professor for North American History at the Free University of Berlin; in 1973 as Senior Fulbright-Hays Lecturer at the University of the Saarland; and in 1983/84 as Dr. Otto Salgo Visiting Professor of American Studies at the Eötvös Lorand University of Budapest. In 1977/78 he was a research fellow of Harvard University's Charles Warren Center for Studies in American History. Contributor of numerous articles to professional journals and composite volumes, he is the editor of *Die Unabhängigkeitserklärung der Vereinigten Staaten* (1964, 1965) and *American Foreign Relations in the Twentieth Century* (1967); the co-editor of *New Opportunities in a New Nation: The Development of New York After the Revolution* (1982); and the author of *Isolationism in America, 1935-1941* (1966, 1969, 1990), and *The United States and Germany: A Diplomatic History* (1984, 1985).